1963

THOUGHT IN PROSE

THOUGHT

PRENTICE-HALL, INC.

IN PROSE

Edited by

Richard S. Beal

BOSTON UNIVERSITY

Jacob Korg

UNIVERSITY OF WASHINGTON

ENGLEWOOD CLIFFS, N. J. • 1958

Preface

This anthology grows out of the conviction that the main business of freshman English is writing, but that learning to write well cannot be divorced from reading good prose. Beyond mechanical competence, freshman English aims at a kind of writing which requires the student to examine his own experience and ideas, to be receptive to the experience and ideas of others, and to be aware of the variety of uses to which skillful writers put language. An anthology which provides essays close to the student's personal experience, which presents a diversity of opinion about some of the recurrent questions of liberal education, and which makes available selected readings on writing and thinking can do much to develop the kind of inquiring mind which is necessary for good writing.

Many anthologies offered for freshman English have either emphasized the study of rhetorical types, focused on various aspects of communication, or offered loosely organized reading in liberal education. In spite of their virtues they seem only partial approaches to the student's writing problem. The rhetorical text saps much of the vitality from the course, and reduces writing to a purely technical matter, without encouraging those habits of inquiry and self-examination which are indispensable to mature writing. The communications reader turns attention from the task of developing writing skill toward an interest in the operation of language. For these reasons, our sympathies lie generally with a third kind of anthology. While we believe that helping the student to widen and improve his background and his critical tastes is a legitimate aim of freshman English, we are convinced that this aim should not and need not be achieved at the expense of the basic writing objectives of the course. We have tried, therefore, to provide an anthology which respects both aims.

Criteria. Throughout our selections, we have applied certain criteria to individual selections and to the whole. In individual selections, we have tried to find expository prose of high quality, varied in style and difficulty, and representative of the various rhetorical methods and aims, but consistently within the serious student's understanding. We have ruled out many provocative and informative pieces because they seemed to us to lack clarity to the uninitiated, or because their supporting detail seemed beyond the province of the freshman English course. Except in a few instances we have consistently preferred the experienced and skilled writer as writer—the artist, the historian, the critic, the philosopher addressing laymen—to the social scientist or other specialist.

Because we believe that in general those selections which the student can grasp as a whole at a single assignment are more likely to suggest usable writing techniques to him, we have preferred selections ranging from two

v

to four thousand words. This length makes practical the use of many of the selections for the study of types and rhetorical methods if the instructor desires, as well as making possible the serious comparison of pieces comparable or contrasting in form and theme. Pieces of this length constitute approximately sixty per cent of the anthology. The remaining selections are divided about equally between longer and shorter pieces.

Organization. In the organization of the whole, we have tried to move, in general, from autobiographical, descriptive, and relatively simple explanatory writing, to more complex expository problems and evaluations. In the early selections, we have tried to provide readings which will encourage the student to examine and draw upon his own experience and observation, help him see something of the variety of language in the hands of skilled writers, and point up for him the need for interpretation, organization, and unity in all writing. Within the seven major sections of the anthology, we have arranged the selections in twenty-one closely related groups which provide contexts for the individual selections. We believe such contexts will be provocative of a wide variety of both rhetorical and thematic comparisons, but we think of them as guiding suggestions only, realizing that to many instructors, other patterns and lines of relationship will seem more apt to their intention.

At the end of each selection we have placed brief suggestions for discussion, rhetorical analysis, and writing. In the first appendix we have included a discussion of the methods and aims of prose, together with lists of selections particularly useful in teaching the several methods and aims. Thus, the instructor who prefers this approach, or wishes to use it as an occasional supplement to other approaches, may easily do so. Brief biographical notes have been included in the second appendix.

Acknowledgments. Such an anthology as this could not have been compiled without the interest and aid of our colleagues, both within the English departments of our own universities and at other universities. To all those who have been so generous with suggestions and good advice, we extend our sincere appreciation. We regret only that practical considerations have many times made it impossible to follow some of the most provocative suggestions for improvement. We should like to acknowledge our especial indebtedness to several colleagues who have helped in various ways: to Morton Berman, Albert Gilman, and Robert H. Sproat of Boston University, Wallace W. Douglas and Harrison Hayford of Northwestern University, Richard Condon of University of Southern California, John Weimer of University of Michigan, Laurence Perrine of Southern Methodist University, Paul R. Sullivan of Georgetown University, Glenn Leggett of University of Washington, Edward Stone of Ohio University, and Newman P. Birk of Tufts University. Finally, we owe a heavy debt to Harriette Beal and Cynthia Korg for invaluable assistance in many of the details of preparation.

R. S. B.

J. K.

Contents

INTERPRETING EXPERIENCE

1. The Eye of Memory

2. The Reader as Artist

3. The Uncommon Observer

The Shape of Reality

LANGUAGE, THOUGHT, AND IDEAS

1. The Craft of Writing

2. Writing and Thinking

3.   Examining Ideas

MAN IN SOCIETY

1.   The American Scene

2.   Democracy and Liberty

3.   The Long View

SCIENCE: PRINCIPLES AND PRACTICE

1.   The Scientist and His Method

2.   Science in Action

3.   The Limits and Value of Science

KNOWLEDGE AND VALUE

1.   Philosophy and Knowledge

LITERATURE AND THE ARTS

1. The Nature and Meaning of Art

2. On Music and Painting

3. Prose, Poetry, and Drama

Appendixes

1 Interpreting Experience

1. THE EYE OF MEMORY

Herbert Read The Vale and the Farm*

When I went to school I learned that the Vale in which we lived had once been a lake, but long ago the sea had eaten through the hills in the east and so released the fresh waters, leaving a fertile plain. But such an idea would have seemed strange to my innocent mind, so remote was this menacing sea. Our farm was towards the western end of the Vale, and because all our land was as flat as once the surface of the lake had been, we could see around us the misty hills, the Moors to the north, the Wolds to the south, meeting dimly in the east where they were more distant. This rim of hills was nearest in the south, at least in effect; for as the sun sank in the west the windows of Stamper's farm in the south caught the blazing rays and cast them back at us, continually drawing our eyes in that direction. But we never traveled so far south as those hills; for the Church and the Market, the only outer places of pilgrimage, lay to the north, five or six miles away. By habit we faced north: the south was 'behind.'

I seemed to live, therefore, in a basin, wide and shallow like the milkpans in the dairy; but the even bed of it was checkered with pastures and cornfields, and the rims were the soft blues and purples of the moorlands. This basin was my world, and I had no inkling of any larger world, for no strangers came to us out of it, and we never went into it. Very rarely my Father went to York or Northallerton, to buy a piece of machinery for the farm or to serve on a jury at the Assizes; but only our vague wonder accompanied him, and the toys he brought back with him might have come, like sailors' curios, from Arabia or Cathay. The basin at times was very wide, especially in the clearness of a summer's day; but as dusk fell it would suddenly contract, the misty hills would draw near, and with night they had clasped us close: the center of the world had become a candle shining from the kitchen window. Inside, in the sitting-room where we spent most of our life, a lamp was lit, with a round glass shade like a full yellow moon. There we were bathed before the fire, said our prayers kneeling on the hearthrug, and then disappeared up the steep stairs lighted by a candle to bed; and once there, the world was finally blotted out. I think it returned with the same suddenness, at least in Summer; but the waking world was a new world, a hollow cube with light streaming in from one window across to a large bed holding, as the years went by, first one, then two, and finally three boys, overseen by two Apostles from one wall and adjured from another, above a chest of drawers, by a white pottery plaque within a pink-luster frame, printed with a vignette of an angel blowing a trumpet and the words:

PRAISE YE THE LORD.

Sometimes the child's mind went on living even during the darkness of night, listening to the velvet stillness of the fields. The stillness of a sleeping town, of a village, is nothing to the stillness of a remote farm; for the peace of day in such a place is so kindly that the ear is attuned to the subtlest sounds, and time is slow. If by chance a cow should low in the night it is like the abysmal cry of some hellish beast, bringing woe to the world. And who knows what hellish beasts might roam by night, for in the cave by the Church five miles away they once found the bones of many strange animals, wolves and hyenas, and even the tusks of mammoths. The night-sound that still echoes in my mind, however, is not of this kind: it is gentler and more musical — the distant sound of horse-hooves on the highroad, at first dim and uncertain, but growing louder until they more suddenly cease. To that distant sound, I realized later, I must have come into the world, for the Doctor arrived on horseback at four o'clock one December morning to find me uttering my first shriek.

I think I heard those hooves again the night my father died, but of this I am not certain; perhaps I shall remember when I come to relate that event, for now the memory of those years, which end shortly after my tenth birthday, comes fitfully, when the proper associations are aroused. If only I can recover the sense and uncertainty of those innocent years, years in which we seemed not so much to live as to be lived by forces outside us, by the wind and trees and moving clouds and all the mobile engines of our expanding world — then

I am convinced I shall possess a key to much that has happened to me in this other world of conscious living. The echoes of my life which I find in my early childhood are too many to be dismissed as vain coincidences; but it is perhaps my conscious life which is the echo, the only real experiences in life being those lived with a virgin sensibility — so that we only hear a tone once, only see a color once, see, hear, touch, taste and smell everything but once, the first time. All life is an echo of our first sensations, and we build up our consciousness, our whole mental life, by variations and combinations of these elementary sensations. But it is more complicated than that, for the senses apprehended not only colors and tones and shapes, but also patterns and atmosphere, and our first discovery of these determines the larger patterns and subtler atmospheres of all our subsequent existence.

I have given the impression that the Farm was remote, but this is not strictly true. Not half a mile on each side of us was another farmhouse, and clustering near the one to the east were three or four cottages. We formed, therefore, a little community, remote as such; in Doomsday Book we had been described as a hamlet. The nearest village was two or three miles away, but to the south, so that it did not count for much until we began to go to school, which was not until towards the end of the period of which I write. Northwards our farm road ran through two fields and then joined the highroad running east and west; but eastward this road soon turned into a road running north and south, down which we turned northwards again, to the Church five miles away, and to Kirby, our real metropolis, six miles away.

The farmhouse was a square stone box with a roof of vivid red tiles; its front was to the south, and warm enough to shelter some apricot trees against the wall. But there was no traffic that way: all our exits and entrances were made on the north side, through the kitchen; and I think even our grandest visitors did not disdain that approach. Why should they? On the left as they entered direct into the kitchen was an old oak dresser; on the right a large open fireplace, with a great iron kettle hanging from the reckan, and an oven to the near side of it. A long deal table, glistening with a honey gold sheen from much scrubbing, filled the far side of the room; long benches ran down each side of it. The floor was flagged with stone, each stone neatly outlined with a border of some softer yellow stone, rubbed on after every washing. Sides of bacon and plum dusky hams hung from the beams of the wooden ceiling.

By day it was the scene of intense bustle. The kitchenmaid was down by five o'clock to light the fire; the laborers crept down in stockinged feet and drew on their heavy boots; they lit candles in their horn lanthorns and went out to the cattle. Breakfast was at seven, dinner at twelve, tea at five. Each morning of the week had its appropriate activity: Monday was washing day, Tuesday ironing, Wednesday and Saturday baking, Thursday 'turning out' upstairs and churning, Friday 'turning out' downstairs. Every day there was the milk to skim in the dairy — the dairy was to the left of the kitchen, and as big as any other room in the house. The milk was poured into large flat pans and allowed to settle; it was skimmed with horn scoops, like toothless combs.

At dinner, according to the time of the year, there would be from five to seven farm laborers, the two servant girls, and the family, with whom, for most of the time, there was a governess—a total of from ten to fifteen mouths to feed every day. The bustle reached its height about midday; the men would come in and sit on the dresser, swinging their legs impatiently; when the food was served, they sprang to the benches and ate in solid gusto, like animals. They disappeared as soon as the pudding had been served, some to smoke a pipe in the saddle room, others to do work which could not wait. Then all the clatter of washing up rose and subsided. More peaceful occupations filled the afternoon. The crickets began to sing in the hearth. The kettle boiled for tea. At nightfall a candle was lit, the foreman or the shepherd sat smoking in the armchair at the fireside end of the table. The latch clicked as the others came in one by one and went early to bed.

The kitchen was the scene of many events which afterwards flowed into my mind from the pages of books. Whenever in a tale a belated traveler saw a light and came through the darkness to ask for shelter, it was to this kitchen door. I can no longer identify the particular stories, but they do not belong to this period of childhood so much as to my later boyhood and youth, long after I had left the Farm; and even today my first memories easily usurp the function of the imagination, and clothe in familiar dimensions and patterns, exact and objective, the scenes which the romancer has purposely left vague, Perhaps the effect of all romance depends on this faculty we have of giving our own definition to the fancies of others. A mind without memories means a body without sensibility; our memories make our imaginative life, and it is only as we increase our memories, widening the imbricated shutters which divide our mind from the light, that we find with quick recognition those images of truth which the world is pleased to attribute to our creative gift.

STUDY QUESTIONS

1. *Two of the notable qualities of this description are its restraint and essential simplicity. Read achieves this partly by his choice of details, and partly by his orderly, controlled sentences. Pick out a paragraph and describe the kind of detail that Read uses. Describe his vocabulary and his sentence structure.*

2. *What does the author gain by giving such exact information as to the direction in which certain things lie, the colors of the landscape, the reasons his father went to the city, and the mottoes on the plaque?*

3. *The author is concerned here not only with giving a vivid description but also defining two reasons for the unusual importance of childhood experience. Summarize those two reasons.*

4. *How does the peculiar relation in the author's mind between the kitchen of the farm and scenes in books illustrate the theory of imaginative creation he expresses in the last sentence?*

5. *Nearly everyone retains a vivid memory of the place or places where he spent his childhood. Write a description like this one of a childhood scene you remember, trying to create the general impression of the place through specific details. You may find it useful to follow the organization of Read's description of the farm kitchen.*

6. *Notice that these experiences from real life lead to an interesting general conclusion at the end of the description. Write a theme following this method. Tell some real experience you have had which has led you to some significant conclusion or general observation.*

Dylan Thomas   Reminiscences of Childhood*

J like very much people telling me about their childhood, but they'll have to be quick or else I'll be telling them about mine.

I was born in a large Welsh town at the beginning of the Great War — an ugly, lovely town (or so it was and is to me), crawling, sprawling by a long and splendid curving shore where truant boys and sandfield boys and old men from nowhere, beachcombed, idled and paddled, watched the dockbound ships or the ships steaming away into wonder and India, magic and China, countries bright with oranges and loud with lions; threw stones into the sea for the barking outcast dogs; made castles and forts and harbours and race tracks in the sand; and on Saturday summer afternoons listened to the brass band, watched the Punch and Judy, or hung about on the fringes of the crowd to hear the fierce religious speakers who shouted at the sea, as though it were wicked and wrong to roll in and out like that, white-horsed and full of fishes.

One man, I remember, used to take off his hat and set fire to his hair every now and then, but I do not remember what it proved, if it proved anything at all, except that he was a very interesting man.

This sea-town was my world; outside a strange Wales, coal-pitted, mountained, river-run, full, so far as I knew, of choirs and football teams and sheep and storybook tall hats and red flannel petticoats, moved about its business which was none of mine.

Beyond that unknown Wales with its wild names like peals of bells in the darkness, and its mountain men clothed in the skins of animals perhaps and always singing, lay England which was London and the country called the

* From *Quite Early One Morning,* by Dylan Thomas. Copyright, 1954, by New Directions, reprinted by permission of New Directions.

Front, from which many of our neighbours never came back. It was a country to which only young men travelled.

At the beginning, the only "front" I knew was the little lobby before our front door. I could not understand how so many people never returned from there, but later I grew to know more, though still without understanding, and carried a wooden rifle in the park and shot down the invisible unknown enemy like a flock of wild birds. And the park itself was a world within the world of the sea-town. Quite near where I lived, so near that on summer evenings I could listen in my bed to the voices of older children playing ball on the sloping paper-littered bank, the park was full of terrors and treasures. Though it was only a little park, it held within its borders of old tall trees, notched with our names and shabby from our climbing, as many secret places, caverns and forests, prairies and deserts, as a country somewhere at the end of the sea.

And though we would explore it one day, armed and desperate, from end to end, from the robbers' den to the pirates' cabin, the highwayman's inn to the cattle ranch, or the hidden room in the undergrowth, where we held beetle races, and lit the wood fires and roasted potatoes and talked about Africa, and the makes of motor cars, yet still the next day, it remained as unexplored as the Poles — a country just born and always changing.

There were many secret societies but you could belong only to one; and in blood or red ink, and a rusty pocketknife, with, of course, an instrument to remove stones from horses' feet, you signed your name at the foot of a terrible document, swore death to all the other societies, crossed your heart that you would divulge no secret and that if you did, you would consent to torture by slow fire, and undertook to carry out by yourself a feat of either daring or endurance. You could take your choice: would you climb to the top of the tallest and most dangerous tree, and from there hurl stones and insults at grown-up passers-by, especially postmen, or any other men in uniform? Or would you ring every doorbell in the terrace, not forgetting the doorbell of the man with the red face who kept dogs and ran fast? Or would you swim in the reservoir, which was forbidden and had angry swans, or would you eat a whole old jam jar full of mud?

There were many more alternatives. I chose one of endurance and for half an hour, it may have been longer or shorter, held up off the ground a very heavy broken pram we had found in a bush. I thought my back would break and the half hour felt like a day, but I preferred it to braving the red face and the dogs, or to swallowing tadpoles.

We knew every inhabitant of the park, every regular visitor, every nurse-maid, every gardener, every old man. We knew the hour when the alarming retired policeman came in to look at the dahlias and the hour when the old lady arrived in the Bath chair with six Pekinese, and a pale girl to read aloud to her. I think she read the newspaper, but we always said she read the *Wizard*. The face of the old man who sat summer and winter on the bench looking over the reservoir, I can see clearly now and I wrote a poem long long after I'd left the park and the sea-town called:

THE HUNCHBACK IN THE PARK

The hunchback in the park
A solitary mister
Propped between trees and water
From the opening of the garden lock
That lets the trees and water enter
Until the Sunday sombre ball at dark

Eating bread from a newspaper
Drinking water from the chained cup
That the children filled with gravel
In the fountain basin where I sailed my ship
Slept at night in a dog kennel
But nobody chained him up.

Like the park birds he came early
Like the water he sat down
And Mister they called Hey mister
The truant boys from the town
Running when he had heard them clearly
On out of sound

Past lake and rockery
Laughing when he shook his paper
Hunchbacked in mockery
Through the loud zoo of the willow groves
Dodging the park-keeper
With his stick that picked up leaves.

And the old dog sleeper
Alone between nurses and swans
While the boys among willows
Made the tigers jump out of their eyes
To roar on the rockery stones
And the groves were blue with sailors

Made all day until bell-time
A woman figure without fault
Straight as a young elm
Straight and tall from his crooked bones
That she might stand in the night
After the locks and the chains

All night in the unmade park
After the railings and shrubberies
The birds the grass the trees and the lake
And the wild boys innocent as strawberries
Had followed the hunchback
To his kennel in the dark.

And that park grew up with me; that small world widened as I learned its secrets and boundaries, as I discovered new refuges and ambushes in its woods and jungles; hidden homes and lairs for the multitudes of imagination, for cowboys and Indians, and the tall terrible half-people who rode on nightmares through my bedroom. But it was not the only world — that world of rockery, gravel path, playbank, bowling green, bandstands, reservoir, dahlia garden, where an ancient keeper, known as Smoky, was the whiskered snake in the grass one must keep off. There was another world where with my friends I used to dawdle on half holidays along the bent and Devon-facing seashore, hoping for gold watches or the skull of a sheep or a message in a bottle to be washed up with the tide; and another where we used to wander whistling through the packed streets, stale as station sandwiches, round the impressive gasworks and the slaughter house, past by the blackened monuments and the museum that should have been in a museum. Or we scratched at a kind of cricket on the bald and cindery surface of the recreation ground, or we took a tram that shook like an iron jelly down to the gaunt pier, there to clamber under the pier, hanging perilously on to its skeleton legs or to run along to the end where patient men with the seaward eyes of the dockside unemployed capped and mufflered, dangling from their mouths pipes that had long gone out, angled over the edge for unpleasant tasting fish.

Never was there such a town as ours, I thought, as we fought on the sand-hills with rough boys or dared each other to climb up the scaffolding of half-built houses soon to be called Laburnum Beaches. Never was there such a town, I thought, for the smell of fish and chips on Saturday evenings; for the Saturday afternoon cinema matinees where we shouted and hissed our three-pences away; for the crowds in the streets with leeks in their hats on international nights; for the park, the inexhaustible and mysterious, bushy red-Indian hiding park where the hunchback sat alone and the groves were blue with sailors. The memories of childhood have no order, and so I remember that never was there such a dame school as ours, so firm and kind and smelling of galoshes, with the sweet and fumbled music of the piano lessons drifting down from upstairs to the lonely schoolroom, where only the sometimes tearful wicked sat over undone sums, or to repeat a little crime — the pulling of a girl's hair during geography, the sly shin kick under the table during English literature. Behind the school was a narrow lane where only the oldest and boldest threw pebbles at windows, scuffled and boasted, fibbed about their relations —

"My father's got a chauffeur."

"What's he want a chauffeur for? He hasn't got a car."

"My father's the richest man in the town."

"My father's the richest man in Wales."

"My father owns the world."

And swapped gob-stoppers for slings, old knives for marbles, kite strings for foreign stamps.

The lane was always the place to tell your secrets; if you did not have any, you invented them. Occasionally now I dream that I am turning out of school into the lane of confidences when I say to the boys of my class, "At last, I have a real secret."

"What is it — what is it?"

"I can fly."

And when they do not believe me, I flap my arms and slowly leave the ground only a few inches at first, then gaining air until I fly waving my cap level with the upper windows of the school, peering in until the mistress at the piano screams and the metronome falls to the ground and stops, and there is no more time.

And I fly over the trees and chimneys of my town, over the dockyards skimming the masts and funnels, over Inkerman Street, Sebastopol Street, and the street where all the women wear men's caps, over the trees of the everlasting park, where a brass band shakes the leaves and sends them showering down on to the nurses and the children, the cripples and the idlers, and the gardeners, and the shouting boys: over the yellow seashore, and the stone-chasing dogs, and the old men, and the singing sea.

The memories of childhood have no order, and no end.

STUDY QUESTIONS

1. *Notice that the child's world in this essay is not merely a series of sense impressions, but also includes things he has heard about or read about, which he links, sometimes mistakenly, to the sights and sounds around him. Point out some places where Thomas combines first-hand experiences with information he has learned second-hand.*

2. *Obviously, this account mingles true experiences with imaginary ones, yet the author does not differentiate between them, describing both kinds of experience as though they were true. What does this demand from the reader? What effect does it create?*

3. *Show how the style and organization of the essay reflect Thomas' opinion that "the memories of childhood have no order . . ." This does not mean that the essay is disorderly. Consider, for example, in the paragraph where this opinion is expressed, the repetition of the word "never."*

4. *Compare Thomas' writing with that of Read in the previous description. What differences do you find in vocabulary? In sentences? What effect does Thomas gain by the frequent long sentences whose parts are loosely connected with "and" or "or"?*

5. *Probably every individual remembers very sharply many details of his childhood. Write an essay giving your impression of "the world" in which you first become aware of things and people around you.*

6. *It is also probably true of every child that he lives "in a world of his own" which has little or nothing to do with actuality. Describe some dream, imaginary activity, impossible ambition or misunderstanding (like Thomas' "Front" or "secret society") from your own childhood.*

Winifred Welles   The Attic*

*P*ossibly only a dreamy child can fully grasp — or wants to — the difference between a family storeroom, an attic, and the public secondhand shop, and perhaps the difference is important only to herself. But all old junk, even when it has belonged to strangers, must vibrate in the imagination of sensitive observers with many exquisite overtones. If the junk consists of objects once loved, used, worn, or made by those of one's own blood, they assume an inescapable and tender significance. Even when the object is ludicrous, one's laughter is gentle.

A child wandering among such outcast but still surviving fragments of other times, other lives, sees herself not as an isolated figure, shelterless and undirected, but as a partaker, a marcher in a long processional that has passed under this, her very own roof. Death is diminished for her, and life enlarged. For better or for worse, the incidents of her own hearth reach out and merge in the events of her country's history. She comes to have both a respect and a disregard for Time that are somewhat Chinese. She knows that the past and the future are closely integrated, yet as distinctly separate as the two sides of a medal, and that her appreciation of the present is measured by the strength of her desire to hold that medal in the hollow of her hand, to scrutinize it, to remember, and to dream.

And so the attic in my grandfather's house became more than just another room in the house. It was the very breath and body of the whole eventful rooftree. Like a family memory-book, it contained a keepsake for everybody, from someone's old doll to someone else's rusty sword. There was a bride's bouquet crumbling to dust in a box, and near by, where it had been set on a shelf neatly tied up in a package, was the groom's hat, the crushable kind, and I was endlessly amused pushing it open and smashing it shut.

Backed up against the chimney, accumulating a rich patina of neglect, stood a maple highboy that in the later years of appreciation was borne forth with tenderness and amid a babble of voices. But to me at that time it was no more exciting than several other objects, one afterward identified as a pewter bedpan, or than the round tin tub with flaring sides, or the walking-machine in which a baby had stood, supported on a little wheeled device, to experiment with his first feeble steps. One of the more violent children, it seemed, had walked in it across the porch, straight down the steps and away.

One large square trunk held some of the pretty belongings of a belle of the

* From *The Lost Landscape*, by Winifred Welles. Copyright, 1946, by Henry Holt and Company, Inc. By permission of the publishers.

1870's — pale pink and blue brocades with bustles and pearl trimmings on the bodices, thin silver bangles, rosebud earrings of coral, a feather fan with pearl sticks, and a small black-lace parasol, the ivory handle delicately carved. To complete this gay chapter in her life, as I afterwards learned it downstairs, there should have been one other item that was missing — a pair of slippers with the heels stripped off.

She had had a devoted but jealous beau, evidently a serious fellow who not only writhed at the sight of her dancing with other men but disapproved altogether of the idea of dancing. So, after what must have been rather a high-pitched scene, he stole a pair of her slippers, tore off the heels, and left them in a reproachful little heap outside her door. I used to wonder where the heels were. Had she thrown them away, chagrined? Or did she indignantly bear them off to the shoemaker's to be put back on and to end their days in the polka? ...

The books in the attic had been stacked or piled or shoved in anywhere with no attempt at arrangement. Over on the shelves by the door was an assortment including everyone's primers and grammars, English, Latin, French, and Greek. There were Bibles, of course, ranging in size from one no bigger than your thumb to one so large and bulky that I carried it in my arms when I took it across to the window to read. On the flyleaf of that one, in bold, black handwriting, was a man's name, the year 1629, and the words "Essex, England." The other big books, bound in worn leather, were an Apocrypha with engravings and several volumes of the laws of early Connecticut with very stately lettering. There were sermons and treatises and Sunday-school books. There was a grimly illustrated *Medical History of the Civil War,* in which I could see for myself, if I had doubted it, that "they all had terrible wounds." Two volumes contained startling pictures, and accounts of heroic ladies who went along with their husbands in the Union Army. Their hair hung loosely and untidily on their shoulders, like Indians' locks, whether they were in dashing riding-costume with a seven-shooter at the belt or wore trousers like the men, surmounted by a modest knee-length tunic, and carried a sergeant's straight sword.

Evidently someone in the family, or perhaps more than one, had been interested in all kinds of extraordinary women for a long time. A shabby old book called *A Vindication of the Rights of Women* lay at the bottom of a heap, but it had no pictures, and its long, antique s's made it difficult reading. A fat volume labeled *Eminent Women of the Age* in gold letters was less puzzling. And there were portraits of them all too, everyone from Queen Victoria to Rosa Bonheur, from Julia Ward Howe and Margaret Fuller Ossoli to Mrs. Sigourney. Mrs. Sigourney had lived in Norwich, and I often came on her poems in anthologies or in scrapbooks full of stained clippings.

There was plenty of poetry, both English and American — stout collected works of Tennyson, Byron, and Longfellow, illustrated editions of Whittier and Poe and others. A thin book called *M'Fingal* enchanted me with its humorous pictures. I also dug out of its contents the incredible tale of the British soldiers walking on Beacon Hill at sunset who ran away from June bugs terrified, thinking that they were bullets.

This story, like that one told me by my father of the redcoats who fled in the night from Windham because the bullfrogs sounded like an approaching army, convinced me that the English must be an easily scared nation. But I felt sure that the frogs of Windham had been a mighty race, for the strength of their song was the subject of several legends. These, and many more about all the towns of Connecticut, I found in one book with both covers and some of the pages gone. Somehow such curious trivia lodged in the corners of my mind, like inescapable, queer-shaped pieces of some big picture puzzle that I was trying to reassemble.

I learned that Norwich was once called "The Rose of New England," and that she was famous for the size of her puddings, while New London was noted for that of her dumplings. I often sat wondering what it would have meant to be a guest at tripe suppers, turtle entertainments, or the ordination parties where the clergy displayed such enthusiasm and skill in making punch. But these meditative moments were the mild ones. I read faster when I came to stories of wolves in the swamps around New London, or of the huge black snakes in the Norwich Town meadows, or of the Indians who were everywhere.

Those two chiefs, shrewd Uncas and that other with his rippling, melodic name, Miantonomo, I never forgot. They hated and feared and admired each other for a long time, but it was Uncas who, with the help of the English, finally won out. Proud of his victory, he was no less proud of his enemy, for as he stood over the body of the slain Miantonomo, he drew out his long knife and, slicing off pieces of the still warm flesh, he ate them and said:

"It is good. It is sweet. It will make my heart strong."

It was somewhat disappointing to find that only one witch had been hanged in Connecticut. But she haunted me because she was only a girl, and her name, Alse, suggested nothing evil. And altogether, she, the wolves, the snakes, and the Indian chiefs seemed as mythical to read about as some of the records left as to the behavior of nature itself in the various townships — as, for instance, the mountain in Moodus that "made noises," or "the rock that walked" on the shore near New London, or the island in the Connecticut River that quietly vanished away.

As a contrast to all this wild, dark, mysterious poetry, there were later substantial figures like Sarah Knight, a very lively lady who finally settled down at Norwich. Early in the eighteenth century she journeyed through New England, keeping a journal as she went. Apparently equally afraid of a "hors" or a "cannoo," she nevertheless managed to traverse much earth and water. Among many observant comments on people and towns, she mentioned divorces — "stand aways," she called them — and considered them entirely "too much in vogue" among both the English and the Indians.

Sometimes, in trying moments, she found it restful to set down her thoughts in verse. Her phrase for this was "Composing my Resentments," and she resorted to it late one night in a Connecticut tavern when some quarrelsome topers in the room next to hers kept her too long awake. She lit her candle in despair and wrote:

> I ask thy aid, O potent Rum,
> To charm these wrangling Topers dum.
> Thou hast their giddy brains possesst,
> The man confounded with the Beast—
> And I, poor I, can get no rest.
> Intoxicate them with thy fumes,
> O still their Tongues till morning comes!

The charm worked, for she added that "the dispute soon ended with t'other dram."

Naturally the attic had no scholarly feeling for the sequence of events. On those shelves and in those boxes and trunks, the decades and the centuries all gathered dust impartially together. I, the contented living child, ran my exploring hand along the rows of books, pulling one out here or there, gathering in my variegated store richly and carelessly, much as a magpie picks up sparkling bits of stone, ribbon, or refuse and carries them all home to its nest. If I was interested one minute to think of Lady Fenwick and her crumbling grave on the shore at Saybrook, I was equally so the next to imagine the Duc de Lauzun, that elegant French nobleman, sulking in the village of Lebanon and longing for the gaiety of Newport. That a hundred years and more, brimful of other lives and events, stretched between this lady and this gentleman would not have disconcerted me very much, even had I happened to count them.

In the attic history shrank, but the lives, as I came upon them, seemed distinct and important, each in its own niche. And the place was so cluttered that it took my mind no longer to dart across the decades, and even from war to war, than it took my eyes to glance from the Union soldier's sword across to the cedar-lined medicine chest that had belonged to the Revolutionary doctor. Perhaps the fact that some of my own discarded toys had found their resting-place up here may have assured me that all the other objects in some way belonged to me as well. My own old doll house with one door off, standing as it did beside a broken spinning wheel, perhaps gave me the impression that one was really no more unfamiliar than the other. They were simply companions in disuse. I never seemed to question why either had been saved. I accepted them, as indeed I accepted the whole attic, as a necessary and comprehensible part of the more orderly rooms downstairs — and so too a part of me myself.

STUDY QUESTIONS

1. *How can you explain the paradox that the attic gives the author both "A respect and a disregard for Time"? In the essay find an example of a thing that*

makes her "respect" time, and an example of one that makes her "disregard" it.

2. This selection is a much more straightforward piece of writing than either of the previous two. Examine the method of organization, the details, and the words and sentences, and see if you can explain some of the differences.

3. How did the author of this essay probably learn the stories of the things she found in the attic? Is it possible, by using this inference and other evidence in the essay, to tell what her family was like?

4. What is the author's attitude toward her subject matter? Is there any difference between her treatment of the cannibal Indian and that of the woman poet who was kept awake by her neighbors? Would you call this realistic? In what way is this characteristic of children's thoughts?

5. The last paragraph says there is a connection between the attic and the rest of the house. How would you describe the relationship?

6. Describe some object—a book, a piece of furniture, a picture, for example— that has been in your own family for a long time and describe its history or associations. Or describe your discoveries in rummaging through the accumulated discards of an attic, cellar, or storeroom.

Henry Adams A New England Boyhood*

Boys are wild animals, rich in the treasures of sense, but the New England boy had a wider range of emotions than boys of more equable climates. He felt his nature crudely, as it was meant. To the boy Henry Adams, summer was drunken. Among senses, smell was the strongest — smell of hot pinewoods and sweet-fern in the scorching summer noon; of new-mown hay; of ploughed earth; of box hedges; of peaches, lilacs, syringas; of stables, barns, cow-yards; of salt water and low tide on the marshes; nothing came amiss. Next to smell came taste, and the children knew the taste of everything they saw or touched, from pennyroyal and flagroot to the shell of a pignut and the letters of a spelling-book — the taste of A-B, AB, suddenly revived on the boy's tongue sixty years afterwards. Light, line, and color as sensual pleasures, came later and were as crude as the rest. The New England light is glare, and the atmosphere harshens color. The boy was a full man before he ever knew what was meant by atmosphere; his idea of pleasure in light was the blaze of a New England sun. His idea of color was a peony, with the dew of early morning on its petals. The intense blue of the sea, as he saw it a mile or two away, from the Quincy hills; the cumuli in a June afternoon sky; the strong reds and greens and purples of colored prints and children's picture-books, as the American colors then ran; these were ideals. The opposites or antipathies were the cold grays of November evenings, and the thick, muddy

* From The Education of Henry Adams. Copyright, 1918, by Houghton Mifflin Company. Reprinted by permission of the publishers.

thaws of Boston winter. With such standards, the Bostonian could not but develop a double nature. Life was a double thing. After a January blizzard, the boy who could look with pleasure into the violent snow-glare of the cold white sunshine, with its intense light and shade, scarcely knew what was meant by tone. He could reach it only by education.

Winter and summer, then, were two hostile lives, and bred two separate natures. Winter was always the effort to live; summer was tropical license. Whether the children rolled in the grass, or waded in the brook, or swam in the salt ocean, or sailed in the bay, or fished for smelts in the creeks, or netted minnows in the salt-marshes, or took to the pine-woods and the granite quarries, or chased muskrats and hunted snapping-turtles in the swamps, or mushrooms or nuts on the autumn hills, summer and country were always sensual living, while winter was always compulsory learning. Summer was the multiplicity of nature; winter was school.

The bearing of the two seasons on the education of Henry Adams was no fancy; it was the most decisive force he ever knew; it ran through life, and made the division between its perplexing, warring, irreconcilable problems, irreducible opposites, with growing emphasis to the last year of study. From earliest childhood the boy was accustomed to feel that, for him, life was double. Winter and summer, town and country, law and liberty, were hostile, and the man who pretended they were not, was in his eyes a schoolmaster — that is, a man employed to tell lies to little boys. Though Quincy was but two hours' walk from Beacon Hill, it belonged in a different world. For two hundred years, every Adams, from father to son, had lived within sight of State Street, and sometimes had lived in it, yet none had ever taken kindly to the town, or been taken kindly by it. The boy inherited his double nature. He knew as yet nothing about his great-grandfather, who had died a dozen years before his own birth: he took for granted that any great-grandfather of his must have always been good, and his enemies wicked; but he divined his great-grandfather's character from his own. Never for a moment did he connect the two ideas of Boston and John Adams; they were separate and antagonistic; the idea of John Adams went with Quincy. He knew his grandfather John Quincy Adams only as an old man of seventy-five or eighty who was friendly and gentle with him, but except that he heard his grandfather always called "the President," and his grandmother "the Madam," he had no reason to suppose that his Adams grandfather differed in character from his Brooks grandfather who was equally kind and benevolent. He liked the Adams side best, but for no other reason than that it reminded him of the country, the summer, and the absence of restraint. Yet he felt also that Quincy was in a way inferior to Boston, and that socially Boston looked down on Quincy. The reason was clear enough even to a five-year-old child. Quincy had no Boston style. Little enough style had either; a simpler manner of life and thought could hardly exist, short of cave-dwelling. The flint-and-steel with which his grandfather Adams used to light his own fires in the early morning was still on the mantelpiece of his study. The idea of a livery or even a dress for servants, or of an evening toilette, was next to blasphemy. Bathrooms, water-supplies, lighting, heating, and the whole array of domestic comforts, were unknown at Quincy. Boston had already a bathroom, a water-supply, a furnace, and gas. The superiority of Boston was evident, but a child liked it no better for that.

The magnificence of his grandfather Brooks's house in Pearl Street or South Street has long ago disappeared, but perhaps his country house at Medford may still remain to show what impressed the mind of a boy in 1845 with the idea of city splendor. The President's place at Quincy was the larger and older and far the more interesting of the two; but a boy felt at once its inferiority in fashion. It showed plainly enough its want of wealth. It smacked of colonial age, but not of Boston style or plush curtains. To the end of his life he never quite overcame the prejudice thus drawn in with his childish breath. He never could compel himself to care for nineteenth-century style. He was never able to adopt it, any more than his father or grandfather or great-grandfather had done. Not that he felt it as particularly hostile, for he reconciled himself to much that was worse; but because, for some remote reason, he was born an eighteenth-century child. The old house at Quincy was eighteenth century. What style it had was in its Queen Anne mahogany panels and its Louis Seize chairs and sofas. The panels belonged to an old colonial Vassall who built the house; the furniture had been brought back from Paris in 1789 or 1801 or 1817, along with porcelain and books and much else of old diplomatic remnants; and neither of the two eighteenth-century styles — neither English Queen Anne nor French Louis Seize — was comfortable for a boy, or for any one else. The dark mahogany had been painted white to suit daily life in winter gloom. Nothing seemed to favor, for a child's objects, the older forms. On the contrary, most boys, as well as grown-up people, preferred the new, with good reason, and the child felt himself distinctly at a disadvantage for the taste.

Nor had personal preference any share in his bias. The Brooks grandfather was as amiable and as sympathetic as the Adams grandfather. Both were born in 1767, and both died in 1848. Both were kind to children, and both belonged rather to the eighteenth than to the nineteenth centuries. The child knew no difference between them except that one was associated with winter and the other with summer, one with Boston, the other with Quincy. Even with Medford, the association was hardly easier. Once as a very young boy he was taken to pass a few days with his grandfather Brooks under charge of his aunt, but became so violently homesick that within twenty-four hours he was brought back in disgrace. Yet he could not remember ever being seriously homesick again.

The attachment to Quincy was not altogether sentimental or wholly sympathetic. Quincy was not a bed of thornless roses. Even there the curse of Cain set its mark. There as elsewhere a cruel universe combined to crush a child. As though three or four vigorous brothers and sisters, with the best will, were not enough to crush any child, every one else conspired towards an education which he hated. From cradle to grave this problem of running order through chaos, direction through space, discipline through freedom, unity through multiplicity, has always been, and must always be, the task of education, as it is the moral of religion, philosophy, science, art, politics, and economy; but a boy's will is his life, and he dies when it is broken, as the colt dies in harness, taking a new nature in becoming tame. Rarely has the boy felt kindly towards his tamers. Between him and his master has always been war. Henry Adams never knew a boy of his generation to like a master, and the task of remaining on friendly terms with one's own family, in such a relation, was never easy.

All the more singular it seemed afterwards to him that his first serious contact with the President should have been a struggle of will, in which the old man almost necessarily defeated the boy, but instead of leaving, as usual in such defeats, a lifelong sting, left rather an impression of as fair treatment as could be expected from a natural enemy. The boy met seldom with such restraint. He could not have been much more than six years old at the time — seven at the utmost — and his mother had taken him to Quincy for a long stay with the President during the summer. What became of the rest of the family he quite forgot; but he distinctly remembered standing at the house door one summer morning in a passionate outburst of rebellion against going to school. Naturally his mother was the immediate victim of his rage; that is what mothers are for, and boys also; but in this case the boy had his mother at unfair disadvantage, for she was a guest, and had no means of enforcing obedience. Henry showed a certain tactical ability by refusing to start, and he met all efforts at compulsion by successful, though too vehement protest. He was in a fair way to win, and was holding his own, with sufficient energy, at the bottom of the long staircase which led up to the door of the President's library, when the door opened, and the old man slowly came down. Putting on his hat, he took the boy's hand without a word, and walked with him, paralyzed by awe, up the road to the town. After the first moments of consternation at this interference in a domestic dispute, the boy reflected that an old gentleman close on eighty would never trouble himself to walk near a mile on a hot summer morning over a shadeless road to take a boy to school, and that it would be strange if a lad imbued with the passion of freedom could not find a corner to dodge around, somewhere before reaching the school door. Then and always, the boy insisted that this reasoning justified his apparent submission; but the old man did not stop, and the boy saw all his strategical points turned, one after another, until he found himself seated inside the school, and obviously the centre of curious if not malevolent criticism. Not till then did the President release his hand and depart.

The point was that this act, contrary to the inalienable rights of boys, and nullifying the social compact, ought to have made him dislike his grandfather for life. He could not recall that it had this effect even for a moment. With a certain maturity of mind, the child must have recognized that the President, though a tool of tyranny, had done his disreputable work with a certain intelligence. He had shown no temper, no irritation, no personal feeling, and had made no display of force. Above all, he had held his tongue. During their long walk he had said nothing; he had uttered no syllable of revolting cant about the duty of obedience and the wickedness of resistance to law; he had shown no concern in the matter; hardly even a consciousness of the boy's existence. Probably his mind at that moment was actually troubling itself little about his grandson's iniquities, and much about the iniquities of President Polk, but the boy could scarcely at that age feel the whole satisfaction of thinking that President Polk was to be the vicarious victim of his own sins, and he gave his grandfather credit for intelligent silence. For this forbearance he felt instinctive respect. He admitted force as a form of right; he admitted even temper, under protest; but the seeds of a moral education would at that moment have fallen on the stoniest soil in Quincy, which is, as every one knows, the stoniest glacial and tidal drift known in any Puritan land.

STUDY QUESTIONS

1. *This selection opens with a contrast. To what extent is this pattern of contrast carried through the whole selection?*
2. *Though it is about a child and a child's thoughts, this account tells about some reactions that are obviously those of an adult. Can you pick these out?*
3. *What is the purpose and effect of telling autobiography in the third person, as Henry Adams does?*
4. *What prevented Henry Adams from hating his grandfather as he hated everyone else who tried to discipline him?*
5. *Write a theme describing an incident of family life that made a profound impression on you when you were a child.*
6. *Do you detect any differences between the way of rearing children when Henry Adams was a boy and the present way? Write a theme contrasting and evaluating old-fashioned and modern concepts of child-raising and family life.*

Mark Twain   Steamboat Town*

When I was a boy, there was but one permanent ambition among my comrades in our village on the west bank of the Mississippi River. That was, to be a steamboatman. We had transient ambitions of other sorts, but they were only transient. When a circus came and went, it left us all burning to

*From *Life on the Mississippi*, by Mark Twain. Reprinted by permission of Harper & Brothers.

become clowns; the first negro minstrel show that ever came to our section left us all suffering to try that kind of life; now and then we had a hope that, if we lived and were good, God would permit us to be pirates. These ambitions faded out, each in its turn; but the ambition to be a steamboatman always remained.

Once a day a cheap, gaudy packet arrived upward from St. Louis, and another downward from Keokuk. Before these events, the day was glorious with expectancy; after them, the day was a dead and empty thing. Not only the boys, but the whole village, felt this. After all these years I can picture that old time to myself now, just as it was then: the white town drowsing in the sunshine of a summer's morning; the streets empty, or pretty nearly so; one or two clerks sitting in front of the Water Street stores, with their splint-bottomed chairs tilted back against the walls, chins on breasts, hats slouched over their faces, asleep — with shingle-shavings enough around to show what broke them down; a sow and a litter of pigs loafing along the sidewalk, doing a good business in watermelon rinds and seeds; two or three lonely little freight piles scattered about the "levee"; a pile of "skids" on the slope of the stone-paved wharf, and the fragrant town drunkard asleep in the shadow of them; two or three wood flats at the head of the wharf, but nobody to listen to the peaceful lapping of the wavelets against them; the great Mississippi, the majestic, the magnificent Mississippi, rolling its mile-wide tide along, shining in the sun; the dense forest away on the other side; the "point" above the town, and the "point" below, bounding the river-glimpse and turning it into a sort of sea, and withal a very still and brilliant and lonely one. Presently a film of dark smoke appears above one of those remote "points"; instantly a negro drayman, famous for his quick eye and prodigious voice, lifts up the cry, "S-t-e-a-m-boat a-comin'!" and the scene changes! The town drunkard stirs, the clerks wake up, a furious clatter of drays follows, every house and store pours out a human contribution, and all in a twinkling the dead town is alive and moving. Drays, carts, men, boys, all go hurrying from many quarters to a common center, the wharf. Assembled there, the people fasten their eyes upon the coming boat as upon a wonder they are seeing for the first time. And the boat *is* rather a handsome sight, too. She is long and sharp and trim and pretty; she has two tall, fancy-topped chimneys, with a gilded device of some kind swung between them; a fanciful pilot-house, all glass and "gingerbread," perched on top of the "texas" deck behind them; the paddle-boxes are gorgeous with a picture or with gilded rays above the boat's name; the boiler-deck, the hurricane-deck, and the texas deck are fenced and ornamented with clean white railings; there is a flag gallantly flying from the jack-staff; the furnace doors are open and the fires glaring bravely; the upper decks are black with passengers; the captain stands by the big bell, calm, imposing, the envy of all; great volumes of the blackest smoke are rolling and tumbling out of the chimneys — a husbanded grandeur created with a bit of pitch-pine just before arriving at a town; the crew are grouped on the forecastle; the broad stage is run far out over the port bow, and an envied deck-hand stands picturesquely on the end of it with a coil of rope in his hand; the pent steam is screaming through the gaugecocks; the captain lifts his hand, a bell rings, the wheels stop; then they turn back, churning the water to foam, and the steamer is at rest. Then such a scramble as there is to get aboard, and to get ashore, and to take in freight and to discharge freight, all at one and the same time; and such a yelling and cursing as the mates facilitate it all with! Ten minutes later the steamer is under way again, with no flag on the jack-staff and no black smoke issuing from the chimneys. After ten more minutes the town is dead again, and the town drunkard asleep by the skids once more.

My father was a justice of the peace, and I supposed he possessed the power of life and death over all men, and could hang anybody that offended him. This was distinction enough for me as a general thing; but the desire to be a steamboatman kept intruding, nevertheless. I first wanted to be a cabin-boy, so that I could come out with a white apron on and shake a table-cloth over the side, where all my old comrades could see me: later I thought I would rather be the deck-hand who stood on the end of the stage-plank with the coil of rope in his hand, because he was particularly conspicuous. But these were only day-dreams — they were too heavenly to be contemplated as real possibilities. By and by one of our boys went away. He was not heard of for a long time. At last he turned up as apprentice engineer or "striker" on a steamboat. This thing shook the bottom out of all my Sunday-school teachings. That boy had been notoriously worldly, and I just the reverse; yet he was exalted to this eminence, and I left in obscurity and misery. There was nothing generous about this fellow in his greatness. He would always manage to have a rusty bolt to scrub while his boat tarried at our town, and he would sit on the inside guard and scrub it, where we all could see him and envy him and loathe him. And whenever his boat was laid up he would come home and swell around the town in his blackest and greasiest clothes, so that nobody could help remembering that he was a steamboatman; and he used all sorts of steamboat technicalities in his talk, as if he were so used to them that he forgot common people could not understand them. He would speak of the "labboard" side of a horse in an easy, natural way that would make one wish he was dead. And he was always talking about "St. Looy" like an old citizen; he would refer casually to occasions when he was "coming down Fourth Street," or when he was "passing by the Planter's House," or when there was a fire and he took a turn on the brakes of "the old Big Missouri"; and then he would go on and lie about how many towns the size of ours were burned down there that day. Two or three of the boys had long been persons of consideration among us because they had been to St. Louis once and had a vague general knowledge of its wonders, but the day of their glory was over now. They lapsed into a humble silence, and learned to disappear when the ruthless "cub"-engineer approached. This fellow had money, too, and hair-oil. Also an ignorant silver watch and a showy brass watch-chain. He wore a leather belt and used no suspenders. If ever a youth was cordially admired and hated by his comrades, this one was. No girl could withstand his charms. He "cut out" every boy in the village. When his boat blew up at last, it diffused a tranquil contentment among us such as we had not known for months. But when he came home the next week, alive, renowned, and appeared in church all battered up and bandaged, a shining hero, stared at and wondered over by everybody, it seemed to us that the partiality of Providence for an undeserving reptile had reached a point where it was open to criticism.

This creature's career could produce but one result, and it speedily followed. Boy after boy managed to get on the river. The minister's son became an engineer. The doctor's and the postmaster's sons became "mud clerks"; the wholesale liquor dealer's son became a barkeeper on a boat; four sons of the chief merchant, and two sons of the county judge, became pilots. Pilot was the grandest position of all. The pilot, even in those days of trivial wages, had a princely salary—from a hundred and fifty to two hundred and fifty dollars a month, and no board to pay. Two months of his wages would pay a preacher's salary for a year. Now some of us were left disconsolate. We could not get on the river—at least our parents would not let us.

So, by and by, I ran away. I said I would never come home again till I was a pilot and could come in glory. But somehow I could not manage it. I went meekly aboard a few of the boats that lay packed together like sardines at the long St. Louis wharf, and humbly inquired for the pilots, but got only a cold shoulder and short words from mates and clerks. I had to make the best of this sort of treatment for the time being, but I had comforting daydreams of a future when I should be a great and honored pilot, with plenty of money, and could kill some of these mates and clerks and pay for them.

STUDY QUESTIONS

1. This very concrete description provides some excellent illustrations of some standard principles for the arrangement of details within a paragraph. What principle governs the arrangement of materials in the second paragraph, for example? Examine several other paragraphs and explain the principle of organization in them.

2. Why is the description of the town at the arrival of the steamboat so successful?

3. Note that the description of the steamboat's arrival consists of two contrasting parts. Compare the verbs used in these two sections to see if they add to the contrasting effect.

4. In the description of the boy who succeeded in becoming a steamboatman, what double awareness operates to produce the humor?

5. What is Twain's attitude toward the town he describes?

6. Write a description of some place which, like the town in this description, has a very different appearance on different occasions. Possibilities are a gym when it is empty and when it is being used, a street on a sunny day or in the rain, a shop at a busy time and at a slack one.

Jesse Stuart   Child's Time and Clock Time*

When I was a boy, I knew what a clock was. My mother had one which sat on the mantel and ticked the time away. I was glad I didn't sleep in this room so I wouldn't have to hear it. I didn't like the ticking of a clock. In those days I slept upstairs alone in this very house where we live today.

We had an alarm clock which my father set on a chair by his bed to wake him at four. He would get up, build fires in the fireplace and kitchen stove, feed his hogs, horses, and cows, and then eat his own breakfast and be off before daylight (in winter) to the railroad section four miles away. Dad often walked to work by lantern light or by starlight. Sometimes he went by bright moonlight. But when his alarm clock went off, we could hear the noise all over this house. After this clock's strange mechanical sound, I found it difficult to go to sleep again. I learned at the age of eight that an alarm clock can be an extremely disturbing thing in one's life.

Then Dad had a watch, which kept almost perfect time. He used to have me sit on his lap and show me this timepiece. He told me about what a wonderful thing this watch was, and he taught me to tell time by it. I learned how man measured time before I knew exactly what time was. Time was something to me, when I was a child, like wind and water. Time was flowing and eternal, like an invisible river. We could divide it into seconds, minutes, hours, days, weeks, months, and years, but that didn't bring us any closer to it. There were yesterdays, and time was with us now, and there would be tomorrows.

I had my way of dividing time. I didn't use a watch or a clock. My day started in the early morning when the sun came up. Then there were the hours of light, which were not long enough, and finally nighttime, which I loved for its beauty but hated because it sent me to bed. And there were the four seasons. These were my simple measurements of time. I didn't remember the day of the week nor the hour of the day. These didn't matter.

When I was a boy and played on the W-Hollow hill slopes and down in the valleys by the little streams, when I waded up and down the main W-Hollow stream and pinhooked minnows and killed water snakes with sticks, the only ticking of the seconds I heard was the falling of water over the rocks. This was the soft rhythmical beating of time. This was the noise that time made. When I hunted at night and crept under rock cliffs to get out of a rainstorm, I would lie on dry leaves and listen to raindrops dripping from the rocks to

* Reprinted by permission from *The Year of My Rebirth*, by Jesse Stuart, published by McGraw-Hill Book Company, Inc. Copyright, 1956, Jesse Stuart.

the ground. This was another noise that time made. And when the winds blew, fast or slow, their rhythms recorded the passing of time. When the dark, ugly storm clouds raced across the sky, or when the white thunderheads floated out, lazylike, across the blue, it was the passing of time. All my work and all my play in those days were measured by this sort of time. This was the natural schedule that I grew up by.

The dripping of rain from the rock cliffs or the falling of leaves through the bright air never hurried me. I took my time. I had plenty of it for dreams. The warm winds of summer made me lazy and detached. The autumn winds made me sad. The winter winds shrill and cold, made me hustle. And the soft spring winds stirred me to awareness of life's reawakening. I didn't need a watch in those days. I never was a clock watcher.

In fact I never owned a watch until after I began teaching school. First I borrowed my father's watch. Later I forced myself to wear one until I got used to it. Gradually my watch became a natural part of my clothing which was hard for me to do without. Minutes and seconds began to count. I was on a tight man-made schedule. I couldn't escape it. I not only needed a watch, but I had to have an accurate one like Dad's "railroad" watch. It had to keep the exact time. For trains and planes were usually on schedule and wouldn't wait for me. And at the other end somebody was there to meet me. I had to lecture at a certain hour. I had to be out of the hotel at this or that time of day. That constant tension of man-made time gripped me in a vice.

This is the "tight schedule." It is one in which minutes are big things, hours are actually precious. The watch that keeps perfect time is on the wrist. A man flicks his arm up again and again to keep up with the flow of seconds and minutes.

And then there was my heart. I treated my heart like a clock, too. Not that I remembered it often. No, I never gave it a thought. But I wound it too tight.

Now these tight schedules are fast becoming memories for me, like the old clock that sat on the mantel, the alarm clock on the chair beside my father's bed, and his watch that was inspected by the railroad company so he would be to his work on time. I'm back now on nature's schedule. My timepieces are rain, wind, and the seasons. I can tell by the sun in the morning about what time of day it is. I know the hour certain species of birds get hungry and fly in for their breakfast. I know the time of morning the ground squirrels make a noise about their feeding. I know the time the redbirds sing, for they waken me at four-thirty each morning. Happily, I listen to them and then go back to sleep. I would rather have them wake me with a song at four-thirty than leap up at an alarm clock's buzzing at seven.

I hear time dripping from the cliffs and bluffs to the leaves below. I've about lost the habit of throwing up my arm every few seconds to glance at my watch. I have other ways of telling time. I have the ways of my youth.

STUDY QUESTIONS

1. *How do the different attitudes toward time divide the essay naturally into three sections?*

2. *What contrasts between the child's world and the adult's world are suggested by the different ways of measuring time?*

3. *Compare the children's "original" ideas of time in this essay and the one by Winifred Welles, "The Attic." In what ways do the two agree? In what ways do both disagree with the adult conception of time?*

4. *At the end of the essay, the grown invalid finds that he has begun to measure time by nature, as he did in his childhood. However, in what way is his way of telling time by nature different from the childhood way?*

5. *Note that at the end of the essay the author seems to feel that his childhood self was wiser about this subject than his adult self. Have you ever come to the conclusion that children are more perceptive or more realistic about some things than adults? Write a theme explaining this.*

6. *Would it be possible for you to keep track of time without a watch, by events in your environment? Write a theme arguing that watches are unnecessary, and that people might be better off without them.*

2. THE READER AS ARTIST

Holbrook Jackson   Writer and Reader*

Writer and reader have much in common. They are both performers and each plays a part to himself, and often for himself, whether before an audience or not. If, as Somerset Maugham holds, the writer is 'the Comedian who never loses himself in the part, for he is at the same time spectator and actor,' the same may be claimed for the reader who must involuntarily place himself in the attitude of the writer without losing his own identity, for he is at the same time reader, or spectator, and (by proxy) writer, or actor, as well. When he seeks to unveil the writer he unveils himself and the subsequent revelation is also a creation.

But that after all is only one phase of art. There is artistry in perception, in point of view, and in attitude. To be an artist you must first possess a sensibility which will give distinction and significance to what you perceive, and with that gift and the power to use the results of imagination you remain an artist whether you have a public or not, or whether you make something

* From *The Reading of Books*, by Holbrook Jackson, copyright, 1947, by Charles Scribner's Sons. Reprinted by permission of Charles Scribner's Sons and Faber & Faber, Ltd.

tangible or not; for just as a violinist may perform for himself alone and be an artist, so may a reader become an artist by using books to express himself to himself. When you enjoy, that is absorb, a poetical or prose work, you re-create it for yourself in your own mind. It becomes your own.

If writing, therefore, is existence to the writer (that is to say, the point at which expression and consciousness merge), if the writer writes to become himself or to discover himself, for becoming and discovering are allied, so also is reading to the reader. The reader reads to express, to discover, to become, but books not pens and paper are the media of his art. The reader has many other points of resemblance to the writer; one of the most important is that both are subject to the same general conditions of life. Their responses to these conditions are different not in kind but in depth and quality of expres-sion; the same degree of response existing between reader and reader, as, indeed, between artist and artist. There are no means of measuring degrees of aesthetic experience, but we all know that they exist. Everyone to a greater or lesser degree is conditioned intellectually and emotionally by his environ-ment and the differences between creation and absorption are technical. Reading as well as writing is a part of the technique of the art of literature. One may write books, another read them, and some do both; but the unre-solved intentions and the immeasurable qualities of the processes are iden-tical.[1] ...

Reading is an adventure with some of the characteristics of the chase. Yet when we adventure among masterpieces with the object, say, of tracking down Pater's 'last lurking delicacies of colour and form,' not finally for the sake of their colour and form but for what impelled those qualities, we are explorers rather than hunters, observers rather than devotees. We confer, exchange, and compare ourselves with them. We win most not by absorbing them wholly, nor yet by following them implicitly, but by holding our own and remaining ourselves. Paul Valéry had this sense of exploration centred in self. When he was studying Leonardo da Vinci, he wandered so far into his subject that he did not know how to return but consoled himself with the thought that 'every road leads back to oneself.'[2]

It is only by temporarily losing ourselves that we may hear those inward intimations which are often awakened by a book and are its best reward. For an author can give us little compared with what we may take from him. The best he can do is to make us aware of inward riches which we already possess. 'What the writer does,' says Katharine Mansfield, 'is not so much to *solve* the

---

[1] 'A poet may be able to appreciate the merit of each particular Part of his own poem as well, or (if he have a well-disciplined mind) better than any other can do; but the *effect* of the whole as a whole, he cannot from the very nature of things (from the fore-knowledge of each following part, from the parts having been written at different times, from the blending of the pleasures and disgusts of composing with the composi-tion itself, etc.) have the same sensation as the Reader or auditor to whom the whole is new and simultaneous.' S. T. Coleridge, 1811, *Unpublished Letters*. Ed. E. R. Griggs (1932), ii, 64.

[2] *Introduction to the Methods of Leonardo da Vinci*. Trans. McGreevy (1920), 14.

question but to *put* the question.' The skilled reader, in Montaigne's phrase, 'puts his ear close to himself, and holds his breath and listens.'

When Schopenhauer said that reading was merely thinking with other people's brains, he was right. Reading is even further in that direction. It is becoming someone else for the time being and running the risk of remaining so. When we read we do not so much enter into the souls of others; we let them enter into us. We become Shakespeare or his characters—Hamlet, Falstaff, Antony, Touchstone. When we read Schopenhauer we become Schopenhauer, which was probably what Schopenhauer intended. When we read Whitman we may become Whitman, which was what Whitman intended although he seemed to deny it when he said that his best disciple was the one who learnt how to destroy the master. And that also is what all fit readers intend. They do not read in order to become someone else. They read in order to become more fully and more distinctly themselves. They go forth from themselves and after a while they return home having gained something and lost something. Thus reading becomes an experience, and although it may begin by prolongation through the imagination of the author's experience, it ends by becoming a part of the reader's consciousness, by a process of absorption, in itself an experience which can in certain circumstances be as impressive as that which originally inspired the author. Far from being a question of subjection no great book can be adequately appreciated unless it is read with something of the quality that went to its making. We can't all hope to be geniuses, nor is that necessary or desirable, any more than it is necessary or desirable that all readers should become writers: the end of reading is living, not reading or writing. Reading should tune our sensibilities to such a pitch that we are able to respond to the poet in the book and the poet in ourselves: a book is not read until the reader becomes its equal.

The test of such an experience is a desire to prolong it. Every sensitive reading of the kind should be followed by a feeling of satisfaction and reluctance to take up another book. We are content to brood on our new experience and to resent, for the time being, interference with what seems to be an established state of mind. A writer must, therefore, persuade or fight us before we accept him. Cunninghame Graham is convinced that the writer and the reader are sworn foes: 'The writer labouring for bread, for hopes of fame, from idleness, from too much energy or from that uncontrollable dance of St. Vitus in the muscles of the wrist which prompts so many men to write (the Lord knows why), works, blots, corrects, rewrites, revises, and improves; then publishes, and for the most part is incontinently damned. Then comes the reader cavalierly... and gingerly examining the book says it is rubbish, and that he wonders how people who should have something else to do, find time to spend their lives in writing trash.'[3] A writer must batter down the barricades of our prejudices, our criticisms, our resentments, and our

[3] R. B. Cunninghame Graham, *Thirteen Stories* (1900), Pref. ix.

complacencies, which are attempts to maintain our mental and spiritual possessions, and to conserve what we are. Great books are great victories rewarding instead of despoiling the vanquished. We benefit by surrender if we retain our integrity.

STUDY QUESTIONS

1. *In this selection, the author alludes to and quotes extensively from various writers. What, exactly, does he gain by this technique?*

2. *Jackson suggests that the "writer writes to become himself or to discover himself," and that the reader "reads to express, to discover, to become." Using details from the selections which precede and follow this essay, discuss how some of the writers and readers give evidence that this is true or false. In what ways, if any, have any of your own themes, or certain books that you have read, led to any self-discovery in the sense that Jackson means?*

3. *What does Jackson mean when he says that "the end of reading is living, not reading or writing"?*

4. *Jackson is discussing here only certain kinds of reading. What kinds of reading do not fall within his discussion? How and why are they different? Do you think they are less important or more important than the kinds Jackson is discussing?*

5. *Write a paper describing your experience with a book in which the author has succeeded in battering down "the barricades of your prejudices, criticisms, resentments, and complacencies."*

6. *Write a paper organized in a manner similar to that of Jackson's essay in which you explain the approach to and value of a kind of reading different from that which Jackson is discussing.*

Henry Miller On Dictionaries and Encyclopedias*

One morning, scarcely out of bed, I turned to my huge Funk & Wagnall's unabridged dictionary to look up a word which had come to my mind on awakening. As usual, one word led to another, for what is the dictionary if not the subtlest form of "circuit game" masquerading in the guise of a book? With Joe at my side, Joe the eternal sceptic, a discussion ensued which lasted the entire day and night, the search for more and more definitions never slackening. It was because of Joe O'Regan, who had stimulated me so often to question all that I had blindly accepted, that my first suspicions about the value of the dictionary were aroused. Prior to this moment I had taken the dictionary for granted, much as one does the Bible. I had believed,

as everyone does, that in obtaining a definition one got the meaning of, or
shall I say the "truth," about a word. But that day, shifting from derivation
to derivation, thereby stumbling upon the most amazing changes in meaning,
upon contradictions and reversals of earlier meanings, the whole framework
of lexicography began to slither and slide. In reaching the earliest "origin"
of a word I observed that one was up against a stone wall. Surely it was not
possible that the words we were looking up had entered human language at
the points indicated! To get back only as far as Sanskrit, Hebrew or Icelandic
(and what wonderful words stem from the Icelandic!) was nothing, in my
opinion. History had been pushed back more than ten thousand years, and
here were we, stranded at the vestibule, so to speak, of modern times. That so
many words of metaphysical and spiritual connotation, freely employed by
the Greeks, had lost all significance was in itself something to give us pause.
To be brief, it soon became apparent that the meaning of a word changed or
disappeared entirely, or became the very opposite, according to the time, place,
culture of the people using the term. The simple truth that life is what we
make it, how we see it with our whole being, and not what is given factually,
historically, or statistically, applies to language too. The one who seems least
to understand this is the philologist. But let me get on—from dictionary to
encyclopedia . . .

It was only natural, in jumping from meaning to meaning, in observing
the *uses* of the words we were tracking down, that for a fuller, deeper treatment we must have recourse to the encyclopaedia. The defining process, after
all, is one of reference and cross-reference. To know what a specific word
means one has to know the words which, so to speak, hedge it in. The meaning is never directly given; it is inferred, implied, or distilled out. And this
is probably because the original source is never known.

But the encyclopaedia! Ah, there perhaps we would be on firm ground!
We would look up subjects, not words. We would discover whence arose
these mystifying symbols over which men had fought and bled, tortured and
killed one another. Now there is a wonderful article in the Encyclopaedia
Britannica (the celebrated edition) on "Mysteries"[1] and, if one wishes to
pass a pleasant, amusing and instructive day at the library, by all means start
with a word such as "mysteries." It will lead you far and wide, it will send
you home reeling, indifferent to food, sleep and other claims of the autonomic
system. But you will never penetrate the mystery! And if, as the good scholar
usually does, you should be impelled to go from the "authorities" selected
by the encyclopaedic knowalls to other "authorities" on the same subject, you
will soon find your awe and reverence for the accumulated wisdom housed
in encyclopaedias withering and crumbling. It is well that one should become
méfiant in the face of this buried learning. Who, after all, are these pundits
entombed in the encyclopaedias? Are they the *final* authorities? Decidedly
not! The final authority must always be oneself. These wizened pundits have

---

[1] Even Annie Besant, I noticed just the other day, makes mention of this article, in
her book *Esoteric Christianity*.

"labored in the field," and they have garnered much wisdom. But it is neither divine wisdom nor even the sum of human wisdom (on any subject) which they offer us. They have worked like ants and beavers, and usually with as little humor and imagination as these humble creatures. One encyclopaedia selects *its* authorities, another *other* authorities. Authorities are always a drug on the market. When you have done with them you know a little about the subject of your quest and a great deal more about things of no account. More often than not you end up in despair, doubt and confusion. If you gain at all, it is in the sharper use of the questioning faculty, that faculty which Spengler extols and which he distinguishes as the chief contribution made him by Nietzsche.

The more I think of it the more I believe that the unwitting contribution made me by the makers of encyclopedias was to foster the lazy, pleasurable pursuit of learning—the most foolish of all pastimes. To read the encyclopedia was like taking a drug—one of those drugs of which they say that it has no evil effects, is non habit-forming. Like the sound, stable, sensible Chinese of old, I think the use of opium preferable. If one wishes to relax, to enjoy surcease from care, to stimulate the imagination—and what could be more conducive to mental, moral and spiritual health?—then I would say the judicious use of opium is far better than the spurious drug of the encyclopedia.

Looking back upon my days in the library—curious that I do not recall my *first* visit to a library!—I liken them to the days spent by an opium addict in his little cell. I went regularly for my "dose" and I got it. Often I read at random, whatever book came to hand. Sometimes I buried myself in technical works, or in handbooks, or the "curiosa" of literature. There was one shelf in the reading room of the New York 42nd Street library, I recall, which was packed with mythologies (of many countries, many peoples) and which I devoured like a starved rat. Sometimes, impelled as if by an ardent mission, I burrowed in nomenclatures alone. There were other times when it seemed imperative—and indeed it *was* imperative, so deep was my trance—to study the habits of moles or whales, or the thousand and one varieties of ophidians. A word like "ecliptic," encountered for the first time, might set me off on a chase that would last for weeks, leaving me stranded eventually in the stellar depths this side of Scorpio.

STUDY QUESTIONS

1. *What does Miller mean when he says that "to read the encyclopaedia was like taking a drug"? Would he say the same thing of the dictionary? Does the rest of the selection bear out this generalization, or does it contradict it?*

2. *How is the author's statement that life is "what we make it, how we see it with our whole being" related to the ideas of Read and Thomas in the first two selections of this anthology?*

3. *To what extent is it true that the dictionary is a subtle form of "circuit game"? You may want to look ahead at Beardsley's discussion of "contexts and vagueness" in the section on language, thought, and ideas in discussing this question.*

4. *What purpose do you think is served by the kind of random, omnivorous reading among "curiosa," which Miller describes here? Is it as valuable as orderly, well organized reading on selected topics? Why?*

5. *Write a paper describing an experience in which you have tried to find the "truth" about some piece of information.*

6. *Select some word such as "Mysteries" and follow it through, say, the* Oxford English Dictionary *and several encyclopedias. Then write a paper describing what you have discovered.*

H. L. Mencken   I Discover "Huckleberry Finn"*

*J*f I undertook to tell you the effect it ["Huckleberry Finn"] had upon me my talk would sound frantic, and even delirious. Its impact was genuinely terrific. I had not gone further than the first incomparable chapter before I realized, child though I was, that I had entered a domain of new and gorgeous wonders, and thereafter I pressed on steadily to the last word. My gait, of course, was still slow, but it became steadily faster as I proceeded. As the blurbs on the slip-covers of murder mysteries say, I simply couldn't put the book down. After dinner that evening, braving a possible uproar, I took it into the family sitting-room, and resumed it while my father searched the *Evening News* hopefully for reports of the arrest, clubbing and hanging of labor leaders. Anon, he noticed what I was at, and demanded to know the name of the book I was reading. When I held up the green volume his comment was "Well, I'll be durned!"

I sensed instantly that there was no reproof in this, but a kind of shy rejoicing. Then he told me that he had once been a great reader of Mark Twain himself—in his younger days. He had got hold of all the volumes as they came out—"The Innocents" in 1869, when he was still a boy himself; "Roughing It" in 1872, "The Gilded Age" in 1873, "Tom Sawyer" in 1876, "A Tramp Abroad" in 1880, the year of my birth, and so on down to date. (All these far from pristine firsts are still in the Biblioteca Menckeniana in Hollins street, minus a few that were lent to neighbor boys and never returned, and had to be replaced.) My father read them in the halcyon days before children, labor troubles and Grover Cleveland had begun to frazzle him, and he still got them down from the shelf on quiet evenings, after the first-named were packed off to bed. But a man of advancing years and cares had to consider also the sorrows of the world, and so he read in Mark less than aforetime.

As for me, I proceeded to take the whole canon at a gulp—and presently

* Reprinted from *Happy Days*, by H. L. Mencken, by permission of Alfred A. Knopf, Inc. Copyright, 1939, 1940, by Alfred A. Knopf, Inc.

gagged distressfully. "Huckleberry Finn," of course, was as transparent to a boy of eight as to a man of eighty, and almost as pungent and exhilarating, but there were passages in "A Tramp Abroad" that baffled me, and many more in "The Innocents," and a whole swarm in "A Gilded Age." I well recall wrestling with the woodcut by W. F. Brown on page 113 of the "Tramp." It shows five little German girls swinging on a heavy chain stretched between two stone posts on a street in Heilbronn, and the legend under it is "Generations of Bare Feet." That legend is silly, for all the girls have shoes on, but what puzzled me about it was something quite different. It was a confusion between the word *generation* and the word *federation,* which latter was often in my father's speech in those days, for the American Federation of Labor had got under way only a few years before, and was just beginning in earnest to harass and alarm employers. Why I didn't consult the dictionary (or my mother, or my father himself) I simply can't tell you. At eight or nine, I suppose, intelligence is no more than a small spot of light on the floor of a large and murky room. So instead of seeking help I passed on, wondering idiotically what possible relation there could be between a gang of little girls in pigtails and the Haymarket anarchists, and it was six or seven years later before the "Tramp" became clear to me, and began to delight me.

It then had the curious effect of generating in me both a great interest in Germany and a vast contempt for the German language. I was already aware, of course, that the Mencken family was of German origin, for my Grandfather Mencken, in his care for me as *Stammhalter,* did not neglect to describe eloquently its past glories at the German universities, and to expound its connections to the most remote degrees. But my father, who was only half German, had no apparent interest in either the German land or its people, and when he spoke of the latter at all, which was not often, it was usually in sniffish terms. He never visited Germany, and never signified any desire to do so, though I recall my mother suggesting, more than once, that a trip there would be swell. It was "A Tramp Abroad" that made me German-conscious, and I still believe that it is the best guide-book to Germany ever written. Today, of course, it is archaic, but it was still reliable down to 1910, when I made my own first trip. The uproarious essay on "The Awful German Language," which appears at the end of it as an appendix, worked the other way. That is to say, it confirmed my growing feeling, born of my struggles with the conjugations and declensions taught at F. Knapp's Institute, that German was an irrational and even insane tongue, and not worth the sufferings of a freeborn American. These diverse impressions have continued with me ever since. I am still convinced that Germany, in the intervals of peace, is the most pleasant country to travel in ever heard of, and I am still convinced that the German language is of a generally preposterous and malignant character.

"Huck," of course, was my favorite, and I read it over and over. In fact,

I read it regularly not less than annually down to my forties, and only a few months ago I hauled it out and read it once more—and found it as magnificent as ever. Only one other book, down to the beginning of my teens, ever beset me with a force even remotely comparable to its smash, and that was a volume called "Boys' Useful Pastimes," by "Prof. Robert Griffith, A.M., principal of Newton High School." This was given to me by my Grandmother Mencken at Christmas, 1889, and it remained my constant companion for at least six years. The sub-title describes its contents: "Pleasant and profitable amusement for spare hours, comprising chapters on the use and care of tools, and detailed instructions by means of which boys can make with their own hands a large number of toys, household ornaments, scientific appliances, and many pretty, amusing and necessary articles for the playground, the house and out-of-doors." Manual training was still a novelty in those days, and I suspect that the professor was no master of it, for many of his plans and specifications were completely unintelligible to me, and also to all the neighborhood boys who dropped in to help and advise. I doubt, indeed, that any human being on earth, short of an astrophysicist, could have made anything of his directions for building boat models. But in other cases he was relatively explicit and understandable, and my brother Charlie and I, after long efforts, managed to make a steam-engine (or, more accurately, a steam-mill) according to his recipe. The boiler was a baking-powder tin, and the steam, issuing out of a small hole in the top, operated a sort of fan or mill-wheel. How we provided heat to make steam I forget, but I remember clearly that my mother considered the process dangerous, and ordered us to take the engine out of the cellar and keep it in the backyard.

I had no more mechanical skill than a cow, but I also managed to make various other things that the professor described, including a what-not for the parlor (my mother professed to admire it, but never put it into service), a rabbit-trap (set in the backyard, it never caught anything, not even a cat), and a fancy table ornamented with twigs from the pear tree arranged in more or less geometrical designs. "Boys' Useful Pastimes" was printed by A. L. Burt on stout paper, and remains extant to this day—a rather remarkable fact, for other boys often borrowed it, and sometimes they kept it on their workbenches for a long while, and thumbed it diligently. One of those boys was Johnnie Sponsler, whose father kept a store in the Frederick road, very near Hollins street. Johnnie was vastly interested in electricity, as indeed were most other boys of the time, for such things as electric lights, motors, telephones and doorbells were just coming in. He thus made hard use of Professor Griffith's Part VII, which was headed "Scientific Apparatus and Experiments," and included directions for making a static machine, and for electroplating door-keys. He later abandoned the sciences for the postal service, and is now, I believe, retired. "Boys' Useful Pastimes," and my apparent interest in it, may have been responsible for my father's decision to transfer me from F. Knapp's Institute to the Baltimore Polytechnic in 1892.

If so, it did me an evil service in the end, for my native incapacity for mechanics made my studies at the Polytechnic a sheer waste of time, though I managed somehow to pass the examinations, even in such abysmal subjects as steam engineering.

The influence of "Huck Finn" was immensely more powerful and durable. It not only reinforced my native aversion to the common run of boys' books; it also set me upon a systematic exploration of all the volumes in the old secretary, and before I finished with them I had looked into every one of them, including even Brother Schultz's sombre history of Freemasonry in Maryland. How many were actually intelligible to a boy of eight, nine, ten? I should say about a fourth. I managed to get through most of Dickens, but only by dint of hard labor, and it was not until I discovered Thackeray, at fourteen, that the English novel really began to lift me. George Eliot floored me as effectively as a text in Hittite, and to the present day I have never read "Adam Bede" or "Daniel Deronda" or "The Mill on the Floss," or developed any desire to do so. So far as I am concerned, they will remain mere names to the end of the chapter, and as hollow and insignificant as the names of Gog and Magog.

But I plowed through Chambers' Encyclopedia relentlessly, beginning with the shortest articles and gradually working my way into the longer ones. The kitchen-midden of irrelevant and incredible information that still burdens me had its origins in those pages, and I almost wore them out acquiring it. I read, too, the whole of Lossing, nearly all of Charlotte M. Yonge, and even some of Duyckinck, perhaps the dullest historian ever catalogued by faunal naturalists on this or any other earth. My brother Charlie and I enjoyed "Our Living World" chiefly because of the colored pictures, but I also read long stretches of it, and astonished my father by calling off the names of nearly all the wild beasts when the circus visited Baltimore in 1889. Finally, I recall reading both "Life Among the Mormons" and "One Thousand Proofs That the Earth Is Not a Globe."

Thus launched upon the career of a bookworm, I presently began to reach out right and left for more fodder. When the Enoch Pratt Free Library of Baltimore opened a branch in Hollins street, in March, 1886, I was still a shade too young to be excited, but I had a card before I was nine, and began an almost daily harrying of the virgins at the delivery desk. In 1888 my father subscribed to *Once-a-Week,* the predecessor of *Collier's,* and a little while later there began to come with it a long series of cheap reprints of contemporary classics, running from Tennyson's poems to Justin M'Carthy's "History of Our Own Times"; and simultaneously there appeared from parts unknown a similar series of cheap reprints of scientific papers, including some of Herbert Spencer. I read them all, sometimes with shivers of puzzlement and sometimes with delight, but always calling for more. I began to inhabit a world that was two-thirds letterpress and only one-third trees, fields, streets and people. I acquired round shoulders, spindly shanks, and a despondent view of humanity. I read everything that I could find in English, taking in some of it but boggling most of it.

This madness ran on until I reached adolescence, and began to distinguish between one necktie and another, and to notice the curiously divergent shapes, dispositions and aromas of girls. Then, gradually, I began to let up.

But to this day I am still what might be called a reader, and have a high regard for authors.

STUDY QUESTIONS

1. *What is notable or unusual about the vocabulary used by Mencken? Compare it to that of Miller in the preceding selection.*
2. *On what principle is this selection organized? Are discussions like those of the author's confusion between generation and federation irrelevant digressions?*
3. *To what extent is the random reading of Mencken pretty much like that described by Miller in the preceding selection? Is Mencken's attitude toward it the same? Explain.*
4. *Is any progress observable in the kind of reading Mencken did?*
5. *Does Mencken's choice of reading matter show any particular tastes? How do you account for his liking or disliking certain books? Is this related to Holbrook Jackson's thesis that the reader "discovers himself"?*
6. *Write a theme relating your experiences with a book which you read as a child and which you think has had a lasting influence on you.*

Graham Greene   The Lost Childhood*

Perhaps it is only in childhood that books have any deep influence on our lives. In later life we admire, we are entertained, we may modify some views we already hold, but we are more likely to find in books merely a confirmation of what is in our minds already: as in a love affair it is our own features that we see reflected flatteringly back.

But in childhood all books are books of divination, telling us about the future, and like the fortune teller who sees a long journey in the cards or death by water they influence the future. I suppose that is why books excited us so much. What do we ever get nowadays from reading to equal the excitement and the revelation in those first fourteen years? Of course I should be interested to hear that a new novel by Mr. E. M. Forster was going to appear this spring, but I could never compare that mild expectation of civilized pleasure with the missed heartbeat, the appalled glee I felt when I found on a library shelf a novel by Rider Haggard, Percy Westerman, Captain Brereton or Stanley Weyman which I had not read before. No, it is in those early years that I would look for the crisis, the moment when life took a new slant in its journey towards death.

I remember distinctly the suddenness with which a key turned in a lock and I found I could read—not just the sentences in a reading book with the syllables coupled like railway carriages, but a real book. It was paper-covered with the picture of a boy, bound and gagged, dangling at the end of a rope inside a well with the water rising above his waist—an adventure of Dixon Brett, detective. All a long summer holiday I kept my secret, as I believed: I did not want anybody to know that I could read. I suppose I half consciously realized even then that this was the dangerous moment. I was safe so long as I could not read—the wheels had not begun to turn, but now the future stood around on bookshelves everywhere waiting for the child to choose—the life of a chartered accountant perhaps, a colonial civil servant, a planter in China, a steady job in a bank, happiness and misery, eventually one particular form of death, for surely we choose our death much as we choose our job. It grows out of our acts and our evasions, out of our fears and out of our moments of courage. I suppose my mother must have discovered my secret, for on the journey home I was presented for the train with another real book, a copy of Ballantyne's *Coral Island* with only a single picture to look at, a coloured frontispiece. But I would admit nothing. All the long journey I stared at the one picture and never opened the book.

But there on the shelves at home (so many shelves for we were a large family) the books waited—one book in particular, but before I reach that one down let me take a few others at random from the shelf. Each was a crystal in which the child dreamed that he saw life moving. Here in a cover stamped dramatically in several colours was Captain Gilson's *The Pirate Aeroplane*. I must have read that book six times at least—the story of a lost civilization in the Sahara and of a villainous Yankee pirate with an aeroplane like a box kite and bombs the size of tennis balls who held the golden city to ransom. It was saved by the hero, a young subaltern who crept up to the pirate camp to put the aeroplane out of action. He was captured and watched his enemies dig his grave. He was to be shot at dawn, and to pass the time and keep his mind from uncomfortable thoughts the amiable Yankee pirate played cards with him—the mild nursery game of Kuhn Kan. The memory of that nocturnal game on the edge of life haunted me for years, until I set it to rest at last in one of my own novels with a game of poker played in remotely similar circumstances.

And here is *Sophy of Kravonia* by Anthony Hope—the story of a kitchen-maid who became a queen. One of the first films I ever saw, about 1911, was made from that book, and I can hear still the rumble of the Queen's guns crossing the high Kravonian pass beaten hollowly out on a single piano. Then

there was Stanley Weyman's *The Story of Francis Cludde,* and above all
other books at that time of my life, *King Solomon's Mines.*

This book did not perhaps provide the crisis, but it certainly influenced
the future. If it had not been for that romantic tale of Allan Quatermain,
Sir Henry Curtis, Captain Good, and, above all, the ancient witch Gagool,
would I at nineteen have studied the appointments list of the Colonial
Office and very nearly picked on the Nigerian Navy for a career? And later,
when surely I ought to have known better, the odd African fixation remained.
In 1935 I found myself sick with fever on a camp bed in a Liberian native's
hut with a candle going out in an empty whiskey bottle and a rat moving in
the shadows. Wasn't it the incurable fascination of Gagool with her bare yellow skull, the wrinkled scalp that moved and contracted like the hood of a
cobra, that led me to work all through 1942 in a little stuffy office in Freetown,
Sierra Leone? There is not much in common between the land of the
Kukuanas, behind the desert and the mountain range of Sheba's Breast, and
a tin-roofed house on a bit of swamp where the vultures moved like domestic
turkeys and the pi-dogs kept me awake on moonlight nights with their wail-
ing, and the white women yellowed by atebrin drove by to the club; but the
two belonged at any rate to the same continent, and, however distantly, to
the same region of the imagination—the region of uncertainty, of not knowing the way about. Once I came a little nearer to Gagool and her witch-
hunters, one night in Zigita on the Liberian side of the French Guinea
border, when my servants sat in their shuttered hut with their hands over
their eyes and someone beat a drum and a whole town stayed behind closed
doors while the big bush devil—whom it would mean blindness to see—
moved between the huts.

But *King Solomon's Mines* could not finally satisfy. It was not the right
answer. The key did not quite fit. Gagool I could recognize—didn't she
wait for me in dreams every night in the passage by the linen cupboard, near
the nursery door? and she continues to wait, when the mind is sick or tired,
though now she is dressed in the theological garments of Despair and speaks
in Spenser's accents:

> The longer life, I wote the greater sin,
> The greater sin, the greater punishment.

Yes, Gagool has remained a permanent part of the imagination, but Quatermain and Curtis—weren't they, even when I was only ten years old, a little
too good to be true? They were men of such unyielding integrity (they
would only admit to a fault in order to show how it might be overcome) that
the wavering personality of a child could not rest for long against those
monumental shoulders. A child, after all, knows most of the game—it is only
an attitude to it that he lacks. He is quite well aware of cowardice, shame,
deception, disappointment. Sir Henry Curtis perched upon a rock bleeding
from a dozen wounds but fighting on with the remnant of the Greys against

the hordes of Twala was too heroic. These men were like Platonic ideas: they were not life as one had already begun to know it.

But when—perhaps I was fourteen by that time—I took Miss Marjorie Bowen's *The Viper of Milan* from the library shelf, the future for better or worse really struck. From that moment I began to write. All the other possible futures slid away: the potential civil servant, the don, the clerk had to look for other incarnations. Imitation after imitation of Miss Bowen's magnificent novel went into exercise books—stories of sixteenth-century Italy or twelfth-century England marked with enormous brutality and a despairing romanticism. It was as if I had been supplied once and for all with a subject.

Why? On the surface *The Viper of Milan* is only the story of a war between Gian Galeazzo Visconti, Duke of Milan, and Mastino della Scala, Duke of Verona, told with zest and cunning and an amazing pictorial sense. Why did it creep in and colour and explain the terrible living world of the stone stairs and the never quiet dormitory? It was no good in that real world to dream that one would ever be a Sir Henry Curtis, but della Scala who at last turned from an honesty that never paid and betrayed his friends and died dishonoured and a failure even at treachery—it was easier for a child to escape behind his mask. As for Visconti, with his beauty, his patience and his genius for evil, I had watched him pass by many a time in his black Sunday suit smelling of mothballs. His name was Carter. He exercised terror from a distance like a snowcloud over the young fields. Goodness has only once found a perfect incarnation in a human body and never will again, but evil can always find a home there. Human nature is not black and white but black and grey. I read all that in *The Viper of Milan* and I looked round and I saw that it was so.

There was another theme I found there. At the end of *The Viper of Milan* —you will remember if you have once read it—comes the great scene of complete success—della Scala is dead, Ferrara, Verona, Novara, Mantua have all fallen, the messengers pour in with news of fresh victories, the whole world outside is cracking up, and Visconti sits and jokes in the wine light. I was not on the classical side or I would have discovered, I suppose, in Greek literature instead of in Miss Bowen's novel the sense of doom that lies over success—the feeling that the pendulum is about to swing. That too made sense; one looked around and saw the doomed everywhere—the champion runner who one day would sag over the tape; the head of the school who would atone, poor devil, during forty dreary undistinguished years; the scholar . . . and when success began to touch oneself too, however mildly, one could only pray that failure would not be held off for too long.

One had lived for fourteen years in a wild jungle country without a map, but now the paths had been traced and naturally one had to follow them. But I think it was Miss Bowen's apparent zest that made me want to write. One could not read her without believing that to write was to live and to enjoy, and before one had discovered one's mistake it was too late—the first book one does enjoy. Anyway she had given me my pattern—religion might later explain it to me in other terms, but the pattern was already there— perfect evil walking the world where perfect good can never walk again, and only the pendulum ensures that after all in the end justice is done. Man is never satisfied, and often I have wished that my hand had not moved further than *King Solomon's Mines,* and that the future I had taken down from the nursery shelf had been a district office in Sierra Leone and twelve tours of malarial duty and a finishing dose of blackwater fever when the danger of retirement approached. What is the good of wishing? The books are always there, the moment of crisis waits, and now our children in their turn are taking down the future and opening the pages. In his poem "Germinal" A.E. wrote:

> In ancient shadows and twilights
>   Where childhood had stayed,
> The world's great sorrows were born
>   And its heroes were made.
> In the lost boyhood of Judas
>   Christ was betrayed.

STUDY QUESTIONS

1. *What does Greene mean by saying that in childhood all books are "books of divination"?*
2. *In what way did his reading merge with the outside world he experienced, even when he was an adult?*
3. *What did* The Viper of Milan *supply that Greene did not find in* King Solomon's Mines?
4. *Is it fair to conclude, from Greene's report of his own experience, that "trash" can feed a child's imagination just as effectively as carefully-chosen reading matter?*
5. *Write a theme describing some of the books you read as a child, and explaining why you think you remember them.*
6. *Can you attribute some of your present interests, as Greene does, to the influence of books or movies you encountered when you were very young? If so, write a theme describing this situation.*

Phyllis McGinley   The Consolations of Illiteracy *

There is something to be said for a bad education. By any standards mine was deplorable; and I deplored it for years, in private and in public. I flaunted it as if it were a medal, a kind of cultural Purple Heart which both excused my deficiencies and lent luster to my mild achievements. But as time goes on I murmur against it less. I find that even ignorance has its brighter side.

For if I grew up no better instructed about the world of books than was Columbus about global geography, I had in store for me, as he did, the splendors of discovery. There is such a thing as a literary landscape; to that, to nearly the whole length and breadth of classic English writing, I came as an astonished stranger. No one who first enters that country on a conducted tour can have any notion what it is like to travel it alone, on foot, and at his own pace.

I am not exaggerating. My education really was bad. As a child I lived on a ranch in Colorado with the nearest one-room schoolhouse four miles away and the roads nearly impassable in winter. Sometimes there was no teacher for the school, sometimes my brother and I were the only pupils. If there was a public library within practical distance I never learned of it. We were a reading family but my father's library ran chiefly to history and law and the collected works of Bulwer-Lytton. I wolfed down what I could but found a good deal of it indigestible. In my teens neither the public high school of a very small Western town nor the decorous boarding school I later attended made much effort to mend the damage. It seems to me now that we were always having to make reports on "Ivanhoe" or repeat from memory passages from Burke's "Speech on Conciliation." I think in two separate English classes we spent most of the year parsing "Snowbound."

However, it was at college I seriously managed to learn nothing. My alma mater was one of those universities founded and supplied by the state which in the West everybody attends as automatically as kindergarten. There are —or were then—no entrance examinations. Anybody could come and everybody did, for the proms and the football games; and they sat under a faculty which for relentless mediocrity must have outstripped any in the land. So by putting my mind to it, I was able to emerge from four years there quite uncorrupted by knowledge. Let me amend that to literary knowledge. Somewhere along the line, out of a jumble of courses in Sociology, Household

Chemistry, Hygiene, Beginner's German, I remember picking up bits and pieces of learning designed to enrich my life: the Theory of Refrigeration; the fact that Old German and Anglo-Saxon were two languages balefully akin and equally revolting; and the law about no offspring's having eyes darker than the eyes of the darker of his two parents. I had also, in one semester, been made to bolt Shakespeare entire, including the sonnets; and the result of such forced feeding had left me with an acute allergy to the Bard I was years getting over. Otherwise, few Great Books had impinged on my life. Through a complicated system of juggling credits and wheedling heads of departments, I had been able to evade even the Standard General Survey of English Literature.

I had read things, of course. I was even considered quite a bookworm by my sorority sisters, who had given up going to the library after polishing off "The Wizard of Oz." But it was the contemporaries who occupied me. I had read Mencken but not Marlowe, Atherton but not Austen, Hoffenstein but not Herrick, Shaw but not Swift, Kipling but not Keats, Millay but not Marvell. Unbelievable as it may seem to an undergraduate, I had never even read A. E. Housman. Although I had scribbled verses in my notebooks during geology lectures, I had not so much as heard of Herbert or Donne or Gay or Prior or Hopkins. I had shunned Chaucer and avoided Dryden. Oliver Goldsmith I knew by hearsay as the author of a dull novel called "The Vicar of Wakefield." Milton had written solely in order to plague the young with "Il Penseroso." I hadn't read "Vanity Fair" or "Ethan Frome" or "Essay on Man" or "Anna Karenina" or "The Hound of Heaven" or "The Dubliners." (Joyce was a contemporary but the furore over "Ulysses" was a mist that obscured his younger work.) Almost none of the alleged classics, under whose burden the student is supposed to bow, had I peered into either for pleasure or for credit.

As a consequence, although I came to them late, I came to them without prejudice. We met on a basis completely friendly; and I do not think the well-educated can always claim as much.

I commiserate, indeed, with people for whom "Silas Marner" was once required reading. They tell me it left permanent scars on their childhood; and I am certain they could not approach George Eliot as openmindedly as I did, only a year or two ago, when I tried "Adam Bede" as one might try for the first time an olive. "But it's magnificent!" I went around exclaiming to my friends. "I've been deceived! You told me Eliot was dull."

I pity the unlucky ones who wrote compositions on "Richardson as the Father of the English Novel." They could never come, relaxed and amused, upon "Pamela" as if it were a brand-new book. The literate may cherish as dearly as I do such disparate joys as "The Deserted Village" or "Pride and Prejudice" or "Old Curiosity Shop" or "The Bostonians." I do not think, however, they feel the same proprietary delight as I do toward them. Behind those pages, for me, hovers no specter of the classroom and the looseleaf note-book. Each is my own discovery.

Often such discoveries have been embarrassing. Once I had begun to read for pleasure in a century not my own, I kept stumbling across treasures new to me only. I remember when I first pulled "Cranford" out of a boarding-house bookcase shortly after I had left college. For weeks I kept buttonholing my friends to insist they taste with me that remarkable and charming tidbit written by some unheard-of wit who signed herself simply "Mrs. Gaskell." And I recall how I blushed to learn they had nearly all read it—and disliked it—as juniors. Although I no longer go about beating the drum for each masterpiece I unearth, neither am I apologetic about someone's having been there before me. After all, Cortez (or Balboa, if one insists on being literal) must have known, when he surveyed the Pacific from that peak in Darien, that generations of Indians had seen it earlier. But the view was new to him. His discovery was important because it came at the right time in his career.

So mine have come. There are books that one needs maturity to enjoy just as there are books an adult can come on too late to savor. I have never, for instance, been able to get through "Wuthering Heights." That I should have read before I was sixteen. I shall never even *try* "Treasure Island," which I missed at twelve.

On the other hand, no child can possibly appreciate "Huckleberry Finn." That is not to say he can find no pleasure in it. He can and does. But it takes a grown-up to realize its wry and wonderful bouquet. Imagine opening it for the first time at forty! That was my reward for an underprivileged youth. For that Mark Twain shall have my heart and hand forever in spite of what he said about Jane Austen. "It's a pity they let her die a natural death," he wrote to William Dean Howells. Perhaps the young Samuel Clemens read her as part of a prescribed curriculum. Otherwise how could even that opinionated and undereducated genius have so misjudged an ironic talent more towering than his own? Had I been younger than thirty when I first happened on Miss Austen I might have found her dry. Had I read her much later I might have been too dry, myself. Her season suited me.

For no matter how enchanting to the young are the realms of gold, maturity makes one a better traveler there. Do not misunderstand me. I wish with all my heart that I had taken to the road earlier—I do not boast because I was provincial so long. But since I began the journey late, I make use of what advantages I have. So for one thing, I capitalize on my lack of impatience. I am not on fire to see everything at once. There is no goal I must reach by any sunset. And how fresh all the landscape is to me! I wander as far afield as I care to, one range of hills opens out into another which I shall explore in due time. I move forward or backward. I retrace my steps when I please. I fall in love with the formal grandeur of the eighteenth century and stop there for as many months as the mood holds. Boswell's "London Journal" leads me back into Johnson himself and into the whole great age. I read Pope and Gray and Goldsmith and backward still through Richardson and Fielding. I read the letters and diaries of Miss Burney because Dr. Johnson calls her his "dear little Fanny." (The view there is unimportant but amusing.) And that leads me forward once more to Jane Austen. I could not proceed at a pace so leisurely were I twenty once more and in haste to keep up with the fashionable cults. I go where I like. I read Gibbon one week and Sarah Orne Jewett the next, with catholic pleasure. Henry James entertains me not because he is in the mode but because he is enthralling, and I continue to prefer "The Bostonians" to "The Golden Bowl." I do not need to praise Kafka; and I can keep Montaigne and Clarence Day and Coleridge on the same bedside stand.

Because I am grown-up I am under no compulsion from either the critics or the professors to like *anything*. If I try "Tristram Shandy" and find it heavy going, I admit it and never open the second volume. If I do not agree with the world that "Moby Dick" is the Great American Novel, studded with the richest possible symbolism, I need not pretend to enjoy Melville. I think Trollope dull. That is nothing against Trollope; I need not dwell in the country he has invented.

And it is wonderful to be a member of no party! I pick my own way among the landmarks. No Baedeker distracts me from the scenery. I can be behind-times enough to like Tennyson and Browning. I can prefer Crashaw to Donne and Willa Cather to Ronald Firbank. I can read (and disagree with) Virginia Woolf on Monday and on Tuesday begin an amiable quarrel with Newman; nor do I find it a dizzy flight. And so much still to see! Peak upon peak unfolds. But there are also delightful little fenced fields and flowery culverts where I can rest when I do not wish to climb. I have not yet read "War and Peace." But then I've never read anything by Rider Haggard, either, or Wilkie Collins, or anything of Mary Webb's except "Precious Bane." I haven't read Pepys's Diary or Katherine Mansfield's. I have "The House of Seven Gables" ahead of me, and I have also "Our Mutual Friend."

For of all my discoveries, nearly the most breathless was Dickens, himself. How many of the educated can even suspect the delights of such a delayed encounter? I think we owned a "Collected Works" when I was a child. But I had tried "David Copperfield" too early and had believed all my life that he was not for me. One night last winter I was sleepless and somehow without a book . From our own shelves I took down "Little Dorrit," which people tell me now is one of the least beguiling of the lot. But Keats first looking on his Homer could have been no more dazzled than I first poring on my Boz. I felt as a treasure-hunter might feel had he tripped over the locked chest that belonged to Captain Kidd. "Oh, my America, my new-found land!" How many novels were there? Thirty-odd? And every one of them still to be possessed! I got as drunk on Dickens for a while as I used to on the Cavalier poets when I first discovered *them.* I read in quick succession, "Great Expectations," "Martin Chuzzlewit," "Oliver Twist," "The Pickwick Papers," the very "David Copperfield" which had once put me off, and then the preposterous, magnificent, exasperating, ridiculous, and utterly engrossing "Bleak House." I stopped there for fear I should have a surfeit; but it's consoling to know the rest of the novels are there waiting for me, none of them grown stale or too familiar for enjoyment.

There is still much to deplore about my education. I shall never read Latin verse in the original or have a taste for the Brontës, and those are crippling lacks. But all handicaps have compensations and I have learned to accept both cheerfully. To have first met Dickens, Austen, and Mark Twain when I was capable of giving them the full court curtsy is beatitude enough for any reader. Blessed are the illiterate, for they shall inherit the Word!

STUDY QUESTIONS

1. *Is there any evidence here for concluding that Miss McGinley's education was not as bad as she claims it was? Or, at least, that it compares favorably with the education of others?*

2. *The real point of this essay is not a message about literature or Miss McGinley, but about something else. How would you express the main idea in a single sentence?*

3. *Can you shed any light on the reason why people dislike books they have to read in school, when they apparently enjoy the same books read independently? Is this a necessary evil? Is there any remedy for it?*

4. *How does Miss McGinley's early reading experience differ from that of Miller, Mencken, and Greene? Does the difference derive from a difference in the books available to her, or from a difference in her attitude towards them?*

5. *Have you ever had the experience of liking a classroom topic better when you came across it out of class? Possibilities here, in addition to books, are a foreign language, a scientific or mechanical principle, a skill such as drawing or playing a musical instrument. Write a theme describing this situation, and explaining the contrasting feelings you had.*

6. *Is there something generally considered necessary or desirable which you have missed learning, and which you think you are better off for not knowing? Possibilities are swimming, dancing, doing arithmetic, playing baseball, sewing, cooking. Write a theme explaining why, contrary to expectation, you are actually lucky not to know or be able to do something most people would consider an accomplishment.*

3. THE UNCOMMON OBSERVER

George Orwell Visiting a Coal Mine *

When you go down a coal mine it is important to try and get to the coal face when the "fillers" are at work. This is not easy, because when the mine is working visitors are a nuisance and are not encouraged, but if you go at any other time, it is possible to come away with a totally wrong impression. On a Sunday, for instance, a mine seems almost peaceful. The time to go there is when the machines are roaring and the air is black with coal dust, and when you can actually see what the miners have to do. At those times the place is like hell, or at any rate like my own mental picture of hell. Most of the things one imagines in hell are there—heat, noise, confusion, darkness, foul air, and, above all, unbearably cramped space. Everything except the fire, for there is no fire down there except the feeble beams of Davy lamps and electric torches which scarcely penetrate the clouds of coal dust.

When you have finally got there—and getting there is a job in itself: I will explain that in a moment—you crawl through the last line of pit props and see opposite you a shiny black wall three or four feet high. This is the coal face. Overhead is the smooth ceiling made by the rock from which the coal has been cut; underneath is the rock again, so that the gallery you are in is only as high as the ledge of coal itself, probably not much more than a yard. The first impression of all, overmastering everything else for a while, is the frightful, deafening din from the conveyor belt which carries the coal away. You cannot see very far, because the fog of coal dust throws back the beam of your lamp, but you can see on either side of you the line of half-naked kneeling men, one to every four or five yards, driving their shovels under the fallen coal and flinging it swiftly over their left shoulders. They are feeding it on to the conveyor belt, a moving rubber belt a couple of feet wide which runs a yard or two behind them. Down this belt a glittering river of coal races constantly. In a big mine it is carrying away several tons of coal every minute. It bears it off to some place in the main roads where it is shot into tubs holding half a ton, and thence dragged to the cages and hoisted to the outer air.

* From *The Orwell Reader*, "Fiction, Essays, and Reportage," by George Orwell, ©, 1956, by Harcourt, Brace and Company, Inc. Reprinted by permission of Harcourt, Brace and Company, Inc. and Martin Secker & Warburg, Ltd.

It is impossible to watch the "fillers" at work without feeling a pang of envy for their toughness. It is a dreadful job that they do, an almost super-human job by the standards of an ordinary person. For they are not only shifting monstrous quantities of coal, they are also doing it in a position that doubles or trebles the work. They have got to remain kneeling all the while—they could hardly rise from their knees without hitting the ceiling—and you can easily see by trying it what a tremendous effort this means. Shoveling is comparatively easy when you are standing up, because you can use your knee and thigh to drive the shovel along; kneeling down, the whole of the strain is thrown upon your arm and belly muscles. And the other conditions do not exactly make things easier. There is the heat—it varies, but in some mines it is suffocating—and the coal dust that stuffs up your throat and nostrils and collects along your eyelids, and the unending rattle of the conveyor belt, which in that confined space is rather like the rattle of a machine gun. But the fillers look and work as though they were made of iron. They really do look like iron—hammered iron statues—under the smooth coat of coal dust which clings to them from head to foot. It is only when you see miners down the mine and naked that you realize what splendid men they are. Most of them are small (big men are at a disadvantage in that job) but nearly all of them have the most noble bodies: wide shoulders tapering to slender supple waists, and small pronounced buttocks and sinewy thighs, with not an ounce of waste flesh anywhere. In the hotter mines they wear only a pair of thin drawers, clogs and knee-pads; in the hottest mines of all, only the clogs and knee-pads. You can hardly tell by the look of them whether they are young or old. They may be any age up to sixty or even sixty-five, but when they are black and naked they all look alike. No one could do their work who had not a young man's body, and a figure fit for a guardsman at that; just a few pounds of extra flesh on the waistline, and the constant bending would be impossible. You can never forget that spectacle once you have seen it—the line of bowed, kneeling figures, sooty black all over, driving their huge shovels under the coal with stupendous force and speed. They are on the job for seven and a half hours, theoretically without a break, for there is no time "off." Actually they snatch a quarter of an hour or so at some time during the shift to eat the food they have brought with them, usually a hunk of bread and dripping and a bottle of cold tea. The first time I was watching the "fillers" at work I put my hand upon some dreadful slimy thing among the coal dust. It was a chewed quid of tobacco. Nearly all the miners chew tobacco, which is said to be good against thirst.

Probably you have to go down several coal mines before you can get much grasp of the processes that are going on round you. This is chiefly because the mere effort of getting from place to place makes it difficult to notice any-thing else. In some ways it is even disappointing, or at least is unlike what you have expected. You get into the cage, which is a steel box about as wide as a telephone box and two or three times as long. It holds ten men, but they pack it like pilchards in a tin, and a tall man cannot stand upright in it. The steel door shuts upon you, and somebody working the winding gear above drops you into the void. You have the usual momentary qualm in your belly and a bursting sensation in the ears, but not much sensation of movement till you get near the bottom, when the cage slows down so abruptly that you could swear it is going upward again. In the middle of the run the cage probably touches sixty miles an hour; in some of the deeper mines it touches even more. When you crawl out at the bottom you are perhaps four hundred yards under ground. That is to say you have a tolerable-sized mountain on top of you; hundreds of yards of solid rock, bones of extinct beasts, subsoil, flints, roots of growing things, green grass and cows grazing on it—all this suspended over your head and held back only by wooden props as thick as the calf of your leg. But because of the speed at which the cage has brought you down, and the complete blackness through which you have traveled, you hardly feel yourself deeper down than you would at the bottom of the Piccadilly tube.

What *is* surprising, on the other hand, is the immense horizontal distances that have to be traveled underground. Before I had been down a mine I had vaguely imagined the miner stepping out of the cage and getting to work on a ledge of coal a few yards away. I had not realized that before he even gets to his work he may have to creep through passages as long as from London Bridge to Oxford Circus. In the beginning, of course, a mine shaft is sunk somewhere near a seam of coal. But as that seam is worked out and fresh seams are followed up, the workings get farther and farther from the pit bottom. If it is a mile from the pit bottom to the coal face, that is probably an average distance; three miles is a fairly normal one; there are even said to be a few mines where it is as much as five miles. But these distances bear no relation to distances above ground. For in all that mile or three miles as it may be, there is hardly anywhere outside the main road, and not many places even there, where a man can stand upright.

You do not notice the effect of this till you have gone a few hundred yards. You start off, stooping slightly, down the dim-lit gallery, eight or ten feet wide and about five high, with the walls built up with slabs of shale, like the stone walls in Derbyshire. Every yard or two there are wooden props holding up the beams and girders; some of the girders have buckled into fantastic curves under which you have to duck. Usually it is bad going underfoot—thick dust or jagged chunks of shale, and in some mines where there is water it is as mucky as a farmyard. Also there is the track for the coal tubs, like a miniature railway track with sleepers a foot or two apart, which is tiresome to walk on. Everything is gray with shale dust; there is a dusty fiery smell which seems to be the same in all mines. You see mysterious machines of which you never learn the purpose, and bundles of tools slung together on wires, and sometimes mice darting away from the beam of the lamps.

They are surprisingly common, especially in mines where there are or have been horses. It would be interesting to know how they got there in the first place; possibly by falling down the shaft—for they say a mouse can fall any distance uninjured, owing to its surface area being so large relative to its weight. You press yourself against the wall to make way for lines of tubs jolting slowly toward the shaft, drawn by an endless steel cable operated from the surface. You creep through sacking curtains and thick wooden doors which, when they are opened, let out fierce blasts of air. These doors are an important part of the ventilation system. The exhausted air is sucked out of one shaft by means of fans, and the fresh air enters the other of its own accord. But if left to itself the air will take the shortest way round, leaving the deeper workings unventilated; so all short-cuts have to be partitioned off.

At the start to walk stooping is rather a joke, but it is a joke that soon wears off. I am handicapped by being exceptionally tall, but when the roof falls to four feet or less it is a tough job for anybody except a dwarf or a child. You have not only got to bend double, you have also got to keep your head up all the while so as to see the beams and girders and dodge them when they come. You have, therefore, a constant crick in the neck, but this is nothing to the pain in your knees and thighs. After half a mile it becomes (I am not exaggerating) an unbearable agony. You begin to wonder whether you will ever get to the end—still more, how on earth you are going to get back. Your pace grows slower and slower. You come to a stretch of a couple of hundred yards where it is all exceptionally low and you have to work yourself along in a squatting position. Then suddenly the roof opens out to a mysterious height—scene of an old fall of rock, probably—and for twenty whole yards you can stand upright. The relief is overwhelming. But after this there is another low stretch of a hundred yards and then a succession of beams which you have to crawl under. You go down on all fours; even this is a relief after the squatting business. But when you come to the end of the beams and try to get up again, you find that your knees have temporarily struck work and refuse to lift you. You call a halt, ignominiously, and say that you would like to rest for a minute or two. Your guide (a miner) is sympathetic. He knows that your muscles are not the same as his. "Only another four hundred yards," he says encouragingly; you feel that he might as well say another four hundred miles. But finally you do somehow creep as far as the coal face. You have gone a mile and taken the best part of an hour; a miner would do it in not much more than twenty minutes. Having got there, you have to sprawl in the coal dust and get your strength back for several minutes before you can even watch the work in progress with any kind of intelligence.

Coming back is worse than going, not only because you are already tired out but because the journey back to the shaft is probably slightly uphill. You get through the low places at the speed of a tortoise, and you have no shame now about calling a halt when your knees give way. Even the lamp you are carrying becomes a nuisance and probably when you stumble you drop it; whereupon, if it is a Davy lamp, it goes out. Ducking the beams becomes more and more of an effort, and sometimes you forget to duck. You try walking head down as the miners do, and then you bang your backbone. Even the miners bang their backbones fairly often. This is the reason why in very hot mines, where it is necessary to go about half naked, most of the miners have what they call "buttons down the back" — that is, a permanent scab on each vertebra. When the track is downhill the miners sometimes fit their clogs, which are hollow underneath, on the trolley rails and slide down. In mines where the "traveling" is very bad all the miners carry sticks about two and a half feet long, hollowed out below the handle. In normal places you keep your hand on top of the stick and in the low places you slide your hand down into the hollow. These sticks are a great help, and the wooden crash-helmets — a comparatively recent invention — are a godsend. They look like a French or Italian steel helmet, but they are made of some kind of pith and very light, and so strong that you can take a violent blow on the head without feeling it. When finally you get back to the surface you have been perhaps three hours underground and traveled two miles, and you are more exhausted than you would be by a twenty-five-mile walk above ground. For a week afterward your thighs are so stiff that coming downstairs is quite a difficult feat; you have to work your way down in a peculiar sidelong manner, without bending the knees. Your miner friends notice the stiffness of your walk and chaff you about it. ("How'd ta like to work down pit, eh?" etc.). Yet even a miner who has been long away from work — from illness, for instance — when he comes back to the pit, suffers badly for the first few days.

STUDY QUESTIONS

1. *Describe the order in which the elements of this description are arranged. Could they have been logically arranged otherwise? What are the advantages of Orwell's arrangement for his purpose?*
2. *What particularly effective and expressive comparisons does Orwell use?*
3. *What effect does Orwell gain by stressing the lowness of the ceiling in a mine, the kneeling position in which the miners work, the long "traveling" distance?*
4. *What would you say was Orwell's attitude toward his subject? Does it promote or interfere with a fair and objective description?*
5. *Write a theme describing some job or activity you are familiar with, being sure to give an outsider an accurate idea of the problems involved in it.*
6. *Write a theme describing some unusual place or scene you have visited. Plan your description by asking yourself what aspects of the subject the general reader is likely to be most curious about, and eliminate everything not peculiar to the subject.*

Lafcadio Hearn Creole Carrier-Girl*

Those who believe that great physical endurance and physical energy cannot exist in the tropics do not know the Creole carrier-girl.

At a very early age — perhaps at five years — she learns to carry small articles upon her head — a bowl of rice — a dobanne, or red earthen decanter, full of water — even an orange on a plate; and before long she is able to balance these perfectly without using her hands to steady them. (I have often seen children actually run with cans of water upon their heads, and never spill a drop.) At nine or ten she is able to carry thus a tolerably heavy basket, or a trait (a wooden tray with deep outward sloping sides) containing a weight of from twenty to thirty pounds; and is able to accompany her mother, sister, or cousin on long peddling journeys — walking barefoot twelve and fifteen miles a day. At sixteen or seventeen she is a tall robust girl — lithe, vigorous, tough — all tendon and hard flesh; — she carries a tray or a basket of the largest size, and a burden of one hundred and twenty to one hundred and fifty pounds weight; — she can now earn about thirty francs (about six dollars) a month, *by walking fifty miles a day*, as an itinerant seller.

Among her class there are figures to make you dream of Atalanta; — and all, whether ugly or attractive as to feature, are finely shapen as to body and limb. Brought into existence by extraordinary necessities of environment, the type is a peculiarly local one — a type of human thoroughbred representing the true secret of grace: economy of force. There are no corpulent porteuses for the long interior routes; all are built lightly and firmly as racers. There are no old porteuses; — to do the work even at forty signifies a constitution of astounding solidity. After the full force of youth and health is spent, the poor carrier must seek lighter labor; — she can no longer compete with the girls. For in this calling the young body is taxed to its utmost capacity of strength, endurance, and rapid motion.

As a general rule, the weight is such that no well-freighted porteuse can, unassisted, either "load" or "unload" (châgé or déchâgé, in Creole phrase); the effort to do so would burst a blood vessel, wrench a nerve, rupture a muscle. She cannot even sit down under her burden without risk of breaking her neck; absolute perfection of the balance is necessary for self-preservation. A case came under my own observation of a woman rupturing a muscle in her arm through careless haste in the mere act of aiding another to unload.

And no one not a brute will ever refuse to aid a woman to lift or to relieve

* From *Two Years in the French West Indies*, 1890.

herself of her burden; — you may see the wealthiest merchant, the proudest
planter, gladly do it; — the meanness of refusing, or of making any conditions
for the performance of his little kindness has only been imagined in those
strange Stories of Devils wherewith the oral and uncollected literature of the
Creole abounds.

Preparing for her journey, the young màchanne (marchande) puts on the
poorest and briefest chemise in her possession, and the most worn of her light
calico robes. These are all she wears. The robe is drawn upward and forward, so as to reach a little below the knee, and is confined thus by a waist-
string, or a long kerchief bound tightly round the loins. Instead of a Madras
or painted turban-kerchief, she binds a plain mouchoir neatly and closely
about her head; and if her hair be long, it is combed back and gathered into a
loop behind. Then, with a second mouchoir of coarser quality she makes a
pad, or, as she calls it, tòche, by winding the kerchief round her fingers as you
would coil up a piece of string; — and the soft mass, flattened with a patting
of the hand, is placed upon her head, over the coiffure. On this the great
loaded trait is poised.

She wears no shoes! To wear shoes and do her work swiftly and well in
such a land of mountains would be impossible. She must climb thousands
and descend thousands of feet every day — march up and down slopes so steep
that the horses of the country all break down after a few years of similar
journeying. The girl invariably outlasts the horse — though carrying an equal
weight. Shoes, unless extraordinarily well made, would shift place a little
with every change from ascent to descent, or the reverse, during the march —
would yield and loosen with the ever-varying strain — would compress the
toes — produce corns, bunions, raw places by rubbing, and soon cripple the
porteuse. Remember, she has to walk perhaps fifty miles between dawn and
dark, under a sun to which a single hour's exposure, without the protection of
an umbrella, is perilous to any European or American — the terrible sun of the
tropics! Sandals are the only conceivable footgear suited to such a calling as
hers; but she needs no sandals: the soles of her feet are toughened so as to
feel no asperities, and present to sharp pebbles a surface at once yielding
and resisting, like a cushion of solid caoutchouc.

Besides her load, she carries only a canvas purse tied to her girdle on the
right side, and on the left a very small bottle of rum, or white tafia — usually
the latter, because it is so cheap. ... For she may not always find the Gouyave
Water to drink — the cold clear pure stream conveyed to the fountains of
Saint Pierre from the highest mountains by a beautiful and marvelous plan of
hydraulic engineering: she will have to drink betimes the common spring-
water of the bamboo-fountains on the remoter high-roads; and this may cause
dysentery if swallowed without a spoonful of spirits. Therefore she never
travels without a little liquor.

... So! — She is ready: "Châgé moin, souplè, chè!" She bends to lift the end
of the heavy trait: some one takes the other — yon! — dè! — toua! — it is on her

head. Perhaps she winces an instant; — the weight is not perfectly balanced; she settles it with her hands — gets it in the exact place. Then, all steady — lithe, light, half naked — away she moves with a long springy step. So even her walk that the burden never sways; yet so rapid her motion that however good a walker you may fancy yourself to be you will tire out after a sustained effort of fifteen minutes to follow her uphill. Fifteen minutes! — and she can keep up that pace without slackening — save for a minute to eat and drink at midday — for at least twelve hours and fifty-six minutes, the extreme length of a West Indian day. She starts before dawn; tries to reach her resting-place by sunset; after dark, like all her people, she is afraid of meeting zombis.

Let me give you some idea of her average speed under an average weight of one hundred and twenty-five pounds — estimates based partly upon my own observations, partly upon the declarations of the trustworthy merchants who employ her, and partly on the assertion of habitants of the burghs or cities named — all of which statements perfectly agree. From Saint Pierre to Basse-Point, by the national road, the distance is a trifle less than twenty-seven kilometres and three quarters. She makes the transit easily in three hours and a half; and returns in the afternoon, after an absence of scarcely more than eight hours. From Saint Pierre to Morne Rouge — two thousand feet up in the mountains (an ascent so abrupt that no one able to pay carriage-fare dreams of attempting to walk it) — the distance is seven kilometres and three quarters. She makes it in little more than an hour. But this represents only the beginning of her journey. She passes on to Grande Anse, twenty-one and three-quarter kilometres away. But she does not rest there: she returns at the same pace, and reaches Saint Pierre before dark. From Saint Pierre to Gros-Morne the distance to be twice traversed by her is more than thirty-two kilometres. A journey of sixty-four kilometres — daily, perhaps — forty miles! And there are many màchannes who make yet longer trips — trips of three or four days' duration; — these rest at villages upon their route. . . .

Forty to fifty miles a day, always under a weight of more than a hundred pounds — for when the trait has been emptied she puts in stones for ballast; — carrying her employer's merchandise and money over the mountain ranges, beyond the peaks, across the ravines, through the tropical forest, sometimes through by-ways haunted by the fer-de-lance — and this in summer or winter, the season of rains or the season of heat, the time of fevers or the time of hur-ricanes, at a franc a day! . . . How does she live upon it?

There are twenty sous to the franc. The girl leaves Saint Pierre with her load at early morning. At the second village, Morne Rouge, she halts to buy one, two, or three biscuits at a sou apiece; and reaching Ajoupa-Bouillon later in the forenoon, she may buy another biscuit or two. Altogether she may be expected to eat five sous of biscuit or bread before reaching the Grande Anse, where she probably has a meal waiting for her. This ought to cost her ten sous — especially if there be meat in her ragoût: which represents a total expense of fifteen sous for eatables. Then there is the additional cost of the cheap liquor, which she must mix with her drinking water, as it would be more than dangerous to swallow pure cold water in her heated condition; two or three sous more. This almost makes the franc. But such a hasty and really erroneous estimate does not include expenses of lodging and clothing; — she may sleep on the bare floor sometimes, and twenty francs a year may keep her in clothes; but she must rent the floor and pay for the clothes out of that franc. As a matter of fact she not only does all this upon her twenty sous a day, but can even economize something which will enable her, when her youth and force decline, to start in business for herself. And her economy will not seem so wonderful when I assure you that thousands of men here — huge men muscled like bulls and lions — live upon an average expenditure of five sous a day. One sou of bread, two sous of manioc flour, one sou of dried codfish, one sou of tafia: such is their meal.

There are women carriers who earn more than a franc a day — women with a particular talent for selling, who are paid on commission — from ten to fifteen per cent. These eventually make themselves independent in many instances; — they continue to sell and bargain in person, but hire a young girl to carry the goods.

STUDY QUESTIONS

1. *Writing in 1890, Hearn marvels in this selection at the beauty and accomplishment of the Creole carrier-girls, and seems to idealize their way of life. Compare this with Orwell's attitude toward the work of the coal-miner. Would it have been possible for Orwell to describe his visit to the coal mine in such a way that the reader would have felt that the miners' life was good? Is one of these descriptions more "objective" than the other?*

2. *Examine the vocabulary of Hearn and that of Orwell. If you did not know the dates of these selections, could you place one as earlier than the other on the basis of vocabulary?*

3. *What is the logic of organization in this selection? What effect would be produced if the discussion of the girls' pay had been placed first? If the discussion of preparation for the journey had been placed first?*

4. *Analyze the description of the carrier-girl's preparation for the journey. What proportion of the detail given actually paints the picture of the girl, and what proportion provides explanation for her preparation and dress?*

5. *Observe some kind of worker closely, and write a description of his preparation for his work, or for his execution of the job. Consider, for example, a carpenter, bricklayer, bulldozer operator, or some similar skilled workman.*

6. *Compare Orwell's description of the miners and Hearn's description of the carrier-girls in some detail and write an analysis of the differences in attitude of the two authors towards their subjects.*

Samuel Butler Dr. Skinner*

Dr. Skinner had been a burning and a shining light in every position he had filled from his boyhood upwards. He was a very great genius. Everyone knew this; they said, indeed, that he was one of the few people to whom the word genius could be applied without exaggeration. Had he not taken I don't know how many University Scholarships in his freshman's year? Had he not been afterwards Senior Wrangler, First Chancellor's Medallist and I do not know how many more things besides? And then, he was such a wonderful speaker; at the Union Debating Club he had been without a rival, and had, of course, been president; his moral character — a point on which so many geniuses were weak — was absolutely irreproachable; foremost of all, however, among his many great qualities, and perhaps more remarkable even than his genius was what biographers have called "the simple-minded and childlike earnestness of his character," an earnestness which might be perceived by the solemnity with which he spoke even about trifles. It is hardly necessary to say he was on the Liberal side in politics.

His personal appearance was not particularly prepossessing. He was about the middle height, portly, and had a couple of fierce grey eyes, that flashed fire from beneath a pair of great, bushy, beetling eyebrows and overawed all who came near him. It was in respect of his personal appearance, however, that, if he was vulnerable at all, his weak place was to be found. His hair when he was a young man was red, but after he had taken his degree he had a brain fever which caused him to have his head shaved; when he reappeared he did so wearing a wig, and one which was a good deal further off red than his own hair had been. He not only had never discarded his wig, but year by year it had edged itself a little more and a little more off red, till by the time he was forty, there was not a trace of red remaining, and his wig was brown.

When Dr. Skinner was a very young man, hardly more than five-and-twenty, the head-mastership of the Roughborough Grammar School had fallen vacant, and he had been unhesitatingly appointed. The result justified the selection. Dr. Skinner's pupils distinguished themselves at whichever University they went to. He moulded their minds after the model of his own, and stamped an impression upon them which was indelible in after-life; whatever else a Roughborough man might be, he was sure to make everyone feel that he was a God-fearing earnest Christian and a Liberal, if not a Radical, in politics. Some boys, of course, were incapable of appreciating the

* From *The Way of All Flesh*, 1903, ch. xxvii. Reprinted by permission of E. P. Dutton, Inc. New York; Jonathan Cape, Ltd; and the Executors of Samuel Butler.

beauty and loftiness of Dr. Skinner's nature. Some such boys, alas! there will be in every school; upon them Dr. Skinner's hand was very properly a heavy one. His hand was against them, and theirs against him during the whole time of the connection between them. They not only disliked him, but they hated all that he more especially embodied, and throughout their lives disliked all that reminded them of him. Such boys, however, were in a minority, the spirit of the place being decidedly Skinnerian.

I once had the honour of playing a game of chess with this great man. It was during the Christmas holidays, and I had come down to Roughborough for a few days to see Alethea Pontifex (who was then living there) on business. It was very gracious of him to take notice of me, for if I was a light of literature at all it was of the very lightest kind.

It is true that in the intervals of business I had written a good deal, but my works had been almost exclusively for the stage, and for those theatres that devoted themselves to extravaganza and burlesque. I had written many pieces of this description, full of puns and comic songs, and they had had a fair success, but my best piece had been a treatment of English history during the Reformation period, in the course of which I had introduced Cranmer, Sir Thomas More, Henry the Eighth, Catherine of Arragon, and Thomas Crom-well (in his youth better known as the *Malleus Monachorum*), and had made them dance a breakdown. I had also dramatised "The Pilgrim's Progress" for a Christmas Pantomime, and made an important scene of Vanity Fair, with Mr. Greatheart, Apollyon, Christiana, Mercy, and Hopeful as the principal characters. The orchestra played music taken from Handel's best known works, but the time was a good deal altered, and altogether the tunes were not exactly as Handel left them. Mr. Greatheart was very stout and he had a red nose; he wore a capacious waistcoat, and a shirt with a huge frill down the middle of the front. Hopeful was up to as much mischief as I could give him; he wore the costume of a young swell of the period, and had a cigar in his mouth which was continually going out.

Christiana did not wear much of anything: indeed it was said that the dress which the Stage Manager had originally proposed for her had been considered inadequate even by the Lord Chamberlain, but this is not the case. With all these delinquencies upon my mind it was natural that I should feel convinced of sin while playing chess (which I hate) with the great Dr. Skinner of Roughborough — the historian of Athens and editor of Demosthenes. Dr. Skinner, moreover, was one of those who pride themselves on being able to set people at their ease at once, and I had been sitting on the edge of my chair all the evening. But I have always been very easily overawed by a schoolmaster.

The game had been a long one, and at half-past nine, when supper came in, we had each of us a few pieces remaining. "What will you take for supper, Dr. Skinner?" said Mrs. Skinner in a silvery voice.

He made no answer for some time, but at last in a tone of almost super-human solemnity, he said, first, "Nothing," and then, "Nothing whatever."

By and by, however, I had a sense come over me as though I were nearer the consummation of all things than I had ever yet been. The room seemed to grow dark, as an expression came over Dr. Skinner's face, which showed that he was about to speak. The expression gathered force, the room grew darker and darker. "Stay," he at length added, and I felt that here at any rate was an end to a suspense which was rapidly becoming unbearable. "Stay — I may presently take a glass of cold water — and a small piece of bread and butter."

As he said the word "butter" his voice sank to a hardly audible whisper; then there was a sigh as though of relief when the sentence was concluded, and the universe this time was safe.

Another ten minutes of solemn silence finished the game. The Doctor rose briskly from his seat and placed himself at the supper table. "Mrs. Skinner," he exclaimed jauntily, "what are those mysterious-looking objects surrounded by potatoes?"

"Those are oysters, Dr. Skinner."

"Give me some, and give Overton some."

And so on till he had eaten a good plate of oysters, a scallop shell of minced veal nicely browned, some apple tart, and a hunk of bread and cheese. This was the small piece of bread and butter.

The cloth was now removed and tumblers with teaspoons in them, a lemon or two and a jug of boiling water were placed upon the table. Then the great man unbent. His face beamed.

"And what shall it be to drink?" he exclaimed persuasively. "Shall it be brandy and water? No. It shall be gin and water. Gin is the more wholesome liquor."

So gin it was, hot and stiff, too.

Who can wonder at him or do anything but pity him? Was he not head-master of Roughborough School? To whom had he owed money at any time? Whose ox had he taken, whose ass had he taken, or whom had he defrauded? What whisper had ever been breathed against his moral character? If he had become rich it was by the most honourable of all means — his literary attainments; over and above his great works of scholarship, his "Meditations upon the Epistle and Character of St. Jude" had placed him among the most popular of English theologians; it was so exhaustive that no one who bought it need ever meditate upon the subject again — indeed it exhausted all who had anything to do with it. He had made £5000 by this work alone, and would very likely make another £5000 before he died. A man who had done all this and wanted a piece of bread and butter had a right to announce the fact with some pomp and circumstance. Nor should his words be taken without searching for what he used to call a "deeper and more hidden meaning."

Those who searched for this even in his lightest utterances would not be without their reward. They would find that "bread and butter" was Skinnerese for oyster-patties and apple tart, and "gin hot" the true translation of water.

But independently of their money value, his works had made him a lasting name in literature. So probably Gallio was under the impression that his fame would rest upon the treatises on natural history which we gather from Seneca that he compiled, and which for aught we know may have contained a complete theory of evolution; but the treatises are all gone and Gallio has become immortal for the very last reason in the world that he expected, and for the very last reason that would have flattered his vanity. He has become immortal because he cared nothing about the most important movement with which he was ever brought into connection (I wish people who are in search of immortality would lay the lesson to heart and not make so much noise about important movements), and so, if Dr. Skinner becomes immortal, it will probably be for some reason very different from the one which he so fondly imagined.

Could it be expected to enter into the head of such a man as this that in reality he was making his money by corrupting youth; that it was his paid profession to make the worse appear the better reason in the eyes of those who were too young and inexperienced to be able to find him out; that he kept out of the sight of those whom he professed to teach material points of the argument, for the production of which they had a right to rely upon the honour of anyone who made professions of sincerity; that he was a passionate, half-turkey-cock, half-gander of a man whose sallow, bilious face and hobble-gobble voice could scare the timid, but who would take to his heels readily enough if he were met firmly; that his "Meditations on St. Jude," such as they were, were cribbed without acknowledgment, and would have been beneath contempt if so many people did not believe them to have been written honestly? Mrs. Skinner might have perhaps kept him a little more in his proper place if she had thought it worth while to try, but she had enough to attend to in looking after her household and seeing that the boys were well fed and, if they were ill, properly looked after — which she took good care they were.

STUDY QUESTIONS

1. *Orwell and Hearn, in their descriptions, have been concerned to depict types, rather than individuals. To what extent is Butler picturing Dr. Skinner as an individual, and to what extent is he using him as a type? What kinds of details are common to the three descriptions? What kinds are different?*
2. *In what way does Dr. Skinner's wig reflect something about his character in general?*
3. *Why do you think the narrator feels Dr. Skinner should be pitied?*

4. *What is the leading trait of character stressed in this description?*

5. *How would you summarize Butler's attitude toward Dr. Skinner? In doing this, you will want to examine the tone of the selection, noting where it is ironic, matter-of-fact, and indignant.*

6. *Write a description of a person you know who has some marked trait of character. Try to use Butler's method of projecting his character through his speech, actions, dress and other outward signs, instead of telling the reader directly what it is.*

John Richard Green Elizabeth *

Εngland's one hope lay in the character of her Queen. Elizabeth was now in her twenty-fifth year. Personally she had more than her mother's beauty; her figure was commanding, her face long but queenly and intelligent, her eyes quick and fine. She had grown up amidst the liberal culture of Henry's court, a bold horsewoman, a good shot, a graceful dancer, a skilled musician, and an accomplished scholar. She studied every morning the Greek Testament, and followed this by the tragedies of Sophocles or orations of Demosthenes, and could "rub up her rusty Greek" at need to bandy pedantry with a Vice-Chancellor. But she was far from being a mere pedant. The new literature which was springing up around her found constant welcome in her court. She spoke Italian and French as fluently as her mother-tongue. She was familiar with Ariosto and Tasso. Even amidst the affectation and love of anagrams and puerilities which sullied her later years, she listened with delight to the *Faerie Queene*, and found a smile for "Master Spenser" when he appeared in her presence. Her moral temper recalled in its strange contrasts the mixed blood within her veins. She was at once the daughter of Henry and of Anne Boleyn. From her father she inherited her frank and hearty address, her love of popularity and of free intercourse with the people, her dauntless courage and her amazing self-confidence. Her harsh, manlike voice, her impetuous will, her pride, her furious outbursts of anger came to her with her Tudor blood. She rated great nobles as if they were schoolboys; she met the insolence of Essex with a box on the ear; she would break now and then into the gravest deliberations to swear at her ministers like a fishwife. But strangely in contrast with the violent outlines of her Tudor temper stood the sensuous, self-indulgent nature she derived from Anne Boleyn. Splendor and pleasure were with Elizabeth the very air she breathed. Her delight was to move in perpetual progresses from castle to castle through a series of gorgeous pageants, fanciful and extravagant as a caliph's dream. She loved gaiety and laughter and wit. A happy retort or a finished compliment

* From *A Short History of the English People*, 1874.

never failed to win her favor. She hoarded jewels. Her dresses were innumerable. Her vanity remained, even to old age, the vanity of a coquette in her teens. No adulation was too fulsome for her, no flattery of her beauty too gross. "To see her was heaven," Hatton told her, "the lack of her was hell." She would play with her rings that her courtiers might note the delicacy of her hands, or dance a coranto that the French ambassador, hidden dexterously behind a curtain, might report her sprightliness to his master. Her levity, her frivolous laughter, her unwomanly jests gave color to a thousand scandals. Her character in fact, like her portraits, was utterly without shade. Of womanly reserve or self-restraint she knew nothing. No instinct of delicacy veiled the voluptuous temper which had broken out in the romps of her girlhood and showed itself almost ostentatiously throughout her later life. Personal beauty in a man was a sure passport to her liking. She patted handsome young squires on the neck when they knelt to kiss her hand, and fondled her "sweet Robin," Lord Leicester, in the face of the court.

It was no wonder that the statesmen whom she outwitted held Elizabeth almost to the last to be little more than a frivolous woman, or that Philip of Spain wondered how "a wanton" could hold in check the policy of the Escurial. But the Elizabeth whom they saw was far from being all of Elizabeth. The wilfulness of Henry, the triviality of Anne Boleyn played over the surface of a nature hard as steel, a temper purely intellectual, the very type of reason untouched by imagination or passion. Luxurious and pleasure-loving as she seemed, Elizabeth lived simply and frugally, and she worked hard. Her vanity and caprice had no weight whatever with her in state affairs. The coquette of the presence-chamber became the coolest and hardest of politicians at the council-board. Fresh from the flattery of her courtiers, she would tolerate no flattery in the closet; she was herself plain and downright of speech with her counsellors, and she looked for a corresponding plainness of speech in return. If any trace of her sex lingered in her actual statesmanship, it was seen in the simplicity and tenacity of purpose that often underlies a woman's fluctuations of feeling. It was this in part which gave her her marked superiority over the statesmen of her time. No nobler group of ministers ever gathered round a council-board than those who gathered round the council-board of Elizabeth. But she was the instrument of none. She listened, she weighed, she used or put by the counsels of each in turn, but her policy as a whole was her own. It was a policy, not of genius, but of good sense. Her aims were simple and obvious: to preserve her throne, to keep England out of war, to restore civil and religious order. Something of womanly caution and timidity perhaps backed the passionless indifference with which she set aside the larger schemes of ambition which were ever opening before her eyes. She was resolute in her refusal of the Low Countries. She rejected with a laugh the offers of the Protestants to make her "head of the religion" and "mistress of the seas." But her amazing success in the end sprang mainly from this wise limitation of her aims. She had a finer sense than any of her counsellors of her real resources; she knew instinctively how far she could go, and what she could do. Her cold, critical intellect was never swayed by enthusiasm or by panic either to exaggerate or to underestimate her risks or her power.

STUDY QUESTIONS

1. *Like Butler's description of Dr. Skinner, this is a description of an individual. Would it be fair to say that its purpose was more exclusively to give a portrait of an individual than Butler's selection? Explain the reasons for your answer.*
2. *Would you describe Green's portrait of Elizabeth as "objective" as compared with the descriptions in the preceding selections? Is it a balanced picture of Elizabeth, or is it generally favorable or unfavorable to her?*
3. *What kinds of sources would Green have depended upon for his information about Elizabeth? How would you check his "accuracy"?*
4. *To what extent is Green's description dependent upon checkable fact? To what extent is it dependent upon generalization about Elizabeth's actions and temperament?*
5. *Write a description of some historical figure based upon your reading of two or three articles in encyclopedias or similar sources.*
6. *Read the articles on Elizabeth in several encyclopedias or history books and write an evaluation of Green's "accuracy."*

R. P. T. Coffin Whistling Wings*

When the stars are their highest, and the cocks still in the depths of sleep, all male Merrymeeting souls go out by lanternlight to the bay. The frost is pretty sure to be sifted by this time. The men and boys walk through the dust of diamonds. The last pale frostflowers crumble under their feet. Pines loom larger than life among the stars.

Some people say that Merrymeeting Bay gets its name from the meeting of the five rivers that unite to form this sweet inland sea, the Kennebec, the Androscoggin, the Abagadasset, the Cathance, and East River. The Atlantic comes in too, to lend its zest and spice, all the way up from Popham to Gardiner, at flood tide. But any man will tell you that the name comes from the fact that the bay is one of the purlieus of Paradise. It borders on Eden all the way, and a man can feel the breath of the angels all over its blue waves. The five rivers wind into it through marshes where the tall grass furnishes enough cover for all the male habitants of the United States, from

* From *Kennebec, Cradle of Americans* by Robert P. T. Coffin. Copyright, 1937, by Rinehart & Company, Inc. Reprinted by permission of Rinehart & Company, Inc.

knee pants up to the trousers of the grandfather. Give every American male a shotgun, unlimited shells, and hipboots, and let them all loose there without women to complicate their days, and they would live in peace to the end of their time. They could return noontimes now and then, to propagate. But they would go right back again to the peaceful business of life. For wild rice grows all around the bay, and all the ducks from the Western Hemisphere sooner or later come there to spoon up its grains from the water and give a man a chance at getting his living on the wing, as his ancestors did when men covered their nakedness with beards and lived in caves. Merrymeeting is a return to an ancient religion, in which men send missiles up as prayers into the sky.

There is no farmer within fifty miles of Merrymeeting who is not a hunter when the leaves turn. A man may be the meanest of Yankees, and slave all his life and slave-drive his woman and his children all the months but October and November. He may bury his money in an old-fashioned wallet under the stones of his pasture wall. But when the duck season comes, he digs out his silver dollars and moldy bills and gets him cartridges and a twelve-gauge and goes after his share of the bay's harvest. For this is another crop that Kennebec men count on, along with alewives and smelts and potatoes and pumpkins — ducks and geese. For two months all other business stops, and men go down and wade and lie in wait, wet themselves to their skins, see dawn come up, run and fall, swim and sink and mire themselves, and rejoice like ancient strong men and like boys. Merrymeeting means renewing one's youth like the eagle's, the youth of man's days and of the race's.

The men and boys creep under the night to their chosen gunning floats and blinds. A Kennebec farmer's stone walls may be so tumble-down that a two weeks' lamb can step through them. But he will work like a Trojan and build himself a duck blind which is as fine a bit of stonework as an old fort builder could ask for. His pumpkins may be choked down to the size of cucumbers by ragweed and smartweed, but he will have his house of brush firm around him. His plow may rust, but his gunning float will be shipshape and neat as a new pin.

The men stow their gear in the light of the lanterns, and they scull to their places under the stars. They untangle the wooden tollers, masterpieces whittled from white pine with a jacknife, the work of many loving hours by winter lamplight, which they have dug out from under the hay in the barns. They rig anchors and set them out. The subdued quacking of live decoys crackles around them. The live ones are hitched to an anchor and put out in the river too. The men climb into their blinds and stow the lanterns between their thighs. They smoke and tell stories of fabulous hunts in other years, hold their guns ready and wait for the dawn. Philosophy may come out of hiding at such a zero hour, and men who are usually silent may put into one sentence the art of getting along for a whole lifetime in good health.

The dark thins out at last. The air pinches up and grows colder. A shrewd wind starts to blow from nowhere. The plumes of grass begin to show up on the night. The wind tapers off to nothing. The silence is all at once so deep a man can hear his heart. Breaths quicken as they come and go. The frost fog begins to flake and ascend.

A single gun goes off far away like a call to prayer. A sudden arrow with all its barbs alive slants down through the dark gray. The men throw their guns to their shoulders, wait till the ducks skim the water, and then turn into volcanoes. Flash on flash of yellow fire, they give them the left barrel, the right barrel, both barrels together. The boys rise up on their haunches and let go, and come back after each kick for more. The sound is deafening. The whole of Merrymeeting Bay turns into an earthquake, as the dawn sweeps through the great pines. Guns roar, ducks squawk. Sharp bodies hurtle over with taut wings that bite into the air, flame jets, and the lovely wings that can think in every feather crumple and shatter, and the arcs of flight are broken. The wounded ducks strike the water on paths of crystal, dive and go under.

Then the boats and the dogs put out. The bay grows alive with men. Gunning floats slip past with boughs over the bow and men blowing off steam behind. The whole high sky is laced with chevrons of the risen fowl. The sun strikes them while the bay is still only the gray of dawn. The whistle of wild wings is a continuous treble music between the bass chords of the guns.

And the hunters gather in their treasure, still warm and resilient with life. They pick up the banquets they have brought down, and hang them like chains about their necks. The sun comes above the pines like a vast bubble of pitch on a Maine spruce tree. The men stagger home muddy and un-combed of hair and beard, their eyes are like burnt holes in a blanket. They walk half asleep. Their sons totter beside them loaded with tollers, live and wooden. The males go back to their farmhouses, a sight to make she-folks weep. They carry hours of hard work and tens of thousands of feathers that she-folks must pluck off. But the hunters have proved themselves men, they have got their dinner in the ancient manner, and they keel over on their beds like lords of creation, like the gods they are.

Now that the rest of the nation has learned about the taste of the Kennebec River which their fathers before them had on their tongues in Kennebec ice, now that Maine has become the holiday of most Americans, outlanders have discovered the wild geese and ducks of Merrymeeting. They come, too, now, in armies of khaki and brown flannel and canvas. They come with dogs that have been lapped in velvet and luxury. They come clean-shorn with the light of prosperity and Wall Street on their jaws. They come with guns that are machines for raking all the horizons with destruction. They come spruce and neat and polished, and unbelieving. And after one night on Merrymeet-ing, they are blood brothers of the men of the Kennebec. They come back unshaven and dirty and coarse. And they have turned back five thousand stale years of indoor living. They have fallen in love with the stars and running waters, with maple trees and the white dawn, in the only right way for men to fall in love with them, by being out among them and drinking them in through the skin. They come home with a life redder in them for the strength and wonder of the Kennebec.

This is one crop that the Kennebec still raises. Manhood that is rooted in hunting. Feasting that whistles on wings.

STUDY QUESTIONS

1. *This selection is unusual because it makes far more use than prose usually does of the sound of words. Point out some examples of alliteration, assonance and strong rhythm. What quality is produced by the use of devices like these?*

2. *Point out, in the passage beginning, "A single gun . . ." the words that describe sensations of sound, feeling and sight. How many different senses does the author appeal to?*

3. *Point out the particularly vigorous and expressive verbs in the section that describes action.*

4. *The author consciously uses various sentence patterns for effect. What is the effect of the short sentences in the paragraph beginning "The dark . . . out at last." Can you point out another, similar effect? What is the effect of the parallel sentences, all beginning with the words, "They come . . ." in the paragraph before the last?*

5. *What is the contrast in the two paragraphs beginning "There is no farmer within fifty miles of Merrymeeting . . ."? How is this contrast used again in the paragraph beginning, "Now that the rest of the nation . . ."?*

6. *This description is not solid and thorough, but creates atmosphere through a number of vivid and incomplete impressions. Write a description of this kind, making sure:*

   a) *that your subject has created a strong impression of you*

   b) *that you convey the details through a particularly vivid vocabulary.*

Robert Louis Stevenson The Old Pacific Capital*

The Bay of Monterey has been compared by no less a person than General Sherman to a bent fishing-hook; and the comparison, if less important than the march through Georgia, still shows the eye of a soldier for topography. Santa Cruz sits exposed at the shank; the mouth of the Salinas river is at the middle of the bend; and Monterey itself is cosily ensconced beside the barb. Thus the ancient capital of California faces across the bay, while the Pacific Ocean, though hidden by low hills and forests, bombards her left

---

* From "The Old Pacific Capital," first published in *Frazer's Magazine,* November, 1880.

flank and rear with never-dying surf. In front of the town, the long line of seabeach trends north and north-west, and then westward to enclose the bay. The waves which lap so quietly about the jetties of Monterey grow louder and larger in the distance; you can see the breakers leaping high and white by day; at night, the outline of the shore is traced in transparent silver by the moonlight and the flying foam; and from all round, even in quiet weather, the low, distant, thrilling roar of the Pacific hangs over the coast and the adjacent country like smoke above a battle.

These long beaches are enticing to the idle man. It would be hard to find a walk more solitary and at the same time more exciting to the mind. Crowds of ducks and sea-gulls hover over the sea. Sandpipers trot in and out by troops after the retiring waves, trilling together in a chorus of infinitesimal song. Strange sea-tangles, new to the European eye, the bones of whales, or sometimes a whole whale's carcase, white with carrion-gulls and poisoning the wind, lie scattered here and there along the sands. The waves come in slowly, vast and green, curve their translucent necks, and burst with a surprising uproar, that runs, waxing and waning, up and down the long keyboard of the beach. The foam of these great ruins mounts in an instant to the ridge of the sand glacis, swiftly fleets back again, and is met and buried by the next breaker. The interest is perpetually fresh. On no other coast that I know shall you enjoy, in calm, sunny weather, such a spectacle of Ocean's greatness, such beauty of changing colour, or such degrees of thunder in the sound. The very air is more than usually salt by this Homeric deep.

Inshore, a tract of sand-hills borders on the beach. Here and there a lagoon, more or less brackish, attracts the birds and hunters. A rough, spotty undergrowth partially conceals the sand. The crouching, hardy, live-oaks flourish singly or in thickets — the kind of wood for murderers to crawl among — and here and there the skirts of the forest extend downward from the hills with a floor of turf and aisles of pine-trees hung with Spaniard's Beard. Through this quaint desert the railway cars drew near to Monterey from the junction at Salina City — though that and so many other things are now for ever altered — and it was from here that you had the first view of the old township lying in the sands, its white windmills bickering in the chill, perpetual wind, and the first fogs of the evening drawing drearily around it from the sea.

The one common note of all this country is the haunting presence of the ocean. A great faint sound of breakers follows you high up into the inland cañons; the roar of water dwells in the clean, empty rooms of Monterey as in a shell upon the chimney; go where you will, you have but to pause and listen to hear the voice of the Pacific. You pass out of the town to the southwest, and mount the hill among pine woods. Glade, thicket, and grove surround you. You follow winding sandy tracks that lead nowhither. You see a deer; a multitude of quail arises. But the sound of the sea still follows you as you advance, like that of wind among the trees, only harsher and stranger to the ear; and when at length you gain the summit, out breaks on every hand

and with freshened vigour, that same unending, distant, whispering rumble of the ocean; for now you are on the top of the Monterey peninsula, and the noise no longer only mounts to you from behind along the beach towards Santa Cruz, but from your right also, round by Chinatown and Pinos lighthouse, and from down before you to the mouth of the Carmello river. The whole woodland is begirt with thundering surges. The silence that immediately surrounds you where you stand is not so much broken as it is haunted by this distant, circling rumour. It sets your senses upon edge; you strain your attention; you are clearly and unusually conscious of small sounds near at hand; you walk listening like an Indian hunter; and that voice of the Pacific is a sort of disquieting company to you in your walk....

The woods and the Pacific rule between them the climate of this seaboard region. On the streets of Monterey, when the air does not smell salt from the one, it will be blowing perfumed from the resinous treetops of the other. For days together a hot, dry air will overhand the town, close as from an oven, yet healthful and aromatic in the nostrils. The cause is not far to seek, for the woods are afire, and the hot wind is blowing from the hills. These fires are one of the great dangers in California. I have seen from Monterey as many as three at the same time, by day a cloud of smoke, by night a red coal of conflagration in the distance. A little thing will start them, and, if the wind be favourable, they gallop over miles of country faster than a horse. The inhabitants must turn out and work like demons, for it is not only the pleasant groves that are destroyed; the climate and the soil are equally at stake, and these fires prevent the rains of the next winter and dry up perennial fountains. California has been a land of promise in its time, like Palestine; but if the woods continue so swiftly to perish, it may become, like Palestine, a land of desolation.

To visit the woods while they are languidly burning is a strange piece of experience. The fire passes through the underbrush at a run. Every here and there a tree flares up instantaneously from root to summit, scattering tufts of flame, and is quenched, it seems, as quickly. But this last is only in semblance. For after this first squib-like conflagration of the dry moss and twigs, there remains behind a deep-rooted and consuming fire in the very entrails of the tree. The resin of the pitch-pine is principally condensed at the base of the bole and in the spreading roots. Thus, after the light, showy, skirmishing flames, which are only as the match to the explosion, have already scampered down the wind into the distance, the true harm is but beginning for this giant of the woods. You may approach the tree from one side, and see it, scorched indeed from top to bottom, but apparently survivor of the peril. Make the circuit, and there, on the other side of the column, is a clear mass of living coal, spreading like an ulcer; while underground, to their most extended fibre, the roots are being eaten out by fire, and the smoke is rising through the fissures to the surface. A little while, and, without a nod of warning, the huge pine-tree snaps off short across the ground and falls prostrate with a crash. Meanwhile the fire continues its silent business; the roots are reduced to a fine ash; and long afterwards, if you pass by, you will find the earth pierced with radiating galleries, and preserving the design of all these subterranean spurs, as though it were the mould for a new tree instead of the print of an old one. These pitch-pines of Monterey are, with the single exception of the Monterey cypress, the most fantastic of forest trees. No words can give an idea of the contortion of their growth; they might figure without change in a circle of the nether hell as Dante pictured it; and at the rate at which trees grow, and at which forest fires spring up and gallop through the hills of California, we may look forward to a time when there will not be one of them left standing in that land of their nativity. At least they have not so much to fear from the axe, but perish by what may be called a natural although violent death; while it is man in his short-sighted greed that robs the country of the nobler red-wood. Yet a little while and perhaps all the hills of sea-board California may be as bald as Tamalpais. . . .

But it is the Pacific that exercises the most direct and obvious power upon the climate. At sunset, for months together, vast, wet, melancholy fogs arise and come shoreward from the ocean. From the hill-top above Monterey the scene is often noble, although it is always sad. The upper air is still bright with sunlight; a glow still rests upon the Gabelano Peak; but the fogs are in possession of the lower levels; they crawl in scarves among the sandhills; they float, a little higher, in clouds of a gigantic size and often of a wild configuration; to the south, where they have struck the seaward shoulder of the mountains of Santa Lucia, they double back and spire up skyward like smoke. Where their shadow touches, colour dies out of the world. The air grows chill and deadly as they advance. The trade-wind freshens, the trees begin to sigh, and all the windmills in Monterey are whirling and creaking and filling their cisterns with the brackish water of the sands. It takes but a little while till the invasion is complete. The sea, in its lighter order, has submerged the earth. Monterey is curtained in for the night in thick, wet, salt, and frigid clouds, so to remain till day returns; and before the sun's rays they slowly disperse and retreat in broken squadrons to the bosom of the sea. And yet often when the fog is thickest and most chill, a few steps out of the town and up the slope, the night will be dry and warm and full of inland perfume.

STUDY QUESTIONS

1. *What principle controls the order or arrangement of parts in this description?*
2. *What verbs are particularly effective in the descriptions of the sea and the fire? Compare Stevenson's use of verbs with that of Coffin in the preceding selection.*
3. *What are the unifying elements in this description?*
4. *In the last paragraph, Stevenson seems to see Monterey as occupying an ambiguous or contradictory position. Exactly what feeling is delicately suggested by it?*

5. *Write a description of a city or town, or part of one, that you found interesting and remember well.*

6. *Make it a point to observe some place or area very carefully in order to write a clear and thorough description of it. Notice all the details about it that seem significant, and decide what dominant impression the place makes upon an observer. Then write a description in which you try to make your reader able to visualize what you have seen, and also convey the feeling or quality of the place. Good subjects for this exercise are rooms in homes, streets, public places. Avoid subjects that seem to have no particular personality.*

Albert Camus   The Wind at Djémila*

There are certain places that kill the spirit within a man so that a truth may be born, a truth that is its own denial. When I went to Djémila, there was wind and sun — but that comes later. First I should say that a deep, heavy, flawless silence hangs over the place, a silence balanced against the bird-cries, the felt-like sounds of a three-holed flute, the stamping of goats, the shuffle of movement that emphasizes the quiet desolation. Now and then, far away on the edge of the plateau, a dry clacking whirr marks the sudden flight of a bird bursting from its hiding place among the stones. Every road in the city, every path winding among the ruins, the wide streets paved with flagstones, the huge public square lying between the arch of triumph and the temple in the hill — all lead toward the ravines that close in on Djémila from all sides. Djémila, its buildings spread out like a card game under a limitless sky. In the old ruined city, confronted by nothing but dead stones and emptiness, as the day wanes and the mountains loom larger in the purple shadows of dusk, you find the essence of your soul. The wind blows on the plateau, and in the great confusion of wind and sun that mixes light with the ruins, something happens that brings you face to face with yourself, in the solitude and silence of the lifeless city.

It takes a long time to go to Djémila. It is not a place where the traveller stops to rest and then goes on. The road to Djémila leads nowhere, opens on no country; you go there so you can return. The dead city lies at the end of a long sinuous road which, because it promises to end around every curve, seems much the longer. Finally, on a high plateau splattered with color, sunk between the high mountains, the yellow skeleton of Djémila appears like a forest of bones. Among its scattered trees and dry grass, in the midst of the hills and dry stones, the city lies hopeless, ugly, negative.

Our group of visitors wandered through its arid splendor all day. Little

* From *Noces* by Albert Camus. Translation by Georges Joyaux and used by his permission. Reprinted by permission of Librairie Gallimard, Paris, and of Alfred A. Knopf, Inc., authorized publishers of Camus in American translation.

by little the dry wind, hardly perceptible at the beginning of the afternoon, grew stronger and stronger until it seemed to fill the landscape. It blew from an opening in the mountains far to the east, ran across the rim of the horizon, and cascaded into the city among the stones and sun, whistling through the ruins, swirling about the columns, spreading out with a shout into the square. I felt myself bending before it like the mast of a ship; it tore the flesh from the bones, burned the eyes, chapped the lips, shrivelled the skin. Rubbed smooth by the gale, stunned with the effort of resistance, I lost consciousness of my body — like a pebble polished by the tides I was polished by the wind, ground down to my soul. I seemed to be floating in an earth-force, until finally the pulse of the wind fused with the pulse of my blood and the beating of my heart merged with the great clangorous rhythm of nature around me. The wind carved me in the shape of the stripped, barren land; in its embrace I was a stone among stones, an impersonal thing, alone like a column or an olive tree in the wind and sky.

The violent bath of sun and wind wore down the feeling of life within me until there was only a weak flutter of wings beneath the surface, only a spark of protest, only a faint rebelliousness of spirit. Cut adrift, blown out to the four corners of the world, I was of the wind and in the wind, part of the broken columns and the arch, of the flagstones warm in the sun, of the pale mountains looming over the deserted city — apart, separate, alienated from the world and from myself.

I know that I exist, I am conscious of the present moment. I can be sure of nothing more. Like a man imprisoned for life in a bare cell, knowing that tomorrow will be the same as today, and all tomorrows after, I know only the present and the now — there is nothing to wait for, no future. This truth I found in the dry landscape and wind of Djémila, a truth that came from the land itself, a touch of solitude, detachment, and death common to us both. As I stood among the columns and their oblique shadows, problems of life and death plummeted out of my mind like wounded birds from the air. When night came, stifling the sounds and lights of the town under the ashy blackness falling from the sky, I was alone and abandoned, defenseless against an inner voice that whispered, No, there is nothing.

Few people realize that there is a refusal to accept things which has nothing to do with renouncing them. What do we mean when we say *future, improvement, progress*? I do not understand the words. I refuse obstinately to believe that there is a *later* in the world because I refuse to renounce the richness of the present moment. I can find no pleasure in believing, as some do, that death is a door that opens on another life; to me it is always closed. I cannot say, as some do, that death is a valley one must cross; to me it is a horrible, ignoble adventure. All that people say about death is simply an attempt to lighten the load of life they carry, but as I watch the heavy flight of the birds above Djémila, I realize that life is a burden that I do not want to lose. Nothing beyond the present concerns me, nothing beyond death. There is still too much youth in my blood for me to speak of death with assurance, but when the time comes to face its silence, I know what I shall say — that death is death, and nothing more, a step not toward something but away from something.

A man lives with a few familiar ideas, two or three at most, and here and there, in contact with the world and men, they are polished, shaped, changed. It takes years for a man to evolve an idea that he can call his own, one he can speak of with authority. A man in his youth looks the world in the face; as he grows older he steps aside to see it in profile. So it is with death. A young man has not yet had time to shape and polish his concept of death and nothingness, though he recognizes how horrible it is and fears it with the physical fear of an animal who does not want to lose the sun. But youth has no illusions, and has neither the time nor the sense of pity needed to construct them. I found the idea and meaning of death at Djémila, in the solemn, dismal cry of stone rising from the serrated land, in the gravelike dusk of the falling sun. From the winds of Djémila I learned that men must find how to look facts in the face, so that they can regain the lost innocence and shining certainty with which ancient men saw death. In recognizing and clasping death, man regains his youth. (But not through illness, a contemptible nostrum against death, an apprenticeship of self-pity to prepare man for death, a feeble attempt to shield him from the inevitability of death.) This I learned at Djémila, that the only way to live is with a real understanding of the meaning of death — that it is a separation from what you have in the here and now, that in dying you lose the world of the present moment, and that beyond that there is nothing.

It is surprising that we have opinions about so many things and yet so few about death. We say, "It is good," or "It is evil." We fear it, or we welcome it. Because it is a plain and simple thing we find it incomprehensible. We can no more discuss it or define it than we can discuss or define a color—what is *blue*, and what is *death?* I have seen dogs die, and a few people; all I remember is that I did not like to touch them. And though I may say to myself, "I must die," the words mean nothing. I cannot really believe it, and I have only the experience of seeing others die to give it any meaning. But when I think of flowers, smiles, young girls, the world around me, I do not want to die. I know then that I fear death because I am jealous of life. I envy those who will live after I am dead, those for whom flowers and smiles and desires will have full meaning in terms of flesh and blood and feeling. I enjoy life too much to be unselfish, and I care little about eternity. Yet I know that someday they will say to me as I lie there with fear in my guts and my life cupped in my hands, "You are brave and must know the truth—you are going to die...." I do not know what death is, but the thought of its blankness brings angry blood beating in my head and the urge to smash the world into bits. *End*

But men die, nevertheless. The doctor says, "When you are cured—"

and then you die. I do not like to be lied to. There are times when the world lies, and times when it tells the truth—Djémila told the truth, a sad insistent truth. I prefer to see death clearly, to look at it plainly, in the full heat of my enjoyment of life and horror of death. I am afraid of death only because it will separate me from the world of the living, because I am attached to the here and now. To lose a fear of death, we must create in ourselves a consciousness of what death really is, we must feel an awareness of the life, the body, and the instant that we lose when we die. Beyond that there is nothing. The lonely song I heard in the wind on the hills of Djémila drove this bitter truth deeper into my mind.

In the evening we climbed the slopes leading toward the town, listening to the guide, "Here is the old pagan city—this section, lying outside, is where the Christians lived. Later we shall see—" Men and societies rose and fell in this land; conquering armies marked it with changing civilizations, measuring greatness by the boundaries of empire. Only the ruins survive. Djémila is a denial of all their aspirations, for this skeleton of a city, with the white pigeons wheeling above the square in the dusk, is a symbol of defeat. The great cry of stone that the city utters, among the hills and the silence, is a clear cry of poetry—of indifference, loneliness, despair—the true signs of a beauty that tightens the heart. As Djémila faded behind me — with its lonely sky, the birdsongs on the far plateau, the sudden scamperings of goats on the flanks of the hills — I knew that there in the relaxed and sonorous dusk I had looked at the live face of a God on his altar.

STUDY QUESTIONS

1. *Would you call this description prevailingly objective or subjective? Is it more or less objective than the description of Coffin and Stevenson? Why?*

2. *Point out some of the striking comparisons that help to convey Camus's feeling about the town he is describing.*

3. *In what way does Djémila reflect for Camus the condition of human life in general? What was the "truth" that was born in the author as the result of his visit to Djémila?*

4. *What relations do you see between Camus' statement that "A man lives with a few familiar ideas, two or three at most, and here and there, in contact with the world and men, they are polished, shaped, changed," and the generalizations which Read and Thomas make in the first two selections of this anthology? As you read ahead in the selections under "The Shape of Reality," consider the extent to which these ideas are related to some of the ideas in those selections.*

5. *Do you think another person might have reacted to Djémila in a less pessimistic way? If you disagree with Camus' view, write a theme explaining your disagreement, and suggesting what other attitudes toward such a place as Djémila might be possible.*

6. *Write an "interpretation" of a place you have visited that seemed to you especially typical or meaningful.*

4. THE SHAPE OF REALITY

George Henry Lewes The Principle of Vision*

*I*nsight is the first condition of Art. Yet many a man who has never been beyond his village will be silent about that which he knows well, and will fancy himself called upon to speak of the tropics or the Andes — on the reports of others. Never having seen a greater man than the parson and the squire — and not having seen into them — he selects Cromwell, and Plato, Raphael and Napoleon, as his models, in the vain belief that these impressive personalities will make his work impressive. Of course, I am speaking figuratively. By "never having been beyond his village," I understand a mental no less than topographical limitation. The penetrating sympathy of genius will, even from a village, traverse the whole world. What I mean is, that unless by personal experience, no matter through what avenues, a man has gained clear insight into the facts of life, he cannot successfully place them before us; and whatever insight he *has* gained, be it of important or of unimportant facts, will be of value if truly reproduced. No sunset is precisely similar to another, no two souls are affected by it in a precisely similar way. Thus may the commonest phenomenon have a novelty. To the eye that can read aright there is an infinite variety even in the most ordinary human being. But to the careless, indiscriminating eye all individuality is merged in a misty generality. Nature and men yield nothing new to such a mind. Of what avail is it for a man to walk out into the tremulous mist of morning, to watch the slow sunset, and wait for the rising stars, if he can tell us nothing about these but what others have already told us — if he feels nothing but what others have already felt? Let a man look for himself and tell truly what he sees. We will listen to that. We must listen to it, for its very authenticity has the subtle power of compulsion. What others have seen and felt we can learn better from their own lips....

Perception, as distinguished from sensation, is the presentation before consciousness of the details which once were present in conjunction with the object at this moment affecting sense. These details are inferred to be still in conjunction with the object, although not revealed to sense. Thus, when an apple is perceived by me, who merely see it, all that sense reports

* From "The Principles of Success in Literature," first published in *Fortnightly Review,* 1865.

is of a certain coloured surface: the roundness, the firmness, the fragrance, and taste of the apple are not present to sense, but are made present to consiousness by the act of perception. The eye sees a certain coloured surface; the mind sees at the same instant many other co-existent but unapparent facts — it reinstates in their due order these unapparent facts. Were it not for this mental vision supplying the deficiencies of ocular vision, the coloured surface would be an enigma. But the suggestion of sense rapidly recalls the experiences previously associated with the object. The apparent facts disclose the facts that are unapparent.

Inference is only a higher form of the same process. We look from the window, see the dripping leaves and the wet ground, and infer that rain has fallen. It is on inferences of this kind that all knowledge depends. The extension of the known to the unknown, of the apparent to the unapparent, gives us science. Except in the grandeur of its sweep, the mind pursues the same course in the interpretation of geological facts as in the interpretation of the ordinary incidents of daily experience. To read the pages of the great Stone Book, and to perceive from the wet streets that rain has fallen, are forms of the same intellectual process. In the one case the inference traverses immeasurable spaces of time, connecting the apparent facts with causes (unapparent facts) similar to those which have been associated in experience with such results; in the other case the inference connects wet streets and swollen gutters with causes which have been associated in experience with such results. Let the inference span with its mighty arch a myriad of years, or link together the events of a few minutes, in each case the arch rises from the ground of familiar facts, and reaches an antecedent which is known to be a cause capable of producing them....

In general, men are passive under sense and the routine of habitual inferences. They are unable to free themselves from the importunities of the apparent facts and apparent relations which solicit their attention; and when they make room for unapparent facts, it is only for those which are familiar to their minds. Hence they can see little more than what they have been taught to see; they can only think what they have been taught to think. For independent vision, and original conception, we must go to children and men of genius. The spontaneity of the one is the power of the other. Ordinary men live among marvels and feel no wonder, grow familiar with objects and learn nothing new about them. Then comes an independent mind which *sees*; and it surprises us to find how servile we have been to habit and opinion, how blind to what we also might have seen, had we used our eyes. The link, so long hidden, has now been made visible to us. We hasten to make it visible to others. But the flash of light which revealed that obscured object does not help us to discover others. Darkness still conceals much that we do not even suspect. We continue our routine. We always think our views correct and complete; if we thought otherwise they would cease to be our views; and when the man of keener insight discloses our error, and reveals relations hitherto unsuspected, we learn to see with his eyes, and exclaim: "Now surely we have got the truth."

STUDY QUESTIONS

1. Lewes' insistence that art depends upon the uniqueness with which each man sees reality is frequently held to be one of the basic principles of good writing. To what extent have the writers in the section entitled "The Uncommon Observer" demonstrated "insight" in their writing? To what extent have they written about things within their own experience?

2. What is the difference, according to Lewes, between "sensation" and "perception"? Between "perception" and "inference"?

3. This short selection provides a convenient and useful example of simple definition of terms. What methods does Lewes use to define such terms as "sensation," "perception," and "inference"?

4. Why do we not ordinarily "perceive" as well as we might?

5. Write a description following Lewes' suggestion about "perception." Take some object or place that is familiar to you, and examine it as though you were seeing it for the first time, with the mind as well as the eye. Then organize your results into a written description.

6. Do you agree with Lewes that one must actually undergo a particular experience to write about it convincingly? If you do not, accept his challenge by writing an account of a place or experience of which you do not have first-hand knowledge, trying to make it as authentic as you can. If you do agree with Lewes, write an expository theme supported by examples, explaining the problems into which you think a writer will fall if he tries to write about experiences he has not had.

Bernard DeVoto   The Value of Observation*

Skill develops from controlled, corrected repetitions of an act for which one has some knack. Skill is a product of experience and criticism and intelligence. Analysis cannot much transcend those truisms. Between the amateur and the professional, between the duffer and the expert, between the novice and the veteran there is a difference not only in degree but in kind. The skillful man is, within the function of his skill, a different integration, a different nervous and muscular and psychological organization. He has specialized responses of great intricacy. His associative faculties have patterns of screening, acceptance and rejection, analysis and sifting, evaluation and selective adjustment much too complex for conscious direction. Yet as

* From *Across the Wide Missouri* by Bernard DeVoto. Copyright, 1947, by Houghton Mifflin Company. Reprinted by permission of the publishers.

the patterns of appraisal and adjustment exert their automatic and perhaps metabolic energy, they are accompanied by a conscious process fully as complex. A tennis player or a watchmaker or an airplane pilot is an automatism but he is also criticism and wisdom.

It is hardly too much to say that a mountain man's life was skill. He not only worked in the wilderness, he also lived there and he did so from sun to sun by the exercise of total skill. It was probably as intricate a skill as any ever developed by any way of working or living anywhere. Certainly it was the most complex of the wilderness crafts practiced on this continent. The mountains, the aridity, the distances, and the climates imposed severities far greater than those laid on forest-runners, rivermen, or any other of our symbolic pioneers. Mountain craft developed out of the crafts which earlier pioneers had acquired and, like its predecessors, incorporated Indian crafts, but it had a unique integration of its own. It had specific crafts, technologies, theorems and rationales and rules of thumb, codes of operating procedure — but it was a pattern of total behavior.

Treatises could be written on the specific details; we lack space even for generalizations. Why do you follow the ridges into or out of unfamiliar country? What do you do for a companion who has collapsed from want of water while crossing a desert? How do you get meat when you find yourself without gunpowder in a country barren of game? What tribe of Indians made this trail, how many were in the band, what errand were they on, were they going to or coming back from it, how far from home were they, were their horses laden, how many horses did they have and why, how many squaws accompanied them, what mood were they in? Also, how old is the trail, where are those Indians now, and what does the product of these answers require of you? Prodigies of such sign-reading are recorded by impressed greenhorns, travelers, and army men, and the exercise of critical reference and deduction which they exhibit would seem prodigious if it were not routine. But reading formal sign, however impressive to Doctor Watson or Captain Frémont, is less impressive than the interpretation of observed circumstances too minute to be called sign. A branch floats down a stream — is this natural, or the work of animals, or of Indians or trappers? Another branch or a bush or even a pebble is out of place — why? On the limits of the plain, blurred by heat mirage, or against the gloom of distant cottonwoods, or across an angle of sky between branches or where hill and mountain meet, there is a tenth of a second of what may have been movement — did men or animals make it, and, if animals, why? Buffalo are moving downwind, an elk is in an unlikely place or posture, too many magpies are hollering, a wolf's howl is off key — what does it mean?

Such minutiae could be extended indefinitely. As the trapper's mind is dealing with them, it is simultaneously performing a still more complex judgement on the countryside, the route across it, and the weather. It is recording the immediate details in relation to the remembered and the forecast.

A ten-mile traverse is in relation to a goal a hundred miles, or five hundred miles away: there are economies of time, effort, comfort, and horseflesh on any of which success or even survival may depend. Modify the reading further, in relation to season, to Indians, to what has happened. Modify it again in relation to stream flow, storms past, storms indicated. Again in relation to the meat supply. To the state of the grass. To the equipment on hand.... You are two thousand miles from depots of supply and from help in time of trouble.

All this (with much more) is a continuous reference and checking along the margin or in the background of the trapper's consciousness while he practices his crafts as hunter, wrangler, furrier, freighter, tanner, cordwainer, smith, gunmaker, dowser, merchant. The result is a high-level integration of faculties. The mountain man had mastered his conditions — how well is apparent as soon as soldiers, goldseekers, or emigrants come into his country and suffer where he has lived comfortably and die where he has been in no danger. He had no faculties or intelligence that the soldier or the goldseeker lacked; he had none that you and I lack. He had only skill. A skill so effective that, living in an Indian country, he made a more successful adaptation to it than the Indian — and this without reference to his superior material equipment. There was no craft and no skill at which the mountain man did not come to excel the Indian. He saw, smelled, and heard just as far and no farther. But there is something after all in the laborious accretion that convolutes the forebrain and increases the cultural heritage, for he made more of it.

STUDY QUESTIONS

1. *What is the difference, according to DeVoto, between "skill" and "a knack"?*
2. *What qualities possessed by the mountain men would be useful in writing a description? Which would be useful to a detective? To a poker player?*
3. *What connection is there between the opinion expressed in DeVoto's last sentence and the theory of evolution?*
4. *What possible reason may be given for the fact that the mountaineers adapted to their environment even more successfully than the Indians, who grew up in it?*
5. *Describe some activity which requires what DeVoto calls "the exercise of critical reference and deduction." Examples would be playing a game like bridge or checkers, predicting the weather, finding out why a car won't start.*
6. *Tell how you made (or could have made) an elaborate deduction from a small clue.*

John Steinbeck and Edward F. Ricketts

Observation and Interpretation*

𝒯he design of a book is the pattern of a reality controlled and shaped by the mind of the writer. This is completely understood about poetry or fiction, but it is too seldom realized about books of fact. And yet the impulse which drives a man to poetry will send another man into the tide pools and force him to try to report what he finds there. Why is an expedition to Tibet undertaken, or a sea bottom dredged? Why do men, sitting at the microscope, examine the calcareous plates of a sea-cucumber, and, finding a new arrangement and number, feel an exaltation and give the new species a name, and write about it possessively? It would be good to know the impulse truly, not to be confused by the "services to science" platitudes or the other little mazes into which we entice our minds so that they will not know what we are doing.

We have a book to write about the Gulf of California. We could do one of several things about its design. But we have decided to let it form itself: its boundaries a boat and a sea; its duration a six weeks' charter time; its subject everything we could see and think and even imagine; its limits — our own without reservation.

We made a trip into the Gulf; sometimes we dignified it by calling it an expedition. Once it was called the Sea of Cortez, and that is a better-sounding and a more exciting name. We stopped in many little harbors and near barren coasts to collect and preserve the marine invertebrates of the littoral. One of the reasons we gave ourselves for this trip — and when we used this reason, we called the trip an expedition -- was to observe the distribution of invertebrates, to see and to record their kinds and numbers, how they lived together, what they ate, and how they reproduced. That plan was simple, straight-forward, and only a part of the truth. But we did tell the truth to ourselves. We were curious. Our curiosity was not limited, but was as wide and horizonless as that of Darwin or Agassiz or Linnaeus or Pliny. We wanted to see everything our eyes would accommodate, to think what we could, and, out of our seeing and thinking, to build some kind of structure in modeled imitation of the observed reality. We knew that what we would see and record and construct would be warped, as all knowledge patterns are warped, first, by the collective pleasure and stream of our time and race, second by the thrust of our individual personalities. But knowing this, we might not fall into too many holes — we might maintain some balance between our warp and the separate thing, the external reality. The oneness of these two might take its contribution from both. For example: the Mexican sierra has "XVII-15-IX" spines in the dorsal fin. These can easily be counted. But if the sierra strikes hard on the line so that our hands are burned, if the fish sounds and nearly escapes and finally comes in over the rail, his colors pulsing and his tail beating the air, a whole new relational externality has come into being — an entity which is more than the sum of the fish plus the fisherman. The only way to count the spines of the sierra unaffected by this second relational reality is to sit in a laboratory, open an evil-smelling jar, remove a stiff colorless fish from formalin solution, count the spines, and write the truth "D. XVII-15-IX." There you have recorded a reality which cannot be assailed — probably the least important reality concerning either the fish or yourself.

It is good to know what you are doing. The man with his pickled fish has set down one truth and has recorded in his experience many lies. The fish is not that color, that texture, that dead, nor does he smell that way.

Such things we had considered in the months of planning our expedition and we were determined not to let a passion for unassailable little truths draw in the horizons and crowd the sky down on us. We knew that what seemed to us true could be only relatively true anyway. There is no other kind of observation. The man with his pickled fish has sacrificed a great observation about himself, the fish, and the focal point, which is his thought on both the sierra and himself.

We suppose this was the mental provisioning of our expedition. We said, "Let's go wide open. Let's see what we see, record what we find, and not fool ourselves with conventional scientific strictures. We could not observe a completely objective Sea of Cortez anyway, for in that lonely and uninhabited Gulf our boat and ourselves would change in the moment we entered. By going there, we would bring a new factor to the Gulf. Let us consider that factor and not be betrayed by this myth of permanent objective reality. If it exists at all, it is only available in pickled tatters or in distorted flashes. Let us go," we said, "into the Sea of Cortez, realizing that we become forever a part of it; that our rubber boots slogging through a flat of eelgrass, that the rocks we turn over in a tide pool, make us truly and permanently a factor in the ecology of the region. We shall take something away from it, but we shall leave something too." And if we seem a small factor in a huge pattern, nevertheless it is of relative importance. We take a tiny colony of soft corals from a rock in a little water world. And that isn't terribly important to the tide pool. Fifty miles away the Japanese shrimp boats are dredging with overlapping scoops, bringing up tons of shrimps, rapidly destroying the species so that it may never come back, and with the species destroying the ecological balance of the whole region. That isn't very important in the world. And six thousand miles away the great bombs are falling on London and the stars are not moved thereby. None of it is important or all of it is.

We determined to go doubly open so that in the end we could, if we wished, describe the sierra thus: "D. XVII-15-IX; A. II-15-IX," but also we could see the fish alive and swimming, feel it plunge against the lines, drag it threshing over the rail, and even finally eat it. And there is no reason why either approach should be inaccurate. Spine-count description need not suffer because another approach is also used. Perhaps out of the two approaches, we thought, there might emerge a picture more complete and even more accurate than either alone could produce. And so we went.

STUDY QUESTIONS

1. The opening generalization of this selection, that "the design of a book is the pattern of a reality controlled and shaped by the mind of the writer," is a thesis implicit in a number of selections in the whole first section of this anthology. Explain how it seems to be implied in the selections by Herbert Read, Graham Greene, George Orwell, Lafcadio Hearn, or others. What implications does this generalization have for the problem of organizing a theme?
2. The authors state that "all knowledge patterns are warped." Does this mean that the scientist cannot provide us with an "objective" description of reality?
3. What different kinds of "truth" do the authors discuss in this selection?
4. Explain in your own words what you think the authors mean by "reality."
5. Observe some object or place, record the checkable truths about it, and then write two brief descriptions, one in which you try to present these truths with the greatest possible objectivity, and the other in which you present it in terms of your interpreted sense perceptions.
6. Select one of the descriptions from the group entitled "The Uncommon Observer," such as that of coal mines by Orwell, or of Monterey by Stevenson; read in an encyclopedia some equivalent account of it; and write a paper describing the relative degree of "objectivity" in the two accounts.

David Daiches The Literary Use of Language*

*L*ife is a jungle of events whose meanings are at once too casual (and to that extent insignificant) and too full of possible implication (without offering us any guidance as to which implication or set of implications we should choose). The skilled storyteller makes those meanings at once more significant and less confused. He chooses or invents a tractable piece of life and proceeds both to define its meaning more precisely than the meaning of

* From *A Study of Literature* by David Daiches. Reprinted by permission of the Cornell University Press.

any event in real life can be known (Can we even talk of the "meaning" of events in real life, unless we mean simply their causes and effects?) and to enrich its meaning in a wholly unique manner. Is it possible simultaneously to define a meaning more precisely and to enrich it? We can see that this is possible if we consider what the skillful writer of fiction (and, indeed, of any kind of creative literature) actually does.

Let us take a very simple example. Consider that a journalist has been asked to stand for a while in a city street and then write up an account of the street and what took place there. As soon as he begins to write he will have to make his own definition of his subject. What in fact is meant by "the street and what took place there"? To define even the street requires a choice: is it simply the thoroughfare leading from one place to another, or are we to include the buildings which flank it, and if we include the buildings what aspects of them are we to include? A street, in fact, can be considered in an indefinite number of ways. As for defining "what took place there," we strike here immediately the problem of selection. Clearly, it would be physically impossible as well as wholly pointless for the writer to give an account of every single event which in fact occurred while he was there, or even of every single event which he observed. Our journalist would have to select from among the plethora of events — the actions and gestures of people, the movement of traffic, all the innumerable activities of city life — what he considered of importance or of interest on some standard or other. He would have to define "street" and "what took place there" before writing or in the process of writing. And he would have to make up his mind about his perspective. Should he try to get closer to some things than to others; should he vary the distance at which he stood from people and things, or maintain a simple gradation from foreground to background? These and other questions he will have to answer, consciously or unconsciously, in presenting us with a verbal picture of that street at that time. Having done so, he will have presented to us aspects of a situation which we can recognize as one which we either have known or might have known. If he can use the language with any ability at all, even if he can put together a number of sentences which say, however badly or crudely, what he saw (or rather, what he thought he saw) that he considered worth mentioning, we shall be able to recognize his account as corresponding to something of which we have had experience — assuming, of course, that we are products of the same civilization and are familiar with that kind of city street. That is to say, we should *recognize* the description as, in a general sort of way at least, true. The writer, without using any other skill than is required of a reasonably competent journalist, would have defined his subject intelligibly and recognizably. Out of the moving chaos of reality he will have isolated a static picture, which a certain class of readers would consent to, as reflecting in some sense an actual state of affairs.

Our journalist might do more than that. He might manage to convey to readers who have not had experience of that kind of city street at all a sense of the authenticity of his picture. He can do this by "style," by the selection and organization of his imagery, by using words in such a way that the reader is persuaded into recognizing not what he has seen but what he might have seen. The first stage is where we recognize what we know, the second is where we recognize what we might have known, and there is a third — where, while we recognize what we have known or might have known, we at the same time see, and know to be authentic, what we should never have seen for ourselves. The interesting fact is that where a writer succeeds in making authentic a picture of a kind that his readers might not have seen, he will very probably be doing more — he will be giving them at the same time a new insight which coexists with the feeling of recognition. This is because "style," that way of writing which makes convincing in its own right what would otherwise be merely recognizable, can rarely do this without going further. For such a style is the result of the ability to choose and order words in such a way that what is described becomes not merely something existing, something which happens to be in a particular place at a particular time, but something that is linked with man's wider fate, that suggests, and keeps on suggesting the more we read, ever wider categories of experiences until there is included something with which we can make contact, which touches what we, too, find recognizable. And then it becomes irrelevant whether what is described exists in fact in the real world or not. The mere journalist drops his words one by one, and there they lie, in the order in which he dropped them, specific but still, corresponding accurately enough to what the author intends to say, but having no further life of their own. But the true creative writer drops his words into our mind like stones in a pool, and the ever-widening circles of meaning eventually ring round and encompass the store of our own experience. And — to continue the metaphor — in doing so they provide a new context for familiar things, and what has been lying half dead in our mind and imagination takes on new life in virtue of its new context, so that we not only recognize what we feel we knew but see the familiar take on rich and exciting new meanings.

If, therefore, the journalist who described what went on in a particular city street during a given period of time had the literary skill (and the initial combination of feeling for life and feeling for language which alone can make such a skill *realizable*) to present his observations in such a way that when he wrote of businessmen entering and leaving the bank, children coming home from school, housewives out shopping, loiterers, barking dogs, lumbering busses, or whatever else he cared to note, he was able to convey to the reader something of the tragedy or the comedy of human affairs, wringing some human insight out of these multifarious incidents so that the reader not only sees what he already knew or even admits as authentic what he did not know, but sees simultaneously what he knew and what he never saw before, recognizes the picture in the light of his deepest, half-intuitive know-

ledge of what man's experience is and can be and at the same time see it
as a new illumination — if he can do this, then he has moved from journalism
into art. He has shown that he can make the means of expression comment
on what is expressed so as simultaneously to define and expand his subject
matter: define it by using words that block off the wrong meanings, which
show with complete compulsion that what is meant is *this* rather than *that*,
and expand it by choosing and arranging words and larger units of expression
so that they set going the appropriate overtones and suggestions which help
to elevate a description of people's behavior to an account of man's fate.

STUDY QUESTIONS

1. *What differences or similarities are there between Daiches' description of the
   functions of the storyteller, and Steinbeck and Ricketts' description of their
   intention in* The Sea of Cortez?
2. *What three decisions does the writer have to make in order to give an account
   of something from real life?*
3. *What, according to Daiches, is the difference between the subject matter of
   the journalist and the subject matter of the artist?*
4. *What are Daiches' three stages of the transcription of life?*
5. *Write a theme about a familiar subject or experience which you think will
   enable the reader to recognize what you are describing, and at the same time
   provide him with an insight into it which he probably could not have achieved
   himself. The subject should, naturally, be something you are familiar with.
   Your superior insight should depend, not on special information which you
   happen to possess, but on your special interest in or understanding of the
   subject.*
6. *Transcribe some actual experience, aiming to give your reader a fair and accurate impression of it by omitting irrelevancies and stressing the main features*

2 Language, Thought, and Ideas

1. THE CRAFT OF WRITING

Harold Whitehall Writing and Speech*

All of us have a grammar. The fact that we use and understand English
in daily affairs means that we use and understand, for the most part unconsciously, the major grammatical patterns of our language. Yet because of
the effects of education, many of us have come to think of a relatively formal
written English and its reflection among those who "speak by the book" as
the only genuine English, and to consider its grammar as the only acceptable
English grammar. That is by no means true. The basic form of present-day
American English is the patterned, rhythmed, and segmented code of voice
signals called *speech* — speech as used in everyday conversation by highly
educated people (*cultivated speech*), by the general run of our population
(*common speech*), or by some rural persons in such geographically isolated
areas as the Ozark Plateau, the Appalachian Mountains, or the woodland
areas of northern New England (*folk speech*). From the code of speech, the
language of formal writing is something of an abstraction, differing in details
of grammar and vocabulary and lacking clear indication of the bodily

* From *Structural Essentials of English*, copyright, 1951, by Harold Whitehall. Copyright, 1954, 1956, by Harcourt, Brace and Company, Inc. Reprinted by permission of
Harcourt, Brace and Company, Inc.

gestures and meaningful qualities of the voice which accompany ordinary conversation. Thus, serious written English may be regarded as a rather artificial dialect of our language. To acquire that dialect, the would-be writer needs to know a good deal about its structural details, and particularly about those in which it differs from the less formal varieties of speech.

Even a moment's reflection will show that the spoken American language is backed by expressive features lacking in the written language: the rise or fall of the voice at the ends of phrases and sentences; the application of vocal loudness to this or that word or part of a word; the use of gesture; the meaningful rasp or liquidity, shouting or muting, drawling or clipping, whining or breaking, melody or whispering imparted to the quality of the voice. Written English, lacking clear indication of such features, must be so managed that it compensates for what it lacks. It must be more carefully organized than speech in order to overcome its communicative deficiencies as compared with speech. In speech, we safeguard meaning by the use of intonation, stress, gesture, and voice qualities. In writing, we must deal with our medium in such a way that the meaning cannot possibly be misunderstood. In the absence of an actual hearer capable of interrupting and demanding further explanation, a clear writer is always conscious of "a reader over his shoulder." All this despite the fact that writing, being permanent, as compared with speech, which is evanescent, allows not only reading but also rereading.

Nor is this all. If written English is somewhat abstract, somewhat artificial, it is also generalized — national, not geographically or socially limited in scope. We must realize that comparatively few of us make use in our day-to-day affairs of a generalized spoken American English that is at all comparable with it. Such a language — a Received Standard Spoken English — exists, but not for the most part in this country where the practical need for it is slight. It exists in England, where the practical need for it is great. In England, many people still start their linguistic careers speaking one or another of the regional dialects, dialects so different from each other in vocabulary and grammar, so quilt-crazy in their distribution, that they form real barriers to generalized, national communication. Yet, in a modern, democratic country, general communication is a necessity. For that reason, Englishmen are willing to accept the notion both of a generalized spoken and a generalized written form of expression on a level above the dialects, and are willing to make the effort of learning them in school and elsewhere. We would be equally willing if our everyday speech happened to resemble this specimen from the English county of Lancaster:

> "Nay! my heart misgi'es me! There's summat abeawt this neet's wark as is noan jannock. Look thee here! Yon chap's noan t' first sheep theaw's lifted tax-free fro't' mooar, an' aw've niver been one to worrit abeawt it, that aw hav'nt. But toneet, someheaw, it's noan t'same. There's summat beawn't 'appen—aw con feel it i' my booans. This een, an unconny wind

wor burrin' i't'ling, an' not a cleawd i't' sky; an' whin aw went deawn to' t'well for watter, t'bats wor flyin' reawn it in a widdershins ring. Mark my words, there's mooar to coom."

In the United States, our language situation is quite different. Ours is probably the only country on earth in which three thousand miles of travel will bring no difficulty of spoken communication. We do have, of course, regional and social differences of language. The speech of Maine does not coincide in all points with that of Texas, nor the speech of Georgia with that of Minnesota. The speech of cultivated people in urban centers is not precisely that of the general mass of our citizens, nor that of rural residents of limited education in geographically secluded areas. Yet, unless we deliberately choose to emphasize disparities for social or other reasons, our regional and social speech differences create no great barriers to the free exchange of opinions and ideas. They consist of flavoring rather than substance.

Precisely for that reason, pressures for the adoption of a generalized national spoken American English comparable in acceptance and prestige with Received Standard Spoken British have proved largely unavailing. In American life, one may use cultivated or common speech Southern, cultivated or common speech Northeastern, or cultivated or common speech North Middle Western, without encountering any great practical disadvantage. Our standards of speech are mainly regional standards, and most of us, in actual fact, speak some kind of a patois in which one or another of the cultivated or common speech regional varieties of American English blends quite happily with elements absorbed from reading and the educational process. We are very fortunate in this — fortunate that American historical and sociological conditions have removed difficulties of spoken communication found in most other parts of the world.

In a lesser sense, however, our good fortune is something of a misfortune. Because an American can understand other Americans no matter what regional or social class they come from, he is apt to underestimate the necessity for a generalized and abstract written American English. Because he finds no pressing reason for standardizing his speech, he is likely to misunderstand the necessity for standardizing his writing. He would like to write as he speaks. Moreover, the differences between the various regional and social varieties of American speech, being slight, are often of so subtle a nature that he tends to find difficulty in discriminating them. Slight as they are, when transferred to writing they are sufficient to make a reader pause, to induce a momentary feeling of unfamiliarity, to interrupt his consideration of the *matter* of expression by unwittingly calling attention to the *manner* of expression. Outside frankly literary writing (particularly the writing of poetry), such pauses, such unfamiliarities, such interruptions will hinder rather than help the writer's communicative purpose. If writing must be generalized, it must be generalized with a good reason: to speak with a local accent is not disadvantageous; to write serious prose with a local accent definitely is.

The moral of all this is clear. To gain command of serious written English is to acquire, quite deliberately, an abstract and generalized variety of the language differing by nature and purpose from any social or regional variety whatsoever. It is to sacrifice the local for the general, the spontaneous for the permanent. It is to bring to the study of written American English something of the perspective we normally reserve for the study of foreign languages. It is to master a set of grammatical and vocabulary patterns not because they are "correct" but because experience has proved them efficient in the communicative activity of writing.

The word "correct" is deliberately introduced here. The clear distinctions between spoken and written language mentioned in the paragraphs above have been all too often masked by the pernicious doctrine of "correctness." Perhaps that is to be expected. Without the flexible medium of language, a human society in human terms would be impossible. Without language, there could be no continuous record of experience, no diversification of labor, no great social institutions — the humanity of man could never have been achieved. But social activities breed social rituals and social judgments. Because language is *the* basic social instrument, it has inevitably acquired social attitudes so complex and variegated that they have often been allowed to obscure its primary communicative function. For far too many of us, knowledge of language is confused with knowledge of judgments on language that are socially acceptable. Education in the English language has become, for the most part, education in linguistic niceties — a poor substitute for that real linguistic education which ought to show us the major and minor patterns of our language, the way in which they interlock in function, the ways in which they can be manipulated for effective expression. As a result, the instrument of communication which should be every man's servant has become most men's master. This need not be so. Our self-confidence is immediately bolstered, our attitudes towards the study of writing techniques tremendously improved, once we realize that the difficulties of writing English do not spring from faulty nurture, restricted intelligence, or beyond-the-tracks environment but from the necessary change-over from one kind of English to another — that they are neither unpardonable nor irremediable.

Such is the milieu of the written English with which this little book is concerned. No matter what irrationalities surround the details and the perspectives by which English is normally viewed, the fact that it has so admirably served and is still serving the needs of many fine writers guarantees that it is neither an impossible nor an unworthy instrument of human expression. Let us admit that all languages, spoken or written, are man-made things, that their weaknesses as well as their strengths are implicit in their human origin. Let us admit that the world has never known either a faultless language nor one constructed on what to us seems a strictly logical system. The proper approach to written English is first to understand what the medium is; then to concede its limitations and to use its strengths to the best possible

effect. Every communicative medium has a set of resistances that the communicator must overcome. Marble is hard; paint relatively unmanageable;
music barely descriptive. No small part of any kind of composition is contributed directly by tensions set up between the craftsman's demands on his
medium on the one hand and its inherent resistances on the other. To this,
the science, craft, and art of expression in written American English is no
exception.

STUDY QUESTIONS

1. *This brief introductory chapter from Harold Whitehall's* Structural Essentials
   of English *offers a good insight into some of the reasons for the difficulties
   we all experience in learning to write well. Can you point out some examples
   of "grammatical and vocabulary patterns" which seem to you to occur in
   writing but not in speech?*
2. *How does the dialect situation in England differ from that in the United
   States? What bearing does this have on the kind of standard English people
   learn in schools in the two countries?*
3. *What is the difference between "just talk" and responsible writing? Why
   can they not be the same?*
4. *In the next to the last paragraph of this selection, Whitehall opposes the
   doctrine of "correctness." Why, in his view, is this doctrine "pernicious"?
   Does Whitehall argue here that one need not learn what are usually referred
   to as "correct" patterns of writing and speech? If not, precisely what is his
   point?*
5. *Whitehall develops this selection largely by using comparisons and contrasts.
   Point out the various comparisons which he uses.*
6. *Note carefully the description of differences between speech and writing
   outlined in the second paragraph of this selection. Then study some simple
   piece of writing—this selection for example—and describe the means by which
   the writer has tried to be conscious of "a reader over his shoulder."*

Wendell Johnson You Can't Write Writing*

*T*his discussion is not designed to take the place of a textbook for the teaching of effective communicative writings, but it is offered in the hope
that a brief statement of a few simple principles upon which such writing
is based might serve at least to raise the question as to why these principles
are not more adequately taught by English instructors.

The first of these principles has already been given in the statement that
clearness depends upon, and can be measured in terms of, the degree of

* From *Language, Meaning, and Maturity,* Harper & Brothers, 1954. Copyright S.
I. Hayakawa, 1954. Reprinted by the kind permission of the author.

agreement between the writer and his readers as to what the words of the
writer represent. Simply by striving for a high degree of such agreement,
the writer discovers, in some measure, his ingenuity in achieving it. He
discovers the usefulness of conditional and quantifying terms, the confusion
created by leaving out significantly differentiating details, the degree to which
the meaning of a term varies from context to context, and the kinds of differences he must allow for among his readers' habits of interpreting words.
He learns to rely less on the dictionary and more on the linguistic habits of
the people for whom he writes. He discovers that literary posing, pleasurable
as it may be, usually can be enjoyed only at the expense of effective communication — that Chesterton's paradoxes or Paul de Kruif's chronic astonishment are more titillating than informative. He discovers that there are various
levels of abstraction, and that if he goes systematically from lower to higher
levels he can use so-called abstract words and still be reasonably clear.

Above all, perhaps, he discovers the basic significance of order, or relations,
or structure, or organization. This matter of structural relationships has wide
ramifications, and no writer ever exhausts it, but the student quickly grasps
some of its more obvious aspects, if he is striving for agreement between himself and his reader. It does not take him long to understand that the organization of what he writes should correspond to the organization of what he is
writing about if the reader is to follow him readily. The graduate students
with whom I work frequently have difficulty organizing their descriptions of
experimental techniques or procedures, and I have found that it is more
helpful to refer them to a cookbook than to a textbook on composition. By
examining a cookbook they see at once that the organization of a description
of procedure is determined simply by the order of the events that make up the
procedure. First you do *a*, and then *b*, and then *c*, and you write it in that
order because you do it in that order. This simple principle of order is
fundamental in practically all descriptive, narrative, and expository writing,
and it is obvious to anyone who is attempting to be considerate of the reader.

One might suppose that graduate students would know this, but in spite
of the years they have spent in English courses most of them seem not to
have learned much about it. The more significant fact is that, as a rule, they
learn quite readily to apply this simple principle, once it is clearly explained
and demonstrated to them. In this case, certainly, one can make a tree that
either God or the English teachers forgot to make.

One aspect of organization that seems to have eluded practically all
graduate students is that involved in the making of transitions. Even those
who have been taught how to lay beads in a row have not been taught how to
string them. Just as the order of what one writes is determined by the order
of the parts or events involved in what one is writing about, so the ways in
which transitions are made in the writing are determined by the ways in
which the parts or events are related in the realities one is describing, nar-
rating, or explaining. The ability to move from one sentence or paragraph or

chapter to the next, in such a way as to blend them into a unified whole, is largely dependent upon an understanding of the reasons for going from one to the next, of why one statement should follow another instead of the reverse, of why one should say, "It follows, then," rather than "But." And these reasons are found in the character of the relations existing among the details of that about which the writing is being done. This becomes obvious to one who is not trying to write writing, but who is attempting, rather, to write-about-something-for-someone.

Another principle underlying communicative writing is that clarity is a prerequisite to validity. It is to be considered that statements that flow beautifully and are grammatically superb may be, also, utterly devoid of factual meaning, or meaningful but vague, or precise but invalid. For writing to be effective, in the sense in which I am using this term, it may or may not be grammatically correct, but it must be both clear and valid. It can be clear without having validity, but if it is unclear its validity cannot well be determined. It must, then, first of all, be clear; it must be that before the question of its validity can even be raised. We ask the writer, "What do you mean?" before we ask, "How do you know?" Until we reach agreement as to precisely what he is writing about, we cannot possibly reach agreement as to whether, or in what degree, his statements are true.

Only to the extent that the various readers of a statement agree as to the specific conditions or observations required for ascertaining its validity can the question of its validity have meaning. And the extent to which the readers of the statement agree on these conditions is, of course, indicative of the extent to which the statement is clear. If a statement is such that its readers do not agree at all as to how it might be verified or refuted, the statement may be "beautiful" or "rich in meaning" or grammatically irreproachable, but it is also, from the point of view of scientific courses such as I am teaching, nonsense. It cannot be demonstrated to be valid or invalid, and is meaningful, therefore, to its author, possibly to his English teacher, and perhaps to his psychiatrist.

My graduate students have not learned this, either. They show this in a particularly disturbing manner when they first attempt to state the topics or problems they propose to investigate in undertaking their theses. They quite characteristically propose problems which preclude the possibility of clear discussion. They propose questions for investigation, for which they desire to obtain precise answers, but which are so stated as to be unanswerable. Apparently they have never been taught that one cannot get a precise answer to a vague question — that the terminology of the question limits the clarity and thus the validity of the answer. Many students are so befuddled on this point that they do not recognize any relation at all between clarity and validity. They actually assume, for example, that they can ask, "What causes personality maladjustments?" without specifying what they mean by "causes," or by "personality," or by "maladjustments," or what observations one is to make in order to comply with their definition of "what." Many of them appear to have been taught that to eliminate the vagueness of a question or statement is to destroy its "richness of meaning" — that for a statement to be "full of meaning" it must not mean anything in particular!

Even though they have been so taught, and come, therefore, to the graduate college quite untrained in the writing of valid statements, they can be taught, to a considerable degree, to gauge the validity of what they write. They can be trained to do this by being trained, first, to write clearly. For when a statement is made clearly — when there is reasonable agreement among its readers as to what it represents in the realm of fact — its validity can be judged, or a procedure for determining its degree of validity can be devised.

In summary, then, what graduate students, as I know them, have not been well taught — and what, in my judgment, their English instructors should have been able to teach them, because the students do learn readily — is the ability to write a clear, organized, unified, and valid document. They have been made familiar with grammar, for the most part, and they have picked up a few tricks of literary flavoring. The grammar can be used to advantage; most of the literary condiments have to be chucked....

My own narrow concern with all this lies in the fact that the ineffectiveness of the English instruction in our schools makes for a serious difficulty in the graduate college in all its branches. But the problem has an importance far more vast than this fact could ever give to it. For the ability of the individual, and of groups of individuals, to use language clearly and with validity is basic to personal efficiency and general development — it is basic to sanity itself — and it is fundamental to intelligent social organization and to the adequate management of national and international problems. The teachers of English in our schools and universities have been and are being entrusted with the heavy responsibility of training the members of our society in the effective communicative use of our language. It is not a responsibility that they can meet appropriately merely by teaching the formalism of grammar, or superciliously disclaim by asserting that effective writing is an art and cannot be taught.

Effective writing is a human necessity in anything resembling a democratic culture, and this becomes increasingly true as the culture becomes increasingly complex. If the effective use of language cannot be taught, or if it is not to be taught to a far greater extent than it has been, we may well have occasion to despair of the grand experiment dreamed by Voltaire, championed by Washington and Franklin, and cherished by the American people through many generations. And if we must despair of that, then truly, even if you do learn to speak correct English, it may well not seem to matter very much "who you talk it to." For when the people cannot adequately speak or write their language, there arise strong men to speak and write it for them — and "at" them.

The issues of which I write are by no means to be regarded as academic issues. We are a symbolic class of life. To say that we are human is to say, above all and with incalculable significance, that our problems, as individuals, as groups, and as a world culture, are symbolic problems. They are problems that center around the symbols of government, the symbols of finance and general economy, of social status, of power and prestige, of class and race. They are the problems involved in the great institutionalized symbol systems of the Church, the Law, the State. They are problems of meaning, of evaluation, of orientation, processes which, on human levels, are predominantly symbolic in character. It is not the vestige of some forebear's whim that the whole structure of our educational system is founded squarely on the three R's, for reading, writing, and the use of numbers are forms of behavior in the absence of which *human* society would disintegrate and vanish. The degree to which these forms of behavior are cultivated and made adequate determines, more than does anything else, the degree to which a symbolic class of life may escape the threat of self-destruction and achieve cultural maturity. Our maladjustment, no less than our genius, as individuals and as groups, lies in our way of responding to and with symbols.

The place of the teacher of English in the structure of a symbolic society is, thus and indeed, not one to be occupied by petulant little men engrossed in verbal "fancy work." It is not too much to say that our possibilities for progress are determined, and limited, by those who instruct us in the use of our language. This view is as disheartening, perhaps, as it is challenging, but the more challenging it is to some, the less disheartening it need be to others.

STUDY QUESTIONS

1. *What are the three requirements Johnson makes of a good paper?*
2. *Johnson is speaking here of what might be called objective expository writing. To what extent are his demands and his criteria for good writing equally applicable to all kinds of writing?*
3. *Johnson thinks that a statement cannot communicate unless reader and author agree on the meaning of the terms in it. Is this necessarily true in every case? Consider, for example, some of the autobiographical and descriptive selections in Section I.*
4. *What, according to Johnson, is the relationship between clarity and validity?*
5. *Write a theme giving some examples and explaining more fully what Johnson means by his observation that the problems faced by men are "symbolic problems." Good examples for this would be problems of meaning, feeling or interpretation which have been important in history.*
6. *Do you think Johnson may be exaggerating when he says that our possibilities for progress depend upon teachers of language? Write a theme describing others who are, to some extent, responsible for progress, being sure that by "progress" you mean the same thing as Johnson.*

Samuel Eliot Morison   History as a Literary Art*

*T*here are no special rules for writing history; any good manual of rhetoric or teacher of composition will supply the rules for writing English. But what terrible stuff passes for English in Ph.D. dissertations, monographs, and articles in historical reviews! Long, involved sentences that one has to read two or three times in order to grasp their meaning; poverty in vocabulary, ineptness of expression, weakness in paragraph structure, frequent misuse of words, and, of late, the introduction of pseudo-scientific and psychological jargon. There is no fundamental cure for this except better teaching of English in our schools and colleges, and by every teacher, whatever his other subject may be. If historical writing is infinitely better in France than in America, and far better in the British Isles and Canada than in the United States, it is because every French and British teacher of history drills his pupils in their mother tongue, requiring a constant stream of essays and reports, and criticizing written work not only as history but as literature. The American university teacher who gives honor grades to students who have not yet learned to write English, for industrious compilations of facts or feats of memory, is wanting in professional pride or competency.

Of course, what we should all like to attain in writing history is style. "The sense for style," says Whitehead in his *Aims of Education*, "is an aesthetic sense, based on admiration for the direct attainment of a foreseen end, simply and without waste. Style in art, style in literature, style in science, style in logic, style in practical execution, have fundamentally the same aesthetic qualities, namely attainment and restraint. Style, in its finest sense, is the last acquirement of the educated mind; it is also the most useful. It pervades the whole being.... Style is the ultimate morality of mind."

Unfortunately, there is no royal road to style. It cannot be attained by mere industry; it can never be achieved through imitation, although it may be promoted by example. Reading the greatest literary artists among historians will help; but do not forget that what was acceptable style in 1850 might seem turgid today. We can still read Macaulay with admiration and pleasure, we can still learn paragraph structure and other things from Macaulay, but anyone who tried to imitate Macaulay today would be a pompous ass.

Just as Voltaire's ideal curé advises his flock not to worry about going to heaven, but to do right and probably by God's grace they will get there; so the young writer of history had better concentrate on day-by-day improve-

---

* Reprinted from *By Land and By Sea*, by Samuel Eliot Morison, by permission of Alfred A. Knopf, Inc. Copyright, 1951, by Priscilla B. Morison.

ment in craftsmanship. Then perhaps he may find some day that his prose appeals to a large popular audience; that, in other words, he has achieved style through simple, honest, straightforward writing.

A few hints as to the craft may be useful to budding historians. First and foremost, *get writing!* Young scholars generally wish to secure the last fact before writing anything, like General McClellan refusing to advance (as people said) until the last mule was shod. It is a terrible strain, isn't it, to sit down at a desk with your notes all neatly docketed, and begin to write? You pretend to your wife that you mustn't be interrupted; but, actually, you welcome a ring of the telephone, a knock at the door, or a bellow from the baby as an excuse to break off. Finally, after smoking sundry cigarettes and pacing about the house two or three times, you commit a lame paragraph or two to paper. By the time you get to the third, one bit of information you want is lacking. What a relief! Now you must go back to the library or the archives to do some more digging. That's where you are happy! And what you turn up there leads to more questions and prolongs the delicious process of research. Half the pleas I have heard from graduate students for more time or another grant-in-aid are mere excuses to postpone the painful drudgery of writing.

There is the "indispensablest beauty in knowing how to get done," said Carlyle. In every research there comes a point, which you should recognize like a call of conscience, when you must get down to writing. And when you once are writing, go on writing as long as you can; there will be plenty of time later to shove in the footnotes or return to the library for extra information. Above all, *start* writing. Nothing is more pathetic than the "gonna" historian, who from graduate school on is always "gonna" write a magnum opus but never completes his research on the subject, and dies without anything to show for a lifetime's work.

Dictation is usually fatal to good historical writing. Write out your first draft in longhand or, if you compose easily on the typewriter, type it out yourself, revise with pencil or pen, and have it retyped clean. Don't stop to consult your notes for every clause or sentence; it is better to get what you have to say clearly in your mind and dash it off; then, after you have it down, return to your notes and compose your next few pages or paragraphs. After a little experience you may well find that you think best with your fingers on the typewriter keys or your fountain pen poised over the paper. For me, the mere writing of a few words seems to point up vague thoughts and make jumbled facts array themselves in neat order. Whichever method you choose, composing before you write or as you write, do not return to your raw material or verify facts and quotations or insert footnotes until you have written a substantial amount, an amount that will increase with practice. It is significant that two of our greatest American historians, Prescott and Parkman, were nearly blind during a good part of their active careers. They had to have the sources read to them and turn the matter over and over in their minds before they could give anything out; and when they gave, *they gave!*

Now, the purpose of this quick, warm synthesis between research, thinking, and writing is to attain the three prime qualities of historical composition — clarity, vigor, and objectivity. You must think about your facts, analyze your material, and decide exactly what you mean before you can write it so that the average reader will understand. Do not fall into the fallacy of supposing that "facts speak for themselves." Most of the facts that you excavate, like other relics of past human activity, are dumb things; it is for you to make them speak by proper selection, arrangement, and emphasis. Dump your entire collection of facts on paper, and the result will be unreadable if not incomprehensible.

So, too, with vigor. If your whole paragraph or chapter is but a hypothesis, say so at the beginning, but do not bore and confuse the reader with numerous "buts," "excepts," "perhapses," "howevers," and "possiblys." Use direct rather than indirect statements, the active rather than the passive voice, and make every sentence and paragraph an organic whole. Above all, if you are writing historical narrative, make it move. Do not take time out in the middle of a political or military campaign to introduce special developments or literary trends, as McMaster did to the confusion of his readers. Place those admittedly important matters in a chapter or chapters by themselves so that your reader's attention will not be lost by constant interruption.

That brings us to the third essential quality — objectivity. Keep the reader constantly in mind. You are not writing history for yourself or for the professors who are supposed to know more about it than you do. Assume that you are writing for intelligent people who know nothing about your particular subject but whom you wish to interest and attract. I once asked the late Senator Beveridge why his *Life of John Marshall*, despite its great length and scholarly apparatus, was so popular. He replied: "The trouble with you professors of history is that you write for each other. I write for people almost completely ignorant of American history, as I was when I began my research."

A few more details. Even if the work you are writing does not call for footnotes, keep them in your copy until the last draft, for they will enable you to check up on your facts, statements, and quotations. And since accuracy is the prime virtue of the historian, this checking must be done, either by the author or by someone else. You will be surprised by the mistakes that creep in between a first rough draft and a final typed copy. And the better you write, the more your critics will enjoy finding misquotations and inaccuracies.

The matter of handling quotations seems to be a difficult one for young historians. There is nothing that adds so much to the charm and effectiveness of a history as good quotations from the sources, especially if the period be somewhat remote. But there is nothing so disgusting to the reader as long, tedious, broken quotations in small print, especially those in which, to make sense, the author has to interpolate words in brackets. Young writers are prone to use quotations in places where their own words would be better, and to incorporate in the text source excerpts that belong in footnotes or appendices. Avoid ending chapters with quotations, and never close your book with one.

Above all, do not be afraid to revise and rewrite. Reading aloud is a good test — historians' wives have to stand a lot of that! A candid friend who is not a historian and so represents the audience you are trying to reach, is perhaps the best "dog" to try it on. Even if he has little critical sense, it is encouraging to have him stay awake. My good friend Lucien Price years ago listened with a pained expression to a bit of my early work. "Now, just what do you mean by that?" he asked after a long, involved, pedantic, and quote-larded paragraph. I told him in words of one syllable, or perhaps two. "Fine!" said he, "I understand that. Now write down what you said; throw the other away!"

STUDY QUESTIONS

1. To what extent is Morison's idea that the writer must make the facts speak for themselves by "proper selection, arrangement, and emphasis" similar to ideas you have met previously in Steinbeck's "Observation and Interpretation"? In Daiches' "The Literary Use of Language"?

2. As far as you can tell from what Morison says in this selection, would he agree or disagree with Johnson's criteria for good writing? Does he establish other criteria which Johnson does not describe?

3. What does Morison mean by "objectivity" in this selection?

4. To what extent does Morison make writing a matter of character rather than skill? What is the meaning of the sentence quoted from Whitehead, "Style is the ultimate morality of the mind"?

5. Morison does not recommend dictation, but at the end, he describes a situation in which he succeeded in saying something he had not succeeded in writing. How do you explain this apparent inconsistency?

6. Write a theme describing some experience you have had in writing, or trying to write a theme or assignment—not this one. You may find it useful to organize this in terms of the criteria which you were trying to meet, or the steps which you had to take in writing the paper.

William Hazlitt On Familiar Style *

It is not easy to write a familiar style. Many people mistake a familiar for a vulgar style, and suppose that to write without affectation is to write at random. On the contrary, there is nothing that requires more precision, and, if I may so so, purity of expression, than the style I am speaking of. It utterly rejects not only all unmeaning pomp, but all low, cant phrases, and loose, unconnected, *slipshod* allusions. It is not to take the first word that offers, but the best word in common use; it is not to throw words together in any combinations we please, but to follow and avail ourselves of the true idiom of the language. To write a genuine familiar or truly English style is to write as any one would speak in common conversation who had a thorough command and choice of words, or who could discourse with ease, force, and perspicuity, setting aside all pedantic and oratorical flourishes. Or, to give another illustration, to write naturally is the same thing in regard to common conversation as to read naturally is in regard to common speech. It does not follow that it is an easy thing to give the true accent and inflection to the words you utter, because you do not attempt to rise above the level of ordinary life and colloquial speaking. You do not assume, indeed, the solemnity of the pulpit, or the tone of stage-declamation; neither are you at liberty to gabble on at a venture, without emphasis or discretion, or to resort to vulgar dialect or clownish pronunciation. You must steer a middle course. You are tied down to a given and appropriate articulation, which is determined by the habitual associations between sense and sound, and which you can only hit by entering into the author's meaning, as you must find the proper words and style to express yourself by fixing your thoughts on the subject you have to write about. Any one may mouth out a passage with a theatrical cadence, or get upon stilts to tell his thoughts; but to write or speak with propriety and simplicity is a more difficult task. Thus it is easy to affect a pompous style, to use a word twice as big as the thing you want to express: it is not so easy to pitch upon the very word that exactly fits it. Out of eight or ten words equally common, equally intelligible, with nearly equal pretensions, it is a matter of some nicety and discrimination to pick out the very one the preferableness of which is scarcely perceptible, but decisive. The reason why I object to Dr. Johnson's style is that there is no discrimination, no selection, no variety in it. He uses none but "tall, opaque words," taken from the "first row of the rubric" — words with the greatest number of syllables, or Latin phrases with merely English terminations. If a fine style depended on this sort of arbitrary pretension, it would be fair to judge of an author's elegance by the measurement

* From *Table Talk*, 1821-24.

of his words and the substitution of foreign circumlocutions (with no precise associations) for the mother-tongue.[1] How simple is it to be dignified without ease, to be pompous without meaning! Surely it is but a mechanical rule for avoiding what is low, to be always pedantic and affected. It is clear you cannot use a vulgar English word if you never use a common English word at all. A fine tact is shown in adhering to those which are perfectly common, and yet never falling into any expressions which are debased by disgusting circumstances, or which owe their signification and point to technical or professional allusions. A truly natural or familiar style can never be quaint or vulgar, for this reason, that it is of universal force and applicability, and that quaintness and vulgarity arise out of the immediate connection of certain words with coarse and disagreeable or with confined ideas. The last form what we understand by *cant* or *slang* phrases. — To give an example of what is not very clear in the general statement. I should say that the phrase *To cut with a knife*, or *To cut a piece of wood*, is perfectly free from vulgarity, because it is perfectly common; but to *cut an acquaintance* is not quite un-exceptionable, because it is not perfectly common or intelligible, and has hardly yet escaped out of the limits of slang phraseology. I should hardly, therefore, use the word in this sense without putting it in italics as a license of expression, to be received *cum grano salis*. All provincial or bye-phrases come under the same mark of reprobation — all such as the writer transfers to the page from his fireside or a particular *coterie*, or that he invents for his own sole use and convenience. I conceive that words are like money, not the worse for being common, but that it is the stamp of custom alone that gives them circulation or value. I am fastidious in this respect, and would almost as soon coin the currency of the realm as counterfeit the King's English. I never invented or gave a new and unauthorised meaning to any word but one single one (the term *impersonal* applied to feelings), and that was in an abstruse metaphysical discussion to express a very difficult distinction. I have been (I know) loudly accused of revelling in vulgarisms and broken English. I cannot speak to that point; but so far I plead guilty to the determined use of acknowl-edged idioms and common elliptical expressions. I am not sure that the critics in question know the one from the other, that is, can distinguish any medium between formal pedantry and the most barbarous solecism. As an author I endeavour to employ plain words and popular modes of construction, as, were I a chapman and dealer, I should common weights and measures.

The proper force of words lies not in the words themselves, but in their application. A word may be a fine-sounding word, of an unusual length, and very imposing from its learning and novelty, and yet in the connection in which it is introduced may be quite pointless and irrelevant. It is not pomp or pretension, but the adaptation of the expression to the idea, that clenches a

---

[1] I have heard of such a thing as an author who makes it a rule never to admit a monosyllable into his vapid verse. Yet the charm and sweetness of Marlowe's lines de-pended often on their being made up almost entirely of monosyllables. [Author.]

writer's meaning: — as it is not the size or glossiness of the materials, but their being fitted each to its place, that gives strength to the arch; or as the pegs and nails are as necessary to the support of the building as the larger timbers, and more so than the mere showy, unsubstantial ornaments. I hate anything that occupies more space than it is worth. I hate to see a load of bandboxes go along the street, and I hate to see a parcel of big words without anything in them. A person who does not deliberately dispose of all his thoughts alike in cumbrous draperies and flimsy disguises may strike out twenty varieties of familiar everyday language, each coming somewhat nearer to the feeling he wants to convey, and at last not hit upon that particular and only one which may be said to be identical with the exact impression in his mind. This would seem to show that Mr. Cobbett is hardly right in saying that the first word that occurs is always the best. It may be a very good one; and yet a better may present itself on reflection or from time to time. It should be suggested naturally, however, and spontaneously, from a fresh and lively conception of the subject. We seldom succeed by trying at improvement, or by merely substituting one word for another that we are not satisfied with, as we cannot recollect the name of a place or person by merely plaguing ourselves about it. We wander farther from the point by persisting in a wrong scent; but it starts up accidentally in the memory when we least expected it, by touching some link in the chain of previous association.

There are those who hoard up and make a cautious display of nothing but rich and rare phraseology — ancient medals, obscure coins, and Spanish pieces of eight. They are very curious to inspect, but I myself would neither offer nor take them in the course of exchange. A sprinkling of archaisms is not amiss, but a tissue of obsolete expressions is more fit *for keep than wear*. I do not say I would not use any phrase that had been brought into fashion before the middle or the end of the last century, but I should be shy of using any that had not been employed by any approved author during the whole of that time. Words, like clothes, get old-fashioned, or mean and ridiculous, when they have been for some time laid aside. Mr. Lamb is the only imitator of old English style I can read with pleasure; and he is so thoroughly imbued with the spirit of his authors that the idea of imitation is almost done away. There is an inward unction, a marrowy vein, both in the thought and feeling, an intuition, deep and lively, of his subject, that carries off any quaintness or awkwardness arising from an antiquated style and dress. The matter is completely his own, though the manner is assumed. Perhaps his ideas are altogether so marked and individual as to require their point and pungency to be neutralised by the affectation of a singular but traditional form of convey-ance. Tricked out in the prevailing costume, they would probably seem more startling and out of the way. The old English authors, Burton, Fuller, Coryate, Sir Thomas Browne, are a kind of mediators between us and the more eccentric and whimsical modern, reconciling us to his peculiarities. I do not, however, know how far this is the case or not, till he condescends to

write like one of us. I must confess that what I like best of his papers under
the signature of Elia (still I do not presume, amidst such excellence, to decide
what is most excellent) is the account of "Mrs. Battle's Opinions on Whist,"
which is also the most free from obsolete allusions and turns of expression —

> A well of native English undefiled.

To those acquainted with his admired prototypes, these *Essays* of the ingenious and highly gifted author have the same sort of charm and relish that
Erasmus's *Colloquies* or a fine piece of modern Latin have to the classical
scholar. Certainly, I do not know any borrowed pencil that has more power
or felicity of execution than the one of which I have here been speaking.

It is as easy to write a gaudy style without ideas as it is to spread a pallet of
showy colours or to smear in a flaunting transparency. "What do you read?"
"Words, words, words." — "What is the matter?" "Nothing," it might be
answered. The florid style is the reverse of the familiar. The last is employed
as an unvarnished medium to convey ideas; the first is resorted to as a
spangled veil to conceal the want of them. When there is nothing to be set
down but words, it costs little to have them fine. Look through the dictionary,
and cull out a *florilegium*, rival the *tulippomania*. *Rouge* high enough, and
never mind the natural complexion. The vulgar, who are not in the secret,
will admire the look of preternatural health and vigour; and the fashionable,
who regard only appearances, will be delighted with the imposition. Keep
to your sounding generalities, your tinkling phrases, and all will be well.
Swell out an unmeaning truism to a perfect tympany of style. A thought, a
distinction is the rock on which all this brittle cargo of verbiage splits at once.
Such writers have merely *verbal* imaginations, that retain nothing but words.
Or their puny thoughts have dragon-wings, all green and gold. They soar
far above the vulgar failing of the *Sermo humi obrepens* — their most ordinary
speech is never short of an hyperbole, splendid, imposing, vague, incomprehensible, magniloquent, a cento of sounding common-places. If some of us,
whose "ambition is more lowly," pry a little too narrowly into nooks and
corners to pick up a number of "unconsidered trifles," they never once direct
their eyes or lift their hands to seize on any but the most gorgeous, tarnished,
threadbare, patchwork set of phrases, the left-off finery of poetic extravagance,
transmitted down through successive generations of barren pretenders. If
they criticize actors and actresses, a huddled phantasmagoria of feathers,
spangles, floods of light, and oceans of sound float before their morbid sense,
which they paint in the style of Ancient Pistol. Not a glimpse can you get of
the merits or defects of the performers: they are hidden in a profusion of
barbarous epithets and wilful rodomontade. Our hypercritics are not thinking
of these little fantoccini beings —

> That strut and fret their hour upon the stage—

but of tall phantoms of words, abstractions, *genera* and *species*, sweeping clauses, periods that unite the Poles, forced alliterations, astounding antitheses —

And on their pens *Fustian* sits plumed.

If they describe kings and queens, it is an Eastern pageant. The Coronation at either House is nothing to it. We get at four repeated images — a curtain, a throne, a sceptre, and a footstool. These are with them the wardrobe of a lofty imagination; and they turn their servile strains to servile uses. Do we read a description of pictures? It is not a reflection of tones and hues which "nature's own sweet and cunning hand laid on," but piles of precious stones, rubies, pearls, emeralds, Golconda's mines, and all the blazonry of art. Such persons are in fact besotted with words, and their brains are turned with the glittering but empty and sterile phantoms of things. Personifications, capital letters, seas of sunbeams, visions of glory, shining inscriptions, the figures of a transparency, Britannia with her shield, or Hope leaning on an anchor, make up their stock-in-trade. They may be considered as *hieroglyphical* writers. Images stand out in their minds isolated and important merely in themselves, without any groundwork of feeling — there is no context in their imaginations. Words affect them in the same way, by the mere sound, that is, by their possible, not by their actual application to the subject in hand. They are fascinated by first appearances, and have no sense of consequences. Nothing more is meant by them than meets the ear: they understand or feel nothing more than meets their eye. The web and texture of the universe, and of the heart of man, is a mystery to them: they have no faculty that strikes a chord in unison with it. They cannot get beyond the daubings of fancy, the varnish of sentiment. Objects are not linked to feelings, words to things, but images revolve in splendid mockery, words represent themselves in their strange rhapsodies. The categories of such a mind are pride and ignorance — pride in outside show, to which they sacrifice everything, and ignorance of the true worth and hidden structure both of words and things. With a sovereign contempt for what is familiar and natural, they are the slaves of vulgar affectation — of a routine of high-flown phrases. Scorning to imitate realities, they are unable to invent anything, to strike out one original idea. They are not copyists of nature, it is true; but they are the poorest of all plagiarists, the plagiarists of words. All is far-fetched, dear-bought, artificial, oriental in subject and allusion; all is mechanical, conventional, vapid, formal, pedantic in style and execution. They startle and confound the understanding of the reader by the remoteness and obscurity of their illustrations; they soothe the ear by the monotony of the same everlasting round of circuitous metaphors. They are the *mock-school* in poetry and prose. They flounder about between fustian in expression and bathos in sentiment. They tantalise the fancy, but never reach the head nor touch the heart. Their Temple of Fame is like a shadowy structure raised by Dulness to Vanity, or like Cowper's description of the Empress of Russia's palace of ice, "as worthless as in show 'twas glittering" —

It smiled, and it was cold!

STUDY QUESTIONS

1. *What is one specific reason Hazlitt gives that explains why it is easier to write a high-flown style like Johnson's than what he calls the "familiar style"?*

2. *Why, exactly, does Hazlitt disapprove of the expression, "to cut an acquaintance"? What general standard for choosing words does this suggest?*

3. *In the analogy between language and money, Hazlitt points out three resemblances. What are they?*

4. *Toward the end, Hazlitt often slips into irony, and the reader is likely to misunderstand him unless he is aware of this. Define irony clearly, and then identify the sentences that are ironic.*

5. *Write a discussion of Hazlitt's own choice of words and expressions, remembering that this essay is about a hundred and fifty years old, and making allowances for some of its old-fashioned qualities. Consider, in particular, the following words: solecism, alliteration, antithesis, fantoccini, preferableness, fastidious, elliptical, antiquated. If you want to find out whether one or another of these words would have been familiar to Hazlitt's readers, look it up in the* New English Dictionary.

6. *Write a theme discussing the variations and abuses of present-day speech and writing. Good material for this can usually be found in sports articles, in the writing of "intimate" newspaper columnists, in the dialogue of comic strips, stories and novels, and in the speech of people who come from another part of the country.*

Marchette Chute Getting at the Truth*

This is a rather presumptuous title for a biographer to use, since truth is a very large word. In the sense that it means the reality about a human being it is probably impossible for a biographer to achieve. In the sense that it means a reasonable presentation of all the available facts it is more nearly possible, but even this limited goal is harder to reach than it appears to be. A biographer needs to be both humble and cautious when he remembers the nature of the material he is working with, for a historical fact is rather like the flamingo that Alice in Wonderland tried to use as a croquet mallet. As soon as she got its neck nicely straightened out and was ready to hit the ball, it would turn and look at her with puzzled expression, and any biographer knows that what is called a "fact" has a way of doing the same.

*"Getting at the Truth" by Marchette Chute, from *The Saturday Review*, September 19, 1953. Reprinted by permission.

Here is a small example. When I was writing my forthcoming biography, "Ben Jonson of Westminster," I wanted to give a paragraph or two to Sir Philip Sidney, who had a great influence on Jonson. No one thinks of Sidney without thinking of chivalry, and to underline the point I intended to use a story that Sir Fulke Greville told of him. Sidney died of gangrene, from a musket shot that shattered his thigh, and Greville says that Sidney failed to put on his leg armor while preparing for battle because the marshal of the camp was not wearing leg armor and Sidney was unwilling to do anything that would give him a special advantage.

The story is so characteristic both of Sidney himself and of the misplaced high-mindedness of late Renaissance chivalry that I wanted to use it, and since Sir Fulke Greville was one of Sidney's closest friends the information seemed to be reliable enough. But it is always well to check each piece of information as thoroughly as possible and so I consulted another account of Sidney written by a contemporary, this time a doctor who knew the family fairly well. The doctor, Thomas Moffet, mentioned the episode but he said that Sidney left off his leg armor because he was in a hurry.

The information was beginning to twist in my hand and could no longer be trusted. So I consulted still another contemporary who had mentioned the episode, to see which of the two he agreed with. This was Sir John Smythe, a military expert who brought out his book a few years after Sidney's death. Sir John was an old-fashioned conservative who advocated the use of heavy armor even on horseback, and he deplored the current craze for leaving off leg protection, "the imitating of which ... cost that noble and worthy gentleman Sir Philip Sidney his life."

So here I was with three entirely different reasons why Sidney left off his leg armor, all advanced by careful writers who were contemporaries of his. The flamingo had a legitimate reason for looking around with a puzzled expression.

The only thing to do in a case like this is to examine the point of view of the three men who are supplying the conflicting evidence. Sir Fulke Greville was trying to prove a thesis: that his beloved friend had an extremely chivalric nature. Sir John Smythe also was trying to prove a thesis: that the advocates of light arming followed a theory that could lead to disaster. Only the doctor, Thomas Moffet, was not trying to prove a thesis. He was not using his own explanation to reinforce some point he wanted to make. He did not want anything except to set down on paper what he believed to be the facts; and since we do not have Sidney's own explanation of why he did not put on leg armor, the chances are that Dr. Moffet is the safest man to trust.

For Moffet was without desire. Nothing can so quickly blur and distort the facts as desire — the wish to use the facts for some purpose of your own — and nothing can so surely destroy the truth. As soon as the witness wants to prove something he is no longer impartial and his evidence is no longer to be trusted.

The only safe way to study contemporary testimony is to bear constantly in mind this possibility of prejudice and to put almost as much attention on the writer himself as on what he has written. For instance, Sir Anthony Weldon's description of the Court of King James is lively enough and often used as source material; but a note from the publisher admits that the pamphlet was issued as a warning to anyone who wished to "side with this bloody house" of Stuart. The publisher, at any rate, did not consider Weldon an impartial witness. At about the same time Arthur Wilson published his history of Great Britain, which contained an irresistibly vivid account of the agonized death of the Countess of Somerset. Wilson sounds reasonably impartial; but his patron was the Earl of Essex, who had good reason to hate that particular countess, and there is evidence that he invented the whole scene to gratify his patron.

Sometimes a writer will contradict what he has already written, and in that case the only thing to do is to investigate what has changed his point of view. For instance, in 1608 Captain John Smith issued a description of his capture by Powhatan, and he made it clear that the Indian chief had treated him with unwavering courtesy and hospitality. In 1624 the story was repeated in Smith's "General History of Virginia," but the writer's circumstances had changed. Smith needed money, "having a prince's mind imprisoned in a poor man's purse," and, he wanted the book to be profitable. Powhatan's daughter, the princess Pocahontas, had recently been in the news, for her visit to England had aroused a great deal of interest among the sort of people that Smith hoped would buy his book. So Smith supplied a new version of the story, in which the once-hospitable Powhatan would have permitted the hero's brains to be dashed out if Pocahontas had not saved his life. It was the second story that achieved fame, and of course it may have been true. But it is impossible to trust it because the desire of the writer is so obviously involved; as Smith said in his prospectus, he needed money and hoped that the book would give "satisfaction."

It might seem that there was an easy way for a biographer to avoid the use of this kind of prejudiced testimony. All he has to do is to construct his biography from evidence that cannot be tampered with — from parish records, legal documents, bills, accounts, court records, and so on. Out of these solid gray blocks of impersonal evidence it should surely be possible to construct a road that will lead straight to the truth and that will never bend itself to the misleading curve of personal desire.

This might be so if the only problem involved were the reliability of the material. But there is another kind of desire that is much more subtle, much more pervasive, and much more dangerous than the occasional distortions of fact that contemporary writers may have permitted themselves to make; and this kind of desire can destroy the truth of a biography even if every individual fact in it is as solid and as uncompromising as rock. Even if the road is built of the best and most reliable materials it can still curve away from the truth because of this other desire that threatens it: the desire of the biographer himself.

A biographer is not a court record or a legal document. He is a human being, writing about another human being, and his own temperament, his own point of view, and his own frame of reference are unconsciously imposed upon the man he is writing about. Even if the biographer is free from Captain Smith's temptation — the need for making money — and wants to write nothing but the literal truth, he is still handicapped by the fact that there is no such thing as a completely objective human being.

An illustration of what can happen if the point of view is sufficiently strong is the curious conclusion that the nineteenth-century biographers reached about William Shakespeare. Shakespeare joined a company of London actors in 1594, was listed as an actor in 1598 and 1603, and was still listed as one of the "men actors" in the company in 1609. Shortly before he joined this company Shakespeare dedicated two narrative poems to the Earl of Southampton, and several years after Shakespeare died his collected plays were dedicated to the Earl of Pembroke. This was his only relationship with either of the two noblemen, and there is nothing to connect him with them during the fifteen years in which he belonged to the same acting company and during which he wrote nearly all his plays.

But here the desire of the biographers entered in. They had been reared in the strict code of nineteenth-century gentility and they accepted two ideas without question. One was that there are few things more important than an English lord; the other was that there are few things less important than a mere actor. They already knew the undeniable fact that Shakespeare was one of the greatest men who ever lived; and while they could not go quite so far as to claim him as an actual member of the nobility, it was clear to them that he must have been the treasured friend of both the Earl of Southampton and the Earl of Pembroke and that he must have written his plays either while basking in their exalted company or while he was roaming the green countryside by the waters of the river Avon. (It is another basic conviction of the English gentleman that there is nothing so inspiring as nature.) The notion that Shakespeare had spent all these years as the working member of a company of London actors was so abhorrent that it was never seriously considered. It could not be so; therefore it was not.

These biographers did their work well. When New South Wales built its beautiful memorial library to Shakespeare, it was the coat of arms of the Earl of Southampton that alternated with that of royalty in dignified splendor over the bookshelves. Shakespeare had been re-created in the image of desire, and desire will always ignore whatever is not relevant to its purpose. Because the English gentlemen did not like Shakespeare's background it was explained away as though it had never existed, and Shakespeare ceased to be an actor because so lowly a trade was not suited to so great a man.

All this is not to say that a biography should be lacking in a point of view. If it does not have a point of view it will be nothing more than a kind of expanded article for an encyclopedia—a string of facts arranged in chronological order with no claim to being a real biography at all. A biography must have a point of view and it must have a frame of reference. But it should be a point of view and a frame of reference implicit in the material itself and not imposed upon it.

It might seem that the ideal biographical system, if it could be achieved, would be to go through the years of research without feeling any kind of emotion. The biographer would be a kind of fact-finding machine and then suddenly, after his years of research, a kind of total vision would fall upon him and he would transcribe it in his best and most persuasive English for a waiting public. But research is fortunately not done by machinery, nor are visions likely to descend in that helpful manner. They are the product not only of many facts but also of much thinking, and it is only when the biographer begins to get emotional in his thinking that he ought to beware.

It is easy enough to make good resolutions in advance, but a biographer cannot altogether control his sense of excitement when the climax of his years of research draws near and he begins to see the pieces fall into place. Almost without his volition, A, B, and D fit together and start to form a pattern, and it is almost impossible for the biographer not to start searching for C. Something turns up that looks remarkably like C, and with a little trimming of the edges and the ignoring of one very slight discrepancy it will fill the place allotted for C magnificently.

It is at this point that the biographer ought to take a deep breath and sit on his hands until he has had time to calm down. He has no real, fundamental reason to believe that his discovery is C, except for the fact that he wants it to be. He is like a man looking for a missing piece in a difficult jigsaw puzzle, who has found one so nearly the right shape that he cannot resist the desire to jam it into place.

If the biographer had refused to be tempted by his supposed discovery of C and had gone on with his research, he might have found not only the connecting, illuminating fact he needed but much more besides. He is not going to look for it now. Desire has blocked the way. And by so much his biography will fall short of what might have been the truth.

It would not be accurate to say that a biographer should be wholly lacking in desire. Curiosity is a form of desire. So is the final wish to get the material down on paper in a form that will be fair to the reader's interest and worthy of the subject. But a subconscious desire to push the facts around is one of the most dangerous things a biographer can encounter, and all the more dangerous because it is so difficult to know when he is encountering it.

The reason Alice had so much trouble with her flamingo is that the average flamingo does not wish to be used as a croquet mallet. It has other purposes in view. The same thing is true of a fact, which can be just as self-willed as a flamingo and has its own kind of stubborn integrity. To try to force a series of facts into a previously desired arrangement is a form of misuse to which no self-respecting fact will willingly submit itself. The best and only way to treat it is to leave it alone and be willing to follow where it leads, rather than to press your own wishes upon it.

To put the whole thing into a single sentence: you will never succeed in getting at the truth if you think you know, ahead of time, what the truth ought to be.

STUDY QUESTIONS

1. *How do you suppose Miss Chute gathered the information that enabled her to evaluate the opinions about Sidney's leg-armor?*

2. *Notice how great a proportion of this essay is devoted to the rather complicated examples the author is compelled to use. What is the proportion? Could she have accomplished her purpose without these examples?*

3. *Compare Miss Chute's procedure in learning the facts with Dewey's account of "reflective thinking" in "What is Thinking?"*

4. *Compare Miss Chute's opinion about the role of emotion in research with La Farge's opinion on the same subject.*

5. *Have you ever had to resort to complicated and troublesome methods to learn some necessary facts—something in connection with registration, the time of a train or plane departure, the facts about a possible job, or about a person? If you have had an experience of this sort, write a theme describing your difficulties and the moral and emotional situation surrounding them.*

6. *One of the most common mistakes among readers is that of accepting a statement of fact or opinion just because it is in print. A good remedy for this is reading two biographical accounts of some person in whom you are interested and comparing the differences in attitude, interpretation, and even in facts that will emerge. Read accounts of some historical figure in two or three encyclopedias and write a report comparing the accounts.*

Robert E. Sherwood   A Speech Is Written*

As I have said, Hopkins did not originate policy and then convince Roosevelt it was right. He had too much intelligence as well as respect for his Chief to attempt the role of mastermind. He made it his job to provide a sounding board for discussions of the best means of attaining the goals that the President set for himself. Roosevelt liked to think out loud, but his greatest difficulty was finding a listener who was both understanding and entirely trustworthy. That was Hopkins — and this was the process that

* From *Roosevelt and Hopkins* by Robert E. Sherwood. Copyright, 1948, by Robert E. Sherwood. Reprinted by permission of Harper & Brothers, publishers.

Rosenman and I watched over and over again in the preparation of the speeches and messages in which Roosevelt made known his policies to the nation and to the world. The work that was put in on these speeches was prodigious, for Roosevelt with his acute sense of history knew that all of those words would constitute the bulk of the estate that he would leave to posterity and that his ultimate measurement would depend on the reconciliation of what he said with what he did. Therefore, utmost importance was attached to his public utterances and utmost care exercised in their preparation. In the previous chapter I have mentioned the Cleveland speech which took a night and a day to prepare, but such speed in preparation was unusual, even for a campaign speech, which was necessarily a creature of the moment. The important speeches sometimes required a week or more of hard labor, with a considerable amount of planning before the intensive work started. I don't know what was the record number of distinct drafts of a single speech but it must have been well over twelve, and in the final draft there might not be one sentence that had survived from the first draft. There were of course numerous routine speeches of a ceremonial nature which were not considered of major significance — but, in wartime, even in these Roosevelt was aware that he had a world audience and that everything he said might be material for the propaganda which flooded the air waves. If such a speech were opening a Bond Drive, a first draft would be prepared in the Treasury Department; if it were launching a new campaign for funds for the Red Cross, the Community Chest, National Brotherhood Week, etc., the organization concerned would send in suggestions as to what it wanted the President to say. This submitted material was almost always so rhetorical, so studiously literary, that it did not sound at all like Roosevelt's normal style and it had to be subjected to the process of simplification or even oversimplification that he demanded. He was happiest when he could express himself in the homeliest, even tritest phrases, such as "common or garden," "clear as crystal," "rule of thumb," "neither here nor there," "armchair strategists," or "simple as ABC."

When he wanted to give a speech for some important purpose, whether it was connected with a special occasion or not, he would discuss it first at length with Hopkins, Rosenman and me, telling us what particular points he wanted to make, what sort of audience he wished primarily to reach and what the maximum word limit was to be (he generally put it far too low). He would dictate pages and pages, approaching his main topic, sometimes hitting it squarely on the nose with terrific impact, sometimes rambling so far away from it that he couldn't get back, in which case he would say, "Well — something along those lines — you boys can fix it up." I think he greatly enjoyed these sessions, when he felt free to say anything he pleased, uttering all kinds of personal insults, with the knowledge that none of it need appear in the final version. When he stopped dictating, because another appointment was due or it was time to go to bed, we would go to the Cabinet Room in the West Wing and start reading through all the assembled material.

The President kept a special "Speech Folder" into which he put newspaper clippings that he had marked, indicating either his approval of some sentiment expressed or indignation that such falsehood should get into print (he could not always remember what the marking signified). There were also all sorts of letters from all sorts of people, known and unknown, containing suggestions as to what he should say, and there were random bits of his own dictation, thoughts that had suddenly occurred to him during preceding days and weeks which might be useful sometime. All of this material was sifted, and added to the newly dictated material with the aid of scissors and paste and a few connecting clauses, until something resembling a coherent speech was put together and fair copies of it made. It was generally two or three times too long. When the President was free to see us again, we handed him this draft and he looked immediately at the last page to see its number, whereupon he announced that at least ninety-two per cent of it must be cut. He then started to read through it, pausing frequently to dictate "Insert A," "Insert G," etc. Each time he decided to dictate something he said, "Grace — take a law," a line he gladly borrowed from the Kaufman-Hart-Rodgers musical show, "I'd Rather Be Right," in which George M. Cohan played the part of Franklin D. Roosevelt. The President himself had never seen this show but he enjoyed what he heard about it.

When he had finished dictating inserts, the speech was far longer than it had been and farther from any coherent form. We then returned to the Cabinet Room and started a second draft. This process went on day and night. Sometimes, while the work was in progress, events would intervene— for instance: on a Sunday evening in July, 1943, we were at Shangri-la finishing up a speech devoted primarily to home-front problems—price stabilization, rationing, manpower, etc.—when news came of the fall of Benito Mussolini, and the speech had to be started all over again; this however, was a pleasure for all.

Most of Roosevelt's work on speeches was done during the evening. We would gather for the standard cocktail ceremony in the Oval Study at 7:15. The President sat behind his desk, the tray before him. He mixed the ingredients with the deliberation of an alchemist but with what appeared to be a certain lack of precision since he carried on a steady conversation while doing it. His bourbon old-fashioneds were excellent, but I did not care for his Martinis, in which he used two kinds of vermouth (when he had them) and sometimes a dash of absinthe. Hopkins occasionally talked him into making Scotch whisky sours, although he didn't really like them. The usual canapés of cream cheese or fish paste on small circles of toast were served, also popcorn. Roosevelt was an extremely mild drinker—he did not have wine with meals except at large, formal dinners, and I don't recall ever having seen him drink brandy or other liqueurs or a highball; but he certainly loved the cocktail period and the stream of small talk that went with it.

After dinner he sat on the couch to the left of the fireplace, his feet up on the stool specially built for him, and started reading the latest speech draft. Grace Tully sat next to him, taking more dictation until Dorothy Brady or Toinette Bachelder came in to relieve her. Sometimes Roosevelt read the speech out loud, to see how it sounded, for every word was judged not by its appearance in print but by its effectiveness over the radio. About 10 o'clock, a tray with drinks was brought in. The President sometimes had a glass of beer but more often a horse's neck (ginger ale and lemon peel). He was by now yawning and losing interest in the speech and he usually went to bed before eleven. During these evening sessions, the telephone almost never rang. Now and then a dispatch might be brought in, which Roosevelt would read and pass on to Hopkins without a word or a change of expression, but otherwise one would have thought this house the most peaceful, remote retreat in a war-wracked world.

After leaving the Study, we would spend most of the night in the Cabinet Room producing another draft which would go to the President with his breakfast in the morning. Sometimes we would send a call for help to Archibald MacLeish, Librarian of Congress, who would come in late at night to help bring a diffuse speech into focus. More than once, before the White House windows were blacked out after Pearl Harbor, Mrs. Roosevelt saw the lights burning in the Cabinet Room at 3:00 A.M. and telephoned down to tell us we were working too hard and should go to bed. Of course, the fact was that she herself was sitting up working at that hour.

We had to get up early in the morning to be ready for summons in case the President wanted to work on the speech before his first appointment. We generally had breakfast on trays in Hopkins' room and it was rarely a cheerful gathering. The draft that had been completed a few hours previously looked awful in the morning light and the judgment on it that we most often expressed was, "I only hope that the reputation of Franklin Delano Roosevelt does not depend on this terrible speech."

After the session in the President's bedroom, Rosenman and I went over to the Cabinet Room to await the summons. The signal bells announced the President's approach to his office and we stood by the French windows leading out to the colonnade and watched him go by in his armless, cushionless, uncomfortable wheelchair, pushed by his Negro valet, Chief Petty Officer Arthur Prettyman. Accompanying him was the detail of Secret Service men, some of them carrying the large, overflowing wire baskets of papers on which he had been working the night before and the dispatches that had come in that morning. When Fala came abreast of the wheelchair as it rolled along, Roosevelt would reach down and scratch his neck. This progress to the day's work by a crippled man was a sight to stir the most torpid imagination; for here was a clear glimpse of the Roosevelt that the people believed him to be—the chin up, the cigarette holder tilted at what was always described as "a jaunty angle" and the air of irrepressible confidence that whatever problems the day might bring, he would find a way to handle them. The fact that this confidence was not always justified made it none the less authentic and reassuring.

When I saw the President go by on these mornings, I felt that nobody who worked for him had a right to feel tired. That was not an unusual feeling: it went all through the wartime Administration in Washington, extending to all sorts of people, some of whom disagreed with him politically and most of whom never laid eyes on him. It was, I think, Henry Pringle who, when working in a government agency shortly after Pearl Harbor, suggested as a wall slogan for bureaucrats' offices: EXHAUSTION IS NOT ENOUGH!

The speeches had to be checked and counterchecked with various departments and agencies, most of all with the Army and Navy; many speeches that were sent over to the War Department came back with corrections and suggestions penciled in the handwriting of General Marshall. The work of the so-called "ghost writers" consisted largely of the painstaking, arduous verification of facts and figures. We felt, "*The New York Times* can make mistakes the *World Almanac* can make mistakes—but the President of the United States must not make mistakes." This constant thought imposed a harrowing responsibility. After 1940, the White House had its resident statistician— Isador Lubin, the Commissioner of Labor Statistics, who was constantly available and incalculably valuable to Roosevelt and to Hopkins in checking every decimal point.

Although the speeches were usually seen in advance by the War and Navy Departments and sometimes (though not always) by the State Department, they were kept otherwise under close wraps of secrecy. There were always various eminent officials who wanted to know what the President was going to say. They were particularly anxious to make sure that he was going to include the several pages of material that they had submitted on their own particular departments. They knew they could get nowhere with Hopkins in their quest of inside information; so they concentrated on Rosenman, who would fob them off with the misstatement that, "The President is weighing that in his mind right now." We used to derive enjoyment from the thought of various important personages around Washington listening to the Presidential broadcasts and then, as the strains of "The Star Spangled Banner" broke out at the finish, cursing, "He didn't use a *word* of that stuff that I sent him." It was even more enjoyable to picture the amazed expression of some anonymous citizen in Council Bluffs who had written a letter to the President and then heard something from that letter incorporated in a Fireside Chat.

On the final two days of preparation of a speech Roosevelt would really buckle down to serious work and then what had seemed a formless, aimless mess of words would begin to assume tautness and sharpness. He studied every implication for its effect on various groups in the nation and on allies and enemies and neutrals. He paid a great deal of attention to the punctuation, not for its correctness but for its aid or hindrance to him in reading the speech aloud. Grace Tully liked to insert a great many commas, and the President loved to strike them out. He once said to her, "Grace! How many times do I have to tell you not to waste the taxpayers' commas?" He liked dashes, which were visual aids, and hated semicolons and parentheses. I don't think he ever used the sonorous phrase, "And I quote—" If he had to have quotation marks, he did not refer to them, knowing they would appear in the printed version.

In the final draft of a speech, every word was counted and Roosevelt finally decided the precise number that he would be able to crowd into thirty minutes. His sense of timing was phenomenal. His normal rate was 100 words a minute, but he would say, "There are some paragraphs in this speech that I can take quickly so I can handle a total of 3,150 words"—and that did not mean 3,162. At other times, he would feel that he had to be deliberate in his delivery and the words would have to be cut to 2,800. This cutting was the most difficult work of all because, by the time we had come to the ninth or tenth draft, we felt sure the speech had been boiled down to the ultimate monosyllable. Roosevelt's estimates were rarely off more than a split second on his broadcasts. Speeches before audiences were difficult to estimate, of course, because crowd responses are unpredictable, but he was generally accurate even on these. In the Teamsters' speech, the roars of laughter and applause were so frequent and prolonged that the speech ran some fifteen minutes overtime, but that did not upset Roosevelt at all despite the fact that, since it was a campaign speech, the Democratic National Committee had to pay the heavy excess charges.

When a speech was finally closed up, about six o'clock in the evening, the President was wheeled over to Dr. McIntire's office for the sinus treatments that were a regular part of his day. Then he went upstairs for cocktails and dinner, after which he chatted or worked on his correspondence or his stamp albums, without seeming to give much attention to the final reading copy of his speech which was typed on special limp paper, to avoid rustling noises as he turned the pages, and bound in a black leather loose-leaf folder. But when he started to broadcast he seemed to know it by heart. When he looked down at his manuscript, he was usually not looking at the words he was then speaking but at the next paragraph to determine where he would put his pauses and which of his large assortment of inflections he would employ. As one who has had considerable experience in the theater, I marveled at the unfailing precision with which he made his points, his grace in reconciling the sublime with the ridiculous, as though he had been rehearsing these lines for weeks and delivering them before audiences for months. Those who worked with him on speeches were all too well aware that he was no slave to his prepared text. He could and did ad-lib at will, and that was something which always amused him greatly. During the days of preparation, Hopkins, Rosenman and I would sometimes unite in opposition to some line, usually of a jocose nature, which the President wanted to include. It was our duty to make every effort to avoid being yes men and so we kept at him until we had persuaded him that the line should be cut out; but, if he really liked it well enough, he would keep it in mind and then ad-lib it, and later would be full of apologies to us for his "unfortunate slip of the tongue." He was almost always immensely good humored about the arguments we offered him—he liked to appear persecuted and complain that "They won't let me say anything of my own in my own speech." There were times, however, when he was worn out and angered by something else and then he would be cantankerous with us because we were the only convenient targets; we learned that on such occasions it was best to shut up and to revive our arguments later after he had had some rest and felt more amiable. Referring again to my experience in the theater, I can testify that he was normally the most untemperamental genius I have ever encountered. That is one of the reasons why he was able to sleep so well at night.

STUDY QUESTIONS

1. *Break down the process described here into its four most important steps. Does the complexity of this procedure mean that writing of this kind must be done by a staff, or does it have any bearing on the problems of the individual writer?*

2. *Point out the passages that are devoted primarily to characterization rather than to the business of writing speeches. Are they merely digressive, or do they have some connection with the main topic?*

3. *Can the time limit described by Sherwood be considered an advantage? Would these speeches have been better if there had been less time for their preparation? More time? If Roosevelt had done all the writing himself?*

4. *Did President Roosevelt's delegation of much of the writing task to subordinates mean that the final product was not his? In what way did his position as a writer differ from that of the average writer? In what other situations might a procedure like Roosevelt's be followed?*

5. *Sherwood observes elsewhere in the book from which this selection was taken that Roosevelt gave a great deal of attention to his speeches in a time of war, when he might have been expected to be concerned with such decisive events as battles and alliances. What conclusions about the role of language in history are suggested by the observation? What has the importance of language, communication and ideas been in history, or in some historical situation you are familiar with?*

6. *Describe the steps in some fairly elaborate operation you have taken part in, such as a camping trip, the arranging of a social function, writing a long term report, running an experiment, or building or making something that took several days or weeks.*

2. WRITING AND THINKING

Charles Morris A Primer of Semantics*

Man is unique among living beings in the extent to which he lives in a world of signs. This is the sea in which the human fish swims. This is its natural element. Other animals, to be sure, respond to some things as signs of other things, and kinship with the rest of life is never lost. But what to other animals is incidental and episodical is to man essential and continual. While other organisms steer themselves by the signs which the world provides, the human being changes himself and changes the world by the signs he himself produces. Individual men and women differ in this respect as in all others, but with respect to the production of signs for the regulation of their own lives human beings differ from all other living beings. In shaping himself by the signs he produces man is unique. The measure of his signs is the measure of his freedom.

This is why the study of signs is of such crucial importance, and why it must assume a central place in the science of man. Some call this study "semantics," some "significs," some "semiotic." Some like it hot and some like it cold. But whatever it is called and whatever its temperature, it is pivotal for our task. So we must square accounts with it. In another book, *Signs, Language, and Behavior,* I have given the colder account appropriate to a science of signs. Here we need only the essentials, and warm enough to keep us on the hunt for ourselves. A primer to prime us.

Never before in history has there been a greater interest in learning about signs. It is revealing that the periods of maximum interest in this study have been times of pervasive social change, such as the period of Confucius, or the Hellenistic period of declining Greece, or the centuries when the feudal structure of medieval Europe was falling away before the rising commercial and industrial middle class. In such periods the symbols under which men have lived together begin to lose their clarity and persuasiveness, and the new symbols appropriate to a changed society have not been found. Communication is no longer easy communion, for emerging meanings clash with older ones. Language becomes ineffectual and the cultural symbols a problem because they no longer can be taken for granted. Men pay conscious

* From *The Open Self,* by Charles Morris. Copyright, 1948, by Prentice-Hall, Inc.

attention to their signs when they no longer serve them well, just as they pay attention to their food when their stomachs hurt. In this sense the current vogue of semantics is a crisis phenomenon, a sign that all is not well with our signs.

But it is more than that. For the study of man has forced the scientist himself to scale this wall. And for a simple reason. Put a hungry animal before food it likes and it will in all but the rarest cases simply start to eat. But put a hungry man before food he likes, and he may simply start to eat, or if he is a Gandhi at a certain moment in his life he may not eat at all, or if he is a Balinese he will not eat unless he is permitted to eat with his right hand, or if he is a pious Christian or Jew he will not eat until a blessing has been said. There is no simple "law" of human behavior which states that a hungry person will eat food placed before him, no automatic "response" to a given "stimulus." Ordinarily we would explain this by saying that what a person does may depend on his ideas and ideals. The more cautious scientist, seeking for something that can be objectively observed, hits upon signs; he will say that how a person responds to something is in part dependent on how this something is signified. Signs intervene in almost everything men and women do. This means that the scientist has to gain knowledge of signs in order to build a science of man. For the sake of science itself it proves necessary to add a study of signs to the study of bodies, physical environments, and cultures.

But this study is also needed by the individual trying to become what he really is. For not only must a person understand how signs work if he is to understand how he acts, but he needs this knowledge in order to work effectively upon himself. Since the unique thing about the human being is that how he will act toward something is largely dependent on how he signifies that something, signs are the tool of tools for man-making. For man works on himself by his ideas and ideals, and these require signs for their operation, perhaps for their very existence. That is another reason why the study of signs is not a fad. And a good ground for adding this instrument to our pack.

THE VARIETIES OF SIGNS

The ring of an alarm-clock. Time to get up. A glance out the window to see what the day's weather will be. A look in the mirror for a report on how one is faring. A shave or a careful hair-do, and the right clothes, so that one will be judged as one wishes to be judged. Pressure on oranges to select a good one. The smell of an egg, just to be sure. A hasty note to the milkman. A choice of busses by the numbers they carry. Scrutiny of black-on-white newspaper marks. A day of talking and being talked to. Constant attention to the material upon which one is working in the office or factory—or to clouds and animals and grain if the work is away from the city. Flowers at dinner, or a pat on the face, or a scowl. Movies or the theatre. Or a book.

Or more talk. Then talking to oneself in falling asleep. And dreams to finish the day's unfinished business. Then another morning. The alarm-clock again.

Signs, signs, signs! From sounds, sights, tastes, feels, odors. From things, from persons, from oneself. Take them away and we would be more humanly naked than if we walked the streets without clothes.

What do all these events have in common that causes us to lump them together as signs? One core similarity: *they all influence the way we tend to react toward something other than themselves.* The alarm tells us the time, the sight of our face in the mirror informs us about our appearance, the newspaper tells us what has happened in the world, the pressure from the oranges or the odor of eggs determines which one we will select, the note to the milkman tells him how we wish him to act. The appearances of the sky or the words of the weather report influence the way we will dress, the way we will behave outdoors. We do not put on our raincoats indoors nor raise an umbrella between us and the newspaper. We eat not the menu but rather what its printed words stand for. Signs denote something other than themselves, other things or other aspects of the thing of which they are a part. The marks on the newspaper stand for happenings in China; the rate of our pulse beat stands for the condition of our heart. Signs influence our beliefs, our preferences, our feelings, our actions with respect to what they signify. They dispose us to react to something other than themselves in one way rather than another.

Just what happens to us when something is a sign is a complex puzzle, but one we do not here have to unscramble. Some persons would say that the sign causes in us an idea or a thought of something else, makes us conscious of something else. Other persons distrust this manner of talking, and prefer to say that the sign sets up some physiological or neural process in us, and so changes us that we tend to react differently to something else than we would have done if the sign had not occurred. We do not have to decide which account is correct or whether both are correct. For both agree that the sign does influence our reactions, does dispose us to act differently than we would otherwise act, does make us different from what we would otherwise have been. No one denies that signs and ideas are closely connected. To concentrate on signs may not tell the whole story, but it is good science, and it cannot lead us far astray. And for our purposes it is sufficient to regard a sign as anything which disposes us to react in a certain way to something other than itself.

It is obvious at once that there are different kinds of signs, since we are disposed by signs to react in very different ways. Some signs mainly report, tell us what to expect, prepare us to encounter one kind of thing rather than another. The weather report is an example, or the numbers on the bus which report the route and destination of the bus. Such signs may be called desig-native signs.

Other signs, however, influence our reactions in another way: they dispose us to look with favor or disfavor upon something, to slant our preferences, to select or reject this rather than that. They do not report what we can observe by our senses and instruments, but chronicle the goodness or badness of things. A certain odor disposes us to reject the odoriferous egg—or to offer it to someone we dislike. If we are told that there are oranges in the next room we expect round orange-colored fruit of a certain size and taste. If we are told merely that there is something good in the next room we are not informed what kind of thing is there, but we are inclined to seek it out, to pay attention to it, to favor it . If we are told that the orange on the table in the next room is better than the orange on the window-sill we both expect oranges and are disposed to prefer the one to the other. Signs which influence our preferences in this way we shall call appraisive signs.

There is still another main kind of sign, a sign which disposes us to react to something by a definite course of action. These signs have a command quality, an imperative tone. They tell us not what exists, or what to like or dislike, but what to do. Such signs we shall call prescriptive. The note to the milkman tells him what to do, disposes him to leave a definite assortment of milk and cream and butter. We command ourselves in the same way. When we tell ourselves that we must buy a refill for our pens that write in the stratosphere or under the shower we are setting in motion a course of action in ourselves, prescribing to ourselves what is to be done when we pass Penman's store.

The first lesson with respect to signs is to distinguish their designative, appraisive, and prescriptive elements. Most signs have all these facets: they are pure as seldom as selves are pure. Pure or impure, the distinctions are important. It makes a great difference whether "all men are equal" designates that persons are identical, or whether it appraises all men as equal in dignity, or whether it prescribes that we extend equal opportunities to all persons. We must know our signs. That is a prescription, of course. But not pure.

THE LEVELS OF SIGNS

The second lesson concerning signs is to distinguish their levels. And this in two senses. Originally signs are about what is not a sign. But then there arise signs about signs, and even signs about signs that are about signs. A picture of our friend is not our friend, and the words "picture of our friend" are not a picture of our friend, nor our friend. This seems simple enough to fool no one, but it does. We constantly confuse these levels, believe we are talking about things when we are talking about signs. To call the villain in a play a good villain means that the portrayal of a villain by the actor is good, not that villainy is good. If a philosopher tells us that only actualities are real we have to make sure whether he is disclosing to us how he uses words or making a statement about the world's furniture. The "determinism" attributed to science frequently harbors the same confusion: to say that something "must" happen is merely to say that the statement describing the happening is a logical consequence of our present knowledge; the "must" signifies primarily a relation between signs; as our knowledge (and skill) changes, the "musts" change. So it is easy to be tricked, easy to confuse words and things, easy to believe that wherever there is a word a thing is named. In the extreme cases we are victims of sign-magic; in the less extreme ones we are guilty of sign-confusion.

Signs have levels in a second sense, levels of complexity. There are signs which occur independently of language, there are language signs, and there are signs which while not language signs depend on such signs for their meaning. Let us call these in order pre-language, language, and post-language signs. The alarm-clock will redeem itself by serving as an example. Dogs can be trained to seek food in a certain place when the alarm sounds; the alarm is then to them a sign—but a pre-language sign since it is not dependent on language. Our word "alarm-clock" is a sign in the English language, and so a language sign. But the alarm-clock itself may become a sign in a still more complicated sense. For we talk about it to its face and it then gains a new meaning even though it can't talk back. Suppose for example we tell an alarm clock that it is the great curse of our life, getting us up earlier than we wish, sending us off into a day's activity we did not like. Then the clock itself may become a sign with all such meanings. It is not now a word in the English language, but it has taken on meanings first carried by words. It is a post-language sign in that sense. One can imagine that hoboes might set up an Alarm Clock on a pedestal in each of their jungles as a Symbol of the Industrial Age of Work—designative, negatively appraisive, and negatively prescriptive post-language symbols. Dogs cannot do this, not even the easygoing hobo dogs.

Language in this way gives to events in our world and in ourselves a meaning they would not otherwise have. The world and our bodies say different things to us because we have talked to them. And so we act differently to them. Language is a wondrous human work. How we talk is a momentous matter.

A language is social and has a vocabulary and a grammar. As social, language signs affect all those who share the signs in a similar way, awaken in them similar expectations, similar preferences, similar types of conduct. In having a grammatical structure a language permits a great variety of sign combinations, and so makes it possible to form new ideas and new ideals from old ones. As signs producible by those who share the language, language to some degree frees individuals from the simpler pre-language signs which the world and the body provide, and floods the world and the body with new meanings. The more we determine by our signs how we shall behave to things, the freer we are from their brute domination.

Language is not found among the animals, nor its products. It is the mark of man. It marks, as George Mead has shown, the transition from body to selfhood. We are talked into selfhood. It is in talk that we celebrate our selfhood. Through talk we advance our selfhood. Man, Ernst Cassirer tells us in his *Essay on Man,* is the *animal symbolicum.*

THE USES OF SIGNS

There is still a third lesson to be conned: the multiplicity of the ways signs can be used. The language of our daily life uses all kinds of signs for all kinds of purposes. It is a jack-of-all-trades tool, the tool of tools. We could get along without it as little as we could get along without our nervous systems. But special jobs need specialized tools, and specialized forms of language have been developed for better performance of specific tasks. Ways of Talking have appeared. The talk of scientists, the talk of artists, the talk of religious men. Many more, of course. But these are central, and sufficient to impress upon us the richness of the forms of symbolism which human living has engendered.

The language of science is a specialization of ordinary language for the purpose of accurately designating what has happened, what is happening, what will happen. The task of the scientist is to inform us truly about such matters, to give us reliable information as to what occurs under what conditions. We need such knowledge to determine correctly our expectations. Because to believe is so easy, and because our wishes so easily compel our beliefs, we need persons with special training, special methods, special caution to examine the evidence for our beliefs, and to give us sound data upon which to build new beliefs. Science lends a note of intellectual asceticism to our beliefs; as scientists we rein our preferences and plan-making, and pause for a moment before evidence. We ask the scientist to give us warranted statements, not to tell us what to like to dislike, or what to do. We may be stirred by what he says but we do not ask him to say it stirringly. We expect him to prune his language, to adapt it to his unique task of giving us "the facts." We want his statements designatively precise, accurate, reliable, cold—just because life is so warm.

Not so with art and the artist. The talk of paintings, novels, poetry, music, the dance, the theatre is slanted, biased, unneutral. It may be warmly or coldly for something, or warmly or coldly against it, but in any case it is for or against. The language is highly appraisive, and plays on our likes and dislikes. Appraisive of anything whatsoever, from dimples to deeds to death. Filled with the likes and dislikes of the artist, filled with himself, filled with ourselves. The artist may and does make statements, may even include statements of science among his means. But we go to him not primarily for his statements but for his appraisals. Partly of course to find an expression of our individual likes and dislikes—the pessimists will linger longest among the poets of despair, and the optimists among the poets of affirmation. But partly to sample alien and strange likes and dislikes, to try out via the artist's signs new ways of being biased. For the high mission of the artist is to explore novel ways of being for and against, and to let us share his explorations through the specialized language which he has created. In this way we live vicariously, seeing things as others have seen them, standing as they stood before things, and falling as they fell. And in so living vicariously we enjoy our characteristic appraisals, test them, gain material for their transformation, perhaps repudiate them. That is why we honor the artist for his work as we honor the scientist for his. We do not choose between them because we need them both.

But at times we must decide to do something—or do nothing. Having learned what we may expect, made our commitments and chosen sides, we must play the game. And here too signs suggest the answers. There are specialized signs for prescribing what precisely we are to do, the language of the ought, the language of imperative tone. The most comprehensive form of this language occurs in the religions, most comprehensive because the religions prescribe an overall pattern for our lives, a path to follow to the end. Just as the artist informs as well as appraises, so the religious prophet appraises as well as prescribes. He sets before us in his words and in his life an ideal of selfhood. But he does more. He tells us by word and deed how to realize this ideal; he prescribes a technique for living. Become such and such a kind of person, and become it in such and such a way: this is the religious imperative.

The religions speak in commandments, and their commands vary with the personality ideals they proclaim as good. But they all tell us how the burden of the complex self may be carried, and lost. The ways of salvation are ways of annihilation, ways of using up our lives. We turn to the prophets for hints of an appropriate ideal for our ultimate allegiance and for instructions as to how we may attain the self we finally choose to become. As we listen to them we try out symbolically possible costumes of selfhood. We may or may not find the one that fits us well. Our individual differences work here as they do in our reactions to art. But the prophets give us material for our widest orientation and our total integration. We select and reject; but we are grateful. Rejections are as basic to life as acceptances. They are the heads and the tails of the coin of choice. We honor the prophet even when we reject him. For we need him in the making of ourselves, need him as we need the scientist and the artist.

THE PITFALLS OF SIGNS

Signs are sign-posts, oases, and springboards. They point out what things are where, they allow us to delight in our achievements and aspirations, they fling us into the wide sea of endeavor. They come upon us from everywhere. From the words of other persons, from our non-human environment, from the monuments of our culture, from every nook and cranny of our bodies. We are in a sense always reading—reading persons, reading things, reading books, reading ourselves. Signs press upon every phase of ourselves, checking some motivations and releasing others, influencing our opinions, slanting our likes and dislikes, coloring our attitude to ourselves, inciting us to one course of action rather than another. They intervene between almost every human need and its satisfaction.

Yet the process is not one-way, not alone from outward to inward. If we are pressed upon by signs we also press upon signs. If signs sometimes serve to drive us mad by their pressure they are also tools for relieving our anxieties, tools for a greater sanity. If they are ropes which bind us they are also knives to cut to freedom.

The point is to master signs instead of being mastered by them. We do this by knowing about them. We ascend to higher levels of language and talk about talking itself. We stand at our own center, and demand of signs that they show their credentials. We avoid being taken in by giving out. In this way we work upon signs through other signs. We sharpen our tool of tools.

Yet the pitfalls of signs are numerous, easy to discern but hard to avoid.

There is the Pitfall of Over-Generalization. To generalize is to say something that applies more than once. It is easy to generalize, necessary in the economy of thought, but fraught with peril. Seductively simple to go from "this" to "some" to "most" to "all." Perilous if (but only if) we omit the qualifying conditions. "Men are more straightforward than women"—instead of "Men of such and such a sort under such and such cultural conditions are more straightforward than such and such women under such conditions." "Buddhism is the best religion"—instead of "Buddhism is for certain persons under certain historical and cultural conditions the best religious alternative." "Men of x inches in height should weigh y pounds"—instead of "Men of such and such bodily build in such and such a society average y pounds and should for most purposes keep their weight in the neighborhood of y pounds."

It is hard to find, and to keep in mind, the qualifications required for sound generalization. The refinement of knowledge is in large part the finding of such qualifications, and accurate knowledge is as difficult as it is rare. That is why we have science. And why Whitehead's advice should be pinned on our walls: "Seek simplicity, but distrust it." But it is also hard to avoid Undue Generalization because we bludgeon others by our generalizations; we keep silent on the qualifications because to admit them would weaken our case. If we want to make all men Buddhists we shall hardly qualify our appraisal of Buddhism as "the best religion." The sins of our generalizations reflect our general sinfulness. It is well to remember this in our statements. And for the statements of others, this motto is good: "Listen to their generalizations—but qualify them." Unless you give out counter-signs, you will be taken in by signs. Hypnotism supplies the evidence.

Then there is the Pitfall of Perfect Communication. Because other persons make the same sounds or write the same words that we do we assume that what they signify to them is exactly what they signify to us. We fail to realize that communication is a matter of degree. It is true that most words in a language have a common core of meaning for those who share the language; if this is not true there is in fact no language. But a common core is compatible with different fringes. Not all blondes dress alike. Not all who use the words "democracy," "freedom," "liberalism," "communism," "fascism," mean exactly the same thing by these words; and in some cases the common core of meaning is very small indeed. If "democracy," for instance, stands for the sum total of ways Americans now behave, then to advocate any change in these ways of acting is to oppose democracy; but if "democracy" stands for a certain ideal that is partly realized and partly unrealized, then those who advocate certain changes are the friends of democracy while those who oppose any change are its enemies. If two persons used this term in these different ways, and each assumed Perfect Communication, they would be talking at cross purposes and without mutual understanding. Each would be for democracy in one sense of the term and against it in the other. A group of clergymen not long ago battled several days over whether the leaders of their meeting were or were not Communists. It took two days to find out they meant different things by the term. They never got to the problems that had provoked the meeting. Perhaps some of them did not want to. For we always use the good words for our friends and the bad words for our enemies.

This pit is deep. It is sometimes said that education is at fault, that we must all be given identical meanings so that communication will be perfect. But this is too simple in theory and too hard in practice. Persons of different temperaments and different experiences inevitably develop different fringe meanings for their words. "Sociability" will become a positively appraisive term for [some] and negatively appraisive for [others]; or if this does not occur, the forms of sociability approved by the one will be different from the forms of sociability approved by the other. Education cannot stop this growth and variation of meaning. What it could do is to develop techniques by which we can find out in a given discussion what someone does mean by the terms he uses, and techniques by which we can in a given discussion make clear what we ourselves mean. If we concentrate on how to improve each instance of communication we need not worry so much about the differences and changes of meaning. One device is to give concrete illustrations of what one is talking about—instances of a democratic society, instances of a free man, instances of a liberal society, instances of a Communist. And demand of one's opponent in the boxing-ring of discussion similar concrete instances. It would be even better in discussions to lay aside all Great Words. But that is perhaps asking too much of human nature—under present historical conditions.

A third major pitfall is Gullibility. We are gullible before the signs of others, and gullible-plus before our own signs. Signs dispose us to act in certain ways, and if we are not on our guard they jerk us into puppet-action when they appear. We are told that war is inevitable because human nature is unchangeable; we nod in assent and prepare our youngsters for the cannon. We are told that we are queer; and we stick out a puppet-tongue at our own uniqueness. We are told that we ought to be fatter or slimmer or stronger; and we worry ourselves into the offered coat even if it is a plaster cast. But above all we are gullible to our own remarks. For most of our lives are spent in trying to keep a high opinion of ourselves. We do this in amazing ways. We almost break an arm to pat ourselves on the back. There is hardly a thing we say that is not aimed at signifying ourselves in a good light. Since we are often afraid to meet ourselves, afraid we will disturb our precariously attained equilibrium, we fall hard for every good thing we manage to say about ourselves. And so remain stalemated and unachieved.

The antidote to the poison of Gullibility is evidence. We must inquire into the reliability of what is said, assess appraisals in terms of actual needs, demand that prescriptions fit the persons prescribed for. The comfortable security that will warm [one person] will incline [another] to manic outbursts; and the weights that [some people] lift with delight will break the spirit—if not the back—of [others]. Openness to evidence requires, however, flexibility in ourselves, courage to delay commitments, knowledge of individual differences, active scrutiny of signs. The process is circular. Only as we lift the masks of signs can we lift the masks of ourselves. But only as we grow into what we deeply are, and cast off false images of ourself, can we become puppeteers and not puppets in the theatre of signs. Each step taken in one direction frees the other foot for its step forward. This is the way we move, and the only way.

THE DYNAMICS OF IDEAS

The human cousin of the apes talks a lot, and in talking lays monkey-traps for himself. But he can also talk himself into ways out of them. And into other things. Into cities like New York, or monasteries high in the Hindu Kush; into gigantic wars or consumers' cooperatives; into jet-planes or cameras which stop motion; into the rough togs of the mountaineer or the sleek perfumed slimness of night-club Eve; into Stravinsky's *Rite of Spring* or Bach's *Mass in B-Minor;* into the planned cruelty of sadistic torture or the deliberate construction of untried mathematical systems. The ways from the body's substructures to the superstructures of historical man are fantastically numerous and complex. But they all pass through the crossroads of talk.

For the self's superstructure is built on the framework of ideas. And the large ideas come through talking, talking to others in the first place, talking then to oneself, until finally events in the self and objects in the world take on, as post-language signs, meanings which they otherwise would not have. There arise in this way thinking persons and patterns of culture, the inward and the outward man, each endlessly transforming the other.

It is important to see the central role which ideas have in the development of the human self and society. If times before ours have overstressed the importance of ideas, recent emphasis upon irrationalism and determinism and sin too easily belittles them. The production of the atom bomb is a large enough event to correct the picture. For the production of atomic energy was impossible until men had thought in certain ways and verified their thoughts. Thought piled on thought, junk-piles of discarded thoughts, a few thoughts standing firm and suggesting new thoughts, a network of thoughts stretching over centuries of thinking men and women — surely this is more amazing than the energy output of the bomb itself. And without this thought no bomb. And with it the bomb and incredible energy sources. The tactics of war have changed and new social institutions become necessary. Every ideal must now feel the impact of these ideas. Men could blow the earth to bits if they wished. Or build a society such as never has appeared on the earth. All because of ideas. Ideas are the atom bombs of human culture. And ideas come from thinking-talking-writing persons.

The idea of atomic energy is simply a dramatic instance of what has always occurred. Ideas of planting crops, of domesticating animals, of making fire were equally momentous. Men moved from one region of the earth partly because they had ideas that there were other regions; Columbus sailed west because of the idea that the earth was round; we take to the air because of ideas our ancestors gained about the flight of birds. No insight is possible into the ways of man that leaves out his ideas. And a science of man which is aware of the role of signs in human history must be cautious in its large predictions. For it cannot tell in advance what ideas men are yet to think. And so not what men are yet to be.

Not much is known about the appearance of new ideas. As the science of signs develops we can expect growing insight into the process. A new idea involves the production of a new sign. The signs which a person produces are parts of his behavior. Because words about food have been trained into his food-seeking activity, he tends when seeking food to produce signs of food. The way we talk is bent according to our needs. We talk about food because of hunger; we talk about cancer because we wish to avoid it in ourselves and in others. How we talk is largely limited by the signs available in our community; our talk is for the most part socially stereotyped; our ideas must utilize the ideas already available.

But language leaves open the possibility of novel combination of signs, and because our urges are many and our tendencies to action complex, we occasionally produce a number of signs in a novel combination, and so a new idea. If this idea gets by the protective defenses of the self and society, and sustains itself in the face of evidence, it is then itself a factor which can enter into new combinations. And so on and on. In some such way ideas accumulate, fertilize, engender new offspring, much as parents make surprising children, or chemical elements compound with novel properties.

Since ideas are so dependent on language and its products, and since all sorts of people can be trained to talk, ideas do not belong to any one kind of person. There are geniuses and nitwits among [all types of people]. The best advice to all of them is to try out novel combinations of such ideas as they have available — to become chemists experimenting with sign compounds. In this way they combine their tendencies to behavior in novel ways. In experimenting with signs they are experimenting with themselves. But here again we meet with circular processes. For the anxious and inflexible self fears new ideas because it fears itself. Only the self that is willing to dare change can think creatively. Once more we find ourselves forced to assume responsibility for ourselves. Knowledge of signs helps, but it is not enough. The burden of the ideal cannot be evaded.

STUDY QUESTIONS

1. *Morris helps to explain the important differences between human language and the "language" of animals. What are these differences?*

2. *Morris distinguishes three kinds of signs—designative, appraisive, and prescriptive. Define each of these. Find essays in this anthology which illustrate the various uses. In what parts of a newspaper would you expect to find each?*

3. *Various writers on semantics have suggested other classifications of language use. Can you think of uses of language besides the three which Morris has defined?*

4. *Look through the advertisements of a newspaper or magazine to find illustrations of Morris' "pitfalls" in the use of signs. Which of these seem to you the most common? What do you think is most important to be wary of in your own writing? Why is it important to consider Whitehead's advice to "seek simplicity, but distrust it"?*

5. *Explain how ideas come through talking. Think back to Jackson's "Writer and Reader" in Section I of this anthology: is Morris' notion that ideas come through talking similar to or different from Jackson's notion that in reading and writing one discovers himself? How does Morris account for the development of new ideas in the history of mankind? How is this related to Lewes' ideas about "insight" and "perception"?*

6. *The importance of designative and prescriptive signs is generally acknowledged. But would it be possible for civilization to survive without the kind of signs Morris calls "appraisive"? Explain how the disappearance of appraisive signs would affect some area where they are now used, such as advertising, religion, courtship, art, or literature.*

Monroe Beardsley On Contexts and Vagueness *

MEANING AND CONTEXT

One of the fundamental facts about words is that the most useful ones in our language have many meanings. That is partly why they are so useful: they work overtime (but, as we shall see, not for nothing). Think of all the various things we mean by the word "foot" on different occasions: one of the lower extremities of the human body, a measure of verse, the ground about a tree, twelve inches, the floor in front of the stairs. The same is true of nearly every common noun or verb. The editors of *The American College Dictionary*, in their preliminary investigation of words most frequently used, found 55 distinct senses of the word "point" in 1,100 occurrences of the word, and they distinguished 109 different senses of the word "run."

Considering the number of ways of taking a particular word, the task of speaking clearly and being understood would seem pretty hopeless if it were not for another very important fact about language. Though a word may have many senses, these senses can be controlled, up to a point, by the *context* in which the word is used. When we find the word in a particular verbal setting — that is, take it with the words that come before and after it in a discourse — we can usually decide quite definitely which of the many senses of the word is relevant. If a poet says his verse has three feet, it doesn't occur to you that he could mean it's a yard long or is three-legged (unless perhaps you are a critic planning to puncture the poet with a pun about his "limping verse"). The context rules out these maverick senses quite decisively.

We might be puzzled if we read in a newspaper that "in the suicide's pocket the police found a large envelope full of bills." In this sentence, as it stands, the word "bills" can easily be taken in two very different senses. But if the context were expanded so as to read, "The police were surprised to find in the suicide's pocket a large envelope full of bills of various denominations," we should understand that "bills" meant *paper money,* and we might wonder whether it was indeed suicide or accident. Or if the context were expanded differently, so as to read, "The police were surprised to find in the suicide's pocket a large envelope full of unpaid bills," we should understand that "bills" meant *requests for payment of a debt,* and we might wonder whether that explains the suicide.

This is a rather simple illustration of the way in which the context of a

* Reprinted by permission from *Thinking Straight*, 2nd Ed., pp. 153-159; 167-173. Copyright, 1956, by Prentice-Hall, Inc., Englewood Cliffs, N. J.

word helps to pick out one of its senses and fix that sense. But of course "context" is used broadly here: it may be the rest of a sentence (the *immediate* context), a page, a whole book, or a newspaper file. A "shady street" is one thing; a "shady neighborhood" is something else. The word "strike" means one action on the front page of a paper and another action on the sports page; the words "liberal" and "patriotic" mean certain attitudes in *The New York Times* and mostly different ones in *The Chicago Tribune*. When some time ago a British physicist announced with pleasure that the hydrogen bomb is "safe," his statement caused gasps of surprise; in the technical talk of atomic scientists, "safe" apparently means that it couldn't set off a chain reaction that might destroy the earth itself. This is not the way the man in the street uses the word.

Many common words like "line," "pipe," "base," "stock," and "head," have acquired many serviceable meanings in different occupational contexts — say, in the shoptalk of plumbers, pitchers, or plastic engineers. Think of what the word "wing" means to a birdwatcher, an airman, a stagehand, a general, or an architect. But just because these meanings are so completely distinct — no one can confuse the wing of an airplane with the wing of a house — it is easy to control them by very light contextual pressure. A word or two makes it clear that it is the airman's wing rather than the architect's that is referred to. But when the differences between the senses of a word are slighter and subtler (they may be even more important, however), the most careful management of the context may be required to get and keep one sense in focus. The exact meaning of a word like "middle class" or "evolution" or "justice" may depend upon the whole book in which it appears.

That is why it is often easy to misrepresent what someone has said by quoting some of his remarks out of their context. The words may not, strictly speaking, be *mis*quoted, but their meaning has been changed. The political candidate's promise to obtain peace or balance the budget is echoed and attacked by his opponent — who is careful to leave out the conditions and qualifications that originally surrounded it. Even if a writer is scrupulous enough to put in dots to indicate that something has been left out, he may not be *quite* scrupulous enough to stick to the original meaning. You have seen advertisements of a new play, with a few words from a review. The phrase "... emotional subtlety ... (Bridgeport *Post*)" may be from a sentence that goes: "It has all the emotional subtlety of a barroom brawl." The phrase "... great drama ... (New Haven *Register*)" may be from a sentence that goes: "No doubt it was considered a great drama when it first appeared in 1927, but ..." And this is nothing to what a professional wiretapper can do if he records a telephone conversation and picks out words to rerecord on a new tape.

Representative Wayne L. Hays, a member of the Special House Committee set up by the 83rd Congress to investigate tax-exempt foundations, frequently argued during the committee's hearings that the "research directors" of the committee were willing to make judgments on passages torn out of contexts that might change their meaning considerably. He finally made a dramatic demonstration of this by producing three paragraphs which the associate research director testified were "closely comparable" with, and parallel to, Communist literature that he had read. They were excerpts from two papal encyclicals.

A loose and sloppy writer lays himself open particularly to accidental mis-quotation, but any writer would find it very hard to write a paragraph that is proof against a deliberate and skillful excerpt-lifter. Dean Sturges of the Yale Law School perhaps came as close as anyone can when, in 1949, the Harvard Law School *Record* asked him for an appropriate comment on the Harvard Law School's decision to admit women students for the first time. Dean Sturges is reported to have sent the following telegram:

YALE LAW FACULTY AND STUDENT BODY DEEPLY MOVED. FEEL IT QUITE POSSIBLE HARVARD MAY MAKE CONTRIBUTION TO WOMANHOOD. DOUBT MANY ADVERSE CONSEQUENCES HARVARD FACULTY OR STUDENT BODY. WE HAVE ALWAYS FOLLOWED WITH GENUINE INTEREST LONG STRUGGLE HARVARD LIBERALS IN THIS MATTER. OUR MANY GENERATIONS OF WOMEN GRADUATES ARE OF COURSE A PRIDE AND JOY. BEST WISHES.

Try digging a quotable compliment out of that.

The importance of context in the interpretation of meaning varies from one discourse to another. In a technical article on mathematics or physics, most sentences can stand pretty much on their own feet and be well understood apart from their context. Scientific terms are designed to resist the influence of context so that they can pass from one context to another without changing their meaning. But sentences in ordinary discourse that contain pronouns often lean on other sentences that contain the antecedents of those pronouns. Moreover, some words in our language — and they are among the most useful, but the trickiest, ones — are so adaptable to their context, like chameleons, that they take most of their character from it, and when they are considered apart from any context, they have only the most indefinite meaning. Words like "efficient," "dangerous," "internal," "successful," "free," tell us very little unless we are told, for example, the *purpose* for which it is efficient, or the *standards* in terms of which the success is judged. Contexts like "freehanded," "free lunch," "free love," "free will," "freeborn," "free association," help to limit the word "free" to a somewhat more definite range of meaning, but even in such cases we often feel that we don't know exactly what the word "free" means unless the context provides answers to the questions: "Free *from* what?" "Free *for* what?" "Free *to do* what?"

Another thing that shows the importance of context is the fact that when people use the wrong word we sometimes know what word should have been used. When Mrs. Malaprop says, "I would by no means wish a daughter of mine to be a progeny of learning... I would have her instructed in geometry, that she might know something of the contagious countries," we understand what she thought she was saying because the context so clearly tells us what words are called for if the sentences are to make sense. A malapropism is a word that is wrongly used in a sentence in place of another word that sounds somewhat like it. And if we couldn't tell from the context what the appropriate word would be, we could never recognize a malapropism.

But of course it would be a mistake to overemphasize contextual influence and say that a word *never* has the same meaning in two different contexts. If this were true, language would be even more difficult to manage than it is now. A person who says, "I believe in the dictionary" and later "I believe in the Bible" is presumably using the word "believe" in the same sense in both contexts. Perhaps sometimes when we say that a word is used twice in the same sense we ignore slight differences that could be important for one purpose or another. It is a good idea to keep in mind that a change in context *may* make a change in the sense, but it doesn't seem that it *must*. In the present paragraph the word "context" has, up to this point, been used three times, in three slightly different (immediate) contexts; but it has about the same meaning each time.

It is only when the context is considerably different that the meaning is likely to change. A person who says, "I believe in the dictionary," and, later, "I don't believe in ghosts," is using the word "believe" in two very different senses. But in each of these contexts it can have only one possible meaning, and when the whole context is taken into account there *may* be no question what that meaning is. "I believe in a federal world government" means about the same as "I believe *there should be* a federal world government." "I believe in extrasensory perception" means about the same as "I believe *there is such a thing as* extrasensory perception." "I believe in woman's intuition" means about the same as "I believe *that some of the things that* women intuit *are true.*"

When a word can have different meanings in different kinds of context, we can say that it has variable meaning. Its meaning *varies*, and it therefore has a variety of senses when it appears in the dictionary. Some words are more variable than others. But the variable meaning of words doesn't ordinarily give us any trouble so long as there is enough contextual control. The trouble arises when the context is not complete enough to rule out all but one possible meaning. If I say, "Henry rents the house," there is no way for you to tell from the sentence itself whether Henry rents the house *from* someone or *to* someone. When a word can have one (but not both) of two (or more) meanings in a certain context, we shall say that the word is ambiguous *in that context*.

The ambiguity of a word is always relative to a context: no word is ambiguous *in itself*. Some words like "freedom," "religion," "democracy," are ambiguous in quite a few contexts, and that is why you have to be careful in interpreting and in using them. Sometimes such words are said to be "meaningless," but the trouble with them is just the opposite: they have so many subtly different meanings that it takes a good deal of skill — more than most writers command — to keep their meanings well under control. And when the writer fails in this task, it is up to the reader. Other words, such as the common nouns, are variable in meaning but are hardly ever ambiguous. It takes a good deal of ingenuity to write a medium-sized sentence in which the word "foot" is ambiguous.

A case of ambiguity, as we have defined it, is a case where there is some *doubt* about the way a discourse is to be interpreted, and you have to choose between alternative readings. Unfortunately, this is not the way the word "ambiguity" is always used. When A. E. Housman, in his poem "To an Athlete Dying Young," writes,

> Home they brought him, shoulder high,
> Townsman of a stiller town,

the word "town" has at least two meanings: the young man's village is quieter for the funeral than it was on the day everyone cheered his victory, and also he is now among the noiseless dead. But "town" is not ambiguous here. It has *both* meanings at once, and there is no uncertainty about them at all.

This sort of double meaning, or multiple meaning as it may be called, is also characteristic of one type of pun. There is the old pun, for example, about the two women leaning out of their windows across an alley and shouting at each other angrily: they can never come to an agreement because they are arguing from different premises. Another type of pun is built on *homonyms*, that is, words that have the same sound but different senses ("boy," "buoy"; "recede," "reseed"; "bier," "beer"; "air," "heir"). If you want to call homonyms the same word because they have the same sound, you would then have to say that such words have an even more variable meaning than we supposed. On the whole, we may as well call them different words if they are spelt differently, and then we shall not need to say any more about homonyms, except to note that they can give rise to the sort of pun made by Macbeth when he says he will plant circumstantial evidence on the grooms:

> "If he do bleed,
> I'll *gild* the faces of the grooms withal,
> For it must seem their *guilt*."

This sort of double entendre, whether in pun or poem, is sometimes called "ambiguity," but it is a very different thing from ambiguity in the sense in which we are using the term. The distinction can be clarified by means of some terms that come up later (in Chapter 6). The important thing at the moment is to note that there is a difference. The high-pressure context of a poem can squeeze many senses, all at once, out of some of its words; this is the multiple meaning of poetic discourse. But we have ambiguity, in the strict sense, when the context is too loose and flabby to hold the words steadily to *any* definite sense. The poet has managed to say several things at once; the ambiguous writer has not quite succeeded in saying anything.

A statement is either true or false; it can't be half-and-half. (A "half-truth" is false.) And an object is either an airplane or it is not; it can't be more or less an airplane. "True" and "airplane" are *either-or* words, but many other words in our language are not either-or words, but *more-or-less* words. A piece of bread can be more or less stale, an argument more or less convincing, a person more or less rich, tired, or bald. These words refer to qualities that vary in degree or amount. They are terms of comparison, or *comparative terms.* Under this label we shall include all words about which it makes sense to ask: How much? or How many? You can ask, "How rich is the Aga Khan?" or "How stale is the bread?" You can't ask, "How airplane is this object?" and when people ask, as they occasionally do, "How true is this statement?" this seems to be a loose colloquial way of asking, not how *true* it is, but how much *evidence* there is for it — which is quite a different thing.

Most of our common comparative terms are also used to classify things. We speak of bread as being more or less stale; but also, in terms of its degree of staleness, we divide bread into *stale* bread and *fresh* bread. If a person is rich enough, we call him "rich," and make a threefold division here between the rich, the poor, and the ones who are neither. If a person loses enough hair, we call him "bald"; if a tire loses enough air, we call it "flat"; and if a driver has enough accidents, we call him "unsafe."

The word "enough" is a key word here, for it leads us to ask questions like this: Exactly *how* dry must bread be in order to be stale? How much money must a man have in order to be rich? How many hairs must a man lose in order to be bald? How many accidents must a driver have, and how serious must they be, if he is to be considered unsafe?

These are all natural questions, and the important point about language that we want to be clear about here is just that *they have no answers.* We have never come to any agreement, tacit or explicit, about these words; there is simply no general rule according to which anyone with less than 196 hairs is bald, or anyone with more than $17,412.35 is rich. How old is middle-aged? Where does red leave off and orange begin? How cold is a cold shoulder? We have never drawn a line at any particular place, and so there is no definite line: this is what we mean when we say that a word is *vague.*

A vague word refers to a certain range of variation in intensity or quantity. Think of a sort of scale, ranging, say, from people with no money to the person who has the most, or from people with no hair to people with bushy tresses, or from bread right out of the oven to bread that has been around for months. In the case of a vague word, there is always a certain part of the scale to which the word definitely, and by universal agreement, applies: anyone who has twenty millions is surely rich, anyone with nothing but a slight fringe of hair is bald, and bread that has begun to mold is definitely stale. Moreover, there is always a certain part of the scale to which the word definitely does *not* apply: a person with only forty-five dollars is *not* rich; a person with hair covering the top of his head is certainly *not* bald; and bread that is only an hour old is *not* stale.

But in between these two parts of the scale there is a *doubtful area* where we have not decided whether to apply the word or not. There will be border-line savings accounts, heads of hair, and loaves of bread that you can describe either way, just as there are people you don't know whether to call "middle-aged" or not. If the word were *precise*, it would be defined so as to draw a sharp line. It is just the nature of a vague word that the line it draws is fuzzy.

As you can see, vagueness is a very different sort of thing from ambiguity. In ambiguity you have a choice between two distinct senses of a word, which may be as unrelated as plane geometry and marital disorders (as in two senses of "triangle"), only there is no way to decide how to choose. In vagueness, you know what the sense is all right, but you don't know *how much* there is of the quality referred to. Thus a word that has several meanings may be vague in some senses but not in others (compare "cold war" and "cold shoulder," "hot jazz" and "hot air"). And even when there is no question about the sense of a word, its doubtful area may shift from context to context. A large child is not the same as a large elephant; in both of these contexts the word is vague, but the doubtful area for children would be in pounds, and for elephants in hundreds of pounds. Compare "hot day," "hot bath," "hot oven" and "hot star," in each of these contexts "hot" means a different degree of temperature, and some of these "hot"s are fuzzier than others: "It's a hot day" is very loosely used, but when the cook book advises a "hot oven" for popovers, this has a pretty definite agreed-upon meaning.

So far, we have defined the word "vague" in such a way that only comparative terms are vague. But it is useful to broaden this a little further. Some words that are not comparative words themselves are defined in terms of other words that *are* comparative words. "Explosion" means "a rapid combustion"; thus, so long as there is no general rule that specifies *how* rapid a combustion must be before it is to be called an explosion, the word "explosion" is vague in *one* respect. Similarly, "democracy," in some of its senses, is vague in some respects. When you want to know whether a given word is vague, then, ask yourself, first, whether there is any question of *degree* involved in applying the word, and second, whether the degree involved is anywhere precisely specified.

It is important to realize that vague words can be very useful. In fact, some of them are useful *because* they are vague: it is handy to be able to report that the room was "crowded," without having to calculate the number of people per square foot; it is equally handy for us to be able to speak of the "context" of a word, without having to specify exactly and for all cases exactly how many words before and after a given word we shall include in its context.

As for most other vague words, if we haven't bothered to make them precise it may be simply that we haven't needed to do so. A vague word is useful so long as it marks *some* distinction: that is, as long as we can point out something to which the word surely applies (the New England town meeting is definitely a democracy, in one sense of this word) and something to which the word surely does not apply (the Franco government in Spain is definitely *not* a democracy, in the same sense of this word).

Or take another example. The words "good taste" and "bad taste" are vague: how bad does taste have to be before it is "bad"? When the Senate Judiciary Subcommittee on Juvenile Delinquency was investigating comic books, in the spring of 1954, it was struck by a comic book whose cover showed a man with a bloody axe in one hand, holding up a severed woman's head in the other. The publisher of this comic book, who was testifying, cited it as an example of "good taste." Senator Kefauver, somewhat taken aback, asked the logically correct question to discover whether the publisher really meant anything by this description: how would the cover have to look if it were in *bad* taste? "It would be in bad taste," replied the publisher, "if the head were held a little higher, with the blood dripping out." This showed that he was drawing *some* line, though perhaps a rather odd one, and hence that "good taste" at least meant *something* to him.

Vague words get us into trouble only when we don't notice that they are vague. We expect too much of them, and they let us down. We think there must be a sharp line between "neutrality" and "involvement," when in fact there is just a blurry no man's land. Sheep and goats, chairs and tables, males and females can be separated from each other in a way that will satisfy nearly everyone, for these words have highly determinate meanings. Moreover, nature and human workmanship have provided us with easily distinguishable things instead of borderline cases. But two heads of hair may differ by a single hair, two bank accounts by less than a dollar, and the ages of two people by a few minutes. In such cases, there will be heads of hair, bank accounts, and people's ages that we won't have any generally agreed upon way of describing.

And this is why it is essential for words to be reasonably precise when questions of truth and falsity arise. The main counts of the Government's indictment of Professor Owen Lattimore accused him of "following the Communist line" and being a "promoter of Communist interests." These counts were thrown out by the Court of Appeals on the ground of vagueness, in keeping with the Sixth Amendment, which specifies that a person has a right to know what crime he is accused of before he can be tried. If the words used to describe the crime are not clear, how can he know what he is being tried for, and how can he defend himself? And how can the jury be expected to decide objectively whether he is guilty of it or not?

But of course, no matter how vague a word may be, we can always make it as precise as we wish for particular purposes and in particular contexts. We *can* draw a sharp line when we want to. A herring is a large sardine; that is a vague way of talking. For its convenience, however, the Food and Drug Administration calls a sardine a "herring" only when it is at least nine inches long. That is fairly precise. In common speech, the words "urban" and "rural" are vague. But the United States Census makes a sharper distinction: if a town has a population of 2,500 or more it is "urban," if not, it is "rural." "High-income group" is vague, but Congress, in a particular act, may arbitrarily draw the line at $25,000. This is a perfectly sensible procedure. Of course, it will always sound odd to say that a person making $25,000 a year is in a "high-income group," whereas a person making $24,999.99 is not. But you have to draw the line *somewhere* if you draw it at all. Where the scale is in terms of pennies, any particular place to draw the line will seem arbitrary.

Sometimes the line drawn may, in fact, be *too* arbitrary for the purpose at hand. If a great deal hinges on the distinction, it may be more than such a slight difference will bear. It doesn't seem fair to pass a student who gets 60 and fail a student who gets 59; we don't feel sure enough about the accuracy of tests and grades to make such an important result depend upon such a minute difference. This is why some educators prefer to use a vaguer scale, such as A, B, C, or Pass, High Pass, Honors, for grading students. Precision is always relative to what we want to do with it. Unnecessary precision is pedantic and fussy, like honing a razor to cut butter. Still, to develop skill in careful thinking, it is sometimes useful to practice a little pedantry. If you know how to make precise distinctions, you are free to decide, in a given case, just how far you ought to go. Each case is different, and only by studying it carefully can you determine what degree of vagueness is probably safe and perhaps desirable.

We would have little trouble in handling vague words, once we understood their habits, if it were not for one ingenious way of misusing them that may impose upon our thinking when we are off guard. It consists in arguing that there is no difference, or no important difference, between two things because the apparent difference is made up of a whole series of small differences. It doesn't matter much whether you smoke ten cigarettes a day or eleven, it doesn't matter much whether you smoke eleven or twelve, and so on. Someone might argue that therefore it doesn't matter whether you smoke ten or forty: there is no difference between heavy smoking and light smoking because any attempt to draw the line, say between thirteen and fourteen, is arbitrary. The amount of freedom you enjoy in one country only differs in degree from the amount of freedom you enjoy in another country; sometimes people argue that since it is only a difference of degree, it is therefore not much of a difference at all: "they are both about the same."

This sort of argument commits the black-or-white fallacy. It is a subtle attempt to paralyze choice by belittling an important difference. It is especially plausible when the distinctions are vague. The prefix "crypto-" has in recent years been used to great advantage in muddling people's thinking about political attitudes. As it is sometimes loosely used, a man can apparently be a disguised, or "crypto-" Communist without knowing it, or, indeed, without doing anything about it. According to this line of thought, a Democrat is a "crypto-liberal," a liberal is a "crypto-socialist," a socialist is a "crypto-communist," and a communist is a traitor; therefore Democrats are traitors, or practically traitors. When put in such a bare form, without any fancy trimmings, this argument doesn't look as though it would fool anyone. But it has been a staple commodity with some rabble rousers, who have done their best to make it appear that there is no important difference between both ends of their equation.

The same method of reasoning sometimes turns up in discussions of the degree of economic difficulty the United States economy may be undergoing at a certain time. There is "inventory correction," "rolling adjustment," "recession," and "depression," and (because the black-or-white fallacy works both ways) there may be an attempt to play down the differences by those who want to show that current troubles are *worse* than they really are (hardly distinguishable from a small depression) and at the same time by those who want to show that current troubles are *not as bad* as they really are (merely a sizeable inventory correction). The only way to get a proper perspective on the situation, and escape both fallacious arguments, is to insist on some definite distinctions between these various ills. For example, let's not call it a depression unless it involves a downward movement on the part of nearly every economic index, and unemployment of at least five million over a period of at least two years. If that seems *too* fine a line, it is easy enough to relax it. But at least we can keep the discussion from bogging down in a mushy terminology like "crypto-depression."

The black-or-white argument is a favorite with extremists, who are blind to the differences between shades of gray because to them the only "real" difference is between black and white. On a scale of cigarette smoking or civil liberty the *big* differences are made up of many *small* differences, but that doesn't make the big difference any less big. There are differences in *kind* and there are differences in *degree*, but some differences in degree are, from a practical point of view, just as crucial as differences in kind. We succeed only in drugging our thinking when we allow these differences to be smudged over by verbal trickery.

STUDY QUESTIONS

1. *What is meant by context? Is the context of a particular word always language, or can other media act as contexts? How many other kinds of context that would have some effect on the meaning of words can you name?*

2. *Beardsley points out that in most cases the meaning of a word depends to a considerable extent on factors outside itself. Is this a desirable state of affairs? Would it not be better to have a language in which each word was assigned a definite and unchanging meaning? Are there any such languages?*

3. *What is the difference between* vagueness *and* ambiguity *of language?*

4. *To what extent does the ordinary dictionary help to solve some of the problems of meaning discussed here? Do the experiences of Henry Miller in "On Dictionaries and Encyclopedias" throw any light on this problem?*

5. *From the point of view of the writer, are the problems of words discussed by Beardsley more important in one of the uses of language described by Morris than in others? Or are they equally important but somewhat different in the various kinds? Explain.*

6. *Among the following words, which would you call vague and which would you call definite: immoral, civilization, homicidal, criminal (adjective), benefactor, contributor, subscriber, alteration, destruction, improvement. Write a short theme on any group of these explaining why some of them are vaguer in meaning than others.*

Max Black Emotive Language *

Personal and impersonal aspects of utterance. We have already said that any utterance normally gives some information about the speaker himself, as well as other matters. Let us, therefore, refer to the personal and impersonal aspects of an utterance. By the first term we shall mean the information given about the speaker, and more especially about the attitudes, feelings, and wishes that caused him to make the utterance; by the second, whatever other information may be conveyed by the utterance. The personal aspects may be further divided into expressive and dynamic aspects. The utterance is expressive insofar as it is caused by the speaker's feelings or attitudes, *without any desired effect on a hearer.* An involuntary cry of pain or joy is markedly expressive in this sense. The utterance is dynamic insofar as it is caused by the speaker's desire to produce actions or other effects in a hearer; a command or a question is markedly dynamic in this sense. Actual utterances vary widely in the relative importance of their expressive, dynamic, and impersonal apects.

Statement and suggestion. No human speaker explicitly symbolizes all that he conveys to the hearer; we must constantly "read between the lines." One important consequence of this has already been mentioned. A speaker very rarely says: "I want you to feel that I am a thoroughly likable person of the sort you can trust; I am not much interested in tariffs (or whatever it may be) except insofar as some knowledge of this subject is necessary to persuade you to trust me." Such devastating frankness would be self-defeating, but many a speaker talks in such a way as to convey the same impression. Intelligent understanding of the utterance requires an awareness of much

* Reprinted by permission from *Critical Thinking*, 2nd Ed., by Max Black, pp. 166-176. Copyright, 1952, by Prentice-Hall, Inc., Englewood Cliffs, N. J.

more than is "said in so many words." The *general setting* of the utterance (whether it is predominantly "scientific" or "poetic," intended to produce approval, result in actions, and so on) is not usually symbolized explicitly.

Let us examine a striking instance of "reading between the lines." In answering a letter not long ago, a certain Senator began his reply with the words "My dear Wop" — an action that led to considerable indignation on the part of his correspondent and many of the lady's sympathizers. Furious letters were written to Congress and the newspapers, and the Senator's action was denounced at meetings of protest as "undemocratic" and "un-American."

Why all this fuss about three words? A foreigner, not thoroughly familiar with the subtleties of the American language, would find on enquiry, that "Wop" means about the same as "Italian" or "person of Italian origin." "Well, well," he might wonder, in his naive way, "is it so insulting to an American to be accused of having Italian ancestors?" The answer, of course, is that "Wop" is a term of powerful *abuse,* conventionally used as a way of expressing a high degree of contempt for the person addressed. The three words might be expanded in some such way as this: "Madam, the usual rules of politeness require me to use the words 'My dear so-and-so.' I show my contempt for you and your opinions by refusing even to call you by your name. I am pretty sure that you can't be an American; I suspect that you are of Italian origin; and I regard Italians in general as inferior and degenerate."

Yet the abusive Senator did not *say* all this "in so many words" — even though much of it is quite clearly understood by his readers. Offense is properly taken at the insulting suggestions of the utterance, rather than at its explicitly formulated content.

The unformulated implications and suggestions of an utterance are not always abusive. Often we convey feelings of approval, enjoyment, or appreciation by gesture, tone of voice, and choice of words. The means employed are so flexible and variable that usually we are hardly aware of them, even while constantly responding to their influence. A large part of the information conveyed by utterance is *suggested, not stated.*

When a purported fact, a wish, a judgment of value, and so forth, are conveyed by means of a symbol conventionally used for that purpose we shall say the fact, wish, and so on, has been stated; when information is conveyed by means not conventionally reserved for that purpose we shall say that that information has been suggested. Thus, a statement is an explicitly formulated assertion, command, desire, judgment, and so forth, while a suggestion is conveyed, though not explicitly formulated. (It is, however, hard to draw a sharp line between suggestion and statement, as here defined. Sometimes, of course, there can be no doubt at all that an important part of a given utterance has been suggested, though not explicitly symbolized. The man who asks "When did you start smoking so heavily?" has not *actually* said "You are smoking heavily.")

All human languages rely, to an astonishing degree, on what is understood, though not said "in so many words." It has been reported of the Eskimos that "Their phrases are as sober as their faces. A gleam in an Eskimo's eye tells you more than half a dozen of our sentences concerning desire, repugnance, or another emotion. Each Eskimo's word is like that gleam: it suggests at once what has happened and what is to come...." (Gontran de Poncins, *Kabloona,* page 247.) The more articulate languages of Western civilization, though not as suggestive as those of the Eskimo, still retain enormous suggestive power.

Emotive and neutral language. Among the most effective suggestions conveyed in human utterance are those expressive of the speaker's *feelings* (and especially feelings of approval or disapproval). Not only *feelings* are conveyed by suggestion: Any statement about "impersonal" matters of fact makes use of tacit assumptions, which are suggested, not stated. Nevertheless, the uses of suggestion to communicate the nature of a speaker's feelings are particularly important, for the following reasons:

1. Suggested feelings concerning a person or object can powerfully influence people's opinions. To call a man a "Red" is already to turn an audience against him; to call him a "dirty Red," in certain contexts, is practically to condemn him outright. Such "name calling" is usually more successful than explicit statement or reasoned argument.

2. Feelings, especially strong feelings, concerning a person or object spontaneously find expression in the use of "satisfying" symbols. (All praise and abuse tends to become poetic.) An angry man tends to *show* his anger rather than talk *about* it: thus the means by which he expresses his feelings will be a suggestion, not a statement. In general, suggestion is a very "natural" way of conveying a feeling.

Much attention has accordingly been given, in recent times, to the use of those signs that particularly lend themselves to the expression and communication of feelings. Such symbols are termed emotive, and are contrasted with neutral symbols. An emotive word, then, is one expressive of strong feelings (especially of approval or disapproval) on the part of the speaker. The use of emotive words has a tendency to produce similar feelings in the hearer.

The English language has a few words reserved for the expression of feeling and used for no other purpose — exclamations like "Shame!" "Hurrah!" "Encore!" While these words are highly emotive according to our definition, they express very generalized feelings. For this reason (and because they are so seldom used in discourse) they have negligible influence in determining people's views concerning *specific* topics.

If an advertiser wants to predispose the man in the street in favor of his product, he will probably adopt more subtle means to recommend it. Suppose he is selling a dentifrice consisting of powdered beef bone (an actual case): the slogan "Hurrah for powdered beef bone!" is unlikely to enlist many customers for the new product, even though repeated thousands of times in newspaper advertisements and on the radio. For the words "powdered beef bone" have suggestions that are unfavorable to the advertiser's purpose: we have all seen raw bones, and we are led to think of an unappetizing mess of blood-stained splinters, not at all the sort of stuff we would choose for cleaning the teeth. How much better then from the advertiser's standpoint to label the product "Numin" (the name actually chosen). Instead of the *negative* emotive force of "powdered beef bone," we have a *positive* emotive appeal of the substitute term, "Numin." For the latter has a scientific flavor, as of some new vitamin, and can therefore be relied upon to attract the man in the street.

The device used in this instance to stimulate a favorable reaction to a certain object (the dentifrice) consists in *the choice of a name having agreeable associations.* The English language is very rich in words approximately equivalent in *explicit* meaning, while markedly divergent in their emotive associations and suggestions.

The terms "government official," "bureaucrat," and "public servant" have much the same explicit meaning, yet the first is neutral, the second abusive, and the last honorific. "Liquidation of the opposition" sounds a great deal more agreeable than "torture and murder of the minority." A man may "talk eloquently" or "jabber"; a statesman may "have the gift of compromise" or be a "slippery trimmer"; a friend is "understandably confused," an enemy "has gone a bit off his noodle"; all these examples were in a single newspaper editorial.

The list of examples could be indefinitely extended, for nearly all the words we use are colored with some shade of respect or contempt, and every notion can be so worded as to make its subject seem either admirable or ridiculous.

The expression and influence of attitudes by means of such highly emotive words as those we have cited should be too obvious to escape notice. *But these cases are not exceptional.* The view that only in "propaganda" and abuse is language used emotively is none the less profoundly mistaken for being widely held. We must insist, to the contrary, that language is *normally* used to express attitudes and exert influence as well as to convey explicit statement; it is as much of an exception for language to be "uncolored" or neutral as for matter to be without odor.

Since the emotive and suggestive influence of language is so strong, we must take account of it in our general program of establishing principles and standards of right thinking. (If, on the other hand, we were to neglect these aspects of language, and pay attention only to what is explicitly stated in neutral terms, we should be behaving like a pilot who refused to take account of any part of an iceberg that was not visible above the water.) By discussing a concrete example in detail, we shall now illustrate the types of critical procedure that are appropriate.

ANALYSIS OF A SPECIMEN OF HIGHLY EMOTIVE WRITING.

A recent newspaper editorial opened with this sentence:

(A) "A fabulously rich playboy, who got tired of his ponies, got the idea that he would like to repudiate the free enterprise that privileged his grandfather to endow him with so many million dollars he could never hope to count them."

This passage tells us a good deal more about the editorial writer (or his employer) than about the millionaire who is the target of his abuse. Yet the passage does contain a little *impersonal* information (true or false), and the first step in analysis is to make this context explicit. An experienced journalist who happened to read (A) would immediately "discount" much of what was said. What this probably means, he might comment, is:

(B) "The rich man in question is supporting federal control of industry."

After the invective of (A), this partial translation appears insipid. Clearly the writer had little interest in conveying the information expressed by (B).

We proceed, therefore, to identify the *emotive suggestions* of the original passage. A convenient way of doing this is to begin by picking out (say by underlining) all the words and phrases that make a notable contribution to the total impression intended. After this has been done, we try to state explicitly the nature of the suggestion conveyed in each case. Proceeding in this fashion, we get the following analysis:

Language used	*Suggestion conveyed*
"*playboy*," "*ponies*"	X (the man in question) is an idler and gambler
"*fabulously rich*"	X is excessively wealthy
"*so many million dollars he could never hope to count them*"	
"*got tired of*"	X is irresponsible—makes decisions for no good reason
"*got the idea*"	
"*would like to repudiate*"	
"*privileged*"	X has received special and unearned favors
"*endow*"	

It will be seen that these suggestions reinforce each other in painting the picture of a most unattractive character. The malice of the writer's intention is obvious when the various suggestions are combined in a single explicit statement, in some such fashion as this:

(C) The man in question is an idle gambler, who has far more money than he deserves, and is now irresponsibly using the vast financial power that he did nothing to earn.

This last statement, if made explicitly, might well be libellous and expose its author to a legal suit for damages. Yet even so it would probably be less effective than the hints and innuendoes of the original passage (A). In all such cases the rule holds that the outspoken accusation is less dangerous than the whispered calumny.

A good way of neutralizing the suggestive power of the original passage is to replace the crucial emotive terms and phrases by others having *opposite emotive tendency* (but approximately the same explicit content). In this way we get the following substitute for (A):

> (D) A very wealthy American sportsman has decided to oppose the system of unregulated commercial trading that enabled his grandfather to leave him his large fortune.

(You would do well to compare versions A and D very carefully, in order to decide for yourself whether the latter can be regarded as a "fair translation" of the former.)

It still remains for us to determine whether the suggestions contained in the original passage (and explicitly formulated in C) are to be regarded as justified. *We must guard carefully against assuming that the implicit suggestions of an utterance can be automatically rejected without further examination, just because they are suggested and not explicitly stated.* Such an assumption would be grossly mistaken, for there are many occasions on which the expression of our feelings is perfectly justified.

We take as a second instance of highly emotive language a passage from one of Garrison's addresses to the public:

> I am aware that many object to the severity of my language; but is there not cause for severity? I will be as harsh as truth, and as uncompromising as justice. On this subject, I do not wish to think, or speak, or write, with moderation; No! no! Tell a man whose house is on fire to give a moderate alarm; tell him to moderately rescue his wife from the hands of the ravisher; tell the mother to gradually extricate her babe from the fire into which it has fallen; But urge me not to use moderation in a cause like the present. I am in earnest—I will not equivocate—I will not retreat a single inch,— AND I WILL BE HEARD.

This is the language of a man laboring under strong emotions, conveyed in words well fitted to communicate indignation. Shall we say he is wrong to have the feelings or to attempt to communicate them? Or that he ought to resort to the pallid and ineffective use of "neutral" language? Surely not. But to grant the right of Garrison or anybody else to express feelings and attitudes towards a subject by the most effective means he can find at hand is a very different thing from admitting without further examination that the specific emotion or attitude is justified. The suggestions of eloquence, rhetoric or poetry, insofar as they consist of claims that might be true or false, must submit to enquiries into their evidence, general credibility, consistency; if their moving appeals to our feelings are justified, they should survive such examination without detriment or loss of eloquence.

Returning to our original example, then, we must ask *what evidence is* provided for the claim formulated in (C). In this particular instance, the answer is quickly given: for *no reasons at all* are brought forward in support of the scurrilous accusation. Even while we admit the editorial writer's general privilege of accusing his subject of idleness, irresponsibility, and so forth, in the manner he has chosen, we must object strenuously that in the case at issue his accusation is presented as a bare assertion, destitute of any supporting evidence in its favor. Our summing up of the value of passage (A) might take some such form as this: "The passage is intended to arouse prejudice against its subject, by representing him as idle, irresponsible, and undeservedly wealthy. It appeals successfully to the reader's presumed dislike of these qualities. But it offers no particle of evidence in support of its hostile contention."

SUGGESTED RULES OF PROCEDURE FOR THE CRITICISM OF EMOTIVELY TONED UTTERANCE.

The painstaking analysis illustrated in the last section will be too elaborate for everyday use — life is too short for us to be always ferreting out the full emotive implications of what we read and hear. It is nevertheless of much value as a training in critical awareness of the suggestive overtones of human utterance to perform a few such exercises in great detail. When this is done, the following suggestions for procedure may be helpful:

1. Begin by reading the passage slowly, carefully, and calmly several times, noting any points in the utterance that seem to deserve further examination. (The reader will pardon this insistence on so elementary and obvious a point. Experience shows that once the excitement of the chase has been aroused, there is a tendency to "discover" sinister or profound implications in a passage, before even reading it with any degree of attention!)

2. State the general intention and context of the utterance. [E.g., "This is a report of a new scientific discovery made to an audience thoroughly familiar with the general background, and made by a man who is trying to suppress all that is personal in the circumstances he is describing." Or "This is an advertisement whose main object is to arouse curiosity concerning a mysteriously labelled new product; it is designed to appeal especially to women to make them more receptive to later 'follow-ups.'" It is useful also to try to determine the evidence used in arriving at this verdict concerning the general nature of the symbolic situation.]

3. Extract the words and phrases in the passage that are particularly effective in conveying the desired suggestion. [Crude instances of this, such as those discussed in the last section, are easily detected. More subtle suggestion, e.g., those due to the general style of a passage, may easily escape notice. It is an excellent practice here, as throughout this training, to compare one's results with those of others working independently on the same passage. Hunting down the reasons for disagreement will often bring to light unsuspected resources of the language used.]

4. Make the suggestions of each word explicit, and combine the partial suggestions in a single statement. [This has been illustrated by the analysis preceding version (C) above. You will soon find, on trial, that the suggestions of a word or phrase can be made explicit only in a rough and approxi-

mate way. Paraphrasing the implicit content largely neutralizes its emotive influence. Instead of extracting the implicit content in this way, a useful variation is to rewrite the original passage reversing the emotive effect of the critical terms, as illustrated in statement (D) above.]

5. Formulate, in neutral language, the impersonal content of the original passage. [The products of steps 4 and 5 should together approximate in informative content to the original passage.]

6. Determine the evidence in favor of the original passage, as now elaborated.

STUDY QUESTIONS

1. *How does the fact that language has suggested meaning as well as explicit meaning make the task of using it more complicated than that of using chemical or mathematical symbols?*

2. *What does Black's observation about such synonyms as "government official," "bureaucrat" and "public servant" suggest about synonyms in general? Consider also these pairs of synonyms: thrift, stinginess; proud, vain; speed, haste; clever, intelligent; joy, happiness; sleep, slumber; new, novel.*

3. *What subjects and occasions justify the use of emotive language? Consider, for example, a legislature discussing a tax rise, an address by a candidate for election, a salesman describing his product to a prospect, a paper describing the results of a scientific experiment, a speech at a college commencement ceremony; a doctor describing a patient's condition to him. Specify what sort of feeling would be evoked (if any) in each case.*

4. *Apply Black's six rules for criticism of emotionally toned utterances to the following:*
   Trespassers Will Be Prosecuted
   Trust in God and keep your powder dry.
   Men are born free, but everywhere they are in chains.
   "It is a pleasure for me to address the Ladies' Luncheon Club this afternoon."
   "Good morning, Bill. How's the family?"
   His parents were poor but honest.
   In which of these is the suggested meaning nearly the opposite of the explicit meaning?

5. *Describe a use of language — advertising, poetry, such Biblical texts as the Sermon on the Mount, or political oratory — in which suggested meaning is more important than explicit meaning.*

6. *Examine the writing in some newspaper or magazine you often read to see how important suggestion is in it. Write a theme describing the use of suggestive language in periodicals, telling where it generally appears, where it is appropriate, and giving examples of it from your reading.*

John Dewey   What Is Thinking?*

I. DIFFERENT MEANINGS OF THOUGHT

*N*o one can tell another person in any definite way how he *should* think, any more than how he ought to breathe or to have his blood circulate. But the various ways in which men *do* think can be told and can be described in their general features. Some of these ways are better than others; the reasons why they are better can be set forth. The person who understands what the better ways of thinking are and why they are better can, if he will, change his own personal ways until they become more effective; until, that is to say, they do better the work that thinking can do and that other mental operations cannot do so well. The better way of thinking that is to be considered in this book is called reflective thinking: the kind of thinking that consists in turning a subject over in the mind and giving it serious and consecutive consideration. Before we take up this main theme, we shall, however, first take note briefly of some other mental processes to which the name *thought* is sometimes given.

All the time we are awake and sometimes when we are asleep, something is, as we say, going through our heads. When we are asleep we call that kind of sequence "dreaming." We also have daydreams, reveries, castles built in the air, and mental streams that are even more idle and chaotic. To this uncontrolled coursing of ideas through our heads the name of "thinking" is sometimes given. It is automatic and unregulated. Many a child has attempted to see whether he could not "stop thinking"—that is, stop this procession of mental states through his mind—and in vain. More of our waking life than most of us would care to admit is whiled away in this inconsequential trifling with mental pictures, random recollections, pleasant but unfounded hopes, flitting, half-developed impressions. Hence it is that he who offers "a penny for your thoughts" does not expect to drive any great bargain if his offer is taken; he will only find out what happens to be "going through the mind" and what "goes" in this fashion rarely leaves much that is worth while behind.

In this sense, silly folk and dullards *think*. The story is told of a man in slight repute for intelligence, who, desiring to be chosen selectman in his New England town, addressed a knot of neighbors in this wise: "I hear you don't believe I know enough to hold office. I wish you to understand that I am thinking about something or other most of the time." Now, reflective

* From *How We Think*, 1933, by John Dewey. Reprinted by special permission of D. C. Heath and Company.

thought is like this random coursing of things through the mind in that it consists of a succession of things thought of, but it is unlike in that the mere chance occurrence of any chance "something or other" in an irregular sequence does not suffice. Reflection involves not simply a sequence of ideas, but a *con*-sequence — a consecutive ordering in such a way that each determines the next as its proper outcome, while each outcome in turn leans back on, or refers to, its predecessors. The successive portions of a reflective thought grow out of one another and support one another; they do not come and go in a medley. Each phase is a step from something to something — technically speaking, it is a *term* of thought. Each term leaves a deposit that is utilized in the next term. The stream or flow becomes a train or chain. There are in any reflective thought definite units that are linked together so that there is a sustained movement to a common end.

The second meaning of thinking limits it to things not sensed or directly perceived, to things *not* seen, heard, touched, smelt, or tasted. We ask the man telling a story if he saw a certain incident happen, and his reply may be, "No, I only thought of it." A note of invention, as distinct from faithful record of observation, is present. Most important in this class are successions of imaginative incidents and episodes that have a certain coherence, hang together on a continuous thread, and thus lie between kaleidoscopic flights of fancy and considerations deliberately employed to establish a conclusion. The imaginative stories poured forth by children possess all degrees of internal congruity; some are disjointed, some are articulated. When connected, they simulate reflective thought; indeed, they usually occur in minds of logical capacity. These imaginative enterprises often precede thinking of the close-knit type and prepare the way for it. In this sense, a thought or idea is a mental picture of something not actually present, and thinking is the succession of such pictures.

In contrast, reflective thinking has a purpose beyond the entertainment afforded by the train of agreeable mental inventions and pictures. The train must lead somewhere; it must tend to a conclusion that can be substantiated outside the course of the images. A story of a giant may satisfy merely because of the story itself; a reflective conclusion that a giant lived at a certain date and place on the earth would have to have some justification outside of the chain of ideas in order to be a valid or sound conclusion. This contrasting element is probably best conveyed in the ordinary saying: "Think it *out*." The phrase suggests an entanglement to be straightened out, something obscure to be cleared up through the application of thought. There is a goal to be reached, and this end sets a task that controls the sequence of ideas.

A third meaning of thought is practically synonymous with *belief*. "I think it is going to be colder tomorrow," or "I think Hungary is larger than Jugo-Slavia" is equivalent to "I believe so-and-so." When we say, "Men used to think the world was flat," we obviously refer to a belief that was held by our ancestors. This meaning of thought is narrower than those previously mentioned. A belief refers to something beyond itself by which its value is tested; it makes an assertion about some matter of fact or some principle or law. It means that a specified state of fact or law is accepted or rejected, that it is something proper to be affirmed or at least acquiesced in. It is hardly necessary to lay stress upon the importance of belief. It covers all the matters of which we have no sure knowledge and yet which we are sufficiently confident of to act upon and also the matters that we now accept as certainly true, as knowledge, but which nevertheless may be questioned in the future — just as much that passed as knowledge in the past has now passed into the limbo of mere opinion or of error.

There is nothing in the mere fact of thought as identical with belief that reveals whether the belief is well founded or not. Two different men say, "I believe the world is spherical." One man, if challenged, could produce little or no evidence for thinking as he does. It is an idea that he has picked up from others and that he accepts because the idea is generally current, not because he has examined into the matter and not because his own mind has taken any active part in reaching and framing the belief.

Such "thoughts" grow up unconsciously. They are picked up — we know not how. From obscure sources and by unnoticed channels they insinuate themselves into the mind and become unconsciously a part of our mental furniture. Tradition, instruction, imitation — all of which depend upon authority in some form, or appeal to our own advantage, or fall in with a strong passion — are responsible for them. Such thoughts are prejudices; that is, prejudgments, not conclusions reached as the result of personal mental activity, such as observing, collecting, and examining evidence. Even when they happen to be correct, their correctness is a matter of accident as far as the person who entertains them is concerned.

Thus we are brought again, by way of contrast, to the particular kind of thinking that we are to study in this volume, *reflective thinking*. Thought, in the two first senses mentioned, may be harmful to the mind because it distracts attention from the real world, and because it may be a waste of time. On the other hand, if indulged in judiciously these thoughts may afford genuine enjoyment and also be a source of needed recreation. But in either case they can make no claim to truth; they cannot hold themselves up as something that the mind should accept, assert, and be willing to act upon. They may involve a kind of emotional commitment, but not intellectual and practical commitment. Beliefs, on the other hand, do involve precisely this commitment and consequently sooner or later they demand our investigation to find out upon what grounds they rest. To think of a cloud as a whale or a camel — in the sense of to "fancy" — does not commit one to the conclusion that the person having the idea would ride the camel or extract oil from the whale. But when Columbus "thought" the world was round, in the sense of "believed it to be so," he and his followers were thereby committed to a series of other beliefs and actions: to beliefs about routes to India, about what would happen if ships traveled far westward on the Atlantic, etc., precisely as thinking that the world was flat had committed those who held it to belief in the impossibility of circumnavigation, and in the limitation of the earth to regions in the small civilized part of it Europeans were already acquainted with, etc.

The earlier thought, belief in the flatness of the earth, had some foundation in evidence; it rested upon what men could see easily within the limits of their vision. But this evidence was not further looked into; it was not checked by considering other evidence; there was no search for new evidence. Ultimately the belief rested on laziness, inertia, custom, absence of courage and energy in investigation. The later belief rests upon careful and extensive study, upon purposeful widening of the area of observation, upon reasoning out the conclusions of alternative conceptions to see what would follow in case one or the other were adopted for belief. As distinct from the first kind of thinking there was an orderly chain of ideas; as distinct from the second, there was a controlling purpose and end; as distinct from the third, there was personal examination, scrutiny, inquiry.

Because Columbus did not accept unhesitatingly the current traditional theory, because he doubted and inquired, he arrived at his thought. Skeptical of what, from long habit, seemed most certain, and credulous of what seemed impossible, he went on thinking until he could produce evidence for both his confidence and his disbelief. Even if his conclusion had finally turned out wrong, it would have been a different sort of belief from those it antagonized, because it was reached by a different method. *Active, persistent, and careful consideration of any belief or supposed form of knowledge in the light of the grounds that support it and the further conclusions to which it tends* constitutes reflective thought. Any one of the first three kinds of thought may elicit this type; but once begun, it includes a conscious and voluntary effort to establish belief upon a firm basis of evidence and rationality.

II. THE CENTRAL FACTOR IN THINKING

There are, however, no sharp lines of demarcation between the various operations just outlined. The problem of attaining correct habits of reflection would be much easier than it is, did not the different modes of thinking blend insensibly into one another. So far, we have considered rather extreme instances of each kind in order to get the field clearly before us. Let us now reverse this operation; let us consider a rudimentary case of thinking, lying between careful examination of evidence and a mere irresponsible stream of fancies. A man is walking on a warm day. The sky was clear the last time he observed it; but presently he notes, while occupied primarily with other things, that the air is cooler. It occurs to him that it is probably going to rain; looking up, he sees a dark cloud between him and the sun, and he then quickens his steps. What, if anything, in such a situation can be called thought? Neither the act of walking nor the noting of the cold is a thought. Walking is one direction of activity; looking and noting are other modes of activity. The likelihood that it will rain is, however, something *suggested*. The pedestrian *feels* the cold; first he *thinks* of clouds, then he looks and perceives them, and then he thinks of something he does not see: a storm. This *suggested possibility* is the idea, the thought. If it is believed in as a genuine possibility which may occur, it is the kind of thought which falls within the scope of knowledge and which requires reflective consideration.

Up to a certain point there is the same sort of situation as when one who looks at a cloud is reminded of a human figure and face. Thinking in both of these cases (the cases of belief and of fancy) involves noting or perceiving a fact, followed by something else that is not observed but that is brought to mind, suggested by the thing seen. One thing reminds us, as we say, of the other. Side by side, however, with this factor of agreement in the two cases of suggestion is a factor of marked disagreement. We do not *believe* in the face suggested by the cloud; we do not consider at all the probability of its being a fact. There is no *reflective* thought. The danger of rain, on the contrary, presents itself to us as a genuine possibility — a fact of the same nature as the observed coolness. Put differently, we do not regard the cloud as meaning or indicating a face, but merely as suggesting it, while we do consider that the coolness may *mean* rain. In the first case, on seeing an object, we just happen, as we say, to think of something else; in the second, we consider the *possibility and nature of the connection between the object seen and the object suggested*. The seen thing is regarded as in some way *the ground or basis of belief* in the suggested thing; it possesses the quality of *evidence*.

This function whereby one thing signifies or indicates another, thus leading us to consider how far the one may be regarded as warrant for belief in the other, is, then, the central factor in all reflective or distinctively intellectual thinking. By calling up various situations to which such terms as *signifies* and *indicates* apply, the student will realize for himself the actual facts denoted. Synonyms for these terms are: points to, tells of, betokens, prognosticates, represents, stands for, implies.[1] We also say one thing portends another, is ominous of another, or a symptom of it, or a key to it, or (if the connection is quite obscure) that it gives a hint, clue, or intimation. Reflection is not identical with the mere fact that one thing indicates, means, another thing. It commences when we begin to inquire into the reliability,

[1] *Implies* is more often used when a principle or general truth brings about belief in some other truth; the other phrases are more frequently used to denote the cases in which a fact or event leads us to believe in some other fact or in a law.

the worth, of any particular indication; when we try to test its value and see what guarantee there is that the existing data *really* point to the idea that is suggested in such a way as to *justify* acceptance of the latter.

Reflection thus implies that something is believed in (or disbelieved in), not on its own direct account, but through something else which stands as witness, evidence, proof, voucher, warrant; that is, as *ground of belief*. At one time, rain is actually felt or directly experienced; at another time, we *infer* that it has rained from the appearance of the grass and trees, or that it is going to rain because of the condition of the air or the state of the barometer. At one time, we see a man (or suppose we do) without any intermediary fact; at another time, we are not quite sure what we see, and hunt for accompanying facts that will serve as signs, indications, tokens of what we are to believe.

Thinking, for the purposes of this inquiry, is accordingly defined as *that operation in which present facts suggest other facts (or truths) in such a way as to induce belief in what is suggested on the ground of real relation in the things themselves,* a relation between what suggests and what is suggested. A cloud *suggests* a weasel or a whale; it does not *mean* the latter, because there is no tie, or bond, in the things themselves between what is seen and what is suggested. Ashes not merely suggest a previous fire, but they signify there has been a fire, because ashes are produced by combustion and, if they are genuine ashes, only by combustion. It is an objective connection, the link in actual things, that makes one thing the ground, warrant, evidence, for believing in something else.

III. PHASES OF REFLECTIVE THINKING

We may carry our account further by noting that *reflective* thinking, in distinction from other operations to which we apply the name of thought, involves (1) a state of doubt, hesitation, perplexity, mental difficulty, in which thinking originates, and (2) an act of searching, hunting, inquiring, to find material that will resolve the doubt, settle and dispose of the perplexity.

In our illustration, the shock of coolness generated confusion and suspended belief, at least momentarily. Because it was unexpected, it was a shock or an interruption needing to be accounted for, identified, or placed. To say that the abrupt occurrence of the change of temperature constitutes a problem may sound forced and artificial; but if we are willing to extend the meaning of the word *problem* to whatever — no matter how slight and commonplace in character — perplexes and challenges the mind so that it makes belief at all uncertain, there is a genuine problem, or question, involved in an experience of sudden change.

The turning of the head, the lifting of the eyes, the scanning of the heavens, are activities adapted to bring to recognition facts that will answer the question presented by the sudden coolness. The facts as they first presented themselves were perplexing; they suggested, however, clouds. The act of looking was an act to discover whether this suggested explanation held good. It may again seem forced to speak of this looking, almost automatic, as an act of research, or inquiry. But once more, if we are willing to generalize our conceptions of our mental operations to include the trivial and ordinary as well as the technical and recondite, there is no good reason for refusing to give this title to the act of looking. For the result of the act is to bring facts before the mind that enable a person to reach a conclusion on the basis of evidence. In so far, then, as the act of looking was deliberate, was performed with the intention of getting an external basis on which to rest a belief, it exemplifies in an elementary way the operation of hunting, searching, inquiring, involved in any reflective operation.

Another instance, commonplace also, yet not quite so trivial, may enforce this lesson. A man traveling in an unfamiliar region comes to a branching of the road. Having no sure knowledge to fall back upon, he is brought to a standstill of hesitation and suspense. Which road is right? And how shall his perplexity be resolved? There are but two alternatives: he must either blindly and arbitrarily take his course, trusting to luck for the outcome, or he must discover grounds for the conclusion that a given road is right. Any attempt to decide the matter by thinking will involve inquiring into other facts, whether brought to mind by memory, or by further observation, or by both. The perplexed wayfarer must carefully scrutinize what is before him and he must cudgel his memory. He looks for evidence that will support belief in favor of either of the roads — for evidence that will weight down one suggestion. He may climb a tree; he may go first in this direction, then in that, looking, in either case, for signs, clues, indications. He wants something in the nature of a signboard or a map, and *his reflection is aimed at the discovery of facts that will serve this purpose.*

The foregoing illustration may be generalized. Thinking begins in what may fairly enough be called a *forked-road* situation, a situation that is ambiguous, that presents a dilemma, that proposes alternatives. As long as our activity glides smoothly along from one thing to another, or as long as we permit our imagination to entertain fancies at pleasure, there is no call for reflection. Difficulty or obstruction in the way of reaching a belief brings us, however, to a pause. In the suspense of uncertainty, we metaphorically climb a tree; we try to find some standpoint from which we may survey additional facts and, getting a more commanding view of the situation, decide how the facts stand related to one another.

Demand for the solution of a perplexity is the steadying and guiding factor in the entire process of reflection. Where there is no question of a problem to be solved or a difficulty to be surmounted, the course of suggestions flows on at random; we have the first type of thought described. If the stream of suggestions is controlled simply by their emotional congruity, their fitting agreeably into a single picture or story, we have the second type. But a question to be answered, an ambiguity to be resolved, sets up an end and holds the current of ideas to a definite channel. Every suggested conclusion is tested by its reference to this regulating end, by its pertinence to the problem in hand. This need of straightening out a perplexity also controls the kind of inquiry undertaken. A traveler whose end is the most beautiful path will look for other signs and will test suggestions on another basis than if he wishes to discover the way to a given city. *The nature of the problem fixes the end of thought,* and *the end controls the process of thinking.*

IV.   SUMMARY

We may recapitulate by saying that the origin of thinking is some perplexity, confusion, or doubt. Thinking is not a case of spontaneous combustion; it does not occur just on "general principles." There is something that occasions and evokes it. General appeals to a child (or a grown-up) to think, irrespective of the existence in his own experience of some difficulty that troubles him and disturbs his equilibrium, are as futile as advice to lift himself by his bootstraps.

Given a difficulty, the next step is suggestion of some way out — the formation of some tentative plan or project, the entertaining of some theory that will account for the peculiarities in question, the consideration of some solution for the problem. The data at hand cannot supply the solution; they can only suggest it. What, then, are the sources of the suggestion? Clearly, past experience and a fund of relevant knowledge at one's command. If the person has had some acquaintance with similar situations, if he has dealt with material of the same sort before, suggestions more or less apt and helpful will arise. But unless there has been some analogous experience, confusion remains mere confusion. Even when a child (or a grown-up) has a problem, it is wholly futile to urge him to think when he has no prior experiences that involve some of the same conditions.

There may, however, be a state of perplexity and also previous experience out of which suggestions emerge, and yet thinking need not be reflective. For the person may not be sufficiently *critical* about the ideas that occur to him. He may jump at a conclusion without weighing the grounds on which it rests; he may forego or unduly shorten the act of hunting, inquiring; he may take the first "answer," or solution, that comes to him because of mental sloth, torpor, impatience to get something settled. One can think reflectively only when one is willing to endure suspense and to undergo the trouble of searching. To many persons both suspense of judgement and intellectual search are disagreeable; they want to get them ended as soon as possible. They cultivate an over-positive and dogmatic habit of mind, or feel perhaps that a condition of doubt will be regarded as evidence of mental inferiority. It is at the point where examination and test enter into investigation that the difference between reflective thought and bad thinking comes in. To be genuinely thoughtful, we must be willing to sustain and protract that state of doubt which is the stimulus to thorough inquiry, so as not to accept an idea or make positive assertion of a belief until justifying reasons have been found.

STUDY QUESTIONS

1. What is the difference between mere "thinking" in the ordinary use of the term, and "reflection"? What is the role of doubt in thinking?
2. Why would Columbus' opinion about the shape of the earth have been different in value from earlier opinions, even if it had turned out to be wrong?
3. What part does memory seem to play in the examples given by Dewey?
4. This selection provides an example both of definition and of process. Outline the steps Dewey takes in defining "thinking" and explain the methods he uses. Discuss the factors which make Dewey's explanation of the "phases of reflective thinking" a clear explanation of process.
5. Describe some case in which you found yourself in what Dewey calls a "forked-road situation," and tell how you resolved the problem.
6. Tell how you examined or tested an opinion you had, and were forced to change your mind about it. Be sure to take some relatively simple and concrete example, and to tell exactly what facts or ideas led you to your new opinion.

Newman and Genevieve Birk

Persuasion by Logical Argument*

The closely organized logical argument usually follows a basic plan of this kind: (1) The writer or speaker states the question clearly and fairly, defining any terms that might be ambiguous, and limiting the argument to the specific issues which he regards as important; he may in this preliminary step of his argument consider the history of the question and its present significance. (2) He states his position and supports that position by citing facts and authorities, and by reasoning from the evidence he presents. (3) He recognizes and refutes any outstanding arguments against his ideas. (4) He summarizes his argument and emphasizes the merits of his position or his proposal. Less formal arguments are likely to include these four steps too, but to follow a more personal, less orderly plan.

The writer of convincing argument must have studied his subject thoroughly. He must know exactly what the major issues are, so that he will not waste words in arguing trivial side issues or points on which there is general agreement. He must have not merely facts and authorities to support his position, but trustworthy, representative, up-to-date facts and reputable authorities. He must know his subject well enough to know more than one

* From *Understanding and Using English* by Newman P. Birk and Genevieve Birk, revised edition, 1958. Copyright, 1958, by The Odyssey Press, Inc. Reprinted by the kind permission of the authors and the publishers.

side of it. Argument, unlike some other kinds of persuasion, assumes opposition; understanding that opposition, being able to concede its strength on some points, but also to demonstrate its weakness on vital points, may be a large part of successful argumentation. In order to see weaknesses in the opposition, and in order to evaluate his own evidence and to arrive at sound conclusions, the writer needs, in addition to knowledge, skill in logical reasoning.

The reader of argument also needs this skill. If he is a critical reader, he will ask two questions about a piece of argumentative prose: Is the evidence good? Is the reasoning sound? In answering the first question he will be helped immeasurably, of course, if he has read and thought about the subject, if he himself has some command of the facts and some acquaintance with the recognized authorities in the field. But without this knowledge he still can make valid judgments about the evidence on which the writer's conclusions are based. He can see how well the writer's statements are substantiated. Some of them may be unsubstantiated, or practically so: "leading scientists agree," or "as psychologists tell us," or "the facts are well known," or "experiments have proved" is not equivalent to quoting scientists, psychologists, facts, or results of specific experiments. Some statements may have unreliable substantiation because the sources are unauthoritative or prejudiced: "the Podunk *Post-Examiner* of April 10, 1958, says..."; "the last issue of *Popular Reading* contains an article which settles this issue for all time"; "John Smith's authoritative study [written in 1935] says the last word on college football"; "the *Democratic Digest* gives an impartial account of the political situation." The reader can also recognize the citing of irrelevant authority — Thomas Jefferson, for example, quoted to support an argument against national health insurance; or a famous chemist quoted on old age pensions, or a prominent businessman on modern art. Persons competent in one field are not necessarily authorities in another. Finally, a reader can make some judgment of the evidence by asking himself how much of it there is, and whether the writer seems to have minimized or ignored evidence on the other side.

In answering the second question — Is the reasoning sound? — the reader is aided by a knowledge of logic. Frequently, while reading or listening to argument, one has an elusive sense of illogic in the thinking, a feeling of something's-wrong-but-I-can't-put-my-finger-on-it. A knowledge of the two kinds of logical thinking called *induction* and *deduction*, and of the common errors in logic, called *fallacies*, makes it easier to detect weaknesses in reasoning and also to recognize and to practice sound reasoning.

A. INDUCTION

Induction is the kind of reasoning by which we examine a number of particulars or specific instances and on the basis of them arrive at a conclusion. The scientific method is inductive when the scientist observes a recurrent phenomenon and arrives at the conclusion or hypothesis that under certain conditions this phenomenon will always take place; if in the course of time further observation supports his hypothesis and if no exceptions are observed, his conclusion is generally accepted as truth and is sometimes called a law. In everyday living, too, we arrive at conclusions by induction. Every cat we encounter has claws; we conclude that all cats have claws. Every rose we smell is fragrant; we conclude that all roses are fragrant. An acquaintance has, on various occasions, paid back money he has borrowed; we conclude that he is frequently out of funds but that he pays his debts. Every Saturday morning for six weeks the new paper boy is late in delivering the paper; we conclude that he sleeps on Saturday mornings and we no longer look for the paper before nine o'clock. In each case we have reasoned inductively from a number of instances; we have moved from an observation of some things to a generalization about all things in the same category.

Occasionally, in restricted situations, it is possible to examine every instance. For example, a teacher may note that student A is present in class today, student B is present, C is present, and so on through the whole class list; by simple counting, the teacher can conclude that all members of the class are present today. Ordinarily, though, it is impossible to examine every instance — the claws of every cat, for example, or the nervous system of every cockroach, or every case of diphtheria, or every ruptured appendix, or the opinion of every voter. One must make an inductive jump from the instances he can know to a conclusion embracing things of the same sort that he cannot know. Inductive reasoning arrives, therefore, not at "truth" or "law," but at probability. The probability grows stronger and the induction becomes sounder when a substantial number of instances are examined, when the instances examined are typical, and when the exceptions, if any, are infrequent and explainable.

A conclusion based on too few instances or on untypical instances is called a *hasty generalization*. It is the most common fallacy in inductive reasoning, and is responsible for much misinformation and prejudice: "Negroes are lazy." "Why do you say that?" "Well we had a Negro cook who was the laziest mortal I ever saw, and look at Bob Jones — he doesn't even try to get a job." The speaker is, of course, generalizing on the basis of only two examples, assuming that these examples are typical, and ignoring the countless exceptions. The hasty generalization may also occur in scientific research; further research may reveal exceptions which modify or invalidate the earlier conclusion.

Cause-effect induction is reasoning about why things happen and about the relationship between them. We observe effects and arrive at a conclusion about their cause; or we observe a set of circumstances (causes) and draw a conclusion about their effects; or we observe some effects and reason from them that there will be other effects. A doctor examines a patient, learns his symptoms, and from the data makes a diagnosis; he has started with the effects of the illness and reasoned to the cause of them. In cause-to-effect thinking the process is reversed because we can see the causes and, usually with the help of past inductions, can predict the effects. A student visits football practice two days before the opening game; he observes that two players are fighting on the field, that the captain and the coach are on bad terms, that the team's best passer is on the bench with a broken arm, and that the backfield is slow; seeing these causes, he predicts that this will not be a successful team. Effect-to-effect thinking is chain reasoning which also usually relies on past inductions: "That little accident [cause] smashed the right front fender [observed effect]; Father will be angry and will make me pay for a new fender [futher effect reasoned on the basis of past instances]; I won't be able to take Jane to the prom [ultimate effect]."

A great deal of scientific investigation deals with causal relationships; that is, with observing and describing those orderly connections between elements and events in the universe, on the basis of which causes can be assigned and effects predicted with accuracy. In our daily thinking, too, we make numerous cause-effect inductions, many of which, however, lack scientific exactitude; they need to be verified before they can be held as logical conclusions. The following effect-to-cause inductions are fairly typical of the kind of reasoning we hear and perhaps do every day. During a storm, the back door slams with such force that the glass breaks; we assume that the wind blew the door. A friend is obviously depressed on the day grades come out; we say that he is badly disappointed in his grades. An engagement is broken a month after the engaged girl's family loses its money; we conclude that the engagement was broken for that reason. All these inductions need further verification, for the cause in each case may well be different from the one assigned; the door may have been slammed by a member of the family who is happy to have the storm blamed for it; the friend may be depressed and the engagement may have been broken for any number of reasons.

These examples illustrate two common fallacies in cause-effect induction. The first fallacy is oversimplifying, and attributing to a single cause effects which actually have complex causes. "I failed the course because the teacher was unreasonably hard" is sometimes an example of this oversimplification. Other familiar examples are: "The atomic bomb won World War II"; "The Hoover administration was responsible for the depression of the nineteen thirties"; "The reason for the high cost of living is the high wages paid to labor."

Often closely related to oversimplification of the cause is the logical fallacy of seeing a cause-effect relationship between events which have only an accidental time relationship. This fallacy is called *post hoc ergo propter hoc*, Latin for "after that therefore because of that." A common instance of this reasoning is a statement like "I won't vote for the Democrats again. Six months after they got into office the city taxes went up two dollars." It is possible, of course, that the Democrats were responsible for the tax increase; but it is also possible that any administration would have found higher taxes necessary. Asserting without proof a cause-effect relationship simply because one event follows another is as illogical as asserting that breakfast causes lunch. Many superstitions are maintained by this *post hoc ergo propter hoc* thinking. A superstitious person walks under a ladder, and an hour later, for reasons entirely unrelated to that incident, has a quarrel with a good friend; he forgets or ignores the real causes of the quarrel, falls into the logical confusion of after-I-walked-under-the-ladder-therefore-because-I-walked-under-the-ladder, and is confirmed in his original faulty induction that walking under ladders brings bad luck.

Induction by analogy occurs when one observes that two things are similar in some ways, and then reasons, from the observed likenesses, that they are also similar in other ways. For example, Sir Isaac Newton observed that certain combustible substances — oils, turpentine, camphor, etc. — had refractive powers two or three times greater than might be expected from their densities. He reasoned by analogy that the diamond, with its very high refractive powers, was also combustible. This inference was correct.

Reasoning from analogy is dangerous, however, and argument by analogy alone is seldom convincing, because analogous situations or objects have differences as well as similarities and the differences may outweigh the similarities. Sir David Brewster, a nineteenth-century physicist and biographer of Sir Isaac Newton, pointed out that if Newton had reasoned from analogy the combustibility of greenockite and octahedrite, which also have high refractive powers, he would have been wrong. His reasoning about the diamond simply happened to be right. Long observation of Mars has given astronomers a body of data from which they have arrived inductively at a number of conclusions about that planet. Some people have reasoned by analogy that since Mars has atmosphere, temperatures, and seasonal changes comparable to earth's, it must also have life like ours. This conclusion is questionable; it disregards the observed differences between the two planets.

Analogy is not logical proof. In informative writing it is, as we have said earlier, a useful method of clarifying a difficult subject. Skillful analogy also has great persuasive power. But it should be used in conjunction with, not as a substitute for, more strictly logical reasoning; and it is effective only when the similarities are striking and the differences slight between the things being compared. The following induction by analogy is weak because the comparison is far-fetched and the differences are glaring:

> Even the most durable machines break down if they are worked constantly for long periods of time. Their parts wear out; they become inefficient. Are students supposed to be stronger than machines? Do they deserve less attention and care? We should have shorter assignments and longer vacations.

The following famous passage illustrates effective analogy. The comparison is used not to prove, but to describe and to persuade:

> In the field of world policy I would dedicate this Nation to the policy of the good neighbor — the neighbor who resolutely respects himself and because he does so, respects the rights of others — the neighbor who respects

his obligations and respects the sanctity of his agreements in and with a world of neighbors. — Franklin D. Roosevelt, *First Inaugural Address.*

B. DEDUCTION

Inductive reasoning, as we have seen, moves from individual circumstances or instances to a conclusion; this conclusion, unless every possible instance has been examined, expresses probability; the probability is as strong as the weight of evidence which supports it. Deduction is reasoning from stated propositions or premises to a conclusion. If the conclusion follows logically from the premises and if the premises are true, deduction arrives at proof or certainty.

> All men are mortal.
> John is a man.
> Therefore John is mortal.

The statement above is a *syllogism,* the pattern in which, in formal logic, a deductive argument is expressed. The syllogism consists of three statements — two premises and a conclusion. It contains three and only three main terms, each of which appears twice, but not twice in the same statement. The terms are given these names: the *major term* is the predicate of the conclusion; the *minor term* is the subject of the conclusion; and the *middle term* appears in both premises. The major term in the syllogism above is "mortal," and the premise in which it appears is called the *major premise.* The minor term is "John," and the premise in which it appears is called the *minor premise.* The middle term, "man/men," appears in both premises.

Diagraming the syllogism sometimes makes the relationship of statements clearer:

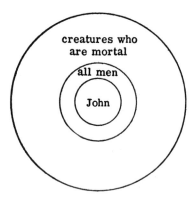

If all men are included in the larger group of mortal things (major premise), and if John is included in the group of all men (minor premise), then John is inevitably included in the group of those who are mortal (conclusion).

There are four patterns of the syllogism, in which the terms have different positions. In the following examples, the middle term (the term which appears in both premises) is printed in capital letters to show its position in the four patterns or "figures" of the syllogism:

Figure 1:   All DOGS are carnivorous.
            My cocker is a DOG.
            Therefore my cocker is carnivorous.

Figure 2:   No thief CAN BE TRUSTED.
            All good men CAN BE TRUSTED.
            Therefore no good men are thieves.

Figure 3:   Every COLLEGE STUDENT has great opportunities.
            Some COLLEGE STUDENTS are poor.
            Therefore some poor people have great opportunities.

Figure 4:   Most people devote themselves to MATERIAL GAIN.
            MATERIAL GAIN is not a worthy goal in life.
            Therefore most people do not devote themselves to a worthy goal
            in life.

When a syllogism has any of these four relationships between terms and between premises and conclusion, its argument is said to be *valid*. It is worth noting here that a "valid" argument is not necessarily *factually true*. For example, for some readers, the conclusions in the second and fourth syllogism above will seem untrue because one or both of the two premises seem untrue. Perhaps the point will be clearer if we look at more obvious examples:

Major premise: All Irishmen have hot tempers.
Minor premise: He is Irish.
Conclusion: Therefore he is hot tempered.

Major premise: Poisonous snakes should be killed.
Minor premise: Garter snakes are poisonous.
Conclusion: Therefore garter snakes should be killed.

These two arguments are "valid" because they have the logical form of Figure 1 of the syllogism. However, the conclusions are unreliable because the major premise of the first syllogism is a hasty generalization, and the minor premise of the second syllogism is a misstatement of fact. In judging the truth or reliability of a deductive argument, one must ask two questions: Are the premises true? Is the argument valid? If the answer to both questions is "yes," the deduction can be accepted as true.[1]

C. FALLACIES

We have mentioned earlier the common fallacies in inductive reasoning: hasty generalization, oversimplification of complex causes, *post hoc ergo*

---

[1] True premises and a valid argument can produce only a true conclusion. Untrue premises, as we have seen, can produce questionable or untrue conclusions. But it may be worth noting that a conclusion may happen to be true even though it is drawn from false premises: All cats are birds; all pigeons are cats; therefore all pigeons are birds. The conclusion here is true for reasons other than those stated in the premises.

propter hoc argument, and faulty analogy. The most common fallacies in deductive argument come from the faulty relationship of parts of the syllogism. Such fallacies sometimes produce a slippery illogic in the reasoning, difficult to detect. For example, in the first figure of the syllogism illustrated on page 154, the subject of the major premise is the predicate of the minor premise; the form of the syllogism is *All X is Y; Z is X; therefore Z is Y.* In the following syllogism of the same pattern, the terms are shifted:

All tigers are felines. (*X is Y*)
My cat is a feline. (*Z is Y*)
Therefore my cat is a tiger. (∴ *Z is X*)

The illogic here is made apparent by the absurdity of the conclusion; but it may not be so apparent in a similarly constructed syllogism:

All communists say Russia doesn't want war.
He says Russia doesn't want war.
Therefore he is a communist.

Diagraming such arguments is a good way of seeing why they are invalid:

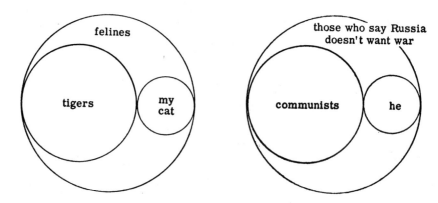

My cat and *he* are in the large circles of *felines* and *those who say Russia doesn't want war,* but not necessarily in the smaller circles of *tigers* and *communists.* There is no established relationship between the terms (tigers and my cat; communists and he) except the fact that they are both members of a larger group.

Another fallacy is in conclusions drawn from negative premises. If one premise is negative, the conclusion must be negative in a valid argument; if both premises are negative, no conclusion can be drawn.

Valid: All those attending the meeting are freshmen.
           John is not a freshman.
           Therefore John is not attending the meeting.

Invalid: No freshmen are attending the meeting.
           John is not a freshman.
           Therefore John is attending the meeting.

No conclusion can be drawn from the last two negative premises; John may or may not be attending the meeting.

In a valid argument, the conclusion follows inevitably from the premises. *Non-sequitur* (Latin for "it does not follow") is the fallacy of leaping to a conclusion not warranted by the premises. Drawing a conclusion from negative premises is one form of *non-sequitur*. Other examples are:

> Anyone who works hard deserves a vacation now and then.
> I work hard.
> Therefore my parents should give me a trip to Bermuda.

> Men who have made sacrifices for their country should be honored.
> I have made sacrifices for my country.
> Therefore I should be President.

The faults in the two preceding syllogisms are closely related to another fallacy of logical relationship — *the shifting of the meaning of terms between the major and the minor premise.* The shifted meaning is equivalent to a fourth term in the syllogism. For example:

> Man is the only creature capable of reason.
> Mary is not a man.
> Therefore Mary is incapable of reason.

The meaning of *man* has been shifted from *mankind* in the major premise to *male* in the minor premise. Other examples of shifted meanings are:

> Men who have devoted themselves to the service of the community should
>   hold public office.
> I have devoted myself to the service of the community by running a bakery
>   for fifteen years.
> Therefore I should hold public office.

> Government employees who are sympathetic with Russian policy should be
>   discharged.
> This government employee belonged in 1943 to an organization which was
>   friendly toward Russia.
> Therefore he should be discharged.

We seldom encounter the complete syllogism except in discussions of logic and in very formal argument. More usual is a reduced form of the syllogism in which one or two of the three parts, though implied, are not stated. The reduced syllogism is called an *enthymeme.* Sometimes in the enthymeme the conclusion of the syllogism is omitted because it is obvious: *Students who are found cheating on examinations fail the course; Clarence has been found cheating on an examination;* [the obvious omitted conclusion: therefore Clarence will fail the course]. Sometimes the minor premise is omitted for the same reason: *I like candidates who speak their minds; I'm going to vote for you* [omitted premise: you speak your mind]; Sometimes both the minor premise and the conclusion are omitted because the major premise adequately communicates them: *I date only men who have cars;* [omitted: you don't have a car; therefore I won't have a date with you]. Most frequently the major premise is omitted because the communicator assumes (often wrongly) that it is universally accepted and so does not require proof or even statement. One of the most useful skills of the hearer or reader of argument, therefore, is the ability to supply the omitted major premise. By recognizing that premise and examining it critically, he can better judge the reliability of the argument. The enthymemes below are familiar informal arguments; the major premise on which each one is based is put in brackets.

> Jim must have been in a fight; he has a black eye. [Major premise: All black eyes are the result of fights.]

> So he forgot he made the appointment. What can you expect? He's a college professor. [Major premise: College professors usually forget appointments. Or, College professors are absent-minded.]

> He must be a grind! He got all A's last semester. [Students who get A records are grinds.]

> He can't be a good doctor. He's in favor of socialized medicine. [No good doctor is in favor of socialized medicine.]

> You're crazy, saying the meat tastes spoiled. I got it at the store just an hour ago. [Meat is always fresh when it is bought at stores.]

> What a coward. He's a conscientious objector, you know. [All conscientious objectors are cowards.]

> Naturally he's a delinquent. He reads ten comic books a week. [Reading comics always produces delinquency.]

> Of course it's true; I read it in the paper. [Everything printed in the newspapers is true.]

> They won't be happy together; he's two years younger than she. [Marriages are always unhappy if the man is younger than the woman.]

> I think they'll be very nice neighbors. They have a new Cadillac. [People are nice neighbors if they have a new Cadillac.]

> We're not talking about the same girl. The one I knew last summer had blond hair. [Once a blonde always a blonde.]

> His mother has trained him to be neat around the house; he'll make a wonderful husband. [Any man who is neat around the house is a wonderful husband; also, a man trained by his mother to be neat around the house will continue to be neat when he is married.]

Two other logical fallacies, not peculiar to induction or to deduction, but involving the quality of the whole argument, are *begging the question* and *ignoring the question.*

Begging the question is assuming, without proof, the truth of a proposition which actually needs proof. If an arguer says, "This senseless language requirement should be abolished," he is, with the word *senseless,* begging the question; the question is whether or not the language requirement is senseless;

if it is, it should of course be abolished; simply calling it senseless is not a logical argument in its disfavor. "This corrupt political machine should be replaced by good government" is another example of begging the question. No proof is offered that the government under attack is a "corrupt political machine," or that the government supported by the speaker will be "good." Both propositions are simply assumed. *Arguing in a circle* is one form of begging the question:

> People who are poor lack ambition because if they didn't lack ambition they wouldn't be poor.

> The study of literature is worthwhile because literature is a worthwhile subject.

Such argument in a circle is sometimes baffling, particularly when the argument is long and the circular motion is therefore difficult to detect. What the arguer in a circle does, technically, is offer as proof of his first proposition a second proposition which can be proved only by proving the first.

Ignoring the question is diverting attention from the real issues, or shifting the argument to some other ground. It has many forms. Name-calling, introducing irrelevant facts, and using other devices of charged language may be means of ignoring the real question. Sometimes a new argument is introduced in an effort to obscure the original issue: "I told you, Dorothy, I can't afford to buy you a coat this winter." "I don't see why not. Susan Jones has a new coat. I should think you'd want me to be well dressed. It's a good thing someone in this family takes some pride in appearance. You haven't even shaved today." Arguing that an accused murderess should be acquitted because she is the mother of three children, and that a candidate should be mayor because he is a veteran of two wars are examples of ignoring the question by shifting from the central issues; the questions here are "Did she commit the murder?" and "Will he make a good mayor?" What is called argument *ad hominem* (to the man) is a way of ignoring the question by a shift from reasonable consideration of a measure to an attack on the character of the opponent; his ancestry, his religion, the fact that his first wife divorced him, that his son was arrested for speeding, etc. may be introduced to appeal to prejudice while the real question — the merits and defects of the measure itself — is ignored.

D. THE TEXTURE OF LOGICAL THOUGHT

Although we have separated induction and deduction for purposes of discussion, the two processes work together in most acts of reasoning. A simple illustration of the interplay between them is this: A friend asks you one afternoon to go with him to a movie at the neighborhood theatre. You say, "No; it's Saturday." Behind your refusal lies an induction, based on instances in your own experience, that on Saturday afternoons many school children attend this theatre and are very noisy. You make a quick deduction: Every Saturday afternoon this theatre is full of noisy school children; this is

Saturday; therefore the theatre will be full of noisy school children. Another inductive-deductive process also takes place. You have arrived at the generalization that you do not enjoy a movie if you cannot hear all of it. You reason: I do not want to go to a movie if I cannot hear all of it; I will not be able to hear all of it today (because of the noise of the children); therefore I do not want to go to this movie on this day. Still another reasoning process about your relationship with the friend who has asked you to go to the movie may occur. From your past experience with him you may have induced: Jack is not offended if for some good reason I refuse his invitations. Now you may deduce: I am refusing this invitation for a good reason; therefore Jack will not be offended. In this kind of thinking, the inductions and deductions are almost automatic. In more complex reasoning they are formulated only after conscious and disciplined thought.

We have said earlier that induction is important in scientific thinking: it enables human beings to arrive at generalizations and hypotheses about the world they live in, to see cause-effect relationships, and, on the basis of established probabilities, to make predictions and produce effects by controlling causes. As a science advances and its inductive hypotheses are further substantiated, the substantiated hypotheses supply premises from which deductive conclusions are drawn. One kind of reasoning leads to, supports, and leads back to the other. In the same way, in a logical argument, observed instances have perhaps led the speaker or writer inductively to the position he takes in the argument. From his inductions he may reason deductively about what should be done in a particular situation.

Closely interwoven though the two kinds of reasoning are, it is useful to have some knowledge of their differences, of the different kinds of reliability they can arrive at, and of the common fallacies in each kind of thinking. Being able to reduce a confusing argument to syllogistic form will enable one to see more clearly its premises and its validity. Being alert to hasty generalization, to faulty cause-effect reasoning, to conclusions which do not follow the premises, to question-begging and to ignoring of the question will help one judge the soundness of an argument. A knowledge of the processes of reasoning, in short, provides instruments of analysis with which one can better examine the texture of his own argument and the arguments of others.

E. TONE

In persuasion by logical argument, the writer may be formal or informal in his attitude toward his audience; but he is usually less concerned with getting their liking than with winning their respect. For this respect, he depends largely on the quality of the argument itself. If he presents the issues fairly; if he is reasonable in considering opposing points of view; if his evidence is good and and his thinking clear and sound; if he respects the intelligence of his audience and assumes that they will not be convinced by slippery illogic and devices like arguments *ad hominem,* he will almost certainly gain a respectful hearing for what he has to say.

As a rule, the most skillful argument is reasonable in tone as well as in thought; it gives the impression of trying to arrive at truth, not merely to win a case; it is good tempered, and free from dogmatism and conceit. Fighting-mad arguments and dogmatic statements do sometimes affect already-sympathetic or prejudiced audiences; but they are likely to alienate and offend an impartial audience. Benjamin Franklin, wise in argument and diplomacy, wrote in his autobiography:

> I made it a rule to forbear all direct contradiction to the sentiments of others, and all positive assertion of my own. I even forbade myself . . . the use of every word or expression in the language that imported a fix'd opinion, such as *certainly, undoubtedly,* etc., and I adopted, instead of them, *I conceive, I apprehend,* or *I imagine* a thing to be so or so; or it *so appears to me at present.* When another asserted something that I thought an error, I deny'd myself the pleasure of contradicting him abruptly, and of showing immediately some absurdity in his proposition; and in answering I began by observing that in certain cases of circumstances his opinion would be right, but in the present case there *appear'd* or *seem'd* to me some difference, etc. I soon found the advantage of this change in my manner; the conversations I engag'd in went on more pleasantly. The modest way in which I propos'd my opinions procur'd them a readier reception and less contradiction; I had less mortification when I was found to be in the wrong, and I more easily prevail'd with others to give up their mistakes and join with me when I happened to be in the right.
>
> And this mode, which I at first put on with some violence to natural inclination, became at length so easy, and so habitual to me, that perhaps for these fifty years past no one has ever heard a dogmatical expression escape me. And to this habit (after my character of integrity) I think it principally owing that I had early so much weight with my fellow-citizens when I proposed new institutions, or alterations in the old, and so much influence in public councils when I became a member; for I was but a bad speaker, never eloquent, subject to much hesitation in my choice of words, hardly correct in language, and yet I generally carried my points.

STUDY QUESTIONS

1. *What, according to the authors, are the steps in formal logical argument? How does such argument differ from other kinds of persuasion? What questions will the critical reader of argument ask himself?*

2. *Define "induction" and "deduction." What are the strengths and weaknesses of each of these? How often will you find one or the other used exclusively? In what kinds of writing will you find the heaviest reliance upon induction? Upon deduction?*

3. *What four factors determine the validity of deductive reasoning? Define and give two or three examples of the enthymeme other than those examples in the text.*

4. List the fallacies of reasoning which the authors define and be prepared to cite
   an example of each from your reading or from arguments in which you have
   engaged with your friends.

5. Set down in outline form the steps of an argument on some controversial issue.
   Then write a paper, filling in this outline with the necessary details or explanations to make it an effective piece of writing.

6. Examine one or more editorials in a newspaper or magazine, being on the
   watch for the kinds of fallacies which the Birks have discussed. Write a paper
   defining and illustrating the fallacies which appear, and evaluating the editorials in the light of your findings.

3. EXAMINING IDEAS

Zechariah Chafee, Jr. The Inquiring Mind*

*K*nowledge is not a series of propositions to be absorbed, but a series of
problems to be solved. Or rather I should say, to be partly solved, for
all the answers are incomplete and tentative. This view of life is in no way
original, but it is frequently ignored. From the fact that reading, writing, and
arithmetic are the bases of education and were long the only education for
most persons, we have unfortunately been led to regard them as typical of *all*
education. We feel that knowledge is something that has been settled by
others and given us to learn, just as we learned the multiplication table.

Nevertheless, outside the field of such established facts as the three R's
there lies a much vaster area, and with it citizens must acquaint themselves
if democratic government is to manage our modern industrial civilization
successfully. Knowledge of this vaster area cannot be obtained merely from
what others tell us; it must come from what we find out ourselves by asking
and answering questions. Therefore, the true type of education is not the
certainty of the multiplication table, but the incomplete approximation of the
square root of two, or better yet, the undiscoverable ratio between the circum-
ference and the diameter of a circle. (How strange that such a common fact
should be so complex!) Indeed, we may eventually come to take as our typical
fact the square root of minus one, which, although we call it an imaginary
quantity, forms a necessary element of many of the electrical calculations
that make possible the ordinary operations of our daily lives. In school

* From *The Inquiring Mind* by Zechariah Chafee, Jr. Copyright, 1928, by Harcourt, Brace and Company, Inc. Reprinted by permission of Harcourt, Brace and Company, Inc. and by permission of the estate of Zechariah Chafee, Jr.

geometries the propositions are printed in large type and the originals are tucked away in the back in small print. Some day we shall realize that the propositions are far less important than the originals.

II

The fruitfulness of this method of constant inquiry is demonstrated by the experience of Darwin. His voyage around the world brought him into contact with many interesting facts which he recorded faithfully, but he was not content to rest with the acquisition of facts. He began to ask himself a question that he could not answer. Soon after his return to England he opened his notebook on the origin of species, in which he preserved all the information he could find for the sake of answering that one question. His method of using books he learned from Buckle, who used to jot down on the fly-leaf of every book he read references to passages in it which he thought might prove serviceable to him. "How do you know," Darwin asked, "which passages to select?" Buckle replied that he did not know, that a sort of instinct guided him. When the thinker has formulated his problem, the facts he meets are bound to shape themselves with regard to it, just as a magnet throws all the iron filings brought near it into one pattern.

Darwin asked himself one question, and spent the rest of his life answering it. Pasteur propounded a succession of riddles, and his earlier problems offered little prospect that their solution would aid mankind. What relation to human happiness was there in his first riddle, the difference in the deflection of light through the crystals formed by tartaric and paratartaric acids, a difference which apparently concerns nobody? From this he passed to the even more useless problem of the possibility of spontaneous generation. Yet this led to the question of fermentation, and from the diseases of beverages he turned to explain those of animals and men. The possession of theoretical knowledge, indeed, seems almost sure to create opportunities for its practical use.

This progress from the theoretical to the practical was reversed in the riddles that beset Kepler, the forerunner of Newton. Finding himself financially prosperous, he decided to place some well-filled casks in his cellar. They must be made of wood, and wood was expensive. Hence a problem, quite independent of the pleasures of theory, but all-important to the economical head of a household: how to get the greatest cubical content of wine into the minimum amount of wood. Should the cask be apple-shaped, pear-shaped, or lemon-shaped? We can imagine him out in his orchard laying boards in various positions on temporary frames and then generalizing his results in mathematical formulae. They developed into his book on the measurement of casks, and became the foundation of infinitesimal calculus, the basis of all our pure and applied science today.

Einstein at five years old was, as he lay in his cot, given a compass by his father. The remembrance of the swinging needle remained with him, suggesting invisible forces, which later he was to explore in electromagnetic waves and gravitation. At twenty-two, struggling with poverty as a private tutor, a friend obtained for him a position as examiner of patents in the Swiss Patent Office. Instead of repining at this job as five years' enslavement, he made his experience in varied fields of invention interlock so widely with the solution of theoretical problems that before he left he published in quick succession the first series of his dissertations on the theory of relativity. To the inquiring mind, all experience is gathered into the solution of over-mastering problems.

Nor need my illustrations be limited to the non-human sciences. Frederick William Maitland, the English legal historian, became interested in a German treatise on the political theories of the Middle Ages. What could be more alien to the twentieth century than medieval doctrines of the relation between the empire, the church, and the guilds? Yet Maitland's attitude was, "Today we study the day before yesterday, in order that yesterday may not paralyze today, and today may not paralyze tomorrow." He began to inquire into the nature of groups of human beings, incorporated and unincorporated. Is such a group merely an aggregation of human beings, or is it in itself a person? Facts accumulated in his mind, he cross-examined documents like a string of hostile witnesses, he talked about his problem, he wrote to America, to men he had never seen, for data about our corporations. And somehow the problem of the Middle Ages became the problem of the great unincorporated groups of today: the Roman Catholic Church; the trade unions—Chief Justice Taft's decision in the Coronado case on the possibility of suing the United Mine Workers of America is just this question; the New Jersey corporation doing business in states where it owes none of its legal existence to the local legislature; the nature of that most powerful of groups, the state itself. Is the state only a sort of glorified public service company, as Maitland's followers would have it, that sells police protection and schooling to its citizens as a trolley company sells rides? Or is it, as the other side contends, a sort of ethical culture society to lead us onward and upward toward the light? Whichever of these two views we take of the state, whether it is an organization for specific business services to the community or an inspirer of souls, why does it haggle over the settlement of its contracts, impose double taxation, deny all responsibility when its mail-trucks run over us, refuse to be sued in its own courts, and in general fall far below the standards of fair dealing which it imposes upon every taxicab driver or keeper of a restaurant?

The old system of water-tight compartments into which knowledge was supposed to be divided, and each of which had to be entered separately, is breaking down. The late Jacques Loeb, whose vital personality was hard to explain by his own mechanistic doctrines, once remarked: "People ask me, 'Why are you studying mathematics? Why are you learning physics? Aren't you a physiologist?' and I say, 'I don't know.' Then, 'Aren't you a chemist?' or 'Aren't you a biologist?' I don't understand these questions. I am preoccupied with problems." Problems—the material for solving them must be drawn from every available source! No place, then, for jealousy between workers in sharply demarcated fields. As H. G. Wells says in *Joan and Peter*, "All good work is one."

STUDY QUESTIONS

1. *What relations do you see between Chafee's discussion of "the inquiring mind" and Dewey's discussion of "reflective thinking"? Does the process of inquiry which Chafee recommends depend most heavily upon inductive or deductive thinking, or upon both?*

2. *How is knowledge in general different from such elements of knowledge as reading, writing, and arithmetic?*

3. *Judging from the examples given by Chafee, what is the relationship between the theoretical and the practical? Which should come first in the study of a particular subject? What are the advantages of assembling facts from many fields as opposed to those of specializing in a single one?*

4. *What attitude on the part of students does Chafee seem to be recommending? Does he suggest that information given by teachers and textbooks be considered subject to skepticism? Does he suggest that the major principles of particular fields be constantly re-examined?*

5. *This selection provides a clear illustration of the development of an abstract concept—that of the "inquiring mind"—by a series of examples. Select some similar concept and write a paper in which you explain or support it by two or three carefully selected and developed examples.*

6. *Have you ever had the experience of finding that a fact or principle you had learned in connection with one subject unexpectedly became useful in connection with another? If so, write a theme describing this experience.*

Everett Dean Martin

The Educational Value of Doubt*

Professor Dewey somewhere speaks of education as freeing the mind of "bunk." It is a large task. No one wholly succeeds. I never saw a completely "debunked" individual. Strive as we may to eradicate it, there is always in our thinking an amount of error, of wish-fancy accepted as objective fact, of exaggeration, special pleading, self-justification. Many of our beliefs are not founded in reason at all, but are demanded by some unconscious and repressed impulse in our nature. Men make a virtue of their faith

---

* Reprinted from *The Meaning of a Liberal Education* by Everett Dean Martin. By permission of W. W. Norton and Company, Inc. Copyright, 1954, by Mrs. Daphne Mason.

when in fact they are *victims* of it; they can no more help believing certain things than a neurotic can stop a compulsive habit.

It is said that it is easy to doubt and that to believe is an accomplishment. It is not so. It is easier to believe than to doubt. The things we must train ourselves to doubt are as a rule just the things we wish to believe. It is children and savages and the illiterate who have the most implicit faith. It is said that unbelief is sin. This is not so; it is nobler to doubt than to believe, for to doubt is often to take sides with fact against oneself. Nietzsche said that this trait is characteristic of "higher men." It was Huxley, as I remember it, who considered that man could in nothing fall so low as when he deliberately took refuge in the absurd. Even with a rationalist like Huxley doubt is not merely a function of the intellect. Under certain circumstances it is a moral necessity.

The pursuit of knowledge is not the same, however, as scrupulous avoidance of error. He who strives to do his own thinking must accept responsibility for himself. He must expect that he will make mistakes. He may end in total failure. He must take his chances and be willing to pay the cost of his adventure. I know professional scholars who are so afraid they may write or say something which their colleagues will show to be wrong that they never express an opinion of their own or commit themselves to any down-right statement. Such equivocation and qualifying — playing safe — is not what I mean by doubt. I do not mean merely that one should be always on guard against the possibility of error, but that one should learn to hold all one's beliefs with a half-amused lightheartedness. Most minds are loaded down with the seriousness of their convictions. Solemnity in the presence of our eternal verities is awkwardness, and makes us always a little ridiculous, giving us the appearance of one about to shake hands with the President. Why not enjoy the humor of the situation? Our great truths may all the while be "spoofing" us. It will do no harm to give them a sly wink now and then.

Crowd men have no sense of humor. It is very difficult to educate solemn and opinionated people. Like Omar, they always come out by that same door wherein they went. I have known students to complete a course of study having learned nothing, because of their disinclination to consider any fact which might cause them to surrender some belief about religion or economic theory with which they entered. Whoever leaves an institution of learning with the same general outlook on life that he had when he first came might better have employed his time otherwise. He is not a student; he is a church-member....

The significant thing is not the particular belief which a man gives up or retains but the manner in which he believes what he does believe. Change the latter and you change a basic habit pattern; you change the man.

Not all scepticism has educational value. There is a kind of doubting which is merely the negative response of the unteachable, the suspiciousness of the wilfully ignorant, the refusal of the incurious to examine disturbing and challenging evidence. There are, as an eighteenth century philosopher said, minds that are moulded to the form of one idea. Many people, after they have accepted one idea, tame it and keep it as a sort of watch-dog to frighten all other ideas away. This refusal to be convinced may appear to be scepticism; it is only stubbornness. The late Mr. Bryan and his followers were very sceptical of evolution. But this hostile attitude is very different from the scepticism of those scientists who hold that the theory is a mere working hypothesis which is yet to be confirmed. The scepticism of ignorance is motivated by the desire to save an old faith. Savages have been known to exhibit this incredulity toward certain aspects of our more advanced knowledge. If you were to tell the natives of Borneo that there is no dragon in the sky which eats up the moon during an eclipse, that there are no spirits and no magic, I imagine they would laugh in your face and think you a fool. Many a discovery and invention has been greeted by a grinning and incredulous public even in civilized society. The scepticism which has value is that which leads one on to further study and investigation. And it is characterized by intellectual modesty.

Philosophic doubt is not the pitiable condition of the soul that timid spirits imagine. It is not pessimism or cynicism, but a healthy and cheerful habit. It gives peace of mind. Men who stop pretending can sleep o' nights. There is a certain scepticism which is in no sense the spirit that denies. It is a frank recognition of the things as they come. It is almost a test of a man's honesty, among those who have stopped to think about the nature and limitations of our knowledge. Certainly cultivated people do not exhibit the same degree of cock-sureness as do the ignorant. People think the old saying about "doubting the intelligence that doubts" is funny. Popular audiences will always laugh at it. But why not? It is a platitude that the more a man learns the more he realizes how little he knows. Existence is filled with inscrutable mystery. To none of the profound questions that we ask of it is there any final answer. We must be satisfied ultimately with surmise, with symbol and poetic fancy. Speculations about the soul, God, the ultimate nature of reality and the course of destiny, and as to whether existence has any meaning or purpose beyond our own, or whether our life itself is worthwhile — all these speculations and many others of similar nature lead to no conclusions in fact, and we return always to the point from which we started. The very terms in which we put such questions are often meaningless when closely examined by the intellect, and the answer to them is determined by our own moods.

There is a general belief that science can answer the riddle. But science is only one possible view of things, the one best adapted to the needs of creatures like ourselves. It cannot deal with questions of value. It can tell us how things operate, their relative mass and positions in space and time, but it cannot tell us what they are in themselves, nor why they exist nor anything about their goodness or beauty. The more exact scientific knowledge becomes, the more closely it approaches mathematics. Pure mathematics deals only with abstractions and logical relations and can dismiss the whole world of objects. Science presupposes the data of experience and the validity of its own logical principles. It substitutes its mechanized order of things for things as we experience them.

Human reasoning is partial in all its processes. We think successfully about things when we ignore all the aspects or qualities of them except those which are relevant to the purpose at hand. The H_2O-ness of water is no more the ultimate nature of water than is its wetness, or its thirst quenching quality. That it is H_2O is only one of the things that may be said about water. Now if we add together bits of onesided and partial scientific knowledge, we do not thereby gain a sum total which is the equivalent of reality as a whole. We have a useful instrument for dealing with our environment, because in thought we have greatly simplified it by ignoring in each instance all that is irrelevant. But what we now have is a universe of discourse, a human construction which is what it is because we are always more interested in some aspects of things than in others.

All our ideas are views — they have been likened to snapshots. The world of which we are part is in flux. It comes to us as process, and our intellect does not grasp the movement any more than we can restore the movement of a man running by adding together a series of photographs. The movement always takes place between the pictures. Intellect is an instrument, not a mirror. Our world is not reducible to a form of thought, and when men speak of truth, reality, cause, substance, they are really only saying what they mean by certain words. The world, as James said, has its meanings for us because we are interested spectators, and so far as we can see none of these meanings are final. Whitehead and others have shown that some of the basic concepts of physical science which have held sway since the seventeenth century are now subject to revision. Santayana says that knowledge is faith — animal faith. It would be strange if it were otherwise, if hairy little creatures such as we are, whose ancestors lived in trees and made queer guttural noises, should so organize human discourse as to be able to say the last word about reality as a whole. It is well that we should marvel at our achievements of knowledge, for they are man's noblest work; but let us remember that human reason, itself a phase and part of the process of nature, can only view the whole process from its own partial standpoint, and that is enough unless we aspire to infallibility.

Man is a disputatious animal who loves to speak like Sir Oracle. Uneducated people, ashamed of their ignorance, commit themselves hastily and cling to their commitments, for to change one's mind is an admission that one was mistaken. We wish to be vindicated as having all along been in the right. Hence, it is more natural to contend for a principle than to test a hypothesis. The ego becomes identified with certain convictions. We feel ourselves personally injured if our convictions are subjected to criticism. We are not ordinarily grateful to the person who points out our errors and sets us right. But if our education is to proceed, we must get over our delusion of infallibility.

This fiction of infallibility is very common, and those who have not learned to doubt this fiction, who are sure that they have the truth and are on the side of the right are as a rule the more ignorant and provincial elements of the population. It is no accident that Fundamentalism, prohibition, and other forms of moral regulation exist in inverse ratio to urbanity and have their strongholds in rural communities. People to whom it never occurs to ask how they know so clearly they are right when better informed people have doubts on the subject, are the ones who naturally strive to coerce their neighbors. To many minds there are no social or moral problems. The answer is always known by the crusader. It is very simple. To him there can be no two opinions. The standards which prevail in his own parish, the self-expression of his own type, are the will of God. Principles of right and wrong are known immediately without reflection or regard to the situations where they are to be applied; they are revealed to conscience. "Right is right and wrong is wrong everywhere and forever the same!" . . .

I am not asserting dogmatically that we cannot know truth or the nature of reality. I am not suggesting that we cannot be educated without ending in universal scepticism or agnostic negation. It seems to me that we have, or can have, such knowledge as will make our intellects fairly adequate instruments in the performance of their proper functions. But I do not see what such functioning has to do with ascribing finality to our beliefs or trying to legislate for all possible worlds. I am not suggesting an attitude of despair in the pursuit of truth, but am trying to state the very reason for any learning at all, for what is the use of it if we know it all before we start?

Education may not end in doubt, but it ends when a man stops doubting. But why speak of the end of a process that should continue through life? As I see it, the process is more often discontinued at the point of some fictitious certainty than in any moment of doubt. Doubt, the willingness to admit that conjecture is subject to revision, is a spur to learning. The recognition that our truths are not copies of eternal realities but are human creations designed to meet human needs, puts one in a teachable frame of mind. And the discovery that thinking may be creative makes intellectual activity interesting. . . .

If it is true that men can only be made to act under the lash of blind faith and enthusiasm, then the estate of man is a sorry one indeed. For most of the things done will end in tragic failure. It is only the conceit of ignorance to believe that the world can be straightened once for all by people who do not know what they are doing. Moreover, to say that ignorance is necessary to the accomplishment of good is to say, that ignorance is desirable and better for man than knowledge. There have been those who held such a view. Obscurantists always hold it. It is the philosophy of pessimism, and it is interesting to note that it is the believer and the devotee, the man of action and not the gentle doubter who finally ends in pessimism.

For want of intelligence the devotees of causes have been the mischief makers in all times. We cannot always know who does the most good in the world, but the evil that men do lives after them and it is sometimes possible to estimate the amount of harm done. Who has done the most harm in human history, the sceptics or the believers, the devotees of causes or the devotees of culture and urbanity? St. Bernard with his crusade, or Abelard with his doubts? The men who conducted the Inquisition, or the men who doubted the doctrine of the Trinity? Calvin and the obscurantists on both sides of the Reformation, or Erasmus and the Humanists? Cromwell and his Puritans or Voltaire and the Deists? Robespierre or Goethe?

The devotees to causes have kept human life in turmoil. If the immorality they would cure has slain its thousands, their "morality" has slain its tens of thousands. In most cases the strife has been useless and for causes that might have been won in other ways, really won. The devotee of a cause requires little provocation to practice persecution, and only the opportunity to play the tyrant.

Doubt not only has educational value: it preserves social sanity. I would suggest as part of everyone's education the reading of such authors as Lucian, Epicurus, Abelard, Hobbes, Montaigne, Rabelais, Erasmus, Lessing, Voltaire, Hume and Anatole France. There is no blood on these men's hands. They have quietly smiled in the face of bigotry and superstition. In their words there is laughter and there is light. Perhaps no one of them ever intended to be a liberator of mankind. They merely thought and spoke as free spirits, and their very presence puts sham and cant and unction and coercion and mistaken zeal to shame. They have done more for freedom and truth than all the armies of crusading devotees.

STUDY QUESTIONS

1. *Explain Martin's paradoxical opinions that doubt is the way to knowledge and modesty the way to power.*
2. *Explain what is meant by Martin's statement, "All our ideas are views. . ."*
3. *Is it fair to conclude that, if Martin is right, and nothing can finally be known, education is largely a waste of time?*
4. *To what extent do Martin and John Stuart Mill agree on the value of doubt?*
5. *Do you agree with Martin that the "gentle doubters" of the world have done more good than the "devotees of causes"? Write a theme explaining and defending your point of view.*
6. *Write a theme about some important question about which you are still in doubt, explaining the issue, and telling why you have not reached a definite decision. Or, if you disagree with Martin, describe a question which you have definitely decided in your own mind, and explain why you feel you are better off for having settled your doubts.*

Jacques Barzun The Teaching Process*

J t is over a quarter of a century since I first obeyed the summons to teach and I can only hope the habit has not become a compulsion. "Oh to sit next a man who has spent his life in trying to educate others!" groaned Oscar Wilde. My belief is that the last thing a good teacher wants to do is to teach outside the classroom; certainly my own vision of bliss halfway through a term is solitary confinement in a soundproof cell. But feeling this way, I often wonder what originally made the impulse to teach take root. In the lives of so many good men one reads that they "drifted into teaching." They drift out again. It is clear that teachers are born, not made, and circumstances usually permit rather than compel. It is impossible to think of William James *not* teaching or of his brother Henry consenting to give a simple explanation. For many people, doing is far easier than talking about it.

From which I conclude that the teaching impulse goes something like this: a fellow human being is puzzled or stymied. He wants to open a door or spell "accommodate." The would-be helper has two choices. He can open the door, spell the word; or he can show his pupil how to do it for himself. The second way is harder and takes more time, but a strong instinct in the born teacher makes him prefer it. It seems somehow to turn an accident into an opportunity for permanent creation. The raw material is what the learner can do, and upon this the teacher-artist builds by the familiar process of taking apart and putting together. He must break down the new and puzzling situation into simpler bits and lead the beginner in the right order from one bit to the next. What the simpler bits and the right order are no one can know ahead of time. They vary for each individual and the teacher must grope around until he finds a "first step" that the particular pupil can manage. In any school subject, of course, this technique does not stop with the opening of a door. The need for it goes on and on — as it seems, forever — and it takes the stubbornness of a saint coupled with the imagination of a demon for a teacher to pursue his art of improvisation gracefully, unwearyingly, endlessly.

Nor is this a purely mental task. All the while, the teacher must keep his charge's feelings in good order. A rattled student can do nothing and a muddled teacher will rattle or dishearten almost any student. The teacher must not talk too much or too fast, must not trip over his own tongue, must not think out loud, must not forget, in short, that he is handling a pair of runaway horses — the pupil and a dramatic situation.

* From *Teacher in America* by Jacques Barzun, by permission of Little, Brown & Company, and Atlantic Monthly Press. Copyright, 1944, 1945, by Jacques Barzun.

Patience is a quality proverbially required for good teaching, but it is not surprising that many good teachers turn out to be impatient people — though not with their students. Their stock of forbearance gives out before they get home. What sustains them in class is that the situation is always changing. Three successive failures to do one thing may all seem identical to the by-stander, but the good teacher will notice a change, a progression, or else the clear sign that the attempt must be postponed until some other preliminary progress has been made.

It is obvious that the relation of teacher to pupil is an emotional one and most complex and unstable besides. To begin with, the motives, the forces that make teaching "go," are different on both sides of the desk. The pupil has some curiosity and he wants to know what grownups know. The master has curiosity also, but it is chiefly about the way the pupil's mind — or hand — works. Remembering his own efforts and the pleasure of discovery, the master finds a satisfaction which I have called artistic in seeing how a new human being will meet and make his own some part of our culture — our ways, our thoughts, even our errors and superstitions. This interest, how-ever, does not last forever. As the master grows away from his own learning period, he also finds that mankind repeats itself. Fewer and fewer students appear new and original. They make the same mistakes at the same places and never seem to go very far into a subject which, for him, is still an ex-panding universe. Hence young teachers are best; they are the most energetic, most intuitive, and the least resented.

For side by side with his eagerness, the pupil feels resentment arising from the fact that the grownup who teaches him appears to know it all. There is, incidentally, no worse professional disease for the teacher than the habit of putting questions with a half-smile that says "I know that one, and I will tell it you: come along, my pretty." Telling and questioning must not be put-up jobs designed to make the teacher feel good about himself. It is as bad as the Jehovah complex among doctors. Even under the best conditions of fair play and deliberate spontaneity, the pupil, while needing and wanting knowledge, will hate and resist it. This resistance often makes one feel that the human mind is made of some wonderfully tough rubber, which you can stretch a little by pulling hard, but which snaps back into shape the moment you let go.

It is exasperating, but consider how the student feels, subjected to daily and hourly stretching. "Here am I," he thinks, "with my brains nicely organized — with everything, if not in its place, at least in a place where I can find it — and you come along with a new and strange item that you want to force into my previous arrangement. Naturally I resist. You persist. I begin to dislike you. But at the same time, you show me aspects of this new fact or idea which in spite of myself mesh in with my existing desires. You seem to know the contents of my mind. You show me the proper place for your contribution to my stock of knowledge. Finally, there is brooding over us a vague threat of disgrace for me if I do not accept your offering and keep it and show you that I still have it when you — dreadful thought! — *examine* me. So I give in, I shut my eyes and swallow. I write little notes about it to myself, and with luck the burr sticks: I have learned something. Thanks to you? Well, not exactly. Thanks to you and thanks to me. I shall always be grateful for your efforts, but do not expect me to love you, at least not for a long, long time. When I am fully formed and somewhat battered by the world and yet not too displeased with myself, I shall generously believe that I owe it all to you. It will be an exaggeration on the other side, just as my present dislike is an injustice. Strike an average between the two and that will be a fair measure of my debt."

At any stage in learning, this inner dialogue between opposite feelings goes on. It should go on. Teaching is possible only because there is a dialogue and one part of the mind can be used to rearrange the other. The whole secret of teaching — and it is no secret — consists in splitting the opposition, downing the conservatives by making an alliance with the radicals. It goes without saying that I am not using these words here in their workaday sense. My meaning applies to the multiplication table as well as to anything else. The conservative part of the pupil's mind is passive, stubborn, mute; but his radical minority, that is, his curiosity and his desire to grow up, may be aroused to action. The move forward is generally short; then the conservatives return to power; they preserve, they feel pride of ownership in the new acquisition and begin to think they had it as a birthright. This rhythmical action is one reason why teaching and learning must not go on all the time, nor at an accelerated pace: time and rest are needed for absorption. Psychologists confirm the fact when they tell us that it is really in summer that our muscles learn how to skate, and in winter how to swim.

If I have dwelt on the emotions of teaching and being taught, it is because many people believe that schooling only engages the mind — and only temporarily at that. "I've forgotten," says the average man, "all I ever learned at school." And he mentally contrasts this happy oblivion with the fact that he still knows how to open oysters and ride a bicycle. But my description of teaching applies equally to physical things and to metaphysical. We may forget the substance of American History but we are probably scarred for life by the form and feeling of it as imparted by book and teacher. Why is it that the businessman's economics and the well-bred woman's taste in art are normally twenty-five years behind the times? It is that one's lifelong opinions are those picked up before maturity — at school and college.

This is why a "teacher's influence," if he does exert one, is not so big a joke as it seems. Notice in the lives of distinguished men how invariably there is a Mr. Bowles or a Dr. Tompkins or a Professor Clunk — whom no one ever heard of, but who is "remembered" for inspiring, guiding, and teaching decisively at the critical time. We can all see the mark left by a teacher in physical arts like tennis or music. The pupils of Leopold Auer or Tobias Matthay can be recognized at forty paces by their posture and even in a dark room by the sound they make. For in these disciplines the teacher usually falls back on direct imitation: "Hold your hand like this," or more simply, "Watch me." Well, much good teaching is of the "watch me" order, but the more abstract the knowledge, the less easy it is to imitate the teacher, and the genuine student wants to do the real thing in a real way *by himself*.

Consequently, the whole aim of good teaching is to turn the young learner, by nature a little copycat, into an independent, self-propelling creature, who cannot merely learn but study — that is, work as his own boss to the limit of his powers. This is to turn pupils into students, and it can be done on any rung of the ladder of learning. When I was a child, the multiplication table was taught from a printed sheet which had to be memorized one "square" at a time — the one's and the two's and so on up to nine. It never occurred to the teacher to show us how the answers could be arrived at also by addition, which we already knew. No one said, "Look: if four times four is sixteen, you ought to be able to figure out, without aid from memory, what five times four is, because that amounts to four more one's added to the sixteen." This would at first have been puzzling, *more* complicated and difficult than memory work, but once explained and grasped, it would have been an instrument for learning and checking the whole business of multiplication. We could temporarily have dispensed with the teacher and cut loose from the printed table.[1]

This is another way of saying that the only thing worth teaching anybody is a principle. Naturally principles involve facts and some facts must be learned "bare" because they do not rest on any principle. The capital of Alaska is Juneau and, so far as I know, that is all there is to it; but a European child ought not to learn that Washington is the capital of the United States without fixing firmly in his mind the relation between the city and the man who led his countrymen to freedom. That would be missing an association, which is the germ of a principle. And just as a complex athletic feat is made possible by rapid and accurate co-ordination, so all valuable learning hangs together and *works* by associations which make sense.

Since associations are rooted in habit and habits in feelings, we can see that anything which makes school seem a nightmare or a joke, which brands the teacher as a fool, or a fraud, is the archenemy of all learning. It so happens that there is one professional disease, or rather vice, which generates precisely this feeling and whose consequences are therefore fatal. I refer to Hokum and I hasten to explain what I mean. Hokum is the counterfeit of true intellectual currency. It is words without meaning, verbal filler, artificial

---

[1] I find that General Grant complained of the same thing: "Both winters were spent in going over the same old arithmetic which I knew every word of before and repeating 'A noun is the name of a thing,' which I had also heard my Georgetown teachers repeat until I had come to believe it." (*Memoirs*, New York, 1894, p .20.)

apples of knowledge. From the necessities of the case, nine tenths of all teaching is done with words, whence the ever-present temptation of hokum.

Words should point to things, seen or unseen. But they can also be used to wrap up emptiness of heart and lack of thought. The student accepts some pompous, false, meaningless formula, and passes it back on demand, to be rewarded with — appropriately enough — a passing grade. All the dull second-rate opinions, all the definitions that don't define, all the moral platitudes that "sound good," all the conventional adjectives ("gentle Shakespeare"), all the pretenses that a teacher makes about the feelings of his students towards him and vice versa, all the intimations that something must be learned because it has somehow got lodged among learnable things (like the Binomial Theorem or the date of Magna Carta) — all this in all its forms gives off the atmosphere of hokum, which healthy people everywhere find absolutely unbreathable.

In a modern play, I think by A. A. Milne, this schoolmarm vice has been caught and set down in a brief dialogue which goes something like this:—

GOVERNESS. Recite.
PUPIL. "The Battle of Blenheim." (*Long pause*)
GOVERNESS. By?
PUPIL. (*silence*).
GOVERNESS. By Robert Southey.
PUPIL. By Robert Southey.
GOVERNESS. Who was Robert Southey?
PUPIL. (*pause*). I don't know.
GOVERNESS. One of our greatest poets. Begin again.
PUPIL. The Battle of Blenheim by Robert Southey one of our greatest poets.

As this example shows, hokum is subtle and I will forbear to analyze it. It hides in the porous part of solid learning and vitiates it by making it stupid and ridiculous. I remember once giving a short quiz to a class of young women who had been reading about the Renaissance. I asked for some "identification" of names and put Petrarch in the list. One girl, who had evidently read a textbook, wrote down: "Petrarch — the vanguard of the new emphasis." I spent a good hour trying to explain why this parroting of opinion was not only not "correct" but blind hokum, hokum absolute. It was not an easy job because so many teachers and books deal exclusively in that cheap commodity. The child's instinct is first to believe the Word, spoken or printed; then with growing good sense to disbelieve it, but to trust to its hokum value for getting through by "satisfying" the teacher. Great heavens, what satisfactions!

To carry my anecdote one step further, I believe I made a lifelong friend and a convert to decent learning by persuading my student that almost any honest mistake would have been truer than the absurdity she was palming off. She might better have been trivial: "Petrarch was an Italian"; or flippant: "Wrote poems to a girl named Laura"; or downright mistaken: "Also spelled Plutarch," rather than do what she did. My difficulty — and this is the important point — was in convincing her that I meant what I said, in breaking down the strongest superstition of the young, which is that everybody but themselves prefers make-believe and lives by it.

STUDY QUESTIONS

1. *Explain why Barzun conceives teaching to be not "a purely mental task." In what way is good teaching a "permanent creation"?*

2. *According to Barzun, what is the natural emotional relationship between student and teacher? Do you agree with him that this attitude is natural?*

3. *What, according to Barzun's clearly implied distinction, is the difference between a "pupil" and a "student"?*

4. *Barzun has had considerable success in writing for laymen on a variety of humane subjects. Examine this selection and be prepared to point out qualities of style which may have contributed to the success of his writing.*

5. *Write a theme describing a relationship you have had with a teacher, and telling whether or not you felt the relationship promoted the learning process.*

6. *Write a theme filling the gap deliberately left by Barzun at the place where he feels it is best not to explain what he means by "hokum." Tell what you think he means by this word, analyzing the characteristics and purposes of hokum, and giving any examples you have noted in your own experience.*

Gilbert Highet The Tutorial Method*

The methods of tutoring a single pupil or a small group vary as widely as subjects and individuals. But the principle is nearly always the same. The pupil prepares a body of work by himself. He takes it for criticism and correction to the tutor, who then goes over it with the greatest possible thoroughness, criticizing everything from the general conception to the tiniest detail. The pupil learns from three different activities: first, from doing his own work alone; second, from observing the mistakes he has missed, *and also* from defending himself on points where he believes he is right; third, from looking over the completed and corrected work and comparing it with the original assignment and his first draft. The first of these is the work of creation, the second is criticism, the third is appreciation of wholeness. It is the tutor's main task to see that the individual activities are not really separate: they must mesh together and work into a larger scheme, covering as much of the subject as the pupil needs.

In music, for example, a teacher may very well start his pupil with the elements — reading the notes, singing the simple scale, hitting the basic

* From *The Art of Teaching* by Gilbert Highet, by permission of Alfred A. Knopf, Inc. Copyright, 1950, by Gilbert Highet.

rhythms — and may carry her through progressively difficult exercises, week by week, planned to train her in breathing, tone-control, rapidity of utterance, and richness of overtones, while avoiding or eliminating the too numerous vices of young singers — blaring, trembling, hooting, and panting. Easy songs will be followed by longer and more complex ones, until at last, years later than the first lesson, he will be teaching her a group of Ravel songs and an entire part from *The Magic Flute.* (Yet he himself may not be a singer at all, far less a coloratura soprano.) If he manages this successfully, he will be a fine teacher. He will have solved the two most difficult of the teacher's problems, which are to plan the complete development of a single individual's learning, from beginnings to maturity, and to guide the pupil over the inevitable periods of discouragement by pointing back to the ground traversed and forward to the hopeful future.

The lessons assigned must not only be interconnected. They must be varied, to sustain the pupil's interest and encourage its multiple growth. There is a story that Caffarelli, the eunuch who became one of the finest sopranos of the baroque age, was tutored by a single faultless but relentless Italian master, who kept him at one single page of exercises for five years, and then dismissed him, saying: "You may go: you are the greatest singer in Europe." Certainly the unhappy creature became one of the finest singers in history. He could sing melodies more purely and sweetly, and execute difficult runs more flexibly and gracefully, than any modern opera star. But his teacher took a chance which was quite unwarrantable, and which might not have succeeded with anyone except a eunuch. Most pupils, all pupils but a very few, would have demanded proof of their progress, in the shape of new assignments, fresh challenges, a change of any kind. Disciplined monotony is good training, but it easily becomes mechanical repetition; and by mechanical repetition nothing higher than card-tricks and juggling can ever (with the rarest and most laborious exceptions) be learnt or taught.

The tutorial system is not very widespread. It flourishes at Oxford and Cambridge. It has been tried at Harvard, but because of the expense of time and effort it has not been entirely successful. At a number of universities it exists in an altered form in the graduate schools; for instance, in the small classes called seminars, where a student reads a carefully prepared report on a special problem he has chosen, defends his conclusions against the criticisms of the other members of the class, and, with further criticism as well as positive suggestions from the professor in charge, builds his paper up into part of a book-length piece of research. A professor who advises a graduate student on a thesis which takes a year or more to write, who sees every chapter in draft and talks over every problem as it emerges, is really tutoring him too, on a rather high level. But as far as I know, the intense and exhausting, but rewarding, relationship which was expressed by the American statesman in the phrase "a simple bench, Mark Hopkins on one end and I on the other" exists only in Oxford and Cambridge Universities.

I passed through it both as a pupil and as a tutor. From both ends, it was one of the best experiences of my life. It worked in this way when I was a student: I was paired off with one other youth, taking the same courses as myself. We were told to come to Mr. Harnish's room at five every Tuesday and Friday. For Tuesday I was invited to write an essay on a part of the field we were both studying. It was considerably ahead of the lectures we were attending meanwhile, and it took longer to do than I expected. However, I finished it about three on Tuesday morning, and read it to Mr. Harnish that evening. Dick listened. Mr. Harnish lay in his armchair smoking, with his eyes closed and an odd expression of mingled interest, pain, apprehension, and hope on his face. After I had finished, he looked into the fire for a minute or two without speaking. (Those were always uncomfortable moments, but one learned a good deal from them.) Then he began to ask me questions about my essay, page by page, paragraph by paragraph, word by word. What was my authority for the statement about the Allies on the first page? Yes, it was in all the books on the subject, but what was the original evidence? Didn't that deserve more careful analysis? What other interpretations of it were possible? Did I know who had proposed them? Shouldn't they have been given more attention in view of recent discoveries? And on page 5, what was the original text of the illustrative quotation? Was that the usual translation? How could the version I offered be justified? Let's look it up now and see. (Dick was brought in at this point, and we engaged in a three-sided argument.) The third page was a rehash of the Tuskar theory, wasn't it? What were the real weaknesses in that theory? And so on through the whole essay.

After that, Hr. Harnish took the essay as a whole and pointed out the omissions, calling on me to justify them or suggest how they could be filled in. He finished off by a few airy references to pieces of research just concluded, to arguments carried on last week at the Philobiblian Society, and to Caversham's new book on the subject, look at it some time, won't you? and for next week you might write about Mumble Mumble; and so shoved us off towards the Buttery and a well-earned glass of sherry.

That was Tuesday. On Friday Dick read an essay of his own, while I listened in silence and then heard Mr. Harnish dissecting it in the same way. Next week, the same. By the end of the term we had each written eight essays and heard eight more, all in the same field, about which we were also reading books and attending lectures. Eight weeks is a short term, but at the end of such an intensive stretch we knew that particular field fairly well.

At an earlier stage, while we were studying language and literature, our class did a piece of translation twice a week: German prose into English, English prose into Spanish, Russian verse into English verse, English lyrics into Latin lyrics, whatever we were studying, and usually made as difficult as the traffic would bear. Sometimes alone, sometimes with another man, we would take the composition to the tutor concerned, who went over it literally word by word, criticizing our choice of meter and vocabulary, making alternative suggestions for awkward phrases, checking the rhythm, occasionally wincing and writing: (!) in the margin for a real boner, and finally discussing the expressiveness and grace of the whole rendering. Then he usually gave us a version of the same piece done by himself, which we copied out or excerpted as we wished, and which for beauty and skill it was difficult not to admire. Once a week or so, at this stage, six or eight of us would gather in his room to read shorter essays on special subjects, which he would criticize hand-running, less intensively than Hr. Harnish was to do at a later stage, but in such a way as to throw out more numerous suggestions to stir up our diverse interests. After you have read one essay on Luther in the Peasants' War, and listened to five others on Erasmus and the Reformation, the tragic career of Ulrich von Hutten, Peter Canisius and the Jesuits in Germany, the Anabaptists of Münster, and the intrigues of emperor and pope, you have learned something about the German Reformation.

And while I am taking examples from my own experience (although they are a little altered), let me pay a debt of thanks to the schoolmaster who taught me Greek. He used the tutorial system because I was his only pupil; and what is more, he gave up half his lunch-hour to do it. We were both doing Greek as an extra: I because I liked the idea of learning the language written in the queer but charming letters; and he because — I don't know: he was a dour quiet Scotsman who seldom showed enthusiasm for anything but his garden. Perhaps he wanted a pupil who might go on to the university and do him credit; probably he liked teaching enough to give up spare time to it if he had a willing learner; certainly he liked Greek literature, for he introduced me to the best in it. Whatever his motives were, he tutored me kindly but relentlessly. I stood beside him at his desk (sometimes cocking an ear to the yells of my friends playing after-lunch football outside) and translated my daily stint of Homer, line by line. He missed nothing, not the smallest γε. He insisted on a straight literal translation, which was the best level for a beginner — like Charles Lamb's Mrs. Battle, he loved "a clear fire, a clean hearth, and the rigour of the game" — and if I finished ahead of time, I didn't pack up and go. No, I was made to push on into the unknown, and translate the next page or so unprepared and unseen. Buchanan helped now and then with the hard words. The rest of the time he stood there, stiff and silent, smelling of pipe-smoke and damp tweeds and garden mixtures, and, for one small boy who scarcely understood, representing the long and noble tradition of exact scholarship and sound teaching. Now I offer him this tribute, regretting only that it comes too late.

STUDY QUESTIONS

1. *What is Highet's evaluation of the teaching method he describes? Would you say that he felt the same way about it when he was experiencing it? If you think he has changed his mind about it, explain what may have led to this change.*

2. *What signs does Highet give which show that he attributes importance to the residence requirements of university education?*

3. *Do you think Highet seems to regard teaching as (in Barzun's words) "a purely mental task"? Do he and Barzun seem to have different opinions about this aspect of the subject?*

4. *Both this and the preceding selection by Barzun provide examples of exposition of process. How do the principles of organization in the two differ? Is one more clear than the other? Is one more "lively" than the other? Defend your evaluations.*

5. *Write a theme describing the ways in which the experience of a student under the tutorial method differs from that of a student taking part in ordinary class work.*

6. *Would you like to see the kind of teaching described by Highet more widely adopted in American colleges and universities? Write a theme explaining your answer to this question.*

John Henry Newman Knowledge and Learning *

I suppose the *primâ-facie* view which the public at large would take of a University, considering it as a place of Education, is nothing more or less than a place for acquiring a great deal of knowledge on a great many subjects. Memory is one of the first developed of mental faculties; a boy's business when he goes to school is to learn, that is, to store up things in his memory. For some years his intellect is little more than an instrument for taking in facts, or a receptacle for storing them; he welcomes them as fast as they come to him; he lives on what is without; he has his eyes ever about him; he has a lively susceptibility of impressions; he imbibes information of every kind; and little does he make his own in a true sense of the word, living rather upon his neighbors all around him. He has opinions, religious, political, and literary, and, for a boy, is very positive in them and sure about them; but he gets them from his schoolfellows, or his masters, or his parents, as the case may be. Such as he is in his other relations, such also is he in his school exercises; his mind is observant, sharp, ready, retentive; he is almost passive in the acquisition of knowledge. I say this in no disparagement of the idea of a clever boy. Geography, chronology, history, language, natural history, he heaps up the matter of these studies as treasures for a future day. It is the seven years of plenty with him; he gathers in by handfuls, like the Egyptians, without counting; and though, as time goes on, there is exercise for his argumentative powers in the Elements of Mathematics, and for his taste in the Poets and Orators, still, while at school, or at least, till quite the last years of his time, he acquires, and little more; and

* From *The Idea of a University*, 1852.

when he is leaving for the University, he is mainly the creature of foreign influences and circumstances, and made up of accidents, homogeneous or not, as the case may be. Moreover, the moral habits, which are a boy's praise, encourage and assist this result; that is, diligence, assiduity, regularity, despatch, persevering application; for these are the direct conditions of acquisition, and naturally lead to it. Acquirements, again, are emphatically producible, and at a moment; they are a something to show, both for master and scholar; an audience, even though ignorant themselves of the subjects of an examination, can comprehend when questions are answered and when they are not. Here again is a reason why mental culture is in the minds of men identified with the acquisition of knowledge.

The same notion possesses the public mind, when it passes on from the thought of a school to that of a University: and with the best of reasons so far as this, that there is no true culture without acquirements, and that philosophy presupposes knowledge. It requires a great deal of reading, or a wide range of information, to warrant us in putting forth our opinions on any serious subject; and without such learning the most original mind may be able indeed to dazzle, to amuse, to refute, to perplex, but not to come to any useful result or any trustworthy conclusion. There are indeed persons who profess a different view of the matter, and even act upon it. Every now and then you will find a person of vigorous or fertile mind, who relies upon his own resources, despises all former authors, and gives the world, with the utmost fearlessness, his views upon religion, or history, or any other popular subject. And his works may sell for a while; he may get a name in his day; but this will be all. His readers are sure to find on the long run that his doctrines are mere theories, and not the expression of facts, that they are chaff instead of bread, and then his popularity drops as suddenly as it rose.

Knowledge then is the indispensable condition of expansion of mind, and the instrument of attaining to it; this cannot be denied, it is ever to be insisted on; I begin with it as a first principle; however, the very truth of it carries men too far, and confirms to them the notion that it is the whole of the matter. A narrow mind is thought to be that which contains little knowledge; and an enlarged mind, that which holds a great deal; and what seems to put the matter beyond dispute is, the fact of the great number of studies which are pursued in a University, by its very profession. Lectures are given on every kind of subject; examinations are held; prizes awarded. There are moral, metaphysical, physical Professors; Professors of languages, of history, of mathematics, of experimental science. Lists of questions are published, wonderful for their range and depth, variety and difficulty; treatises are written, which carry upon their very face the evidence of extensive reading or multifarious information; what then is wanting for mental culture to a person of large reading and scientific attainments? what is grasp of mind but acquirement? where shall philosophical repose be found, but in the consciousness and enjoyment of large intellectual possessions?

And yet this notion is, I conceive, a mistake, and my present business is to show that it is one, and that the end of a Liberal Education is not mere knowledge, or knowledge considered in its *matter;* and I shall best attain my object, by actually setting down some cases, which will be generally granted to be instances of the process of enlightenment or enlargement of mind, and others which are not, and thus, by the comparison, you will be able to judge for yourselves, Gentlemen, whether Knowledge, that is, acquirement, is after all the real principle of the enlargement, or whether that principle is not rather something beyond it.

For instance, let a person, whose experience has hitherto been confined to the more calm and unpretending scenery of these islands, ... go for the first time into parts where physical nature puts on her wilder and more awful forms, whether at home or abroad, as into mountainous districts; or let one, who has ever lived in a quiet village, go for the first time to a great metropolis, — then I suppose he will have a sensation which perhaps he never had before. He has a feeling not in addition or increase of former feelings, but of something different in its nature. He will perhaps be borne forward, and find for a time that he has lost his bearings. He has made a certain progress, and he has a consciousness of mental enlargement; he does not stand where he did, he has a new centre, and a range of thoughts to which he was before a stranger.

Again, the view of the heavens which the telescope opens upon us, if allowed to fill and possess the mind, may almost whirl it round and make it dizzy. It brings in a flood of ideas, and is rightly called an intellectual enlargement, whatever is meant by the term.

And so again, the sight of beasts of prey and other foreign animals, their strangeness, the originality (if I may use the term) of their forms and gestures and habits and their variety and independence of each other, throw us out of ourselves into another creation, and as if under another Creator, if I may so express the temptation which may come on the mind. We seem to have new faculties, or a new exercise for our faculties, by this addition to our knowledge; like a prisoner, who, having been accustomed to wear manacles or fetters, suddenly finds his arms and legs free.

Hence Physical Science generally, in all its departments, as bringing before us the exuberant riches and resources, yet the orderly course of the Universe, elevates and excites the student, and at first, I may say, almost takes away his breath, while in time it exercises a tranquilizing influence upon him.

Again, the study of history is said to enlarge and enlighten the mind, and why? because, as I conceive, it gives it a power of judging of passing events, and of all events, and a conscious superiority over them, which before it did not possess.

And in like manner, what is called seeing the world, entering into active life, going into society, travelling, gaining acquaintance with the various classes of the community, coming into contact with the principles and modes of thought of various parties, interests, and races, their views, aims, habits and manners, their religious creeds and forms of worship, — gaining experience how various yet how alike men are, how low-minded, how bad, how opposed, yet how confident in their opinions; all this exerts a perceptible influence upon the mind, which it is impossible to mistake, be it good or be it bad, and is popularly called its enlargement.

And then again, the first time the mind comes across the arguments and speculations of unbelievers, and feels what a novel light they cast upon what he has hitherto accounted sacred; and still more, if it gives into them and embraces them, and throws off as so much prejudice what it has hitherto held, and, as if waking from a dream, begins to realize to its imagination that there is now no such thing as law and the transgression of law, that sin is a phantom, and punishment a bugbear, that it is free to sin, free to enjoy the world and the flesh; and still further, when it does enjoy them, and reflects that it may think and hold just what it will, that "the world is all before it where to choose," and what system to build up as its own private persuasion; when this torrent of wilful thoughts rushes over and inundates it, who will deny that the fruit of the tree of knowledge, or what the mind takes for knowledge, has made it one of the gods, with a sense of expansion and elevation, — an intoxication in reality, still, so far as the subjective state of the mind goes, an illumination? Hence the fanaticism of individuals or nations, who suddenly cast off their Maker. Their eyes are opened; and, like the judgment-stricken king in the Tragedy, they see two suns, and a magic universe, out of which they look back upon their former state of faith and innocence with a sort of contempt and indignation, as if they were then but fools, and the dupes of imposture.

On the other hand, Religion has its own enlargement, and an enlargement, not of tumult, but of peace. It is often remarked of uneducated persons, who have hitherto thought little of the unseen world, that, on their turning to God, looking into themselves, regulating their hearts, reforming their conduct, and meditating on death and judgment, heaven and hell, they seem to become, in point of intellect, different beings from what they were. Before, they took things as they came, and thought no more of one thing than another. But now every event has a meaning; they have their own estimate of whatever happens to them; they are mindful of times and seasons, and compare the present with the past; and the world, no longer dull, monotonous, unprofitable, and hopeless, is a various and complicated drama, with parts and an object, and an awful moral.

Now from these instances, to which many more might be added, it is plain, first, that the communication of knowledge certainly is either a condition or the means of that sense of enlargement or enlightenment, of which at this day we hear so much in certain quarters: this cannot be denied; but next, it is equally plain, that such communication is not the whole of the process. The enlargement consists, not merely in the passive reception into the mind of a number of ideas hitherto unknown to it, but in the mind's energetic and simultaneous action upon and towards and among those new ideas, which are rushing in upon it. It is the action of a formative power, reducing to order and meaning the matter of our acquirements; it is a making the objects of our knowledge subjectively our own, or, to use a familiar word, it is a digestion of what we receive, into the substance of our previous state of thought; and without this no enlargement is said to follow. There is no enlargement, unless there be a comparison of ideas one with another, as they come before the mind, and a systematizing of them. We feel our minds to be growing and expanding *then,* when we not only learn, but refer what we learn to what we know already. It is not the mere addition to our knowledge that is the illumination; but the locomotion, the movement onwards, of that mental centre, to which both what we know, and what we are learning, the accumulating mass of our acquirements, gravitates. And therefore a truly great intellect, and recognized to be such by the common opinion of mankind, such as the intellect of Aristotle, or of St. Thomas, or of Newton, or of Goethe,...is one which takes a connected view of old and new, past and present, far and near, and which has an insight into the influence of all these one on another; without which there is no whole, and no centre. It possesses the knowledge, not only of things, but also of their mutual and true relations; knowledge, not merely considered as acquirement but as philosophy.

Accordingly, when this analytical, distributive, harmonizing process is away, the mind experiences no enlargement, and is not reckoned as enlightened or comprehensive, whatever it may add to its knowledge. For instance, a great memory, as I have already said, does not make a philosopher, any more than a dictionary can be called a grammar. There are men who embrace in their minds a vast multitude of ideas, but with little sensibility about their real relations towards each other. These may be antiquarians, annalists, naturalists; they may be learned in the law; they may be versed in statistics; they are most useful in their own place; I should shrink from speaking disrespectfully of them; still, there is nothing in such attainments to guarantee the absence of narrowness of mind. If they are nothing more than well-read men, or men of information, they have not what specially deserves the name of culture of mind, or fulfills the type of Liberal Education.

In like manner, we sometimes fall in with persons who have seen much of the world, and of the men who, in their day, have played a conspicuous part in it, but who generalize nothing, and have no observation, in the true sense of the word. They abound in information in detail, curious and entertaining, about men and things; and, having lived under the influence of no very clear or settled principles, religious or political, they speak of every one and every thing, only as so many phenomena, which are complete in themselves, and lead to nothing, not discussing them, or teaching any truth, or instructing the hearer, but simply talking. No one would say that these persons, well informed as they are, had attained to any great culture of intellect or to philosophy.

The case is the same still more strikingly where the persons in question are beyond dispute men of inferior powers and deficient education. Perhaps they have been much in foreign countries, and they receive, in a passive, otiose, unfruitful way, the various facts which are forced upon them there. Seafaring men, for example, range from one end of the earth to the other; but the multiplicity of external objects, which they have encountered, forms no symmetrical and consistent picture upon their imagination; they see the tapestry of human life, as it were on the wrong side, and it tells no story. They sleep, and they rise up, and they find themselves, now in Europe, now in Asia; they see visions of great cities and wild regions; they are in the marts of commerce, or amid the islands of the South; they gaze on Pompey's Pillar, or on the Andes; and nothing which meets them carries them forward or backward, to any idea beyond itself. Nothing has a drift or relation; nothing has a history or a promise. Every thing stands by itself, and comes and goes in its turn, like the shifting scenes of a show, which leave the spectator where he was. Perhaps you are near such a man on a particular occasion, and expect him to be shocked or perplexed at something which occurs; but one thing is much the same to him as another, or, if he is perplexed, it is as not knowing what to say, whether it is right to admire, or to ridicule, or to disapprove, while conscious that some expression of opinion is expected from him; for in fact he has no standard of judgment at all, and no landmarks to guide him to a conclusion. Such is mere acquisition, and, I repeat, no one would dream of calling it philosophy.

Instances, such as these, confirm, by the contrast, the conclusion I have already drawn from those which preceded them. That only is true enlargement of mind which is the power of viewing many things at once as one whole, of referring them severally to their true place in the universal system, of understanding their respective values, and determining their mutual dependence. Thus is that form of Universal Knowledge, of which I have on a former occasion spoken, set up in the individual intellect, and constitutes its perfection. Possessed of this real illumination, the mind never views any part of the extended subject-matter of Knowledge without recollecting that it is but a part, or without the associations which spring from this recollection. It makes every thing in some sort lead to every thing else; it would communicate the image of the whole to every separate portion, till that whole becomes in imagination like a spirit, every where pervading and penetrating its component parts, and giving them one definite meaning. Just as our bodily organs, when mentioned, recall their function in the body, as the word "creation" suggests the Creator, and "subjects" a sovereign, so, in the mind of the Philosopher, as we are abstractedly conceiving of him, the elements of the physical and moral world, sciences, arts, pursuits, ranks, offices, events, opinions, individualities, are all viewed as one, with correlative functions, and as gradually by successive combinations converging, one and all, to the true centre.

To have even a portion of this illuminative reason and true philosophy is the highest state to which nature can aspire, in the way of intellect; it puts the mind above the influences of chance and necessity, above anxiety, suspense, unsettlement, and superstition, which is the lot of the many. Men, whose minds are possessed with some one object, take exaggerated views of its importance, are feverish in the pursuit of it, make it the measure of things which are utterly foreign to it, and are startled and despond if it happens to fail them. They are ever in alarm or in transport. Those on the other hand who have no object or principle whatever to hold by, lose their way, every step they take. They are thrown out, and do not know what to think or say, at every fresh juncture; they have no view of persons, or occurrences, or facts, which come suddenly upon them, and they hang upon the opinion of others, for want of internal resources. But the intellect, which has been disciplined to the perfection of its powers, which knows, and thinks while it knows, which has learned to leaven the dense mass of facts and events with the elastic force of reason, such an intellect cannot be partial, cannot be exclusive, cannot be impetuous, cannot be at a loss, cannot but be patient, collected, and majestically calm, because it discerns the end in every beginning, the origin in every end, the law in every interruption, the limit in each delay; because it ever knows where it stands, and how its path lies from one point to another. It is the $\tau\epsilon\tau\rho\acute{\alpha}\gamma\omega\nu\circ\varsigma$ of the Peripatetic,[1] and has the "nil admirari"[2] of the Stoic,—

> Felix qui potuit rerum cognoscere causas,
> Atque metus omnes, et inexorabile fatum
> Subjecit pedibus, strepitumque Acherontis avari.[3]

There are men who, when in difficulties, originate at the moment vast ideas or dazzling projects; who, under the influence of excitement, are able to cast a light, almost as if from inspiration, on a subject or course of action which comes before them; who have a sudden presence of mind equal to any emergency, rising with the occasion, and an undaunted magnanimous bearing, and an energy and keenness which is but made intense by opposition. This is genius, this is heroism; it is the exhibition of a natural gift, which no culture can teach, at which no Institution can aim; here, on the contrary, we are concerned, not with mere nature, but with training and teaching. That perfection of the Intellect, which is the result of Education, and its *beau ideal*, to be imparted to individuals in their respective measures, is the clear, calm, accurate vision and comprehension of all things, as far as the finite mind can embrace them, each in its place, and with its own characteristics upon it. It is almost prophetic from its knowledge of history; it is almost heart-searching from its knowledge of human nature; it has almost supernatural charity from its freedom from littleness and prejudice; it has almost the repose of faith, because nothing can startle it; it has almost the beauty and harmony of heavenly contemplation, so intimate is it with the eternal order of things and the music of the spheres.

---

[1] An allusion to Aristotle's *Ethics*—the good and *foursquare* man.
[2] To be amazed at nothing.
[3] Happy the man who can understand nature's causes, and thus spurn all fear and inexorable fate and the roar of greedy Acheron.

STUDY QUESTIONS

1. *Exactly what does Newman mean by the phrase "enlargement of the mind"? How does a man whose mind has undergone this process differ from others?*

2. *How does Newman help to explain why the mere accumulation of facts or information is not education? Newman's discussion is very closely related to the ideas of both Chafee and Martin. In what way does he add depth and complexity to those ideas?*

3. *Newman's discussion suggests that a man who undertakes education must have certain capacities to begin with. What are they? How does Newman rank them in value?*

4. *What was Newman's objection to the popular education of his day? Exactly what advantage does he see in the kind of education that requires residence as compared with the kind that requires the passing of examinations? To what extent would Barzun and Highet agree with Newman?*

5. *Write a theme explaining your own educational aims.*

6. *Much of contemporary education is based on a point of view directly opposed to Newman's. Write a theme criticizing his opinions, showing why they are impractical or unrealistic.*

3 Man in Society

1. THE AMERICAN SCENE

D. W. Brogan The New American*

What is this new man, the new American? Here we move into deep
waters of sociological theory in which I can hardly keep afloat, much
less swim. Is the new American society producing a new American or a new
myth about the new American? Maybe a new American; but some of the
reasons advanced are not totally convincing. The new American may be
conformist, but was the old often nonconformist? I wrote in the first edition
of this book that "any well-established village in New England or the northern Middle West could afford a town drunkard, a town atheist and a few
Democrats." It can now afford more than one town drunkard (called "alco-
holics," of course), being a Democrat is less bold today than it was; some of
the nicest people are Democrats; but a town atheist? "There are no atheists
in the foxholes," and America is now in a foxhole that she may have to
inhabit for a generation. The consequence of this predicament is that refusal
to give lip service, at least, to the American religion is a kind of treason and
is punished as it was in the America of a century ago.

* From *The American Character* by D. W. Brogan, by permission of Alfred A.
Knopf, Inc. Copyright, 1956, by Denis W. Brogan.

It is not the social coercion of the real dissenter, the man who by his action or inaction condemns the faith of his neighbors, that is the new thing. (All that need be said on democratic conformity was said by Tocqueville.) What is new is the increasing condemnation of the man who conforms *too* vigorously, who pursues happiness in indisputably American terms, but pursues it with too little regard for his neighbor's comfort. Of course he *is* in competition with them, but he mustn't rub that fact in or rejoice too much in victory. He must win without showing it and, to be able to win, he must not antagonize the other runners, who will gang up on him if he does. The race is still to the swift but mere swiftness is not enough if its too ostentatious display leads to some other competitor's bumping or spiking, with the approval of the other competitors — and the spectators. So far this new-found consideration may be only skin deep; it may be only a tactic, but it is interesting that it is a tactic.[1]

It is, on the surface, a long way from the traditional pioneer; it may be more than a change of methods; it may be a change of spirit. And yet, and yet! By European standards, what is still notable about American life is that competition, even by the new, softer, more formally amiable methods, is the accepted way of life. So is the lavishness of the prizes; so is the acceptance of the fact that not everybody can answer the $64,000 question — and the absence of jealousy of the winners. This absence of jealousy, this conviction that the game is worth playing and the results not cooked, is one of the chief sources of American wealth, well-being, and political stability. No one (hardly anyone, Negroes excepted) feels automatically excluded from the pursuit of happiness. Even the Negroes feel less excluded than they did. There is consequently a universal acceptance of the legitimacy of the political authority of "We, the People of the United States," that startles and impresses European visitors like Père Bruckberger. In this very important sense, a more perfect union has been attained than is known in any country in Europe and which pleases or angers European visitors in accordance with their personal temperaments and doctrines.

There is, of course, a danger or a promise that the formal good manners of the American acquisitive society will in fact weaken the acquisitive motive and habit. Not only can no one be rich on the old scale (taxes see to that), but achievement in the field of production is not admired as it was in the older, simpler, cruder American society. No great business magnate will ever know the free command of wealth that Rockefeller and Carnegie knew; the admiration, just short of worship, that Edison and Henry Ford I knew.

---

[1] How far the new spirit has gone is illustrated by the innocent remark of an Irish-American contractor, specializing in pulling down buildings and excavating foundations, traditionally tough trades. Mr. Howard Collins notes the change. " 'When I started in this business, everybody was a roughneck. Talked dirty, dressed dirty, lived dirty. Now the men come to work in nice clothes, drive nice cars, live in nice houses, have nice families. Funny thing that's happened in this country—nobody *has* to be tough any more.' " *The New Yorker*, December 31, 1955.

Whether the lessened rewards will begin to eat into the will to "succeed" of the young American we do not yet know. The old battle of the strong had the attractions of battle. The modern business career is more like the peace-time career of the professional soldier than the bloody campaigns that brought the Robber Barons to the top. It is not insignificant that the services of the Robber Barons are now better appreciated when (outside Texas) they are, as a breed, almost extinct.

In discussing this question we are all at school to Mr. David Riesman, and if the "inner directed" are indeed in retreat, are becoming un-American, the United States may be moving nearer the Soviet Union than it realizes, for Communism, too, professes to create a new man as unlike the conscience-driven heroes of Dostoievsky as the modern dweller in the executive suite, in gray flannel, is unlike such flamboyant pirates as Jim Fisk. If it is no longer a matter of "keeping up with the Joneses," but of everybody keeping up with everybody else, it is possible that the American people will end up going round, in happy harmony, a mulberry bush that isn't there. And against such a danger a great deal of modern American religiosity is less than no safeguard.

It is not only a matter of adjusting to the great, anonymous, self-governing, mass-owned corporations to whose service and promises so many young Americans gladly give themselves. It is a matter of adjusting to a world in which mass organizations are the normal centers of life for more and more millions of human beings. It can be asserted that the United States must adjust or perish. And one aspect of that adjustment is the immense growth of the armed forces and of the economic units serving them. Millions of Americans in 1939 had little or nothing to do with the government of the United States. Millions of Americans in 1944 looked forward to a near and victorious future in which they would have nothing to do with that government. They were disillusioned. From that disillusion has come much of what has most disturbed the outside world in contemporary America, McCarthyism, "sounding-off" by cabinet officers, senators, generals, columnists, threats of atomic war, brisk denunciation of allies and the like. The Americans are forced to live not only in a world they have not made, but in a world that they definitely thought they had killed in its cradle. No wonder the average American is uneasy, ready to believe that the cause of all his discontents is treason or folly in his rulers, unwilling to accept the fact that the world was not made exclusively by or for Americans. Great wonder that, with all these natural grounds for resentment of the human situation, he has *not* revolted against prudence or duty, that he has accepted leadership every time that it has been offered, has, in such different activities as the Marshall Plan and the Korean War, given the world a lead and an example, has, with a readiness totally unforeseen in 1939 and only barely hoped for in 1944, risen to his duty. Those who expected much from the American people have not been disappointed.

There are other ways in which they have not been disappointed. Despite

setbacks like the revival of lynching in Mississippi, the frenzies provoked by
the threat of desegregation in southern schools, the revival of the most farcical
and odious doctrines of race supremacy, in no field of human relations has
the United States made more progress than in its dealing with Negro
Americans. The churches, laggard enough in 1939, have in many cases
been pioneers — above all, the Catholic Church, where bishops have shown
that there is something to be said for a church in which authority does not
come from the grass roots; grass roots are sometimes poisoned.

American trade unions are not led by or composed of angels. But they have
proved a great stabilizing force and if the American economic system, called,
a little naïvely, the "free-enterprise system," has secured such universal
acceptance, it is in part due to the integration of the American worker in
American industrial society by the trade unions.

In the same way, the social services, so bitterly opposed, open as some are
to grave and increasing abuse, have made the government of the United
States something less remote, less merely demanding than it was. The woes
of the farmer may be real, but it is significant that he turns, simply and
candidly, to the government to keep him in the state to which he thinks he is
entitled. This is a change from the days of "root, hog, or die," but it represents
less a change in attitude than an acceptance of the fact that the urbanization
of the American society makes certain proud old agricultural attitudes very
expensive. The American farmer, in his rugged way, would rather have
money without control, and he may get it. But he is not yet ready to join a
kolkhoz to get a living.

There are other changes whose consequences no one, at any rate not I,
can foresee. What is to become of the equality between the sexes in an
economy that both imposes the draft and pours the horn of plenty of veterans'
benefits solely on the male part of the population? What is to become of the
school system when its task changes from that of adjusting the young to a new
society to giving them intellectual tools to run it? What is to become of a
society that can afford leisure on an unprecedented scale and may have to
find uses for free men and citizens, deprived of their social utility by automa-
tion? No one knows and, final blessing, no one in America really thinks that
he knows. Free from ideological baggage, the hopeful American plunges
rather than strides forward. After all, said Cromwell, no man goes as far as
the man who does not know where he is going. The American may be going
to hell in a wheelbarrow or in a flying saucer. If he is, we'll all go with him.
But I suspect that, humanly speaking, heaven's his destination. He won't
quite get there, but he'll go far and fare better than if he doubted the general
wisdom of his course. When ex-President Jackson was being buried, a visitor
asked one of his slaves if he thought that General Jackson (like many soldier
Presidents, a belated convert to formal Christianity) would go to heaven.
"He will if he wants to." General Jackson was and is a symbol of the
American.

STUDY QUESTIONS

1. The degree to which the portrayal of such an abstraction as "the new American" is convincing will depend largely upon the skill with which the writer draws concrete details to the support of his generalizations. How skillful has Brogan been in this? Do you accept his generalizations about "the new American"? What concrete details can you think of that seem to contradict his generalizations? Do these make his portrayal an "inaccurate" one? How accurate can such portrayals be?

2. What is the great change in the acquisitive drive of Americans that Brogan sees as a future possibility? What signs does Brogan see which indicate that Americans are genuinely united?

3. What is the post-war development in America that seems particularly significant to Brogan?

4. What relation do you find between Brogan's observation that overt competition is taboo in America, and Ortega y Gasset's view that the mass man loves comfort and the feeling that he is the equal of everyone?

5. Can you give further examples of the increasing participation of Americans in mass organizations and enterprises, such as Federal housing and power, social security, and military service? Do you think that individuality is compromised by this sort of activity?

6. Write a paper describing some type or kind of person—the college Freshman, the science instructor, the small town store-owner—in which you draw a series of generalizations about the type and support them with carefully selected detail.

C. Wright Mills   White Collar People*

The white-collar people slipped quietly into modern society. Whatever history they have had is a history without events; whatever common interests they have do not lead to unity; whatever future they have will not be of their own making. If they aspire at all it is to a middle course, at a time when no middle course is available, and hence to an illusory course in an imaginary society. Internally, they are split, fragmented; externally, they are dependent on larger forces. Even if they gained the will to act, their actions, being unorganized, would be less a movement than a tangle of unconnected contests. As a group, they do not threaten anyone; as individuals, they do not practice an independent way of life. So before an adequate idea of them could be formed, they have been taken for granted as familiar actors of the urban mass.

Yet it is to this white-collar world that one must look for much that is

* From White Collar by C. Wright Mills. © 1951, by Oxford University Press, Inc. Reprinted by permission.

characteristic of twentieth-century existence. By their rise to numerical importance, the white-collar people have upset the nineteenth-century expectation that society would be divided between entrepreneurs and wage workers. By their mass way of life, they have transformed the tang and feel of the American experience. They carry, in a most revealing way, many of those psychological themes that characterize our epoch, and, in one way or another, every general theory of the main drift has had to take account of them. For above all else they are a new cast of actors, performing the major routines of twentieth-century society:

At the top of the white-collar world, the old captain of industry hands over his tasks to the manager of the corporation. Alongside the politician, with his string tie and ready tongue, the salaried bureaucrat, with brief case and slide rule, rises into political view. These top managers now command hierarchies of anonymous middle managers, floorwalkers, salaried foremen, county agents, federal inspectors, and police investigators trained in the law.

In the established professions, the doctor, lawyer, engineer, once was free and named on his own shingle; in the new white-collar world, the salaried specialists of the clinic, the junior partners in the law factory, the captive engineers of the corporation have begun to challenge free professional leadership. The old professions of medicine and law are still at the top of the professional world, but now all around them are men and women of new skills. There are a dozen kinds of social engineers and mechanical technicians, a multitude of girl Fridays, laboratory assistants, registered and unregistered nurses, draftsmen, statisticians, social workers.

In the salesrooms, which sometimes seem to coincide with the new society as a whole, are the stationary salesgirls in the department store, the mobile salesmen of insurance, the absentee salesmen — ad-men helping others sell from a distance. At the top are the prima donnas, the vice presidents who say that they are "merely salesmen, although perhaps a little more creative than others," and at the bottom, the five-and-dime clerks, selling commodities at a fixed price, hoping soon to leave the job for marriage.

In the enormous file of the office, in all the calculating rooms, accountants and purchasing agents replace the man who did his own figuring. And in the lower reaches of the white-collar world, office operatives grind along, loading and emptying the filing system; there are private secretaries and typists, entry clerks, billing clerks, corresponding clerks — a thousand kinds of clerks; the operators of light machinery, comptometers, dictaphones, addressographs; and the receptionists to let you in or keep you out.

The nineteenth-century farmer and businessman were generally thought to be stalwart individuals — their own men, men who could quickly grow to be almost as big as anyone else. The twentieth-century white-collar man has never been independent as the farmer used to be, nor as hopeful of the main chance as the businessman. He is always somebody's man, the corporation's, the government's, the army's; and he is seen as the man who does not rise.

The decline of the free entrepreneur and the rise of the dependent employee on the American scene has paralleled the decline of the independent individual and the rise of the little man in the American mind.

In a world crowded with big ugly forces, the white-collar man is readily assumed to possess all the supposed virtues of the small creature. He may be at the bottom of the social world, but he is, at the same time, gratifyingly middle class. It is easy as well as safe to sympathize with his troubles; he can do little or nothing about them. Other social actors threaten to become big and aggressive, to act out of selfish interests and deal in politics. The big businessman continues his big-business-as-usual through the normal rhythm of slump and war and boom; the big labor man, lifting his shaggy eyebrows, holds up the nation until his demands are met; the big farmer cultivates the Senate to see that big farmers get theirs. But not the white-collar man. He is more often pitiful than tragic, as he is seen collectively, fighting impersonal inflation, living out in slow misery his yearning for the quick American climb. He is pushed by forces beyond his control, pulled into movements he does not understand; he gets into situations in which his is the most helpless position. The white-collar man is the hero as victim, the small creature who is acted upon but who does not act, who works along unnoticed in somebody's office or store, never talking loud, never talking back, never taking a stand.

When the focus shifts from the generalized Little Man to specific white-collar types whom the public encounters, the images become diverse and often unsympathetic. Sympathy itself often carries a sharp patronizing edge; the word "clerk," for example, is likely to be preceded by "merely." Who talks willingly to the insurance agent, opens the door to the bill collector? "Everybody knows how rude and nasty salesgirls can be." Schoolteachers are standard subjects for businessmen's jokes. The housewife's opinion of private secretaries is not often friendly — indeed, much of white-collar fiction capitalizes on her hostility to "the office wife."

These are images of specific white-collar types seen from above. But from below, for two generations sons and daughters of the poor have looked forward eagerly to becoming even "mere" clerks. Parents have sacrificed to have even one child finish high school, business school, or college so that he could be the assistant to the executive, do the filing, type the letter, teach school, work in the government office, do something requiring technical skills: hold a white-collar job. In serious literature white-collar images are often subjects for lamentation; in popular writing they are often targets of aspiration.

Images of American types have not been built carefully by piecing together live experience. Here, as elsewhere, they have been made up out of tradition and schoolbook and the early, easy drift of the unalerted mind. And they have been reinforced and even created, especially in white-collar times, by the editorial machinery of popular amusement and mass communications.

Manipulations by professional image-makers are effective because their audiences do not or cannot know personally all the people they want to talk about or be like, and because they have an unconscious need to believe in certain types. In their need and inexperience, such audiences snatch and hold to the glimpses of types that are frozen into the language with which they see the world. Even when they meet the people behind the types face to face, previous images, linked deeply with feeling, blind them to what stands before them. Experience is trapped by false images, even as reality itself sometimes seems to imitate the soap opera and the publicity release.

Perhaps the most cherished national images are sentimental versions of historical types that no longer exist, if indeed they ever did. Underpinning many standard images of The American is the myth, in the words of the eminent historian, A. M. Schlesinger, Sr., of the "long tutelage to the soil" which, as "the chief formative influence," results in "courage, creative energy and resourcefulness. . . ." According to this idea, which clearly bears a nineteenth-century trademark, The American possesses magical independence, homely ingenuity, great capacity for work, all of which virtues he attained while struggling to subdue the vast continent.

One hundred years ago, when three-fourths of the people were farmers, there may have been some justification for engraving such an image and calling it The American. But since then, farmers have declined to scarcely more than one-tenth of the occupied populace, and new classes of salaried employees and wage-workers have risen. Deep-going historic changes resulting in wide diversities have long challenged the nationalistic historian who would cling to The American as a single type of ingenious farmer-artisan. In so far as universals can be found in life and character in America, they are due less to any common tutelage of the soil than to the leveling influences of urban civilization, and above all, to the standardization of the big technology and of the media of mass communication.

America is neither the nation of horse-traders and master builders of economic theory, nor the nation of go-getting, claim-jumping, cattle-rustling pioneers of frontier mythology. Nor have the traits rightly or wrongly associated with such historic types carried over into the contemporary population to any noticeable degree. Only a fraction of this population consists of free private enterprisers in any economic sense; there are now four times as many wage-workers and salary workers as independent entrepreneurs. "The struggle for life," William Dean Howells wrote in the 'nineties, "has changed from a free fight to an encounter of disciplined forces, and the free fighters that are left get ground to pieces. . . ."

If it is assumed that white-collar employees represent some sort of continuity with the old middle class of entrepreneurs, then it may be said that for the last hundred years the middle classes have been facing the slow expropriation of their holdings, and that for the last twenty years they have faced the spectre of unemployment. Both assertions rest on facts, but the facts have not been experienced by the middle class as a *double* crisis. The property question is not an issue to the new middle class of the present generation. That was fought out, and lost, before World War I, by the old middle class. The centralization of small properties is a development that has affected each generation back to our great-grandfathers, reaching its climax in the Progressive Era. It has been a secular trend of too slow a tempo to be felt as a continuing crisis by middle-class men and women, who often seem to have become more commodity-minded than property-minded. Yet history is not always enacted consciously; if expropriation is not felt as crisis, still it is a basic fact in the ways of life and the aspirations of the new middle class; and the facts of unemployment *are* felt as fears, hanging over the white-collar world.

By examining white-collar life, it is possible to learn something about what is becoming more typically "American" than the frontier character probably ever was. What must be grasped is the picture of society as a great salesroom, an enormous file, an incorporated brain, a new universe of management and manipulation. By understanding these diverse white-collar worlds, one can also understand better the shape and meaning of modern society as a whole, as well as the simple hopes and complex anxieties that grip all the people who are sweating it out in the middle of the twentieth century.

The troubles that confront the white-collar people are the troubles of all men and women living in the twentieth century. If these troubles seem particularly bitter to the new middle strata, perhaps that is because for a brief time these people felt themselves immune to troubles.

Before the First World War there were fewer little men, and in their brief monopoly of high-school education they were in fact protected from many of the sharper edges of the workings of capitalist progress. They were free to entertain deep illusions about their individual abilities and about the collective trustworthiness of the system. As their number has grown, however, they have become increasingly subject to wage-worker conditions. Especially since the Great Depression have white-collar people come up against all the old problems of capitalist society. They have been racked by slump and war and even by boom. They have learned about impersonal unemployment in depressions and about impersonal death by technological violence in war. And in good times, as prices rose faster than salaries, the money they thought they were making was silently taken away from them.

The material hardship of nineteenth-century industrial workers finds its parallel on the psychological level among twentieth-century white-collar employees. The new Little Man seems to have no firm roots, no sure loyalties to sustain his life and give it a center. He is not aware of having any history, his past being as brief as it is unheroic; he has lived through no golden age he can recall in time of trouble. Perhaps because he does not know where he is going, he is in a frantic hurry; perhaps because he does not know what frightens him, he is paralyzed with fear. This is especially a feature of his political life, where the paralysis results in the most profound apathy of modern times.

The uneasiness, the malaise of our time, is due to this root fact: in our politics and economy, in family life and religion — in practically every sphere of our existence — the certainties of the eighteenth and nineteenth centuries have disintegrated or been destroyed and, at the same time, no new sanctions or justifications for the new routines we live, and must live, have taken hold. So there is no acceptance and there is no rejection, no sweeping hope and no sweeping rebellion. There is no plan of life. Among white-collar people, the malaise is deep-rooted; for the absence of any order of belief has left them morally defenseless as individuals and politically impotent as a group. Newly created in a harsh time of creation, white-collar man has no culture to lean upon except the contents of a mass society that has shaped him and seeks to manipulate him to its alien ends. For security's sake, he must strain to attach himself somewhere, but no communities or organizations seem to be thoroughly his. This isolated position makes him excellent material for synthetic molding at the hands of popular culture — print, film, radio, and television. As a metropolitan dweller, he is especially open to the focused onslaught of all the manufactured loyalties and distractions that are contrived and urgently pressed upon those who live in worlds they never made.

In the case of the white-collar man, the alienation of the wage-worker from the products of his work is carried one step nearer to its Kafka-like completion. The salaried employee does not make anything, although he may handle much that he greatly desires but cannot have. No product of craftsmanship can be his to contemplate with pleasure as it is being created and after it is made. Being alienated from any product of his labor, and going year after year through the same paper routine, he turns his leisure all the more frenziedly to the *ersatz* diversion that is sold him, and partakes of the synthetic excitement that neither eases nor releases. He is bored at work and restless at play, and this terrible alternation wears him out.

In his work he often clashes with customer and superior, and must almost always be the standardized loser: he must smile and be personable, standing behind the counter, or waiting in the outer office. In many strata of white-collar employment, such traits as courtesy, helpfulness, and kindness, once intimate, are now part of the impersonal means of livelihood. Self-alienation is thus an accompaniment of his alienated labor.

When white-collar people get jobs, they sell not only their time and energy but their personalities as well. They sell by the week or month their smiles and their kindly gestures, and they must practice the prompt repression of resentment and aggression. For these intimate traits are of commercial relevance and required for the more efficient and profitable distribution, of goods and services. Here are the new little Machiavellians, practicing their personal crafts for hire and for the profit of others, according to rules laid down by those above them.

In the eighteenth and nineteenth centuries, rationality was identified with freedom. The ideas of Freud about the individual, and of Marx about society, were strengthened by the assumption of the coincidence of freedom and rationality. Now rationality seems to have taken on a new form, to have its seat not in individual men, but in social institutions which by their bureaucratic planning and mathematical foresight usurp both freedom and rationality from the little individual men caught in them. The calculating hierarchies of department store and industrial corporation, of rationalized office and governmental bureau, lay out the gray ways of work and stereotype the permitted initiatives. And in all this bureaucratic usurpation of freedom and of rationality, the white-collar people are the interchangeable parts of the big chains of authority that bind the society together.

White-collar people, always visible but rarely seen, are politically voiceless. Stray politicians wandering in the political arena without party may put "white collar" people alongside businessmen, farmers, and wage-workers in their broadside appeals, but no platform of either major party has yet referred to them directly. Who fears the clerk? Neither *Alice Adams* nor *Kitty Foyle* could be a *Grapes of Wrath* for the "share-croppers in the dust bowl of business."

But while practical politicians, still living in the ideological air of the nineteenth century, have paid little attention to the new middle class, theoreticians of the left have vigorously claimed the salaried employee as a potential proletarian, and theoreticians of the right and center have hailed him as a sign of the continuing bulk and vigor of the middle class. Stray heretics from both camps have even thought, from time to time, that the higher-ups of the white-collar world might form a center of initiative for new political beginnings. In Germany, the "black-coated worker" was one of the harps that Hitler played on his way to power. In England, the party of labor is thought to have won electoral socialism by capturing the votes of the suburban salaried workers.

To the question, what political direction will the white-collar people take, there are as many answers as there are theorists. Yet to the observer of American materials, the political problem posed by these people is not so much what the direction may be as whether they will take any political direction at all.

Between the little man's consciousness and the issues of our epoch there seems to be a veil of indifference. His will seems numbed, his spirit meager. Other men of other strata are also politically indifferent, but electoral victories are imputed to them; they do have tireless pressure groups and excited captains who work in and around the hubs of power, to whom, it may be imagined, they have delegated their enthusiasms for public affairs. But white-collar people are scattered along the rims of all the wheels of power; no one is enthusiastic about them and, like political eunuchs, they themselves are without potency and without enthusiasm for the urgent political clash.

Estranged from community and society in a context of distrust and manipulation; alienated from work and, on the personality market, from self;

expropriated of individual rationality, and politically apathetic—these are the new little people, the unwilling vanguard of modern society. These are some of the circumstances for the acceptance of which their hopeful training has quite unprepared them.

STUDY QUESTIONS

1. *What historical developments (some of them not mentioned here by Mills) produced the large class of white collar workers? Why is the white-collar worker at a disadvantage in the social and economic arena?*

2. *Is the white-collar worker more like an entrepreneur or a factory worker? How useful are appearances in deciding this question?*

3. *What does Mills feel to be the main cause of the unfortunate position of the white-collar class as opposed to other classes?*

4. *Compare Mills' analysis of "white collar people" in this selection with Brogan's analysis of the "new American." To what extent do they contradict each other? Agree with each other? Is one more "objective" or "accurate" than the other? To what extent are all authors writing on such subjects controlling and shaping reality in the fashion which Steinbeck describes in "Observation and Writing"?*

5. *Do you think Mills' picture of the life of the white-collar worker is unduly pessimistic? If so, write a theme telling the other side, and showing how he is better off than workers at other times or in other classes?*

6. *In what ways are white-collar people characteristic of their time, and representative of the "psychological themes" of our age?*

H. L. Mencken   American Culture*

The capital defect in the culture of These States is the lack of a civilized aristocracy, secure in its position, animated by an intelligent curiosity, skeptical of all facile generalizations, superior to the sentimentality of the mob, and delighting in the battle of ideas for its own sake. The word I use, despite the qualifying adjective, has got itself meanings, of course, that I by no means intend to convey. Any mention of an aristocracy, to a public fed upon democratic fustian, is bound to bring up images of stockbrokers' wives lolling obscenely in opera boxes, or of haughty Englishmen slaughtering whole generations of grouse in an inordinate and incomprehensible manner, or of bogus counts coming over to work their magic upon the daughters of breakfast-food and bathtub kings. This misconception belongs to the general American tradition. Its depth and extent are constantly revealed by the naïve assumption that the so-called fashionable folk of the large cities—chiefly

* From *A Mencken Chrestomathy* by H. L. Mencken, by permission of Alfred A. Knopf, Inc. Copyright, 1920, 1949, by Alfred A. Knopf, Inc.

wealthy industrials in the interior-decorator and country-club stage of culture — constitute an aristocracy, and by the scarcely less remarkable assumption that the peerage of England is identical with the gentry — that is, that such men as Lord Northcliffe, Lord Riddel and even Lord Reading were English gentlemen.

Here, as always, the worshiper is the father of the gods, and no less when they are evil than when they are benign. The inferior man must find himself superiors, that he may marvel at his political equality with them, and in the absence of recognizable superiors *de facto* he creates superiors *de jure*. The sublime principle of one man, one vote must be translated into terms of dollars, diamonds, fashionable intelligence; the equality of all men before the law must have clear and dramatic proofs. Sometimes, perhaps, the thing goes further and is more subtle. The inferior man needs an aristocracy to demonstrate, not only his mere equality, but also his actual superiority. The society columns in the newspapers may have some such origin. They may visualize once more the accomplished journalist's understanding of the mob mind that he plays upon so skillfully, as upon some immense and cacophonous organ, always going *fortissimo*. What the inferior man and his wife see in the sinister revels of those brummagem first families, I suspect, is often a massive witness to their own higher rectitude — in brief, to their firmer grasp upon the immutable axioms of Christian virtue, the one sound boast of the nether nine-tenths of humanity in every land under the cross.

But this bugaboo aristocracy is actually bogus, and the evidence of its bogusness lies in the fact that it is insecure. One gets into it only onerously, but out of it very easily. Entrance is effected by dint of a long and bitter struggle, and the chief incidents of that struggle are almost intolerable humiliations. The aspirant must school and steel himself to sniffs and sneers; he must see the door slammed upon him a hundred times before ever it is thrown open to him. To get in at all he must show a talent for abasement — and abasement makes him timorous. Worse, that timorousness is not cured when he succeeds at last. On the contrary, it is made even more tremulous, for what he faces within the gates is a scheme of things made up almost wholly of harsh and often unintelligible taboos, and the penalty for violating even the least of them is swift and disastrous. He must exhibit exactly the right social habits, appetites and prejudices, public and private. He must harbor exactly the right enthusiasms and indignations. He must have a hearty taste for exactly the right sports and games. His attitude toward the fine arts must be properly tolerant and yet not a shade too eager. He must read and like exactly the right books, pamphlets and public journals. He must put up at the right hotels when he travels. His wife must patronize the right milliners. He himself must stick to the right haberdashery. He must live in the right neighborhood. He must even embrace the right doctrines of religion. It would ruin him, for all society column purposes, to move to Union Hill, N. J., or to drink coffee from his saucer, or to marry a chambermaid with a gold tooth, or to join the Seventh Day Adventists. Within the boundaries of his curious order he is worse fettered than a monk in a cell. Its obscure conception of propriety, its nebulous notion that this or that is honorable, hampers him in every direction, and very narrowly. What he resigns when he enters, even when he makes his first deprecating knock at the door, is every right to attack the ideas that happen to prevail within. Such as they are, he must accept them without question. And as they shift and change he must shift and change with them, silently and quickly.

Obviously, that order cannot constitute a genuine aristocracy, in any rational sense. A genuine aristocracy is grounded upon very much different principles. Its first and most salient character is its interior security, and the chief visible evidence of that security is the freedom that goes with it — not only freedom in act, the divine right of the aristocrat to do what he damn well pleases, so long as he does not violate the primary guarantees and obligations of his class, but also and more importantly freedom in thought, the liberty to try and err, the right to be his own man. It is the instinct of a true aristocracy, not to punish eccentricity by expulsion, but to throw a mantle of protection about it — to safeguard it from the suspicions and resentments of the lower orders. Those lower orders are inert, timid, inhospitable to ideas, hostile to changes, faithful to a few maudlin superstitions. All progress goes on on the higher levels. It is there that salient personalities, made secure by artificial immunities, may oscillate most widely from the normal track. It is within that entrenched fold, out of reach of the immemorial certainties of the mob, that extraordinary men of the lower orders may find their city of refuge, and breathe a clear air. This, indeed, is at once the hall-mark and the justification of a genuine aristocracy — that it is beyond responsibility to the general masses of men, and hence superior to both their degraded longings and their no less degraded aversions. It is nothing if it is not autonomous, curious, venturesome, courageous, and everything if it is. It is the custodian of the qualities that make for change and experiment; it is the class that organizes danger to the service of the race; it pays for its high prerogatives by standing in the forefront of the fray.

No such aristocracy, it must be plain, is now on view in the United States. The makings of one were visible in the Virginia of the Eighteenth Century, but with Jefferson and Washington the promise died. In New England, it seems to me, there was never anything of the sort, either in being or in nascency: there was only a theocracy that degenerated very quickly into a plutocracy on the one hand and a caste of sterile pedants on the other — the passion for God splitting into a lust for dollars and a weakness for mere words. Despite the common notion to the contrary — a notion generated by confusing literacy with intelligence — the New England of the great days never showed any genuine enthusiasm for ideas. It began its history as a slaughterhouse of ideas, and it is today not easily distinguishable from a cold-storage plant. Its celebrated adventures in mysticism, once apparently so bold and significant, are now seen to have been little more than an elaborate hocus-pocus — respectable Unitarians shocking the peasantry and scaring the horned cattle in the fields by masquerading in the robes of Rosicrucians. The notions that it embraced in those austere and far-off days were stale, and when it had finished with them they were dead. So in politics. Since the Civil War it has produced fewer political ideas, as political ideas run in the Republic, than any average county in Kansas or Nebraska. Appomattox seemed to be a victory for New England idealism. It was actually a victory for the New England plutocracy, and that plutocracy has dominated thought above the Housatonic ever since. The sect of professional idealists has so far dwindled that it has ceased to be of any importance, even as an opposition. When the plutocracy is challenged now, it is challenged by the proletariat.

Well, what is on view in New England is on view in all other parts of the nation, sometimes with ameliorations, but usually with the colors merely exaggerated. What one beholds, sweeping the eye over the land, is a culture that, like the national literature, is in three layers — the plutocracy on top, a vast mass of undifferentiated human blanks bossed by demagogues at the bottom, and a forlorn *intelligentsia* gasping out a precarious life between. I need not set out at any length, I hope, the intellectual deficiencies of the plutocracy — its utter failure to show anything even remotely resembling the makings of an aristocracy. It is badly educated, it is stupid, it is full of low-caste superstitions and indignations, it is without decent traditions or informing vision; above all, it is extraordinarily lacking in the most elemental independence and courage. Out of this class comes the grotesque fashionable society of our big towns, already described. It shows all the stigmata of inferiority — moral certainty, cruelty, suspicion of ideas, fear. Never does it function more revealingly than in the recurrent *pogroms* against radicalism, *i.e.*, against humorless persons who, like Andrew Jackson, take the platitudes of democracy seriously. And what is the theory at the bottom of all these proceedings? So far as it can be reduced to comprehensible terms it is much less a theory than a fear — a shivering, idiotic, discreditable fear of a mere banshee — an overpowering, paralyzing dread that some extra-eloquent Red, permitted to emit his balderdash unwhipped, may eventually convert a couple of courageous men, and that the courageous men, filled with indignation against the plutocracy, may take to the highroad, burn down a nail-factory or two, and slit the throat of some virtuous profiteer.

Obviously, it is out of reason to look for any hospitality to ideas in a class so extravagantly fearful of even the most palpably absurd of them. Its philosophy is firmly grounded upon the thesis that the existing order must stand forever free from attack, and not only from attack, but also from mere academic criticism, and its ethics are as firmly grounded upon the thesis that every attempt at any such criticism is a proof of moral turpitude. Within its own ranks, protected by what may be regarded as the privilege of the order, there is nothing to take the place of this criticism. In other countries the plutocracy has often produced men of reflective and analytical habit, eager to rationalize its instincts and to bring it into some sort of relationship to the main streams of human thought. The case of David Ricardo at once comes to mind, and there have been many others: John Bright, Richard Cobden, George Grote. But in the United States no such phenomenon has been visible. Nor has the plutocracy ever fostered an inquiring spirit among its intellectual valets and footmen, which is to say, among the gentlemen who compose headlines and leading articles for its newspapers. What chiefly distinguishes the daily press of the United States from the press of all other countries pretending to culture is not its lack of truthfulness or even its lack of dignity and honor, for these deficiencies are common to newspapers every-where, but its incurable fear of ideas, its constant effort to evade the discus-sion of fundamentals by translating all issues into a few elemental fears, its incessant reduction of all reflection to mere emotion. It is, in the true sense, never well-informed. It is seldom intelligent, save in the arts of the mob-master. It is never courageously honest. Held harshly to a rigid correctness of opinion, it sinks rapidly into formalism and feebleness. Its yellow section is perhaps its best section, for there the only vestige of the old free journalist survives. In the more respectable papers one finds only a timid and petulant animosity to all questioning of the existing order, however urbane and sincere — a pervasive and ill-concealed dread that the mob now heated up against the orthodox hobgoblins may suddenly begin to unearth hobgoblins of its own, and so run amok.

For it is upon the emotions of the mob, of course, that the whole comedy is played. Theoretically, the mob is the repository of all political wisdom and virtue; actually, it is the ultimate source of all political power. Even the plutocracy cannot make war upon it openly, or forget the least of its weak-nesses. The business of keeping it in order must be done discreetly, warily, with delicate technique. In the main that business consists in keeping alive its deep-seated fears — of strange faces, of unfamiliar ideas, of unhackneyed gestures, of untested liberties and responsibilities. The one permanent emo-tion of the inferior man, as of all the simpler mammals, is fear — fear of the unknown, the complex, the inexplicable. What he wants beyond everything else is security. His instincts incline him toward a society so organized that it will protect him at all hazards, and not only against perils to his hide but also against assaults upon his mind — against the need to grapple with un-accustomed problems, to weigh ideas, to think things out for himself, to scrutinize the platitudes upon which his everyday thinking is based.

STUDY QUESTIONS

1. *Why, according to Mencken, does not the class that is the subject of newspaper society columns constitute a genuine aristocracy? What standards does Mencken set for a genuine aristocracy?*

2. *What is the basis of Mencken's criticism of the press? Do you think his criticism is valid? Explain your reasons.*

3. *Compare Mencken's vocabulary and his general approach to his subject with those of Brogan and Mills. Are there significant differences? If so what are they?*

4. *To what extent does Mencken agree with Rossiter?*

5. *This essay of Mencken's was written in 1920. How well does it apply to the contemporary scene? Give some current examples of the conditions described here, or, if you feel that America has changed considerably since 1920, explain the differences.*

6. *Do you agree with Mencken that the lack of an aristocracy is a serious deficiency?*

David Riesman   Americans and Kwakiutls*

Moralists are constantly complaining that the ruling vice of the present time is pride. This is true in one sense, for indeed everybody thinks that he is better than his neighbor or refuses to obey his superior; but it is extremely false in another, for the same man who cannot endure subordination or equality has so contemptible an opinion of himself that he thinks he is born only to indulge in vulgar pleasures. He willingly takes up with low desires without daring to embark on lofty enterprises, of which he scarcely dreams.

Thus, far from thinking that humility ought to be preached to our contemporaries, I would have endeavors made to give them a more enlarged idea of themselves and of their kind. Humility is unwholesome to them; what they most want is, in my opinion, pride.

Tocqueville, Democracy in America

Ruth Benedict's book, *Patterns of Culture*, describes in vivid detail three primitive societies: the Pueblo (Zuñi) Indians of the southwest, the people of the Island of Dobu in the Pacific, and the Kwakiutl Indians of the northwest coast of America.[1]

The Pueblo Indians are pictured as a peaceable, cooperative society, in which no one wishes to be thought a great man and everyone wishes to be thought a good fellow. Sexual relations evoke little jealousy or other violent response; infidelity is not severely punished. Death, too, is taken in stride, with little violent emotion; in general, emotion is subdued. While there are considerable variations in economic status, there is little display of economic power and even less of political power; there is a spirit of cooperation with family and community.

The Dobu, by contrast, are portrayed as virtually a society of paranoids in

---

* From *The Lonely Crowd, A Study of the Changing American Character* by David Riesman, with Nathan Glazer and Reuel Denny. Reprinted by permission of Yale University Press. Copyright, 1950, 1953, by Yale University Press.

[1] *Patterns of Culture* (Boston, Houghton Mifflin, 1934; reprinted New York, Pelican Books, 1946).

which each man's hand is against his neighbor's in sorcery, theft, and abuse; in which husband and wife alternate as captives of the spouse's kin; and in which infidelity is deeply resented. Dobuan economic life is built on sharp practice in inter-island trading, on an intense feeling for property rights, and on a hope of getting something for nothing through theft, magic, and fraud.

The third society, the Kwakiutl, is also intensely rivalrous. But the rivalry consists primarily in conspicuous consumption, typified by feasts called "potlatches," at which chiefs outdo each other in providing food and in burning up the blankets and sheets of copper which are the main counters of wealth in the society; sometimes even a house or a canoe is sent up in flames in a final bid for glory. Indeed, the society is a caricature of Veblen's conspicuous consumption; certainly, the potlatches of the Kwakiutl chiefs serve "as the legitimate channel by which the community's surplus product has been drained off and consumed, to the greater spiritual comfort of all parties concerned." Veblen was, in fact, familiar with these northwest-coast "coming-out parties."

I have asked students who have read Ruth Benedict's book which of these three cultures in their opinion most closely resembles the obviously more complex culture of the United States. The great majority see Americans as Kwakiutls. They emphasize American business rivalry, sex and status jealousy, and power drive. They see Americans as individualists, primarily interested in the display of wealth and station.

A minority of students, usually the more politically radical, say that America is more like Dobu. They emphasize the sharp practice of American business life, point to great jealousy and bitterness in family relations, and see American politics, domestic and international, as hardly less aggressive than Hobbes's state of nature.

No students I have talked with have argued that there are significant resemblances between the culture of the Hopi and Zuñi Pueblos and American culture — they wish that there were.

Yet when we turn then to examine the culture patterns of these very students, we see little evidence either of Dobu or Kwakiutl ways. The wealthy students go to great lengths not to be conspicuous — things are very different from the coon-coated days of the 20's. The proper uniform is one of purposeful shabbiness. In fact, none among the students except a very rare Lucullus dares to be thought uppity. Just as no modern Vanderbilt says "the public be damned," so no modern parent would say: "Where Vanderbilt sits, there is the head of the table. I teach my son to be rich."[2]

It is, moreover, not only in the virtual disappearance of conspicuous consumption that the students have abandoned Kwakiutl-like modes of life. Other displays of gifts, native or acquired, have also become more subdued. A leading college swimming star told me: "I get sore at the guys I'm competing against. Something's wrong with me. I wish I could be like X who

---

[2] The remark is quoted by Justice Oliver Wendell Holmes, Jr., in "The Soldier's Faith," 1895, reprinted in *Speeches* (Boston, Little, Brown, 1934), p. 56.

really cooperates with the other fellows. He doesn't care so much about winning."

There seems to be a discrepancy between the America that students make for themselves as students and the America they think they will move into when they leave the campus. Their image of the latter is based to a large extent on legends about America that are preserved in our literature. For example, many of our novelists and critics still believe that America, as compared with other cultures, is a materialistic nation of would-be Kwakiutl chiefs. There may have been some truth in this picture in the Gilded Age, though Henry James saw how ambiguous the issue of "materialism" was between America and Europe even then.

The materialism of these older cultures has been hidden by their status systems and by the fact that they had inherited many values from the era dependent on tradition-direction. The European masses simply have not had the money and leisure, until recent years, to duplicate American consumer-ship patterns; when they do, they are, if anything, sometimes more vulgar, more materialistic.

The Europeans, nevertheless, have been only too glad to tell Americans that they were materialistic; and the Americans, feeling themselves *nouveaux riches* during the last century, paid to be told. They still pay: it is not only my students who fail to see that it is the turn of the rest of the world to be *nouveaux riches*, to be excited over the gadgets of an industrial age, while millions of Americans have turned away in boredom from attaching much emotional significance to the consumer-goods frontier.[3]

When, however, I try to point these things out to students who compare Americans with Kwakiutls, they answer that the advertisements show how much emotion is attached to goods consumption. But, when I ask them if they believe the ads themselves, they say scornfully that they do not. And when I ask if they know people who do, they find it hard to give examples, at least in the middle class. (If the advertisements powerfully affected people in the impoverished lower class who had small hope of mobility, there would surely be a revolution!) Yet the advertisements must be reaching somebody, the students insist. Why, I ask, why isn't it possible that advertising as a whole is a fantastic fraud, presenting an image of America taken seriously by no one, least of all by the advertising men who create it? Just as the mass media persuade people that other people think politics is important, so they persuade people that everyone else cannot wait for his new refrigerator or car or suit of clothes. In neither case can people believe that "the others" are as apathetic as they feel themselves to be. And, while their indifference to politics may make people feel on the defensive, their indifference to advertising may allow them to feel superior. In fact, I think that a study of American advertising during the last quarter century would show that the advertising men themselves at least implicitly realize the consumer's loss of

[3] Mary McCarthy's fine article, "America the Beautiful," *Commentary*, IV (1947), 201 takes much the same attitude as the text.

emotional enthusiasm. Where once car and refrigerator advertisements showed the housewife or husband exulting in the new possessions, today it is often only children in the ads who exult over the new Nash their father has just bought. In many contemporary ads the possession itself recedes into the background or is handled abstractly, surrealistically; it no longer throws off sparks or exclamation points; copy itself has become subtler or more matter of fact.

Of course many old-fashioned enthusiasts of consumption remain in America who have not yet been affected by the spread of other-directed consumer sophistication and repression of emotional response. A wonderful example is the small-town Irish mother in the movie, A Letter to Three Wives, whose greatest pride and joy in her dingy railroadside home is the big, shiny, new, not yet paid-for refrigerator. And it may be argued that even middle-class Americans have only covered over their materialism with a veneer of "good taste," without altering their fundamental drives. Nevertheless, the other-directed person, oriented as he is toward people, is simply unable to be as materialistic as many inner-directed people were. For genuine inner-directed materialism — real acquisitive attachment to things — one must go to the Dutch bourgeois or French peasant or others for whom older ways endure.

It is the other-directedness of Americans that has prevented their realizing this; between the advertisers on the one hand and the novelists and intellectuals on the other, they have assumed that other Americans were materialistic, while not giving sufficient credence to their own feelings. Indeed, the paradoxical situation in a stratum which is other-oriented is that people constantly make grave misjudgments as to what others, at least those with whom they are not in peer-group contact, but often also those with whom they spend much time, feel and think.

To be sure, the businessmen themselves often try to act as if it were still possible to be a Kwakiutl chief in the United States. When they write articles or make speeches, they like to talk about free enterprise, about tough competition, about risk-taking. These businessmen, of course, are like World War I Legionnaires, talking about the glorious days of yore. Students and many others believe what the businessmen say on these occasions, but then have little opportunity to watch what they do. Perhaps the businessmen themselves are as much the victims of their own chants and rituals as the Kwakiutls.

Those few students who urge that America resembles Dobu can find little in student life to sustain their view, except perhaps a bit of cheating in love or on examinations. It is rather that they see the "capitalistic system" as a jungle of sharp practice, as if nothing had changed since the days of Mark Twain, Jack London, and Frank Norris. America is to them a land of lynchings, gangsterism, and deception by little foxes and big foxes. Yet, today, only small businessmen (car dealers or furnace repairmen, for instance) have many opportunities for the "wabu-wabu" trading, that is, the sharply manipulative property-pyramiding of the Dobuan canoeists.

If, however, these students turn to social science for their images of power in America, they will very frequently find their own view supported. The scattered remarks on the United States in *Patterns of Culture* are themselves an illustration. My students also read Robert Lynd's chapter on "The Pattern of American Culture" in *Knowledge for What?*[4] While noting contradictory exhortations to amity and brotherhood, Lynd emphasizes business as highly individualistic and politically ruthless; elsewhere he stresses the masterful ambition and conspicuous consumption typified by the older generation of the "X family" of Middletown. Ironically, the outlook of these and other sociological critics of business is confirmed and reflected by those neoclassical economists who construct models for the rational conduct of the firm — wittingly or unwittingly presenting businessmen as dismally "economic men."

Partly as a result of this image of the businessman, many students at privately endowed universities have become reluctant to consider business careers, and, as more and more young people are drawn into the colleges, these attitudes become increasingly widespread. The abler ones want something "higher" and look down their noses at the boys at Wharton or even at the Harvard Business School. Business is thought to be dull and disagreeable as well as morally suspect, and the genuine moral problem involved in career choice — namely, how best to develop one's potentialities for a full existence — is obfuscated by the false, over-dramatized choice of making money (and losing one's soul) in business versus penury (and saving one's soul) in government service or teaching. The notion that business today, especially big business, presents challenging intellectual problems and opportunities and is no more noticeably engaged in Dobuan sharp practice and Kwakiutl rivalry than any other career, seems not to exist even in the minds of students whose fathers are (perhaps woefully inarticulate) businessmen.

It is likely, then, that the students' image of business, and of American life generally, will have some self-confirming effects. Business will be forced to recruit from the less gifted and sensitive, who will not be able to take advantage of the opportunities for personal development business could offer and who, therefore, will not become models for younger men. Moreover, people who expect to meet hostility and calculation in others will justify an anticipatory hostility and calculation in themselves.

To be sure, there are plenty of unlovely, vicious, and mean Americans, in and out of business life; plenty of frightening southern mobs, northern hoodlums, dead-end kids with and without tuxedoes. There are many cultural islands in the United States where Dobu ways abound, just as there are survivals of late nineteenth-century Kwakiutl patterns. But these islands and survivals do not make a system of power, nor are they linked by any conspiracy, fascist or otherwise.

Now, of course, to show that Americans are neither like Kwakiutls nor

[4] Robert S. Lynd, *Knowledge for What?* (Princeton, Princeton University Press, 1939), pp. 54-113.

Dobuans does not prove they are like Zuñi and Hopi Indians. Obviously, in any case, the comparisons must be very rough; from the standpoint of my character types all three tribes, as long as they are in the phase of high population growth potential, would be more or less dependent on tradition-direction. My purpose is to present a parable, not a description. There is evidence, though it is perhaps somewhat understressed by Ruth Benedict, that the Pueblo Indians are actually not so bland and amiable as they seem, that they are, to a degree, antagonistic cooperators, with a good deal of repressed hostility and envy that crops up in dreams and malicious gossip. But this only strengthens the analogy with the middle-class Americans, whose other-directed cooperativeness is also not completely mild but contains repressed antagonistic elements.

Indeed the whole emotional tone of life in the Pueblos reminds me strongly of the American peer-group, with its insulting "You think you're big." While the Kwakiutls pride themselves on their passions that lead them to commit murder, arson, and suicide, the Pueblos frown on any violent emotion.

Ruth Benedict writes:

A good man has . . . "a pleasing address, a yielding disposition, and a generous heart." . . . He should "talk lots, as they say — that is, he should always set people at their ease — and he should without fail co-operate easily with others either in the field or in ritual, never betraying a suspicion of arrogance or a strong emotion."

The quotation brings to mind one of the most striking patterns from our interviews with young people. When we ask them their best trait they are hard pressed for an answer, though they sometimes mention an ability to "get along well with everybody." When we ask them, "What is your worst trait?" the most frequent single answer is "temper." And when we go on to ask, "Is your temper, then, so bad?" it usually turns out that the interviewee has not got much of a temper. If we ask whether his temper has gotten him into much trouble, he can cite little evidence that it has. What may these answers — of course no proper sample — mean? My impression is that temper is considered the worst trait in the society of the glad hand. It is felt as an internal menace to one's cooperative attitude. Moreover, the peer-group regards rage and temper as faintly ridiculous: one must be able to take it with a smile or be charged with something even worse than temper, something no one will accuse himself of even in an interview — a lack of a sense of humor. The inner-directed man may also worry about temper, for instance, if he is religious, but his conscience-stricken inhibitions and reaction-formations leave the emotion still alive, volcano-like, within him — often ready to erupt in political indignation — whereas the other-directed man allows or compels his emotions to heal, though not without leaving scars, in an atmosphere of enforced good fellowship and tolerance.

Many young people today also set themselves an ideal in their sex lives not too different from the Zuñi norm. They feel they ought to take sex with little interpersonal emotion and certainly without jealousy. The word of the wise

to the young — "Don't get involved" — has changed its meaning in a generation. Once it meant: don't get, or get someone, pregnant; don't run afoul of
the law; don't get in the newspapers. Today the injunction seeks to control
the personal experiencing of emotion that might disrupt the camaraderie of
the peer-group.

The chief worry of the Pueblo Indians is directed not to each other's
behavior but to the weather, and their religious ceremonies are primarily
directed toward rain-making. To quiet their anxiety the Indians go through
rituals that must be letter perfect. American young people have no such
single ritual to assure personal or tribal success. However, one can see a
similarity in the tendency to create rituals of a sort in all spheres of life.
People make a ritual out of going to school, out of work, out of having fun,
out of political participation as inside-dopesters or as indignants, as well as out
of countless private compulsions. But the rituals, whether private or public,
have usually to be rationalized as necessary; and since this is not self-evident
and since the sign of success is not so explicit as a downpour of rain, the
American young people can hardly get as much comfort from their rituals as
the Pueblo Indians do from theirs.

The young people who express the views I have described have begun to
pass out of the adolescent peer-groups; they have not yet taken their places
in the adult patterning of American life. What will be the effect of the
discrepancy between their picture of the United States as a place led by
Kwakiutl chiefs, leading Kwakiutl-style followers, and the reality of their
progress along the "Hopi Way"? Will they seek to bring about changes,
through social and political action, that will make America more comfortable
for the tolerant, other-directed types? Or will they seek to adopt more ruthless, Kwakiutl-like behavior as supposedly more compatible with real life?
Or, perchance, will they admit that they, too, are Americans, after all not so
unique, which might require a revision of their images of power, their images
of what Americans in general are like?

Doubtless, all these things can occur, and many more. But there is perhaps
one additional factor which will shape both changing ideology and changing
character. The students, aware of their own repressed competitiveness and
envy, think that others may try to do to them what they themselves would not
dare to do to others. The society *feels* to them like Kwakiutl or even Dobu,
not only because that is the ideology about America they have learned but
also because their own cooperativeness is tinged with an antagonism they have
not yet completely silenced. And perhaps this gives us an answer to a puzzle
about other-directed tolerance: why, if the other-directed person is tolerant, is
he himself so afraid of getting out of line? Can he not depend on the tolerance
of others? It may be that he feels his own tolerance precarious, his dreadful
temper ready to let fly when given permission; if he feels so irritable himself,
no matter how mild his behavior, he must fear the others, no matter how
amiable they, too, may appear.

These students would prefer to live in the Pueblo culture, if they had to choose among the three described by Ruth Benedict. And, while this choice is in itself not to be quarreled with, the important fact is that they do not know that they already are living in such a culture. They want social security, not great achievements. They want approval, not fame. They are not eager to develop talents that might bring them into conflict, whereas the inner-directed young person tended to push himself to the limit of his talents and beyond. Few of them suffer, like youth in the earlier age, because they are "twenty, and so little accomplished." Whereas the inner-directed middle-class boy often had to learn after twenty to adjust, to surrender his adolescent dreams and accept a burgher's modest lot, the other-directed boy never had such dreams. Learning to conform to the group almost as soon as he learns anything, he does not face, at adolescence, the need to choose between his family's world and that of his own generation or between his dreams and a world he never made.

Since, moreover, his adjustment to this group reality begins earlier, it becomes more a matter of conforming character and less a matter of conforming behavior. The popular song, "I don't want to set the world on fire," expresses a typical theme. The Kwakiutl wanted to do just that, literally to set the world on fire. The other-directed person prefers "love" to "glory." As Tocqueville saw, or foresaw: "He willingly takes up with low desires without daring to embark on lofty enterprises, of which he scarcely dreams."

There is a connection between the feeling these students and other young people have about their own fates and the contemporary notions of who runs the country. We have seen that the students feel themselves to be powerless, safe only when performing a ritual in approving company. Though they may seek to preserve emotional independence by not getting involved, this requirement is itself a peer-group mandate. How, then, as they look about them in America, do they explain their powerlessness? Somebody must have what they have not got: their powerlessness must be matched by power somewhere else. They see America as composed of Kwakiutls, not only because of their own residual and repressed Kwakiutl tendencies but even more because of their coerced cooperativeness. Some big chiefs must be doing this to them, they feel. They do not see that, to a great extent, it is they themselves who are doing it, through their own character.

The chiefs have lost the power, but the followers have not gained it. The savage believes that he will secure more power by drinking the blood or shrinking the head of his enemy. But the other-directed person, far from gaining, only becomes weaker from the weakness of his fellows.

STUDY QUESTIONS

1. *How does the author explain the fact that the America the students criticized apparently does not exist?*
2. *Is any strong evidence offered to show that Americans are not as consumption-minded as they believe themselves to be?*

3. *Did the students think of themselves as generally like or generally unlike everyone else? Does this tend to support or contradict Riesman's conclusion?*

4. *What attitude toward power did the students take? Is it a simple or a complicated one?*

5. *To what extent do the attitudes and feelings described seem to you to be authentic? Write a theme examining Riesman's generalizations in the light of your knowledge of actual students and their opinions.*

6. *Write a theme describing the prevalent attitude among a group you know well on some fundamental question such as wealth, sex, honesty, dating, parental control, or family life.*

2. DEMOCRACY AND LIBERTY

Carl L. Becker   The Ideal Democracy*

$\mathcal{D}$emocracy, like liberty or science or progress, is a word with which we are all so familiar that we rarely take the trouble to ask what we mean by it. It is a term, as the devotees of semantics say, which has no "referent" — there is no precise or palpable thing or object which we all think of when the word is pronounced. On the contrary, it is a word which connotes different things to different people, a kind of conceptual Gladstone bag which, with a little manipulation, can be made to accommodate almost any collection of social facts we may wish to carry about in it. In it we can as easily pack a dictatorship as any other form of government. We have only to stretch the concept to include any form of government supported by a majority of the people, for whatever reasons and by whatever means of expressing assent, and before we know it the empire of Napoleon, the Soviet regime of Stalin, and the Fascist systems of Mussolini and Hitler are all safely in the bag. But if this is what we mean by democracy, then virtually all forms of government are democratic, since virtually all governments, except in times of revolution, rest upon the explicit or implicit consent of the people. In order to discuss democracy intelligently it will be necessary, therefore, to define it, to attach to the word a sufficiently precise meaning to avoid the confusion which is not infrequently the chief result of such discussions.

All human institutions, we are told, have their ideal forms laid away in heaven, and we do not need to be told that the actual institutions conform but indifferently to these ideal counterparts. It would be possible then

* From *Modern Democracy* by Carl Becker. Reprinted by permission of Yale University Press. Copyright, 1941, by Yale University Press.

to define democracy either in terms of the ideal or in terms of the real form — to define it as government of the people, by the people, for the people; or to define it as government of the people, by the politicians, for whatever pressure groups can get their interests taken care of. But as a historian, I am naturally disposed to be satisfied with the meaning which, in the history of politics, men have commonly attributed to the word — a meaning, needless to say, which derives partly from the experience and partly from the aspirations of mankind. So regarded, the term democracy refers primarily to a form of government, and it has always meant government by the many as opposed to government by the one — government by the people as opposed to government by a tyrant, a dictator, or an absolute monarch. This is the most general meaning of the word as men have commonly understood it.

In this antithesis there are, however, certain implications, always tacitly understood, which give a more precise meaning to the term. Peisistratus, for example, was supported by a majority of the people, but his government was never regarded as a democracy for all that. Caesar's power derived from a popular mandate, conveyed through established republican forms, but that did not make his government any less a dictatorship. Napoleon called his government a democratic empire, but no one, least of all Napoleon himself, doubted that he had destroyed the last vestiges of the democratic republic. Since the Greeks first used the term, the essential test of democratic government has always been this: the source of political authority must be and remain in the people and not in the ruler. A democratic government has always meant one in which the citizens, or a sufficient number of them to represent more or less effectively the common will, freely act from time to time, and according to established forms, to appoint or recall the magistrates and to enact or revoke the laws by which the community is governed. This I take to be the meaning which history has impressed upon the term democracy as a form of government. It is, therefore, the meaning which I attach to it in these lectures.

The most obvious political fact of our time is that democracy as thus defined has suffered an astounding decline in prestige. Fifty years ago it was not impossible to regard democratic government, and the liberties that went with it, as a permanent conquest of the human spirit. In 1886 Andrew Carnegie published a book entitled *Triumphant Democracy*. Written without fear and without research, the book was not an achievement of the highest intellectual distinction perhaps; but the title at least expressed well enough the prevailing conviction — the conviction that democracy had fought the good fight, had won the decisive battles, and would inevitably, through its inherent merits, presently banish from the world the most flagrant political and social evils which from time immemorial had afflicted mankind. This conviction could no doubt be most easily entertained in the United States, where even the tradition of other forms of government was too remote and alien to color our native optimism. But even in Europe the downright skeptics, such as Lecky, were thought to be perverse, and so hardheaded a historian as J. B. Bury could proclaim with confidence that the long struggle for freedom of thought had finally been won.

I do not need to tell you that within a brief twenty years the prevailing optimism of that time has been quite dispelled. One European country after another has, willingly enough it seems, abandoned whatever democratic institutions it formerly enjoyed for some form of dictatorship. The spokesmen of Fascism and Communism announce with confidence that democracy, a sentimental aberration which the world has outgrown, is done for; and even the friends of democracy support it with declining conviction. They tell us that democracy, so far from being triumphant, is "at the crossroads" or "in retreat," and that its future is by no means assured. What are we to think of this sudden reversal in fortune and prestige? How explain it? What to do about it?

II

One of the presuppositions of modern thought is that institutions, in order to be understood, must be seen in relation to the conditions of time and place in which they appear. It is a little difficult for us to look at democracy in this way. We are so immersed in its present fortunes that we commonly see it only as a "close-up," filling the screen to the exclusion of other things to which it is in fact related. In order to form an objective judgment of its nature and significance, we must therefore first of all get it in proper perspective. Let us then, in imagination, remove from the immediate present scene to some cool high place where we can survey at a glance five or six thousand years of history, and note the part which democracy has played in human civilization. The view, if we have been accustomed to take democratic institutions for granted, is a bit bleak and disheartening. For we see at once that in all this long time, over the habitable globe, the great majority of the human race has neither known nor apparently much cared for our favorite institutions.

Civilization was already old when democracy made its first notable appearance among the small city states of ancient Greece, where it flourished brilliantly for a brief century or two and then disappeared. At about the same time something that might be called democracy appeared in Rome and other Italian cities, but even in Rome it did not survive the conquest of the world by the Roman Republic, except as a form of local administration in the cities of the empire. In the twelfth and thirteenth centuries certain favorably placed medieval cities enjoyed a measure of self-government, but in most instances it was soon replaced by the dictatorship of military conquerors, the oligarchic control of a few families, or the encroaching power of autocratic kings. The oldest democracy of modern times is the Swiss Confederation, the next oldest is the Dutch Republic. Parliamentary government in England does not antedate the late seventeenth century, the great American experiment is scarcely older. Not until the nineteenth century did democratic government make its way in any considerable part of the world — in the great states of continental Europe, in South America, in Canada and Australia, in South Africa and Japan.

From this brief survey it is obvious that, taking the experience of mankind as a test, democracy has as yet had but a limited and temporary success. There must be a reason for this significant fact. The reason is that democratic government is a species of social luxury, at best a delicate and precarious adventure which depends for success upon the validity of certain assumptions about the capacities and virtues of men, and upon the presence of certain material and intellectual conditions favorable to the exercise of these capacities and virtues. Let us take the material conditions first.

It is a striking fact that until recently democracy never flourished except in very small states — for the most part in cities. It is true that in both the Persian and the Roman empires a measure of self-government was accorded to local communities, but only in respect to purely local affairs; in no large state as a whole was democratic government found to be practicable. One essential reason is that until recently the means of communication were too slow and uncertain to create the necessary solidarity of interest and similarity of information over large areas. The principle of representation was well enough known to the Greeks, but in practice it proved impracticable except in limited areas and for special occasions. As late as the eighteenth century it was still the common opinion that the republican form of government, although the best ideally, was unsuited to large countries, even to a country no larger than France. This was the view of Montesquieu, and even of Rousseau. The view persisted into the nineteenth century, and English conservatives, who were opposed to the extension of the suffrage in England, consoled themselves with the notion that the American Civil War would confirm it — would demonstrate that government by and for the people would perish, if not from off the earth at least from large countries. If their hopes were confounded the reason is that the means of communication, figuratively speaking, were making large countries small. It is not altogether fanciful to suppose that, but for the railroad and the telegraph, the United States would today be divided into many small republics maneuvering for advantage and employing war and diplomacy for maintaining an unstable balance of power.

If one of the conditions essential to the success of democratic government is mobility, ease of communication, another is a certain measure of economic security. Democracy does not flourish in communities on the verge of destitution. In ancient and medieval times democratic government appeared for the most part in cities, the centers of prosperity. Farmers in the early Roman Republic and in the Swiss Cantons were not wealthy to be sure, but equality of possessions and of opportunity gave them a certain economic security. In medieval cities political privilege was confined to the prosperous merchants and craftsmen, and in Athens and the later Roman Republic democratic government was found to be workable only on condition that the poor citizens were subsidized by the government or paid for attending the assemblies and the law courts.

In modern times democratic institutions have, generally speaking, been most successful in new countries, such as the United States, Canada, and Australia, where the conditions of life have been easy for the people; and in European countries more or less in proportion to their industrial prosperity. In European countries, indeed, there has been a close correlation between the development of the industrial revolution and the emergence of democratic institutions. Holland and England, the first countries to experience the industrial revolution, were the first also (apart from Switzerland, where certain peculiar conditions obtained) to adopt democratic institutions; and as the industrial revolution spread to France, Belgium, Germany, and Italy, these countries in turn adopted at least a measure of democratic government. Democracy is in some sense an economic luxury, and it may be said that in modern times it has been a function of the development of new and potentially rich countries, or of the industrial revolution which suddenly dowered Europe with unaccustomed wealth. Now that prosperity is disappearing round every next corner, democracy works less well than it did.

So much for the material conditions essential for the success of democratic government. Supposing these conditions to exist, democratic government implies in addition the presence of certain capacities and virtues in its citizens. These capacities and virtues are bound up with the assumptions on which democracy rests, and are available only in so far as the assumptions are valid. The primary assumption of democratic government is that its citizens are capable of managing their own affairs. But life in any community involves a conflict of individual and class interests, and a corresponding divergence of opinion as to the measures to be adopted for the common good. The divergent opinions must be somehow reconciled, the conflict of interests somehow compromised. It must then be an assumption of democratic government that its citizens are rational creatures, sufficiently so at least to understand the interests in conflict; and it must be an assumption that they are men of good will, sufficiently so toward each other at least to make those concessions of individual and class interest required for effecting workable compromises. The citizens of a democracy should be, as Pericles said the citizens of Athens were, if not all originators at least all sound judges of good policy.

These are what may be called the minimum assumptions and the necessary conditions of democratic government anywhere and at any time. They may be noted to best advantage, not in any state, but in small groups within the state — in clubs and similar private associations of congenial and like-minded people united for a specific purpose. In such associations the membership is limited and select. The members are, or may easily become, all acquainted with each other. Everyone knows, or may easily find out, what is being done and who is doing it. There will of course be differences of opinion, and there may be disintegrating squabbles and intrigues. But on the whole, ends and means being specific and well understood, the problems of government are few and superficial; there is plenty of time for discussion; and since intelligence and good will can generally be taken for granted there is the disposition to make reasonable concessions and compromises. The analogy must be taken for what it is worth. States may not be the mystical blind Molochs of German philosophy, but any state is far more complex and intangible than a private association, and there is little resemblance between such associations and the democracies of modern times. Other things equal, the resemblance is closest in very small states, and it is in connection with the small city states of ancient Greece that the resemblance can best be noted.

The Greek states were limited in size, not as is often thought solely or even chiefly by the physiography of the country, but by some instinctive feeling of the Greek mind that a state is necessarily a natural association of people bound together by ties of kinship and a common tradition of rights and obligations. There must then, as Aristotle said, be a limit:

> For if the citizens of a state are to judge and distribute offices according to merit, they must know each other's characters; where they do not possess this knowledge, both the elections to offices and the decisions in the law courts will go wrong. Where the population is very large they are manifestly settled by haphazard, which clearly ought not to be. Besides, in overpopulous states foreigners and metics will readily acquire citizenship, for who will find them out?

It obviously did not occur to Aristotle that metics and foreigners should be free to acquire citizenship. It did not occur to him, or to any Greek of his time, or to the merchants of the self-governing medieval city, that a state should be composed of all the people inhabiting a given territory. A state was rather an incorporated body of people within, but distinct from, the population of the community.

Ancient and medieval democracies had thus something of the character of a private association. They were, so to speak, purely pragmatic phenomena, arising under very special conditions, and regarded as the most convenient way of managing the affairs of people bound together by community of interest and for the achievement of specific ends. There is no suggestion in Aristotle that democracy (polity) is intrinsically a superior form of government, no suggestion that it derives from a special ideology of its own. If it rests upon any superiority other than convenience, it is the superiority which it shares with any Greek state, that is to say, the superiority of Greek over barbarian civilization. In Aristotle's philosophy it is indeed difficult to find any clear-cut distinction between the democratic form of government and the state itself; the state, if it be worthy of the name, is always, whatever the form of government, "the government of freemen and equals," and in any state it is always necessary that "the freemen who compose the bulk of the people should have absolute power in some things." In Aristotle's philosophy the distinction between good and bad in politics is not between good and bad types of government, but between the good and the bad form of each type. Any type of government — monarchy, aristocracy, polity — is good provided the rulers aim at the good of all rather than at the good of the class to which they belong. From Aristotle's point of view neither democracy nor dictatorship is good or bad in itself, but only in the measure that it achieves, or fails to achieve, the aim of every good state, which is that "the inhabitants of it should be happy." It did not occur to Aristotle that democracy (polity), being in some special sense in harmony with the nature of man, was everywhere applicable, and therefore destined by fate or the gods to carry throughout the world a superior form of civilization.

It is in this respect chiefly that modern democracy differs from earlier forms. It rests upon something more than the minimum assumptions. It is reinforced by a full-blown ideology which, by endowing the individual with natural and imprescriptible rights, sets the democratic form of government off from all others as the one which alone can achieve the good life. What then are the essential tenets of the modern democratic faith?

III

The liberal democratic faith, as expressed in the works of eighteenth- and early nineteenth-century writers, is one of the formulations of the modern doctrine of progress. It will be well, therefore, to note briefly the historical antecedents of that doctrine.

In the long history of man on earth there comes a time when he remembers something of what has been, anticipates something that will be, knows the country he has traversed, wonders what lies beyond — the moment when he becomes aware of himself as a lonely, differentiated item in the world. Sooner or later there emerges for him the most devastating of all facts, namely, that in an indifferent universe which alone endures, he alone aspires, endeavors to attain, and attains only to be defeated in the end. From that moment his immediate experience ceases to be adequate, and he endeavors to project himself beyond it by creating ideal worlds of semblance, Utopias of other time or place in which all has been, may be, or will be well.

In ancient times Utopia was most easily projected into the unknown past, pushed back to the beginning of things — to the time of P'an Ku and the celestial emperors, to the Garden of Eden, or the reign of King Chronos when men lived like gods free from toil and grief. From this happy state of first created things there had obviously been a decline and fall, occasioned by disobedience and human frailty, and decreed as punishment by fate or the angry gods. The mind of man was therefore afflicted with pessimism, a sense of guilt for having betrayed the divine purpose, a feeling of inadequacy for bringing the world back to its original state of innocence and purity. To men who felt insecure in a changing world, and helpless in a world always changing for the worse, the future had little to offer. It could be regarded for the most part only with resignation, mitigated by individual penance or well-doing, or the hope of some miraculous intervention by the gods, or the return of the god-like kings, to set things right again, yet with little hope that from this setting right there would not be another falling away.

This pervasive pessimism was gradually dispelled in the Western world, partly by the Christian religion, chiefly by the secular intellectual revolution occurring roughly between the fifteenth and the eighteenth centuries. The Christian religion gave assurance that the lost golden age of the past would be restored for the virtuous in the future, and by proclaiming the supreme worth of the individual in the eyes of God enabled men to look forward with hope to the good life after death in the Heavenly City. Meantime, the secular intellectual revolution, centering in the matter-of-fact study of history and science, gradually emancipated the minds of men from resignation to fate and the angry gods. Accumulated knowledge of history, filling in time past with a continuous succession of credible events, banished all lost golden ages to the realm of myth, and enabled men to live without distress in a changing world since it could be regarded as not necessarily changing for the worse. At the same time, a more competent observation and measurement of the action of material things disclosed an outer world of nature, indifferent to man indeed, yet behaving, not as the unpredictable sport of the gods, but in ways understandable to human reason and therefore ultimately subject to man's control.

Thus the conditions were fulfilled which made it possible for men to conceive of Utopia, neither as a lost golden age of the past nor as a Heavenly City after death prepared by the gods for the virtuous, but as a future state on earth of man's own devising. In a world of nature that could be regarded as amenable to man's control, and in a world of changing social relations that need not be regarded as an inevitable decline and fall from original perfection, it was possible to formulate the modern doctrine of progress: the idea that, by deliberate intention and rational direction, men can set the terms and indefinitely improve the conditions of their mundane existence.

The eighteenth century was the moment in history when men first fully realized the engaging implications of this resplendent idea, the moment when, not yet having been brought to the harsh appraisal of experience, it could be accepted with unclouded optimism. Never had the universe seemed less mysterious, more open and visible, more eager to yield its secrets to common-sense questions. Never had the nature of man seemed less perverse, or the mind of man more pliable to the pressure of rational persuasion. The essential reason for this confident optimism is that the marvels of scientific discovery disclosed to the men of that time a God who still functioned but was no longer angry. God the Father could be conceived as a beneficent First Cause who, having performed his essential task of creation, had withdrawn from the affairs of men, leaving them competently prepared and fully instructed for the task of achieving their own salvation. In one tremendous sentence Rousseau expressed the eighteenth-century world view of the universe and man's place in it. "Is it simple," he exclaimed, "is it natural that God should have gone in search of Moses in order to speak to Jean Jacques Rousseau?"

God had indeed spoken to Rousseau, he had spoken to all men, but his revelation was contained, not in Holy Writ interpreted by Holy Church, but in the great Book of Nature which was open for all men to read. To this open book of nature men would go when they wanted to know what God had said to them. Here they would find recorded the laws of nature and of nature's God, disclosing a universe constructed according to a rational plan; and that men might read these laws aright they had been endowed with reason, a bit of the universal intelligence placed within the individual to make manifest to him the universal reason implicit in things and events. "Natural law," as Volney so clearly and confidently put it, "is the regular and constant order of facts by which God rules the universe; the order which his wisdom presents to the sense and reason of men, to serve them as an equal and common rule of conduct, and to guide them, without distinction of race or sect, toward perfection and happiness." Thus God had devised a planned economy, and had endowed men with the capacity for managing it: to bring his ideas, his conduct, and his institutions into harmony with the universal laws of nature was man's simple allotted task.

At all times political theory must accommodate itself in some fashion to the prevailing world view, and liberal-democratic political theory was no exception to this rule. From time immemorial authority and obedience had been the cardinal concepts both of the prevailing world view and of political and social theory. From time immemorial men had been regarded as subject to overruling authority — the authority of the gods, and the authority of kings who were themselves gods, or descended from gods, or endowed with divine authority to rule in place of gods; and from time immemorial obedience to such divine authority was thought to be the primary obligation of men. Even the Greeks, who were so little afraid of their gods that they could hob-nob with them in the most friendly and engaging way, regarded mortals as subject to them; and when they lost faith in the gods they deified the state as the highest good and subordinated the individual to it. But the eighteenth-century world view, making man the measure of all things, mitigated if it did not destroy this sharp contrast between authority and obedience. God still reigned but he did not govern. He had, so to speak, granted his subjects a constitution and authorized them to interpret it as they would in the supreme court of reason. Men were still subject to an overruling authority, but the subjection could be regarded as voluntary because self-imposed, and self-imposed because obedience was exacted by nothing more oppressive than their own rational intelligence.

Liberal-democratic political theory readily accommodated itself to this change in the world view. The voice of the people was now identified with the voice of God, and all authority was derived from it. The individual instead of the state or the prince was now deified and endowed with imprescriptible rights; and since ignorance or neglect of the rights of man was the chief cause of social evils, the first task of political science was to define these rights, the second to devise a form of government suited to guarantee them. The imprescriptible rights of man were easily defined, since they were self-evident: "All men are created equal, [and] are endowed by their Creator with certain inalienable rights, among which are life, liberty, and the pursuit of happiness." From this it followed that all just governments would remove those artificial restraints which impaired these rights, thereby liberating those natural impulses with which God had endowed the individual as a guide to thought and conduct. In the intellectual realm, freedom of thought and the competition of diverse opinion would disclose the truth, which all men, being rational creatures, would progressively recognize and willingly follow. In the economic realm, freedom of enterprise would disclose the natural aptitudes of each individual, and the ensuing competition of interests would stimulate effort, and thereby result in the maximum of material advantage for all. Liberty of the individual from social constraint thus turned out to be not only an inherent natural right but also a preordained natural mechanism for bringing about the material and moral progress of mankind. Men had only to follow reason and self-interest: something not themselves, God and Nature, would do whatever else was necessary for righteousness.

The modern liberal-democracy is associated with an ideology which rests upon something more than the minimum assumptions essential to any democratic government. It rests upon a philosophy of universally valid ends and means. Its fundamental assumption is the worth and dignity and creative capacity of the individual, so that the chief aim of government is the maximum of individual self-direction, the chief means to that end the minimum of compulsion by the state. Ideally considered, means and ends are conjoined in the concept of freedom: freedom of thought, so that the truth may prevail; freedom of occupation, so that careers may be open to talent; freedom of self-government, so that no one may be compelled against his will.

STUDY QUESTIONS

1. *In this, a part of the first chapter of his* Modern Democracy, *Becker is concerned primarily to define the ideal democracy. In the later chapters of his book he defines "the reality," and describes what he conceives to be the "dilemma" of modern democracy. What devices does he use to define the ideal democracy in this selection? To what extent does he evaluate as well as define?*

2. *Study the skillful organization of this essay. Select one section and examine the paragraphs noting transitions between paragraphs and sections, and the use of initial and final sentences in paragraphs.*

3. *What aspect of his general subject does Becker consider in each of the three major sections of this selection?*

4. *What material conditions does Becker think necessary for democracy? What assumptions does it make about its citizens? What does Becker mean when he says that modern democracy is "one of the formulations of the modern doctrine of progress"?*

5. *Becker's style has been often praised as a model of clarity and precision. Examine this selection, considering vocabulary and sentence structure as well as paragraphing, and be prepared to explain what characteristics contribute to its clarity.*

6. *Write a paper defining the ideal concept of something, say a college, government by town meeting, capitalism or some similar abstraction.*

Edward Hallett Carr

From Individualism to Mass Democracy*

The problem of political organization in the new society is to adapt to the mass civilization of the twentieth century conceptions of democracy formed in earlier and highly individualistic periods of history. The proclamation by the French revolution of popular sovereignty was a serious challenge to institutions which had grown up under quite different auspices and influences. It is no accident that Athenian democracy, which has been commonly regarded as the source and exemplar of democratic institutions, was the creation and prerogative of a limited and privileged group of the population. It is no accident that Locke, the founder of the modern democratic tradition, was the chosen philosopher and prophet of the eighteenth-century English Whig oligarchy. It is no accident that the magnificent structure of British nineteenth-century liberal democracy was built up on a highly restrictive property franchise. History points unmistakably to the fact that political democracy, in the forms in which it has hitherto been known, flourishes best where some of the people, but not all the people, are free and equal; and, since this conclusion is incompatible with the conditions of the new society and repugnant to the contemporary conscience, the task of saving democracy in our time is the task of reconciling it with the postulate of popular sovereignty and mass civilization.

Modern democracy, as it grew up and spread from its focus in western Europe over the past three centuries, rested on three main propositions: first, that the individual conscience is the ultimate source of decisions about what is right and wrong; second, that there exists between different individuals a

* From *The New Society* by Edward Hallett Carr, by permission of Macmillan & Co. Ltd. and of St. Martin's Press, copyright 1951.

fundamental harmony of interests strong enough to enable them to live peacefully together in society; third, that where action has to be taken in the name of society, rational discussion between individuals is the best method of reaching a decision on that action. Modern democracy is, in virtue of its origins, individualist, optimistic and rational. The three main propositions on which it is based have all been seriously challenged in the contemporary world. . . .

The prominent rôle assigned to reason in the original democratic scheme provides perhaps the most convincing explanation why democracy has hitherto always seemed to flourish best with a restrictive franchise. Much has been written in recent years of the decline of reason, and of respect for reason, in human affairs, when sometimes what has really happened has been the abandonment of the highly simplified eighteenth-century view of reason in favour of a subtler and more sophisticated analysis. But it is none the less true that the epoch-making changes in our attitude towards reason provide a key to some of the profoundest problems of contemporary democracy.

First of all, the notion that men of intelligence and good will were likely by process of rational discussion to reach a correct opinion on controversial political questions could be valid only in an age when such questions were comparatively few and simple enough to be accessible to the educated layman. It implicitly denied that any specialized knowledge was required to solve political problems. This hypothesis was perhaps tenable so long as the state was not required to intervene in economic issues, and the questions on which decisions had to be taken turned on matters of practical detail or general political principles. In the first half of the twentieth century these conditions had everywhere ceased to exist. In Great Britain major issues of a highly controversial character like the return to the gold standard in 1925 or the acceptance of the American loan in 1946 were of a kind in which no opinion seriously counted except that of the trained expert in possession of a vast array of facts and figures, some of them probably not available to the public. In such matters the ordinary citizen could not even have an intelligent opinion on the question who were the best experts to consult. The only rôle he could hope to play was to exercise his hunch at the election by choosing the right leader to consult the right experts about vital, though probably still unformulated, issues of policy which would ultimately affect his daily life.

At this initial stage of the argument reason itself is not dethroned from its supreme rôle in the decision of political issues. The citizen is merely asked to surrender his right of decision to the superior reason of the expert. At the second stage of the argument reason itself is used to dethrone reason. The social psychologist, employing rational methods of investigation, discovers that men in the mass are often most effectively moved by non-rational emotions such as admiration, envy, hatred, and can be most effectively reached not by rational argument, but by emotional appeals to eye and ear, or by sheer repetition. Propaganda is as essential a function of mass democracy as advertising of mass production. The political organizer takes a leaf out of the book of the commercial advertiser and sells the leader or the candidate to the voter by the same methods used to sell patent medicines or refrigerators. The appeal is no longer to the reason of the citizen, but to his gullibility. A more recent phenomenon has been the emergence of what Max Weber called the "charismatic leader" as the expression of the general will. The retreat from individualism seemed to issue at last — and not alone in the so-called totalitarian countries — in the exaltation of a single individual leader who personified and resumed within himself the qualities and aspirations of the "little man," of the ordinary individual lost and bewildered in the new mass society. But the principal qualification of the leader is no longer his capacity to reason correctly on political or economic issues, or even his capacity to choose the best experts to reason for him, but a good public face, a convincing voice, a sympathetic fireside manner on the radio; and these qualities are deliberately built up for him by his publicity agents. In this picture of the techniques of contemporary democracy, the party headquarters, the directing brain at the centre, still operates rationally, but uses irrational rather than rational means to achieve its ends — means which are, moreover, not merely irrational but largely irrelevant to the purposes to be pursued or to the decisions to be taken.

The third stage of the argument reaches deeper levels. Hegel, drawing out the philosophical implications of Rousseau's doctrine, had identified the course of history with universal reason, to which the individual reason stood in the same relation as the individual will to Rousseau's general will. Individual reason had been the corner-stone of individualist democracy. Marx took Hegel's collective reason to make it the corner-stone of the new mass democracy. Marx purported to reject the metaphysical character of Hegel's thought. But, equally with Hegel, he conceived of history pursuing a rational course, which could be analysed and even predicted in terms of reason. Hegel had spoken of the cunning of reason in history, using individuals to achieve purposes of which they themselves were unconscious. Marx would have rejected the turn of phrase as metaphysical. But his conception of history as a continuous process of class struggle contained elements of determinism which revealed its Hegelian ancestry, at any rate on one side. Marx remained a thorough-going rationalist. But the reason whose validity he accepted was collective rather than individual.

Marx played, however, a far more important part in what has been called "the flight from reason" than by the mere exaltation of the collective over the individual. By his vigorous assertion that "being determines consciousness, not consciousness being," that thinking is conditioned by the social environment of the thinker, and that ideas are the superstructure of a totality whose foundation is formed by the material conditions of life, Marx presented a clear challenge to what had hitherto been regarded as the sovereign or autonomous human reason. The actors who played significant parts in the historical drama were playing parts already written for them: this indeed was what made them significant. The function of individual reason was to identify itself with the universal reason which determined the course of history and to make itself the agent and executor of this universal reason. Some such view is indeed involved in any attempt to trace back historical events to underlying social causes; and Marx — and still more Engels — hedged a little in later years about the rôle of the individual in history. But the extraordinary vigour and conviction with which he drove home his main argument, and the political theory which he founded on it, give him a leading place among those nineteenth-century thinkers who shattered the comfortable belief of the Age of Enlightenment in the decisive power of individual reason in shaping the course of history.

Marx's keenest polemics were those directed to prove the "conditioned" character of the thinking of his opponents and particularly of the capitalist ruling class of the most advanced countries of his day. If they thought as they did it was because, as members of a class, "being" determined their "consciousness," and their ideas necessarily lacked any independent objectivity and validity. Hegel, as a good conservative, had exempted the current reality of the Prussian from the operation of the dialectic which had destroyed successively so many earlier historical forms. Marx, as a revolutionary, admitted no such absolute in the present, but only in the future. The proletariat, whose victory would automatically abolish classes, was alone the basis of absolute value; and collective proletarian thinking had thus an objectivity which was denied to the thinking of other classes. Marx's willingness, like that of Hegel, to admit an absolute as the culminating point of his dialectical process was, however, an element of inconsistency in his system; and, just as Marx was far more concerned to dissect capitalism than to provide a blueprint for socialism, so his use of the dialectic to lay bare the conditioned thinking of his opponents lay far nearer to his heart, and was far more effective, than his enunciation of the objective and absolute values of the proletariat. Marx's writings gave a powerful impetus to all forms of relativism. It seemed less important, at a time when the proletarian revolution was as yet nowhere in sight, to note his admission of absolute truth as a prerogative of the proletariat. The proletariat was for Marx the collective repository of Rousseau's infallible general will.

Another thinker of the later nineteenth century also helped to mould the climate of political opinion. Like Darwin, Freud was a scientist without pretensions to be a philosopher or, still less, a political thinker. But in the flight from reason at the end of the nineteenth century, he played the same popular rôle as Darwin had played a generation earlier in the philosophy of *laissez-faire*. Freud demonstrated that the fundamental attitudes of human beings in action and thought are largely determined at levels beneath that of consciousness, and that the supposedly rational explanations of those attitudes which we offer to ourselves and others are artificial and erroneous "rationalizations" of processes which we have failed to understand. Reason is given to us, Freud seems to say, not to direct our thought and action, but to camouflage the hidden forces which do direct it. This is a still more devastating version of the Marxist thesis of substructure and superstructure. The substructure of reality resides in the unconscious: what appears above the surface is no more than the reflexion, seen in a distorting ideological mirror, of what goes on underneath. The political conclusion from all this — Freud himself drew none — is that any attempt to appeal to the reason of the ordinary man is waste of time, or is useful merely as camouflage to conceal the real nature of the process of persuasion; the appeal must be made to those subconscious strata which are decisive for thought and action. The debunking of ideology undertaken by the political science of Marx is repeated in a far more drastic and far-reaching way by the psychological science of Freud and his successors.

By the middle of the nineteenth century, therefore, the propositions of Locke on which the theory of liberal democracy were founded had all been subjected to fundamental attack, and the attack broadened and deepened as the century went on. Individualism began to give way to collectivism both in economic organization and in the forms and practice of mass democracy: the age of mass civilization had begun. The alleged harmony of interests between individuals was replaced by the naked struggle between powerful classes and organized interest groups. The belief in the settlement of issues by rational discussion was undermined, first, by recognition of the complex and technical character of the issues involved, later and more seriously, by recognition that rational arguments were merely the conditioned reflection of the class interests of those who put them forward, and, last and most seriously of all, by the discovery that the democratic voter, like other human beings, is most effectively reached not by arguments directed to his reason, but by appeals directed to his irrational, subconscious prejudices. The picture of democracy which emerged from these criticisms was the picture of an arena where powerful interest-groups struggled for the mastery. The leaders themselves were often the spokesmen and instruments of historical processes which they did not fully understand; their followers consisted of voters recruited and marshalled for purposes of which they were wholly unconscious by all the subtle techniques of modern psychological science and modern commercial advertising.

The picture is overdrawn. But we shall not begin to understand the problems of mass democracy unless we recognize the serious elements of truth in it, unless we recognize how far we have moved away from the conceptions and from the conditions out of which the democratic tradition was born. From the conception of democracy as a select society of free individuals, enjoying equal rights and periodically electing to manage the affairs of the society, a small number of their peers, who deliberate together and decide by rational argument on the course to pursue (the assumption being that the course which appeals to the majority is likely to be the most rational), we have passed to the current reality of mass democracy. The typical mass democracy of today is a vast society of individuals, stratified by widely different social and economic backgrounds into a series of groups or classes, enjoying equal political rights the exercise of which is organized through two or more closely integrated political machines called parties. Between the parties and individual citizens stand an indeterminate number of entities variously known as unions, associations, lobbies or pressure-groups devoted to the promotion of some economic interest, or of some social or humanitarian cause in which keen critics usually detect a latent and perhaps unconscious interest. At the first stage of the democratic process, these associations and groups form a sort of exchange and mart where votes are traded for support of particular policies; the more votes such a group controls the better its chance of having its views incorporated in the party platform. At the second stage, when these bargains have been made, the party as a united entity "goes to the country" and endeavors by every form of political propaganda to win the support of the unattached voter. At the third stage, when the election has been decided, the parties once more dispute or bargain together, in the light of the votes cast, on the policies to be put into effect; the details of procedure at this third stage differ considerably in different democratic countries in accordance with varying constitutional requirements and party structures. What is important to note is that the first and third stages are fierce matters of bargaining. At the second stage, where the mass persuasion of the electorate is at issue, the methods employed now commonly approximate more and more closely to those of commercial advertisers, who, on the advice of modern psychologists, find the appeal to fear, envy or self-aggrandizement more effective than the appeal to reason. Certainly in the United States, where contemporary large-scale democracy has worked most successfully and where the strongest confidence is felt in its survival, experienced practitioners of politics would give little encouragement to the idea that rational argument exercises a major influence on the democratic process. We have returned to a barely disguised struggle of interest-groups in which the arguments used are for the most part no more than a rationalization of the interests concerned, and the rôle of persuasion is played by carefully calculated appeals to the irrational subconscious.

This discussion is intended to show not that mass democracy is more corrupt or less efficient than other forms of government (this I do not believe), but that mass democracy is a new phenomenon — a creation of the last half-century — which it is inappropriate and misleading to consider in terms of the philosophy of Locke or of the liberal democracy of the nineteenth century. It is new, because the new democratic society consists no longer of a homogeneous closed society of equal and economically secure individuals mutually recognizing one another's rights, but of ill co-ordinated, highly stratified masses of people of whom a large majority are primarily occupied with the daily struggle for existence. It is new, because the new democratic state can no longer be content to hold the ring in the strife of private economic interests, but must enter the arena at every moment and take the initiative in urgent issues of economic policy which affect the daily life of all the citizens, and especially of the least secure. It is new, because the old rationalist assumptions of Locke and of liberal democracy have broken down under the weight both of changed material conditions and of new scientific insights and inventions, and the leaders of the new democracy are concerned no longer primarily with the reflexion of opinion, but with the moulding and manipulation of opinion. To speak today of the defence of democracy as if we were defending something which we knew and had possessed for many decades or many centuries is self-deception and sham. . . .

STUDY QUESTIONS

1. *How well do Carr and Becker agree as to the fundamental nature of democracy?*
2. *Explain what is meant by the term "universal reason" as it is used in this selection. What are the relative roles of reason and emotion in the history of democracy given by Carr?*
3. *How is present-day democracy different from what democracy was originally supposed to be, according to Carr's account?*
4. *Is Carr's writing as lucid as Becker's? How is it organized? Are there significant differences in organization, paragraphing, sentences, or vocabulary? Does the fact that Carr is advancing an explanation of a contemporary situation rather than explaining an ideal make his job more complex?*
5. *If Carr is right about the changes in democracy, what bearing do these changes have upon the traditional element of democracy? To what extent are the principles of the American Revolution, the French Revolution, the democratic state of Athens, and of such documents as the Constitution and the Declaration of Independence relevant to present-day mass democracy?*
6. *Is Carr correct in contending that underground and irrational forces are the real moving powers of today's democracy? Write a theme which examines this point of view, using some contemporary political development as an example.*

Sidney Hook The Hero and Democracy*

𝒥 f the hero is defined as an event-making individual who redetermines the
course of history, it follows at once that a democratic community must
be eternally on guard against him.

This simple, and to some unwelcome, conclusion is involved in the very
conception of a democratic society. For in such a society leadership cannot
arrogate to itself heroic power. At legally determined intervals government
must draw its sanction from the *freely given consent* of the governed. And
so long as that consent is *freely* given, that is, after the opposition has been
heard, the policy or action agreed upon becomes the one for which the
community is responsible even though the leadership may have initiated it.[1]

The problem of leadership in a democracy is highly complex. Its importance warrants further clarification. Our reflections in this chapter, as
distinct from the others, will be normative. They will involve judgments
of value concerning democracy and democracy's good.

An old Chinese proverb tells us "the great man is a public misfortune."
The sentiment aptly expresses the experience and wisdom of a peace-loving
race. Were the victims of great men's glory to speak, not only in China but
almost anywhere, they would echo this homely judgment with sighs and
tears and curses. For on the whole, heroes in history have carved out their
paths of greatness by wars, conquests, revolutions, and holy crusades.

And yet this Chinese proverb epitomizes only past history, and not all of
that. A great man may sometimes be a public fortune. His absence is far
from being a sign that we shall be spared great misfortunes. Indeed, in face
of calamity the people pray for a deliverer. Among the calamities they
pray to be delivered from may be the rule of an earlier deliverer. If we were
to conclude from the evil things great men have done that their greatness is
the source of their evil, we should have to condemn all talent and capacity
because they are often abused.

Great men, then, may be good men. And still a democracy must be suspicious of them! For essential to democracy is the participation of the
governed in determining their own welfare. This participation is coupled
with the *hope* that the governed will select and elect their governors wisely,

* From *Hero in History* by Sidney Hook, by permission of The Humanities Press,
Inc. Copyright, 1943, by Sidney Hook.

[1] For further amplification of the meaning of "freely given consent," see Chapter
thirteen of my *Reason, Social Myths and Democracy*, New York, 1941; also "The
Philosophical Presuppositions of Democracy," *Ethics*, April 1942.

that is, in such a way as to gratify as many of their needs and wants as the situation permits. But more important than this hope, which is sometimes sadly at variance with the facts, is the belief that it is more worthy of men to decide their own fate than to let others decide it for them.

The hero in a democratic community — the potentially event-making man — may sincerely believe that he accepts its underlying philosophy. But sooner or later he finds himself straining against two features of the democratic process. The first is the principle of majority rule, especially when he is convinced that the majority is wrong on a matter of great import. The second is the slowness of its operation even when he believes the majority is right.

No one believes in majority rule as a reasonable principle of decision in a family of small children, a prison, or an institution for the feeble-minded. To the extent that we accept majority rule as an essential feature of democracy, we are committed to the well-grounded belief that, on the whole, men are not infants, cretins, or criminals. But although men are capable of rationality, reason in human affairs is so much a matter of weighing interests, and interests so often are at variance with each other, that the majority's reason may be the minority's disaster. This proves that the principle of majority rule is not sufficient for democracy, not that it is unnecessary. Nor does it prove that certain rights are inalienable and absolute, for not one such right can be mentioned which under certain circumstances may not need to be abridged in the interest of other rights.

What is necessary in addition to the principle of majority rule is the recognition by every group interest in society of the legitimacy of any group interest, provided the group in question accepts the methods of *free* inquiry and democratic decision as principles of negotiating conflicts of interest. Even so the majority may be mistaken and unjust, even as the man who follows the lead of evidence may sometimes be mistaken while the man who acts blindly may be right. But the majority that provides a minority with the possibility of becoming a majority through the education of citizens by public opposition has gone as far as it can politically to meet legitimate grievance. Under the conditions indicated, the democrat who enjoys freedom of agitation must abide by the decision of the majority even when he believes it to be wrong.

This does not *in principle* justify toleration of a minority whose actual program calls for the overthrow of democratic political institutions by force of arms. Any particular minority may be tolerated on grounds of prudence or expediency, for example, where it is opposed to another minority, more dangerous at the moment, or where its suppression is likely to establish a precedent that may be extended to other minorities who are genuinely devoted to democratic processes.

The "potential hero" in a democracy sees what others do not. His will to action is stronger. His knowledge of what must be done to realize what he sees is surer. For these reasons, he finds himself, more likely than not, in a minority. His sense of his vocation impels him to fight for his insight. His loyalty to the democratic ideal compels him to make this insight the common faith of the majority. If the latter remain stubbornly intractable, his chances of heroic action, as a democrat, are lost. The hero fades into history as a "village Hampden."

Superior talent and strong vision, however, press for expression. So far as the hero does not renounce politics as a sphere of activity, his task becomes to get himself accepted by a majority. For, as a democrat, he does not dare to admit to himself or to others that he wants to make himself independent of the majority. In pursuit of a majority, he may seek to win it, broadly speaking, by the patient methods of education, relying upon the inherent reasonableness of his vision to make its way.

Insofar as he does this, and only so far, democracy is safe from the hero. This means that he courts failure. But the hero may master the arts of the demagogue and use the very instruments of democracy to debase its quality. Yet as long as democratic controls are not abolished, the hero as demagogue must still build up, cajole, and cater to the majority. He acquires a contempt for the group he leads by virtue of the methods by which he corrupts them. In the process, if his own will and insight grow uncertain and cloudy, he becomes just another politician. He is a hero who has missed his chance. But where his will and insight remain firm, the hero as demagogue must "fool" his following into accepting them. He must develop a public platform, on the basis of which he solicits confidence, and a secret program in whose behalf he uses the confidence so won. He becomes a threat to democracy. The greater his faith in himself, the more disinterested his intentions, the more fateful the issue to which his heroic vision drives him, the more insidious is the menace to the whole rationale of democracy. Particularly so if the hero or potential event-making character believes himself to be the indispensable instrument of his vision.

Until now we have assumed that the standpoint of the hero is one that cannot recommend itself to the majority in the light of free discussion and intelligent inquiry and that if it is adopted it is only in virtue of chicanery and demagogic fraud. Let us now assume that the majority is properly persuaded that the hero is right. The latter may still regard the processes of democracy as a fetter upon his calling. For these processes grind too slowly, and many things will not wait. If he is confident that he knows the community's good, and convinced that it hangs in the balance, the hero is tempted to confront it with a *fait accompli*. Well-intentioned opposition that delays and obstructs appears to him as objective betrayal, and can easily be pilloried as such. And he knows that, if he succeeds, a great deal will be forgiven him.

But need a democracy move slowly? No, for its pace can be accelerated by delegation of power to the leader or hero. Yet in the best of situations, this only mitigates the dangers of delay; it does not eliminate them. For a democracy cannot in advance delegate all its powers and remain a democracy.

And the crucial situation is always one that involves the undelegated powers. Since power cannot in a democracy be delegated in perpetuity, the crucial situation may arise just when the delegation of power is up for *renewal*. Again, the delegation of power is always requested in a moment of crisis or emergency. But who is to determine when the moment is here?

The hero always presses for greater powers. It is natural to his vocation that he should do so. He is as eager to accept new powers as he is reluctant to surrender them after they are granted. And it is true that, in a troubled world, no democratic community can survive for long unless it entrusts its leaders with great powers. At the same time, what it gives with reluctance, it must take back with eagerness. The timing is all—and it is not likely that the hero and the community will agree on what time it is.

There cannot be any guarantee that a leader will not usurp delegated power to carry out a heroic event-making task. But a democracy would be foolish to refuse delegation of power for this reason if the situation is so crucial that decisive action must be taken at once. On the other hand, there may be no evidence that delegated powers will be abused. Nonetheless, a democracy would be foolish not to withdraw them promptly when the emergency is over, for they are a standing temptation to abuse and usurpation.

A democracy is imperiled not alone by its heroes, necessary as they may sometimes be for survival. It is imperiled by any group of its citizens who are more attached to the advantages or privileges they enjoy under democracy, or hope it will bring, than they are to the democratic process of bringing them about. For these groups, which set greater store on peace or prosperity or social status than they do on the methods of democracy to preserve (or modify) them, are the ones which feel justified in calling in the hero to cherish their "goods" even at the cost of democracy. An instructive example is furnished by conservative classes in western Europe who, convinced that democratic legislation had unjustly abridged the privileges of property, opened the gates to Mussolini and Hitler. True, their profession of democratic allegiance was merely lip service to begin with. But not so for the large numbers of the middle classes and even workers who constituted the mass base of Fascism. Security, fixed prices, employment meant more to them than democracy. They were to learn that when democracy goes, the goods for which it is sacrificed, without becoming more certain, are degraded in quality.

If we were to list as heroes the event-making men of the past, we should find few of them in the histories of democratic societies. It is in conformity with the genius of democratic society that this should be so.

There is great wisdom in the notorious political ingratitude of democratic communities. They usually refuse to glorify their leaders until they are dead. And the best reason for honoring these leaders is that they did not yield to the temptations of power, or that they were prepared to step down from positions of power even when they were convinced that they were right and the majority wrong.

Great men do not ask permission to be born. Nor do they ask permission of democracies to lead them. They find their own way to the tasks they feel called to fulfill, unless crushed by a hostile environment or isolated by the tide of events. Democracies do not have to seek these heroes when it seeks leaders. For if they exist, they will make themselves heard. A democracy must always be girded to protect itself against them even as it uses them, relying not on *their* intentions, which are always honorable but not infrequently messianic, but on the mechanisms of its own democratic institutions, on the plurality of centers of power and interest, and on the spirit of its education and morale.

In a democratic community education must pitch the ideal of the hero in a different key from that of the event-making man. The heroes in a democracy should be the great figures in the Pantheon of thought, the men of ideas, of social vision, of scientific achievement and artistic power. For it is these men who mould the intellectual ideals and social attitudes of the citizens, who without knowledge, quickened perception, and educated taste cannot realize the promise of democracy. If we are earnest in our belief in democracy, we must recognize that it is those who are affected by a basic policy who must pass upon it, either directly or indirectly. And if they are to pass upon it intelligently, know when to delegate power or withdraw it, and enhance the quality of political life by their participation, they must develop a sensitiveness to what is significant and what is trivial, an indifference to rhetorical bombast but a keen interest in what it conceals, an ability to isolate relevant issues and to weigh the available evidence.

The statesman in a democracy exercises his leadership by *proposing* a policy. But whether it is adopted and why depends upon the representatives of the democratic community who are chosen by individuals themselves potentially representatives. A successful democracy, therefore, may honor its statesmen; but it must honor its teachers more — whether they be prophets, scientists, poets, jurists, or philosophers. The true hero of democracy, then, should be not the soldier or the political leader, great as their services may be, but the teacher — the Jeffersons, Holmes, Deweys, Whitmans, and all others who have given the people vision, method, and knowledge.

It is the task of a democratic society to break down the invidious distinctions reflected in current linguistic usage between the hero and the masses or the average man. This can be accomplished in part by reinterpreting the meaning of the word "hero," and by recognizing that "heroes" can be made by fitting social opportunities more skillfully to specific talents. What we call "the average man" is not a biological but a social phenomenon. Human capacities are much more diversified than our social arrangements take note of.

Where we restrict social opportunities, so that only a few types of excellence are recognized, in respect to them the great mass of individuals, despite their differences, will appear as the dull, gray average. If, however, we extend social opportunities so that each person's specific talents have a stimulus to development and expression, we increase the range of possibility of distinctively significant work. From this point of view, a hero is any individual who does his work well and makes a unique contribution to the public good. It is sheer prejudice to believe that the grandeur and nobility associated with the heroic life can be found only in careers that reck little of human blood and suffering. Daily toil on any level has its own occasions of struggle, victory, and quiet death. A democracy should contrive its affairs, not to give one or a few the chance to reach heroic stature, but rather to take as a regulative ideal the slogan, "every man a hero."

We call this a "regulative ideal" because it would be Utopian to imagine that it could ever be literally embodied. As a regulative ideal it gives direction to policies that enable society to make the best of whatever powers are available to men.

What are the powers available to men? They are theoretically limited but practically indefinite. In the absence of an environment that encourages their expression, no one can speak with dogmatism about their nature and specific form. Nor can we be certain of the precise limit of human power without allowing for the willed effort that enables the runner to clear a hurdle that until then had been an insuperable obstacle.

A democracy should encourage the belief that all are called and all may be chosen. All may be chosen because a wisely contrived society will take as a point of departure the rich possibilities that nature herself gives through the spontaneous variations in the powers and capacities of men. These variations are the source and promise of new shoots of personality and value. The belief that all may be chosen, acted upon in a co-operating environment, may inspire the added increment of effort that often transforms promise into achievement.

Our conception of a democracy without event-making figures runs counter to a plausible but fundamentally mistaken critique of democracy developed by a notable school of Italian theorists — Mosca, Pareto, and Michels.[2] These men in different ways seek to establish the impossibility of democracy. Their chief argument is that all political rule involves organization and that all organization, no matter how democratic its mythology, sooner or later comes under the effective control of a minority élite. The history of societies, despite the succession of different political *forms*, is in substance nothing but the succession of different political élites. Democracy is a political form that conceals both the conflicts of interest between the governing élite and the governed and the fact that these conflicts are always undemocratically resolved in favor of the former. To the extent that these élites make history, their outstanding leaders are heroes or event-making figures even in a democracy.

The whole force of this argument rests upon a failure to understand the

2 I have previously expounded and criticized the doctrines of this school from a somewhat different point of view in my *Reason, Social Myths and Democracy*, pp. 119 ff., New York, 1940.

nature of ideals, including political ideals. In addition, the critique overlooks the fact that the problems of political power are always *specific* and that they allow choices between courses of conduct that strengthen or weaken, extend or diminish particular political ideals. Finally, it underestimates the tremendous differences between societies, all of which fall short in varying degrees of the defined ideal of democracy, and the crucial importance of institutions in the never-ending process of realizing ideals.

In virtue of the nature of things and men, no ideal can be perfectly embodied. There is no such thing as absolute health, absolute wisdom, absolute democracy, an absolutely honest man — or an absolutely fat one. Yet when we employ these ideals intelligently we can order a series of flesh and blood men in such a way as to distinguish between them in respect to their being healthier, wiser, or fatter. And so with states. There is no absolutely democratic state, but we can tell when states are more democratic or less democratic. Ideals, in short, are functional. They are principles of organization and reorganization but cannot be identified with any particular organization as it exists at any place and time.

If we define a democratic society as one in which the government rests upon the freely given consent of the governed[3] it is obvious that no society is a perfect democracy, even one in which the members are so few that they can all meet in one place without delegating power to representatives. For we never can be sure that consent is freely given, that is, not in bondage to ignorance, rhetoric, or passion. Further, the division of labor requires that decisions be carried out by individuals and not by the assembly. There can be no guarantee that these decisions as well as the discretionary powers they entail will be carried out in the same spirit as that in which they were authorized.

What follows? That democracy is impossible? No more so than that a man cannot be healthy because he cannot enjoy perfect health. The defects when recognized become problems to be remedied by actions, institutions, checks, and restraints that are themselves informed by the principle or ideal of democracy. The remedies are of course imperfect, fallible, and unguaranteed. But we do not therefore reject them. We continue to improve them — if we are democrats. And we test by the fruits of the process the validity of the unrealizable democratic principle that serves as our functional guide.

Mosca, Pareto, and Michels make much of the fact that when power is delegated in a democracy and when political organizations arise, as they must in a society sufficiently complex, the decisions of the government may reflect the interests of the governors more than the interests of the governed. This is indisputably true.

What follows? Not that democracy is impossible but that it is difficult. It is more difficult under certain social and historical conditions than under others. But as long as we hold to democratic principles, again the remedies consist in thinking up of specific mechanisms, devices, and checks which (1) increase the *participation* of the governed in the processes of government,

---

[3] For a detailed analysis of this definition, see *ibid*, p. 285.

(2) decrease the *concentrations* of powers — educational, religious, economic, political — in the hands of the governors, and (3) provide for the renewal or withdrawal of the mandates of power by the governed. Again, the remedies may be defective. But if we believe that those whose interests are affected by the policies of government should have a voice in determining those policies, either directly, or indirectly by controlling the makers of policy, the *direction* which the never-ending task of democratizing the social process must take is clear. Whether it does take that direction depends greatly upon us.

That there will always be a governing élite to administer government is true. There will also always be a medical élite to minister to our health. The governing élite will always have more power for good or evil than the medical élite. But it need not be more permanent or even as permanent as the medical élite. So long as the governing élite operates within a framework of a democracy, we have a choice between élites. Where élites must contend with out-élites, the victor must pay a price to the governed for victory. How high the price is depends in part at least on how much the governed ask.[4]

The great limitation of the thought of Mosca, Pareto, and Michels is their failure to appreciate the differential advantages of the specific institutions available in a democracy that enable us both to select élites and to curb them. They overlook the concrete ways in which the governed through pressure groups, strikes, public debates, committee hearings, radio discussion, letters and telegrams to newspapers and their representatives, petitions, mass meetings, primaries, and elections actually contribute to moulding the basic policies and decisions of the government in a democracy.[5]

The crux of the issue raised by the contention that democracy is impossible because power is exercised by an organized minority may best be met by asking the following questions: Can a democracy get rid of its ruling élite? Can a democracy rid itself of a governing élite more easily or at a lesser cost than a nondemocratic society? There can hardly be any doubt about the answers. The evidence of politics and history shows that democracy can and has rid itself of governing élites, and that it can do so more easily than is generally possible in nondemocratic societies. That in consequence one élite is replaced by another is a feature of the political process in a complex society, not an indictment of democracy or a proof of its impossibility. Sufficient unto the day is the problem thereof!

Behind the facade of logical argument in the writings of Mosca, Pareto, and Michels are two significant assumptions. The first is that human nature has a fixed and unalterable character from which it can be predicted that democracy in action must fail, not in the innocent sense that a perfect

---

[4] "For the working masses every 'final victory' proclaimed by their victorious leaders, even if it is a real step forward, can be only another starting point in their endless struggle *for more and always more*." Max Nomad, in his "Masters—Old and New," *The Making of Society*, edited by V. F. Calverton, p. 892.

[5] *Cf.* the brief but excellent discussion of Glenn Morrow in *Ethics*, April 1942, pp. 299 *ff.*; also Arthur Bentley's important but neglected study, *The Process of Government*, Chicago, 1908.

democracy cannot be realized, but in the sense that a working democracy *cannot be bettered* from the standpoint of its own ideal. The second assumption is that the amount of freedom and democracy in a society is determined by a *law already known*. Both assumptions are false.

So far as the position of these social philosophers is based upon the constancy of human nature, their entire political wisdom consists in framing a simple alternative to man — rule or be ruled! But one does not have to be a Utopian to maintain that nothing in human nature limits us to this simple alternative. For other alternatives must be taken together with it. Who is to rule? Over what? For how long? Under what conditions and restrictions? Here is the place for intelligence, experiment, critical adaptation, and political discovery.

The amount and quality of freedom and democracy in a society are determined by many things — economic organization, education, tradition, religion, to name only a few. *But they depend just as much upon our willingness to fight for them as upon any other thing.*

Democracy is difficult, and it is made more difficult because many who call themselves democrats are totalitarians in disguise. The moral is not to call off the struggle but to struggle all the more.

STUDY QUESTIONS

1. *In what ways are the impulses of the "hero" and the principles of democracy opposed to each other?*
2. *At what point does Hook set the limits of liberty for minorities in a democracy? Are these limits different from those set by Mill in "On Liberty"?*
3. *How is the "governing élite" in a democracy different from that in other forms of government?*
4. *How does Hook counter the argument that even when a government is elected, as in a democracy, its actions may reflect its own interests rather than those of the people it governs?*
5. *Do you agree with Hook that the relationship between the leader and the led is essentially the same in a democracy and other forms of government?*
6. *Examine Hook's generalizations about the methods and temptations of the democratic hero in the light of the career of some democratic leader.*

John Milton FROM Areopagitica*

I deny not, but that it is of greatest concernment in the Church and Commonwealth, to have a vigilant eye how books demean themselves as well as men; and thereafter to confine, imprison, and do sharpest justice on

* First published in 1644.

them as malefactors. For books are not absolutely dead things, but do contain a potency of life in them to be as active as that soul was whose progeny they are; nay, they do preserve as in a vial the purest efficacy and extraction of that living intellect that bred them. I know they are as lively, and as vigorously productive, as those fabulous dragon's teeth; and being sown up and down, may chance to spring up armed men. And yet, on the other hand, unless wariness be used, as good almost kill a man as kill a good book. Who kills a man kills a reasonable creature, God's image; but he who destroys a good book, kills reason itself, kills the image of God, as it were in the eye. Many a man lives a burden to the earth; but a good book is the precious life-blood of a master spirit, embalmed and treasured up on purpose to a life beyond life. 'Tis true, no age can restore a life, whereof perhaps there is no great loss; and revolutions of ages do not oft recover the loss of a rejected truth, for the want of which whole nations fare the worse.

We should be wary therefore what persecution we raise against the living labours of public men, how we spill that seasoned life of man, preserved and stored up in books; since we see a kind of homicide may be thus committed, sometimes a martyrdom, and if it extend to the whole impression, a kind of massacre; whereof the execution ends not in the slaying of an elemental life, but strikes at that ethereal and fifth essence, the breath of reason itself, slays an immortality rather than a life. . . .

Good and evil we know in the field of this world grow up together almost inseparably; and the knowledge of good is so involved and interwoven with the knowledge of evil, and in so many cunning resemblances hardly to be discerned, that those confused seeds which were imposed upon Psyche as an incessant labour to cull out, and sort asunder, were not more intermixed. It was from out the rind of one apple tasted, that the knowledge of good and evil, as two twins cleaving together, leaped forth into the world. And perhaps this is that doom which Adam fell into of knowing good and evil, that is to say of knowing good by evil. As therefore the state of man now is; what wisdom can there be to choose, what continence to forbear without the knowledge of evil? He that can apprehend and consider vice with all her baits and seeming pleasures, and yet abstain, and yet distinguish, and yet prefer that which is truly better, he is the true warfaring Christian.

I cannot praise a fugitive and cloistered virtue, unexercised and unbreathed, that never sallies out and sees her adversary, but slinks out of the race, where that immortal garland is to be run for, not without dust and heat. Assuredly we bring not innocence into the world, we bring impurity much rather; that which purifies us is trial, and trial is by what is contrary. That virtue therefore which is but a youngling in the contemplation of evil, and knows not the utmost that vice promises to her followers, and rejects it, is but a blank virtue, not a pure; her whiteness is but an excremental whiteness. Which was the reason why our sage and serious poet Spenser, whom I dare be known to think a better teacher than Scotus or Aquinas, describing true temperance under the person of Guion, brings him in with his palmer through the cave of Mammon, and the bower of earthly bliss, that he might see and know, and yet abstain. Since therefore the knowledge and survey of vice is in this world so necessary to the constituting of human virtue, and the scanning of error to the confirmation of truth, how can we more safely, and with less danger, scout into the regions of sin and falsity than by reading all manner of tractates and hearing all manner of reason? And this is the benefit which may be had of books promiscuously read. . . .

Seeing, therefore, that those books, and those in great abundance, which are likeliest to taint both life and doctrine, cannot be suppressed without the fall of learning and of all ability in disputation, and that these books of either sort are most and soonest catching to the learned, from whom to the common people whatever is heretical or dissolute may quickly be conveyed, and that evil manners are as perfectly learnt without books a thousand other ways which cannot be stopped, and evil doctrine not with books can propagate, except a teacher guide, which he might also do without writing, and so beyond prohibiting, I am not able to unfold, how this cautelous enterprise of licensing can be exempted from the number of vain and impossible attempts. And he who were pleasantly disposed could not well avoid to liken it to the exploit of that gallant man who thought to pound up the crows by shutting his park gate.

Besides another inconvenience, if learned men be the first receivers out of books and dispreaders both of vice and error, how shall the licensers themselves be confided in, unless we can confer upon them, or they assume to themselves above all others in the land, the grace of infallibility and uncorruptedness? And again, if it be true that a wise man, like a good refiner, can gather gold out of the drossiest volume, and that a fool will be a fool with the best book, yea or without book; there is no reason that we should deprive a wise man of any advantage to his wisdom, while we seek to restrain from a fool, that which being restrained will be no hindrance to his folly. For if there should be so much exactness always used to keep that from him which is unfit for his reading, we should in the judgment of Aristotle not only, but of Solomon and of our Saviour, not vouchsafe him good precepts, and by consequence not willingly admit him to good books; as being certain that a wise man will make better use of an idle pamphlet, than a fool will do of sacred Scripture. . . .

If we think to regulate printing, thereby to rectify manners, we must regulate all recreations and pastimes, all that is delightful to man. No music must be heard, no song be set or sung, but what is grave and Doric. There must be licensing dancers, that no gesture, motion, or deportment be taught our youth but what by their allowance shall be thought honest; for such Plato was provided of. It will ask more than the work of twenty licensers to examine all the lutes, the violins, and the guitars in every house; they must not be suffered to prattle as they do, but must be licensed what they may say. And who shall silence all the airs and madrigals that whisper softness in chambers? The windows also, and the balconies must be thought on; there are shrewd books, with dangerous frontispieces, set to sale; who shall prohibit them, shall twenty licensers? The villages also must have their visitors to inquire what lectures the bagpipe and the rebeck reads, even to the ballatry and the gamut of every municipal fiddler, for these are the countryman's Arcadias, and his Monte Mayors.

Next, what more national corruption, for which England hears ill abroad, than household gluttony: who shall be the rectors of our daily rioting? And what shall be done to inhibit the multitudes that frequent those houses where drunkenness is sold and harboured? Our garments also should be referred to the licensing of some more sober workmasters to see them cut into a less wanton garb. Who shall regulate all the mixed conversation of our youth, male and female together, as is the fashion of this country? Who shall still appoint what shall be discoursed, what presumed, and no further? Lastly, who shall forbid and separate all idle resort, all evil company? These things will be, and must be; but how they shall be least hurtful, how least enticing, herein consists the grave and governing wisdom of a state.

To sequester out of the world into Atlantic and Utopian politics, which never can be drawn into use, will not mend our condition; but to ordain wisely as in this world of evil, in the midst whereof God hath placed us unavoidably. Nor is it Plato's licensing of books will do this, which necessarily pulls along with it so many other kinds of licensing, as will make us all both ridiculous and weary, and yet frustrate; but those unwritten, or at least unconstraining, laws of virtuous education, religious and civil nurture, which Plato there mentions as the bonds and ligaments of the commonwealth, the pillars and the sustainers of every written statute; these they be which will bear chief sway in such matters as these, when all licensing will be easily eluded. Impunity and remissness, for certain, are the bane of a commonwealth; but here the great art lies, to discern in what the law is to bid restraint and punishment, and in what things persuasion only is to work.

If every action, which is good or evil in man at ripe years, were to be under pittance and prescription and compulsion, what were virtue but a name, what praise could be then due to well-doing, what gramercy to be sober, just, or continent? Many there be that complain of divine Providence for suffering Adam to transgress; foolish tongues! When God gave him reason, he gave him freedom to choose, for reason is but choosing; he had been else a mere artificial Adam, such an Adam as he is in the motions. We ourselves esteem not of that obedience, or love, or gift, which is of force: God therefore left him free, set before him a provoking object, ever almost in his eyes; herein consisted his merit, herein the right of his reward, the praise of his abstinence. Wherefore did he create passions within us, pleasures round about us, but that these rightly tempered are the very ingredients of virtue?

They are not skillful considerers of human things, who imagine to remove sin by removing the matter of sin; for, besides that it is a huge heap increasing under the very act of diminishing, though some part of it may for a time be withdrawn from some persons, it cannot from all, in such a universal thing as books are; and when this is done, yet the sin remains entire. Though ye take from a covetous man all his treasure, he has yet one jewel left, ye cannot bereave him of his covetousness. Banish all objects of lust, shut up all youth in the severest discipline that can be exercised in any hermitage, ye cannot make them chaste, that came not thither so; such great care and wisdom is required to the right managing of this point. Suppose we could expel sin by this means; look how much we thus expel of sin, so much we expel of virtue: for the matter of them both is the same; remove that, and ye remove them both alike.

This justifies the high providence of God, who, though he command us temperance, justice, continence, yet pours out before us, even to a profuseness, all desirable things, and gives us minds that can wander beyond all limit and satiety. Why should we then affect a rigour contrary to the manner of God and of nature, by abridging or scanting those means, which books freely permitted are, both to the trial of virtue and the exercise of truth? It would be better done, to learn that the law must needs be frivolous, which goes to restrain things, uncertainly and yet equally working to good and to evil. And were I the chooser, a dram of well-doing should be preferred before many times as much the forcible hindrance of evil-doing. For God sure esteems the growth and completing of one virtuous person more than the restraint of ten vicious.

STUDY QUESTIONS

1. *This is a brief selection from Milton's famous prose pamphlet written in 1644 as an argument against the restriction of freedom of the press. It is powerfully persuasive argument by one of the masters of English prose, but it clearly belongs to an earlier period. What stylistic characteristics—vocabulary, sentence patterns, figures of speech—mark it off from the prose of such writers as Mill in the 19th century, or Becker in our own century?*

2. *Why does Milton say that it is a worse crime to "kill" a book by suppressing or destroying it, than to kill a man?*

3. *What is the logic of Milton's argument that it is important to read books that are wrong and evil as well as others?*

4. *What reasons does Milton give for arguing that censorship is impractical? What is the view of human nature which is the basis of Milton's point of view?*

5. *Do you agree with Milton that an extreme degree of freedom of the press is desirable? If you believe that certain kinds of censorship are justified, write a theme explaining your opinion.*

6. *Are you acquainted with any incidents or institutions involving censorship that existed or exist in the United States? Write a theme describing one of them and evaluating it against Milton's principles.*

John Stuart Mill On Liberty*

The subject of this Essay is not the so-called Liberty of the Will, so un-fortunately opposed to the misnamed doctrine of Philosophical Necessity; but Civil, or Social Liberty: the nature and limits of the power which can be legitimately exercised by society over the individual. A question seldom stated, and hardly ever discussed, in general terms, but which profoundly influences the practical controversies of the age by its latent presence, and is likely soon to make itself recognized as the vital question of the future. It is so far from being new, that, in a certain sense, it has divided mankind, almost from the remotest ages; but in the stage of progress into which the more civilized portions of the species have now entered, it presents itself under new conditions, and requires a different and more fundamental treatment.

The struggle between Liberty and Authority is the most conspicuous feature in the portions of history with which we are earliest familiar, par-ticularly in that of Greece, Rome, and England. But in old times this contest was between subjects, or some classes of subjects, and the government. By liberty, was meant protection against the tyranny of the political rulers. The rulers were conceived (except in some of the popular governments of Greece) as in a necessarily antagonistic position to the people whom they ruled. They consisted of a governing One, or a governing tribe or caste, who derived their authority from inheritance or conquest; who, at all events, did not hold it at the pleasure of the governed, and whose supremacy men did not venture, perhaps did not desire, to contest, whatever precautions might be taken against its oppressive exercise. Their power was regarded as necessary, but also as highly dangerous; as a weapon which they would attempt to use against their subjects, no less than against external enemies. To prevent the weaker mem-bers of the community from being preyed upon by innumerable vultures, it was needful that there should be an animal of prey stronger than the rest, commissioned to keep them down. But as the king of vultures would be no less bent upon preying on the flock than any of the minor harpies, it was indispensable to be in a perpetual attitude of defence against his beak and claws. The aim, therefore, of patriots, was to set limits to the power which the ruler should be suffered to exercise over the community; and this limita-tion was what they meant by liberty. It was attempted in two ways. First, by obtaining a recognition of certain immunities, called political liberties or rights, which it was to be regarded as a breach of duty in the ruler to infringe, and which, if he did infringe, specific resistance, or general rebellion, was

* First published in 1859.

held to be justifiable. A second, and generally a later expedient, was the establishment of constitutional checks; by which the consent of the community, or of a body of some sort supposed to represent its interests, was made a necessary condition to some of the more important acts of the governing power. To the first of these modes of limitation, the ruling power, in most European countries, was compelled, more or less, to submit. It was not so with the second; and to attain this, or when already in some degree possessed, to attain it more completely, became everywhere the principal object of the lovers of liberty. And so long as mankind were content to combat one enemy by another, and to be ruled by a master, on condition of being guaranteed more or less efficaciously against his tyranny, they did not carry their aspirations beyond this point.

A time, however, came, in the progress of human affairs, when men ceased to think it a necessity of nature that their governors should be an independent power, opposed in interest to themselves. It appeared to them much better that the various magistrates of the State should be their tenants or delegates, revocable at their pleasure. In that way alone, it seemed, could they have complete security that the powers of government would never be abused to their disadvantage. By degrees, this new demand for elective and temporary rulers became the prominent object of the exertions of the popular party, wherever any such party existed; and superseded, to a considerable extent, the previous efforts to limit the power of rulers. As the struggle proceeded for making the ruling power emanate from the periodical choice of the ruled, some persons began to think that too much importance had been attached to the limitation of the power itself. *That* (it might seem) was a resource against rulers whose interests were habitually opposed to those of the people. What was now wanted was, that the rulers should be identified with the people; that their interest and will should be the interest and will of the nation. The nation did not need to be protected against its own will. There was no fear of its tyrannizing over itself. Let the rulers be effectually responsible to it, promptly removable by it, and it could afford to trust them with power of which it could itself dictate the use to be made. Their power was but the nation's own power, concentrated, and in a form convenient for exercise. This mode of thought, or rather perhaps of feeling, was common among the last generation of European liberalism, in the Continental section of which, it still apparently predominates. Those who admit any limit to what a government may do, except in the case of such governments as they think ought not to exist, stand out as brilliant exceptions among the political thinkers of the Continent. A similar tone of sentiment might by this time have been prevalent in our own country, if the circumstances which for a time encouraged it had continued unaltered.

But, in political and philosophical theories, as well as in persons, success discloses faults and infirmities which failure might have concealed from observation. The notion, that the people have no need to limit their power over themselves, might seem axiomatic, when popular government was a thing only dreamed about, or read of as having existed at some distant period of the past. Neither was that notion necessarily disturbed by such temporary aberrations as those of the French Revolution, the worst of which were the work of an usurping few, and which, in any case, belonged, not to the permanent working of popular institutions, but to a sudden and convulsive outbreak against monarchical and aristocratic despotism. In time, however, a democratic republic came to occupy a large portion of the earth's surface, and made itself felt as one of the most powerful members of the community of nations; and elective and responsible government became subject to the observations and criticisms which wait upon a great existing fact. It was now perceived that such phrases as "self-government," and "the power of the people over themselves," do not express the true state of the case. The "people" who exercise the power, are not always the same people with those over whom it is exercised; and the self-government spoken of, is not the government of each by himself, but of each by all the rest. The will of the people, moreover, practically means, the will of the most numerous or the most active *part* of the people; the majority, or those who succeed in making themselves accepted as the majority: the people, consequently, *may* desire to oppress a part of their number; and precautions are as much needed against this, as against any other abuse of power. The limitation, therefore, of the power of government over individuals, loses none of its importance when the holders of powers are regularly accountable to the community, that is, to the strongest party therein. This view of things, recommending itself equally to the intelligence of thinkers and to the inclination of those important classes in European society to whose real or supposed interests democracy is adverse, has had no difficulty in establishing itself; and in political speculations "the tyranny of the majority" is now generally included among the evils against which society requires to be on its guard.

Like other tyrannies, the tyranny of the majority was at first, and is still vulgarly, held in dread, chiefly as operating through the acts of the public authorities. But reflecting persons perceived that when society is itself the tyrant — society collectively, over the separate individuals who compose it —its means of tyrannizing are not restricted to the acts which it may do by the hands of its political functionaries. Society can and does execute its own mandates: and if it issues wrong mandates instead of right, or any mandates at all in things with which it ought not to meddle, it practises a social tyranny more formidable than many kinds of political oppression, since, though not usually upheld by such extreme penalties, it leaves fewer means of escape, penetrating much more deeply into the details of life, and enslaving the soul itself. Protection, therefore, against the tyranny of the magistrate is not enough; there needs protection also against the tyranny of the prevailing opinion and feeling; against the tendency of society to impose, by other means than civil penalties, its own ideas and practices as rules of conduct on those who dissent from them; to fetter the development, and, if possible, prevent the formation, of any individuality not in harmony with its ways, and compel all characters to fashion themselves upon the model of its own. There is a limit to the legitimate interference of collective opinion with individual independence; and to find that limit, and maintain it against encroachment, is as indispensable to a good condition of human affairs, as protection against political despotism.

But though this proposition is not likely to be contested in general terms, the practical question, where to place the limit — how to make the fitting adjustment between individual independence and social control — is a subject on which nearly everything remains to be done. All that makes existence valuable to any one, depends on the enforcement of restraints upon the actions of other people. Some rules of conduct, therefore, must be imposed, by law in the first place, and by opinion on many things which are not fit subjects for the operation of law. What these rules should be, is the principal question in human affairs; but if we except a few of the most obvious cases, it is one of those which least progress has been made in resolving. No two ages, and scarcely any two countries, have decided it alike; and the decision of one age or country is a wonder to another. Yet the people of any given age and country no more suspect any difficulty in it, than if it were a subject on which mankind had always been agreed. The rules which obtain among themselves appear to them self-evident and self-justifying. This all but universal illusion is one of the examples of the magical influence of custom, which is not only, as the proverb says, a second nature, but is continually mistaken for the first. The effect of custom, in preventing any misgiving respecting the rules of conduct which mankind impose on one another, is all the more complete because the subject is one on which it is not generally considered necessary that reasons should be given, either by one person to others, or by each to himself. People are accustomed to believe, and have been encouraged in the belief by some who aspire to the character of philosophers, that their feelings, on subjects of this nature, are better than reasons, and render reasons unnecessary. The practical principle which guides them to their opinions on the regulation of human conduct, is the feeling in each person's mind that everybody should be required to act as he, and those with whom he sympathizes, would like them to act. No one, indeed, acknowledges to himself that his standard of judgment is his own liking; but an opinion on a point of conduct, not supported by reasons, can only count as one person's preference; and if the reasons, when given, are a mere appeal to a similar preference felt by other people, it is still only many people's liking instead of one. To an ordinary man, however, his own preference, thus supported, is not only a perfectly satisfactory reason, but the only one he generally has for any of his notions of morality, taste, or propriety, which are not expressly written in his religious creed; and his chief guide in the interpretation even of that. Men's opinions, accordingly, on what is laudable or blameable, are affected by all the multifarious causes which influence their wishes in regard to the conduct of others, and which are as numerous as those which determine their wishes on any other subject. Sometimes their reason — at other times their prejudices or superstitions: often their social affections, not seldom their antisocial ones, their envy or jealousy, their arrogance or contemptuousness: but most commonly, their desires or fears for themselves — their legitimate or illegitimate self-interest. Wherever there is an ascendant class, a large portion of the morality of the country emanates from its class interests, and its feelings of class superiority. The morality between Spartans and Helots, between planters and negroes, between princes and subjects, between nobles and roturiers, between men and women, has been for the most part the creation of these class interests and feelings: and the sentiments thus generated, react in turn upon the moral feelings of the members of the ascendant class, in their relations among themselves. Where, on the other hand, a class, formerly ascendant, has lost its ascendancy, or where its ascendancy is unpopular, the prevailing moral sentiments frequently bear the impress of an impatient dislike of superiority. Another grand determining principle of the rules of conduct, both in act and forbearance, which have been enforced by law or opinion, has been the servility of mankind towards the supposed preferences or aversions of their temporal masters, or of their gods. This servility, though essentially selfish, is not hypocrisy; it gives rise to perfectly genuine sentiments of abhorrence; it made men burn magicians and heretics. Among so many baser influences, the general and obvious interests of society have of course had a share, and a large one, in the direction of the moral sentiments: less, however, as a matter of reason, and on their own account, than as a consequence of the sympathies and antipathies which grew out of them: and sympathies and antipathies which had little or nothing to do with the interests of society, have made themselves felt in the establishment of moralities with quite as great force.

The likings and dislikings of society, or of some powerful portion of it, are thus the main thing which has practically determined the rules laid down for general observance, under the penalties of law or opinion. And in general, those who have been in advance of society in thought and feeling, have left this condition of things unassailed in principle, however they may have come into conflict with it in some of its details. They have occupied themselves rather in inquiring what things society ought to like or dislike, than in questioning whether its likings or dislikings should be a law to individuals. They preferred endeavoring to alter the feelings of mankind on the particular points on which they were themselves heretical, rather than make common cause in defence of freedom, with heretics generally. The only case in which the higher ground has been taken on principle and maintained with consistency, by any but an individual here and there, is that of religious belief: a case instructive in many ways, and not least so as forming a most striking instance of the fallibility of what is called the moral sense: for the *odium theologicum*,[1] in a sincere bigot, is one of the most unequivocal cases of moral feeling. Those who first broke the yoke of what called itself the Universal Church, were in general as little willing to permit difference of religious opinion as that church itself. But when the heat of the conflict was over, without giving a complete victory to any party, and each church or sect was reduced to limit its hopes to retaining possession of the ground it already occupied; minorities, seeing that they had no chance of becoming majorities, were under the necessity of pleading to those whom they could not convert, for permission to differ. It is accordingly on this battle-field, almost solely, that the rights of the individual against society have been asserted on broad grounds of principle, and the claim of society to exercise authority over dissentients openly controverted. The great writers to whom the world owes what religious liberty it possesses, have mostly asserted freedom of conscience as an indefeasible right, and denied absolutely that a human being is accountable to others for his religious belief. Yet so natural to mankind is intolerance in whatever they really care about, that religious freedom has hardly anywhere been practically realized, except where religious indifference, which dislikes to have its peace disturbed by theological quarrels, has added its weight to the scale. In the minds of almost all religious persons, even in the most tolerant countries, the duty of toleration is admitted with tacit reserves. One person will bear with dissent in matters of church government, but not of dogma; another can tolerate everybody, short of a Papist or an Unitarian; another, every one who believes in revealed religion; a few extend their charity a little further, but stop at the belief in a God and in a future state. Wherever the sentiment of the majority is still genuine and intense, it is found to have abated little of its claim to be obeyed.

In England, from the peculiar circumstances of our political history, though the yoke of opinion is perhaps heavier, that of law is lighter, than in most other countries of Europe; and there is considerable jealousy of direct interference, by the legislative or the executive power, with private conduct; not so much from any just regard for the independence of the individual, as from the still subsisting habit of looking on the government as representing an opposite interest to the public. The majority have not yet learnt to feel the power of the government their power, or its opinions their opinions. When they do so, individual liberty will probably be as much exposed to invasion from the government, as it already is from public opinion. But, as yet, there is a considerable amount of feeling ready to be called forth against any attempt of the law to control individuals in things in which they have not hitherto been accustomed to be controlled by it; and this with very little discrimination as to whether the matter is, or is not, within the legitimate sphere of legal control; insomuch that the feeling, highly salutary on the whole, is perhaps quite as often misplaced as well grounded in the particular instances of its application. There is, in fact, no recognized principle by which the propriety or impropriety of government interference is customarily

---

[1] Detestation felt by one theologian or sect for another.

tested. People decide according to their personal preferences. Some, whenever they see any good to be done, or evil to be remedied, would willingly instigate the government to undertake the business; while others prefer to bear almost any amount of social evil, rather than add one to the departments of human interests amenable to governmental control. And men range themselves on one or the other side in any particular case, according to this general direction of their sentiments; or according to the degree of interest which they feel in the particular thing it is proposed that the government should do; or according to the belief they entertain that the government would, or would not, do it in the manner they prefer; but very rarely on account of any opinion to which they consistently adhere, as to what things are fit to be done by a government. And it seems to me that, in consequence of this absence of rule or principle, one side is at present as often wrong as the other; the interference of government is, with about equal frequency, improperly invoked and improperly condemned.

The object of this Essay is to assert one very simple principle, as entitled to govern absolutely the dealings of society with the individual in the way of compulsion and control, whether the means used be physical force in the form of legal penalties, or the moral coercion of public opinion. That principle is, that the sole end for which mankind are warranted, individually or collectively, in interfering with the liberty of action of any of their number, is self-protection. That the only purpose for which power can be rightfully exercised over any member of a civilized community, against his will, is to prevent harm to others. His own good, either physical or moral, is not a sufficient warrant. He cannot rightfully be compelled to do or forbear because it will be better for him to do so, because it will make him happier, because, in the opinions of others, to do so would be wise, or even right. These are good reasons for remonstrating with him, or reasoning with him, or persuading him, or entreating him, but not for compelling him, or visiting him with any evil, in case he do otherwise. To justify that, the conduct from which it is desired to deter him must be calculated to produce evil to some one else. The only part of the conduct of any one, for which he is amenable to society, is that which concerns others. In the part which merely concerns himself, his independence is, of right, absolute. Over himself, over his own body and mind, the individual is sovereign.

It is, perhaps, hardly necessary to say that this doctrine is meant to apply only to human beings in the maturity of their faculties. We are not speaking of children, or of young persons below the age which the law may fix as that of manhood or womanhood. Those who are still in a state to require being taken care of by others, must be protected against their own actions as well as against external injury. For the same reason, we may leave out of consideration those backward states of society in which the race itself may be considered as in its nonage. The early difficulties in the way of spontaneous progress are so great, that there is seldom any choice of means for overcoming them; and a ruler full of the spirit of improvement is warranted in the use of any expedients that will attain an end, perhaps otherwise unattainable. Despotism is a legitimate mode of government in dealing with barbarians, provided the end be their improvement, and the means justified by actually effecting that end. Liberty, as a principle, has no application to any state of things anterior to the time when mankind have become capable of being improved by free and equal discussion. Until then, there is nothing for them but implicit obedience to an Akbar or a Charlemagne, if they are so fortunate as to find one. But as soon as mankind have attained the capacity of being guided to their own improvement by conviction or persuasion (a period long since reached in all nations with whom we need here concern ourselves), compulsion, either in the direct form or in that of pains and penalties for non-compliance, is no longer admissible as a means to their own good, and justifiable only for the security of others.

It is proper to state that I forego any advantage which could be derived to my argument from the idea of abstract right, as a thing independent of utility. I regard utility as the ultimate appeal on all ethical questions; but it must be utility in the largest sense, grounded on the permanent interests of man as a progressive being. Those interests, I contend, authorize the subjection of individual spontaneity to external control, only in respect to those actions of each, which concern the interest of other people. If any one does an act hurtful to others there is a *primâ facie* case for punishing him, by law, or, where legal penalties are not safely applicable, by general disapprobation. There are also many positive acts for the benefit of others, which he may rightfully be compelled to perform; such as, to give evidence in a court of justice; to bear his fair share in the common defence, or in any other joint work necessary to the interest of the society of which he enjoys the protection; and to perform certain acts of individual beneficence, such as saving a fellow creature's life, or interposing to protect the defenceless against ill-usage, things which whenever it is obviously a man's duty to do, he may rightfully be made responsible to society for not doing. A person may cause evil to others not only by his actions but by his inaction, and in either case he is justly accountable to them for the injury. The latter case, it is true, requires a much more cautious exercise of compulsion than the former. To make any one answerable for doing evil to others, is the rule; to make him answerable for not preventing evil, is, comparatively speaking, the exception. Yet there are many cases clear enough and grave enough to justify that exception. In all things which regard the external relations of the individual, he is *de jure* amenable to those whose interests are concerned, and if need be, to society as their protector. There are often good reasons for not holding him to the responsibility; but these reasons must arise from the special expediences of the case: either because it is a kind of case in which he is on the whole likely to act better, when left to his own discretion, than when controlled in any way in which society have it in their power to control him; or because the attempt to exercise control would produce other evils, greater than those which it would prevent. When such reasons as these preclude the enforcement of responsibility, the conscience of the agent himself should step into the vacant judgment-seat, and protect those interests of others which have no external protection; judging himself all the more rigidly, because the case does not admit of his being made accountable to the judgment of his fellow-creatures.

But there is a sphere of action in which society, as distinguished from the individual, has, if any, only an indirect interest; comprehending all that portion of a person's life and conduct which affects only himself, or, if it also affects others, only with their free, voluntary, and undeceived consent and participation. When I say only himself, I mean directly, and in the first instance: for whatever affects himself, may affect others *through* himself; and the objection which may be grounded on this contingency, will receive consideration in the sequel. This, then, is the appropriate region of human liberty. It comprises, first, the inward domain of consciousness; demanding liberty of conscience, in the most comprehensive sense; liberty of thought and feeling; absolute freedom of opinion and sentiment on all subjects, practical or speculative, scientific, moral, or theological. The liberty of expressing and publishing opinions may seem to fall under a different principle, since it belongs to that part of the conduct of an individual which concerns other people; but, being almost of as much importance as the liberty of thought itself, and resting in great part on the same reasons, is practically inseparable from it. Secondly, the principle requires liberty of tastes and pursuits; of framing the plan of our life to suit our own character; of doing as we like, subject to such consequences as may follow; without impediment from our fellow-creatures, so long as what we do does not harm them, even though they should think our conduct foolish, perverse, or wrong. Thirdly, from this liberty of each individual, follows the liberty, within the same limits, of combination among individuals; freedom to unite, for any purpose not involving harm to others: the persons combining being supposed to be of full age, and not forced or deceived.

No society in which these liberties are not, on the whole, respected, is free, whatever may be its form of government; and none is completely free in which they do not exist absolute and unqualified. The only freedom which deserves the name, is that of pursuing our own good in our own way, so long as we do not attempt to deprive others of theirs, or impede their efforts to obtain it. Each is the proper guardian of his own health, whether bodily, or mental and spiritual. Mankind are greater gainers by suffering each other to live as seems good to themselves, than by compelling each to live as seems good to the rest.

Though this doctrine is anything but new, and, to some persons, may have the air of a truism, there is no doctrine which stands more directly opposed to the general tendency of existing opinion and practice. Society has expended fully as much effort in the attempt (according to its lights) to compel people to conform to its notions of personal, as of social excellence. The ancient commonwealths thought themselves entitled to practise, and the ancient philosophers countenanced, the regulation of every part of private conduct by public authority, on the ground that the State had a deep interest in the whole bodily and mental discipline of every one of its citizens; a mode of thinking which may have been admissible in small republics surrounded by powerful enemies, in constant peril of being subverted by foreign attack or internal commotion, and to which even a short interval of relaxed energy and self-command might so easily be fatal, that they could not afford to wait for the salutary permanent effects of freedom. In the modern world, the greater size of political communities, and above all, the separation between the spiritual and temporal authority (which placed the direction of men's consciences in other hands than those which controlled their worldly affairs), prevented so great an interference by law in the details of private life; but the engines of moral repression have been wielded more strenuously against divergence from the reigning opinion in self-regarding, than even in social matters; religion, the most powerful of the elements which have entered into the formation of moral feeling, having almost always been governed either by the ambition of a hierarchy, seeking control over every department of human conduct, or by the spirit of Puritanism. And some of those modern reformers who have placed themselves in strongest opposition to the religions of the past, have been noway behind either churches or sects in their assertion of the right of spiritual domination: M. Comte, in particular, whose social system, as unfolded in his *Traité de Politique Positive,* aims at establishing (though by moral more than by legal appliances) a despotism of society over the individual, surpassing anything contemplated in the political ideal of the most rigid disciplinarian among the ancient philosophers.

Apart from the peculiar tenets of individual thinkers, there is also in the world at large an increasing inclination to stretch unduly the powers of society over the individual, both by the force of opinion and even by that of legislation: and as the tendency of all the changes taking place in the world is to strengthen society, and diminish the power of the individual, this encroachment is not one of the evils which tend spontaneously to disappear, but, on the contrary, to grow more and more formidable. The disposition of mankind, whether as rulers or as fellow-citizens, to impose their own opinions and inclinations as a rule of conduct on others, is so energetically supported by some of the best and by some of the worst feelings incident to human nature, that it is hardly ever kept under restraint by anything but want of power; and as the power is not declining, but growing, unless a strong barrier of moral conviction can be raised against the mischief, we must expect, in the present circumstances of the world, to see it increase....

STUDY QUESTIONS

1. *What does Mill mean by "the tyranny of the majority"?*
2. *What two central principles here does Mill fail to support by logic or evidence? Why has Mill failed to support them in this way? Is it possible for them to be denied? If so, under what conditions?*

3. Do you believe Mill should have included "property" together with "mind and body" among the things over which the individual has sovereignty? Why?

4. Mill says that the usual way of judging the rival claims of collective welfare and individual liberty has been by "likings and dislikings," but he does not say why he thinks this method is a poor one. Why is it subject to criticism? Can anything be said in its defence?

5. Write a theme showing how some particular historical event reflected the issues Mill deals with here. Possibilities would be the trial of Socrates, the migration of colonists to America, the Scopes trial, or any case in which individual and collective wills clashed with each other.

6. Write a theme discussing the validity of one of the following in the light of Mill's principle that the individual should be sovereign over his own mind and body: compulsory schooling; compulsory military service; the pledge of allegiance to the flag in schools; the requirement that government workers take loyalty oaths; routine vaccination of school children.

Henry David Thoreau

FROM On the Duty of Civil Disobedience*

I heartily accept the motto, — "That government is best which governs least"; and I should like to see it acted up to more rapidly and systematically. Carried out, it finally amounts to this, which also I believe, — "That government is best which governs not at all"; and when men are prepared for it, that will be the kind of government which they will have. Government is at best but an expedient; but most governments are usually, and all governments are sometimes, inexpedient. The objections which have been brought against a standing army, and they are many and weighty, and deserve to prevail, may also at last be brought against a standing government. The standing army is only an arm of the standing government. The government itself, which is only the mode which the people have chosen to execute their will, is equally liable to be abused and perverted before the people can act through it. Witness the present Mexican war, the work of comparatively a few individuals using the standing government as their tool; for, in the outset, the people would not have consented to this measure.

This American government, — what is it but a tradition, though a recent one, endeavoring to transmit itself unimpaired to posterity, but each instant losing some of its integrity? It has not the vitality and force of a single living man; for a single man can bend it to his will. It is a sort of wooden gun to the people themselves. But it is not the less necessary for this; for the people must have some complicated machinery or other, and hear its din, to satisfy that idea of government which they have. Governments show us how suc-

* First published in 1849.

cessfully men can be imposed on, even impose on themselves, for their own advantage. It is excellent, we must all allow. Yet this government never of itself furthered any enterprise, but by the alacrity with which it got out of its way. *It* does not keep the country free. *It* does not settle the West. *It* does not educate. The character inherent in the American people has done all that has been accomplished; and it would have done somewhat more, if the government had not sometimes got in its way. For government is an expedient by which men would fain succeed in letting one another alone; and, as has been said, when it is most expedient, the governed are most let alone by it. Trade and commerce, if they were not made of India-rubber, would never manage to bounce over the obstacles which legislators are continually putting in their way; and, if one were to judge these men wholly by the effects of their actions and not partly by their intentions, they would deserve to be classed and punished with those mischievous persons who put obstructions on the railroads.

But, to speak practically and as a citizen, unlike those who call themselves no-government men, I ask for, not at once no government, but *at once* a better government. Let every man make known what kind of government would command his respect, and that will be one step toward obtaining it.

After all, the practical reason why, when the power is once in the hands of the people, a majority are permitted, and for a long period continue, to rule is not because they are most likely to be in the right, nor because this seems fairest to the minority, but because they are physically the strongest. But a government in which the majority rule in all cases cannot be based on justice, even as far as men understand it. Can there not be a government in which majorities do not virtually decide right and wrong, but conscience? — in which majorities decide only those questions to which the rule of expediency is applicable? Must the citizen ever for a moment, or in the least degree, resign his conscience to the legislator? Why has every man a conscience, then? I think that we should be men first, and subjects afterward. It is not desirable to cultivate a respect for the law, so much as for the right. The only obligation which I have a right to assume is to do at any time what I think right. It is truly enough said, that a corporation has no conscience; but a corporation of conscientious men is a corporation *with* a conscience. Law never made men a whit more just; and, by means of their respect for it, even the well-disposed are daily made the agents of injustice. A common and natural result of an undue respect for law, is that you may see a file of soldiers, colonel, captain, corporal, privates, powder-monkeys, and all, marching in admirable order over hill and dale to the wars, against their wills, ay, against their common sense and consciences, which makes it very steep marching indeed, and produces a palpitation of the heart. They have no doubt that it is a damnable business in which they are concerned; they are all peaceably inclined. Now, what are they? Men at all? or small movable forts and magazines, at the service of some unscrupulous man in power? Visit the Navy-Yard, and behold a marine, such a man as an American government can make, or such as it can make a man with its black arts,— a mere shadow and reminiscence of humanity, a man laid out alive and standing, and already, as one may say, buried under arms with funeral accompaniments, . . .

The mass of men serve the state thus, not as men mainly, but as machines, with their bodies. They are the standing army, and the militia, jailors, constables, posse comitatus, etc. In most cases there is no free exercise whatever of the judgment or of the moral sense; but they put themselves on a level with wood and earth and stones; and wooden men can perhaps be manufactured that will serve the purpose as well. Such command no more respect than men of straw or a lump of dirt. They have the same sort of worth only as horses and dogs. Yet such as these even are commonly esteemed good citizens. Others—as most legislators, politicians, lawyers, ministers, and office-holders—serve the state chiefly with their heads; and, as they rarely make any moral distinctions, they are as likely to serve the Devil, without *intending* it, as God. A very few, as heroes, patriots, martyrs, reformers in the great sense, and *men*, serve the state with their consciences also, and so necessarily resist it for the most part; and they are commonly treated as enemies by it. . . .

How does it become a man to behave toward this American government to-day? I answer, that he cannot without disgrace be associated with it. I cannot for an instant recognize that political organization as *my* government which is the *slave's* government also.

All men recognize the right of revolution; that is, the right to refuse allegiance to, and to resist, the government, when its tyranny or its inefficiency are great and unendurable. But almost all say that such is not the case now. But such was the case, they think in the Revolution of '75. If one were to tell me that this was a bad government because it taxed certain foreign commodities brought to its ports, it is most probable that I should not make an ado about it, for I can do without them. All machines have their friction . . . But when the friction comes to have its machine, and oppression and robbery are organized, I say, let us not have such a machine any longer. In other words, when a sixth of the population of a nation which has undertaken to be the refuge of liberty are slaves, and a whole country is unjustly overrun and conquered by a foreign army, and subjected to military law, I think that it is not too soon for honest men to rebel and revolutionize. What makes this duty the more urgent is the fact that the country so overrun is not our own, but ours is the invading army. . . .

Practically speaking, the opponents to a reform in Massachusetts are not a hundred thousand politicians at the South, but a hundred thousand merchants and farmers here, who are more interested in commerce and agriculture than they are in humanity, and are not prepared to do justice to the slave and to Mexico, *cost what it may*. I quarrel not with far-off foes, but with those who, near at home, coöperate with, and do the bidding of, those far away, and without whom the latter would be harmless. We are accustomed to say, that the mass of men are unprepared; but improvement is slow, because the few are not materially wiser or better than the many. It is not so important that many should be as good as you, as that there be some absolute goodness somewhere; for that will leaven the whole lump. There are thousands who are *in opinion* opposed to slavery and to the war, who yet in effect do nothing to put an end to them; who, esteeming themselves children of Washington and Franklin, sit down with their hands in their pockets, and say that they know not what to do, and do nothing; who even postpone the question of freedom to the question of free-trade, and quietly read the prices-current along with the latest advices from Mexico, after dinner, and, it may be, fall asleep over them both. What is the price-current of an honest man and patriot to-day? They hesitate, and they regret, and sometimes they petition; but they do nothing in earnest and with effect. They will wait, well disposed, for others to remedy the evil, that they may no longer have it to regret. At most, they give only a cheap vote, and a feeble countenance and God-speed, to the right, as it goes by them. There are nine hundred and ninety-nine patrons of virtue to one virtuous man. But it is easier to deal with the real possessor of a thing than with the temporary guardian of it....

Unjust laws exist: shall we be content to obey them, or shall we endeavor to amend them, and obey them until we have succeeded, or shall we transgress them at once? Men generally, under such a government as this, think that they ought to wait until they have persuaded the majority to alter them. They think that, if they should resist, the remedy would be worse than the evil. But it is the fault of the government itself that the remedy *is* worse than the evil. *It* makes it worse. Why is it not more apt to anticipate and provide for reform? Why does it not cherish its wise minority? Why does it cry and resist before it is hurt? Why does it not encourage its citizens to be on the alert to point out its faults, and *do* better than it would have them? Why does it always crucify Christ, and excommunicate Copernicus and Luther, and pronounce Washington and Franklin rebels? ...

I do not hesitate to say, that those who call themselves Abolitionists should at once effectually withdraw their support, both in person and property, from the government of Massachusetts and not wait till they constitute a majority of one, before they suffer the right to prevail through them. I think that it is enough if they have God on their side, without waiting for that other one. Moreover, any man more right than his neighbors constitutes a majority of one already.

I meet this American government, or its representative, the state government, directly, and face to face, once a year—no more—in the person of its tax-gatherer; this is the only mode in which a man situated as I am necessarily meets it; and it then says distinctly, Recognize me; and the simplest, most effectual, and, in the present posture of affairs, the indispensablest mode of treating with it on this head, of expressing your little satisfaction with and love for it, is to deny it then. My civil neighbor, the tax-gatherer, is the very man I have to deal with,— for it is, after all, with men and not with parchment that I quarrel,— and he has voluntarily chosen to be an agent of the government. How shall he ever know well what he is and does as an officer of the government, or as a man, until he is obliged to consider whether he shall treat me, his neighbor, for whom he has respect, as a neighbor and well-disposed man, or as a maniac and disturber of the peace, and see if he can get over this obstruction to his neighborliness without a ruder and more impetuous thought of speech corresponding with his action. I know this well, and if one thousand, if one hundred, if ten men whom I could name,— if ten *honest* men only,— ay if *one* HONEST man, in this State of Massachusetts, *ceasing to hold slaves,* were actually to withdraw from this copartnership, and be locked up in the county jail therefor, it would be the abolition of slavery in America. For it matters not how small the beginning may seem to be: what is once well done is done forever....

Under a government which imprisons any unjustly, the true place for a just man is also a prison. The proper place to-day, the only place which Massachusetts has provided for her freer and less desponding spirits, is in her prisons, to be put out and locked out of the State by her own act, as they have already put themselves out by their principles. It is there that the fugitive slave, and the Mexican prisoner on parole, and the Indian come to plead the wrongs of his race should find them; on that separate, but more free and honorable ground, where the State places those who are not *with* her, but *against* her, — the only house in a slave State in which a free man can abide with honor. If any think that their influence would be lost there, and their voices no longer afflict the ear of the State, that they would not be as an enemy within its walls, they do not know by how much truth is stronger than error, nor how much more eloquently and effectively he can combat injustice who has experienced a little in his own person. Cast your whole vote, not a strip of paper merely, but your whole influence. A minority is powerless while it conforms to the majority; it is not even a minority then; but it is irresistible when it clogs by its whole weight. If the alternative is to keep all just men in prison, or give up war and slavery, the State will not hesitate which to choose. If a thousand men were not to pay their tax-bills this year, that would not be a violent and bloody measure, as it would be to pay them, and enable the State to commit violence and shed innocent blood. This is, in fact, the definition of a peaceable revolution, if any such is possible. If the tax-gatherer, or any other public officer, asks me, as one has done, "But what shall I do?" my answer is, "If you really wish to do any-thing, resign your office." When the subject has refused allegiance, and the officer has resigned his office, then the revolution is accomplished. But even suppose blood should flow. Is there not a sort of blood shed when the conscience is wounded? Through this wound a man's real manhood and immortality flow out, and he bleeds to an everlasting death. I see this blood flowing now....

The authority of government, even such as I am willing to submit to,— for I will cheerfully obey those who know and can do better than I, and in many things even those who neither know nor can do so well,— is still an impure one: to be strictly just, it must have the sanction and consent of the governed. It can have no pure right over my person and property but what I concede to it. The progress from an absolute to a limited monarchy, from a limited monarchy to a democracy, is a progress toward a true respect for the individual. Even the Chinese philosopher was wise enough to regard the individual as the basis of the empire. Is a democracy, such as we know it, the last improvement possible in government? Is it not possible to take a step further towards recognizing and organizing the rights of man? There will never be a really free and enlightened State until the State comes to recognize the individual as a higher and independent power, from which all its own power and authority are derived, and treats him accordingly. I please myself with imagining a State at last which can afford to be just to all men, and to treat the individual with respect as a neighbor; which even would not think it inconsistent with its own repose if a few were to live aloof from it, not meddling with it, nor embraced by it, who fulfilled all the duties of neighbors and fellow-men. A State which bore this kind of fruit, and suffered it to drop off as fast as it ripened, would prepare the way for a still more perfect and glorious State, which also I have imagined, but not yet anywhere seen.

STUDY QUESTIONS

1. *This is an edited version of Thoreau's famous essay, but his essential thesis and reasoning is preserved. What is his view of the relation between the people and the government? How pertinent to contemporary issues is his view?*

2. *What is the fundamental principle underlying Thoreau's objection to slavery, and to obedience to a government which condones it?*

3. *What method does Thoreau suggest for reforming the government? What does this method assume about the nature of the government that is to be reformed? Would the method work against a government that made use of violence and suppression?*

4. *Thoreau is, of course, dealing with a serious question here, but there are places where he uses satire and mockery to make his point. Locate some of these passages, and discuss their effectiveness.*

5. *Is Thoreau's idea that liberty is found in anarchy a sound one? Is he right in believing that "that government is best which governs not at all"?*

6. *Are there any dangers in Thoreau's method of civil disobedience? Or do you believe that it is, on the whole, a sound one for the citizens of a democracy to use in reforming their government?*

3. THE LONG VIEW

C. E. Ayres Society in the Light of Reason*

To regulate society by the laws of science is a laudable ambition — theoretically. The idea is a captivating one. Like the theory of the order of nature which needs only to be let alone to realize the kingdom of heaven upon earth, it has a certain esthetic charm. It would be nice if things were like that. We can stamp out a disease by discovering its cause, as for instance mosquito bites, and then eliminating mosquitoes. Why not stamp out crime by the same process? Crime, let us say, is a product of poverty. We have, then, only to stamp out poverty to prevent all crime. There is only one flaw in this reasoning, and that is that poverty is not like mosquitoes, something which can be extirpated, leaving all the rest of the visible world very much as it was before, but minus mosquitoes and minus yellow fever. Poverty is a very extensive and ancient institution. It is the nether boundary of affluence. Stamp out poverty and you stamp out affluence as well. Cut away both, and you have amputated civilization. In a very real sense, poverty is one of the elements which constitute civilization. So is crime. Crime is the nether boundary of moral and civic rectitude. Eliminate it and you eliminate civic virtue. There is no such thing as decency when there is no such thing as vice. In fine, the disagreeable aspects of civilization are just as much a part of the order of nature and just as definitely ordered by whatever laws there are as any other aspect.

Scientifically speaking, this is also true of mosquitoes — which only means that we do not exterminate mosquitoes as the result of scientific insights. We were resolved upon it for reasons of our own as an expression of our prejudice against dying of yellow fever before we knew that mosquitoes have any connection with that malady. Science applies only the means of achievement. The problems of civilization, on the other hand, are questions of what we want to achieve. Science has devised no technique for solving them. Whatever passed for solutions in former times was a product of the folk-ways, that is, of customs and habits that had always in some fashion got established. Reasoning from the past, the inference is that we can break away from one set of habits and the "superstitions" associated with them only by falling into

* From *Science, the False Messiah* by C. E. Ayres, copyright, 1927, 1954, used by special permission of the publishers, The Bobbs-Merrill Company, Inc.

another set of habits. What place is there for science in this cycle? In such a medium science can be effective only by abandoning its character of technician-in-chief to the mechanical arts and assuming the pontifical robes of folklore. In that character it can pour the anointing oil upon some "newly" established scheme of folkways. It can reveal our "infant industries" as the order of nature, and itself as a new and sublimer conception of God as the invisible hand. All this is quite effective — as a means of lending countenance to commerce. But it is not science in the "modern" sense; it is folklore in a very ancient sense indeed. On the other hand — and this is the real tragedy of science — to be itself it must put off its robes of omniscience and repair to the machine shop. There it can be modern, and efficient, and mechanical. But there, alas, it can do or say nothing that is in the remotest degree applicable to the problems of civilization.

We are just beginning to find this out. A generation or two ago, we began to realize that our infant industries were becoming lusty enough to tyrannize over the whole family. Simultaneously it occurred to us that human sympathies must have played a large part in the "intellectual" process by which the eighteenth century philosophers hit on commerce and manufacture as those departments of life most beloved of God the Invisible King. We could not accuse those grand old scholars of that kind of personal interest which was only too evident in the special pleading of public-be-damned business men. So we called theirs "unconscious bias" and when we had dissected it out, we labeled it "preconception." With these things in mind we determined that industry may require regulation after all; and we proceeded to regulate it with minds well cleared of the *laissez-faire* preconceptions of an older and less scientific day. Our procedure should be based on facts; and we went on to produce them in what is now generally known as the "era of muckraking." The stench was very great. We were therefore led to assume that the method was effective. We were at long last truly scientific. We were not formulating theories; we were exposing facts.

To our dismay and chagrin, however, all has not worked out precisely as our scientific calculations led us to expect. Gradually it began to appear that facts, even the most factual facts, are not self-operating. They require to be cranked up by some human driver before they will go anywhere; and this driver may be so very human as to influence the direction they are given. We could no doubt control our industries. But what is control? No one could possibly advocate a blind control which would exterminate all commercial combinations evenly and impartially, leaving nothing in the land but isolated business men. What we required was judicious control in the best interest of society. But the best interest of society, like prejudice against yellow fever, is a matter of tradition, and traditions are always subject to interpretation. In short, we found that the most eloquent facts mean different things to different men, and that what happened as a result of our determination to control our new stalwart industries was very largely affected by the human predilections of nine elderly men upon the Supreme Court of the United States. Preconceptions might be supplanted by facts in our array of evidence; but they could hardly be excluded from the breast of even the most august court. Some members of the court might be quite up-to-the-minute public-be-damned men of the world in their attitude toward these matters. Others might be sincere antiquarians, gentle and bookish octogenarians of pre-Adamite philosophy. Others might be warm-hearted sympathizers with the under-dog of the modern proletariat. But none could be scientific. That would be impossible. Moralists say that to understand everything is to forgive everything. Perhaps. But in science the rule is to know all the facts and to have no opinion. Opinion is a substitute for facts. It is the point at which facts leave off. Now facts or not, opinion or not, a court has got to get something done. It has got to exercise control. It has got to exceed facts by proceeding to acts. Those acts will be human acts in spite of everything facts can do. They will be based on the facts; but they will be the effect of those inanimate facts upon human preconceptions.

Thus we have discovered the human equation in social control. We have learned to our sorrow that facts propose but courts dispose. In the meantime, however, we have been more impressed than ever by the methods and techniques of science. The period of greatest social disillusionment — the period of great reforms gone awry and ending in international and industrial strife upon an unprecedented scale — has also been the period of greatest scientific achievement. The oldest and best established sciences, which we had almost begun to address in the past tense, have suddenly revolutionized their fundamental laws; while the newer ones, such as the various branches of biology, have made equally rapid strides toward maturity. More than ever before we feel now that science is mighty and will prevail. Consequently we have been more strongly convinced than ever that what is wrong with our social science is an insufficiency of science. In our chagrin over the persistence of human factors in the conduct of civilization, we have turned for compensation to a refurbishing of inanimate facts.

These facts are to be of various kinds; but especially they are to be psychological. The reason for this is that psychology is the science of the human equation. We have high hopes that by approaching these problems of civilization with a real scientific knowledge of the springs of sentiment in the human heart, we can dispose of them scientifically, consulting the heart only in the laboratories of psychology. In this fashion we shall be able to circumvent the preconceptions which so often influence even social scientists in the statement of their laws. We shall analyze preconceptions and provide against them. We shall similarly analyze the motives by which men in society are moved. The soft spot in eighteenth century philosophy was the theory of motives. Adam Smith and the others supposed men to be moved by quite simple considerations of economic self-interest. But later psychology has showed their economic man, their Robinson Crusoe on his desert isle, to be a far more complicated creature than they supposed. Very well; let modern psychology go on and exhibit the true economic man in all his complexity of motive. When it has finished, we shall have a sound scientific basis upon which to solve the problems of civilization. Social science, as we say so often now-a-days, waits upon psychology.

This is a large responsibility for psychology, which has its own preconceptions to deal with. In particular, it has been very much occupied with getting rid of the preconception that psychology is the description of the soul. As any one can see, the soul is a perfect stormcenter of preconceptions. To be scientific, psychology also has to be objective, to deal only in established facts, to avoid ancient beliefs. Consequently psychology has become a laboratory science, and has more and more excluded from consideration anything which can not be examined with instruments. The result of this has been, as every one knows, that psychology has become more and more a branch of biology and less and less a department of philosophy. The more it has had to say about "the organism as a whole," the less it has cared to hazard an opinion about man, the mysterious author of civilization.

Surely there is no reason for disparaging the science of the organism. If psychology and neurology between them succeed in unraveling the structure and working of the nervous system, we may be in a position to cure many diseases which now resist all treatment. This will be no small gain. But curing epilepsy and preventing dementia praecox are very different matters from solving the mysteries of human motives, just as different as stopping yellow fever and preventing crime. Psychology may become more scientific by such procedure. It may even become — what William James hardly dared to hope — a regular branch of science. But it does so at the cost of ceasing to peer into the human soul. The more it knows of reflexes and secretions, the less it is able to choose among them. If "all human behavior results from conditioned reflexes," what conditioned reflexes should Supreme Court judges have? This, it will be seen, is not a scientific question.

If we turn the searchlight of science from the human organism to man-in-society, the result is just the same. We get an accurate, detailed, and very disillusioning picture of how our vaunted civilization works. But we get no help. The fundamental "law" of social psychology seems to be that all human behavior is formed by pre-existing human behavior. This is the law of continuity. In adopting such a statement social psychology moved over into the neighborhood of anthropology just as psychology has courted physiology. Anthropology is the natural history of civilization. Instead of reflexes and secretions, it deals with folkways and folklore. The problems of anthropology are to identify the folkways and folklore of any given people as psychologists identify conditioned reflexes, and to trace them to their historic source. The fundamental law of anthropology is that all culture comes from culture, the law of continuity in another form. Anthropology is a science. The anthropologist may be able, by amassing tremendous quantities of evidence, to prove that a given culture trait, such as jazz music, was derived from such and such a source. He may prove that it comes from negro folk music, and that this came from ancient African ceremonials connected with tribal life in the African jungle. This enables us to make whatever inferences we like. We may then proceed to exterminate jazz by exterminating the negro race, or more humanely by making all colored people deaf-mutes and forbidding the publication and performance of tainted works. But there is no scientific authority for such procedure. The whole meaning of the law of continuity is that to science all culture is alike, just as to science all microbes are alike. Invidious discriminations among them are due to human prejudice. So are invidious discriminations among folkways.

But anthropology, which seems to be the end of the series of sciences to which we can appeal, is rather less amenable than the others to human use. This array of sciences suggests the experience of the old woman whose pig refused to get over the stile. She appealed to a stick to beat the pig, and then to a fire to burn the stick, and then to water to quench the fire, and then to an ox to drink the water, and then to a butcher to kill the ox, and then to a rope to hang the butcher, and then to a rat to gnaw the rope, and finally to a cat to kill the rat. The cat, it will be remembered, made conditions. But they were conditions with which the old lady was able to comply, so that very shortly the cat began to kill the rat, the rat began to gnaw the rope, and so on with the inevitable salubrious result. The appeal to reason in the manner of modern science has led from pillar to post and seems to end with the science which reveals the inmost mysteries of civilization. But unlike the cat, that one is less open to persuasion than all the others. Most sciences maintain an attitude of benevolent neutrality toward human aspirations. If we want to arrive at certain ends, science has nothing to say against it, and may be able to provide a vehicle. We can still hope for some other science to provide the signboards directing us where to go — until we reach anthropology. There we learn all too clearly that whither we go and why are matters toward which science may display a polite curiosity; but they are no more to be extracted from science than heavenly salvation. The whole meaning of the law of continuity is that they have got to come from us, from our pre-existing organized behavior. In short, human life moves by preconceptions and can proceed in no other way. This is what we learn from science.

Whether any advantage comes of finding out such things is an open question. We have a saying that knowledge is power. It is one of our favorite preconceptions in this scientific age. No doubt there is some truth in it. Obviously many different kinds of knowledge lend power to many arms. But here we are dealing with an extraordinary bit of knowledge: the

knowledge that in civilization folkways are power. What power is lent by
the knowledge that where human aspirations are concerned knowledge is
impotent, and to whose arm? Perhaps some scientists can answer this
question, and perhaps not.

STUDY QUESTIONS

1. *In what way, according to Ayres, is the problem of eliminating mosquitoes
   different from the problem of eliminating poverty? Is Ayres' argument persuasive? Is it logically sound?*
2. *Ayres says that scientific knowledge can guide the formation of customs only
   if it becomes "folklore." What is there about "folklore" that cannot co-exist
   with science?*
3. *What reason does Ayres give for the failure of psychology to operate as a guide
   for the social sciences? Do you agree with his reasoning?*
4. *Does Ayres' conclusion about the limitation of science as a guide to society
   have any bearing on the problem of free will?*
5. *To what extent is Ayres analyzing and evaluating a situation in this selection,
   and to what extent is he attempting to persuade his audience? Upon what
   evidence do you base your answer?*
6. *Do you think that Ayres has underestimated the potential of the social sciences
   as a source of knowledge? Explain how some social science has made a contribution to the rational guidance of society.*

Clinton Rossiter

The Conservative View of Man and Society*

The Conservative holds definite opinions about man's nature, his capacity
for self-government, his relations with other men, the kind of life he
should lead, and the rights he may properly claim. On these opinions rests
the whole Conservative tradition.

Man, says the Conservative, is a composite of good and evil, a blend of
ennobling excellencies and degrading imperfections. He is not perfect; he is
not perfectible. If educated properly, placed in a favorable environment, and
held in restraint by tradition and authority, he may display innate qualities of
rationality, sociability, industry, decency, and love of liberty. Never, no
matter how he is educated or situated or restrained, will he throw off completely his other innate qualities of irrationality, selfishness, laziness, depravity, and corruptibility. Man's nature is essentially immutable, and the
immutable strain is one of deep-seated wickedness. Although some Con-

* Reprinted from *Conservatism in America* by Clinton Rossiter, by permission of
Alfred A. Knopf, Inc. Copyright, 1955, by Clinton Rossiter.

servatives find support for their skeptical view of man in recent experiments in psychology, most continue to rely on religious teaching and the study of history. Those who are Christians, and most Conservatives are, prefer to call the motivation for iniquitous and irrational behavior by its proper name: Original Sin.

The Conservative is often accused of putting too much stress on man's wickedness and irrationality and of overlooking his many good qualities, especially his capacity for reason. The Conservative's answer is candid enough. He is well aware of man's potentialities, but he must counter the optimism of the liberal and radical with certain cheerless reminders that are no less true for telling only half the truth: that evil exists independently of social or economic maladjustments; that we must search for the source of our discontents in defective human nature rather than in a defective social order; and that man, far from being malleable, is subject to cultural alteration only slowly and to a limited degree. The Conservative therefore considers it his stern duty to call attention, as did John Adams, to "the general frailty and depravity of human nature."

This view of human nature is saved from churlish cynicism by two splendid beliefs. First, man is touched with eternity. He has a precious soul; he is a religious entity. His urges toward sin are matched, and with God's grace are over-matched if never finally beaten down, by his aspiration for good. For this reason, the Conservative asserts, man is an object of reverence, and a recognition of man's heaven-ordained shortcomings serves only to deepen this reverence. Second, to quote from Burke, the father of all Conservatives, "The nature of man is intricate." The confession of an eminent psychologist, Gardner Murphy, "Not much, I believe, is known about man," is applauded by the Conservative, who then adds: "Not much, I believe, will ever be known about him." Man is a mysterious and complex being, and no amount of psychological research will ever solve the mystery or unravel the complexity.

No truth about human nature and capabilities is more important than this: man can govern himself, but there is no certainty that he will; free government is possible but far from inevitable. Man will need all the help he can get from education, religion, tradition, and institutions if he is to enjoy even a limited success in his experiments in self-government. He must be counseled, encouraged, informed, and checked. Above all, he must realize that the collective wisdom of the community, itself the union of countless partial and imperfect wisdoms like his own, is alone equal to this mightiest of social tasks. A clear recognition of man's conditional capacity for ruling himself and others is the first requisite of constitution-making.

Conservatism holds out obstinately against two popular beliefs about human relations in modern society: individualism and equality. Putting off a discussion of the Conservative and individualism for a few pages, let us hear what he has to say about the explosive question of equality.

Each man is equal to every other man in only one meaningful sense: he is a man, a physical and spiritual entity, and is thus entitled by God and nature to be treated as end rather than means. From the basic fact of moral equality come several secondary equalities that the modern Conservative recognizes, more eloquently in public than in private: equality of opportunity, the right of each individual to exploit his own talents up to their natural limits; equality before the law, the right to justice on the same terms as other men; and political equality, which takes the form of universal suffrage. Beyond this the Conservative is unwilling to go. Recognizing the infinite variety among men in talent, taste, appearance, intelligence, and virtue, he is candid enough to assert that this variety extends vertically as well as horizontally. Men are grossly unequal — and, what is more, can never be made equal — in all qualities of mind, body, and spirit.

The good society rests solidly on this great truth. The social order is organized in such a way as to take advantage of ineradicable natural distinctions among men. It exhibits a class structure in which there are several quite distinct levels, most men find their level early and stay in it without rancor, and equality of opportunity keeps the way at least partially open to ascent and decline. At the same time, the social order aims to temper those distinctions that are not natural. It recognizes the inevitability and indeed the necessity of orders and classes, but it insists that all privileges, ranks, and other visible signs of inequality be as natural and functional as possible. The Conservative, of course — and this point is of decisive importance — is much more inclined than other men to consider artificial distinctions as natural. Equity rather than equality is the mark of his society; the reconciliation rather than the abolition of classes is his constant aim. When he is forced to choose between liberty and equality, he throws his support unhesitatingly to liberty. Indeed, the preference for liberty over equality lies at the root of the Conservative tradition.

While Conservatism has retreated some distance from Burke and Adams under the pressures of modern democracy, it has refused to yield one salient: the belief in a ruling and serving aristocracy. "If there is any one point," Gertrude Himmelfarb writes, "any single empirical test, by which conservatism can be distinguished from liberalism, it is a respect for aristocracy and aristocratic institutions. Every tenet of liberalism repudiates the idea of a fixed aristocracy; every tenet of conservatism affirms it." If it is no longer good form to use the word *aristocracy* in political debate, nor good sense to expect that an aristocracy can be "fixed" to the extent that it was one hundred and fifty years ago, the Conservative is still moved powerfully by the urge to seek out the best men and place them in positions of authority. He continues to assert the beneficence of an aristocracy of talent and virtue, one that is trained for special service and thus entitled to special consideration. He continues to believe that it takes more than one generation to make a genuine aristocrat.

The world being what it is today, the Conservative spends a good deal of his time in the pulpit exhorting his fellow men to live godly, righteous, and sober lives. He does not do this gladly, for he is not by nature a Puritan, but the times seem to have made him our leading "moral athlete."

Man, the Conservative asserts, is stamped with sin and carnality, but he is also blessed with higher aspirations. If human nature in general can never be much improved, each individual may nevertheless bring his own savage and selfish impulses under control. It is his duty to himself, his fellows, and God to do just this — to shun vice, cultivate virtue, and submit to the guidance of what Lincoln called "the better angels of our nature." Only thus, through the moral striving of many men, can free government be secured and society be made stable.

What virtues must the individual cultivate? The Conservative of the tower, the Conservative of the field, the Conservative of the market place, and the Conservative of the assembly each give a somewhat different answer to this question, yet all agree to this catalogue of primary virtues: wisdom, justice, temperance, and courage; industry, frugality, piety, and honesty; contentment, obedience, compassion, and good manners. The good man is peaceful but not resigned and is conservative through habit and choice rather than sloth and cowardice. He assumes that duty comes before pleasure, self-sacrifice before self-indulgence. Believing that the test of life is accomplishment rather than enjoyment, he takes pride in doing a good job in the station to which he has been called. He is alert to the identity and malignity of the vices he must shun: ignorance, injustice, intemperance, and cowardice; laziness, luxury, selfishness, and dishonesty; envy, disobedience, violence, and bad manners. And he is aware, too, of the larger implications of his own life of virtue: self-government is for moral men; those who would be free must be virtuous.

Education starts a man on the road that leads through virtue to freedom. Only through education — in family, church, and school — can children be shaped into civilized men. Only through education can man's vices, which are tough, be brought under control and his virtues, which are frail, be nourished into robust health. The instruments of education should teach a man to think, survive, ply a trade, and enjoy his leisure. Their great mission, however, is to act as a conserving, civilizing force: to convey to each man his share of the inherited wisdom of the race, to train him to lead a moral, self-disciplined life, and to foster a love of order and respect for authority.

The Conservative's understanding of the mission of education explains his profound mistrust of modern theories, most of which, he feels, are grounded in a clear misreading of the nature and needs of children. The school has always been a conservative force in society, and the Conservative means to keep it that way. He admits that there is a stage in the education of some individuals — those who are to go on to leadership — when self-development and self-expression should get prime consideration. First things must come first, however, and before this stage is reached, the individual must be taught his community's values and be integrated into its structure.

Before we can describe the Conservative consensus on freedom and responsibility, we must learn more of the circumstances in which men can enjoy the one because they accept the other.

The Conservative's best thoughts are directed to society and the social process. The key points of his social theory appear to be these:

Society is a living organism with roots deep in the past. The true community, the Conservative likes to say, is a tree, not a machine. It rose to its present strength and glory through centuries of growth, and men must forbear to think of it as a mechanical contrivance that can be dismantled and reassembled in one generation. Prescription, not fiat, is the chief creative force in the social process.

Society is cellular. It is not an agglomeration of lonely individuals, but a grand, complex union of functional groups. Man is a social animal whose best interests are served by co-operating with other men. Indeed, he has no real meaning except as contributing member of one or more of these intrinsic groups: family, church, local community, and, at certain stages of historical development, occupational association. The group is important not only because it gives life, work, comfort, and spiritual support to the individual, but because it joins with thousands of other groups to form the one really stubborn roadblock against the march of the all-powerful state. The Conservative is careful not to ride the cellular analogy too hard, for he is aware that it can lead to a social theory in which man loses all dignity and personality.

In addition to the intrinsic groups, a healthy society will display a balanced combination of "institutions": constitution, common law, monarchy or presidency, legislature, courts, civil service, armed services and subdivisions, colleges, schools, forms of property, corporations, co-operatives, trade unions, guilds, fraternal orders, and dozens of other instrumentalities and understandings that mold the lives of men. Such symbols of national unity and continuity as anthems, flags, rituals, battlefields, monuments, and pantheons of heroes are equally dear to the Conservative heart. All men are stanch defenders of the institutions that meet their practical and spiritual needs, but the Conservative places special trust in them. "Individuals may form communities," Disraeli warned, "but it is institutions alone that can create a nation."

Society is a unity. In the healthy community all these groups and institutions fit together into a harmonious unity, and attempts to reshape one part of society must inevitably disturb other parts. The Conservative, though something of a pluralist, never loses sight of the ultimate unity into which all groups and institutions must merge. He sees the social structure not as a series of neat strata laid one on top of another, but, in Coleridge's phrase, as "an indissoluble blending and interfusion of persons from top to bottom."

Society cannot be static. Change is the rule of life, for societies as for men. A community cannot stand still; it must develop or decline. "Society must alter," Russell Kirk acknowledges in *The Conservative Mind*, "for slow change is the means of its conservation, like the human body's perpetual renewal." In recognizing this great truth, the Conservative shows himself to be neither a reactionary nor stand-patter. Yet he is just as emphatically not a liberal or radical, and he therefore sets severe conditions upon social change, especially if it is to be worked by active reform. Change, he insists, must never be taken for its own sake; must have preservation, if possible even restoration, as its central object; be severely limited in scope and purpose; be a response to an undoubted social need — for example, the renovation or elimination of an institution that is plainly obsolete; be worked out by slow and careful stages; represent progress, "a change for the better"; be brought off under Conservative auspices, or with Conservatives intervening at the decisive moment; and finally, in Disraeli's words, "be carried out in deference to the manners, the customs, the laws, the traditions of the people." The essence of Conservatism is the feeling for the possibilities and limits of natural, organic change. In the eloquent phrases of R. J. White, of Cambridge:

> To discover the order which inheres in things rather than to impose an order upon them; to strengthen and perpetuate that order rather than to dispose things anew according to some formula which may be nothing more than a fashion; to legislate along the grain of human nature rather than against it; to pursue limited objectives with a watchful eye; to amend here, to prune there; in short, to preserve the method of nature in the conduct of the state . . . this is Conservatism.

Society must be stable. Although men can never hope to see their community completely stable, they can create an endurable condition of peace and order. To achieve this end, they must work unceasingly for a society that has this ideal appearance:

Common agreement on fundamentals exists among men of all ranks and stations. Loyalty, good will, fraternal sympathy, and a feeling for compromise pervade the political and social scene.

Institutions and groups are in functional adjustment. Political, economic, social, and cultural power is widely diffused among persons, groups, and other instruments; these are held by law, custom, and constitution in a state of operating equilibrium. For every show of power there is corresponding responsibility. A minimum of friction and maximum of accommodation exist between government and group, government and individual, group and individual.

The authority of each group, and especially of the government, is legitimate. The laws honor the traditions of the nation, are adjusted to the capacities of the citizenry, meet the requirements of abstract justice, and satisfy the needs of society. Men obey the laws cheerfully and readily, and they know why they obey them. They know, too, the difference between authority and authoritarianism.

Men are secure; they have a sense of being, belonging, and creating. Their labors are rewarded, their sorrows comforted, their needs satisfied. They have the deep feeling of serenity that arises not merely from material well-being, but from confidence in the future, from daily contact with decent and trustworthy men, and from participation in an even-handed system of justice. Predictability, morality, and equity are important ingredients of their security. Most important, however, is ordered liberty, which makes it possible for men to pursue their talents and tastes within a sheltering order.

Change and reform are sure-footed, discriminating, and respectful of the past. "Men breathe freely," as F. E. Dessauer puts it, "because change is limited.... The changes which are taking place do not frighten the affected." The currents of change are channeled into the stream of progress by institutions and values that have stood the tests of time and service.

Unity, balance, authority, security, continuity — these are the key elements of social stability. In longing for a society in which peace and order reign, the Conservative comes closest to the utopianism that he ridicules in others.

STUDY QUESTIONS

1. How do Rossiter's views contrast with those of Mill on: (a) the nature of man; (b) social equality; (c) social institutions; (d) the past.
2. Would you say, judging from Rossiter's ideas, that the liberal or the conservative lays a greater stress on moral qualities in social and political questions?
3. In what way, according to Rossiter, are the principles of liberty and equality opposed to each other?
4. To what extent do Rossiter's views seem to harmonize with democratic ideals?
5. Analyze the organization and aims of this selection. To what extent do you think it is Rossiter's intention to define the conservative view? To evaluate it? To persuade his reader to accept it? Explain the grounds upon which you base your answer.
6. Do you find Rossiter's description of the conservative society attractive? Write a theme evaluating it, and explaining whether or not you would like to live in such a society.

Jose Ortega y Gasset   The Mass Man*

What is he like, this mass-man who to-day dominates public life, political and non-political, and why is he like it, that is, how has he been produced?

---

* From The Revolt of the Masses by José Ortega y Gasset. Copyright, 1932, by W. W. Norton & Company, Inc. By permission of W. W. Norton & Company, Inc., and George Allen & Unwin, Ltd.

It will be well to answer both questions together, for they throw light on one another. The man who to-day is attempting to take the lead in European existence is very different from the man who directed the XIXth Century, but he was produced and prepared by the XIXth Century. Any keen mind of the years 1820, 1850, and 1880 could by simple *a priori* reasoning, foresee the gravity of the present historical situation, and in fact nothing is happening now which was not foreseen a hundred years ago. "The masses are advancing," said Hegel in apocalyptic fashion. "Without some new spiritual influence, our age, which is a revolutionary age, will produce a catastrophe," was the pronouncement of Comte. "I see the flood-tide of nihilism rising," shrieked Nietzsche from a crag of the Engadine. It is false to say that history cannot be foretold. Numberless times this has been done. If the future offered no opening to prophecy, it could not be understood when fulfilled in the present and on the point of falling back into the past. The idea that the historian is on the reverse side a prophet, sums up the whole philosophy of history. It is true that it is only possible to anticipate the general structure of the future, but that is all that we in truth understand of the past or of the present. Accordingly, if you want a good view of your own age, look at it from far off. From what distance? The answer is simple. Just far enough to prevent you seeing Cleopatra's nose.

What appearance did life present to that multitudinous man who in ever-increasing abundance the XIXth Century kept producing? To start with, an appearance of universal material ease. Never had the average man been able to solve his economic problem with greater facility. Whilst there was a proportionate decrease of great fortunes and life became harder for the individual worker, the middle classes found their economic horizon widened every day. Every day added a new luxury to their standard of life. Every day their position was more secure and more independent of another's will. What before would have been considered one of fortune's gifts, inspiring humble gratitude toward destiny, was converted into a right, not to be grateful for, but to be insisted on.

From 1900 on, the worker likewise begins to extend and assure his existence. Nevertheless, he has to struggle to obtain his end. He does not, like the middle class, find the benefit attentively served up to him by a society and a state which are a marvel of organization. To this ease and security of economic conditions are to be added the physical ones, comfort and public order. Life runs on smooth rails, and there is no likelihood of anything violent or dangerous breaking in on it. Such a free, untrammelled situation was bound to instil into the depths of such souls an idea of existence which might be expressed in the witty and penetrating phrase of an old country like ours: "Wide is Castile." That is to say, in all its primary and decisive aspects, life presented itself to the new man as *exempt from restrictions*. The realisation of this fact and of its importance becomes immediate when we remember that such a freedon of existence was entirely lacking to the common men of the past. On the contrary, for them life was burdensome destiny, economically and physically. From birth, existence meant to them an accumulation of impediments which they were obliged to suffer, without possible solution other than to adapt themselves to them, to settle down in the narrow space they left available.

But still more evident is the contrast of situations, if we pass from the material to the civil and moral. The average man, from the second half of the XIXth Century on, finds no social barriers raised against him. That is to say, that as regards the forms of public life he no longer finds himself from birth confronted with obstacles and limitations. There is nothing to force him to limit his existence. Here again, "Wide is Castile." There are no "estates" or "castes." There are no civil privileges. The ordinary man learns that all men are equal before the law.

Never in the course of history had man been placed in vital surroundings even remotely familiar to those set up by the conditions just mentioned. We are, in fact, confronted with a radical innovation in human destiny, implanted by the XIXth Century. A new stage has been mounted for human existence, new both in the physical and the social aspects. Three principles have made possible this new world: liberal democracy, scientific experiment, and industrialism. The two latter may be summed-up in one word: technicism. Not one of those principles was invented by the XIXth Century; they proceed from the two previous centuries. The glory of the XIXth Century lies not in their discovery, but in their implantation. No one but recognises that fact. But it is not sufficient to recognise it in the abstract, it is necessary to realise its inevitable consequences.

The XIXth Century was of its essence revolutionary. This aspect is not to be looked for in the scenes of the barricades, which are mere incidents, but in the fact that it placed the average man — the great social mass — in conditions of life radically opposed to those by which he had always been surrounded. It turned his public existence upside down. Revolution is not the uprising against pre-existing order, but the setting up of a new order contradictory to the traditional one. Hence there is no exaggeration in saying that the man who is the product of the XIXth Century is, for the effects of public life, a man apart from all other men. The XVIIIth-Century man differs, of course, from the XVIIth-Century man, and this one in turn from his fellow of the XVIth Century, but they are all related, similar, even identical in essentials when confronted with this new man. For the "common" man of all periods "life" had principally meant limitation, obligation, dependence; in a word, pressure. Say oppression, if you like, provided it be understood not only in the juridical and social sense, but also in the cosmic. For it is this latter which has never been lacking up to a hundred years ago, the date at which starts the practically limitless expansion of scientific technique —

physical and administrative. Previously, even for the rich and powerful, the world was a place of poverty, difficulty and danger.[1]

The world which surrounds the new man from his birth does not compel him to limit himself in any fashion, it sets up no veto in opposition to him; on the contrary, it incites his appetite, which in principle can increase indefinitely. Now it turns out — and this is most important — that this world of the XIXth and early XXth Centuries not only has the perfections and the completeness which it actually possesses, but furthermore suggests to those who dwell in it the radical assurance that to-morrow it will be still richer, ampler, more perfect, as if it enjoyed a spontaneous, inexhaustible power of increase. Even to-day, in spite of some signs which are making a tiny breach in that sturdy faith, even to-day, there are few men who doubt that motorcars will in five years' time be more comfortable and cheaper than to-day. They believe in this as they believe that the sun will rise in the morning. The metaphor is an exact one. For, in fact, the common man, finding himself in a world so excellent, technically and socially, believes that it has been produced by nature, and never thinks of the personal efforts of highly-endowed individuals which the creation of this new world presupposed. Still less will he admit the notion that all these facilities still require the support of certain difficult human virtues, the least failure of which would cause the rapid disappearance of the whole magnificent edifice.

This leads us to note down in our psychological chart of the mass-man of to-day two fundamental traits: the free expansion of his vital desires, and therefore, of his personality; and his radical ingratitude towards all that has made possible the ease of his existence. These traits together make up the well-known psychology of the spoilt child. And in fact it would entail no error to use this psychology as a "sight" through which to observe the soul of the masses of to-day. Heir to an ample and generous past — generous both in ideals and in activities — the new commonalty has been spoiled by the world around it. To spoil means to put no limit on caprice, to give one the impression that everything is permitted to him and that he has no obligations. The young child exposed to this regime has no experience of its own limits. By reason of the removal of all external restraint, all clashing with other things, he comes actually to believe that he is the only one that exists, and gets used to not considering others, especially not considering them as superior to himself. This feeling of another's superiority could only be instilled into him by someone who, being stronger than he is, should force him to give up some desire, to restrict himself, to restrain himself. He would then have learned

[1] However rich an individual might be in relation to his fellows, as the world in its totality was poor, the sphere of conveniences and commodities with which his wealth furnished him was very limited. The life of the average man to-day is easier, more convenient and softer than that of the most powerful of another age. What difference does it make to him not to be richer than others if the world is richer and furnishes him with magnificent roads, railways, telegraphs, hotels, personal safety and aspirin?

this fundamental discipline: "Here I end and here begins another more powerful than I am. In the world, apparently, there are two people: I myself and another superior to me." The ordinary man of past times was daily taught this elemental wisdom by the world about him, because it was a world so rudely organised, that catastrophes were frequent, and there was nothing in it certain, abundant, stable. But the new masses find themselves in the presence of a prospect full of possibilities, and furthermore, quite secure with everything ready to their hands, independent of any previous efforts on their part, just as we find the sun in the heavens without our hoisting it up on our shoulders. No human being thanks another for the air he breathes, for no one has produced the air for him; it belongs to the sum-total of what "is there," of which we say "it is natural," because it never fails. And these spoiled masses are unintelligent enough to believe that the material and social organisation, placed at their disposition like the air, is of the same origin, since apparently it never fails them, and is almost as perfect as the natural scheme of things.

My thesis, therefore, is this: the very perfection with which the XIXth Century gave an organisation to certain orders of existence has caused the masses benefited thereby to consider it, not as an organised, but as a natural system. Thus is explained and defined the absurd state of mind revealed by these masses; they are only concerned with their own well-being, and at the same time they remain alien to the cause of that well-being. As they do not see, beyond the benefits of civilisation, marvels of invention and construction which can only be maintained by great effort and foresight, they imagine that their role is limited to demanding these benefits peremptorily, as if they were natural rights. In the disturbances caused by scarcity of food, the mob goes in search of bread, and the means it employs is generally to wreck the bakeries. This may serve as a symbol of the attitude adopted, on a greater and more complicated scale, by the masses of to-day towards the civilisation by which they are supported.

NOBLE LIFE AND COMMON LIFE, OR EFFORT AND INERTIA

To start with, we are what our world invites us to be, and the basic features of our soul are impressed upon it by the form of its surroundings as in a mould. Naturally, for our life is no other than our relations with the world around. The general aspect which it presents to us will form the general aspect of our own life. It is for this reason that I stress so much the observation that the world into which the masses of to-day have been born displays features radically new to history. Whereas in past times life for the average man meant finding all around him difficulties, dangers, want, limitations of his destiny, dependence, the new world appears as a sphere of practically limitless possibilities, safe, and independent of anyone. Based on this primary and lasting impression, the mind of every contemporary man will be formed, just as previous minds were formed on the opposite impression. For that basic impression becomes an interior voice which ceaselessly utters certain words in the depths of each individual, and tenaciously suggests to him a definition of life which is, at the same time, a moral imperative. And if the traditional sentiment whispered: "To live is to feel oneself limited, and therefore to have to count with that which limits us," the newest voice shouts: "To live is to meet with no limitation whatever and, consequently, to abandon oneself calmly to one's self. Practically nothing is impossible, nothing is dangerous, and, in principle, nobody is superior to anybody." This basic experience completely modifies the traditional, persistent structure of the mass-man. For the latter always felt himself, by his nature, confronted with material limitations and higher social powers. Such, in his eyes, was life. If he succeeded in improving his situation, if he climbed the social ladder, he attributed this to a piece of fortune which was favourable to him in particular. And if not to this, then to an enormous effort, of which he knew well what it had cost him. In both cases it was a question of an exception to the general character of life and the world; an exception which, as such, was due to some very special cause.

But the modern mass finds complete freedom as its natural, established condition, without any special cause for it. Nothing from outside incites it to recognise limits to itself, and consequently, to refer at all times to other authorities higher than itself. Until lately, the Chinese peasant believed that the welfare of his existence depended on the private virtues which the Emperor was pleased to possess. Therefore, his life was constantly related to this supreme authority on which it depended. *But the man we are now analysing accustoms himself not to appeal from his own to any authority outside him.* He is satisfied with himself exactly as he is. Ingenuously, without any need of being vain, as the most natural thing in the world, he will tend to consider and affirm as good everything he finds within himself: opinions, appetites, preferences, tastes. Why not, if, as we have seen, nothing and nobody force him to realise that he is a second-class man, subject to many limitations, incapable of creating or conserving that very organisation which gives his life the fullness and contentedness on which he bases this assertion of his personality?

The mass-man would never have accepted authority external to himself had not his surroundings violently forced him to do so. As to-day, his surroundings do not so force him, the everlasting mass-man, true to his character, ceases to appeal to other authority and feels himself lord of his own existence. On the contrary the select man, the excellent man is urged, by interior necessity, to appeal from himself to some standard beyond himself, superior to himself, whose service he freely accepts. Let us recall that at the start we distinguished the excellent man from the common man by saying that the former is the one who makes great demands on himself, and the latter the one who makes no demands on himself, but contents himself with what he is, and is delighted with himself. Contrary to what is usually thought, it is the man of excellence, and not the common man who lives in essential servitude. Life has no savour for him unless he makes it consist in service to something transcendental. Hence he does not look upon the necessity of serving as an oppression. When, by chance, such necessity is lacking, he grows restless and invents some new standard, more difficult, more exigent, with which to coerce himself. This is life lived as a discipline — the noble life. Nobility is defined by the demands it makes on us — by obligations, not by rights. *Noblesse oblige.* "To live as one likes is plebeian; the noble man aspires to order and law" (Goethe). The privileges of nobility are not in their origin concessions or favours; on the contrary, they are conquests. And their maintenance supposes, in principle, that the privileged individual is capable of reconquering them, at any moment, if it were necessary, and anyone were to dispute them. Private rights or *privileges* are not, then, passive possession and mere enjoyment, but they represent the standard attained by personal effort. On the other hand, common rights, such as those "of the man and the citizen," are passive property, pure usufruct and benefit, the generous gift of fate which every man finds before him, and which answers to no effort whatever, unless it be that of breathing and avoiding insanity. I would say, then, that an impersonal right is held, a personal one is upheld.

STUDY QUESTIONS

1. *Is there a parallel between Brogan's observation that overt competition is taboo in America, and Ortega y Gasset's view that the mass man loves comfort and the feeling that he is the equal of anyone? What relationships do you find between Ortega y Gasset's views and C. Wright Mills' description of the white collar class?*

2. *Can you find any evidence in popular magazines or newspapers to support Ortega y Gasset's description of "the mass man"?*

3. *In what way, according to the author, is the nineteenth century man different from those of previous centuries? What are the consequences of the mass man's failure to understand the past?*

4. *To what extent does Ortega y Gasset agree with Rossiter? Is there any difference in their views of human nature?*

5. *Do you think that Ortega's description of the mass man's attitude is fair or unfair? Write a theme evaluating his opinions.*

6. *Can it be argued that the conditions of modern life have improved character, instead of causing it to deteriorate, as Ortega believes they have done?*

Arnold J. Toynbee Civilization on Trial*

O ur present Western outlook on history is an extraordinarily contradictory one. While our historical horizon has been expanding vastly in both the space dimension and the time dimension, our historical vision — what we actually do see, in contrast to what we now could see if we chose — has been contracting rapidly to the narrow field of what a horse sees between its blinkers or what a U-boat commander sees through his periscope.

This is certainly extraordinary; yet it is only one of a number of contradictions of this kind that seem to be characteristic of the times in which we are living. There are other examples that probably loom larger in the minds of most of us. For instance, our world has risen to an unprecedented degree of humanitarian feeling. There is now a recognition of the human rights of people of all classes, nations, and races; yet at the same time we have sunk to perhaps unheard-of depths of class warfare, nationalism, and racialism. These bad passions find vent in cold-blooded, scientifically planned cruelties; and the two incompatible states of mind and standards of conduct are to be seen to-day, side by side, not merely in the same world, but sometimes in the same country and even in the same soul.

Again, we now have an unprecedented power of production side by side with unprecedented shortages. We have invented machines to work for us, but have less spare labour than ever before for human service — even for such an essential and elementary service as helping mothers to look after their babies. We have persistent alternations of widespread unemployment with famines of man-power. Undoubtedly, the contrast between our expanding historical horizon and our contracting historical vision is something characteristic of our age. Yet, looked at in itself, what an astonishing contradiction it is!

Let us remind ourselves first of the recent expansion of our horizon. In space, our Western field of vision has expanded to take in the whole of mankind over all the habitable and traversable surface of this planet, and the whole stellar universe in which this planet is an infinitesimally small speck of dust. In time, our Western field of vision has expanded to take in all the civilizations that have risen and fallen during these last 6000 years; the previous history of the human race back to its genesis between 600,000 and a million years ago; the history of life on this planet back to perhaps 800 million years ago. What a marvellous widening of our historical horizon! Yet, at the

* From *Civilization on Trial* by Arnold J. Toynbee. Copyright, 1948, by Oxford University Press, Inc. Reprinted by permission.

same time, our field of historical vision has been contracting; it has been tending to shrink within the narrow limits in time and space of the particular
republic or kingdom of which each of us happens to be a citizen. The oldest
surviving Western states — say France or England — have so far had no more
than a thousand years of continuous political existence; the largest existing
Western state — say Brazil or the United States — embraces only a very small
fraction of the total inhabited surface of the Earth.

Before the widening of our horizon began — before our Western seamen
circumnavigated the globe, and before our Western cosmogonists and geologists pushed out the bounds of our universe in both time and space — our
prenationalist mediaeval ancestors had a broader and juster historical vision
than we have to-day. For them, history did not mean the history of one's own
parochial community; it meant the history of Israel, Greece, and Rome. And,
even if they were mistaken in believing that the world was created in
4004 B.C., it is at any rate better to look as far back as 4004 B.C. than to look
back no farther than the Declaration of Independence or the voyages of the
Mayflower or Columbus or Hengist and Horsa. (As a matter of fact, 4004 B.C.
happens, though our ancestors did not know this, to be a quite important date;
it approximately marks the first appearance of representatives of the species
of human society called civilizations.)

Again, for our ancestors, Rome and Jerusalem meant much more than
their own home towns. When our Anglo-Saxon ancestors were converted to
Roman Christianity at the end of the sixth century of the Christian era, they
learned Latin, studied the treasures of sacred and profane literature to which
a knowledge of the Latin language gives access, and went on pilgrimages to
Rome and Jerusalem — and this in an age when the difficulties and dangers
of travelling were such as to make modern war-time travelling seem child's
play. Our ancestors seem to have been big-minded, and this is a great intellectual virtue as well as a great moral one, for national histories are unintelligible within their own time limits and space limits.

II

In the time dimension, you cannot understand the history of England if
you begin only at the coming of the English to Britain, any better than you
can understand the history of the United States if you begin only at the
coming of the English to North America. In the space dimension, likewise,
you cannot understand the history of a country if you cut its outlines out of
the map of the world and rule out of consideration anything that has originated outside that particular country's frontiers.

What are the epoch-making events in the national histories of the United
States and the United Kingdom? Working back from the present towards
the past, I should say they were the two world wars, the Industrial Revolution, the Reformation, the Western voyages of discovery, the Renaissance, the
conversion to Christianity. Now I defy anyone to tell the history of either

the United States or the United Kingdom without making these events the cardinal ones, or to explain these events as local American or local English affairs. To explain these major events in the history of any Western country, the smallest unit that one can take into account is the whole of Western Christendom. By Western Christendom I mean the Roman Catholic and Protestant world — the adherents of the Patriarchate of Rome who have maintained their allegiance to the Papacy, together with the former adherents who have repudiated it.

But the history of Western Christendom, too, is unintelligible within its own time limits and space limits. While Western Christendom is a much better unit than the United States or the United Kingdom or France for a historian to operate with, it too turns out, on inspection, to be inadequate. In the time dimension, it goes back only to the close of the Dark Ages following the collapse of the western part of the Roman Empire; that is, it goes back less than 1300 years, and 1300 years is less than a quarter of the 6000 years during which the species of society represented by Western Christendom has been in existence. Western Christendom is a civilization belonging to the third of the three generations of civilizations that there have been so far.

In the space dimension, the narrowness of the limits of Western Christendom is still more striking. If you look at the physical map of the world as a whole, you will see that the small part of it which is dry land consists of a single continent — Asia — which has a number of peninsulas and off-lying islands. Now, what are the farthest limits to which Western Christendom has managed to expand? You will find them at Alaska and Chile on the west and at Finland and Dalmatia on the east. What lies between those four points is Western Christendom's domain at its widest. And what does that domain amount to? Just the tip of Asia's European peninsula, together with a couple of large islands. (By these two large islands, I mean, of course, North and South America.) Even if you add in the outlying and precarious footholds of the Western world in South Africa, Australia, and New Zealand, its total habitable present area amounts to only a very minor part of the total habitable area of the surface of the planet. And you cannot understand the history of Western Christendom within its own geographical limits.

Western Christendom is a product of Christianity, but Christianity did not arise in the Western world; it arose outside the bounds of Western Christendom, in a district that lies today within the domain of a different civilization: Islam. We Western Christians did once try to capture from the Muslims the cradle of our religion in Palestine. If the Crusades had succeeded, Western Christendom would have slightly broadened its footing on the all-important Asiatic mainland. But the Crusades ended in failure.

Western Christendom is merely one of five civilizations that survive in the world to-day; and these are merely five out of about nineteen that one can identify as having come into existence since the first appearance of representatives of this species of society about 6000 years ago.

III

To take the four other surviving civilizations first: if the firmness of a civilization's foothold on the continent — by which I mean the solid land-mass of Asia — may be taken as giving a rough indication of that civilization's relative expectation of life, then the other four surviving civilizations are "better lives" — in the jargon of the life insurance business — than our own Western Christendom.

Our sister civilization, Orthodox Christendom, straddles the continent from the Baltic to the Pacific and from the Mediterranean to the Arctic Ocean: it occupies the northern half of Asia and the eastern half of Asia's European peninsula. Russia overlooks the back doors of all the other civilizations; from White Russia and North-Eastern Siberia she overlooks the Polish and Alaskan back doors of our own Western world; from the Caucasus and Central Asia she overlooks the back doors of the Islamic and Hindu worlds; from Central and Eastern Siberia she overlooks the back door of the Far Eastern world.

Our half-sister civilization, Islam, also has a firm footing on the continent. The domain of Islam stretches from the heart of the Asiatic continent in North-Western China all the way to the west coast of Asia's African peninsula. At Dakar, the Islamic world commands the continental approaches to the straits that divide Asia's African peninsula from the island of South America. Islam also has a firm footing in Asia's Indian peninsula.

As for the Hindu society and the Far Eastern society, it needs no demonstration to show that the 400 million Hindus and the 400 or 500 million Chinese have a firm foothold on the continent.

But we must not exaggerate the importance of any of these surviving civilizations just because, at this moment, they happen to be survivors. If, instead of thinking in terms of "expectation of life," we think in terms of achievement, a rough indication of relative achievement may be found in the giving of birth to individual souls that have conferred lasting blessings on the human race.

Now who are the individuals who are the greatest benefactors of the living generation of mankind? I should say: Confucius and Lao-tse; the Buddha; the Prophets of Israel and Judah; Zoroaster, Jesus, and Muhammad; and Socrates. And not one of these lasting benefactors of mankind happens to be a child of any of the five living civilizations. Confucius and Lao-tse were children of a now extinct Far Eastern civilization of an earlier generation; the Buddha was the child of a now extinct Indian civilization of an earlier generation. Hosea, Zoroaster, Jesus, and Muhammad were children of a now extinct Syrian civilization. Socrates was the child of a now extinct Greek civilization.

Within the last 400 years, all the five surviving civilizations have been brought into contact with each other as a result of the enterprise of two of them: the expansion of Western Christendom from the tip of Asia's European peninsula over the ocean, and the expansion of Orthodox Christendom overland across the whole breadth of the Asiatic continent.

The expansion of Western Christendom displays two special features: being oceanic, it is the only expansion of a civilization to date that has been literally world-wide in the sense of extending over the whole habitable portion of the Earth's surface; and, owing to the "conquest of space and time" by modern mechanical means, the spread of the network of Western material civilization has brought the different parts of the world into far closer physical contact than ever before. But, even in these points, the expansion of the Western civilization differs in degree only, and not in kind, from the contemporary overland expansion of Russian Orthodox Christendom, and from similar expansions of other civilizations at earlier dates.

There are earlier expansions that have made important contributions towards the present unification of mankind — with its corollary, the unification of our vision of human history. The now extinct Syrian civilization was propagated to the Atlantic coasts of Asia's European and African peninsulas westward by the Phoenicians, to the tip of Asia's Indian peninsula south-eastwards by the Himyarites and Nestorians, and to the Pacific north-eastwards by the Manichaeans and Nestorians. It expanded in two directions overseas and in a third direction overland. Any visitor to Peking will have seen a striking monument of the Syrian civilization's overland cultural conquests. In the trilingual inscriptions of the Manchu Dynasty of China at Peking, the Manchu and Mongol texts are inscribed in the Syriac form of our alphabet, not in Chinese characters.

Other examples of the expansion of now extinct civilizations are the propagation of the Greek civilization overseas westwards to Marseilles by the Greeks themselves, overland northwards to the Rhine and Danube by the Romans, and overland eastwards to the interiors of India and China by the Macedonians; and the expansion of the Sumerian civilization in all directions overland from its cradle in 'Iraq.

IV

As a result of these successive expansions of particular civilizations, the whole habitable world has now been unified into a single great society. The movement through which this process has been finally consummated is the modern expansion of Western Christendom. But we have to bear in mind, first, that this expansion of Western Christendom has merely completed the unification of the world and has not been the agency that has produced more than the last stage of the process; and, second, that, though the unification of the world has been finally achieved within a Western framework, the present Western ascendency in the world is certain not to last.

In a unified world, the eighteen non-Western civilizations — four of them living, fourteen of them extinct — will assuredly reassert their influence. And as, in the course of generations and centuries, a unified world gradually works its way toward an equilibrium between its diverse component cultures, the Western component will gradually be relegated to the modest place which is all that it can expect to retain in virtue of its intrinsic worth by comparison with those other cultures — surviving and extinct — which the Western society, through its modern expansion, has brought into association with itself and with one another.

History, seen in this perspective, makes, I feel, the following call upon historians of our generation and of the generations that will come after ours. If we are to perform the full service that we have the power to perform for our fellow human beings — the important service of helping them to find their bearings in a unified world — we must make the necessary effort of imagination and effort of will to break our way out of the prison walls of the local and short-lived histories of our own countries and our own cultures, and we must accustom ourselves to taking a synoptic view of history as a whole.

Our first task is to perceive, and to present to other people, the history of all the known civilizations, surviving and extinct, as a unity. There are, I believe, two ways in which this can be done.

One way is to study the encounters between civilizations, of which I have mentioned four outstanding examples. These encounters between civilizations are historically illuminating, not only because they bring a number of civilizations into a single focus of vision, but also because, out of the encounters between civilizations, the higher religions have been born — the worship, perhaps originally Sumerian, of the Great Mother and her Son who suffers and dies and rises again; Judaism and Zoroastrianism, which sprang from an encounter between the Syrian and Babylonian civilizations; Christianity and Islam, which sprang from an encounter between the Syrian and Greek civilizations; the Mahayana form of Buddhism and Hinduism, which sprang from an encounter between the Indian and Greek civilizations. The future of mankind in this world — if mankind is going to have a future in this world — lies, I believe, with these higher religions that have appeared within the last 4000 years (and all but the first within the last 3000 years), and not with the civilizations whose encounters have provided opportunities for the higher religions to come to birth.

A second way of studying the history of all the known civilizations as a unity is to make a comparative study of their individual histories, looking at them as so many representatives of one particular species of the genus Human Society. If we map out the principal phases in the histories of civilizations — their births, growths, breakdowns, and declines — we can compare their experiences phase by phase; and by this method of study we shall perhaps be able to sort out their common experiences, which are specific, from their unique experiences, which are individual. In this way we may be able to work out a morphology of the species of society called civilizations.

If, by the use of these two methods of study, we can arrive at a unified vision of history, we shall probably find that we need to make very far-going adjustments of the perspective in which the histories of divers civilizations and peoples appear when looked at through our peculiar present-day Western spectacles.

In setting out to adjust our perspective, we shall be wise, I suggest, to proceed simultaneously on two alternative assumptions. One of these alternatives is that the future of mankind may not, after all, be going to be catastrophic and that, even if the Second World War prove not to have been the last, we shall survive the rest of this batch of world wars as we survived the first two bouts, and shall eventually win our way out into calmer waters. The other possibility is that these first two world wars may be merely overtures to some supreme catastrophe that we are going to bring on ourselves.

This second, more unpleasant, alternative has been made a very practical possibility by mankind's unfortunately having discovered how to tap atomic energy before we have succeeded in abolishing the institution of war. Those contradictions and paradoxes in the life of the world in our time, which I took as my starting point, also look like symptoms of serious social and spiritual sickness, and their existence — which is one of the portentous features in the landscape of contemporary history — is another indication that we ought to take the more unpleasant of our alternatives as a serious possibility, and not just as a bad joke.

On either alternative, I suggest that we historians ought to concentrate our own attention — and direct the attention of our listeners and readers — upon the histories of those civilizations and peoples which, in the light of their past performances, seem likely, in a unified world, to come to the front in the long run in one or other of the alternative futures that may be lying in wait for mankind.

V

If the future of mankind in a unified world is going to be on the whole a happy one, then I would prophesy that there is a future in the Old World for the Chinese, and in the island of North America for the *Canadiens*. Whatever the future of mankind in North America, I feel pretty confident that these French-speaking Canadians, at any rate, will be there at the end of the story.

On the assumption that the future of mankind is to be very catastrophic, I should have prophesied, even as lately as a few years ago, that whatever future we might be going to have would lie with the Tibetans and the Eskimos, because each of these peoples occupied, till quite lately, an unusually sheltered position. "Sheltered" means, of course, sheltered from the dangers arising from human folly and wickedness, not sheltered from the rigors of the physical environment. Mankind has been master of its physical environment, sufficiently for practical purposes, since the middle palaeolithic age; since that time, man's only dangers — but these have been deadly dangers — have come from man himself. But the homes of the Tibetans and the Eskimos are sheltered no longer, because we are on the point of managing to fly over the North Pole and over the Himalayas, and both Northern Canada and Tibet would (I think) be likely to be theatres of a future Russo-American war.

If mankind is going to run amok with atom bombs, I personally should look to the Negrito Pygmies of Central Africa to salvage some fraction of the present heritage of mankind. (Their eastern cousins in the Philippines and in the Malay Peninsula would probably perish with the rest of us, as they both live in what have now come to be dangerously exposed positions.)

The African Negritos are said by our anthropologists to have an unexpectedly pure and lofty conception of the nature of God and of God's relation to man. They might be able to give mankind a fresh start; and, though we should then have lost the achievements of the last 6000 to 10,000 years, what are 10,000 years compared to 600,000 or a million years for which the human race has already been in existence?

The extreme possibility of catastrophe is that we might succeed in exterminating the whole human race, African Negritos and all.

On the evidence of the past history of life on this planet, even that is not entirely unlikely. After all, the reign of man on the Earth, if we are right in thinking that man established his present ascendency in the middle palaeolithic age, is so far only about 100,000 years old, and what is that compared to the 500 million or 800 million years during which life has been in existence on the surface of this planet? In the past, other forms of life have enjoyed reigns which have lasted for almost inconceivably longer periods — and which yet at last have come to an end. There was a reign of the giant armored reptiles which may have lasted about 80 million years; say from about the year 130 million to the year 50 million before the present day. But the reptiles' reign came to an end. Long before that — perhaps 300 million years ago — there was a reign of giant armoured fishes — creatures that had already accomplished the tremendous achievement of growing a moving lower jaw. But the reign of the fishes came to an end.

The winged insects are believed to have come into existence about 250 million years ago. Perhaps the higher winged insects — the social insects that have anticipated mankind in creating an institutional life — are still waiting for their reign on Earth to come. If the ants and bees were one day to acquire even that glimmer of intellectual understanding that man has possessed in his day, and if they were then to make their own shot at seeing history in perspective, they might see the advent of the mammals, and the brief reign of the human mammal, as almost irrelevant episodes, "full of sound and fury, signifying nothing."

The challenge to us, in our generation, is to see to it that this interpretation of history shall not become the true one.

STUDY QUESTIONS

1. *Toynbee's description of the narrowing of our historical view implies certain causes that have brought this phenomenon about. What are they?*
2. *What are the criteria Toynbee uses in evaluating the standards of a civilization?*
3. *Although he does not offer any himself, can you think of any reasons to support Toynbee's view that the present dominance of our own culture in the world is certain to be temporary?*
4. *What are the values of following Toynbee's suggestion to look outside the history of our own culture in order to see it in the perspective of other nations and other times?*
5. *Are you satisfied with Toynbee's standards for judging the "life expectancy" of civilizations? Do you think there are other factors that should be taken into consideration?*
6. *Toynbee's description of the place our civilization holds in history may change your feeling about some of the problems within our own culture, such as disarmament, desegregation, civil liberties, war or education. Write a theme explaining how the broad view described by Toynbee has influenced your estimate of some such problem. Or explain why you cannot accept Toynbee's description.*

Herbert J. Muller The Meaning of History*

*T*ime will tell, we say; but we may not be aware of the difference that is made by our very conception of time. To the Greeks and Romans time was characteristically a slow but inexorable enemy of man, telling the destruction of all his work. To the Hindu sage it was static or illusory, resembling a deep pool rather than a flow or a river; so the splash of history made ripples that vanished as they spread, distracting only the foolish. To the modern Westerner, on the contrary, time is all-important. He tells it, keeps it, lives by it punctually. In America he has a passion for making it and saving it (though what he saves it for may not be clear). It has been his great hope, in its promise of ever bigger and better things to come. And if he is now much less hopeful he has a more vivid sense of the horrors that time may bring. For him, in any event, things always keep moving. Time Marches On!

In short, our feeling about time — however vague or unconscious — ultimately involves a philosophy of history. It leads to a momentous question. Given all the drama of human history, what is the plot, the grand design, the final meaning of the whole show? Positivists will tell us that this is a meaningless question. Manifestly we cannot give it a precise, positive answer: we cannot state it in terms that permit either empirical verification or rigorous

---

* From *The Uses of the Past* by Herbert J. Muller. Copyright, 1952, by Oxford University Press, Inc. Reprinted by permission.

logical analysis. But neither can we escape it. Although we naturally come to it as we hope to make sense of history, we are forced to consider it if only because men persist in answering it. Thus Westerners have declared that history is a progress, and in this faith have made extraordinary history. Today Communists are still so positive the drama will have a happy ending, in a classless society, that they threaten to precipitate a war which might make any society impossible, put a literal end to history. Others have therefore been led to reject the whole faith in progress — and their negations may also have positive consequences. Time will tell in any case; but what it will tell depends on what men say and do right now.

This is to reject the Indian view that history is mere appearance or illusion. In certain moods, to be sure, we all know the feeling that the "real" reality is changeless and timeless — the feeling of eternity as a quality of the present, which is perhaps the most valid intimation of immortality. Even so worldly a philosopher as Bertrand Russell has said that "there is some sense, easier to feel than to state, in which Time is an unimportant and superficial characteristic of reality"; and almost all the wise men have agreed that wisdom begins with a realization of its unimportance.[1] Still, Westerners have good reason for sticking to their senses as they do. The very insistence of the Hindu sages on the necessity of renouncing or transcending the temporal world, and their arduous disciplines for shaking off the illusions of sense, indicate that this world is real enough. And as students of history, at any rate, we are bound to take time seriously. The pertinent theories of history concern dramas that are played out in time, by flesh and blood actors, on a real stage. The most common theories involve three main kinds of movement in time — progress, decline, and cycle. Because the idea of progress is so familiar, we may forget that it is a very novel Western idea, only a few centuries old; so we might first consider the alternative theories, which have the prestige of endorsement by the most illustrious thinkers of the past.

As I have already indicated, the theory of decline is the hoariest theory of history. Men used to locate Utopia in the remote past instead of the future — as in the Garden of Eden of Babylonian-Hebrew mythology, or the Golden Age of Hesiod. Even the sophisticated literature of the Greco-Roman world is shot through with the notion that civilization is a disease or degeneration. (Lovejoy and Boas offer a comprehensive account of the early career of this theory in their *Primitivism and Related Ideas in Antiquity*.) Although it was generally assumed that the utopian simple life had actually been lived somewhere, the conceptions of it varied widely. Hedonists pictured it as a carefree life in which men were good and happy; Stoics pictured it as a hard, rugged life that bred the manly virtues wanting in their effete society. Usually

---

[1] A further difficulty with the Western man's common-sense notion of time is that if he begins to think seriously about it, he soon runs into the unthinkable. He cannot really conceive an eternal universe: it must have a beginning, if not an end; yet neither can he conceive of the state before the beginning, or after the end. Time cannot march on forever, but neither can it stop.

primitivism was an earnest criticism and exhortation, implying that man could mend his civilized ways; but the explicit conclusion was usually a gloomy belief that he lacked the sense to do so, implying that civilization is an incurable disease. A similar diversity appears in modern versions. Dostoyevsky and Tolstoy found their ideal in primitive Christianity, and their hope in the Russian peasant; whereas D. H. Lawrence glorified the intuitive, instinctive life or "phallic consciousness," but could never find a satisfactory historical model.

As all this implies, theories of decline cannot be taken seriously as literal outlines of history. There is no evidence whatever of the historical existence of a Garden of Eden or Golden Age, or of an ideal primitive stage in evolution. Such fictions may be useful as metaphors, symbolizing the actual corruptions of civilizations and the natural corruptibility of man, but it is essential to remember that they are fictions, pure and rather too simple. Usually they reflect a shallow view of history, or a sheer ignorance of it.[2]

Hence the deepest thought of antiquity led rather to the conclusion that history is an endless cycle. Aristotle saw a continuous "coming to be and falling away"; he speculated that there had already been countless civilizations, which had passed through a uniform destiny. Stoics and Epicureans alike dwelt on the inevitable recurrences. The rational soul, wrote Marcus Aurelius, "considers the periodic destructions and rebirths of the universe, and reflects that our posterity will see nothing new, and that our ancestors saw nothing greater than we have seen." Or in the words of Ecclesiastes, "The thing that hath been, it is that which shall be; and that which is done is that which shall be done; and there is no new thing under the sun." This theory of cycles has been maintained by such Western thinkers as Bodin, Vico, and Nietzsche, and in our time has been given its most systematic, comprehensive formulation in Spengler's *Decline of the West*. Spengler argued that all civilizations necessarily pass through parallel stages and necessarily die a natural death — unless (like the Aztec) they are prematurely destroyed by accident.

Whether one is comforted or depressed by this fatalistic view of history is presumably a matter of temperament. Most thinkers have chosen to dwell on its pessimistic implications. The cycles appear to be rhymes without reason, even when God is made their author. The eternal inanity of the cosmic process is most conspicuous in the Hindu and Buddhist versions, as summarized by Sir Charles Eliot: "An infinite number of times the Universe has collapsed in flaming or watery ruin, aeons of quiescence follow the col-

[2] A modern version typical of such fictions was a recent speech by the president of an alumni association. He edified the old grads with an account of the golden age of our society, which he dated about 1910—with no hint that this businessman's Eden was breeding its own serpents, and that its fruit was war and depression. Although his speech was no doubt inspired by the beery sentimentality appropriate to alumni reunions, it expressed the sober attitude of many business leaders, congressmen, and newspaper publishers.

lapse, and then the Deity (he has done it an infinite number of times) emits again from himself worlds and souls of the same old kind." Babylonian and Aztec myths likewise stressed the melancholy idea that the cycles are punctuated by universal catastrophes. Men are most disposed to take such a view of history, moreover, when they believe that their society is on the downswing, headed for catastrophe. Like the primitivists, the "cyclists" usually believed that the best days were behind them, and they have even less hope of the future. So we have the curious spectacle of civilized man forever marching with his face turned backward — as no doubt the cave-man looked back to the good old days when men were free to roam instead of being stuck in a damn hole in the ground. And so the theory of cycles has again become seductive, as the men again fear the worst. Spengler, Sorokin, and Toynbee have presented different versions of it, but all agree that the West is on the decline.

The most obvious argument for this theory is its correspondence with the processes of birth, growth, decay, and death in the natural world. Given the fate of all other higher organisms, it seems reasonable to assume that a civilization cannot maintain itself indefinitely, but in time must age and die. Offhand, the theory also corresponds with the actual history of civilizations to date: all but our own have died, or have been dying. (Thus we have unearthed several of Aristotle's "lost" civilizations, such as the ancient Indic and the Minoan, and in the huge statues on Easter Island see evidence that there might once have been a high civilization in the South Pacific area.) Everywhere we find a monotonous recurrence of the basic themes of selfishness and greed, fear and hate. But most pertinent is the evidence of cyclical movements within civilizations, the familiar patterns of rise and fall. In *Configurations of Cultural Growth*, A. L. Kroeber surveys the major cultural achievements of all the great societies; and the most striking fact that emerges from his anthropological study is the fact of configuration and cycle.

About 1400, for example, the notable Dutch-Flemish school of painters arose suddenly, out of nowhere, with the Van Eycks; about 1700 the whole movement ended as suddenly, for Rembrandt, Hals, Teniers, Ruysdael, and the rest had died within a few years of one another; and ever since there has been practically no Dutch-Flemish painting of consequence. So it has been with all the major growths in art, literature, philosophy, and science. This phenomenon of the golden age is so familiar that we may forget how strange it is. All our knowledge of genetics indicates that the appearance of genius in any given society should be more or less constant — yet it never has been. Except for a very few isolated great men, such as John Scotus Erigena, genius has appeared only when there was a movement afoot; most potential greatness evidently goes to waste. And the movements appear to have specific limits as well as potentialities: they move to fulfilment, and then to exhaustion. All this implies a kind of predestination that Kroeber regrets. Nevertheless "the empirical data, over and over again, and with really remarkably few exceptions, compel the conclusion that there are whole arrays of events in the history of culture which are objectively describable only in terms of the metaphors of 'growth,' 'realization,' 'exhaustion,' and 'death,' as our vocabulary stands today."

This much seems clear. The picture as a whole, however, is not at all clear. Although we can make out configurations everywhere, they are irregular in their growth, diverse in their content, and inconstant in their associations. After medieval philosophy reached the end of its development, about 1350, there was no important philosophy in all Europe until the rise of the moderns with Descartes, after 1600; yet this long slump coincided with the Renaissance, a period of abounding intellectual activity. Kroeber's survey indicates that such apparent anomalies are the rule. Ancient Greece has fixed the common notion of a golden age as a rich growth in all fields of art and thought, a whole culture on the surge; but this glory has so profoundly impressed men because it was indeed unique. Thus the splendid Elizabethan Age produced no painting or sculpture to speak of, whereas the splendor of the Italian Renaissance was largely confined to the representative arts. Similarly there are conspicuous gaps in great civilizations. Egypt, Mesopotamia, and Japan produced no significant philosophy, Rome no science, Islam no painting, sculpture, or drama.[3] Furthermore, the golden ages of culture appear to have no necessary connection with national expansion. Greek culture flowered before and after the little city-states had their brief hours of military glory; the Italians made their greatest contributions when their cities were torn by civil war and largely dominated by other countries; the Germans led all Europe under Beethoven, Goethe, and Kant while they were being overrun by Napoleon's armies, and their great creative period was over by 1870, when their great national expansion began.

Altogether, Kroeber can make out no "true law" in cultural history: "nothing cyclical, regularly repetitive, or necessary." And in the history of whole civilizations, regular cycles are still harder to find. Civilizations are much less discrete and homogeneous than the cyclical theory presupposes, and their geographical, political, and cultural components do not have a uniform destiny. (We have already seen that when "Rome" fell, its Eastern Empire lived on.) Historians cannot even agree on their location in time and space — Toynbee makes out at least twice as many civilizations as Spengler did. Neither can they agree on criteria for marking the peak of a society, or on the symptoms of growth and decay. And most dubious are the neat parallels, the efforts to make all societies swing through exactly the same cycle. On

---

3 With Islam, an obvious explanation is the Mohammedan law prohibiting the representation of the human form; but since native sculpture had been dead in this region long before this taboo, its absence might be considered the reason for the taboo. Kroeber warns against the conventional "explanations" in our texts. Although Elizabethan drama, for example, is usually explained by the defeat of the Spanish Armada, it might be as reasonable to explain the defeat by the rise of Elizabethan poetry. The truth probably is that both were manifestations of some deeper cause that has yet to be defined.

the face of it, civilizations start at different points, building on different pasts in different environments, exploiting different possibilities. Spengler, the most systematic exponent of this theory, kept his cycles orderly only by a Teutonic forcing and drilling of the facts, with a ruthless suppression of all unruly facts.

Above all, the *necessity* of the cycles is unproved, and unprovable on the basis of present knowledge. The only cause suggested by Spengler is a biological analogy that cannot bear scientific analysis. "The Biology of the future," he declared, "will undoubtedly find the point of departure for an entirely new formulation of its problems in the concept of the preordained life-span of the genus and species" — a span, he added, which is "a numerical value of almost mystical significance." Mystical is strictly the word for it. Biology gives no signs of accommodating him; and even if it attempted this new departure (or aspired to the exaltation of a capital B) it would not prove his point, since a society is neither a genus nor a species.

What biology still does teach is the theory of evolution; and this brings us back to the modern theory of progress. Although past societies were often complacent enough about their superiority over barbarians, there are only a few scattered hints of any hope for continuous advance. The nearest thing to it was the Hebrew vision of the Messiah, which bred the Christian visions of the Millennium and the Second Coming, but these all depended upon a direct intervention by God; they stirred no hope that man, by his own efforts, could achieve a steady improvement of his earthly condition. Only with the rise of science did men begin to entertain seriously the possibility of progress. At length the possibility was transformed into a gospel, a certainty. History became a success story, of a race that was bound to make good. "Progress is not an accident but a necessity," proclaimed Herbert Spencer. "What we call evil and immorality must disappear. It is certain that man must become perfect.... Always toward perfection is the mighty movement."

Now in the long evolutionary view, reaching back to the caveman and ape-man, there unquestionably has been progress—always granted the assumption that it is worth being a human being. Man has achieved greater mastery of his natural environment, greater freedom of action, and thereupon has discovered the finer possibilities of life implicit in his distinctive power of consciousness. In historic times there have been clear gains in intellectual and spiritual as well as material wealth and power. Christian thinkers who now ridicule the faith in progress forget the assumption of progress in their own concept of "higher" religions, and of the progressive revelations of God through Abraham, Moses, and Christ; and hardly any thinker will deny that the religion of Jesus is loftier than that of Moloch. If all specific gains are disputable, there remains the general advance that man has made, from blind obedience to the totems and taboos of the tribe to conscious, reasoned loyalty to ideals of humanity. All the savagery that persists seems more frightful because it no longer seems inevitable or proper. In general, the tragic failures of civilization have left substantial residues of knowledge, skills, arts, ideas, ideals—of enduring goods that men do not willingly give up, once they are known, but that we are apt to forget because we take them for granted.

Simply as we cherish the possibilities of progress, however, we must severely qualify the popular notions about them. The progress has not been steady or in a straight line: history is not a succession of civilizations rising to ever greater heights, coming ever closer to the distinction of having produced us. The progress has not been progress pure and simple: all the gains in freedom and power have enabled men to do more evil as well as good, to destroy as well as create. Above all, the progress has not been automatic and inevitable: it has resulted from arduous human effort, an "expense of greatness" that has often been squandered by later generations. Hence continued progress is not guaranteed by any known law of nature. Nothing in history assures the success of our civilization; history tells us only that the incalculable possibilities open to us are more likely to be for worse than for better. Nothing in biology assures the indefinite progress or even the indefinite survival of the human race; devolution or extinction has been the common fate of the more complex forms of life, while the simple amoeba is a good bet to last to the end. At that, the exciting story of the evolution of life is a local affair, an interlude confined to a speck in interstellar space. Those who make "emergent evolution" the key to the cosmic plan have little more scientific authority than the Book of Revelation; for our most certain knowledge indicates that all life on this planet is ultimately doomed to extinction, and that its disappearance will make no apparent difference to the universe. The only enduring result of man's works, Santayana has said, is that the earth may cast a slightly different shadow on the moon.

THE OPEN SOCIETY

What, then, is the meaning of history? The answer presumably should come at the end of this work, where conclusions belong. My conclusions were in fact modified during the course of my studies, and will be restated at the end. Yet it would be idle to pretend that we are now to embark on a voyage of exploration, with no idea of our destination. My answer has been implicit in all that I have written so far, and will determine the content of the chapters that follow. It amounts to a basic assumption, a premise that should be laid face up on the table. Briefly, my answer is at once a negation and an affirmation. History has no meaning, in the sense of a clear pattern or determinate plot; but it is not simply meaningless or pointless. It has no certain meaning because man is free to give it various possible meanings.

His freedom is sharply limited, of course. Man has to choose within the conditions imposed by his biological structure, his natural environment, and his cultural heritage. He cannot do whatever he has a mind to, and at that his mind has been largely made up by his ancestors. For such reasons he is always prone to believe that history somehow makes itself, in spite of his efforts, by the automatic operation of natural laws or God's will. Still, at any moment he has a wide range of choices and is willy-nilly making more history, discovering the meanings of his past and determining the meanings of his future. The most significant "facts" he has to face are of man's own making. Marxism, for all its theoretical determinism, is the clearest illustration of how history is made by men's beliefs about what has happened, what is happening, and what should happen.

This insistence on human freedom is not simply cheering. It means that we have to keep making history, instead of leaning on it, and that we can never count on a final solution. It means the constant possibility of foolish or even fatal choices. Yet the dignity of man lies precisely in this power to choose his destiny. We may therefore welcome the conclusion that we cannot foretell the future, even apart from the possibility that it may not bear knowing. Uncertainty is not only the plainest condition of human life but the necessary condition of freedom, of aspiration, of conscience—of all human idealism.

It is the business of the future to be dangerous, Whitehead remarked; and we can always trust it to keep on the job. I again stress the uncertainties, however, because the dangers are always intensified by the pretensions to absolute certainty or finality. These are the ultimate source of corruption, the reason why the best becomes the worst and crusaders for heaven make a hell on earth. And none is more insidious than the principle of historical predestination. Knowing in advance how history is going to turn out, men climb on the bandwagon, ride the wave of the future.[4] They can then indulge any policy, from supine resignation to ruthless violence. So the Communists can justify the most barbarous behavior: like hangmen, they are merely executing "the verdict of history." They corrupt morality at its very base by implying that it is man's duty to fight for the inevitable, or that historic might makes right. Even in self-sacrifice they are profoundly irresponsible. Our business as rational beings is not to argue for what is going to be but to strive for what ought to be, in the consciousness that it will never be all we would like it to be.

Among the possible "meanings" of history — to restate my premises in these terms—the most significant is the growth of this power of self-determination, or freedom to make history. I assume that for interpreting the past and choosing a future we must begin with a full acknowledgment of the claims of reason: a humble reason that makes no claim to finality or metaphysical certitude, because such claims cannot be rationally substantiated, and that

---

[4] James Burnham is especially agile in the performance of this feat. In the name of hard-boiled realism, he has so far ridden at least three waves—the Marxist revolution, the managerial revolution, and the imperial destiny of America. Presumably he has a weather eye open for the next wave; but meanwhile he still tends to deride visionary idealists who are more interested in making history than in predicting it.

recognizes its finiteness and fallibility; a proud reason that nevertheless maintains its authority as the final judge of all claims to truth, insisting that its tested knowledge is no less real and reliable because it is not a knowledge of ultimate reality, and that only by a further exercise of reason can its limitations and its fallacies be clearly discerned. We are not forced to choose between reason and faith in the conventional sense—we may choose between more or less reasonable faiths. The ideal of rationality in turn requires the ideal of freedom, the right to be an individual. A rational person is not merely one who has good habits or right principles, but one who knows what he believes and assumes the intellectual and moral responsibilities of his beliefs; and first he must be free to think for himself, make up his own mind. Although non-rational behavior may exhibit admirable qualities, such as the loyalty, fortitude, and daring found in barbarians, or even in the animal world, these qualities are not wholly admirable, or trustworthy, unless they are conscious, responsible choices. The only possible virtue in being a civilized man instead of a barbarian, an ignoramus, or a moron is in being a free, responsible individual with a mind of one's own.

The best society, accordingly, is that which is most conducive to the growth of such persons. It is what Karl Popper has called the "open society." [5] It is an adventurous society that has broken with the universal, prehistoric custom of regarding ancient customs as magical or sacred, that views its institutions as man-made for human purposes and examines their suitability for these purposes, that welcomes variety and change instead of enforcing rigid conformity, and that accordingly provides its members with personal opportunities and responsibilities beyond mere obedience. It is Athens as opposed to Sparta.

Today it is us; and thereby hangs our tale. Because we have made the farthest advance toward the open society we are likely to feel more impotent than men have ever felt before. The novel idea of progress, or simply of "opportunity," has been so deeply engrained in our everyday thought and feeling that we are incapable of passive acceptance and endurance; in a crisis we take for granted the possibility and the need of "doing something about it." Having accumulated a vast deal of sociological and historical knowledge, we are also more aware of the difficulty of doing anything about it, and are more critical of the simple faiths that once made it easier for men to do or die for God, king, and country. We bear the cross of consciousness. In a fuller consciousness the burden may be eased — and this is the reason for the chapters that follow. Our adventure in freedom is so recent that what appear to be our death rattles may be growing pains. But in any event the pains are unavoidable. For a society as for an individual, the hardest problems begin with freedom. Today the future of the open society is wide open, to triumphs or to disasters of a magnitude hitherto undreamed of.

[5] *The Open Society and Its Enemies*, London, 1945. Popper is somewhat unfair to its enemies, of whom he makes Plato No. 1. Otherwise his book is a cogent argument for the views I am expressing here.

STUDY QUESTIONS

1. *Note how often Muller uses analogies and parallel cases in his discussion. Point out some of these and evaluate their usefulness as rhetorical devices.*

2. *What conclusion does Muller reach about the possibility of finding a pattern or "meaning" in history? What kind of evidence does he use to support his conclusion? Is it convincing?*

3. *What standards of superiority in a civilization does Muller adopt in trying to decide whether or not history represents growth?*

4. *To what extent do Toynbee and Muller agree in their philosophy of history? Are both interpretations plausible? Can both be "right"? Is one in any sense more "useful" than the other?*

5. *Write a theme describing the cultural characteristics of a period of civilization with which you are acquainted. Do you think it was a better period than our own? What comparisons and contrasts can be developed?*

6. *What position do you think our own time holds in historical development? Is it the end of an era? The beginning of one? Does it represent a high stage of development, or only the beginning of one?*

4 Science:
Principles and Practice

1. THE SCIENTIST AND HIS METHOD

Oliver La Farge Scientists Are Lonely Men*

It is not so long ago that, even in my dilettante study of the science of
ethnology, I corresponded with men in Ireland, Sweden, Germany, France,
and Yucatán, and had some discussion with a Chinese. One by one these
interchanges were cut off; in some countries the concept of science is dead,
and even in the free strongholds of Britain and the Americas pure science is
being—must be—set aside in favor of what is immediately useful and urgently
needed. It must hibernate now; for a while all it means is likely to be forgotten.

It has never been well understood. Scientists have never been good at explaining themselves and, frustrated by this, they tend to withdraw into the
esoteric, refer to the public as "laymen," and develop incomprehensible vocab-
ularies from which they draw a naïve, secret-society feeling of superiority.

* Copyright, 1942, by Oliver La Farge. Reprinted by permission of the author.

295

What is the special nature of a scientist as distinguished from a soda-jerker? Not just the externals such as his trick vocabulary, but the human formation within the man? Most of what is written about him is rot; but there is stuff there which a writer can get his teeth into, and it has its vivid direct relation to all that we are fighting for.

The inner nature of science within the scientist is both emotional and intellectual. The emotional element must not be overlooked, for without it there is no sound research on however odd and dull-seeming a subject. As is true of all of us, an emotion shapes and informs the scientist's life; at the same time an intellectual discipline molds his thinking, stamping him with a character as marked as a seaman's although much less widely understood.

To an outsider who does not know of this emotion, the scientist suggests an ant, putting forth great efforts to lug one insignificant and apparently unimportant grain of sand to be added to a pile, and much of the time his struggle seems as pointless as an ant's. I can try to explain why he does it and what the long-term purpose is behind it through an example from my own work. Remember that in this I am not thinking of the rare, fortunate geniuses like the Curies, Darwin, or Newton, who by their own talents and the apex of accumulated thought at which they stood were knowingly in pursuit of great, major discoveries. This is the average scientist, one among thousands, obscure, unimportant, toilsome.

I have put in a good many months of hard work, which ought by usual standards to have been dull but was not, on an investigation as yet unfinished to prove that Kanhobal, spoken by certain Indians in Guatemala, is not a dialect of Jacalteca, but that, on the contrary, Jacalteca is a dialect of Kanhobal. Ridiculous, isn't it? Yet to me the matter is not only serious but exciting. Why?

There is an item of glory. There are half a dozen or so men now living (some now, unfortunately, our enemies) who will pay me attention and respect if I prove my thesis. A slightly larger number, less interested in the details of my work, will give credit to La Farge for having added to the linguistic map of Central America the name of a hitherto unnoted dialect. But not until I have told a good deal more can I explain—as I shall presently —why the notice of so few individuals can constitute a valid glory.

There's the nature of the initial work. I have spent hours, deadly, difficult hours, extracting lists of words, paradigms of verbs, constructions, idioms, and the rest from native informants, often at night in over-ventilated huts while my hands turned blue with cold. (Those mountains are far from tropical.) An illiterate Indian tires quickly when giving linguistic information. He is not accustomed to thinking of words in terms of other words; his command of Spanish is so poor that again and again you labor over misunderstandings; he does not think in our categories of words. Take any schoolchild and ask him how you say, "I go." Then ask him in turn, "Thou goest, he goes, we go." Even the most elementary schooling has taught him, if only from the force of staring resentfully at the printed page, to think in terms of the present tense of a single verb—that is, to conjugate. He will give you, in Spanish for instance, "*Me voy, te vas, se va, nos vamos,*" all in order. Try this on an illiterate Indian. He gives you his equivalent of "I go," follows it perhaps with "thou goest," but the next question reminds him of his son's departure that morning for Ixtatán, so he answers "he sets out," and from that by another mental leap produces "we are traveling." This presents the investigator with a magnificently irregular verb. He starts checking back, and the Indian's mind being set in the new channel, he now gets "I travel" instead of "I go."

There follows an exhausting process of inserting an alien concept into the mind of a man with whom you are communicating tenuously in a language which you speak only pretty well and he quite badly.

Then of course you come to a verb which really is irregular and you mistrust it. Both of you become tired, frustrated, upset. At the end of an hour or so the Indian is worn out, his friendship for you has materially decreased, and you yourself are glad to quit.

Hours and days of this, and it's not enough. I have put my finger upon the village of Santa Eulalia and said, "Here is the true, the classic Kanhobal from which the other dialects diverge." Then I must sample the others; there are at least eight villages which must yield me up fairly complete word-lists and two from which my material should be as complete as from Santa Eulalia. More hours and more days, long horseback trips across the mountains to enter strange, suspicious settlements, sleep on the dirt floor of the schoolhouse, and persuade the astonished yokelry that it is a good idea, a delightful idea, that you should put "The Tongue" into writing. Bad food, a bout of malaria, and the early-morning horror of seeing your beloved horse's neck running blood from vampire bats ("Oh, but, yes, señor, everyone knows that here are very troublesome the vampire bats"), to get the raw material for proving that Jacalteca is a dialect of Kanhobal instead of ...

You bring your hard-won data back to the States and you follow up with a sort of detective-quest for obscure publications and old manuscripts which may show a couple of words of the language as it was spoken a few centuries ago, so that you can get a line on its evolution. With great labor you unearth and read the very little that has been written bearing upon this particular problem.

By now the sheer force of effort expended gives your enterprise value in your own eyes. And you still have a year's work to put all your data in shape, test your conclusions, and demonstrate your proof.

Yet the real emotional drive goes beyond all this. Suppose I complete my work and prove, in fact, that Kanhobal as spoken in Santa Eulalia is a language in its own right and the classic tongue from which Jacalteca has diverged under alien influences, and that, further, I show just where the gradations of speech in the intervening villages fit in. Dear God, what a small, dull grain of sand!

But follow the matter a little farther. Jacalteca being relatively well-known

(I can, offhand, name four men who have given it some study), from it it has been deduced that this whole group of dialects is most closely related to the languages spoken south and east of these mountains. If my theory is correct, the reverse is true—the group belongs to the Northern Division of the Mayan Family. This fact, taken along with others regarding physical appearance, ancient remains, and present culture, leads to a new conclusion about the direction from which these tribes came into the mountains: a fragment of the ancient history of what was once a great, civilized people comes into view. So now my tiny contribution begins to be of help to men working in other branches of anthropology than my own, particularly to the archaeologists; it begins to help toward an eventual understanding of the whole picture in this area: the important question of, not what these people are to-day, but how they got that way and what we can learn from that about all human behavior including our own.

Even carrying the line of research as far as this assumes that my results have been exploited by men of greater attainments than I. Sticking to the linguistic line, an error has been cleared away, an advance has been made in our understanding of the layout and interrelationship of the many languages making up the Mayan Family. With this we come a step nearer to working out the processes by which these languages became different from one another and hence to determining the archaic, ancestral roots of the whole group.

So far as we know at present, there are not less than eight completely unrelated language families in America north of Panama. This is unreasonable: there are hardly that many families among all the peoples of the Old World. Twenty years ago we recognized not eight, but forty. Some day perhaps we shall cut the total to four. The understanding of the Mayan process is a step toward that day; it is unlikely that Mayan will remain an isolated way of speech unconnected with any other. We know now that certain tribes in Wyoming speak languages akin to those of others in Panama; we have charted the big masses and islands of that group of tongues and from the chart begin to see the outlines of great movements and crashing historical events in the dim past. If we should similarly develop a relationship between Mayan and, let's say, the languages of the Mississippi Valley, again we should offer something provocative to the archaeologist, the historian, the student of mankind. Some day we shall show an unquestionable kinship between some of these families and certain languages of the Old World and with it cast a new light on the dim subject of the peopling of the Americas, something to guide our minds back past the Arctic to dark tribes moving blindly from the high plateaus of Asia.

My petty detail has its place in a long project carried out by many men which will serve not only the history of language but the broad scope of history itself. It goes farther than that. The humble Pah-Utes of Nevada speak a tongue related to that which the subtle Montezuma used, the one narrow in scope, evolved only to meet the needs of a primitive people, the other sophisticated, a capable instrument for poetry, for an advanced governmental system, and for philosophical speculation. Men's thoughts make language and their languages make thought. When the matter of the speech of mankind is fully known and laid side by side with all the other knowledges, the philosophers, the men who stand at the gathering-together point of science, will have the means to make man understand himself at last.

Of course no scientist can be continuously aware of such remote possible consequences of his labors; in fact the long goal is so remote that if he kept his eyes on it he would become hopelessly discouraged over the half inch of progress his own life's work will represent. But it was the vision of this which first made him choose his curious career, and it is an emotional sense of the great structure of scientific knowledge to which his little grain will be added which drives him along.

II

I spoke of the item of glory, the half dozen colleagues who will appreciate one's work. To understand that one must first understand the *isolation* of research, a factor which has profound effects upon the scientist's psyche.

The most obvious statement of this is in the public attitude and folk-literature about "professors." The titles and subjects of Ph.D. theses have long been sources of exasperated humor among us; we are all familiar with the writer's device which ascribes to a professorial character an intense interest in some such matter as the development of the molars in pre-Aurignacian man or the religious sanctions of the Levirate in northeastern Australia, the writer's intention being that the reader shall say "Oh God!," smile slightly, and pigeonhole the character. But what do you suppose is the effect of the quite natural public attitude behind these devices upon the man who is excitedly interested in pre-Aurignacian molars and who knows that this is a study of key value in tracing the evolution of *Homo sapiens?*

Occasionally some line of research is taken up and made clear, even fascinating, to the general public, as in Zinsser's *Rats, Lice and History*, or De Kruif's rather Sunday-supplement writings. Usually, as in these cases, they deal with medicine or some other line of work directly resulting in findings of vital interest to the public. Then the ordinary man will consent to understand, if not the steps of the research itself, at least its importance, will grant the excitement, and honor the researcher. When we read Eve Curie's great biography of her parents our approach to it is colored by our knowledge, forty years later, of the importance of their discovery to every one of us. It would have been quite possible at the time for a malicious or merely ignorant writer to have presented that couple as archetypes of the "professor," performing incomprehensible acts of self-immolation in pursuit of an astronomically unimportant what's-it.

Diving to my own experience like a Stuka with a broken wing, I continue to take my examples from my rather shallow linguistic studies because, in its very nature, the kind of thing a linguist studies is so beautifully calculated to arouse the "Oh God!" emotion.

It happened that at the suggestion of my betters I embarked upon an ambitious, general comparative study of the whole Mayan Family. The farther in I got the farther there was to go and the more absorbed I became. Puzzle piled upon puzzle to be worked out and the solution used for getting after the next one, the beginning of order in chaos, the glimpse of understanding at the far end. Memory, reasoning faculties, realism, and imagination were all on the stretch; I was discovering the full reach of whatever mental powers I had. When I say that I became absorbed I mean absorbed; the only way to do such research is to roll in it, become soaked in it, live it, breathe it, have your system so thoroughly permeated with it that at the half glimpse of a fugitive possibility everything you have learned so far and everything you have been holding in suspension is in order and ready to prove or disprove that point. You do not only think about your subject while the documents are spread before you; everyone knows that some of our best reasoning is done when the surface of the mind is occupied with something else and the deep machinery of the brain is free to work unhampered.

One day I was getting aboard a trolley car in New Orleans on my way to Tulane University. As I stepped up I saw that if it were possible to prove that a prefixed s- could change into a prefixed y- a whole series of troublesome phenomena would fall into order. The transition must come through u- and, thought I with a sudden lift of excitement, there may be a breathing associated with u- and that may make the whole thing possible. As I paid the conductor I thought that the evidence I needed might exist in Totonac and Tarascan, non-Mayan languages with which I was not familiar. The possibilities were so tremendous that my heart pounded and I was so preoccupied that I nearly went to sit in the Jim Crow section. Speculation was useless until I could reach the University and dig out the books, so after a while I calmed myself and settled to my morning ration of Popeye, who was then a new discovery too. As a matter of fact, the idea was no good, but the incident is a perfect example of the "professor mind."

Of course, if as I stepped on to the car it had dawned upon me that the reason my girl's behavior last evening had seemed odd was that she had fallen for the Englishman we had met, the incident would not have seemed so funny, although the nature of the absorption, subconscious thinking, and realization would have been the same in both cases.

I lived for a month with the letter *k*. If we have three words in Quiché, one of the major Mayan languages, beginning with *k*, in Kanhobal we are likely to find that one of these begins with *ch*. Moving farther west and north, in Tzeltal one is likely to begin with *k*, one with *ch*, and the one which began with *ch* in Kanhobal to begin with *ts*. In Huasteca, at the extreme northwest, they begin with *k, ts,* and plain *s* respectively. Why don't they all change alike? Which is the original form? Which way do these changes run, or from which point do they run both ways? Until those questions can be answered we cannot even guess at the form of the mother tongue from which these languages diverged, and at that point all investigation halts. Are these k's in Quiché pronounced even faintly unlike? I noticed no difference between the two in Kanhobal, but then I wasn't listening for it. I wished someone properly equipped would go and listen to the Quiché Indians, and wondered if I could talk the University into giving me money enough to do so.

This is enough to give some idea of the nature of my work, and its uselessness for general conversation. My colleagues at Tulane were archaeologists. Shortly after I got up steam they warned me frankly that I had to stop trying to tell them about the variability of k, the history of Puctun t^y, or any similar matter. If I produced any results that they could apply, I could tell them about it; but apart from that I could keep my damned sound-shifts and intransitive infixes to myself; I was driving them nuts. My other friends on the faculty were a philosopher and two English professors; I was pursuing two girls at the time but had not been drawn to either because of intellectual interests in common; my closest friends were two painters and a sculptor. The only person I could talk to was myself.

The cumulative effect of this non-communication was terrific. A strange, mute work, a thing crying aloud for discussion, emotional expression, the check and reassurance of another's point of view, turned in upon myself to boil and fume, throwing upon me the responsibility of being my own sole check, my own impersonal, external critic. When finally I came to New York on vacation I went to see my Uncle John. He doesn't know Indian languages but he is a student of linguistics, and I shall never forget the relief, the reveling pleasure, of pouring my work out to him.

Thus at the vital point of his life-work the scientist is cut off from communication with his fellow-men. Instead, he has the society of two, six, or twenty men and women who are working in his specialty, with whom he corresponds, whose letters he receives like a lover, with whom when he meets them he wallows in an orgy of talk, in the keen pleasure of conclusions and findings compared, matched, checked against one another—the pure joy of being really understood.

The praise and understanding of those two or six become for him the equivalent of public recognition. Around these few close colleagues is the larger group of workers in the same general field. They do not share with one in the steps of one's research, but they can read the results, tell in a general way if they have been soundly reached, and profit by them. To them McGarnigle "has shown" that there are traces of an ancient, dolichocephalic strain among the skeletal remains from Pusilhá, which is something they can use. Largely on the strength of his close colleagues' judgment of him, the word gets around that McGarnigle is a sound man. You can trust his work. He's the fellow you want to have analyze the material if you turn up an interesting bunch of skulls. All told, including men in allied fields who use his findings, some fifty scientists praise him; before them he has achieved international reputation. He will receive honors. It is even remotely possible that he might get a raise in salary.

McGarnigle disinters himself from a sort of fortress made of boxes full of skeletons in the cellar of Podunk University's Hall of Science, and emerges into the light of day to attend a Congress. At the Congress he delivers a paper entitled *Additional Evidence of Dolichocephaly among the Eighth Cycle Maya* before the Section on Physical Anthropology. In the audience are six archaeologists specializing in the Maya field, to whom these findings have a special importance, and twelve physical anthropologists including Gruenwald of Eastern California, who is the only other man working on Maya remains.

After McGarnigle's paper comes Gruenwald's turn. Three other physical anthropologists, engaged in the study of the Greenland Eskimo, the Coastal Chinese, and the Pleistocene Man of Lake Mojave respectively, come in. They slipped out for a quick one while McGarnigle was speaking because his Maya work is not particularly useful to them and they can read the paper later; what is coming next, with its important bearing on method and theory, they would hate to miss.

Gruenwald is presenting a perfectly horrible algebraic formula and a diagram beyond Rube Goldberg's wildest dream, showing *A Formula for Approximating the Original Indices of Artificially Deformed Crania.* (These titles are not mere parodies; they are entirely possible.) The archaeologists depart hastily to hear a paper in their own section on *Indications of an Early Quinary System at Uaxactún.* The formula is intensely exciting to Mc-Garnigle because it was the custom of the ancient Mayas to remodel the heads of their children into shapes which they (erroneously) deemed handsomer than nature's. He and Gruenwald have been corresponding about this; at one point Gruenwald will speak of his colleague's experience in testing the formula; he has been looking forward to this moment for months.

After the day's sessions are over will come something else he has been looking forward to. He and Gruenwald, who have not seen each other in two years, go out and get drunk together. It is not that they never get drunk at home, but that now when in their cups they can be uninhibited, they can talk their own, private, treble-esoteric shop. It is an orgy of release.

III

In the course of their drinking it is likely—if an archaeologist or two from the area joins them it is certain—that the talk will veer from femoral pilasters and alveolar prognathism to personal experiences in remote sections of the Petén jungle. For in my science and a number of others there is yet another frustration.

We go into the field and there we have interesting experiences. The word "adventure" is taboo and "explore" is used very gingerly. But the public mind has been so poisoned by the outpourings of bogus explorers that it is laden with claptrap about big expeditions, dangers, hardships, hostile tribes, the lighting of red flares around the camp to keep the savages at bay, and God knows what rot. (I can speak freely about this because my own expeditions have been so unambitious and in such easy country that I don't come into the subject.) As a matter of fact it is generally true that *for a scientist on an expedition to have an adventure is evidence of a fault in his technique.* He is sent out to gather information, and he has no business getting into "a brush with the natives."

The red-flare, into-the-unknown, hardship-and-danger boys, who manage to find a tribe of pink-and-green Indians, a lost city, or the original, hand-painted descendants of the royal Incas every time they go out, usually succeed in so riling the natives and local whites upon whom scientists must depend if they are to live in the country as to make work in the zones they contaminate difficult for years afterward. The business of their adventures and discoveries is sickening.

I have sat squirming through a lecture in which the lecturer told how he barely escaped with his life after desperate adventures among the Jivaro Indians of Peru, while (a) he showed excellently taken moving pictures of the said adventures, (b) I had recently finished cataloguing a very nice collection of their material brought us by a man who happened, quite casually, to pass through their territory, and (c) three of my friends, boys in their early twenties, were just back from spending their summer vacation among those friendly, kindly warriors.

I have read a thrilling account of an "explorer's" hardships in fighting his way upriver in the jungle, the threat of disease, battles with lianas and thorny bushes, alligators, lions, and jaguars on the banks, deadly snakes in the underbrush, and hostile natives peering menacingly from behind the trees. He embarked upon this wild adventure in order to find a lost city of which he had heard a rumor. He heard his rumor from an archaeologist who had dug there and published an account of it twenty years earlier; maps of the city were already available and specimens from it were on exhibition at Harvard. It lies within one day's travel of the capital of British Honduras, the upriver trip takes four hours in a motor boat, and the few inhabitants of that section are peaceful Negroes who are proud of being British subjects.

The public, innocently, laps up the stuff, and so if one mentions work in the field one meets an expectation which requires that he lie like Munchausen or take a back seat. The men whom I honor myself by calling my colleagues go out alone or in pairs, sometimes in larger groups, not because "there is a blank space on the map which must be filled in" or because "the little we could learn about the Poopidoopi River and its dark inhabitants presented an irresistible challenge and a mystery," but because the logic of their research calls for investigations in a given place, which may be five miles from a resort hotel or five hundred from the nearest human being. Year after year they go out, usually on a shoestring (I have been handed thirteen hundred dollars on which to buy all equipment, get myself from New York to Guatemala, live six months, and return), and they come back with *data*. They suffer from chronic tropical diseases; they occasionally encounter something vaguely resembling a romance; now and then they prevent "a brush with the natives" from arising by mother-wit, tact, and a round of drinks; they carry out careful, exact work while malaria racks them; they suffer from hells of loneliness; and they experience peace and unflawed beauty.

These men by training express themselves in factual, "extensional" terms, which don't make for good adventure stories. They understandably lean over backward to avoid sounding even remotely like the frauds, the "explorers." And then what they have seen and done lacks validity to them if it cannot be told in relation to the purpose and dominant emotion which sent them there. McGarnigle went among the independent Indians of Icaiché because he had heard of a skull kept in one of their temples which, from a crude description, seemed to have certain important characteristics. All his risks and his maneuverings with those tough, explosive Indians centered around the problem of gaining access to that skull. When he tries to tell an attractive girl about his experiences he not only understates, but can't keep from stressing the significance of a skull with a healed, clover-leaf trepan. The girl gladly leaves him for the nearest broker.

The man is isolated all the way round. The snuffy fellow who gives a couple of unlikely courses in the Winter Semester leaves every midyear to spend the next six months in a fabulous wilderness where he is intensely happy. There he is a person of eminence and authority among wild, hardy people; he is a great man, well proven. He knows intimately a world so unlike ours that it seems almost as if he had left this planet when he enters it. There and at home he exercises his mental faculties triumphantly on matters which he knows are important. But he can't make any of this known to anyone outside his own guild. It is small wonder then that he develops a special attitude toward people in general and seems somewhat peculiar. In the face of the evidence, the remarkable thing is that I have found most of my colleagues in my own, small field to be gentlemen and delightful companions.

It is too bad both for the scientists and the public that they are so cut off from each other. The world needs now not the mere knowledges of science, but the way of thought and the discipline. It is the essence of what Hitler has set out to destroy; against it he has waged total war within his own domain. It is more than skepticism, the weighing of evidence, more even than the love of truth. It is the devotion of oneself to an end which is far more important than the individual, the certainty that that end is absolutely good, not only for oneself but for all mankind, and the character to set personal advantage, comfort, and glory aside in the devoted effort to make even a little progress toward it.

STUDY QUESTIONS

1. *What popular misconceptions about scientists are contradicted by the information La Farge gives?*
2. *According to La Farge, what are the scientist's motivations? To what extent do they involve egoism, altruism and curiosity?*
3. *In what ways do the scientist's emotions help him with his work? In what ways are they dangerous or a nuisance?*
4. *How does La Farge help the layman to understand why (a) apparently trivial bits of information may be valuable, and (b) why it is important for scientists to communicate with each other through journals and libraries?*
5. *Write a theme describing the emotions you experienced while performing some dangerous, difficult or trying task.*
6. *Write an essay describing what you consider to be the best personality qualifications for someone interested in being a research scientist.*

Thomas Henry Huxley All Men Are Scientists *

Scientific investigation is not, as many people seem to suppose, some kind of modern black art. You might easily gather this impression from the manner in which many persons speak of scientific inquiry, or talk about inductive and deductive philosophy, or the principles of the "Baconian philosophy." I do protest that, of the vast number of cants in this world, there are none, to my mind, so contemptible as the pseudo-scientific cant which is talked about the "Baconian philosophy."

To hear people talk about the great Chancellor—and a very great man he certainly was,—you would think that it was he who had invented science, and that there was no such thing as sound reasoning before the time of Queen Elizabeth! Of course you say, that cannot possibly be true; you perceive, on a moment's reflection, that such an idea is absurdly wrong....

The method of scientific investigation is nothing but the expression of the necessary mode of working of the human mind. It is simply the mode at which all phenomena are reasoned about, rendered precise and exact. There is no more difference, but there is just the same kind of difference, between the mental operations of a man of science and those of an ordinary person, as there is between the operations and methods of a baker or of a butcher weighing out his goods in common scales, and the operations of a chemist in performing a difficult and complex analysis by means of his balance and finely-graduated weights. It is not that the action of the scales in the one case, and the balance in the other, differ in the principles of their construction or manner of working; but the beam of one is set on an infinitely finer axis

* From *Darwiniana*, 1893.

than the other, and of course turns by the addition of a much smaller weight.

You will understand this better, perhaps, if I give you some familiar example. You have all heard it repeated, I dare say, that men of science work by means of induction and deduction, and that by the help of these operations, they, in a sort of sense, wring from Nature certain other things, which are called natural laws, and causes, and that out of these, by some cunning skill of their own, they build up hypotheses and theories. And it is imagined by many, that the operations of the common mind can be by no means compared with these processes, and that they have to be acquired by a sort of special apprenticeship to the craft. To hear all these large words, you would think that the mind of a man of science must be constituted differently from that of his fellow men; but if you will not be frightened by terms, you will discover that you are quite wrong, and that all these terrible apparatus are being used by yourselves every day and every hour of your lives.

There is a well-known incident in one of Molière's plays, where the author makes the hero express unbounded delight on being told that he had been talking prose during the whole of his life. In the same way, I trust, that you will take comfort, and be delighted with yourselves, on the discovery that you have been acting on the principles of inductive and deductive philosophy during the same period. Probably there is not one who has not in the course of the day had occasion to set in motion a complex train of reasoning, of the very same kind, though differing of course in degree, as that which a scientific man goes through in tracing the causes of natural phenomena.

A very trivial circumstance will serve to exemplify this. Suppose you go into a fruiterer's shop, wanting an apple,—you take up one, and, on biting it, you find it is sour; you look at it, and see that it is hard and green. You take up another one, and that too is hard, green, and sour. The shopman offers you a third; but, before biting it, you examine it, and find that it is hard and green, and you immediately say that you will not have it, as it must be sour, like those that you have already tried.

Nothing can be more simple than that, you think; but if you will take the trouble to analyse and trace out into its logical elements what has been done by the mind, you will be greatly surprised. In the first place, you have performed the operation of induction. You found that, in two experiences, hardness and greenness in apples went together with sourness. It was so in the first case, and it was confirmed by the second. True, it is a very small basis, but still it is enough to make an induction from; you generalize the facts, and you expect to find sourness in apples where you get hardness and greenness. You found upon that a general law, that all hard and green apples are sour; and that, so far as it goes, is a perfect induction. Well, having got your natural law in this way, when you are offered another apple which you find is hard and green, you say, "All hard and green apples are sour; this apple is hard and green, therefore this apple is sour." That train of reasoning is what logicians call a syllogism, and has all its various parts and terms—its major premiss, its minor premiss, and its conclusion. And, by the help of further reasoning, which, if drawn out, would have to be exhibited in two or three other syllogisms, you arrive at your final determination, "I will not have that apple." So that, you see, you have, in the first place, established a law by induction, and upon that you have founded a deduction, and reasoned out the special conclusion of the particular case. Well now, suppose, having got your law, that at some time afterwards, you are discussing the qualities of apples with a friend: you will say to him, "It is a very curious thing,—but I find that all hard and green apples are sour!" Your friend says to you, "But how do you know that?" You at once reply, "Oh, because I have tried them over and over again, and have always found them to be so." Well, if we were talking science instead of common sense, we should call that an experimental verification. And, if still opposed, you go further, and say, "I have heard from the people of Somersetshire and Devonshire, where a large number of apples are grown, that they have observed the same thing. It is also found to be the case in Normandy, and in North America. In short, I find it to be the universal experience of mankind wherever attention has been directed to the subject." Whereupon, your friend, unless he is a very unreasonable man, agrees with you, and is convinced that you are quite right in the conclusion you have drawn. He believes, although perhaps he does not know he believes it, that the more extensive verifications are,—that the more frequently experiments have been made, and results of the same kind arrived at,—that the more varied the conditions under which the same results are attained, the more certain is the ultimate conclusion, and he disputes the question no further. He sees that the experiment has been tried under all sorts of conditions, as to time, place, and people, with the same result; and he says with you, therefore, that the law you have laid down must be a good one, and he must believe it.

In science we do the same thing; — the philosopher exercises precisely the same faculties, though in a much more delicate manner. In scientific inquiry it becomes a matter of duty to expose a supposed law to every possible kind of verification, and to take care, moreover, that this is done intentionally, and not left to a mere accident, as in the case of the apples. And in science, as in common life, our confidence in a law is in exact proportion to the absence of variation in the result of our experimental verifications. For instance, if you let go your grasp of an article you may have in your hand, it will immediately fall to the ground. That is a very common verification of one of the best established laws of nature — that of gravitation. The method by which men of science establish the existence of that law is exactly the same as that by which we have established the trivial proposition about the sourness of hard and green apples. But we believe it in such an extensive, thorough, and unhesitating manner because the universal experience of mankind verifies it, and we can verify it ourselves at any time; and that is the strongest possible foundation on which any natural law can rest.

So much, then, by way of proof that the method of establishing laws in science is exactly the same as that pursued in common life. Let us now turn to another matter (though really it is but another phase of the same question), and that is, the method by which, from the relations of certain phenomena, we prove that some stand in the position of causes towards the others.

I want to put the case clearly before you, and I will therefore show you what I mean by another familiar example. I will suppose that one of you, on coming down in the morning to the parlour of your house, finds that a tea-pot and some spoons which had been left in the room on the previous evening are gone, — the window is open, and you observe the mark of a dirty hand on the window-frame, and perhaps, in addition to that, you notice the impress of a hob-nailed shoe on the gravel outside. All these phenomena have struck your attention instantly, and before two seconds have passed you say, "Oh, somebody has broken open the window, entered the room, and run off with the spoons and the tea-pot!" That speech is out of your mouth in a moment. And you will probably add, "I know there has; I am quite sure of it!" You mean to say exactly what you know; but in reality you are giving expression to what is, in all essential particulars, an hypothesis. You do not *know* it at all; it is nothing but an hypothesis rapidly framed in your own mind. And it is an hypothesis founded on a long train of inductions and deductions.

What are those inductions and deductions, and how have you got at this hypothesis? You have observed, in the first place, that the window is open; but by a train of reasoning involving many inductions and deductions, you have probably arrived long before at the general law — and a very good one it is — that windows do not open of themselves; and you therefore conclude that something has opened the window. A second general law that you have arrived at in the same way is, that tea-pots and spoons do not go out of a window spontaneously, and you are satisfied that, as they are not now where you left them, they have been removed. In the third place, you look at the marks on the window-sill, and the shoe-marks outside, and you say that in all previous experience the former kind of mark has never been produced by anything else but the hand of a human being; and the same experience shows that no other animal but man at present wears shoes with hob-nails in them such as would produce the marks in the gravel. I do not know, even if we could discover any of those "missing links" that are talked about, that they would help us to any other conclusion! At any rate the law which states our present experience is strong enough for my present purpose. You next reach the conclusion, that as these kinds of marks have not been left by any other animals than men, or are liable to be formed in any other way than by a man's hand and shoe, the marks in question have been formed by a man in that way. You have, further, a general law, founded on observation and experience, and that, too, is, I am sorry to say, a very universal and unimpeachable one, — that some men are thieves; and you assume at once from all these premises

— and that is what constitutes your hypothesis — that the man who made the marks outside and on the window-sill, opened the window, got into the room, and stole your tea-pot and spoons. You have now arrived at a *vera causa*; — you have assumed a cause which, it is plain, is competent to produce all the phenomena you have observed. You can explain all these phenomena only by the hypothesis of a thief. But that is a hypothetical conclusion, of the justice of which you have no absolute proof at all; it is only rendered highly probable by a series of inductive and deductive reasonings.

I suppose your first action, assuming that you are a man of ordinary common sense, and that you have established this hypothesis to your own satisfaction, will very likely be to go for the police, and set them on the track of the burglar, with the view to the recovery of your property. But just as you are starting with this object, some person comes in, and on learning what you are about, says, "My good friend, you are going on a great deal too fast. How do you know that the man who really made the marks took the spoons? It might have been a monkey that took them, and the man may have merely looked in afterwards." You would probably reply, "Well, that is all very well, but you see it is contrary to all experience of the way tea-pots and spoons are abstracted; so that, at any rate, your hypothesis is less probable than mine." While you are talking the thing over in this way, another friend arrives. And he might say, "Oh, my dear sir, you are certainly going on a great deal too fast. You are most presumptuous. You admit that all these occurrences took place when you were fast asleep, at a time when you could not possibly have known anything about what was taking place. How do you know that the laws of nature are not suspended during the night? It may be that there has been some kind of supernatural interference in this case." In point of fact, he declares that your hypothesis is one of which you cannot at all demonstrate the truth and that you are by no means sure that the laws of Nature are the same when you are asleep as when you are awake.

Well, now, you cannot at the moment answer that kind of reasoning. You feel that your worthy friend has you somewhat at a disadvantage. You will feel perfectly convinced in your own mind, however, that you are quite right, and you say to him, "My good friend, I can only be guided by the natural probabilities of the case, and if you will be kind enough to stand aside and permit me to pass, I will go and fetch the police." Well, we will suppose that your journey is successful, and that by good luck you meet with a policeman; that eventually the burglar is found with your property on his person, and the marks correspond to his hand and to his boots. Probably any jury would consider those facts a very good experimental verification of your hypothesis, touching the cause of the abnormal phenomena observed in your parlour, and would act accordingly.

Now, in this suppositious case, I have taken phenomena of a very common kind, in order that you might see what are the different steps in an ordinary process of reasoning, if you will only take the trouble to analyze it carefully.

All the operations I have described, you will see, are involved in the mind
of any man of sense in leading him to a conclusion as to the course he should
take in order to make good a robbery and punish the offender. I say that you
are led, in that case, to your conclusion by exactly the same train of reasoning
as that which a man of science pursues when he is endeavouring to discover
the origin and laws of the most occult phenomena. The process is, and always
must be, the same; and precisely the same mode of reasoning was employed by
Newton and Laplace in their endeavours to discover and define the causes of
the movements of the heavenly bodies, as you, with your own common sense,
would employ to detect a burglar. The only difference is, that the nature of
the inquiry being more abstruse, every step has to be most carefully watched,
so that there may not be a single crack or flaw in your hypothesis. A flaw or
crack in many of the hypotheses of daily life may be of little or no moment
as affecting the general correctness of the conclusions at which we may
arrive; but, in a scientific inquiry, a fallacy, great or small, is always of importance, and is sure to be in the long run constantly productive of mischievous, if not fatal results.

Do not allow yourselves to be misled by the common notion that an
hypothesis is untrustworthy simply because it is an hypothesis. It is often
urged, in respect to some scientific conclusion, that, after all, it is only an
hypothesis. But what more have we to guide us in nine-tenths of the most
important affairs of daily life than hypotheses, and often very ill-based ones?
So that in science, where the evidence of any hypothesis is subjected to the
most rigid examination, we may rightly pursue the same course. You may
have hypotheses and hypotheses. A man may say, if he likes, that the moon
is made of green cheese: that is an hypothesis. But another man, who has
devoted a great deal of time and attention to the subject, and availed himself
of the most powerful telescopes and the results of the observations of others,
declares that in his opinion it is probably composed of materials very similar
to those of which our own earth is made up: and that is also only an hypothesis. But I need not tell you that there is an enormous difference in the
value of the two hypotheses. That one which is based on sound scientific
knowledge is sure to have a corresponding value; and that which is a mere
hasty random guess is likely to have but little value. Every great step in our
progress in discovering causes has been made in exactly the same way as that
which I have detailed to you. A person observing the occurrence of certain
facts and phenomena asks, naturally enough, what process, what kind of
operation known to occur in Nature applied to the particular case, will unravel and explain the mystery? Hence you have the scientific hypothesis; and
its value will be proportionate to the care and completeness with which its
basis has been tested and verified. It is in these matters as in the commonest
affairs of practical life: the guess of the fool will be folly, while the guess of
the wise man will contain wisdom. In all cases, you see that the value of the

result depends on the patience and faithfulness with which the investigator applies to his hypothesis every possible kind of verification. . . .

STUDY QUESTIONS

1. *Into what two main parts does this explanation fall? What is the tone of the essay? What sort of an audience do you think it was addressed to? What devices does Huxley use to achieve clarity and the understanding of the reader?*

2. *Define "hypothesis" and "scientific law." What is the difference between a scientific law and a legislative law?*

3. *In the example of the missing spoons and tea-pot, is the friend who objects to the hypothesis proved wrong? What part is played by absolute proof in this and the other examples? Illustrate the difference between a trustworthy hypothesis and an untrustworthy one.*

4. *Summarize the steps in the scientific method as defined by Huxley. Do the examples of scientific thinking given by Huxley reflect the procedure followed by La Farge? Explain.*

5. *Write a theme describing an actual episode in which you unconsciously used the scientific method to arrive at a conclusion about something.*

6. *Note that Huxley insists that the scientific method, if properly followed, and verified under different conditions, produces results which must be accepted. Is Huxley making too strong a claim? Are there exceptions or qualifications that should be pointed out? Have there been any recent developments that might force Huxley to change his opinion? In discussing these points, consider the essays by Cohen and Nagel, Chesterton, and Krutch.*

Henri Poincaré   Mathematical Creation*

*I*t is time to penetrate deeper and to see what goes on in the very soul of the mathematician. For this, I believe, I can do best by recalling memories of my own. But I shall limit myself to telling how I wrote my first memoir on Fuchsian functions. I beg the reader's pardon; I am about to use some technical expressions, but they need not frighten him, for he is not obliged to understand them. I shall say, for example, that I have found the demonstration of such a theorem under such circumstances. This theorem will have a barbarous name, unfamiliar to many, but that is unimportant; what is of interest for the psychologist is not the theorem but the circumstances.

For fifteen days I strove to prove that there could not be any functions like those I have since called Fuchsian functions. I was then very ignorant; every

* From *Foundations of Science*, Science Press, 1913. Reprinted by permission of Jaques Cattell.

day I seated myself at my work table, stayed an hour or two, tried a great number of combinations and reached no results. One evening, contrary to my custom, I drank black coffee and could not sleep. Ideas rose in crowds; I felt them collide until pairs interlocked, so to speak, making a stable combination. By the next morning I had established the existence of a class of Fuchsian functions, those which come from the hypergeometric series; I had only to write out the results, which took but a few hours.

Then I wanted to represent these functions by the quotient of two series; this idea was perfectly conscious and deliberate, the analogy with elliptic functions guided me. I asked myself what properties these series must have if they existed, and I succeeded without difficulty in forming the series I have called theta-Fuchsian.

Just at this time I left Caen, where I was then living, to go on a geologic excursion under the auspices of the school of mines. The changes of travel made me forget my mathematical work. Having reached Coutances, we entered an omnibus to go some place or other. At the moment when I put my foot on the step the idea came to me, without anything in my former thoughts seeming to have paved the way for it, that the transformations I had used to define the Fuchsian functions were identical with those of non-Euclidean geometry. I did not verify the idea; I should not have had time, as, upon taking my seat in the omnibus, I went on with a conversation already commenced, but I felt a perfect certainty. On my return to Caen, for conscience's sake I verified the result at my leisure.

Then I turned my attention to the study of some arithmetical questions apparently without much success and without a suspicion of any connection with my preceding researches. Disgusted with my failure, I went to spend a few days at the seaside, and thought of something else. One morning, walking on the bluff, the idea came to me, with just the same characteristics of brevity, suddenness and immediate certainty, that the arithmetic transformations of indeterminate ternary quadratic forms were identical with those of non-Euclidean geometry.

Returned to Caen, I meditated on this result and deduced the consequences. The example of quadratic forms showed me that there were Fuchsian groups other than those corresponding to the hypergeometric series; I saw that I could apply to them the theory of theta-Fuchsian series and that consequently there existed Fuchsian functions other than those from the hypergeometric series, the ones I then knew. Naturally I set myself to form all these functions. I made a systematic attack upon them and carried all the outworks, one after another. There was one however that still held out, whose fall would involve that of the whole place. But all my efforts only served at first the better to show me the difficulty, which indeed was something. All this work was perfectly conscious.

Thereupon I left for Mont-Valérien, where I was to go through my military service; so I was very differently occupied. One day, going along the street, the solution of the difficulty which had stopped me suddenly appeared to me. I did not try to go deep into it immediately, and only after my service did I again take up the question. I had all the elements and had only to arrange them and put them together. So I wrote out my final memoir at a single stroke and without difficulty.

I shall limit myself to this single example; it is useless to multiply them. In regard to my other researches I would have to say analogous things, and the observations of other mathematicians given in *L'Enseignement Mathématique* would only confirm them.

Most striking at first is this appearance of sudden illumination, a manifest sign of long, unconscious prior work. The rôle of this unconscious work in mathematical invention appears to me incontestable, and traces of it would be found in other cases where it is less evident. Often when one works at a hard question, nothing good is accomplished at the first attack. Then one takes a rest, longer or shorter, and sits down anew to the work. During the first half-hour, as before, nothing is found, and then all of a sudden the decisive idea presents itself to the mind. It might be said that the conscious work has been more fruitful because it has been interrupted and the rest has given back to the mind its force and freshness. But it is more probable that this rest has been filled out with unconscious work and that the result of this work has afterward revealed itself to the geometer just as in the cases I have cited; only the revelation, instead of coming during a walk or a journey, has happened during a period of conscious work, but independently of this work which plays at most a rôle of excitant, as if it were the goad stimulating the results already reached during rest, but remaining unconscious, to assume the conscious form.

There is another remark to be made about the conditions of this unconscious work: it is possible, and of a certainty it is only fruitful, if it is on the one hand preceded and on the other hand followed by a period of conscious work. These sudden inspirations (and the examples already cited sufficiently prove this) never happened except after some days of voluntary effort which has appeared absolutely fruitless and whence nothing good seems to have come, where the way taken seems totally astray. These efforts then have not been as sterile as one thinks; they have set agoing the unconscious machine and without them it would not have moved and would have produced nothing.

The need for the second period of conscious work, after the inspiration, is still easier to understand. It is necessary to put in shape the results of this inspiration, to deduce from them the immediate consequences, to arrange them, to word the demonstrations, but above all is verification necessary. I have spoken of the feeling of absolute certitude accompanying the inspiration; in the cases cited this feeling was no deceiver, nor is it usually. But do not think this is a rule without exception; often this feeling deceives us without being any the less vivid, and we only find it out when we seek to put on foot the demonstration.

STUDY QUESTIONS

1. *Both Huxley and Poincaré presumably based their descriptions of the scientific method on personal experience. What part was played in Poincaré's thinking by the method which Huxley describes? Does Poincaré add elements not discussed by Huxley? Do you think there is a disagreement between them on the nature of the process? On the relative importance of certain aspects?*

2. *Review the experiences narrated by La Farge in his work on Kanhobal and Jacalteca. What similarities do you find between La Farge's experiences and those of Poincaré? What differences?*

3. *To what extent do Poincaré's experiences support the arguments in Chesterton's "The Logic of Elfland"?*

4. *Would it be accurate to call Poincaré's insights "intuitions"? Would it be fair to attribute them to "imagination"? Are they essentially like or unlike the artist's imaginative ordering of experience?*

5. *Have you ever had a sudden and unaccountable flash of insight into a difficult problem? If so, write a theme describing your experience.*

6. *Poincaré does not explain the mental processes that led to the solutions of these problems, because they were unconscious and therefore unknown to him. Is there any explanation of them? Is there any reason why his answers came to him at times when he was least concerned with his problems?*

2. SCIENCE IN ACTION

Fred Hoyle

The Origin of the Earth and the Planets*

I am now going to tell a story. I hope you will find it an interesting story, perhaps even a fascinating one. It is the story of how the Earth itself was born, how it came into being along with the other planets that go to form the retinue of the Sun.

The origin of the planets is one of the high points of the New Cosmology. It affects our whole outlook on life. For instance, the question of whether life

* From *The Nature of the Universe* by Fred Hoyle. Copyright, 1950, by Fred Hoyle. Reprinted by permission of Harper & Brothers, and of Basil Blackwell.

is rare or commonplace in the Universe depends essentially on this issue. I suppose that it is because of its cosmological importance that many people are given so strongly to asserting that the planets originated as bits of material that were torn out of the Sun. For some reason or other this idea has a deep-rooted appeal. So perhaps I had better begin by outlining some of the arguments that show why it must be wrong.

The origin of the solar system can only be understood if we appreciate its scale. As I have said before, this can best be done by thinking of it as a model in which the Sun is represented by a ball about the size of a large grapefruit. On this model the great bulk of the planetary material lies at a hundred yards or more from the Sun. In other words, nearly all the planetary material lies very far out. This simple fact is already the death blow of every theory that seeks for an origin of the planets in the Sun itself. For how could the material have been flung out so far? It was proved, for instance, by H. N. Russell that if Jeans' well-known tidal theory were right, the planets would have to move around the Sun at distances on our model of not more than a few feet. This notion of Jeans', which still seems to be very widely believed, was that the planets were torn out of the Sun by the gravitational pull of a star that passed close by.

Once this difficulty was appreciated, people attached to the planets-from-the-Sun idea shifted their ground. The planets, they said, were not formed with the Sun in a state as it is at present, but at a time when the Sun had a vastly greater size, as it must have had when it was condensing out of the interstellar gas. But it is hard to see how this can help. To make it work at all it would be necessary to demonstrate that a blob of primeval gas — the interstellar gas — could condense in such a way that the great bulk of it went to form a massive inner body — that is to say, the Sun — surrounded at vast distances by a wisp of planetary material. And I do not think that this can be done. At any rate all the attempts that have so far been made to cope with the difficulty seem to me to fall very far short of the mark. Also there is another and perhaps more important reason why our Earth and the planets cannot have originated with the Sun.

I have tried to bring out the dominating cosmic role played by hydrogen, the simplest of the elements. Helium, the next simplest, is produced in appreciable quantities in the inner regions of normal stars like the Sun. But, apart from hydrogen and helium, all other elements are extremely rare, all over the Universe. In the Sun they amount to only about 1 per cent of the total mass. Contrast this with the Earth and the other planets where hydrogen and helium make only about the same contribution as highly complex atoms like iron, calcium, silicon, magnesium, and aluminum. This contrast brings out two important points. First, we see that material torn from the Sun would not be at all suitable for the formation of the planets as we know them. Its composition would be hopelessly wrong. And our second point in this contrast is that it is the Sun that is normal and the Earth that is the freak.

The interstellar gas and most of the stars are composed of material like the Sun, not like the Earth. You must understand that, cosmically speaking, the room you are now sitting in is made of the wrong stuff. You, yourself, are a rarity. You are a cosmic collector's piece.

Here then is a way to approach the problem of the origin of the planets. We must find a source of the strangely complicated rare material out of which the Earth and the planets are made. I will begin by telling you the answer in two sentences. There was once another star moving around the Sun that disintegrated with extreme violence. So great was the explosion that all the remnants were blown a long way from the Sun into space with the exception of a tiny wisp of gas out of which the Earth and the planets have condensed. So the first point to get clear is that the Sun was not always a single star. Before the Earth was born it was one of a pair of stars. As we have said earlier, such a pair is called a binary system.

Now if you pick a star at random the chance that it will be a separate star by itself, as the Sun is at present, is no greater than the chance that it will be a member of a binary system. Let us see what can happen if we suppose that the Sun was at one time a component in such a double system. First we make a choice for the distance between the Sun and the companion star it used to have. It is important to realize that there is practically no restriction on our freedom of choice here, because, as observation by telescope shows, the distance apart of the component stars in a binary may be anywhere in the enormous range from a tenth of a light year down to a fraction of a light minute. The required distance apart of the Sun and its companion star is intermediate between these extremes, being about one light hour. That is to say, on a plan with the Sun represented by our grapefruit the companion star would be about 100 yards away. This value will give you a clue as to how the choice of separation is made; namely, so that in the final outcome the bigger planets will be found to lie at the right distances from the Sun.

The next step is to draw up a set of specifications for the companion star. It must have been appreciably more massive than the Sun. It must have been a very special star. It must have been a star that exploded with extreme violence. It must have been a supernova. Thanks largely to the work of the two Mount Wilson astronomers, Baade and Minkowski, we know a good deal about the explosions of these stars. When one explodes, most of the material — that is to say, considerably more material than there is inside the whole of the Sun — gets blown out into space as a tremendous cloud of fiercely incandescent gas moving at a speed of several million miles an hour. For a few days the accompanying blaze of light is as great as the total radiation by all the 10,000,000,000 or so stars in the Galaxy. It was out of such a holocaust that the Earth and planets were born, and it happened in this way.

Not all of a supernova is blown away as gas in such an explosion. But the dense stellar nucleus that was left over after the explosion of the Sun's companion star did not stay with the Sun. One of the effects of the explosion was to give this stellar nucleus a recoil that broke its gravitational connection with the Sun. It moved off, and is now some unrecognized star lying in some distant part of the Galaxy. But before it left the Sun, and during the last dying stages of the explosion, it puffed out a cloud of gas that the Sun managed to hold on to. In as little as a few centuries this cloud of gas spread out around the Sun and took on the form of a rotating circular disk. As we shall see later, the planets condensed out of the material in this disk. So the real parent of the Earth is not the Sun at all, but some star that is probably unnamed and unseen.

According to the results of Baade and Minkowski the temperature inside a supernova is about 300 times greater than it is at the center of the Sun. At such a temperature all manner of nuclear transmutations occur with great rapidity. The helium-hydrogen reactions which are so important in the Sun are no longer important here. Instead, helium becomes transmuted to elements of what is called high atomic weight; for example, magnesium, aluminum, silicon, iron, lead and uranium, to name only a few. The importance of this is obvious. It means that the companion star's final gift to the Sun was a cloud of gas with just the right kind of composition necessary to account for the constitution of the Earth and the planets.

Before we go on to discuss the condensation of the planets, perhaps I might mention how this general picture of the origin of the planets has arisen. It is really the outcome of developments that started with Jeans' tidal theory. First this was modified and improved by Jeffreys. Then H. N. Russell overthrew both these theories with the sort of criticism I referred to earlier. Lyttleton was the next to take up the problem about fifteen years ago. He was the first to realize for certain that the planetary material cannot have come out of the Sun, and it is to him that we owe the development of the double star idea. Once this stage was reached the remaining steps were more or less inevitable. They arose for the most part through an attempt to put the theory on a firm observational footing.

The final stages in the formation of the planets after the tremendous explosion were comparatively tranquil. A few centuries after the explosion the remnant of the Sun's companion star must have moved far away from the Sun, or at any rate far enough for its effect on the wisp of gas that was captured by the Sun to be unimportant. This wisp of gas then settled down into a flat circular disk that rotated around the Sun—that is to say, it spread around the Sun and then it settled down into the disk. The main part of the gas must have been distributed in the regions where the orbits of the great planets, Jupiter, Saturn, Uranus, and Neptune, now lie. This means that on the model we are using with a grapefruit sun the main part of the disk must have had a diameter of several hundred yards. At its edges the gas would have trailed away very gradually.

But I must now explain how such a rotating disk of gas condensed into the planets as we know them. Once the supernova remnant had receded to an appreciable distance, the temperature of the main bulk of the gas in the disk must have fallen well below the freezing point of water. Many sorts of molecules must then have been formed and, as was pointed out in 1944 by Professor Jeffreys and A. L. Parsons, these molecules must have collected into a swarm of solid bodies by a process very similar to the formation of water drops in the clouds of our own terrestrial atmosphere. But this condensation into solid particles must have been offset to some extent by collisions between the particles themselves, which tend to return material to the gaseous state.

At any particular time there must have been a rough balance between condensation from gas into solid bodies and evaporation that converted solid material back into gas. You might think that this stalemate would have had to go on for ever, and it probably would have done if the raindrop form of condensation were the whole story. But in a situation like this if any particular condensation should ever happen to grow to a certain critical size, which is about 100 miles across, the gravitational pull of the condensation itself would begin to play a dominating role. The gravitational field is, so to speak, able to reach out into the surrounding gas and drag it in onto the condensation. When this happens the rate of condensation is greatly increased. It is this that ensures that such a cloud of gas would form into a few comparatively large bodies rather than into a swarm of much smaller particles. The essential point is that although the chance that a particular body ever grows to the critical size is very small, given sufficient time it will certainly happen in a few cases. The fewer the number of cases the fewer the number of planets into which the material finally condenses. For once the gravitational field of a growing body comes into operation the rate of acquisition of material becomes so large that the first few bodies to attain the critical size then go on to snatch up practically all the material of the disk.

Perhaps you will see this best if I quote one or two of the results calculated for our own solar system. The first condensations to grow large are believed to have taken about 1,000,000,000 years to reach the mass of the Earth. But from this stage only about 100,000 years was needed for such a primordial planet to increase its mass up to the same order as those of the great planets Jupiter, Saturn, Uranus, and Neptune. This shows you the tremendous accelerating effect of this condensation by gravitation.

Now this has an important consequence. It means that the earth can hardly have been formed as a primordial condensation. For a condensation would hardly stop short after taking 1,000,000,000 years to reach the mass of the Earth if it only needed a further 100,000 years to go on and become a great planet. It could, of course, be argued that a condensation stopped short at the mass of the Earth simply because all the gas in its neighborhood had become exhausted. This might be a reasonable argument if we had only one case to explain, but there are five planets — Mercury, Venus, Mars, Pluto, and the Earth — and also about thirty satellites to be accounted for. It would be stretching coincidence much too far to suggest that exhaustion of material was responsible for cessation of growth in all these cases.

Besides, there is another argument that shows the same thing. None of the present planets can have been primordial condensations, not even the great planets. For owing to the rotation of the disk around the Sun, the primordial planets must have acquired axial rotations — that is to say, rotations like the rotation of the Earth around its polar axis. Once the primordial planets had formed into a compact state, their times of rotation must have become less than about seven hours, and as Lyttleton showed in 1938, a solid planet rotating as rapidly as this must break up under the power of its own rotation. The great planets must be the main chunks arising from these processes of break-up. Now in the break-up it is also to be expected that a number of comparatively small blobs become detached from the main bodies as they separate from each other. For the most part, these blobs remained circling around the great planets — and these are the satellites of the planets — their moons we should call them. But a few of the larger blobs seem to have escaped, and these are the five small planets — Venus, Mercury, Mars, Pluto and the Earth. Very probably the Moon was an adjacent blob that became detached along with the Earth. So, to sum up, there were a number of big primordial planets that broke up about 2,500,000,000 years ago, and one of the bits of the debris was our Earth and another the Moon.

This picture of the way the Earth came into being is I think very important to our studies of the interior of the Earth. It affects our views on the probable temperature of the deep interior, suggesting that it may be much less than was formerly believed. It provides interesting possibilities regarding the origin of the Earth's magnetism. It leads to a plausible explanation of the origin of the surface rocks. For the Earth must have originally moved along a highly flattened path that took it into the inner parts of the gaseous disk. Here the material had not been entirely swept up by the primordial condensations, which were formed much farther out from the Sun. So the Earth moved through a medium consisting partly of gas and partly of comparatively small solid bodies. This had two effects: one was to round up the Earth's motion into a nearly circular path that lies well inside the orbits of the great planets, and the other was to modify the surface features of the Earth through the acquisition of various gases and solid bodies. The rocks of the Earth's crust may well have originated in this way. In particular, it is possible that the Earth acquired its radioactive materials during this final stage. Among the gases acquired were probably nitrogen, water, oxygen, and carbon dioxide. The histories of Venus, Mercury, and Mars must have been somewhat different because their orbits took them through different parts of the disk. In particular, Venus seems to have obtained little or no water but very large quantities of carbon dioxide and also possibly nitrogen. Mars, on the other hand, obtained carbon dioxide, and water but not so much water as the Earth. The fate of Pluto we do not know.

By now we've covered enough ground for us to refer back to the end of my first chapter when I said that there are about 1,000,000 planetary systems in the Milky Way in which life may exist. I should like now to tell you how

I made this estimate. It must depend, as you will see, on the frequency of supernova explosions within our Galaxy. No supernova outburst is visible in the Milky Way at the present time. But the gases hurled into space by the supernova observed by the Chinese in A.D. 1054 actually can be seen. It was these gases that furnished Baade and Minkowski with the information I mentioned above. Since A.D. 1054 two other supernovae have also blazed out in the Milky Way, one in 1572 and the other in 1604.

On this basis it is to be expected that on the average one supernova occurs every two or three hundred years. This estimate, as we shall see later, is strongly supported by the observation of supernovae in galaxies other than our own. At this rate there must have been more than 10,000,000 supernova explosions since the oldest stars were born — which was about 4,000,000,000 years ago. Now something like a half of all these supernovae must have been components in binary systems, and must accordingly have given birth to planets in exactly the way we have discussed. So in the past, nearly 10,000,-000 planetary systems, each one similar to the solar system in the essential features of its constructions, must have been formed in the Milky Way.

Next we ask what proportion of these systems would contain a planet on which the physical conditions were suitable for the support of life. I estimate for this about one planetary system in ten, which gives me a final total of about 1,000,000 possible abodes of life within the Milky Way. I will admit that the last bit of calculation is approximate. But even when full allowance is made for all the uncertainties I do not think that the final total could be less than 100,000. Our next question is: will living creatures arise on every planet where favorable physical conditions occur? No certain answer can be given to this, but those best qualified to judge the matter, the biologists, seem to think that life would in fact arise wherever conditions were able to support it. Accepting this, we can proceed with greater assurance. The extremely powerful process of natural selection would come into operation and would shape the evolution of life on each of these distant planets. Would creatures arise having some sort of similarity to those on the Earth? The distinguished biologist C. D. Darlington has shown that this is by no means as unlikely as it seems at first sight. To quote Darlington's own words, "There are such very great advantages in walking on two legs, in carrying one's brain in one's head, in having two eyes on the same eminence at a height of five or six feet, that we might as well take quite seriously the possibility of a pseudo man and a pseudo woman with some physical resemblance to ourselves...."

Let us end by putting all this in another way. I have often seen it stated that our situation on the Earth is providential. The argument goes like this. It is providential that the Earth is of the right size and is at the right distance from the Sun. It is providential that the Sun radiates the right kind of light and heat. It is providential that the right chemical substances occur on the Earth. A long list of this sort of statement could be compiled, and to some people it looks as if there is indeed something very strange and odd about our particular home in the Universe. But I think that this outlook rises from a misunderstanding of the situation. Because if everything was not just right we should not be here. We should be somewhere else.

STUDY QUESTIONS

1. *What evidence does Hoyle give to show that the earth could not have come from the sun? Does it seem convincing? Why?*
2. *Is the opinion that the earth came from a companion star to the sun supported by any evidence? Does this evidence seem convincing?*
3. *What method of organization does Hoyle use in the account of the origin of the earth?*
4. *How do you account for the clarity of Hoyle's style? Are his sentences relatively simple, or complicated? What sort of a vocabulary does he use? Do any unfamiliar words occur? Are his paragraphs generally devoted to one point or to more than one? Do they usually have transitional or introductory phrases or sentences? What use is made of analogies and examples?*
5. *Write an explanation which, like this one, makes a fairly complicated scientific point clear to a lay audience.*
6. *Do you think the new point of view expressed here about the origin of the earth will have any importance outside astronomy? What difference will it make in science? In social studies? In philosophy? In religion? In daily life?*

Loren C. Eiseley Is Man Here to Stay?*

There is a widespread tendency to conceive of the course of evolution as an undeviating upward march from the level of very simple organisms to much more complex ones. We are inclined to think of man as the crown and culmination of this movement and the natural point of origin for any further progress. The syllogism runs something like this: Evolution is an upward movement. Man is the most intelligent form of life on the planet. Therefore he will continue to dominate the earth throughout future time, or he will himself give rise to some more perfect and intellectual species as far superior to us as we are superior to our heavy-browed, lumbering forerunners of the Pleistocene.

This last statement is very significant. In it lies the major source of the confusion we manifest about human destiny. We know that man has moved along a particular line that has led to greater and greater intellectual triumphs. We know his brain has grown and his body has altered. We call this process

* Reprinted with permission from *Scientific American*, November, 1950, Vol. 183, No. 5.

evolution, and we tend not to understand why it cannot go on through an indefinite future. The confusion lies in the fact that we fail to distinguish adequately between progressive evolution in a single family line and those greater movements which adjust life to the rise and fall of continents or the chill winds of geological climate.

There is a pulse in the earth to which life in the long sense adjusts, but it is a rhythm so slow that it is imperceptible in short-line evolution. We can grasp its significance and its indifference to the aspirations of individual life forms only when we call the roll of the ages and note the number of the vanished. Even if we concentrate only upon the Age of Mammals, ignoring the strange departed amphibians of the Paleozoic or the stalking giants of the Age of Reptiles — even then we discover that whole orders and families have passed out of existence. Many of these creatures were highly successful in their day. Yet as one compares the durability of the simpler creatures with that of the more efficient, one may be led to comment cynically that to evolve is to perish.

The subject is a very complex one, of course, because obviously the completely inadaptive organism cannot master a shifting environment. Life must evolve to live. Why, then, are we confronted with the paradox that he who evolves perishes? Are we not the highest animal? And what, among all things that fly or creep or crawl, is more apt to inherit the future than we are?

The one great biological principle that seems to deny man's hopes for continued dominance of the planet is known as the "law of the unspecialized." It is one of the curious ironies of scientific history that the discoverer, or at least the formalizer, of this law was a devout Quaker scientist who put forth his views during the full flush of 19th-century enthusiasm for evolutionary progress. He was Edward Drinker Cope, undoubtedly one of the greatest naturalists America has ever produced.

The gist of Cope's brilliant generalization is that the leaps ahead in evolution generally take off from comparatively unspecialized forms of life, rather than from the most highly developed. In Cope's words: "The highly developed, or specialized types of one geological period have not been the parents of the types of succeeding periods but... the descent has been derived from the less specialized of preceding ages." It is the more adaptable and generally the smaller forms that are best able to meet the onset of new conditions which destroy the already dominant and successful types. The first amphibians arose not from a highly successful fish but from a slow-swimming, foul-water form which had to be peculiarly adaptable. Similarly, the first mammals came not from one of the specialized dragon reptiles but from a smaller and much less specialized reptile which was learning to control its blood temperature. Another climbing, jumping reptile became a bird. All were small, all were the fortunate possessors of traits that offered the potentialities of successful adaptation to new climates or new media.

Every one of these insignificant, stumbling but remarkably endowed creatures founded explosive dynasties. Climbing out of the marshes to the uninhabited air or land, entering into some still region whose previous occupants were dead, they radiated with amazing rapidity into a diversity of forms. The new forms grew ever more specialized as they adapted to the particular niches in the environment that they came to occupy. Many of these specializations are of quite remarkable character. Yet in the long course of evolution they threaten to reduce the adaptability of the form in case it should ever find its particular evolutionary corridor blocked or destroyed. The problem is a little like that presented to an elderly glass-blower, let us say, when glassblowing becomes mechanized. His environmental zone has changed, yet he is old; he is no longer able to master a new field. He is through—and so it may be, in even more brutal ways, in the world of animal life.

Thus the evolutionary paradox becomes plain: The highly and narrowly adapted flourish, but they move in a path which becomes ever more difficult to retrace or break away from as their adaptation becomes perfected. Their proficiency may increase, their numbers may grow. But their perfect adaptation, so necessary for survival, can become a euphemism for death. Climates change, vegetation changes, enemies perfect their weapons, continental icefields advance, indirect competitors may smother the corridor. Sooner or later an impasse develops, an impasse which a small, omnivorous creature that has "specialized" in generalized adaptability and inconspicuousness may escape, but which the perfected evolutionary instrument never can. Consider, for example, the disaster that would overtake an animal like the tubularmouthed anteater if extinction were to overtake the social insects. The anteater could never readjust. He would starve in the midst of food everywhere available to the less specialized.

The question we are mainly interested in is: Is man a specialized or a generalized creature? Are we the refined end-product of an evolutionary line whose genetic plasticity has about reached its limit, or are we the departure point for an undreamed of future? An answer of sorts can be given, but it has to be given with great care and with much attention to precise definition. We will want to ask, first of all, whether there really is such a thing as an "unspecialized" animal. My answer is that there is, and that, furthermore, it robbed our kitty's food dish last night. It is no mere intellectual abstraction.

Probably the major confusion that has developed about Cope's principle of the unspecialized animal is the tendency to imagine it as some kind of inchoate "archetype" creature capable of galloping off in several evolutionary directions at once. No such animal ever existed, and Cope never intended to suggest that it had. The term "unspecialized" is used only in a comparative sense, and in this sense we need not look far, even today, to find examples. The opossum that stole up our back stairway last night and turned the cat's tail into a frightened bush has marched unchanged through 80 million years of geological upheaval. As George Gaylord Simpson observes in his widely read recent book, *The Meaning of Evolution*: "It has been suggested that all animals are now specialized and that the generalized forms on which major evolutionary developments depend are absent. In fact all animals have been more or less specialized, and a really generalized living form is merely a myth or an abstraction. It happens that there are still in existence some of the less specialized — that is, less narrowly adapted and more adaptable — forms from which radiations have occurred and could, as far as we can see, occur again. Opossums are not notably more specialized now than in the Cretaceous and could almost certainly radiate again markedly if available space were to occur again." Nature, in other words, seems to keep available creatures whose life zones are broad enough for renewed experimentation if the need arises.

It is evident, then, that there are two currents in the evolutionary flow, although neither is completely separate from the other. There are times when only a person gifted with foreknowledge of the future could indicate which of these streams means progress. But in general one of the streams is not really progressive. It is simply the perfection of specialization: the creation of the ideally adjusted parasite, of the glowing monster of the abyssal seas, the saber-toothed tiger, the fish with batteries in its belly. All of this is remarkable beyond words, but beneath these superficial diversions a deeper flow has carried life up from the waters, perfected its chemical adjustments, conquered the land, stabilized bodily temperature, developed nervous systems of growing complexity and brought into being the mind, whereby the universe examines itself.

So far this broad upward movement has never retraced its steps. Not that it has not wandered or specialized, or lost itself in peculiar and constricted niches, but once a new level of organization has been attained, it has not been lost, and the old has dwindled in importance. The Crossoptyrigian fishes gave rise to the amphibians and vanished almost totally. The amphibians, making further lung and limb adjustments, then gave rise to the reptiles. The latter then contributed the two great living groups — the mammals and birds. In all these cases it was not the largest or most highly specialized of the new classes that produced the succeeding forms. It was instead the smaller, less spectacular and more adaptable types. Man, who derives from a comparatively generalized and ancient order of mammals, has opened a strange new corridor of existence — the cultural corridor. With the appearance of culture the biologist is confronted with a true innovation.

There exist in various obscure parts of the globe certain ancient and remarkable forms of life. They are, one might say, the immovable immortals. Is that quick-witted, volatile and short-lived parvenu, man, destined to join their company? Has his mastery over environment, the greatest yet achieved by any animal, created the first highly specialized but truly adaptable organism? Does his one great specialization — his brain — mean escape at last from the disasters that have stalked all other forms?

There is a creature something like man that may provide a hint, though it crawls in another shape. Like man, it is an agriculturist and a city builder. It numbers, like man, in the millions, and like man it has mastered the problem of food storage and distribution. In its dark cities it knows something of the common warmth and security, the thrusting back of the harsh natural environment, that man has so recently achieved. This creature is the ant.

You will object at once that ants are physically and mentally remote from men. So they are, but in their tremendous, if minute, activities they have achieved a remarkably humanlike adaptability. The important point is that the ants have led their present lives for more than 80 million years, while man's civilization is scarcely more than 7,000 years old. They are the oldest cosmopolites; they have sheltered longest, grown food, escaped many of the violences of the mammalian world. We shall want to ask just one question: "Have they changed?" It would seem they have changed very little, if at all. They are one of the small "immortals."

The reason for this long life without noticeable change would seem to lie in a perfect environmental balance. Even the creatures' parasites are old. The remarkable instinct-built cities, playing a part roughly equivalent to our own metropolises, have provided shelter, food and protection. The stability of perfect adjustment has set in.

It can justifiably be contended, of course, that man, by reason of his cultural malleability, his ability to invent, to progress, to introduce changes into his environment, is in a much more dynamic and unstable relationship with nature than the social insects. But it is also true that man's cultural proclivities are directed toward making life easier for himself. He prepares food which makes an elaborate dentition superfluous, and which actually encourages its disappearance. His machines transport him with little effort on his own part. His clothing, his air-conditioned houses, his medical devices all protect him from the harsh natural environment that controls the survival and directs the evolution of other animals. As a living organism man is still susceptible in some degree to environmental influences and genetic drift, but natural selection has ceased to operate intensively upon him, except in so far as it may perfect his urban adjustment. To be sure, competition in implements and methods of warfare may well determine the increase or relative decline in significance of particular racial types in given moments of human history. There is nothing in the present life of man, however, to suggest the likelihood of striking increases in brain development or other remarkable innovations in human structure. We may expect at most a few mild changes toward a reduced dentition and other small adjustments if civilization and its luxuries continue.

Man, in other words, gives every sign of having reached by a different road from that of the social insects, an equivalent environmental mastery. It would take a formidable and unforeseen world cataclysm to thrust him once more naked into the wilderness out of which he emerged. It is conceivable that his propensities for destruction may bring about his self-extinction, but because of his worldwide distribution and enormous expansion in numbers this is extremely unlikely.

The 19th century drew from the century before it a concept of human progress which the evidence of the earth's history does not entirely justify. Evolutionists do not see at work any inner perfecting principle that would automatically improve a given organism after it has achieved a certain stability of relationship with its environment. Rather the pace of evolution steadily becomes slower, until the vicissitudes of time demand new adjustments or force the now specialized organism toward extinction.

Darwin, like his 18th-century forerunners, believed in progressive change and predicted that "we may look with some confidence to a future of great length.... All corporeal and mental endowments will tend to progress toward perfection." Yet curiously this quotation lies at the close of a paragraph in which he said: "Of the species now living very few will transmit progeny of any kind to a far distant futurity."

The primate order is old. Man is a comparatively young branch of that order, but his great brain marks him as specialized in a way peculiarly apt to bring an end very soon to his physical modifications and advancement. Indeed, there is evidence that *Homo sapiens* has not altered markedly for perhaps a hundred thousand years. Yet man's strange specialization has introduced a new kind of life into the universe — one capable within limits of ordering its own environment and transmitting that order through social rather than biological heredity.

If man can master quickly his individualistic propensities for destruction, he may be able to become another of the small immortals. Even to this, however, judging by the records of the geological past, there will come an end some day. Sooner or later Cope's law of the unspecialized will have its chance once more.

STUDY QUESTIONS

1. *Both Hoyle and Eiseley are writing scientific exposition for the lay reader. In what respects are their tasks in these two essays similar? In what respects different? Is the thesis of one more subject to verification than that of the other? If so, does this affect the writer's approach in any way?*

2. *Point out a place where Eiseley makes use of deduction. Analogy. What does he gain by using analogy?*

3. *What are the two evolutionary currents he describes?*

4. *What faculty does man possess that makes it seem likely that he will survive abrupt environmental changes, as other specialized creatures have been unable to do?*

5. *Do you agree with Eiseley that man's capacity for self-destruction is not likely to lead to his disappearance? Do you think anything should be added or changed in Eiseley's prediction of man's future?*

6. *Write a theme which, like Eiseley's article, speculates upon one of the unsolved problems of science, making use of whatever evidence is available.*

W. H. Ittelson and F. P. Kilpatrick

Experiments in Perception*

What is perception? How do we see what we see, feel what we feel, hear what we hear? We act in terms of what we perceive; our acts lead to new perceptions; these lead to new acts, and so on in the incredibly complex process that constitutes life. Clearly, then, an understanding of the process by which man becomes aware of himself and his world is basic to any adequate understanding of human behavior. But the problem of explaining how and why we perceive in the way we do is one of the most controversial fields in psychology. We shall describe here some recent experimental work which sheds new light on the problem and points the way to a new theory of perception.

The fact that we see a chair and are then able to go to the place at which we localize it and rest our bodies on a substantial object does not seem particularly amazing or difficult to explain — until we try to explain it. If we accept the prevailing current view that we can never be aware of the world as such, but only of the nervous impulses arising from the impingement of physical forces on sensory receptors, we immediately face the necessity of explaining the correspondence between what we perceive and whatever it is that is there.

An extremely logical, unbeatable — and scientifically useless — answer is simply to say there is no real world, that everything exists in the mind alone. Another approach is to postulate the existence of an external world, to grant that there is some general correspondence between that world and what we perceive and to seek some understandable and useful explanation of why that should be. Most of the prominent theories about perception have grown out of the latter approach. These theories generally agree that even though much of the correspondence may be due to learning, at some basic level there exists an absolute correspondence between what is "out there" and what is in the "mind." But there is a great deal of disagreement concerning the level at which such innately determined correspondence occurs. At one extreme are theorists who believe that the correspondence occurs at the level of simple sensations, such as color, brightness, weight, hardness, and so on, and that out of these sensations are compounded more complex awarenesses, such as the recognition of a pencil or a book. At the other extreme are Gestalt psychologists who feel that complex perceptions such as the form of

---

* Reprinted with permission from *Scientific American*, August, 1951, Vol. 185, No. 2.

an object are the result of an inherent relationship between the properties of the thing perceived and the properties of the brain. All these schools seem to agree, however, that there is some perceptual level at which exists absolute objectivity; that is, a one-to-one correspondence between experience and reality.

This belief is basic to current thinking in many fields. It underlies most theorizing concerning the nature of science, including Percy W. Bridgman's attempt to reach final scientific objectivity in the "observable operation." In psychology one is hard put to find an approach to human behavior which departs from this basic premise. But it leads to dichotomies such as organism v. environment, subjective v. objective. Stimuli or stimulus patterns are treated as though they exist apart from the perceiving organism. Psychologists seek to find mechanical relationships or interactions between the organism and an "objectively defined" environment. They often rule out purposes and values as not belonging in a strictly scientific psychology.

The experiments to be described here arose from a widespread and growing feeling that such dichotomies are false, and that in practice it is impossible to leave values and purposes out of consideration in scientific observation. The experiments were designed to re-examine some of the basic ideas from which these problems stem.

During the past few years Adelbert Ames, Jr., of the Institute for Associated Research in Hanover, N. H., has designed some new ways of studying visual perception. They have resulted in a new conception of the nature of knowing and of observation. This theory neither denies the existence of objects nor proposes that they exist in a given form independently, that is, apart from the perceiving organism. Instead, it suggests that the world each of us knows is a world created in large measure from our experience in dealing with the environment.

Let us illustrate this in specific terms through some of the demonstrations. In one of them the subject sits in a dark room in which he can see only two star points of light. Both are equidistant from the observer, but one is brighter than the other. If the observer closes one eye and keeps his head still, the brighter point of light looks nearer than the dimmer one. Such apparent differences are related not only to brightness but also to direction from the observer. If two points of light of equal brightness are situated near the floor, one about a foot above the other, the upper one will generally be perceived as farther away than the lower one; if they are near the ceiling, the lower one will appear farther away.

A somewhat more complex experiment uses two partly inflated balloons illuminated from a concealed source. The balloons are in fixed positions about one foot apart. Their relative sizes can be varied by means of a lever control connected to a bellows; another lever controls their relative brightness. When the size and brightness of both balloons are the same, an observer looking at them with one eye from 10 feet or more sees them as two glowing spheres at equal distances from him. If the brightnesses are left the same and the relative sizes are changed, the larger balloon appears to nearly all observers somewhat nearer. If the size lever is moved continuously, causing continuous variation in the relative size of the balloons, they appear to move dramatically back and forth through space, even when the observer watches with both eyes open. The result is similar when the sizes are kept equal and the relative brightness is varied.

With the same apparatus the effects of size and brightness may be combined so that they supplement or conflict with each other. When they supplement each other, the variation in apparent distance is much greater than when either size or brightness alone is varied. When they oppose each other, the variation is much less. Most people give more weight to relative size than to relative brightness in judging distance.

These phenomena cannot be explained by referring to "reality," because "reality" and perception do not correspond. They cannot be explained by reference to the pattern in the retina of the eye, because for any given retinal pattern there are an infinite number of brightness-size-distance combinations to which that pattern might be related. When faced with such a situation, in which an unlimited number of possibilities can be related to a given retinal pattern, the organism apparently calls upon its previous experiences and assumes that what has been most probable in the past is most probable in the immediate occasion. When presented with two star-points of different brightness, a person unconsciously "bets" or "assumes" that the two points, being similar, are probably identical (i.e., of equal brightness), and therefore that the one which seems brighter must be nearer. Similarly the observed facts in the case of two star-points placed vertically one above the other suggest that when we look down we assume, on the basis of past experience, that objects in the lower part of the visual field are nearer than objects in the upper part; when we look up, we assume the opposite to be true. An analogous explanation can be made of the role of relative size as an indication of relative distance.

Why do the differences in distance seem so much greater when the relative size of two objects is varied continuously than when the size difference is fixed? This phenomenon, too, apparently is based on experience. It is a fairly common experience, though not usual, to find that two similar objects of different sizes are actually the same distance away from us. But it is rare indeed to see two stationary objects at the same distance, one growing larger and the other smaller; almost always in everyday life when we see two identical or nearly identical objects change relative size they are in motion in relation to each other. Hence under the experimental conditions we are much more likely to assume distance differences in the objects of changing size than in those of fixed size.

Visual perception involves an impression not only of *where* an object is but of *what* it is. From the demonstrations already described we may guess that there is a very strong relationship between localization in space ("thereness") and the assignment of objective properties ("thatness"). This relationship can be demonstrated by a cube experiment.

Two solid white cubes are suspended on wires that are painted black so as to be invisible against a black background. One cube is about 3 feet from the observer and the other about 12 feet. The observer's head is in a headrest so positioned that the cubes are almost in line with each other but he can see both, the nearer cube being slightly to the right. A tiny metal shield is then placed a few inches in front of the left eye. It is just big enough to cut off the view of the far cube from the left eye. The result is that the near cube is seen with both eyes and the far cube with just the right eye. Under these conditions the observer can fix the position of the near cube very well, because he has available all the cues that come from the use of the two eyes. But in the case of the far cube seen with only one eye, localization is much more difficult and uncertain.

Now since the two cubes are almost in line visually, a slight movement of the head to the right will cause the inside vertical edges of the cubes to coincide. Such coincidence of edge is strongly related to an assumption of "togetherness." Hence when the subject moves his head in this way, the uncertainly located distant cube appears to have moved forward to a position even with the nearer cube. Under these conditions not only does the mislocated cube appear smaller, but it appears different in shape, that is, no longer cubical, even though the pattern cast by the cube on the retina of the eye has not changed at all.

The most reasonable explanation of these visual phenomena seems to be that an observer unconsciously relates to the stimulus pattern some sort of weighted average of the past consequences of acting with respect to that pattern. The particular perception "chosen" is the one that has the best predictive value, on the basis of previous experience, for action in carrying out the purposes of the organism. From this one may make two rather crucial deductions: 1) an unfamiliar external configuration which yields the same retinal pattern as one the observer is accustomed to deal with will be perceived as the familiar configuration; 2) when the observer acts on his interpretation of the unfamiliar configuration and finds that he is wrong, his perception will change even though the retinal pattern is unchanged.

Let us illustrate with some actual demonstrations. If an observer in a dark room looks with one eye at two lines of light which are at the same distance and elevation but of different lengths, the longer line will look nearer than the shorter one. Apparently he assumes that the lines are identical and translates the difference in length into a difference in position. If the observer takes a wand with a luminous tip and tries to touch first one line and then the other, he will be unable to do so at first. After repeated practice, however, he can learn to touch the two lines quickly and accurately. At this point he no longer sees the lines as at different distances;

they now look, as they are, the same distance from him. He originally assumed that the two lines were the same length because that seemed the best bet under the circumstances. After he had tested this assumption by purposive action, he shifted to the assumption, less probable in terms of past experience but still possible, that the lines were at the same distance but of different lengths. As his assumption changed, perception did also.

There is another experiment that demonstrates these points even more convincingly. It uses a distorted room in which the floor slopes up to the right of the observer, the rear wall recedes from right to left and the windows are of different sizes and trapezoidal in shape. When the observer looks at this room with one eye from a certain point, the room appears completely normal, as if the floor were level, the rear wall at right angles to the line of sight and the windows rectangular and the same size. Presumably the observer chooses this particular appearance instead of some other because of the assumptions he brings to the occasion. If he now takes a long stick and tries to touch the various parts of the room, he will be unsuccessful, even though he has gone into the situation knowing the true shape of the room. With practice, however, he becomes more and more successful in touching what he wants to touch with the stick. More important, he sees the room more and more in its true shape, even though the stimulus pattern on his retina has remained unchanged.

By means of a piece of apparatus called the "rotating trapezoidal window" it has been possible to extend the investigation to complex perceptual situations involving movement. This device consists of a trapezoidal surface with panes cut in it and shadows painted on it to give the appearance of a window. It is mounted on a rod connected to a motor so that it rotates at a slow constant speed in an upright position about its own axis. When an observer views the rotating surface with one eye from about 10 feet or more or with both eyes from about 25 feet or more, he sees not a rotating trapezoid but an oscillating rectangle. Its speed of movement and its shape appear to vary markedly as it turns. If a small cube is attached by a short rod to the upper part of the short side of the trapezoid, it seems to become detached, sail freely around the front of the trapezoid and attach itself again as the apparatus rotates.

All these experiments, and many more that have been made, suggest strongly that perception is never a sure thing, never an absolute revelation of "what is." Rather, what we see is a prediction — our own personal construction designed to give us the best possible bet for carrying out our purposes in action. We make these bets on the basis of our past experience. When we have a great deal of relevant and consistent experience to relate to stimulus patterns, the probability of success of our prediction (perception) as a guide to action is extremely high, and we tend to have a feeling of surety. When our experience is limited or inconsistent, the reverse holds true. According to the new theory of perception developed from the demonstrations we have described, perception is a functional affair based on action, experience and probability. The thing perceived is an inseparable part of the function of perceiving, which in turn includes all aspects of the total process of living. This view differs from the old rival theories: the thing perceived is neither just a figment of the mind nor an innately determined absolute revelation of a reality postulated to exist apart from the perceiving organism. Object and percept are part and parcel of the same thing.

This conclusion of course has far-reaching implications for many areas of study, for some assumption as to what perception is must underly any philosophy or comprehensive theory of psychology, of science or of knowledge in general. Although the particular investigations involved here are restricted to visual perception, this is only a vehicle which carries us into a basic inquiry of much wider significance.

STUDY QUESTIONS

1. *What possible effects may the results of these experiments have upon philosophical questions? How do they affect the usual meaning of such terms as "accurate observation," "objectivity," "the external world"?*

2. *Do the experiments described here seek to reproduce the usual conditions? If not, what is their value?*

3. *Do these experiments show that perception depends entirely upon the sense and the stimuli they encounter? If not, what do they show?*

4. *What is the "basic inquiry of much wider significance" which is mentioned at the end of the article as the end to which these experiments will lead?*

5. *Observe carefully what Ittelson and Kilpatrick have done to make their account of rather complicated experiments clear and interesting. Then write a theme describing accurately and in detail an experiment you have seen or have carried out yourself, giving the conclusions you drew from it.*

6. *Do the conclusions arrived at here have any effect upon daily life and social affairs? Write a theme applying the principles suggested by these experiments to everyday situations and problems.*

3. THE LIMITS AND VALUE OF SCIENCE

Morris R. Cohen and Ernest Nagel

The Limits and Value of the Scientific Method*

The desire for knowledge for its own sake is more widespread than is generally recognized by anti-intellectualists. It has its roots in the animal curiosity which shows itself in the cosmological questions of children and in the gossip of adults. No ulterior utilitarian motive makes people want to know about the private lives of their neighbors, the great, or the notorious. There is also a certain zest which makes people engage in various intellectual games or exercises in which one is required to find out something. But while the desire to know is wide, it is seldom strong enough to overcome the more powerful organic desires, and few indeed have both the inclination and the ability to face the arduous difficulties of scientific method in more than one special field. The desire to know is not often strong enough to sustain critical inquiry. Men generally are interested in the results, in the story or romance of science, not in the technical methods whereby these results are obtained and their truth continually is tested and qualified. Our first impulse is to accept the plausible as true and to reject the uncongenial as false. We have not the time, inclination, or energy to investigate everything. Indeed, the call to do so is often felt as irksome and joy-killing. And when we are asked to treat our cherished beliefs as mere hypotheses, we rebel as violently as when those dear to us are insulted. This provides the ground for various movements that are hostile to rational scientific procedure (though their promoters do not often admit that it is science to which they are hostile).

Mystics, intuitionists, authoritarians, voluntarists, and fictionalists are all trying to undermine respect for the rational methods of science. These attacks have always met with wide acclaim and are bound to continue to do so, for they strike a responsive note in human nature. Unfortunately they do not offer any reliable alternative method for obtaining verifiable knowledge. The great French writer Pascal opposed to logic the spirit of subtlety or finesse (*esprit géometrique and esprit de finesse*) and urged that the

* From *An Introduction to Logic and Scientific Method* by Morris R. Cohen and Ernest Nagel. Copyright, 1934, by Harcourt, Brace and Company, Inc. Reprinted by permission of Harcourt, Brace and Company, Inc.

heart has its reasons as well as the mind, reasons that cannot be accurately formulated but which subtle spirits apprehend none the less. Men as diverse as James Russell Lowell and George Santayana are agreed that:

> "The soul is oracular still,"

and

> "It is wisdom to trust the heart . . .
> To trust the soul's invincible surmise."

Now it is true that in the absence of omniscience we must trust our soul's surmise; and great men are those whose surmises or intuitions are deep or penetrating. It is only by acting on our surmise that we can procure the evidence in its favor. But only havoc can result from confusing a surmise with a proposition for which there is already evidence. Are all the reasons of the heart sound? Do all oracles tell the truth? The sad history of human experience is distinctly discouraging to any such claim. Mystic intuition may give men absolute subjective certainty, but can give no proof that contrary intuitions are erroneous. It is obvious that when authorities conflict we must weigh the evidence in their favor logically if we are to make a rational choice. Certainly, when a truth is questioned it is no answer to say, "I am convinced," or, "I prefer to rely on this rather than on another authority." The view that physical science is no guide to proof, but is a mere fiction, fails to explain why it has enabled us to anticipate phenomena of nature and to control them. These attacks on scientific method receive a certain color of plausibility because of some indefensible claims made by uncritical enthusiasts. But it is of the essence of scientific method to limit its own pretension. Recognizing that we do not know everything, it does not claim the ability to solve all of our practical problems. It is an error to suppose, as is often done, that science denies the truth of all unverified propositions. For that which is unverified today may be verified tomorrow. We may get at truth by guessing or in other ways. Scientific method, however, is concerned with verification. Admittedly the wisdom of those engaged in this process has not been popularly ranked as high as that of the sage, the prophet, or the poet. Admittedly, also, we know of no way of supplying creative intelligence to those who lack it. Scientists, like all other human beings, may get into ruts and apply their techniques regardless of varying circumstances. There will always be formal procedures which are fruitless. Definitions and formal distinctions may be a sharpening of tools without the wit to use them properly, and statistical information may conform to the highest technical standards and yet be irrelevant and inconclusive. Nevertheless, scientific method is the only way to increase the general body of tested and verified truth and to eliminate arbitrary opinion. It is well to clarify our ideas by asking for the precise meaning of our words, and to try to check our favorite ideas by applying them to accurately formulated propositions.

In raising the question as to the social need for scientific method, it is well to recognize that the suspension of judgment which is essential to that method is difficult or impossible when we are pressed by the demands of immediate action. When my house is on fire, I must act quickly and promptly — I cannot stop to consider the possible causes, nor even to estimate the exact probabilities involved in the various alternative ways of reacting. For this reason, those who are bent upon some specific course of action often despise those devoted to reflection; and certain ultramodernists seem to argue as if the need for action guaranteed the truth of our decision. But the fact that I must either vote for candidate X or refrain from doing so does not of itself give me adequate knowledge. The frequency of our regrets makes this obvious. Wisely ordered society is therefore provided with means for deliberation and reflection *before* the pressure of action becomes irresistible. In order to assure the most thorough investigation, all possible views must be canvassed, and this means toleration of views that are *prima facie* most repugnant to us.

In general the chief social condition of scientific method is a widespread desire for truth that is strong enough to withstand the powerful forces which make us cling tenaciously to old views or else embrace every novelty because it is a change. Those who are engaged in scientific work need not only leisure for reflection and material for their experiments, but also a community that respects the pursuit of truth and allows freedom for the expression of intellectual doubt as to its most sacred or established institutions. Fear of offending established dogmas has been an obstacle to the growth of astronomy and geology and other physical sciences; and the fear of offending patriotic or respected sentiment is perhaps one of the strongest hindrances to scholarly history and social science. On the other hand, when a community indiscriminately acclaims every new doctrine the love of truth becomes subordinated to the desire for novel formulations.

On the whole it may be said that the safety of science depends on there being men who care more for the justice of their methods than for any results obtained by their use. For this reason it is unfortunate when scientific research in the social field is largely in the hands of those not in a favorable position to oppose established or popular opinion.

We may put it the other way by saying that the physical sciences can be more liberal because we are sure that foolish opinions will be readily eliminated by the shock of facts. In the social field, however, no one can tell what harm may come of foolish ideas before the foolishness is finally, if ever, demonstrated. None of the precautions of scientific method can prevent human life from being an adventure, and no scientific investigator knows whether he will reach his goal. But scientific method does enable large numbers to walk with surer step. By analyzing the possibilities of any step or plan, it becomes possible to anticipate the future and adjust ourselves to it in advance. Scientific method thus minimizes the shock of novelty and the uncertainty of life. It enables us to frame policies of action and of moral judgment fit for a wider outlook than those of immediate physical stimulus or organic response.

Scientific method is the only effective way of strengthening the love of truth. It develops the intellectual courage to face difficulties and to overcome illusions that are pleasant temporarily but destructive ultimately. It settles differences without any external force by appealing to our common rational nature. The way of science, even if it is up a steep mountain, is open to all. Hence, while sectarian and partisan faiths are based on personal choice or temperament and divide men, scientific procedure unites men in something nobly devoid of all pettiness. Because it requires detachment, disinterestedness, it is the finest flower and test of a liberal civilization.

STUDY QUESTIONS

1. *The authors do not exclude emotion from scientific inquiry, but they do limit it to particular areas. What emotions do they think proper to scientific inquiry? What emotions do they think dangerous to it?*

2. *To what extent do the authors agree with La Farge in their estimate of the place of emotion in scientific inquiry? With Miss Chute in "Getting at the Truth"?*

3. *In what way is this selection related to G. K. Chesterton's "The Logic of Elfland"?*

4. *According to Cohen and Nagel, there is something (actually, two things) more important about the scientific method than the results it can give. What is it?*

5. *Do you think that Cohen and Nagel over-rate the value of scientific method in the social field? If you do, explain why it is not well adapted to historical, social or political problems. Or, if you agree with them that it is an effective instrument in these fields, write a theme explaining your point of view. In thinking about this question you may wish to consider the point of view expressed by C. E. Ayres in "Society in the Light of Reason."*

6. *Does this essay help to explain, clarify or compromise the supposed conflict between science and religion? Write a theme expressing your opinions on this highly controversial subject.*

Gilbert Keith Chesterton   The Logic of Elfland*

My first and last philosophy, that which I believe in with unbroken certainty, I learnt in the nursery. I generally learnt it from a nurse; that is, from the solemn and star-appointed priestess at once of democracy and tradition. The things I believed most then, the things I believe most now, are the things called fairy tales. They seem to me to be the entirely reasonable things. They are not fantasies: compared with them other things are fantastic.

* By permission of Dodd, Mead & Company from *Orthodoxy*, by G. K. Chesterton. Copyright, 1908, 1935, by G. K. Chesterton. By permission of John Lane the Bodley Head Ltd.

Compared with them religion and rationalism are both abnormal, though religion is abnormally right and rationalism abnormally wrong. Fairyland is nothing but the sunny country of common sense. It is not earth that judges heaven, but heaven that judges earth; so for me at least it was not earth that criticised elfland, but elfland that criticised the earth. I knew the magic beanstalk before I had tasted beans; I was sure of the Man in the Moon before I was certain of the moon. This was at one with all popular tradition. Modern minor poets are naturalists, and talk about the bush or the brook; but the singers of the old epics and fables were supernaturalists, and talked about the gods of brook and bush. That is what the moderns mean when they say that the ancients did not "appreciate Nature," because they said that Nature was divine. Old nurses do not tell children about grass, but about the fairies that dance on the grass; and the old Greeks could not see the trees for the dryads.

But I deal here with what ethic and philosophy come from being fed on fairy tales. If I were describing them in detail I could note many noble and healthy principles that arise from them. There is the chivalrous lesson of "Jack the Giant Killer"; that giants should be killed because they are gigantic. It is a manly mutiny against pride as such. For the rebel is older than all the kingdoms, and the Jacobin has more tradition than the Jacobite. There is the lesson of "Cinderella," which is the same as that of the Magnificat — *exaltavit humiles*. There is the great lesson of "Beauty and the Beast"; that a thing must be loved *before* it is lovable. There is the terrible allegory of the "Sleeping Beauty," which tells how the human creature was blessed with all birthday gifts, yet cursed with death; and how death also may perhaps be softened to a sleep. But I am not concerned with any of the separate statutes of elfland, but with the whole spirit of its law, which I learnt before I could speak, and shall retain when I cannot write. I am concerned with a certain way of looking at life, which was created in me by the fairy tales, but has since been meekly ratified by the mere facts.

It might be stated this way. There are certain sequences or developments (cases of one thing following another), which are, in the true sense of the word, reasonable. They are, in the true sense of the word, necessary. Such are mathematical and merely logical sequences. We in fairyland (who are the most reasonable of all creatures) admit that reason and that necessity. For instance, if the Ugly Sisters are older than Cinderella, it is (in an iron and awful sense) *necessary* that Cinderella is younger than the Ugly Sisters. There is no getting out of it. Haeckel may talk as much fatalism about that fact as he pleases: it really must be. If Jack is the son of a miller, a miller is the father of Jack. Cold reason decrees it from her awful throne: and we in fairyland submit. If the three brothers all ride horses, there are six animals and eighteen legs involved: that is true rationalism, and fairyland is full of it. But as I put my head over the hedge of the elves and began to take notice of the natural world, I observed an extraordinary thing. I observed that learned men in spectacles were talking of the actual things that happened — dawn and death and so on — as if *they* were rational and inevitable. They talked as if the fact that trees bear fruit were just as *necessary* as the fact that two and one trees make three. But it is not. There is an enormous difference by the test of fairyland; which is the test of the imagination. You cannot *imagine* two and one not making three. But you can easily imagine trees not growing fruit; you can imagine them growing golden candlesticks or tigers hanging on by the tail. These men in spectacles spoke much of a man named Newton, who was hit by an apple, and who discovered a law. But they could not be got to see the distinction between a true law, a law of reason, and the mere fact of apples falling. If the apple hit Newton's nose, Newton's nose hit the apple. That is a true necessity: because we cannot conceive the one occurring without the other. But we can quite well conceive the apple not falling on his nose; we can fancy it flying ardently through the air to hit some other nose, of which it had a more definite dislike. We have always in our fairy tales kept this sharp distinction between the science of mental relations, in which there really are laws, and the science of physical facts, in which there are no laws, but only weird repetitions. We believe in bodily miracles, but not in mental impossibilities. We believe that a Bean-stalk climbed up to Heaven; but that does not at all confuse our convictions on the philosophical question of how many beans make five.

Here is the peculiar perfection of tone and truth in the nursery tales. The man of science says, "Cut the stalk, and the apple will fall"; but he says it calmly, as if the one idea really led up to the other. The witch in the fairy tale says, "Blow the horn, and the ogre's castle will fall"; but she does not say it as if it were something in which the effect obviously arose out of the cause. Doubtless she has given the advice to many champions, and has seen many castles fall, but she does not lose either her wonder or her reason. She does not muddle her head until it imagines a necessary mental connection between a horn and a falling tower. But the scientific men do muddle their heads, until they imagine a necessary mental connection between an apple leaving the tree and an apple reaching the ground. They do really talk as if they had found not only a set of marvellous facts, but a truth connecting those facts. They do talk as if the connection of two strange things physically connected them philosophically. They feel that because one incomprehensible thing constantly follows another incomprehensible thing the two together somehow make up a comprehensible thing. Two black riddles make a white answer.

In fairyland we avoid the word "law"; but in the land of science they are singularly fond of it. Thus they will call some interesting conjecture about how forgotten folks pronounced the alphabet, Grimm's Law. But Grimm's Law is far less intellectual than Grimm's Fairy Tales. The tales are, at any rate, certainly tales; while the law is not a law. A law implies that we know the nature of the generalisation and enactment; not merely that we have noticed some of the effects. If there is a law that pick-pockets shall go to prison, it implies that there is an imaginable mental connection between the idea of prison and the idea of picking pockets. And we know what the idea is. We can say why we take liberty from a man who takes liberties. But we cannot say why an egg can turn into a chicken any more than we can say why a bear could turn into a fairy prince. As *ideas*, the egg and the chicken are further off each other than the bear and the prince; for no egg in itself suggests a chicken, whereas some princes do suggest bears. Granted, then, that certain transformations do happen, it is essential that we should regard them in the philosophic manner of fairy tales, not in the unphilosophic manner of science and the "Laws of Nature." When we are asked why eggs turn to birds or fruits fall in autumn, we must answer exactly as the fairy godmother would answer if Cinderella asked her why mice turned to horses or her clothes fell from her at twelve o'clock. We must answer that it is *magic*. It is not a "law," for we do not understand its general formula. It is not a necessity, for though we can count on it happening practically, we have no right to say that it must always happen. It is no argument for unalterable law (as Huxley fancied) that we count on the ordinary course of things. We do not count on it; we bet on it. We risk the remote possibility of a miracle as we do that of a poisoned pancake or a world-destroying comet. We leave it out of account, not because it is a miracle, and therefore an impossibility, but because it is a miracle, and therefore an exception. All the terms used in the science books, "law," "necessity," "order," "tendency," and so on, are really unintellectual, because they assume an inner synthesis which we do not possess. The only words that ever satisfied me as describing Nature are the terms used in the fairy books, "charm," "spell," "enchantment." They express the arbitrariness of the fact and its mystery. A tree grows fruit because it is a *magic* tree. Water runs downhill because it is bewitched. The sun shines because it is bewitched.

I deny altogether that this is fantastic or even mystical. We may have some mysticism later on; but this fairy-tale language about things is simply rational and agnostic. It is the only way I can express in words my clear and definite perception that one thing is quite distinct from another; that there is no logical connection between flying and laying eggs. It is the man who talks about "a law" that he has never seen who is the mystic. Nay, the ordinary scientific man is strictly a sentimentalist. He is a sentimentalist in this essential sense, that he is soaked and swept away by mere associations. He has so often seen birds fly and lay eggs that he feels as if there must be some dreamy, tender connection between the two ideas, whereas there is none. A forlorn lover might be unable to dissociate the moon from lost love; so the materialist is unable to dissociate the moon from the tide. In both cases there is no connection, except that one has seen them together. A sentimentalist might shed tears at the smell of apple-blossom, because, by a dark association of his own, it reminded him of his boyhood. So the materialist professor (though he conceals his tears) is yet a sentimentalist, because, by a dark association of his own, apple-blossoms remind him of apples. But the cool rationalist from fairyland does not see why, in the abstract, the apple tree should not grow crimson tulips; it sometimes does in his country.

This elementary wonder, however, is not a mere fancy derived from the fairy tales; on the contrary, all the fire of the fairy tales is derived from this. Just as we all like love tales because there is an instinct of sex, we all like astonishing tales because they touch the nerve of the ancient instinct of astonishment. This is proved by the fact that when we are very young children we do not need fairy tales: we only need tales. Mere life is interesting enough. A child of seven is excited by being told that Tommy opened a door and saw a dragon. But a child of three is excited by being told that Tommy opened a door. Boys like romantic tales; but babies like realistic tales — because they find them romantic. In fact, a baby is about the only person, I should think, to whom a modern realistic novel could be read without boring him. This proves that even nursery tales only echo an almost pre-natal leap of interest and amazement. These tales say that apples were golden only to refresh the forgotten moment when we found that they were green. They make rivers run with wine only to make us remember, for one wild moment, that they run with water. I have said that this is wholly reasonable and even agnostic. And, indeed, on this point I am all for the higher agnosticism; its better name is Ignorance. We have all read in scientific books, and, indeed, in all romances, the story of the man who has forgotten his name. This man walks about the streets and can see and appreciate everything; only he cannot remember who he is. Well, every man is that man in the story. Every man has forgotten who he is. One may understand the cosmos, but never the ego; the self is more distant than any star. Thou shalt love the Lord thy God; but thou shalt not know thyself. We are all under the same mental calamity; we have all forgotten our names. We have all forgotten what we really are. All that we call common sense and rationality and practicality and positivism only means that for certain dead levels of our life we forget that we have forgotten. All that we call spirit and art and ecstasy only means that for one awful instant we remember that we forget.

STUDY QUESTIONS

1. *Do you think that all of Chesterton's arguments are meant to be taken literally? Or is his real meaning falsified unless the special tone of his essay is taken into account?*

2. *What difference does Chesterton see between the view that sequences of events are "reasonable" or "natural" and the view that they are "necessary" or "inevitable"?*

3. *Chesterton's allusion to Huxley refers to the passage in Huxley's "We are All Scientists" where Huxley defends the hypothesis about the theft of the spoons and the tea-pot on the ground that it corresponds with past experience. Is Chesterton's criticism of Huxley's position justified?*

4. In what way does Chesterton adopt an attitude toward life that is different from that of Huxley? In what way does it correspond with the attitude of Poincaré?

5. Is Chesterton fair in saying that scientific laws are based on the association rather than on the actual connection of events? Defend scientific thought and method against his charges.

6. Or, if you feel that Chesterton has touched a genuine weak spot in scientific theory, write a theme expressing his ideas in a more direct and immediate form.

Joseph Wood Krutch The Colloid and the Crystal*

The first real snow was soon followed by a second. Over the radio the weatherman talked lengthily about cold masses and warm masses, about what was moving out to sea and what wasn't. Did Benjamin Franklin, I wondered, know what he was starting when it first occurred to him to trace by correspondence the course of storms? From my stationary position the most reasonable explanation seemed to be simply that winter had not quite liked the looks of the landscape as she first made it up. She was changing her sheets.

Another forty-eight hours brought one of those nights ideal for frosting the panes. When I came down to breakfast, two of the windows were almost opaque and the others were etched with graceful, fernlike sprays of ice which looked rather like the impressions left in rocks by some of the antediluvian plants, and they were almost as beautiful as anything which the living can achieve. Nothing else which has never lived looks so much as though it were actually informed with life.

I resisted, I am proud to say, the almost universal impulse to scratch my initials into one of the surfaces. The effect, I knew, would not be an improvement. But so, of course, do those less virtuous than I. That indeed is precisely why they scratch. The impulse to mar and to destroy is as ancient and almost as nearly universal as the impulse to create. The one is an easier way than the other of demonstrating power. Why else should anyone not hungry prefer a dead rabbit to a live one? Not even those horrible Dutch painters of bloody still — or shall we say stilled? — lifes can have really believed that their subjects were more beautiful dead.

Indoors it so happened that a Christmas cactus had chosen this moment to bloom. Its lush blossoms, fuchsia-shaped but pure red rather than magenta,

* From The Best of Two Worlds by Joseph Wood Krutch, copyright, 1950, by Joseph Wood Krutch. By permission of William Sloane Associates, Inc. (Copyright, 1950, by Street and Smith Publications, Inc., reprinted by permission of Mademoiselle.)

hung at the drooping ends of strange thick stems and outlined themselves in blood against the glistening background of the frosty pane — jungle flower against frostflower; the warm beauty that breathes and lives and dies competing with the cold beauty that burgeons, not because it wants to, but merely because it is obeying the laws of physics which require that crystals shall take the shape they have always taken since the world began. The effect of red flower against white tracery was almost too theatrical, not quite in good taste perhaps. My eye recoiled in shock and sought through a clear area of the glass the more normal out-of-doors.

On the snow-capped summit of my bird-feeder a chickadee pecked at the new-fallen snow and swallowed a few of the flakes which serve him in lieu of the water he sometimes sadly lacks when there is nothing except ice too solid to be picked at. A downy woodpecker was hammering at a lump of suet and at the coconut full of peanut butter. One nuthatch was dining while the mate waited his — or was it her? — turn. The woodpecker announces the fact that he is a male by the bright red spot on the back of his neck, but to me, at least, the sexes of the nuthatch are indistinguishable. I shall never know whether it is the male or the female who eats first. And that is a pity. If I knew, I could say, like the Ugly Duchess, "and the moral of that is..."

But I soon realized that at the moment the frosted windows were what interested me most — especially the fact that there is no other natural phenomenon in which the lifeless mocks so closely the living. One might almost think that the frostflower had got the idea from the leaf and the branch if one did not know how inconceivably more ancient the first is. No wonder that enthusiastic biologists in the nineteenth century, anxious to conclude that there was no qualitative difference between life and chemical processes, tried to believe that the crystal furnished the link, that its growth was actually the same as the growth of a living organism. But excusable though the fancy was, no one, I think, believes anything of the sort today. Protoplasm is a colloid and the colloids are fundamentally different from the crystalline substances. Instead of crystallizing they jell, and life in its simplest known form is a shapeless blob of rebellious jelly rather than a crystal eternally obeying the most ancient law.

No man ever saw a dinosaur. The last of these giant reptiles was dead eons before the most dubious halfman surveyed the world about him. Not even the dinosaurs ever cast their dim eyes upon many of the still earlier creatures which preceded them. Life changes so rapidly that its later phases know nothing of those which preceded them. But the frostflower is older than the dinosaur, older than the protozoan, older no doubt than the enzyme or the ferment. Yet it is precisely what it has always been. Millions of years before there were any eyes to see it, millions of years before any life existed, it grew in its own special way, crystallized along its preordained lines of cleavage, stretched out its pseudo-branches and pseudo-leaves. It was beautiful before beauty itself existed.

We find it difficult to conceive a world except in terms of purpose, of will, or of intention. At the thought of the something without beginning and presumably without end, of something which is, nevertheless, regular though blind, and organized without any end in view, the mind reels. Constituted as we are it is easier to conceive how the slime floating upon the waters might become in time *homo sapiens* than it is to imagine how so complex a thing as a crystal could have always been and can always remain just what it is — complicated and perfect but without any meaning, even for itself. How can the lifeless even obey a law?

To a mathematical physicist I once confessed somewhat shamefacedly that I had never been able to understand how inanimate nature managed to follow so invariably and so promptly her own laws. If I flip a coin across a table, it will come to rest at a certain point. But before it stops at just that point, many factors must be taken into consideration. There is the question of the strength of the initial impulse, of the exact amount of resistance offered by the friction of that particular table top, and of the density of the air at the moment. It would take a physicist a long time to work out the problem and he could achieve only an approximation at that. Yet presumably the coin will stop exactly where it should. Some very rapid calculations have to be made before it can do so, and they are, presumably, always accurate.

And then, just as I was blushing at what I suppose he must regard as my folly, the mathematician came to my rescue by informing me that Laplace had been puzzled by exactly the same fact. "Nature laughs at the difficulties of integration," he remarked — and by "integration" he meant, of course, the mathematician's word for the process involved when a man solves one of the differential equations to which he has reduced the laws of motion.

When my Christmas cactus blooms so theatrically a few inches in front of the frost-covered pane, it also is obeying laws but obeying them much less rigidly and in a different way. It blooms at about Christmastime because it has got into the habit of doing so, because, one is tempted to say, it wants to. As a matter of fact it was, this year, not a Christmas cactus but a New Year's cactus, and because of this unpredictability I would like to call it "he," not "it." His flowers assume their accustomed shape and take on their accustomed color. But not as the frostflowers follow their predestined pattern. Like me, the cactus has a history which stretches back over a long past full of changes and developments. He has not always been merely obeying fixed laws. He has resisted and rebelled; he has attempted novelties, passed through many phases. Like all living things he has had a will of his own. He has made laws, not merely obeyed them.

"Life," so the platitudinarian is fond of saying, "is strange." But from our standpoint it is not really so strange as those things which have no life and yet nevertheless move in their predestined orbits and "act" though they do not "behave." At the very least one ought to say that if life is strange there is nothing about it more strange than the fact that it has its being in a universe so astonishingly shared on the one hand by "things" and on the other by "creatures," that man himself is both a "thing" which obeys the laws of chemistry or physics and a "creature" who to some extent defies them. No other contrast, certainly not the contrast between the human being and the animal, or the animal and the plant, or even the spirit and the body, is so tremendous as this contrast between what lives and what does not.

To think of the lifeless as merely inert, to make the contrast merely in terms of a negative, is to miss the real strangeness. Not the shapeless stone which seems to be merely waiting to be acted upon but the snowflake or the frostflower is the true representative of the lifeless universe as opposed to ours. They represent plainly, as the stone does not, the fixed and perfect system of organization which includes the sun and its planets, includes therefore this earth itself, but against which life has set up its seemingly puny opposition. Order and obedience are the primary characteristics of that which is not alive. The snowflake eternally obeys its one and only law: "Be thou six pointed"; the planets their one and only: "Travel thou in an ellipse." The astronomer can tell where the North Star will be ten thousand years hence; the botanist cannot tell where the dandelion will bloom tomorrow.

Life is rebellious and anarchial, always testing the supposed immutability of the rules which the nonliving changelessly accepts. Because the snowflake goes on doing as it was told, its story up to the end of time was finished when it first assumed the form which it has kept ever since. But the story of every living thing is still in the telling. It may hope and it may try. Moreover, though it may succeed or fail, it will certainly change. No form of frostflower ever became extinct. Such, if you like, is its glory. But such also is the fact which makes it alien. It may melt but it cannot die.

If I wanted to contemplate what is to me the deepest of all mysteries, I should choose as my object lesson a snowflake under a lens and an amoeba under the microscope. To a detached observer — if one can possibly imagine any observer who *could* be detached when faced with such an ultimate choice — the snowflake would certainly seem the "higher" of the two. Against its intricate glistening perfection one would have to place a shapeless, slightly turbid glob, perpetually oozing out in this direction or that but not suggesting so strongly as the snowflake does, intelligence and plan. Crystal and colloid, the chemist would call them, but what an inconceivable contrast those neutral terms imply! Like the star, the snowflake seems to declare the glory of God, while the promise of the amoeba, given only perhaps to itself, seems only contemptible. But its jelly holds, nevertheless, not only its promise but ours also, while the snowflake represents some achievement which we cannot possibly share. After the passage of billions of years, one can see and be aware of the other, but the relationship can never be reciprocal. Even after these billions of years no aggregate of colloids can be as beautiful as the crystal always was, but it can know, as the crystal cannot, what beauty is.

Even to admire too much or too exclusively the alien kind of beauty is dangerous. Much as I love and am moved by the grand, inanimate forms of nature, I am always shocked and a little frightened by those of her professed lovers to whom landscape is the most important thing, and to whom landscape is merely a matter of forms and colors. If they see or are moved by an animal or flower, it is to them merely a matter of a picturesque completion and their fellow creatures are no more than decorative details. But without some continuous awareness of the two great realms of the inanimate and the animate there can be no love of nature as I understand it, and what is worse, there must be a sort of disloyalty to our cause, to us who are colloid, not crystal. The pantheist who feels the oneness of all living things, I can understand; perhaps indeed he and I are in essential agreement. But the ultimate All is not one thing, but two. And because the alien half is in its way as proud and confident and successful as our half, its fundamental difference may not be disregarded with impunity. Of us and all we stand for, the enemy is not so much death as the not-living, or rather that great system which succeeds without ever having had the need to be alive. The frostflower is not merely a wonder; it is also a threat and a warning. How admirable, it seems to say, not living can be! What triumphs mere immutable law can achieve!

Some of Charles Peirce's strange speculations about the possibility that "natural law" is not law at all but merely a set of habits fixed more firmly than any habits we know anything about in ourselves or in the animals suggest the possibility that the snowflake was not, after all, always inanimate, that it merely surrendered at some time impossibly remote the life which once achieved its perfect organization. Yet even if we can imagine such a thing to be true, it serves only to warn us all the more strongly against the possibility that what we call the living might in the end succumb also to the seduction of the immutably fixed.

No student of the anthill has ever failed to be astonished either into admiration or horror by what is sometimes called the perfection of its society. Though even the anthill can change its ways, though even ant individuals — ridiculous as the conjunction of the two words may seem — can sometimes make choices, the perfection of the techniques, the regularity of the habits almost suggests the possibility that the insect is on its way back to inanition, that, vast as the difference still is, an anthill crystallizes somewhat as a snowflake does. But not even the anthill, nothing else indeed in the whole known universe is so perfectly planned as one of these same snowflakes. Would, then, the ultimately planned society be, like the anthill, one in which no one makes plans, any more than a snowflake does? From the cradle in which it is not really born to the grave where it is only a little deader than it always was, the ant-citizen follows a plan to the making of which he no longer contributes anything.

Perhaps we men represent the ultimate to which the rebellion, begun so long ago in some amoeba-like jelly, can go. And perhaps the inanimate is beginning the slow process of subduing us again. Certainly the psychologist and the philosopher are tending more and more to think of us as creatures who obey laws rather than as creatures of will and responsibility. We are, they say, "conditioned" by this or by that. Even the greatest heroes are studied on the assumption that they can be "accounted for" by something outside themselves. They are, it is explained, "the product of forces." All the emphasis is placed, not upon that power to resist and rebel which we were once supposed to have, but upon the "influences" which "formed us." Men are made by society, not society by men. History as well as character "obeys laws." In their view, we crystallize in obedience to some dictate from without instead of moving in conformity with something within.

And so my eye goes questioningly back to the frosted pane. While I slept the graceful pseudo-fronds crept across the glass, assuming, as life itself does, an intricate organization. "Why live," they seem to say, "when we can be beautiful, complicated, and orderly without the uncertainty and effort required of a living thing? Once we were all that was. Perhaps some day we shall be all that is. Why not join us?"

Last summer no clod or no stone would have been heard if it had asked such a question. The hundreds of things which walked and sang, the millions which crawled and twined were all having their day. What was dead seemed to exist only in order that the living might live upon it. The plants were busy turning the inorganic into green life and the animals were busy turning that green into red. When we moved, we walked mostly upon grass. Our pre-eminence was unchallenged.

On this winter day nothing seems so successful as the frostflower. It thrives on the very thing which has driven some of us indoors or underground and which has been fatal to many. It is having now its hour of triumph, as we before had ours. Like the cactus flower itself, I am a hothouse plant. Even my cats gaze dreamily out of the window at a universe which is no longer theirs.

How are we to resist, if resist we can? This house into which I have withdrawn is merely an expedient and it serves only my mere physical existence. What mental or spiritual convictions, what will to maintain to my own kind of existence can I assert? For me it is not enough merely to say, as I do say, that I shall resist the invitation to submerge myself into a crystalline society and to stop planning in order that I may be planned for. Neither is it enough to go further, as I do go, and to insist that the most important thing about a man is not that part of him which is "the product of forces" but that part, however small it may be, which enables him to become something other than what the most accomplished sociologist, working in conjunction with the most accomplished psychologist, could predict that he would be.

I need, so I am told, a faith, something outside myself to which I can be loyal. And with that I agree, in my own way. I am on what I call "our side," and I know, though vaguely, what I think that is. Wordsworth's God had his dwelling in the light of setting suns. But the God who dwells there seems to me most probably the God of the atom, the star, and the crystal. Mine, if I have one, reveals Himself in another class of phenomena. He makes the grass green and the blood red.

STUDY QUESTIONS

1. *What is the basic principle of organization in this essay? In what ways do the opening three paragraphs suggest the central thesis? What purpose is served by the details of the birds feeding in the fifth paragraph?*

2. *Is the concluding contrast between "last summer" and "this winter day" suggestive of anything beyond the literal comparison? What? What other similar specific contrast does Krutch employ in the essay? What do they contribute to the total effect of the essay?*

3. *Compare this essay in organization, style, and tone with those by Hoyle, Ittelson and Kilpatrick, and Cohen and Nagel.*

4. *What similarities and differences does Krutch perceive between living and non-living things? In what ways do the non-living seem superior? What feelings does the comparison arouse in the author? Why is the frostflower a "threat and a warning"?*

5. *What limitations of science are implicit in Krutch's observations about the predictability of "rebellious and anarchial" life? What similarities and differences do you find between these implications and the ideas of Cohen and Nagel? Of Ayres in "Society in the Light of Reason"?*

6. *Write a theme in which you follow Krutch's method of evolving interesting generalizations and speculations from a familiar and everyday comparison.*

5 Knowledge and Value

1. PHILOSOPHY AND KNOWLEDGE

Bertrand Russell The Value of Philosophy*

Having now come to the end of our brief and very incomplete review of the problems of philosophy, it will be well to consider, in conclusion, what is the value of philosophy and why it ought to be studied. It is the more necessary to consider this question, in view of the fact that many men, under the influence of science or of practical affairs, are inclined to doubt whether philosophy is anything better than innocent but useless trifling, hair-splitting distinctions, and controversies on matters concerning which knowledge is impossible.

This view of philosophy appears to result, partly from a wrong conception of the ends of life, partly from a wrong conception of the kind of goods which philosophy strives to achieve. Physical science, through the medium of inventions, is useful to innumerable people who are wholly ignorant of it; thus the study of physical science is to be recommended, not only, or primarily, because of the effect on the student, but rather because of the effect on mankind in general. This utility does not belong to philosophy. If the study of

* From *The Problems of Philosophy* by Bertrand Russell, by permission of the Oxford University Press.

philosophy has any value at all for others than students of philosophy, it must be only indirectly, through its effects upon the lives of those who study it. It is in these effects, therefore, if anywhere, that the value of philosophy must be primarily sought.

But further, if we are not to fail in our endeavour to determine the value of philosophy, we must first free our minds from the prejudices of what are wrongly called "practical" men. The "practical" man, as this word is often used, is one who recognises only material needs, who realises that men must have food for the body, but is oblivious of the necessity of providing food for the mind. If all men were well off, if poverty and disease had been reduced to their lowest possible point, there would still remain much to be done to produce a valuable society; and even in the existing world the goods of the mind are at least as important as the goods of the body. It is exclusively among the goods of the mind that the value of philosophy is to be found; and only those who are not indifferent to these goods can be persuaded that the study of philosophy is not a waste of time.

Philosophy, like all other studies, aims primarily at knowledge. The knowledge it aims at is the kind of knowledge which gives unity and system to the body of the sciences, and the kind which results from a critical examination of the grounds of our convictions, prejudices, and beliefs. But it cannot be maintained that philosophy has had any very great measure of success in its attempts to provide definite answers to its questions. If you ask a mathematician, a mineralogist, a historian, or any other man of learning, what definite body of truths has been ascertained by his science, his answer will last as long as you are willing to listen. But if you put the same question to a philosopher, he will, if he is candid, have to confess that his study has not achieved positive results such as have been achieved by other sciences. It is true that this is partly accounted for by the fact that, as soon as definite knowledge concerning any subject becomes possible, this subject ceases to be called philosophy, and becomes a separate science. The whole study of the heavens, which now belongs to astronomy, was once included in philosophy; Newton's great work was called "the mathematical principles of natural philosophy." Similarly, the study of the human mind, which was, until very lately, a part of philosophy, has now been separated from philosophy and has become the science of psychology. Thus, to a great extent, the uncertainty of philosophy is more apparent than real: those questions which are already capable of definite answers are placed in the sciences, while those only to which, at present, no definite answer can be given, remain to form the residue which is called philosophy.

This is, however, only a part of the truth concerning the uncertainty of philosophy. There are many questions — and among them those that are of the profoundest interest to our spiritual life — which, so far as we can see, must remain insoluble to the human intellect unless its powers become of quite a different order from what they are now. Has the universe any unity of plan or purpose, or is it a fortuitous concourse of atoms? Is consciousness a permanent part of the universe, giving hope of indefinite growth in wisdom, or is it a transitory accident on a small planet on which life must ultimately become impossible? Are good and evil of importance to the universe or only to man? Such questions are asked by philosophy, and variously answered by various philosophers. But it would seem that, whether answers be otherwise discoverable or not, the answers suggested by philosophy are none of them demonstrably true. Yet, however slight may be the hope of discovering an answer, it is part of the business of philosophy to continue the consideration of such questions, to make us aware of their importance, to examine all the approaches to them, and to keep alive that speculative interest in the universe which is apt to be killed by confining ourselves to definitely ascertainable knowledge.

Many philosophers, it is true, have held that philosophy could establish the truth of certain answers to such fundamental questions. They have supposed that what is of most importance in religious beliefs could be proved by strict demonstration to be true. In order to judge of such attempts, it is necessary to take a survey of human knowledge, and to form an opinion as to its methods and its limitations. On such a subject it would be unwise to pronounce dogmatically; but if the investigations of our previous chapters have not led us astray, we shall be compelled to renounce the hope of finding philosophical proofs of religious beliefs. We cannot, therefore, include as part of the value of philosophy any definite set of answers to such questions. Hence, once more, the value of philosophy must not depend upon any supposed body of definitely ascertainable knowledge to be acquired by those who study it.

The value of philosophy is, in fact, to be sought largely in its very uncertainty. The man who has no tincture of philosophy goes through life imprisoned in the prejudices derived from common sense, from the habitual beliefs of his age or his nation, and from convictions which have grown up in his mind without the co-operation or consent of his deliberate reason. To such a man the world tends to become definite, finite, obvious; common objects rouse no questions, and unfamiliar possibilities are contemptuously rejected. As soon as we begin to philosophise, on the contrary, we find, as we saw in our opening chapters, that even the most everyday things lead to problems to which only very incomplete answers can be given. Philosophy, though unable to tell us with certainty what is the true answer to the doubts which it raises, is able to suggest many possibilities which enlarge our thoughts and free them from the tyranny of custom. Thus, while diminishing our feeling of certainty as to what things are, it greatly increases our knowledge as to what they may be; it removes the somewhat arrogant dogmatism of those who have never travelled into the region of liberating doubt, and it keeps alive our sense of wonder by showing familiar things in an unfamiliar aspect.

Apart from its utility in showing unsuspected possibilities, philosophy has a value — perhaps its chief value — through the greatness of the objects which it contemplates, and the freedom from narrow and personal aims resulting from this contemplation. The life of the instinctive man is shut up within the circle of his private interests: family and friends may be included, but the outer world is not regarded except as it may help or hinder what comes within the circle of instinctive wishes. In such a life there is something feverish and confined, in comparison with which the philosophic life is calm and free. The private world of instinctive interests is a small one, set in the midst of a great and powerful world which must, sooner or later, lay our private world in ruins. Unless we can so enlarge our interests as to include the whole outer world, we remain like a garrison in a beleaguered fortress, knowing that the enemy prevents escape and that ultimate surrender is inevitable. In such a life there is no peace, but a constant strife between the insistence of desire and the powerlessness of will. In one way or another, if our life is to be great and free, we must escape this prison and this strife.

One way of escape is by philosophic contemplation. Philosophic contemplation does not, in its widest survey, divide the universe into two hostile camps — friends and foes, helpful and hostile, good and bad — it views the whole impartially. Philosophic contemplation, when it is unalloyed, does not aim at proving that the rest of the universe is akin to man. All acquisition of knowledge is an enlargement of the Self, but this enlargement is best attained when it is not directly sought. It is obtained when the desire for knowledge is alone operative, by a study which does not wish in advance that its objects should have this or that character, but adapts the Self to the characters which it finds in its objects. This enlargement of Self is not obtained when, taking the Self as it is, we try to show that the world is so similar to this Self that knowledge of it is possible without any admission of what seems alien. The desire to prove this is a form of self-assertion, and like all self-assertion, it is an obstacle to the growth of Self which it desires, and of which the Self knows that it is capable. Self-assertion, in philosophic speculation as elsewhere, views the world as a means to its own ends; thus it makes the world of less account than Self, and the Self sets bounds to the greatness of its goods. In contemplation, on the contrary, we start from the not-Self, and through its greatness the boundaries of Self are enlarged; through the infinity of the universe the mind which contemplates it achieves some share in infinity.

For this reason greatness of soul is not fostered by those philosophies which assimilate the universe to Man. Knowledge is a form of union of Self and not-Self; like all union, it is impaired by dominion, and therefore by any attempt to force the universe into conformity with what we find in ourselves. There is a widespread philosophical tendency towards the view which tells us that man is the measure of all things, that truth is man-made, that space and time and the world of universals are properties of the mind, and that, if there be anything not created by the mind, it is unknowable and of no account for us. This view, if our previous discussions were correct, is untrue; but in addition to being untrue, it has the effect of robbing philosophic contemplation of all that gives it value, since it fetters contemplation to Self. What it calls knowledge is not a union with the not-Self, but a set of prejudices, habits, and desires, making an impenetrable veil between us and the world beyond. The man who finds pleasure in such a theory of knowledge is like the man who never leaves the domestic circle for fear his word might not be law.

The true philosophic contemplation, on the contrary, finds its satisfaction in every enlargement of the not-Self, in everything that magnifies the objects contemplated, and thereby the subject contemplating. Everything, in contemplation, that is personal or private, everything that depends upon habit, self-interest, or desire, distorts the object, and hence impairs the union which the intellect seeks. By thus making a barrier between subject and object, such personal and private things become a prison to the intellect. The free intellect will see as God might see, without a *here* and *now*, without hopes and fears, without the trammels of customary beliefs and traditional prejudices, calmly, dispassionately, in the sole and exclusive desire of knowledge — knowledge as impersonal, as purely contemplative, as it is possible for man to attain. Hence also the free intellect will value more the abstract and universal knowledge into which the accidents of private history do not enter, than the knowledge brought by the senses, and dependent, as such knowledge must be, upon an exclusive and personal point of view and a body whose sense-organs distort as much as they reveal.

The mind which has become accustomed to the freedom and impartiality of philosophic contemplation will preserve something of the same freedom and impartiality in the world of action and emotion. It will view its purposes and desires as parts of the whole, with the absence of insistence that results from seeing them as infinitesimal fragments in a world of which all the rest is unaffected by any one man's deeds. The impartiality which, in contemplation, is the unalloyed desire for truth, is the very same quality of mind which, in action, is justice, and in emotion is that universal love which can be given to all, and not only to those who are judged useful or admirable. Thus contemplation enlarges not only the objects of our thoughts, but also the objects of our actions and our affections: it makes us citizens of the universe, not only of one walled city at war with all the rest. In this citizenship of the universe consists man's true freedom, and his liberation from the thraldom of narrow hopes and fears.

Thus, to sum up our discussion of the value of philosophy: Philosophy is to be studied, not for the sake of any definite answers to its questions, since no definite answers can, as a rule, be known to be true, but rather for the sake of the questions themselves; because these questions enlarge our conception of what is possible, enrich our intellectual imagination, and diminish the dogmatic assurance which closes the mind against speculation; but above all because, through the greatness of the universe which philosophy contemplates, the mind is rendered great, and becomes capable of that union with the universe which constitutes its highest good.

STUDY QUESTIONS

1. Russell opens his discussion by admitting that philosophy does not have the "utility" of physical science and that it is not "practical" in the sense in which that term is frequently used. What does Russell gain by opening with these statements? What does he claim as the principal aim and value of philosophy?
2. How does Russell account for the fact that philosophy is so often unable to give definite answers to the problems it is concerned with? How does Russell show that the "uncertainty" characteristic of philosophy is an advantage?
3. Russell says that philosophy usually contemplates problems of great importance. Is there any relation, however, between philosophy and the trivial everyday problems people have to face?
4. What relation between the Self and the world does philosophy make possible?
5. Does Russell's explanation of the end and nature of philosophy have any bearing upon education? What would education based upon his principles be like?
6. Russell speaks, at the end of this selection, of the value of philosophy in diminishing "the dogmatic assurance which closes the mind against speculation." Note that Martin and several other writers in this anthology have been concerned in one way or another with the need for and the value of cultivating an open mind, of diminishing "dogmatic assurance." Name two or three such writers and summarize their particular concerns.

Barrows Dunham   Then Why Not Every Man?*

When the sun hangs lower than the lowest branches, the world, much wearied, slides out of its day-long rut, and people move by various paths to their release. It has been a hard day, stirred with the little excitements of failure or success: eight hours of one's life, spent (who knows how fruitfully?) in acquiring the means of working another eight.

The man in the street, who is often quoted and has never said a word, is at last — in the street.

He walks past the bank that has his money and keeps it safe from him by closing at three, past the shop windows whose reductions he can't afford, past the bootblack-hatcleaner who beautifies both extremities, past the bars where desperate men are drinking and the literary assassins lurk. He takes a bus or train or trolley, and, after a forgetful interval, he comes home.

And here, if not quite heaven, there is a haven: the loved, enduring sameness which all the motions of his life go to sustain, the immediate hearth of values, the rock and tower whence he looks out, protected, upon the world. He is always building it, in fancy and in fact. Looking backward, he can see

---

* From *Giants in Chains* by Barrows Dunham, by permission of Little, Brown & Company. Copyright, 1953, by Barrows Dunham.

the history of half-unnoticed change through which it has survived and even grown. Looking forward, he can hopefully guess the ampler wage, the more rewarded talent, which is to make all happiness secure. And beyond that, his own ultimate, the very alteration of his being — not storm or terror, he will wish, but a simple leaving off of light.

Doubtless he does not always range through all these notions. Yet in each opening of the door there are the inevitable questions: Are they at home? And well? And happy? If so, then life may wander as it will until another evening and the questions come again.

The man in the street, now the man at home — who is nearer than he to the subtle conflict of permanence and change? Who knows, more than he, what effort it takes to make possession last, to hold within the moving universe some firm abode? Surely he is shrewder than Parmenides, who thought that logic had abolished change; sturdier than Hume, who found in all the fabric of the world mere causeless series of sensations.

And now at home, he shuts the door upon the outer world but not upon philosophy. Seated at table and exercising his right to the day's secrets, he learns everything that happened, what it was and how it felt. Though the notion may not rise into full consciousness, his behavior suggests an understanding that events such as these are what the world is really made of — not the gossip of headlines nor the loud obscurities of commentators, but the effort of people like his wife and children to do what they think ought to be done at the moment they have to do it.

Now, this is a generalization to the effect that history is made by people. It is not particularly a favorite with historians or philosophers, who have their eyes (let us say) upon the splendors and lusts of kings. Nevertheless, it is simple, it is very arguable, and it is in all probability true. The man at home, if modesty did not so shroud him, might marvel how many learned errors he has escaped.

But his acumen is not yet exhausted. For I fancy that as he reads his evening paper, backwards, from the comics through murder, theft, fire, and divorce to the serried horrors of Page One, he rejects this item, accepts that, rather doubts the other, and in general wonders how much correspondence there may be between the story and the event. He began life, to be sure, believing what he was told; but he has learned that many things which are told are erroneous, and that one must do a little testing for oneself. One seldom, perhaps, fully develops the technique of inquiry. One does know, however, that contradictions within a story will destroy it, and that prejudice will tear it loose from the sustaining facts.

These are the rudiments, indeed the essentials, of a theory of knowledge — a theory, that is to say, which should be able to give us the talent of true belief. We all have some impression of what this theory contains, for the total lack of it would leave us helpless; and very probably we all feel that, however much we now know of it, there would be benefit in knowing more.

The man at home, soon to be the man in bed, has thus spent an entire

evening without being released from philosophy. His last reflections are set
by an item in the paper to the effect that a lecturer at the Good Feeling Club
has exhorted the audience not to care for material well-being, which is equally
attainable by rabbits and snakes. But, on this supposition, one has labored
for inferior substance, and all the iterated tasks were frauds. Moreover, shall
one conclude that, in this fragment of the universe, what one buys with so
much toil has really lesser value, while pearls abound for simple taking? That
would be a paradox indeed, to make faint sense of. And thus over the long
day ethics slides her curtain, the first and deepening purple of the night.

PHILOSOPHY AS REFLECTION

Unless I have misconceived the habits of homes and of evenings, I am
entitled to my conclusion that it is very natural for men to philosophize and
that they do it oftener than they know. They do it, moreover, better than they
know, just because they do it naturally. They are not asked to publish their
findings, and hence are not tempted to the platitude and obscurity of official
pronouncements. Nor do they dispense that purchasable comfort which sighs
and lies and lets the misery last.

On the contrary, they are simply trying to make their lives intelligible, a
process they began in their cradles. If they are amateurs rather than profes-
sionals, they are so in a profound sense, namely, that they love understanding.
They practice philosophy in its ancient and traditional form, as reflection.

And what is it to reflect? It is to draw the scattered data of experience into
various unities, to find the likenesses and contrasts, to catch the logic moving
throughout change. A sunrise and a sunset make one day, and of such days
a handful makes a life. Yet in these regularities, dull (it has sometimes
seemed) as the ticking of a clock, lies the vast stretch of objects to be known.

The simplest facts are pregnant with philosophy. Men, it is obvious
enough, are born of their own kind, are reared among men, and die among
men. The relations thus instituted are somewhat shifting, somewhat insecure,
and at their extremes rapturous or tragic. During a lifetime, every man stores
up some knowledge of them and some theories about them. Thus, despite
prejudice and naïveté, every man is, at least in rudiments, a social scientist.

Secondly, men are everywhere and always in some relation with the
physical world, which is the source of food, clothing, shelter, and the innumerable other commodities they need. During a lifetime, they acquire
knowledge and develop theories about this world also. They are, in rather
more than rudiments, physical scientists.

Now, it happens that between these worlds, the physical and the social,
there are many interactions. The technology of producing goods is mainly a
problem in physical science, and the distribution of those goods is mainly
a problem in social science. Nevertheless, the two profoundly influence each
other. Failures in the scheme of distribution will thwart technology and

sometimes bring it to a halt. On the other hand, a failure (and sometimes a great success) in technology will unsettle all social relations. A crisis in either world begets a crisis in the other; and the human race, now master of the atom, stands terrified, knowing that it could be affluent and happy, knowing also that it may perish altogether.

Since in man these two worlds meet with cordiality or with violence, it is clear that there is a kind of knowledge incorporating what is known about society and about physical nature, but larger, more nearly universal than these. It will consist of statements describing the whole complex of relations in which we stand, the welter (as it may appear) of happenings which surge around us, jostling, pushing, driving us upon our destiny. It will consist, further, of statements asserting what goals we seek or ought to seek. And lastly there will be statements composing the master plan by which we are to direct, so far as we may, the whole great process to our human goal.

This congeries of statements — this *system* of them, as we must hope it may become — is philosophy. Its single theme is Man and His Place in Nature. Around this theme are gathered the clusters of knowledge and theory called, in the darkened language of tradition, ontology, epistemology, and ethics. Which words, taken all together, are a deafening way of saying that before mankind attains its ultimate safety, we shall need to know what the world is, how it is known, and to what ends it ought to be controlled.

Generalizations must be large to encompass such subjects. Their very size invites abstractness, as if it were their fate to obscure the labors of lesser but more lively men. This notion is due in part to the fact that the first acknowledged philosophers were leisured aristocrats and the latest are university professors.

It is also due, I fancy, to a certain aloof exercise of philosophical techniques. The thinker, demonstrating his claim to be the "spectator of all time and all existence," abstracts some attribute from the mass and hangs it like a blanket across the stars. Or, preferring the little world to the great, he may show us infinity in the palm of his hand, where the touch is thrilling but the shape is odd.

Though I seem reproachful of these exercises, the truth is that I know them and love them well. They are the sinews of meditation and are no less active for being calm. Scientists, to be sure, have public motion, even hurly-burly, for they are to be found in laboratories, looking through microscopes and into test tubes, and handling with a fine boldness much combustible material. Philosophers are, by habit and by reputation, a much quieter breed. They will be found in armchairs, and, when they are not found in armchairs, they will be found in bed. But this only means that some generalizations can be formulated seated or prone, and perhaps must be formulated that way.

Such, we say, are the habits of philosophers; but I think there are familiar moments when the process shows itself in every life. The mood, which now and then descends, of "What is it all about? What am I doing here?" differs only in precision from Kant's celebrated questions, "What can I know? What ought I to do? What may I hope for?"

It is the genuinely philosophic moods, into which, as most people have it, float scraps of ill-digested sermons, pedagogic homilies, and calendar mottoes. But the authentic content is various insights which experience has suggested and a native intelligence has made shrewd. It is this that gives such pith and pregnancy to folk sayings and emboldens us to hope that the world, which plainly will not be saved by its scientists, will be saved by its people.

PHILOSOPHY AS GUIDE

"Saved by its people"—the phrase suggests that philosophy is more than reflection. For if its people are to save the world by means of some wisdom original with them, they will have to philosophize with a view to guiding their actions. Thus philosophy gives eyes to practice, and practice informs philosophy.

That philosophy is the guide of life is an old boast, not limited to philosophers. It is sententious enough to invite agreement, and it can be made by men whose lives are not conspicuously guided in this way. Yet a precept coined by the richest of Athenian intellects and sanctified by the sufferings of Spinoza will not be much tarnished by inferior use.

There is reason to think, for example, that the philosopher-kings, rather too aristocratically defined by Plato, are an ultimate historical necessity. They will be, not kings, but a commonwealth of knowledgeable persons accustomed to settling problems by general principles. They will appear in that not unimaginable epoch when human science, no longer spent upon fattening an elite, brings treasures to every door.

Meanwhile philosophy needs some effort to make its value known. Part of that value, I suppose, is already recognized in Horace's maxim,

> Aequam memento rebus in arduis
> Servare mentem.

But calm in perplexity and courage under loss are attributes mainly personal. Now that everyone knows how closely each life is linked with others, how impossible the chance of living to oneself, philosophy appears anew, as guide to social action.

For such a use its very substance fits it. That substance, which we have called "Man and His Place in Nature," is also the stuff of politics, for man's political behavior is simply his effort to determine, by conflict as by concord, what his place in nature shall be. To this great theme no science or combination of sciences is adequate, for their generalizations are too small. No art or combination of arts suffices, for their skills govern only segments of the whole. The talent for discussing (so far as may be) all things and all relations, the given and the desired, the means and the end, is philosophy's alone.

If philosophy could not claim leadership by right of content, it would nevertheless acquire it by surrender. The sciences have for many years been as explicit concerning what their content is *not* as concerning what it is. They say, for example, and quite falsely, that they have nothing to do with ethics. The natural sciences say that they have nothing to do with politics — an illusion which not even the hydrogen bomb seems able to explode. And the social sciences, in terror of harboring dangerous knowledge, are beginning to talk as if they had no knowledge at all.

History, however, will not leave undone what scientists are thus neglecting to do. Despite the undoubted possibility, it seems improbable that mankind will permit science to work universal destruction. In conquering at last these lethal uses, mankind will work out the theory and practice which can adapt science entirely to human welfare. The theory and practice thus attained will mark the passage from philosophy militant to philosophy triumphant. I do not suggest that professional philosophers as we now know them are likely to achieve all this, but I do say that it will be achieved and that the men who achieve it may be called philosophers.

STUDY QUESTIONS

1. *Like Russell, Dunham is concerned to define philosophy and to assess its place and value in our lives. But his approach is highly informal compared with that of Russell. Point out significant differences in sentence structure and in vocabulary in the two essays. What other devices does Dunham use to make his writing appealing to the lay reader?*

2. *What kind of reader might prefer Russell? Dunham? Is one of the selections "better" than the other? Is one more informative? More accurate?*

3. *Try to construct a definition of philosophy from Dunham's observations. What is the relation of philosophy to other fields of learning? How does Dunham think the invention of the H-bomb will affect the practice of philosophy?*

4. *Is the "reflection" which Dunham describes like or unlike the "reflective thinking" which Dewey defines in "What is Thinking"?*

5. *In a part of this piece, Dunham shows how philosophy enters into everyday life. Write a theme showing how some field of study in which you are interested is involved in ordinary daily experience. Good possibilities are history, economics, or any of the sciences, though nearly every subject you have studied is also a possibility.*

6. *What was your idea of philosophy prior to reading Russell and Dunham in these selections? Write a paper in which you define your previous conception of philosophy, and assess the contribution which these two selections have made to your understanding.*

Plato   The Allegory of the Cave *

And now, I said, let me show in a figure how far nature is enlightened or unenlightened: — Behold! human beings living in an underground den, which has a mouth open towards the light and reaching all along the den; here they have been from their childhood, and have their legs and necks chained so that they cannot move, and can only see before them, being prevented by the chains from turning round their heads. Above and behind them a fire is blazing at a distance, and between the fire and the prisoners there is a raised way; and you will see, if you look, a low wall built along the way, like the screen which marionette players have in front of them, over which they show the puppets.

I see.

And do you see, I said, men passing along the wall carrying all sorts of vessels, and statues and figures of animals made of wood and stone and various materials, which appear over the wall? Some of them are talking, others silent.

You have shown me a strange image, and they are strange prisoners.

Like ourselves, I replied; and they see only their own shadows, or the shadows of one another, which the fire throws on the opposite wall of the cave?

True, he said; how could they see anything but the shadows if they were never allowed to move their heads?

And of the objects which are being carried in like manner they would only see the shadows?

Yes, he said.

And if they were able to converse with one another, would they not suppose that they were naming what was actually before them?

Very true.

And suppose further that the prison had an echo which came from the other side, would they not be sure to fancy when one of the passers-by spoke that the voice which they heard came from the passing shadow?

No question, he replied.

To them, I said, the truth would be literally nothing but the shadows of the images.

That is certain.

And now look again, and see what will naturally follow if the prisoners are released and disabused of their error. At first, when any of them is liberated

* From *The Republic*, translated by Benjamin Jowett.

and compelled suddenly to stand up and turn his neck round and walk and look towards the light, he will suffer sharp pains; the glare will distress him, and he will be unable to see the realities of which in his former state he had seen the shadows; and then conceive some one saying to him, that what he saw before was an illusion, but that now, when he is approaching nearer to being and his eye is turned towards more real existence, he has a clearer vision, — what will be his reply? And you may further imagine that his instructor is pointing to the objects as they pass and requiring him to name them, — will he not be perplexed? Will he not fancy that the shadows which he formerly saw are truer than the objects which are now shown to him?

Far truer.

And if he is compelled to look straight at the light, will he not have a pain in his eyes which will make him turn away to take refuge in the objects of vision which he can see, and which he will conceive to be in reality clearer than the things which are now being shown to him?

True, he said.

And suppose once more, that he is reluctantly dragged up a steep and rugged ascent, and held fast until he is forced into the presence of the sun himself, is he not likely to be pained and irritated? When he approaches the light his eyes will be dazzled, and he will not be able to see anything at all of what are now called realities.

Not all in a moment, he said.

He will require to grow accustomed to the sight of the upper world. And first he will see the shadows best, next the reflections of men and other objects in the water, and then the objects themselves; then he will gaze upon the light of the moon and the stars and the spangled heaven; and he will see the sky and the stars by night better than the sun or the light of the sun by day?

Certainly.

Last of all he will be able to see the sun, and not mere reflections of him in the water, but he will see him in his own proper place, and not in another; and he will contemplate him as he is.

Certainly.

He will then proceed to argue that this is he who gives the season and the years, and is the guardian of all that is in the visible world, and in a certain way the cause of all things which he and his fellows have been accustomed to behold?

Clearly, he said, he would first see the sun and then reason about him.

And when he remembered his old habitation, and the wisdom of the den and his fellow-prisoners, do you not suppose that he would felicitate himself on the change, and pity them?

Certainly, he would.

And if they were in the habit of conferring honours among themselves on those who were quickest to observe the passing shadows and to remark which of them went before, and which followed after, and which were together;

and who were therefore best able to draw conclusions as to the future, do you think that he would care for such honours and glories, or envy the possessors of them? Would he not say with Homer,

> Better, to be the poor servant of a poor master,

and to endure anything, rather than think as they do and live after their manner?

Yes, he said, I think that he would rather suffer anything than entertain these false notions and live in this miserable manner.

Imagine once more, I said, such an one coming suddenly out of the sun to be replaced in his old situation; would he not be certain to have his eyes full of darkness?

To be sure, he said.

And if there were a contest, and he had to compete in measuring the shadows with the prisoners who had never moved out of the den, while his sight was still weak, and before his eyes had become steady (and the time which would be needed to acquire this new habit of sight might be very considerable) would he not be ridiculous? Men would say of him that up he went and down he came without his eyes; and that it was better not even to think of ascending; and if any one tried to loose another and lead him up to the light, let them only catch the offender, and they would put him to death.

No question, he said.

This entire allegory, I said, you may now append, dear Glaucon, to the previous argument; the prison-house is the world of sight, the light of the fire is the sun, and you will not misapprehend me if you interpret the journey upwards to be the ascent of the soul into the intellectual world according to my poor belief, which, at your desire, I have expressed — whether rightly or wrongly God knows. But, whether true or false, my opinion is that in the world of knowledge the idea of good appears last of all, and is seen only with an effort; and, when seen, is also inferred to be the universal author of all things beautiful and right, parent of light and of the lord of light in this visible world, and the immediate source of reason and truth in the intellectual; and that this is the power upon which he who would act rationally either in public or private life must have his eye fixed.

I agree, he said, as far as I am able to understand you.

Moreover, I said, you must not wonder that those who attain to this beatific vision are unwilling to descend to human affairs; for their souls are ever hastening into the upper world where they desire to dwell; which desire of theirs is very natural, if our allegory may be trusted.

Yes, very natural.

And is there anything surprising in one who passes from divine contemplations to the evil state of man, misbehaving himself in a ridiculous manner; if, while his eyes are blinking and before he has become accustomed to the surrounding darkness, he is compelled to fight in courts of law, or in other places, about the images or the shadows of images of justice, and is endeavouring to meet the conceptions of those who have never yet seen absolute justice?

Anything but surprising, he replied.

Any one who has common sense will remember that the bewilderments of the eyes are of two kinds, and arise from two causes, either from coming out of the light or from going into the light, which is true of the mind's eye, quite as much as of the bodily eye; and he who remembers this when he sees any one whose vision is perplexed and weak, will not be too ready to laugh; he will first ask whether that soul of man has come out of the brighter life, and is unable to see because unaccustomed to the dark, or having turned from darkness to the day is dazzled by excess of light. And he will count the one happy in his condition and state of being, and he will pity the other; or, if he have a mind to laugh at the soul which comes from below into the light, there will be more reason in this than in the laugh which greets him who returns from above out of the light into the den.

That, he said, is a very just distinction.

But then, if I am right, certain professors of education must be wrong when they say that they can put a knowledge into the soul which was not there before, like sight into blind eyes.

They undoubtedly say this, he replied.

Whereas, our argument shows that the power and capacity of learning exists in the soul already; and that just as the eye was unable to turn from darkness to light without the whole body, so too the instrument of knowledge can only by the movement of the whole soul be turned from the world of becoming into that of being, and learn by degrees to endure the sight of being, and of the brightest and best of being, or in other words, of the good.

STUDY QUESTIONS

1. *In this allegory, what does the cave represent? The prison house? The outside sunshine? What advantage does Plato gain from presenting his argument in concrete, figurative language instead of in more abstract terms?*

2. *What is symbolized by the pain experienced by the man who goes into the light for the first time?*

3. *What possibilities of mutual understanding existed between those who remained in the cave and those who were exiled from it?*

4. *Does Plato offer any definite evidence to support his contention that it is better to know reality directly? Or is it supported in other ways?*

5. *What place in this allegory is occupied by the objects and institutions of everyday life that represent justice?*

6. *Since the prisoners of the cave can see only shadows, are not these shadows reality as far as they are concerned? Could they not continue to think and act as they did, as long as none of them could see beyond the shadows?*

Arthur S. Eddington

The Nature of the Physical World*

I have settled down to the task of writing these lectures and have drawn up my chairs to my two tables. Two tables! Yes; there are duplicates of every object about me—two tables, two chairs, two pens.

This is not a very profound beginning to a course which ought to reach transcendent levels of scientific philosophy. But we cannot touch bedrock immediately; we must scratch a bit of the surface of things first. And whenever I begin to scratch the first thing I strike is—my two tables.

One of them has been familiar to me from earliest years. It is a commonplace object of that environment which I call the world. How shall I describe it? It has extension; it is comparatively permanent; it is colored; above all it is substantial. By substantial I do not merely mean that it does not collapse when I lean upon it; I mean that it is constituted of "substance" and by that word I am trying to convey to you some conception of its intrinsic nature. It is a *thing*; not like space, which is a mere negation; nor like time, which is— Heaven knows what! But that will not help you to my meaning because it is the distinctive characteristic of a "thing" to have this substantiality, and I do not think substantiality can be described better than by saying that it is the kind of nature exemplified by an ordinary table. And so we go round in circles. After all if you are a plain common-sense man, not too much worried with scientific scruples, you will be confident that you understand the nature of an ordinary table. I have even heard of plain men who had the idea that they could better understand the mystery of their own nature if scientists would discover a way of explaining it in terms of the easily comprehensible nature of a table.

Table No. 2 is my scientific table. It is a more recent acquaintance and I do not feel so familiar with it. It does not belong to the world previously mentioned—that world which spontaneously appears around me when I open my eyes, though how much of it is objective and how much subjective I do not here consider. It is part of a world which in more devious ways has forced itself on my attention. My scientific table is mostly emptiness. Sparsely scattered in that emptiness are numerous electric charges rushing about with great speed; but their combined bulk amounts to less than a billionth of the bulk of the table itself. Notwithstanding its strange construction it turns out to be an entirely efficient table. It supports my writing paper as satisfactorily as

* From *The Nature of the Physical World* by Sir Arthur S. Eddington, by permission of the Cambridge University Press. Copyright, 1928, by Cambridge University Press.

table No. 1; for when I lay the paper on it the little electric particles with their headlong speed keep on hitting the underside, so that the paper is maintained in shuttlecock fashion at a nearly steady level. If I lean upon this table I shall not go through; or, to be strictly accurate, the chance of my scientific elbow going through my scientific table is so excessively small that it can be neglected in practical life. Reviewing their properties one by one, there seems to be nothing to choose between the two tables for ordinary purposes; but when abnormal circumstances befall, then my scientific table shows to advantage. If the house catches fire my scientific table will dissolve quite naturally into scientific smoke, whereas my familiar table undergoes a metamorphosis of its substantial nature which I can only regard as miraculous.

There is nothing substantial about my second table. It is nearly all empty space—space pervaded, it is true, by fields of force, but these are assigned to the category of "influences," not of "things." Even in the minute part which is not empty we must not transfer the old notion of substance. In dissecting matter into electric charges we have traveled far from that picture of it which first gave rise to the conception of substance, and the meaning of that conception—if it ever had any—has been lost by the way. The whole trend of modern scientific views is to break down the separate categories of "things," "influences," "forms," etc., and to substitute a common background of all experience. Whether we are studying a material object, a magnetic field, a geometrical figure, or a duration of time, our scientific information is summed up in measures; neither the apparatus of measurement nor the mode of using it suggests that there is anything essentially different in these problems. The measures themselves afford no ground for a classification by categories. We feel it necessary to concede some background to the measures—an external world; but the attributes of this world, except in so far as they are reflected in the measures, are outside scientific scrutiny. Science has at last revolted against attaching the exact knowledge contained in these measurements to a traditional picture-gallery of conceptions which convey no authentic information of the background and obtrude irrelevancies into the scheme of knowledge.

I will not here stress further the nonsubstantiality of electrons, since it is scarcely necessary to the present line of thought. Conceive them as substantially as you will, there is a vast difference between my scientific table with its substance (if any) thinly scattered in specks in a region mostly empty and the table of every day conception which we regard as the type of solid reality —an incarnate protest against Berkeleian subjectivism. It makes all the difference in the world whether the paper before me is poised as it were on a swarm of flies and sustained in shuttlecock fashion by a series of tiny blows from the swarm underneath, or whether it is supported because there is substance below it, it being the intrinsic nature of substance to occupy space to the exclusion of other substance; all the difference in conception at least, but no difference to my practical task of writing on the paper.

I need not tell you that modern physics has by delicate test and remorseless logic assured me that my second scientific table is the only one which is really there—wherever "there" may be. On the other hand I need not tell you that modern physics will never succeed in exorcising that first table—strange compound of external nature, mental imagery and inherited prejudice—which lies visible to my eyes and tangible to my grasp. We must bid good-bye to it for the present for we are about to turn from the familiar world to the scientific world revealed by physics. This is, or is intended to be, a wholly external world.

"You speak paradoxically of two worlds. Are they not really two aspects or two interpretations of one and the same world?"

Yes, no doubt they are ultimately to be identified after some fashion. But the process by which the external world of physics is transformed into a world of familiar acquaintance in human consciousness is outside the scope of physics. And so the world studied according to the methods of physics remains detached from the world familiar to consciousness, until after the physicist has finished his labors upon it. Provisionally, therefore, we regard the table which is the subject of physical research as altogether separate from the familiar table, without prejudging the question of their ultimate identification. It is true that the whole scientific inquiry starts from the familiar world and in the end it must return to the familiar world; but the part of the journey over which the physicist has charge is in foreign territory.

Until recently there was a much closer linkage; the physicist used to borrow the raw material of his world from the familiar world, but he does so no longer. His raw materials are aether, electrons, quanta, potentials, Hamiltonian functions, etc., and he is nowadays scrupulously careful to guard these from contamination by conceptions borrowed from the other world. There is a familiar table parallel to the scientific table, but there is no familiar electron, quantum or potential parallel to the scientific electron, quantum or potential. We do not even desire to manufacture a familiar counterpart to these things or, as we should commonly say, to "explain" the electron. After the physicist has quite finished his world-building a linkage or identification is allowed; but premature attempts at linkage have been found to be entirely mischievous.

Science aims at constructing a world which shall be symbolic of the world of commonplace experience. It is not at all necessary that every individual symbol that is used should represent something in common experience or even something explicable in terms of common experience. The man in the street is always making this demand for concrete explanation of the things referred to in science; but of necessity he must be disappointed. It is like our experience in learning to read. That which is written in a book is symbolic of a story in real life. The whole intention of the book is that ultimately a reader will identify some symbol, say BREAD, with one of the conceptions of familiar life. But it is mischievous to attempt such identifications prematurely, before the letters are strung into words and the words into sentences. The symbol A is not the counterpart of anything in familiar life. To the child the letter

A would seem horribly abstract; so we give him a familiar conception along with it. "*A* was an Archer who shot at a frog." This tides over his immediate difficulty; but he cannot make serious progress with word-building so long as Archers, Butchers, Captains dance round the letters. The letters are abstract, and sooner or later he has to realize it. In physics we have outgrown archer and apple-pie definitions of the fundamental symbols. To a request to explain what an electron really is supposed to be we can only answer, "It is part of the A B C of physics."

The external world of physics has thus become a world of shadows. In removing our illusions we have removed the substance for indeed we have seen that substance is one of the greatest of our illusions. Later perhaps we may inquire whether in our zeal to cut out all that is unreal we may not have used the knife too ruthlessly. Perhaps, indeed, reality is a child which cannot survive without its nurse illusion. But if so, that is of little concern to the scientist, who has good and sufficient reasons for pursuing his investigations in the world of shadows and is content to leave to the philosopher the determination of its exact status in regard to reality. In the world of physics we watch a shadowgraph performance of the drama of familiar life. The shadow of my elbow rests on the shadow table as the shadow ink flows over the shadow paper. It is all symbolic, and as a symbol the physicist leaves it. Then comes the alchemist Mind who transmutes the symbols. The sparsely spread nuclei of electric force become a tangible solid; their restless agitation becomes the warmth of summer; the octave of aethereal vibrations becomes a gorgeous rainbow. Nor does the alchemy stop here. In the transmuted world new significances arise which are scarcely to be traced in the world of symbols; so that it becomes a world of beauty and purpose — and, alas, suffering and evil.

The frank realization that physical science is concerned with a world of shadows is one of the most significant of recent advances. I do not mean that physicists are to any extent preoccupied with the philosophical implications of this. From their point of view it is not so much a withdrawal of untenable claims as an assertion of freedom for autonomous development. At the moment I am not insisting on the shadowy and symbolic character of the world of physics because of its bearing on philosophy, but because the aloofness from familiar conceptions will be apparent in the scientific theories I have to describe. If you are not prepared for this aloofness you are likely to be out of sympathy with modern scientific theories, and may even think them ridiculous — as, I daresay, many people do.

It is difficult to school ourselves to treat the physical world as purely symbolic. We are always relapsing and mixing with the symbols incongruous conceptions taken from the world of consciousness. Untaught by long experience we stretch a hand to grasp the shadow, instead of accepting its shadowy nature. Indeed, unless we confine ourselves altogether to mathematical symbolism it is hard to avoid dressing our symbols in deceitful cloth·

ing. When I think of an electron there rises to my mind a hard, red, tiny ball; the proton similarly is neutral gray. Of course the color is absurd — perhaps not more absurd than the rest of the conception — but I am incorrigible. I can well understand that the younger minds are finding these pictures too concrete and are striving to construct the world out of Hamiltonian functions and symbols so far removed from human preconception that they do not even obey the laws of orthodox arithmetic. For myself I find some difficulty in rising to that plane of thought; but I am convinced that it has got to come. . . .

STUDY QUESTIONS

1. *Divide this selection into its main parts. What does Eddington accomplish by opening with the comparison of the two tables? Would his explanation have been clearer if he had outlined his abstract idea first and then used the example of the two tables as illustration?*

2. *What, exactly, does Eddington mean when he says that science aims at constructing a world which is "symbolic of the world of commonplace experience"? Does his comparison of this process with that of learning to read help us to understanding his meaning here? Is it a good comparison? Why?*

3. *What effect does the description of the physical world given by Eddington have upon the possibility of defining such terms as* real *and* reality?

4. *In such a world as Eddington describes, what is the value of "common sense"? What does Eddington mean by suggesting that reality cannot survive without illusion? Is this "common sense"?*

5. *What comfort might a poet, philosopher, theologian, or other person occupied with a non-scientific discipline take in Eddington's description of the natural world?*

6. *Write a vivid and clear account of some piece of scientific knowledge intended for readers to whom this knowledge is unfamiliar.*

George Santayana

Understanding, Imagination, and Mysticism*

When we consider the situation of the human mind in Nature, its limited plasticity and few channels of communication with the outer world, we need not wonder that we grope for light, or that we find incoherence and instability in human systems of ideas. The wonder rather is that we have done so well, that in the chaos of sensations and passions that fills the mind,

* From *Interpretations of Poetry and Religion* by George Santayana, reprinted by permission of Charles Scribner's Sons.

we have found any leisure for self-concentration and reflection, and have succeeded in gathering even a light harvest of experience from our distracted labours. Our occasional madness is less wonderful than our occasional sanity. Relapses into dreams are to be expected in a being whose brief existence is so like a dream; but who could have been sure of this sturdy and indomitable perseverance in the work of reason in spite of all checks and discouragements?

The resources of the mind are not commensurate with its ambition. Of the five senses, three are of little use in the formation of permanent notions: a fourth, sight, is indeed vivid and luminous, but furnishes transcripts of things so highly coloured and deeply modified by the medium of sense, that a long labour of analysis and correction is needed before satisfactory conceptions can be extracted from it. For this labour, however, we are endowed with the requisite instrument. We have memory and we have certain powers of synthesis, abstraction, reproduction, invention, — in a word, we have understanding. But this faculty of understanding has hardly begun its work of deciphering the hieroglyphics of sense and framing an idea of reality, when it is crossed by another faculty — the imagination. Perceptions do not remain in the mind, as would be suggested by the trite simile of the seal and the wax, passive and changeless, until time wear off their sharp edges and make them fade. No, perceptions fall into the brain rather as seeds into a furrowed field or even as sparks into a keg of powder. Each image breeds a hundred more, sometimes slowly and subterraneously, sometimes (when a passionate train is started) with a sudden burst of fancy. The mind, exercised by its own fertility and flooded by its inner lights, has infinite trouble to keep a true reckoning of its outward perceptions. It turns from the frigid problems of observations to its own visions; it forgets to watch the courses of what should be its "pilot stars." Indeed, were it not for the power of convention in which, by a sort of mutual cancellation of errors, the more practical and normal conceptions are enshrined, the imagination would carry men wholly away, — the best men first and the vulgar after them. Even as it is, individuals and ages of fervid imagination usually waste themselves in dreams, and must disappear before the race, saddened and dazed, perhaps, by the memory of those visions, can return to its plodding thoughts.

Five senses, then, to gather a small part of the infinite influences, that vibrate in Nature, a moderate power of understanding to interpret those senses, and an irregular, passionate fancy to overlay that interpretation — such is the endowment of the human mind. And what is its ambition? Nothing less than to construct a picture of all reality, to comprehend its own origin and that of the universe, to discover the laws of both and prophesy their destiny. Is not the disproportion enormous? Are not confusions and profound contradictions to be looked for in an attempt to build so much out of so little?

Yet the metaphysical ambition we speak of cannot be abandoned, because whatever picture of things we may carry about in our heads we are bound to regard as a map of reality; although we may mark certain tracts of it "unexplored country," the very existence of such regions is vouched for only by our representation, and is necessarily believed to correspond to our idea. All we can do is, without abandoning the aspiration to knowledge which is the inalienable birthright of reason, to control as best we may the formation of our conceptions; to arrange them according to their derivation and measure them by their applicability in life, so prudently watching over their growth that we may be spared the deepest of sorrows — to survive the offspring of our own thought.

The inadequacy of each of our faculties is what occasions the intrusion of some other faculty into its field. The defect of sense calls in imagination, the defect of imagination calls in reasoning, the defect of reasoning, divination. If our senses were clairvoyant and able to observe all that is going on in the world, if our instincts were steady, prompting us to adequate reactions upon these observations, the fancy might remain free. We should not need to call upon it to piece out the imperfections of sense and reflection, but we should employ it only in avowed poetry, only in building dream-worlds alongside of the real, not interfering with the latter or confusing it, but repeating its pattern with as many variations as the fertility of our minds could supply. As it is, the imagination is brought into the service of sense and instinct, and made to do the work of intelligence. This substitution is the more readily effected, in that imagination and intelligence do not differ in their origin, but only in their validity. Understanding is an applicable fiction, a kind of wit with a practical use. Common sense and science live in a world of expurgated mythology, such as Plato wished his poets to compose, a world where the objects are imaginative in their origin and essence, but useful, abstract, and beneficent in their suggestions. The sphere of common sense and science is concentric with the sphere of fancy; both move in virtue of the same imaginative impulses. The eventual distinction between intelligence and imagination is ideal; it arises when we discriminate various functions in a life that is dynamically one. Those conceptions which, after they have spontaneously arisen, prove serviceable in practice, and capable of verification in sense, we call ideas of the understanding. The others remain ideas of the imagination. The shortness of life, the distractions of passion, and the misrepresentation to which all transmitted knowledge is subject, have made the testing of ideas by practice extremely slow in the history of mankind. Hence the impurity of our knowledge, its confusion with fancy, and its painful inadequacy to interpret the whole world of human interests. These shortcomings are so many invitations to foreign powers to intervene, so many occasions for new waves of imagination to sweep away the landmarks of our old labour, and flood the whole mind with impetuous dreams.

It is accordingly the profounder minds that commonly yield to the imagination, because it is these minds that are capable of feeling the greatness of the problems of life and the inadequacy of the understanding, with its present resources, to solve them. The same minds are, moreover, often swayed by emotion, by the ever-present desire to find a noble solution to all questions, perhaps a solution already hallowed by authority and intertwined inextricably, for those who have always accepted it, with the sanctions of spiritual life. Such a coveted conclusion may easily be one which the understanding, with its basis in sense and its demand for verification, may not be able to reach. Therefore the impassioned soul must pass beyond the understanding, or else go unsatisfied; and unless it be as disciplined as it is impassioned it will not tolerate dissatisfaction. From what quarter, then, will it draw the wider views, the deeper harmonies, which it craves? Only from the imagination. There is no other faculty left to invoke. The imagination, therefore, must furnish to religion and to metaphysics those large ideas tinctured with passion, those supersensible forms shrouded in awe, in which alone a mind of great sweep and vitality can find its congenial objects. Thus the stone which the builder, understanding, rejected, becomes the chief stone of the corner; the intuitions which science could not use remain the inspiration of poetry and religion.

The imagination, when thus employed to anticipate or correct the conclusions of the understanding, is of course not called imagination by those who appeal to it. The religious teachers call it prophecy or revelation, the philosophers call it a higher reason. But these names are merely eulogistic synonyms for imagination, implying (what is perfectly possible) that the imagination has not misled us. They imply on the contrary that in the given instances the imagination has hit upon an ultimate truth. A prophet, unless he be the merely mechanical vehicle of truths he does not understand, cannot be conceived as anything but a man of imagination, whose visions miraculously mirror the truth. A metaphysician who transcends the intellect by his reason can be conceived only as using his imagination to such good purpose as to divine by it the ideal laws of reality or the ultimate goals of moral effort. His reason is an imagination that succeeds, an intuition that guesses the principle of experience. But if this intuition were of such a nature that experience could verify it, then that higher reason or imagination would be brought down to the level of the understanding; for understanding, as we have defined it, is itself a kind of imagination, an imagination prophetic of experience, a spontaneity of thought by which the science of perception is turned into the art of life. The same absence of verification distinguishes revelation from science; for when the prophecies of faith are verified, the function of faith is gone. Faith and the higher reason of the metaphysicians are therefore forms of imagination believed to be avenues to truth, as dreams or oracles may sometimes be truthful, not because their necessary correspondence to truth can be demonstrated, for then they would be portions of science, but because a man dwelling on those intuitions is conscious of a certain moral transformation, of a certain warmth and energy of life. This emotion, heightening his ideas and giving them power over his will, he calls faith or high philosophy, and under its dominion he is able to face his destiny with enthusiasm, or at least with composure.

The imagination, even when its premonitions are not wholly justified by subsequent experience, has thus a noble rôle to play in the life of man. Without it his thoughts would be not only far too narrow to represent, although it were symbolically, the greatness of the universe, but far too narrow even to render the scope of his own life and the conditions of his practical welfare. Without poetry and religion the history of mankind would have been darker than it is. Not only would emotional life have been poorer, but the public conscience, the national and family spirit, so useful for moral organization and discipline, would hardly have become articulate. By what a complex and uninspired argumentation would the pure moralist have to insist upon those duties which the imagination enforces so powerfully in oaths sworn before the gods, in commandments written by the finger of God upon stone tablets, in visions of hell and heaven, in chivalrous love and loyalty, and in the sense of family dignity and honour? What intricate, what unavailing appeals to positive interests would have to be made before those quick reactions could be secured in large bodies of people which can be produced by the sight of a flag or the sound of a name? The imagination is the great unifier of humanity. Men's perceptions may be various, their powers of understanding very unequal; but the imagination is, as it were, the self-consciousness of instinct, the contribution which the inner capacity and demand of the mind makes to experience. To indulge the imagination is to express the universal self, the common and contagious element in all individuals, that rudimentary potency which they all share. To stimulate the imagination is to produce the deepest, the most pertinacious emotions. To repress it is to chill the soul, so that even the clearest perception of the truth remains without the joy and impetuosity of conviction.

The part played by imagination is thus indispensable; but obviously the necessity and beneficence of this contribution makes the dangers of it correspondingly great. Wielding a great power, exercising an omnipresent function, the imagination may abuse a great force. While its inspirations coincide with what would be the dictates of reason, were reason audible in the world, all is well, and the progress of man is accelerated by his visions; but being a principle *a priori* the imagination is an irresponsible principle; its rightness is an inward rightness, and everything in the real world may turn out to be disposed otherwise than as it would wish. Our imaginative preconceptions are then obstacles to the perception of fact and of rational duty; the faith that stimulated our efforts and increased our momentum, multiplies our wanderings. The too hasty organization of our thoughts becomes the cause of their more prolonged disorganization, for to the natural obscurity of things and the difficulty of making them fit together among themselves, we add the cross lights of our prejudices and the impossibility of fitting reality into the frame we have made for it in our ignorance of its constitution and extent. And as we love our hopes, and detest the experience that seems to contradict them, we add fanaticism to our confusion. The habits of the imagination, in conflict with the facts of sense, thus come to cloud science with passion, with fiction, with sentimental prejudice. Nor is this the end of our troubles. For Imagination herself suffers violence in this struggle; she seeks to reduce herself to conformity with existence, in the hope of vindicating her nominal authority at the price of some concessions. She begins to feign that she demanded nothing but what she finds. Thus she loses her honesty and freedom, becomes a flatterer of things instead of the principle of their ideal correction, and in the attempt to prove herself prophetic and literally valid (as in a moment of infatuation she had fancied herself to be) she forfeits that symbolic truth, that inner propriety, which gave her a moral value. Thus the false steps of the imagination lead to a contorted science and to a servile ideal.

These complications not unnaturally inspire discouragement and a sense of the hopeless relativity of human thought. Indeed, if there be any special endowment of mind and body called human nature, as there seems to be, it is obvious that all human experience must be relative to that. But the truth, the absolute reality, surrounds and precedes these operations of finite faculty. What value, then, we may say, have these various ideals or perceptions, or the conflicts between them? Are not our senses as human, as "subjective" as our wills? Is not the understanding as visionary as the fancy? Does it not transform the Unknowable into as remote a symbol as does the vainest dream?

The answer which a rational philosophy would make to these questions would be a double one. It is true that every idea is equally relative to human nature and that nothing can be represented in the human mind except by the operation of human faculties. But it is not true that all these products of human ideation are of equal value, since they are not equally conducive to human purposes or satisfactory to human demands.

The impulse that would throw over as equally worthless every product of human art, because it is not indistinguishable from some alleged external reality, does not perceive the serious self-contradictions under which it labours. In the first place the notion of an external reality is a human notion; our reason makes that hypothesis, and its verification in our experience is one of the ideals of science, as its validity is one of the assumptions of daily life. In throwing over all human ideas, because they are infected with humanity, all human ideas are being sacrificed to one of them — the idea of an absolute reality. If this idea, being human, deserved that such sacrifices should be made for it, have the other notions of the mind no rights? Furthermore, even if we granted for the sake of argument a reality which our thoughts were essentially helpless to represent, whence comes the duty of our thoughts to represent it? Whence comes the value of this unattainable truth? From an ideal of human reason. We covet truth. So that the attempt to surrender all human science as relative and all human ideals as trivial is founded on a blind belief in one human idea and an absolute surrender to one human passion.

In spite of these contradictions, which only a dispassionate logic could thoroughly unravel, the enthusiast is apt to rush on. The vision of absolute truth and absolute reality intoxicates him, and as he is too subtle a thinker, too inward a man, to accept the content of his senses or the conventions of his intelligence for unqualified verities, he fortifies himself against them with the consciousness of their relativity, and seeks to rise above them in his mediations. But to rise to what? To some more elaborate idea? To some object, like a scientific cosmos or a religious creed, put together by longer and more indirect processes than those of common perception? Surely not. If I renounce my senses and vulgar intellect because they are infected with finitude and smell of humanity, how shall I accept a work of art, a product of reasoning, or an idol made originally with hands and now encrusted all over, like the statue of Glaucus, with traditional accretions? Poetry, science, and religion, in their positive constructions, are more human, more conditioned, than are the senses and the common understanding themselves. The lover of inviolate reality must not look to them. If the data of human knowledge must be rejected as subjective, how much more should we reject the inferences made from those data by human thought. The way of true wisdom, therefore, if true wisdom is to deal with the Absolute, can only lie in abstention: neither the senses nor the common understanding, and much less the superstructure raised upon these by imagination, logic, or tradition, must delude us: we must keep our thoughts fixed upon the inanity of all this in comparison with the unthinkable truth, with the undivided and unimaginable reality. Everything, says the mystic, is nothing, in comparison with the One.

This confusion, the logical contradiction of which we have just seen, may, for lack of a more specific word, be called mysticism. It consists in the surrender of a category of thought on account of the discovery of its relativity. If I saw or reasoned or judged by such a category, I should be seeing, reasoning, or judging in a specific manner, in a manner conditioned by my finite nature. But the specific and the finite, I feel, are odious; let me therefore aspire to see, reason and judge in no specific or finite manner — that is, not to see, reason or judge at all. So I shall be like the Infinite, nay I shall become one with the Infinite and (marvellous thought!) one with the One.

The ideal of mysticism is accordingly exactly contrary to the ideal of reason; instead of perfecting human nature it seeks to abolish it; instead of building a better world, it would undermine the foundations even of the world we have built already; instead of developing our mind to greater scope and precision, it would return to the condition of protoplasm — to the blessed consciousness of an Unutterable Reality. In the primary stages, of course, mysticism does not venture to abolish all our ideas, or to renounce all our categories of thought. Thus many Christian mystics have still clung, out of respect for authority, to traditional theology, and many philosophical mystics have made some room for life and science in the postscripts which they, like

Parmenides, have appended to the blank monism of their systems. But such concessions or hesitations are inconsistent with the mystical spirit which will never be satisfied, if fully developed and fearless, with anything short of Absolute Nothing.

For the very reason, however, that mysticism is a tendency to obliterate distinctions, a partial mysticism often serves to bring out with wonderful intensity those underlying strata of experience which it has not yet decomposed. The razing of the edifice of reason may sometimes discover its foundations. Or the disappearance of one department of activity may throw the mind with greater energy into another. So Spinoza, who combined mysticism in morals with rationalism in science, can bring out the unqualified naturalism of his system with a purity and impressiveness impossible to men who still retain an ideal world, and seek to direct endeavour as well as to describe it. Having renounced all ideal categories, Spinoza has only the material categories left with which to cover the ground. He thus acquires all the concentrated intensity, all the splendid narrowness, which had belonged to Lucretius, while his mystical treatment of the spheres which Lucretius simply ignored, gives him the appearance of a greater profundity. So an ordinary Christian who is mystical, let us say, about time and space, may use his transcendentalism in that sphere to intensify his positivism in theology, and to emphasize his whole-souled surrender to a devout life.

What is impossible is to be a transcendentalist "all 'round." In that case there would be nothing left to transcend; the civil war of the mind would have ended in the extermination of all parties. The art of mysticism is to be mystical in spots and to aim the heavy guns of your transcendental philosophy against those realities or those ideas which you find particularly galling. Planted on your dearest dogma, on your most precious postulate, you may then transcend everything else to your heart's content. You may say with an air of enlightened profundity that nothing is "really" right or wrong, because in Nature all things are regular and necessary, and God cannot act for purposes as if his will were not already accomplished; your mysticism in religion and morals is kept standing, as it were, by the stiff backing which is furnished by your materialistic cosmology. Or you may say with a tone of devout rapture that all sights and sounds are direct messages from Divine Providence to the soul, without any objects "really" existing in space; your mysticism about the world of perception and scientific inference is sustained by the naïve theological dogmas which you substitute for the conceptions of common sense. Yet among these partialities and blind denials a man's positive insight seems to thrive, and he fortifies and concentrates himself on his chosen ground by his arbitrary exclusions. The patient art of rationalizing the various sides of life, the observational as well as the moral, without confusing them, is an art apparently seldom given to the haste and pugnacity of philosophers.

Thus mysticism, although a principle of dissolution, carries with it the safeguard that it can never be consistently applied. We reach it only in exceptional moments of intuition, from which we descend to our pots and pans with habits and instincts virtually unimpaired. Life goes on; virtues and affections endure, none the worse, the mystic feels, for that slight film of unreality which envelops them in a mind not unacquainted with ecstasy. And although mysticism, left free to express itself, can have no other goal than Nirvana, yet moderately indulged in and duly inhibited by a residuum of conventional sanity, it serves to give a touch of strangeness and elevation to the character and to suggest superhuman gifts. It is not, however, in the least superhuman. It is hardly even abnormal, being only an exaggeration of a rational interest in the highest abstractions. The divine, the universal, the absolute, even the One, are legitimate conceptions. They are terms of human thought having as such a meaning in language and a place in speculation. Those who live in the mind, whose passions are only audible in the keen overtones of dialectic, are no doubt exalted and privileged natures, choosing a better part which should not be taken from them. So the poet and the mathematician have their spheres of abstract and delicate labour, in which a liberal legislator would not disturb them. Trouble only arises when the dialectician represents his rational dreams as knowledge of existences, and the mystic his excusable raptures as the only way of life. Poets and mathematicians do not imagine that their pursuits raise them above human limitations and are no part of human life, but rather its only goal and justification. Such a pretension would be regarded as madness in the mathematician or the poet; and is not the mystic as miserably a man? Is he not embodying, at his best, the analytic power of a logician, or the imagination of an enthusiast, and, at his worst, the lowest and most obscure passions of human nature?

Yes, in spite of himself, the mystic remains human. Nothing is more normal than abstraction. A contemplative mind drops easily its practical preoccupations, raises easily into an ideal sympathy with impersonal things. The wheels of the universe have a wonderful magnetism for the human will. Our consciousness likes to lose itself in the music of the spheres, a music that finer ears are sometimes privileged to catch. The better side of mysticism is an aesthetic interest in large unities and cosmic laws. The aesthetic attitude is not the moral, but it is not for that reason illegitimate. It gives us refreshment and a foretaste of that perfect adaptation of things to our faculties and of our faculties to things which, could it extend to every part of experience, would constitute the ideal life. Such happiness is denied us in the concrete; but a hint and example of it may be gathered by an abstracted element of our nature as it travels through an abstracted world. Such an indulgence adds to the value of reality only such value as it may itself have in momentary experience; it may have a doubtful moral effect on the happy dreamer himself. But it serves to keep alive the conviction, which a confused experience might obscure, that perfection is essentially possible; it reminds us, like music, that there are worlds far removed from the actual which are yet living and very near to the heart. Such is the fruit of abstraction when abstraction bears any fruit. If the imagination merely alienates us from reality, without giving us either a model for its correction or a glimpse into its structure, it becomes the refuge of poetical selfishness. Such selfishness is barren, and the fancy, feeding only on itself, grows leaner every day. Mysticism is usually an incurable disease. Facts cannot arouse it, since it never denied them. Reason cannot convince it, for reason is a human faculty, assuming a validity which it cannot prove. The only thing that can kill mysticism is its own uninterrupted progress, by which it gradually devours every function of the soul and at last, by destroying its own natural basis, immolates itself to its inexorable ideal.

Need we ask, after all these reflections, where we should look for that expansion and elevation of the mind which the mystic seeks so passionately and so unintelligently? We can find that expansion, in the first place, in the imagination itself. That is the true realm of man's infinity, where novelty may exist without falsity and perpetual diversity without contradiction. But such exercise of imagination leaves the world of knowledge untouched. Is there no escape from the prison, as the mystic thinks it, of science and history which shall yet not carry us beyond reality? Is there no truth beyond conventional truth, no life behind human existence?

Certainly. Behind the discovered there is the discoverable, beyond the actual, the possible. Science and history are not exhausted. In their determinate directions they are as infinite as fancy in its indetermination. The spectacle which science and history now spread before us is as far beyond the experience of an ephemeral insect as any Absolute can be beyond our own; yet we have put that spectacle together out of just such sensations as the insect may have — out of this sunlight and this buzz and these momentary throbs of existence. The understanding has indeed supervened, but it has supervened not to deny the validity of those sensations, but to combine their messages. We may still continue in the same path, by the indefinite extension of science over a world of experience and of intelligible truth. Is that prospect insufficient for our ambition? With a world so full of stuff before him, I can hardly conceive what morbid instinct can tempt a man to look elsewhere for wider vistas, unless it be unwillingness to endure the sadness and the discipline of the truth.

STUDY QUESTIONS

1. *Santayana is at once a very rewarding and a very difficult writer, and this selection is among the most demanding of those in this anthology. Can you point out sentence patterns and matters of vocabulary which account for this? Could Santayana have made this discussion easier to understand and still have said the "same thing"?*

2. *Style might be defined as "thinking into language." It is, at its best, a reflection of the writer's habits of thought and of his character, rather than merely an*

arbitrary way of saying things. (Compare here Morison's comments on style in his "History as a Literary Art.") What qualities of mind does Santayana's writing suggest?

3. According to Santayana, what is the difference between knowledge obtained through understanding, and knowledge obtained through the imagination?

4. Santayana is very critical of the imagination in this essay. First, list the limitations and dangers he sees involved in its use. Then point out the values which he attributes to it. Explain Santayana's sentence, "The imagination is the great unifier of humanity."

5. What is the "logical contradiction" involved in mysticism? As with imagination, Santayana is critical of mysticism. At the same time, however, he is willing to describe its virtues and uses. What are they?

6. In his complicated discussion of mysticism, Santayana gives no concrete details or examples. Supplement his discussion by taking some specific instance of mysticism with which you are familiar and examining it in the light of his opinions.

2. MORAL LAW AND THE CONDUCT OF LIFE

Dorothy Sayers

The "Laws" of Nature and Opinion*

Much confusion is caused in human affairs by the use of the same word "law" to describe these two very different things: an arbitrary code of behavior based on a consensus of human opinion and a statement of unalterable fact about the nature of the universe. The confusion is at its worst when we come to talk about the "moral law." Professor Macmurray, for example, contrasting the moral law with the law of nature, says, "The essence of . . . a mechanical morality will be the idea that goodness consists in obedience to a moral law. Such a morality is false, because it destroys human spontaneity . . . by subjecting it to an external authority. . . . It is only matter that can be free in obeying laws." What he is doing here is to use the words "law" and "laws" in two different senses. When he speaks of the "laws" governing the behavior of matter, he means statements of observed fact about the nature of the material universe; when he speaks of a moral "law," he means the arbitrary code of behavior established by human opinion.

There is a universal moral law, as distinct from a moral code, which con-

* From *The Mind of the Maker* by Dorothy Sayers. Copyright, 1941, by Dorothy Sayers. Reprinted by permission of Ann Watkins, Inc.

sists of certain statements of fact about the nature of man; and by behaving in conformity with which, man enjoys his true freedom. This is what the Christian Church calls "the natural law." The more closely the moral code agrees with the natural law, the more it makes for freedom in human behavior; the more widely it departs from the natural law, the more it tends to enslave mankind and to produce the catastrophes called "judgments of God."

The universal moral *law* (or natural law of humanity) is discoverable, like any other law of nature, by experience. It cannot be promulgated, it can only be ascertained, because it is a question not of opinion but of fact. When it has been ascertained, a moral *code* can be drawn up to direct human behavior and prevent men, as far as possible, from doing violence in their own nature. No code is necessary to control the behavior of matter, since matter is apparently not tempted to contradict its own nature, but obeys the law of its being in perfect freedom. Man, however, does continually suffer this temptation and frequently yields to it. This contradiction within his own nature is peculiar to man, and is called by the Church "sinfulness"; other psychologists have other names for it.

The moral *code* depends for its validity upon a consensus of human opinion about what man's nature really is, and what it ought to be, when freed from this mysterious self-contradiction and enabled to run true to itself. If there is no agreement about these things, then it is useless to talk of enforcing the moral code. It is idle to complain that a society is infringing a moral code intended to make people behave like St. Francis of Assisi if the society retorts that it does not wish to behave like St. Francis, and considers it more natural and right to behave like the Emperor Caligula. When there is a genuine conflict of opinion, it is necessary to go behind the moral code and appeal to the natural law — to prove, that is, at the bar of experience, that St. Francis does in fact enjoy a freer truth to essential human nature than Caligula, and that a society of Caligulas is more likely to end in catastrophe than a society of Franciscans.

Christian morality comprises both a moral code and a moral law. The Christian code is familiar to us; but we are apt to forget that it is valid or not valid according as Christian opinion is right or wrong about the moral law — that is to say, about the essential facts of human nature. Regulations about doing no murder and refraining from theft and adultery belong to the moral code and are based on certain opinions held by Christians in common about the value of human personality. Such "laws" as these are not statements of fact, but rules of behavior. Societies which do not share Christian opinion about human values are logically quite justified in repudiating the code based upon that opinion. If, however, Christian opinion turns out to be right about the facts of human nature, then the dissenting societies are exposing themselves to that judgment of catastrophe which awaits those who defy the natural law.

At the back of the Christian moral *code* we find a number of pronouncements about the moral *law*, which are not regulations at all, but which purport to be statements of fact about man and the universe, and upon which the whole moral code depends for its authority and its validity in practice. These statements do not rest on human consent; they are either true or false. If they are true, man runs counter to them at his own peril. He may, of course, defy them, as he may defy the law of gravitation by jumping off the Eiffel Tower, but he cannot abolish them by edict. Nor yet can God abolish them, except by breaking up the structure of the universe, so that in this sense they are not arbitrary laws. We may of course argue that the making of this kind of universe, or indeed of any kind of universe, is an arbitrary act; but, given the universe as it stands, the rules that govern it are not freaks of momentary caprice. There is a difference between saying: "If you hold your finger in the fire you will get burned" and saying, "if you whistle at your work I shall beat you, because the noise gets on my nerves." The God of the Christians is too often looked upon as an old gentleman of irritable nerves who beats people for whistling. This is the result of a confusion between arbitrary "law" and the "laws" which are statements of fact. Breach of the first is "punished" by edict; but breach of the second, by judgment.

"For He visits the sins of the fathers upon the children unto the third and fourth generation of them that hate Him, and shows mercy unto thousands of them that love Him and keep His commandments."

Here is a statement of fact, observed by the Jews and noted as such. From its phrasing it might appear an arbitrary expression of personal feeling. But today, we understand more about the mechanism of the universe, and are able to reinterpret the pronouncement by the "laws" of heredity and environment. Defy the commandments of the natural law, and the race will perish in a few generations; co-operate with them, and the race will flourish for ages to come. That is the fact; whether we like it or not, the universe is made that way. This commandment is interesting because it specifically puts forward the moral *law* as the basis of the moral *code*: *because* God has made the world like this and will not alter it, *therefore* you must not worship your own fantasies, but pay allegiance to the truth.

Scattered about the New Testament are other statements concerning the moral law, many of which bear a similar air of being arbitrary, harsh or paradoxical: "Whosoever will save his life shall lose it"; "to him that hath shall be given, but from him that hath not shall be taken away even that which he hath"; "it must needs be that offences come, but woe unto that man by whom the offence cometh"; "there is joy in heaven over one sinner that repenteth more than over ninety and nine just persons that need no repentance"; "it is easier for a camel to go through the eye of a needle than for a rich man to enter into the Kingdom of God"; "it is better for thee to enter halt into life than having two feet to be cast into hell"; "blasphemy against the Holy Ghost shall not be forgiven . . . neither in this world, neither in the world to come."

We may hear a saying such as these a thousand times, and find in it nothing but mystification and unreason; the thousand-and-first time, it falls into our recollection pat upon some vital experience, and we suddenly know it to be a statement of inexorable fact. The parable of the Unjust Steward presents an insoluble enigma when approached by way of *a priori* reasoning; it is only when we have personally wrestled with the oddly dishonest inefficiency of some of the children of light that we recognize its ironical truth to human nature. The cursing of the barren fig-tree looks like an outburst of irrational bad temper, "for it was not yet the time of figs"; till some desperate crisis confronts us with the challenge of that acted parable and we know that we must perform impossibilities or perish.

Of some laws such as these, psychology has already begun to expose the mechanism; on others, the only commentary yet available is that of life and history.

It is essential to our understanding of all doctrine that we shall be able to distinguish between what is presented as personal opinion and what is presented as a judgment of fact. Twenty centuries ago, Aristotle, in his university lectures on poetry, offered certain observations on dramatic structure, which were subsequently codified as the "Rule of the Three Unities." These observations underwent the vicissitudes that attend all formal creeds. There was a period when they were held to be sacrosanct, not because they were a judgment of truth, but because they were the "say-so" of authority; and they were applied as tests automatically, regardless whether the actual plays in question were informed with the vital truth that was the reason behind the rule. Later, there was a reaction against them as against an arbitrary code, and critics of our own time have gone so far as to assert that Aristotle's unities are obsolete. But this is a folly worse than the other. Audiences who have never heard of Aristotle criticize plays every day for their failure to observe the unities. "The story," they say, "didn't seem to hang together; I didn't know whom to be interested in; it began as a drama and ended as a farce. . . . Too many scenes — the curtain was up one minute and down the next; I couldn't keep my attention fixed — all those intervals were so distracting. . . . The story is spread out over the whole Thirty Years' War; it would have been all right for a novel, but it wasn't concentrated enough for the theater; it just seemed to go on and on." What is the use of saying that twentieth-century playwrights should refuse to be bound by the dictum of an ancient Greek professor? They are bound, whether they like it or not, by the fundamental realities of human nature, which have not altered between classical Athens and modern London. Aristotle never offered his "unities" as an *a priori* personal opinion about the abstract ideal of a play: he offered them as observations of fact about the kind of plays which were, in practice, successful. Judging by results, he put forward the observation that the action of a play should be coherent and as concentrated as possible, otherwise — human nature being what it is — the audience would become distracted and bored. That is presented as a statement of fact — and that it is a true statement of fact a melancholy succession of theatrical failures bears witness to this day. It is open to any playwright to reject Aristotle's opinion, but his independence will not profit him if that opinion was based on fact; it is open to any playwright to accept Aristotle's opinion, but he ought to do so, not because it is Aristotle's, but because the facts confirm it.

In a similar way, volumes of angry controversy have been poured out about the Christian creeds, under the impression that they represent, not statements of fact, but arbitrary edicts. The conditions of salvation, for instance, are discussed as though they were conditions for membership in some fantastic club like the Red-Headed League. They do not purport to be anything of the kind. Rightly or wrongly, they purport to be necessary conditions based on the facts of human nature. We are accustomed to find conditions attached to human undertakings, some of which are arbitrary and some not. A regulation that allowed a cook to make omelettes only on condition of first putting on a top hat might conceivably be given the force of law, and penalties might be inflicted for disobedience; but the condition would remain arbitrary and irrational. The law that omelettes can be made only on condition that there shall be a preliminary breaking of eggs is one with which we are sadly familiar. The efforts of idealists to make omelettes without observing that condition are foredoomed to failure by the nature of things. The Christian creeds are too frequently assumed to be in the top-hat category; this is an error; they belong to the category of egg-breaking. Even that most notorious of damnatory clauses which provokes sensitive ecclesiastics to defy the rubric and banish the Athanasian Creed from public recitation does not say that God will refuse to save unbelievers; it is at once less arbitrary and more alarming: "which except a man believe faithfully, he *cannot* be saved." It purports to be a statement of fact. The proper question to be asked about any creed is not, "Is it pleasant?" but, "is it true?" "Christianity has compelled the mind of man not because it is the most cheering view of man's existence but because it is truest to the facts." It is unpleasant to be called sinners, and much nicer to think that we all have hearts of gold — but have we? It is agreeable to suppose that the more scientific knowledge we acquire the happier we shall be — but does it look like it? It is encouraging to feel that progress is making us automatically every day and in every way better, and better, and better — but does history support that view? "We hold these truths to be self-evident: that all men were created equal" — but does the external evidence support this *a priori* assertion? Or does experience rather suggest that man is "very far gone from original righteousness and is of his own nature inclined to evil"?

A creed put forward by authority deserves respect in the measure that we respect the authority's claim to be a judge of truth. If the creed and the authority alike are conceived as being arbitrary, capricious and irrational, we shall continue in a state of terror and bewilderment, since we shall never know from one minute to the next what we are supposed to be doing, or why, or what we have to expect. But a creed that can be shown to have its basis in fact inclines us to trust the judgment of the authority; if in this case and in that it turns out to be correct, we may be disposed to think that it is, on the whole, probable that it is correct about everything. The necessary condition for assessing the value of creeds is that we should fully understand that they claim to be, not idealistic fancies, not arbitrary codes, not abstractions irrelevant to human life and thought, but statements of fact about the universe as we know it. Any witness — however small — to the rationality of a creed assists us to an intelligent apprehension of what it is intended to mean, and enables us to decide whether it is, or is not, as it sets out to be, a witness of universal truth.

STUDY QUESTIONS

1. *This and the next two selections by Westermarck and Melville are all pertinent to the problem of relativity in moral standards. They illustrate not only somewhat differing ideas about this subject, but also differing styles and kinds of writing. As you read them, compare and be prepared to discuss the methods which each writer uses to make his ideas clear. Prepare yourself, also, to summarize briefly the central thesis of each writer and to compare their ideas.*
2. *What is the difference between a moral law and a moral code, according to Mrs. Sayers?*
3. *Do you agree that facts about the nature of man can be learned by experience, and are not subject to opinion?*
4. *How does Mrs. Sayers explain the apparently arbitrary quality of the quotations taken from the Bible?*
5. *What evidence is offered to support Mrs. Sayers' contention that the "Christian creeds" are not arbitrary rules, but inevitable laws resulting from the nature of things?*
6. *Do you agree with Mrs. Sayers that the "moral code" of Christianity harmonizes with "natural law" as she defines it? Write a theme stating her view of this problem and evaluating it.*

Edward Westermarck

The Emotional Origin of Moral Judgments*

Society is the school in which men learn to distinguish between right and wrong. The headmaster is Custom, and the lessons are the same for all. The first moral judgments were pronounced by public opinion; public indignation and public approval are the prototypes of the moral emotions. As regards questions of morality, there was, in early society, practically no difference of opinion; hence a character of universality, or objectivity, was from the very beginning attached to all moral judgments. And when, with advanc-

* From *The Origin and Development of the Moral Ideas* by Edward Westermarck. Reprinted by the kind permission of Hugo E. Pipping.

ing civilization, this unanimity was to some extent disturbed by individuals venturing to dissent from the opinions of the majority, the disagreement was largely due to facts which in no way affected the moral principle, but had reference only to its application.

Most people follow a very simple method in judging of an act. Particular modes of conduct have their traditional labels, many of which are learnt with language itself; and the moral judgment commonly consists simply in labelling the act according to certain obvious characteristics which it presents in common with others belonging to the same group. But a conscientious and intelligent judge proceeds in a different manner. He carefully examines all the details connected with the act, the external and internal conditions under which it was performed, its consequences, its motives; and, since the moral estimate in a large measure depends upon the regard paid to these circumstances, his judgment may differ greatly from that of the man in the street, even though the moral standard which they apply be exactly the same. But to acquire a full insight into all the details which are apt to influence the moral value of an act is in many cases anything but easy, and this naturally increases the disagreement. There is thus in every advanced society a diversity of opinion regarding the moral value of certain modes of conduct which results from circumstances of a purely intellectual character — from the knowledge or ignorance of positive facts, — and involves no discord in principle.

Now it has been assumed by the advocates of various ethical theories that all the differences of moral ideas originate in this way, and that there is some ultimate standard which must be recognised as authoritative by everybody who understands it rightly. According to Bentham, the rectitude of utilitarianism has been contested only by those who have not known their own meaning: —

> When a man attempts to combat the principle of utility . . . his arguments, if they prove anything, prove not that the principle is wrong, but that, according to the applications he supposes to be made of it, it is misapplied.

Mr. Spencer, to whom good conduct is that "which conduces to life in each and all," believes that he has the support of "the true moral consciousness," or "moral consciousness proper," which, whether in harmony or in conflict with the "pro-ethical" sentiment, is vaguely or distinctly recognised as the rightful ruler. Samuel Clarke, the intuitionist, again, is of opinion that if a man endowed with reason denies the eternal and necessary moral differences of things, it is the very same

> . . . as if a man that has the use of his sight, should at the same time as he beholds the sun, deny that there is any such thing as light in the world; or as if a man that understands Geometry or Arithmetick, should deny the most obvious and known proportions of lines or numbers.

In short, all disagreement as to questions of morals is attributed to ignorance or misunderstanding.

The influence of intellectual considerations upon moral judgments is certainly immense. We shall find that the evolution of the moral consciousness to a large extent consists in its development from the unreflecting to the reflecting, from the unenlightened to the enlightened. All higher emotions are determined by cognitions, they arise from "the presentation of determinate objective conditions"; and moral enlightenment implies a true and comprehensive presentation of those objective conditions by which the moral emotions, according to their very nature, are determined. Morality may thus in a much higher degree than, for instance, beauty be a subject of instruction and of profitable discussion, in which persuasion is carried by the representation of existing data. But although in this way many differences may be accorded, there are points in which unanimity cannot be reached even by the most accurate presentation of facts or the subtlest process of reasoning.

Whilst certain phenomena will almost of necessity arouse similar moral emotions in every mind which perceives them clearly, there are others with which the case is different. The emotional constitution of man does not present the same uniformity as the human intellect. Certain cognitions inspire fear in nearly every breast; but there are brave men and cowards in the world, independently of the accuracy with which they realise impending danger. Some cases of suffering can hardly fail to awaken compassion in the most pitiless heart; but the sympathetic dispositions of men vary greatly, both in regard to the beings with whose sufferings they are ready to sympathise, and with reference to the intensity of the emotion. The same holds good for the moral emotions. The existing diversity of opinion as to the rights of different classes of men and of the lower animals, which springs from emotional differences, may no doubt be modified by a clearer insight into certain facts, but no perfect agreement can be expected as long as the conditions under which the emotional dispositions are formed remain unchanged. Whilst an enlightened mind *must* recognise the complete or relative irresponsibility of an animal, a child, or a madman, and *must* be influenced in its moral judgment by the motives of an act — no intellectual enlightenment, no scrutiny of facts, can decide how far the interests of the lower animals should be regarded when conflicting with those of men, or how far a person is bound, or allowed, to promote the welfare of his nation, or his own welfare, at the cost of that of other nations or other individuals. Professor Sidgwick's well known moral axiom, "I ought not to prefer my own lesser good to the greater good of another," would, if explained to a Fuegian or a Hottentot, be regarded by him, not as self-evident, but as simply absurd; nor can it claim general acceptance even among ourselves. Who is that "Another" to whose greater good I ought not to prefer my own lesser good? A fellow-countryman, a savage, a criminal, a bird, a fish — all without distinction? It will, perhaps, be argued that on this, and on all other points of morals, there would be general agreement, if only the moral consciousness of men were sufficiently developed. But then, when speaking of a "sufficiently developed" moral consciousness (beyond insistence upon a full insight into the governing facts of each case), we practically mean nothing else than agreement with our own moral convictions. The expression is faulty and deceptive, because, if intended to mean anything more, it presupposes an objectivity of the moral judgments which they do not possess, and at the same time seems to be proving what it presupposes. We may speak of an intellect as sufficiently developed to grasp a certain truth, because truth is objective; but it is not proved to be objective by the fact that it is recognised as true by a "sufficiently developed" intellect. The objectivity of truth lies in the recognition of facts as true by all who understand them fully, whilst the appeal to a *sufficient* knowledge assumes their objectivity. To the verdict of a perfect intellect, that is, an intellect which knows everything existing, all would submit; but we can form no idea of a moral consciousness which could lay claim to a similar authority. If the believers in an all-good God, who has revealed his will to mankind, maintain that they in this revelation possess a perfect moral standard, and that, consequently, what is in accordance with such a standard must be objectively right, it may be asked what they mean by an "all-good" God. And in their attempt to answer this question, they would inevitably have to assume the objectivity they wanted to prove.

The error we commit by attributing objectivity to moral estimates becomes particularly conspicuous when we consider that these estimates have not only a certain quality, but a certain quantity. There are different degrees of badness and goodness, a duty may be more or less stringent, a merit may be smaller or greater. These quantitative differences are due to the emotional origin of all moral concepts. Emotions vary in intensity almost indefinitely, and the moral emotions form no exception to this rule. Indeed, it may be fairly doubted whether the same mode of conduct ever arouses exactly the same degree of indignation or approval in any two individuals. Many of these differences are of course too subtle to be manifested in the moral judgment; but very frequently the intensity of the emotion is indicated by special words, or by the way in which the judgment is pronounced. It should be noticed, however, that the quantity of the estimate expressed in a moral predicate is not identical with the intensity of the moral emotion which a certain mode of conduct arouses on a special occasion. We are liable to feel more indignant if an injury is committed before our eyes than if we read of it in a newspaper, and yet we admit that the degree of wrongness is in both cases the same. The quantity of moral estimates is determined by the intensity of the emotions which their objects tend to evoke under exactly similar external circumstances.

Beside the relative uniformity of moral opinions, there is another circumstance which tempts us to objectivise moral judgments, namely, the authority which, rightly or wrongly, is ascribed to moral rules. From our earliest childhood we are taught that certain acts *are* right and that others *are* wrong. Owing to their exceptional importance for human welfare, the facts of the moral consciousness are emphasised in a much higher degree than any other subjective facts. We are allowed to have our private opinions about the beauty of things, but we are not so readily allowed to have our private opinions about rights and wrong. The moral rules which are prevalent in the society to which we belong are supported by appeals not only to human, but to divine, authority, and to call in question their validity is to rebel against religion as well as against public opinion. Thus the belief in a moral order of the world has taken hardly less firm hold of the human mind than the belief in a natural order of things. And the moral law has retained its authoritativeness even when the appeal to an external authority has been regarded as inadequate. It filled Kant with the same awe as the star-spangled firmament. According to Butler, conscience is "a faculty in kind and in nature supreme over all others, and which bears its own authority of being so." Its supremacy is said to be "felt and tacitly acknowledged by the worst no less than by the best of men." Adam Smith calls the moral faculties the "viceregents of God within us," who "never fail to punish the violation of them by the torments of inward shame and self-condemnation; and, on the contrary, always reward obedience with tranquility of mind, with contentment, and self-satisfaction." Even Hutcheson, who raises the question why the moral sense should not vary in different men as the palate does, considers it "to be naturally destined to command all the other powers."

Authority is an ambiguous word. It may indicate knowledge of truth, and it may indicate a rightful power to command obedience. The authoritativeness attributed to the moral law has often reference to both kinds of authority. The moral lawgiver lays down his rules in order that they be obeyed. But he is also believed to know what is right and wrong, and his commands are regarded as expressions of moral truths. As we have seen, however, this latter kind of authority involves a false assumption as to the nature of the moral predicates, and it cannot be justly inferred from the power to command. Again, if the notion of an external lawgiver be put aside, the moral law does not generally seem to possess supreme authority in either sense of the word. It does not command obedience in any exceptional degree; few laws are broken more frequently. Nor can the regard for it be called the mainspring of action; it is only one spring out of many, and variable like all others. In some instances it is the ruling power in a man's life, in others it is a voice calling in the desert; and the majority of people seem to be more afraid of the blame or ridicule of their fellowmen, or of the penalties with which the law threatens them, than of the "viceregents of God" in their own hearts. That mankind prefer the possession of virtue to all other enjoyments, and look upon vice as worse than any other misery, is unfortunately an imagination of some moralists who confound men as they are with men as they ought to be.

It is said that the authority of the moral law asserts itself every time the law is broken, that virtue bears in itself its own reward, and vice its own punishment. But, to be sure, conscience is a very unjust retributor. The more a person habituates himself to virtue the more he sharpens its sting, the deeper he sinks in vice the more he blunts it. Whilst the best men have the most sensitive consciences, the worst have hardly any consciences at all. It is argued that the habitual sinner has rid himself of remorse at a great cost; but it may be fairly doubted whether the loss is an adequate penalty for his wickedness. We are reminded that men are rewarded for good and punished for bad acts by the moral feelings of their neighbors. But public opinion and law judge of detected acts only. Their judgment is seldom based upon an exhaustive examination of the case. They often apply a standard which is itself open to criticism. And the feelings with which men regard their fellow-creatures, and which are some of the main sources of human happiness and suffering, have often very little to do with morality. A person is respected or praised, blamed or despised, on other grounds than his character. Nay the admiration which men feel for genius, courage, pluck, strength, or accidental success, is often superior in intensity to the admiration they feel for virtue.

In spite of all this however, the supreme authority assigned to the moral law is not altogether an illusion. It really exists in the minds of the best, and is nominally acknowledged by the many. By this I do not refer to the universal admission that the moral law, whether obeyed or not, ought under all circumstances to be obeyed; for this is the same as to say that what ought to be ought to be. But it is recognised, in theory at least, that morality, either alone or in connection with religion, possesses a higher value than anything else; that rightness and goodness are preferable to all other kinds of mental superiority, as well as of physical excellence. If this theory is not more commonly acted upon, that is due to its being, in most people, much less the outcome of their own feelings than of instruction from the outside. It is ultimately traceable to some great teacher whose own mind was ruled by the ideal of moral perfection, and whose words became sacred on account of his supreme wisdom, like Confucius or Buddha, or on religious grounds, like Jesus. The authority of the moral law is thus only an expression of a strongly developed, overruling moral consciousness. It can hardly, as Mr. Sidgwick maintains, be said to "depend upon" the conception of the objectivity of duty. On the contrary, it must be regarded as a cause of this conception — not only, as has already been pointed out, where it is traceable to some external authority, but where it results from the strength of the individual's own moral emotions. As clearness and distinctness of the conception of an object easily produces the belief in its truth, so the intensity of a moral emotion makes him who feels it disposed to objectivise the moral estimate to which it gives rise, in other words, to assign to it universal validity. The enthusiast is more likely than anybody else to regard his judgments as true, and so is the moral enthusiast with reference to his moral judgments. The intensity of his emotions makes him the victim of an illusion.

The presumed objectivity of moral judgments thus being a chimera, there can be no moral truth in the sense in which this term is generally understood. The ultimate reason for this is, that the moral concepts are based upon emotions, and that contents of an emotion fall entirely outside the category of truth. But it may be true or not that we have a certain emotion, it may be true or not that a given mode of conduct has a tendency to evoke in us moral indignation or moral approval. Hence a moral judgment is true or false according as its subject has or has not that tendency which the predicate attributes to it. If I say that it is wrong to resist evil, and yet resistance to evil has no tendency whatever to call forth in me an emotion of moral disapproval, then my judgment is false.

If there are no general moral truths, the object of scientific ethics cannot be to fix rules for human conduct, the aim of all science being the discovery of some truth. It has been said by Bentham and others that moral principles cannot be proved because they are first principles which are used to prove everything else. But the real reason for their being inaccessible to demonstration is that, owing to their very nature, they can never be true. If the word "Ethics," then, is to be used as the name for a science, the object of that science can only be to study the moral consciousness as a fact.

Ethical subjectivism is commonly held to be a dangerous doctrine, destructive to morality, opening the door to all sorts of libertinism. If that which appears to each man as right or good, stands for that which is right or good; if he is allowed to make his own law, or to make no law at all; then, it is said, everybody has the natural right to follow his caprice and inclinations, and to hinder him from doing so is an infringement on his rights, a constraint with which no one is bound to comply provided that he has the power to evade it. This inference was long ago drawn from the teaching of the Sophists, and it will no doubt be still repeated as an argument against any theorist who dares to assert that nothing can be said to be truly right or wrong.

To this argument may, first, be objected that a scientific theory is not invalidated by the mere fact that it is likely to cause mischief. The unfortunate circumstance that there do exist dangerous things in the world proves that something may be dangerous and yet true. Another question is whether any scientific truth really is mischievous on the whole, although it may cause much discomfort to certain people. I venture to believe that this, at any rate, is not the case with that form of ethical subjectivism which I am here advocating. The charge brought against the Sophists does not at all apply to it. I do not even subscribe to that beautiful modern sophism which admits every man's conscience to be an infallible guide. If we had to recognise, or rather if we did recognise, as right everything which is held to be right by anybody, savage or Christian, criminal or saint, morality would really suffer a serious loss. But we do not, and we cannot, do so. My moral judgments are my own judgments; they spring from my own moral consciousness; they judge of the conduct of other men not from their point of view but from mine, not with primary reference to their opinions about right and wrong, but with reference to my own. Most of us indeed admit that, when judging of an act, we also ought to take into consideration the moral conviction of the agent, and the agreement or disagreement between his doing and his idea of what he ought to do. But although we hold it to be wrong of a person to act against his conscience, we may at the same time blame him for having such a conscience as he has. Ethical subjectivism covers all such cases. It certainly does not allow everybody to follow his own inclinations; nor does it lend sanction to arbitrariness and caprice. Our moral consciousness belongs to our mental constitution, which we cannot change as we please. We approve and we disapprove because we cannot do otherwise. Can we help feeling pain when the fire burns us? Can we help sympathising with our friends? Are these phenomena less necessary or less powerful in their consequences, because they fall within the subjective sphere of experience? So, too, why should the moral law command less obedience because it forms part of our own nature?

Far from being a danger, ethical subjectivism seems to me more likely to be an acquisition for moral practice. Could it be brought home to people that there is no absolute standard in morality, they would perhaps be somewhat more tolerant in their judgments, and more apt to listen to the voice of reason. If the right has an objective existence, the moral consciousness has certainly been playing at blindman's buff ever since it was born, and will continue to do so until the extinction of the human race. But who does admit this? The popular mind is always inclined to believe that it possesses the knowledge of what *is* right and wrong, and to regard public opinion as the reliable guide of conduct. We have, indeed, no reason to regret that there are men who rebel against the established rules of morality; it is more deplorable that the rebels are so few, and that, consequently, the old rules change so slowly. Far above the vulgar idea that the right is a settled something to which everybody has to adjust his opinions, rises the conviction that it has its existence in each individual mind, capable of any expansion, proclaiming its own right to exist, and, if need, be, venturing to make a stand against the whole world. Such a conviction makes for progress.

STUDY QUESTIONS

1. *What evidence does Westermarck offer to show that moral attitudes are essentially emotional? Do you consider the evidence convincing? Has he overlooked evidence which would contradict his thesis?*

2. *How does he explain the fact that moral opinions are, as he observes, relatively uniform?*

3. *What are some of the reasons Westermarck gives for denying that such a concept as "moral truth," which implies an objective morality, can exist? Are his reasons persuasive?*

4. *What does Westermarck mean by the term "ethical subjectivism"? What advantages does he see in it?*

5. *Compare Westermarck's view of moral law with Mrs. Sayers'. Which do you find more persuasive? To what extent is your decision here determined by your own preconceptions?*

6. *Do you agree with Westermarck that conscience is not a sufficient guide for morality? Illustrate your answer with examples drawn from your own experience.*

Herman Melville

Chronometricals and Horologicals *

LECTURE FIRST, BY PLOTINUS PLINLIMMON

(Being not so much the Portal, as part of the temporary Scaffold to the Portal of this New Philosophy).

*F*ew of us doubt, gentlemen, that human life on this earth is but a state of probation; which among other things implies, that here below, we mortals have only to do with things provisional. Accordingly, I hold that all our so-called wisdom is likewise but provisional.

"This preamble laid down, I begin.

"It seems to me, in my visions, that there is a certain most rare order of human souls, which if carefully carried in the body will almost always and everywhere give Heaven's own Truth, with some small grains of variance. For peculiarly coming from God, the sole source of that heavenly truth, and the great Greenwich hill and tower from which the universal meridians are far out into infinity reckoned; such souls seem as London sea-chronometers (*Greek*, time-namers) which as the London ship floats past Greenwich down the Thames, are accurately adjusted by Greenwich time, and if heedfully kept, we still give that same time, even though carried to the Azores. True, in nearly all cases of long, remote voyages — to China, say — chronometers of the best make, and the most carefully treated, will gradually more or less vary from Greenwich time, without the possibility of the error being corrected by direct comparison with their great standard; but skilful and devout observations of the stars by the sextant will serve materially to lessen such errors. And besides, there is such a thing as *rating* a chronometer; that is, having ascertained its degree of organic inaccuracy, however small, then in all subsequent chronometrical calculations, that ascertained loss or gain can be readily added or deducted, as the case may be. Then again, on these long voyages, the chronometer may be corrected by comparing it with the chronometer of some other ship at sea, more recently from home.

"Now in an artificial world like ours, the soul of man is further removed from its God and the Heavenly Truth, than the chronometer carried to China,

* From *Pierre, or the Ambiguities*, 1852.

is from Greenwich. And, as that chronometer, if at all accurate, will pronounce it to be 12 o'clock high-noon, when the China local watches say,
perhaps, it is 12 o'clock midnight; so the chronometric soul, if in this world
true to its great Greenwich in the other, will always, in its so-called intuitions
of right and wrong, be contradicting the mere local standards and watchmaker's brains of this earth.

"Bacon's brains were mere watchmaker's brains; but Christ was a chronometer; and the most exquisitely adjusted and exact one, and the least
affected by all terrestrial jarrings, of any that have ever come to us. And the
reason why his teachings seemed folly to the Jews, was because he carried
that Heaven's time in Jerusalem, while the Jews carried Jerusalem time there.
Did he not expressly say — My wisdom (time) is not of this world? But
whatever is really peculiar in the wisdom of Christ seems precisely the same
folly to-day as it did 1850 years ago. Because, in all that interval his be-
queathed chronometer has still preserved its original Heaven's time, and the
general Jerusalem of this world has likewise carefully preserved its own.

"But though the chronometer carried from Greenwich to China, should
truly exhibit in China what the time may be at Greenwich at any moment;
yet, though thereby it must necessarily contradict China time, it does by no
means thence follow, that with respect to China, the China watches are at all
out of the way. Precisely the reverse. For the fact of that variance is a pre-
sumption that, with respect to China, the Chinese watches must be all right;
and consequently as the China watches are right as to China, so the Greenwich chronometers must be wrong as to China. Besides, of what use to the
Chinaman would a Greenwich chronometer, keeping Greenwich time, be?
Were he thereby to regulate his daily actions, he would be guilty of all
manner of absurdities: — going to bed at noon, say, when his neighbours
would be sitting down to dinner. And thus, though the earthly wisdom of
man be heavenly folly to God; so also, conversely, is the heavenly wisdom of
God an earthly folly to man. Literally speaking, this is so. Nor does the
God at the heavenly Greenwich expect common men to keep Greenwich
wisdom in this remote Chinese world of ours; because such a thing were unprofitable for them here, and, indeed, a falsification of Himself, inasmuch
as in that case, China time would be identical with Greenwich time, which
would make Greenwich time wrong.

"But why then does God now and then send a heavenly chronometer (as a
meteoric stone) into the world, uselessly as it would seem, to give the lie to all
the world's time-keepers? Because He is unwilling to leave man without some
occasional testimony to this: — that though man's Chinese notions of things
may answer well enough here, they are by no means universally applicable,
and that the central Greenwich in which he dwells goes by a somewhat different method from this world. And yet it follows not from this, that God's
truth is one thing and man's truth another; but — as above hinted, and as will
be further elucidated in subsequent lectures — by their very contradictions
they are made to correspond.

"By inference it follows, also, that he who finding in himself a chrono-metrical soul, seeks practically to force that heavenly time upon the earth; in such an attempt he can never succeed, with an absolute and essential success. And as for himself, if he seek to regulate his own daily conduct by it, he will but array all men's earthly time-keepers against him, and thereby work himself woe and death. Both these things are plainly evinced in the character and fate of Christ, and the past and present condition of the religion he taught. But here one thing is to be especially observed. Though Christ encountered woe in both the precept and the practice of his chronometricals, yet did he remain throughout entirely without folly or sin. Whereas, almost invariably, with inferior beings, the absolute effort to live in this world according to the strict letter of the chronometricals is, somehow, apt to involve those inferior beings eventually in strange, *unique* follies and sins, unimagined before. It is the story of the Ephesian matron, allegorised.

"To any earnest man of insight, a faithful contemplation of these ideas concerning Chronometricals and Horologicals, will serve to render provision-ally far less dark some few of the otherwise obscurest things which have hitherto tormented the honest-thinking men of all ages. What man who carries a heavenly soul in him, has not groaned to perceive, that unless he committed a sort of suicide as to the practical things of this world, he never can hope to regulate his earthly conduct by the same heavenly soul? And yet by an infallible instinct he knows, that that monitor cannot be wrong in itself.

"And where is the earnest and righteous philosopher, gentlemen, who look-ing right and left, and up and down, through all the ages of the world, the present included; where is there such an one who has not a thousand times been struck with a sort of infidel idea, that whatever other worlds God may be Lord of, he is not the Lord of this; for else this world would seem to give the lie to Him; so utterly repugnant seem its ways to the instinctively known ways of Heaven. But it is not, and cannot be so; nor will he who regards this chronometrical conceit aright, ever more be conscious of that horrible idea. For he will then see, or seem to see, that this world's seeming incompatibility with God, absolutely results from its meridional correspondence with Him.

"This chronometrical conceit does by no means involve the justification of all the acts which wicked men may perform. For in their wickedness down-right wicked men sin as much against their own horologes, as against the heavenly chronometer. That this is so, their spontaneous liability to remorse does plainly evince. No, this conceit merely goes to show, that for the mass of men, the highest abstract heavenly righteousness is not only impossible, but would be entirely out of place, and positively wrong in a world like this. To turn the left cheek if the right be smitten, is chronometrical; hence, no average son of man ever did such a thing. To give *all* that thou hast to the poor, this too is chronometrical; hence no average son of man ever did such a thing. Nevertheless, if a man gives with a certain self-considerate generosity to the poor; abstains from doing downright ill to any man; does his convenient best in a general way to do good to his whole race; takes watchful loving care

of his wife and children, relatives, and friends; is perfectly tolerant to all
other men's opinions, whatever they may be; is an honest dealer, an honest
citizen, and all that; and more especially if he believe that there is a God
for infidels, as well as for believers, and acts upon that belief; then, though
such a man falls infinitely short of the chronometrical standard, though all his
actions are entirely horologic; — yet such a man need never lastingly despond,
because he is sometimes guilty of some minor offence: — hasty words, im-
pulsively returning a blow, fits of domestic petulance, selfish enjoyment of a
glass of wine while he knows there are those around him who lack a loaf of
bread. I say he need never lastingly despond on account of his perpetual
liability to these things; because *not* to do them, and their like, would be to
be an angel, a chronometer; whereas, he is a man and a horologe.

"Yet does the horologe itself teach, that all liabilities to these things should
be checked as much as possible, though it is certain they can never be utterly
eradicated. They are only to be checked, then, because, if entirely unre-
strained, they would finally run into utter selfishness and human demonism,
which, as before hinted, are not by any means justified by the horologe.

"In short, this chronometrical and horological conceit, in sum, seems to
teach this: — That in things terrestrial (horological) a man must not be
governed by ideas celestial (chronometrical); that certain minor self-renuncia-
tions in this life his own mere instinct for his own everyday general well-
being will teach him to make, but he must by no means make a complete un-
conditional sacrifice of himself in behalf of any other being, or any cause, or
any conceit. (For, does aught else completely and unconditionally sacrifice
itself for him? God's own sun does not abate one tittle of its heat in July,
however you swoon with that heat in the sun. And if it *did* abate its heat on
your behalf, then the wheat and the rye would not ripen; and so, for the
incidental benefit of one, a whole population would suffer.)

"A virtuous expediency, then, seems the highest desirable or attainable
earthly excellence for the mass of men, and is the only earthly excellence that
their Creator intended for them. When they go to heaven, it will be quite
another thing. There, they can freely turn the left cheek, because there the
right cheek will never be smitten. There they can freely give all to the poor,
for *there* there will be no poor to give to. A due appreciation of this matter
will do good to man. For, hitherto, being authoritatively taught by his dog-
matical teachers that he must, while on earth, aim at heaven, and attain it,
too, in all his earthly acts, on pain of eternal wrath; and finding by experience
that this is utterly impossible; in his despair, he is too apt to run clean away
into all manner of moral abandonment, self-deceit, and hypocrisy (cloaked,
however, mostly under an aspect of the most respectable devotion); or else he
openly runs, like a mad dog, into atheism. Whereas, let men be taught those
Chronometricals and Horologicals, and while still retaining every common-
sense incentive to whatever of virtue be practicable and desirable, and having
these incentives strengthened, too, by the consciousness of powers to attain

their mark; then there would be an end to that fatal despair of becoming at all good, which has too often proved the vice-producing result in many minds of the undiluted chronometrical doctrines hitherto taught to mankind. But if any man say, that such a doctrine as this I lay down is false, is impious; I would charitably refer that man to the history of Christendom for the last 1800 years; and ask him, whether, in spite of all the maxims of Christ, that history is not just as full of blood, violence, wrong, and iniquity of every kind, as any previous portion of the world's history? Therefore, it follows, that so far as practical results are concerned — regarded in a purely earthly light — the only great original moral doctrine of Christianity (*i.e.* the chronometrical gratuitous return of good for evil, as distinguished from the horological forgiveness of injuries taught by some of the Pagan philosophers), has been found (horologically) a false one; because after 1800 years' inculcation from tens of thousands of pulpits, it has proved entirely impracticable.

"I but lay down, then, what the best mortal men do daily practise; and what all really wicked men are very far removed from. I present consolation to the earnest man, who, among all his human frailties, is still agonisingly conscious of the beauty of chronometrical excellence. I hold up a practicable virtue to the vicious; and interfere not with the eternal truth, that, sooner or later, in all cases, downright vice is downright woe.

"Moreover: if——"

But here the pamphlet was torn, and came to a most untidy termination.

STUDY QUESTIONS

1. *This selection from Melville's novel* Pierre, or The Ambiguities *is a "lecture" which Melville represents as written by a philosopher named Plotinus Plinlimmon. The lecture deals with one possible view of the paradox of Christian ideals in an unideal world. Explain the main symbols of Melville's allegory. That is, what does he mean by Greenwich time, China time, "chronometers" and "horologicals"?*

2. *Would Melville, agree with Westermarck that concepts of morality are relative? Or would he agree with Mrs. Sayers that natural moral law is an ascertainable fact that can be learned through experience?*

3. *What policy does Melville recommend with regard to moral problems?*

4. *What is the tone of this discussion? Do you think it is appropriate? How does it help or hinder Melville in making his point?*

5. *Some may feel that Melville's analogy, in which time and the various ways it can be kept, stand for moral systems, is unfair and misleading. If that is your opinion, write a theme showing why Melville's analogy is faulty.*

6. *Write a theme giving some examples of the differences in moral ideas to which Melville is referring by his symbols, "China time" and "Greenwich time." What do you think is the significance of these differences?*

John Stuart Mill

The Pleasure Principle *

The creed which accepts as the foundation of morals *utility*, or the *greatest happiness principle*, holds that actions are right in proportion as they tend to promote happiness, wrong as they tend to produce the reverse of happiness. By "happiness" is intended pleasure, and the absence of pain; by "unhappiness," pain, and the privation of pleasure. To give a clear view of the moral standard set up by the theory, much more requires to be said; in particular, what things it includes in the ideas of pain and pleasure; and to what extent this is left an open question. But these supplementary explanations do not affect the theory of life on which this theory of morality is grounded — namely, that pleasure, and freedom from pain, are the only things desirable as ends; and that all desirable things (which are as numerous in the utilitarian as in any other scheme) are desirable either for the pleasure inherent in themselves, or as means to the promotion of pleasure and the prevention of pain.

Now such a theory of life excites in many minds, and among them in some of the most estimable in feeling and purpose, inveterate dislike. To suppose that life has (as they express it) no higher end than pleasure — no better and nobler object of desire and pursuit — they designate as utterly mean and groveling; as a doctrine worthy only of swine, to whom the followers of Epicurus were, at a very early period, contemptuously likened; and modern holders of the doctrine are occasionally made the subject of equally polite comparisons by its German, French, and English assailants.

When thus attacked, the Epicureans have always answered that it is not they but their accusers who represent human nature in a degrading light; since the accusation supposes human beings to be capable of no pleasures except those of which swine are capable. If this supposition were true, the charge could not be gainsaid, but would then be no longer an imputation; for if the sources of pleasure were precisely the same to human beings and to swine, the rule of life which is good enough for the one would be good enough for the other. The comparison of the Epicurean life to that of beasts is felt as degrading, precisely because a beast's pleasures do not satisfy a human being's conceptions of happiness. Human beings have faculties more elevated than the animal appetites, and when once made conscious of them, do not regard anything as happiness which does not include their gratification. I do not, indeed, consider the Epicureans to have been by any means faultless in drawing out their scheme of consequences from the utilitarian principle. To do this in any sufficient manner, many Stoic, as well as Christian elements

* From *Utilitarianism*, 1863

require to be included. But there is no known Epicurean theory of life which does not assign to the pleasures of the intellect, of the feelings and imagination, and of the moral sentiments, a much higher value as pleasures than to those of mere sensation. It must be admitted, however, that utilitarian writers in general have placed the superiority of mental over bodily pleasure chiefly in the greater permanency, safety, uncostliness, etc., of the former — that is, in their circumstantial advantages rather than in their intrinsic nature. And on all these points utilitarians have fully proved their case; but they might have taken the other, and, as it may be called, higher ground, with entire consistency. It is quite compatible with the principle of utility to recognize the fact, that some *kinds* of pleasure are more desirable and more valuable than others. It would be absurd that while, in estimating all other things, quality is considered as well as quantity, the estimation of pleasures should be supposed to depend on quantity alone.

If I am asked what I mean by difference of quality in pleasures, or what makes one pleasure more valuable than another merely as a pleasure, except its being greater in amount, there is but one possible answer. Of two pleasures, if there be one to which all or almost all who have experience of both give a decided preference, irrespective of any feeling of moral obligation to prefer it, that is the more desirable pleasure. If one of the two is, by those who are competently acquainted with both, placed so far above the other that they prefer it, even though knowing it to be attended with a greater amount of discontent, and would not resign it for any quantity of the other pleasure which their nature is capable of, we are justified in ascribing to the preferred enjoyment a superiority in quality, so far outweighing quantity as to render it, in comparison, of small account.

Now it is an unquestionable fact that those who are equally acquainted with, and equally capable of appreciating and enjoying both, do give a most marked preference to the manner of existence which employs their higher faculties. Few human creatures would consent to be changed into any of the lower animals, for a promise of the fullest allowance of a beast's pleasures; no intelligent human being would consent to be a fool, no instructed person would be an ignoramus, no person of feeling and conscience would be selfish and base, even though they should be persuaded that the fool, the dunce, or the rascal is better satisfied with his lot than they are with theirs. They would not resign what they possess more than he for the most complete satisfaction of all the desires which they have in common with him. If they ever fancy they would, it is only in cases of unhappiness so extreme, that to escape from it they would exchange their lot for almost any other, however undesirable in their own eyes. A being of higher faculties requires more to make him happy, is capable probably of more acute suffering, and certainly accessible to it at more points, than one of an inferior type; but in spite of these liabilities, he can never really wish to sink into what he feels to be a lower grade of existence. We may give what explanation we please of this unwillingness:

we may attribute it to pride, a name which is given indiscriminately to some
of the most and to some of the least estimable feelings of which mankind are
capable; we may refer it to the love of liberty and personal independence,
an appeal to which was with the Stoics one of the most effective means for the
inculcation of it; to the love of power, or to the love of excitement, both of
which do really enter into and contribute to it: but its most appropriate
appellation is a sense of dignity, which all human beings possess in one
form or other; and in some, though by no means in exact, proportion to their
higher faculties, and which is so essential a part of the happiness of those in
whom it is strong, that nothing which conflicts with it could be, otherwise
than momentarily, an object of desire to them. Whoever supposes that this
preference takes place at a sacrifice of happiness — that the superior being, in
anything like equal circumstances, is not happier than the inferior — con-
founds the two very different ideas, of *happiness* and *content*. It is indis-
putable that the being whose capacities of enjoyment are low, has the greatest
chance of having them fully satisfied; and a highly endowed being will always
feel that any happiness which he can look for, as the world is constituted, is
imperfect. But he can learn to bear its imperfections, if they are at all bear-
able; and they will not make him envy the being who is indeed unconscious of
the imperfections, but only because he feels not at all the good which those
imperfections qualify. It is better to be a human being dissatisfied than a pig
satisfied; better to be Socrates dissatisfied than a fool satisfied. And if the fool,
or the pig, are of a different opinion, it is because they only know their own
side of the question. The other party to the comparison knows both sides.

It may be objected that many who are capable of the higher pleasures,
occasionally, under the influence of temptation, postpone them to the lower.
But this is quite compatible with a full appreciation of the intrinsic superiority
of the higher. Men often, from infirmity of character, make their election for
the nearer good, though they know it to be the less valuable; and this no less
when the choice is between two bodily pleasures, than when it is between
bodily and mental. They pursue sensual indulgences to the injury of health,
though perfectly aware that health is the greater good. It may be further
objected that many who begin with youthful enthusiasm for everything noble,
as they advance in years sink into indolence and selfishness. But I do not believe that those who undergo this very common change, voluntarily choose the
lower description of pleasures in preference to the higher. I believe that before they devote themselves exclusively to the one, they have already become
incapable of the other. Capacity for the nobler feelings is in most natures a
very tender plant, easily killed, not only by hostile influences, but by mere
want of sustenance; and in the majority of young persons it speedily dies
away if the occupations to which their position in life has devoted them, and
the society into which it has thrown them, are not favorable to keeping that
higher capacity in exercise. Men lose their high aspirations as they lose their
intellectual tastes, because they have not time or opportunity for indulging

them; and they addict themselves to inferior pleasures not because they deliberately prefer them, but because they are either the only ones to which they have access or the only ones which they are any longer capable of enjoying. It may be questioned whether anyone who has remained equally susceptible to both classes of pleasures, ever knowingly and calmly preferred the lower; though many, in all ages, have broken down in an ineffectual attempt to combine both.

From this verdict of the only competent judges I apprehend there can be no appeal. On a question which is the best worth having of two pleasures, or which of two modes of existence is the most grateful to the feelings, apart from its moral attributes and from its consequences, the judgment of those who are qualified by knowledge of both, or, if they differ, that of the majority among them, must be admitted as final. And there need be the less hesitation to accept this judgment respecting the quality of pleasures, since there is no other tribunal to be referred to even on the question of quantity. What means are there of determining which is the acutest of two pains, or the intensest of two pleasurable sensations, except the general suffrage of those who are familiar with both? Neither pains nor pleasures are homogeneous, and pain is always heterogeneous with pleasure. What is there to decide whether a particular pleasure is worth purchasing at the cost of a particular pain, except the feelings and judgment of the experienced? When, therefore, those feelings and judgment declare the pleasures derived from the higher faculties to be preferable *in kind*, apart from the question of intensity, to those of which the animal nature, disjoined from the higher faculties, is susceptible, they are entitled on this subject to the same regard.

I have dwelt on this point, as being a necessary part of a perfectly just conception of utility, or happiness, considered as the directive rule of human conduct. But it is by no means an indispensable condition to the acceptance of the utilitarian standard; for that standard is not the agent's own greater happiness, but the greatest amount of happiness altogether; and if it may possibly be doubted whether a noble character is always the happier for its nobleness, there can be no doubt that it makes other people happier, and that the world in general is immensely a gainer by it. Utilitarianism, therefore, could only attain its end by the general cultivation of nobleness of character, even if each individual were only benefited by the nobleness of others, and his own, so far as happiness is concerned, were a sheer deduction from the benefit. But the bare enunciation of such an absurdity as this last renders refutation superfluous.

According to the "greatest happiness principle," as above explained, the ultimate end, with reference to and for the sake of which all other things are desirable (whether we are considering our own good or that of other people), is an existence exempt as far as possible from pain, and as rich as possible in enjoyments, both in point of quantity and quality; the test of quality, and the rule for measuring it against quantity, being the preference felt by those who in their opportunities of experience, to which must be added their habits of self-consciousness and self-observation, are best furnished with the means of comparison. This, being, according to the utilitarian opinion, the end of human action, is necessarily also the standard of morality; which may accordingly be defined, the rules and precepts for human conduct, by the observance of which an existence such as has been described might be, to the greatest extent possible, secured to all mankind; and not to them only, but, so far as the nature of things admits, to the whole sentient creation.

STUDY QUESTIONS

1. *How does Mill answer the argument that his "greatest happiness principle" is degrading?*
2. *Are you satisfied with Mill's evidence that the pleasures of the intellect and sensibility are higher in quality than those of the body?*
3. *What distinction does Mill make between happiness and contentment?*
4. *How well do Mill's ideas correspond with those of Westermarck? What relation do they have to those of Mrs. Sayers?*
5. *Do you agree with Mill that questions of right and wrong should be decided according to the amount of pleasure and pain that will result? Write a theme defending or attacking this principle.*
6. *Do you think Mill's principle would be desirable or workable on the practical level? Write a theme giving your opinion of it as the basis for a practical morality.*

Walter Pater FROM The Renaissance*

CONCLUSION

Λέγει που Ἡράκλειτος ὅτι πάντα χωρεῖ καὶ οὐδὲν μένει[1]

*T*o regard all things and principles of things as inconsistent modes or fashions has more and more become the tendency of modern thought. Let us begin with that which is without — our physical life. Fix upon it in one of its more exquisite intervals, the moment, for instance, of delicious recoil from the flood of water in summer heat. What is the whole physical life in that moment but a combination of natural elements to which science gives their

---

* First published in 1873.
[1] Λέγει που Ἡράκλειτος, etc., from the *Cratylus* of Plato (402 A). In his *Plato and Platonism*, ch. I, Pater translates: "Heraclitus cries out, All things give way: nothing remaineth" (*Library Ed.*, 14).

names? But these elements, phosphorus and lime and delicate fibres, are present not in the human body alone: we detect them in places most remote from it. Our physical life is a perpetual motion of them—the passage of the blood, the wasting and repairing of the lenses of the eye, the modification of the tissues of the brain by every ray of light and sound—processes which science reduces to simpler and more elementary forces. Like the elements of which we are composed, the action of these forces extends beyond us; it rusts iron and ripens corn. Far out on every side of us those elements are broadcast, driven by many forces; and birth and gesture and death and the springing of violets from the grave are but a few out of ten thousand resultant combinations. That clear, perpetual outline of face and limb is but an image of ours, under which we group them—a design in a web, the actual threads of which pass out beyond it. This at least of flame-like our life has, that it is but the concurrence, renewed from moment to moment, of forces parting sooner or later on their ways.

Or if we begin with the inward world of thought and feeling, the whirlpool is still more rapid, the flame more eager and devouring. There it is no longer the gradual darkening of the eye and fading of colour from the wall,—the movement of the shore-side, where the water flows down indeed, though in apparent rest,—but the race of the mid-stream, a drift of momentary acts of sight and passion and thought. At first sight experience seems to bury us under a flood of external objects, pressing upon us with a sharp and importunate reality, calling us out of ourselves in a thousand forms of action. But when reflection begins to act upon those objects they are dissipated under its influence; the cohesive force seems suspended like a trick of magic; each object is loosed into a group of impressions — colour, odour, texture — in the mind of the observer. And if we continue to dwell in thought on this world, not of objects in the solidity with which language invests them, but of impressions unstable, flickering, inconsistent, which burn and are extinguished with our consciousness of them, it contracts still further; the whole scope of observation is dwarfed to the narrow chamber of the individual mind. Experience, already reduced to a swarm of impressions, is ringed round for each one of us by that thick wall of personality through which no real voice has ever pierced on its way to us, or from us to that which we can only conjecture to be without. Every one of those impressions is the impression of the individual in his isolation, each mind keeping as a solitary prisoner its own dream of a world.

Analysis goes a step farther still, and assures us that those impressions of the individual mind to which, for each one of us, experience dwindles down, are in perpetual flight; that each of them is limited by time, and that as time is infinitely divisible, each of them is infinitely divisible also; all that is actual in it being a single moment, gone while we try to apprehend it, of which it may ever be more truly said that it has ceased to be than that it is. To such a tremulous wisp constantly reforming itself on the stream, to a single sharp impression, with a sense in it, a relic more or less fleeting, of such moments gone by, what is real in our life fines itself down. It is with this movement, with the passage and dissolution of impressions, images, sensations, that analysis leaves off — that continual vanishing away, that strange, perpetual weaving and unweaving of ourselves.

Philosophiren, says Novalis, *ist dephlegmatisiren, vivificiren*.[2] The service of philosophy, of speculative culture, towards the human spirit is to rouse, to startle it into sharp and eager observation. Every moment some form grows perfect in hand or face; some tone on the hills or the sea is choicer than the rest; some mood of passion or insight or intellectual excitement is irresistibly real and attractive for us, — for that moment only. Not the fruit of experience, but experience itself, is the end. A counted number of pulses only is given to us of a variegated, dramatic, life. How may we see in them all that is to be seen in them by the finest sense? How shall we pass most swiftly from point to point, and be present always at the focus where the greatest number of vital forces unite in their purest energy?

To burn always with this hard, gemlike flame, to maintain this ecstasy, is success in life. In a sense it might even be said that our failure is to form habits: for, after all, habit is relative to a stereotyped world, and meantime it is only the roughness of the eye that makes any two persons, things, situations, seem alike. While all melts under our feet, we may well catch at any exquisite passion, or any contribution to knowledge that seems by a lifted horizon to set the spirit free for a moment, or any stirring of the senses, strange dyes, strange colours, and curious odours, or work of the artist's hands, or the face of one's friend. Not to discriminate every moment some passionate attitude in those about us, and in the brilliancy of their gifts some tragic dividing of forces on their ways, is, on this short day of frost and sun, to sleep before evening. With this sense of the splendour of our experience and of its awful brevity, gathering all we are into one desperate effort to see and touch, we shall hardly have time to make theories about the things we see and touch. What we have to do is to be for ever curiously testing new opinions and courting new impressions, never acquiescing in a facile orthodoxy of Comte, or of Hegel, or of our own. Philosophical theories or ideas, as points of view, instruments of criticism, may help us to gather up what might otherwise pass unregarded by us. "Philosophy is the microscope of thought." The theory or idea or system which requires of us the sacrifice of any part of this experience, in consideration of some interest into which we cannot enter, or some abstract theory we have not identified with ourselves, or what is only conventional, has no real claim upon us.

One of the most beautiful passages in the writings of Rousseau is that in the sixth book of the *Confessions*, where he describes the awakening in him of the literary sense. An undefinable taint of death had always clung about him, and now in early manhood he believed himself smitten by mortal disease.

---

[2] *Philosophiren*, etc.: "To philosophize is to throw off inertia, to come to life." Novalis is the pseudonym of Friedrich von Hardenberg (1772-1801), German poet and romanticist.

He asked himself how he might make as much as possible of the interval that remained; and he was not biassed by anything in his previous life when he decided that it must be by intellectual excitement, which he found just then in the clear, fresh writings of Voltaire. Well! we are all *condamnés*, as Victor Hugo says: we are all under sentence of death but with a sort of indefinite reprieve — *les hommes sont tous condamnés à mort avec des sursis indéfinis:* we have an interval, and then our place knows us no more. Some spend this interval in listlessness, some in high passions, the wisest, at least among "the children of this world," in art and song. For our one chance lies in expanding that interval, in getting as many pulsations as possible into the given time. Great passions may give us this quickened sense of life, ecstasy and sorrow of love, the various forms of enthusiastic activity, disinterested or otherwise, which come naturally to many of us. Only be sure it is passion — that it does yield you this fruit of a quickened, multiplied consciousness. Of this wisdom, the poetic passion, the desire of beauty, the love of art for art's sake, has most; for art comes to you professing frankly to give nothing but the highest quality to your moments as they pass, and simply for those moments' sake.

STUDY QUESTIONS

1. *What does Pater think is the relation between the individual and the sensations offered by the world around him? What attitude toward the external world does Pater recommend?*

2. *What is Pater's opinion of habit, theory, and abstraction? Is Pater's idea that we must be "forever curiously testing new opinions and courting new experiences" the kind of process Newman recommends in his "Knowledge Viewed in Relation to Learning" for the "enlargement of the mind"? Is the aim the same? Explain.*

3. *How well do Pater's ideas correspond with those of Mill in "The Pleasure Principle"? Does Pater seem interested in society or in the individual? Which does Mill seem to have in mind?*

4. *Pater is famous for the richness and precision of his style—the care with which he chose his words and wrought his sentences. Although much of his writing now seems to us in some ways overworked, we can learn much from him. What differences do you find between his writing and that of Mill? Do you think there is a basic difference in purpose? Is Pater more concrete and specific? Do you notice any particular differences in sentence structure or vocabulary?*

5. *Write a theme describing some experience which you found enjoyable and significant, and which, as Pater puts it, seemed to give the highest possible quality to some moment.*

6. *Do you think Pater is wrong in saying that we can never appreciate more than a small part of the external world? Write a theme on this question, either supporting Pater or showing how he underestimates man's ability to observe and understand his environment.*

Lionel Trilling The Morality of Inertia*

A theological seminary in New York planned a series of lectures on "The Literary Presentations of Great Moral Issues," and invited me to give one of the talks. Since I have a weakness for the general subject, I was disposed to accept the invitation. But I hesitated over the particular instance, for I was asked to discuss the moral issues in *Ethan Frome*. I had not read Edith Wharton's little novel in a good many years, and I remembered it with no pleasure or admiration. I recalled it as not at all the sort of book that deserved to stand in a list which included *The Brothers Karamazov* and *Billy Budd, Foretopman*. If it presented a moral issue at all, I could not bring to mind what that issue was. And so I postponed my acceptance of the invitation and made it conditional upon my being able to come to terms with the subject assigned to me.

Ethan Frome, when I read it again, turned out to be pretty much as I had recalled it, not a great book or even a fine book, but a factitious book, perhaps even a cruel book. I was puzzled to understand how it ever came to be put on the list, why anyone should want to have it discussed as an example of moral perception. Then I remembered its reputation, which, in America, is very considerable. It is sometimes spoken of as an American classic. It is often assigned to high-school and college students as a text for study.

But the high and solemn repute in which it stands is, I am sure, in large part a mere accident of American culture. *Ethan Frome* appeared in 1911, at a time when, to a degree that we can now only wonder at, American literature was committed to optimism, cheerfulness, and gentility. What William Dean Howells called the "smiling aspects of life" had an importance in the literature of America some fifty years ago which is unmatched in the literature of any other time and place. It was inevitable that those who were critical of the prevailing culture and who wished to foster in America higher and more serious literature should put a heavy stress upon the grimmer aspects of life, that they should equate the smiling aspects with falsehood, the grimmer aspects with truth. For these devoted people, sickened as they were by cheerfulness and hope, the word "stark" seemed to carry the highest possible praise a critical review or a blurb could bestow, with "relentless" and "inevitable" as its proper variants. *Ethan Frome* was admired because it was "stark" — its action, we note, takes place in the New England village of Starkville — and because the fate it describes is *relentless* and *inevitable*.

---

* From *A Gathering of Fugitives* by Lionel Trilling. Copyright, 1956, by Lionel Trilling. Reprinted by permission of The Beacon Press, Inc.

No one would wish to question any high valuation that may be given to the literary representation of unhappy events — except, perhaps, as the high valuation may be a mere cliché of an intellectual class, except as it is supposed to seem the hallmark of the superior sensibility and intelligence of that class. When it is only this, we have the right, and the duty, to look sniffishly at starkness, and relentlessness, and inevitability, to cock a skeptical eye at grimness. And I am quite unable to overcome my belief that *Ethan Frome* enjoys its high reputation because it still satisfies our modern snobbishness about tragedy and pain.

We can never speak of Edith Wharton without some degree of respect. She brought to her novels a strong if limited intelligence, notable powers of observation, and a genuine desire to tell the truth, a desire which in some part she satisfied. But she was a woman in whom we cannot fail to see a limitation of heart, and this limitation makes itself manifest as a literary and moral deficiency of her work, and of *Ethan Frome* especially. It appears in the deadness of her prose, and more flagrantly in the suffering of her characters. Whenever the characters of a story suffer, they do so at the behest of their author — the author is responsible for their suffering and must justify his cruelty by the seriousness of his moral intention. The author of *Ethan Frome,* it seemed to me as I read the book again to test my memory of it, could not lay claim to any such justification. Her intention in writing the story was not adequate to the dreadful fate she contrived for her characters. She indulges herself by what she contrives — she is, as the phrase goes, "merely literary." This is not to say that the merely literary intention does not make its very considerable effects. There is in *Ethan Frome* an image of life-in-death, of hell-on-earth, which is not easily forgotten: the crippled Ethan, and Zeena, his dreadful wife, and Matty, the once charming girl he had loved, now bedridden and querulous with pain, all living out their death in the kitchen of the desolate Frome farm — a perpetuity of suffering memorializes a moment of passion. It is terrible to contemplate, it is unforgettable, but the mind can do nothing with it, can only endure it.

My new reading of the book, then, did not lead me to suppose that it justified its reputation, but only confirmed my recollection that *Ethan Frome* was a dead book, the product of mere will, of the cold hard literary will. What is more, it seemed to me quite unavailable for any moral discourse. In the context of morality, there is nothing to say about *Ethan Frome*. It presents no moral issue at all.

For consider the story it tells. A young man of good and gentle character is the only son of a New England farm couple. He has some intellectual gifts and some desire to know the world, and for a year he is happy attending a technical school. But his father is incapacitated by a farm accident, and Ethan dutifully returns to manage the failing farm and sawmill. His father dies; his mother loses her mental faculties, and during her last illness she is nursed by a female relative whom young Ethan marries, for no other reason than that he is bemused by loneliness. The new wife, Zeena, immediately becomes a shrew, a harridan and a valetudinarian — she lives only to be ill. Because Zeena now must spare herself, the Fromes take into their home a gentle and charming young girl, a destitute cousin of the wife. Ethan and Matty fall in love, innocently but deeply. The wife, perceiving this, plans to send the girl away, her place to be taken by a servant whose wages the husband cannot possibly afford. In despair at the thought of separation Matty and Ethan attempt suicide. They mean to die by sledding down a steep hill and crashing into a great elm at the bottom. Their plan fails: both survive the crash, Ethan to be sorely crippled, Matty to be bedridden in perpetual pain. Now the wife Zeena surrenders her claim to a mysterious pathology and becomes the devoted nurse and jailer of the lovers. The terrible tableau to which I have referred is ready for inspection.

It seemed to me that it was quite impossible to talk about this story. This is not to say that the story is without interest as a story, but what interest it may have does not yield discourse, or at least not moral discourse.

But as I began to explain to the lecture committee why I could not accept the invitation to lecture about the book, it suddenly came over me how very strange a phenomenon the book made — how remarkable it was that a story should place before us the dreadful image of three ruined and tortured lives, showing how their ruin came about, and yet propose no moral issue of any kind. And if *issue* seems to imply something more precisely formulated than we have a right to demand of a story, then it seemed to me no less remarkable that the book had scarcely any moral reverberation, that strange and often beautiful sound we seem to hear generated in the air by a tale of suffering, a sound which is not always music, which does not always have a "meaning," but which yet entrances us, like the random notes of an Aeolian harp, or merely the sound of the wind in the chimney. The moral sound that *Ethan Frome* makes is a dull thud. And this seemed to me so remarkable, indeed, that in the very act of saying why I could not possibly discuss *Ethan Frome*, I found the reason why it must be discussed.

It is, as I have suggested, a very great fault in *Ethan Frome* that it presents no moral issue, sets off no moral reverberation. A certain propriety controls the literary representation of human suffering. This propriety dictates that the representation of pain may not be, as it were, gratuitous; it must not be an end in itself. The naked act of representing, or contemplating, human suffering is a self-indulgence, and it may be a cruelty. Between a tragedy and a spectacle in the Roman circus there is at least this much similarity, that the pleasure both afford derives from observing the pain of others. A tragedy is always on the verge of cruelty. What saves it from the actuality of cruelty is that it has an intention beyond itself. This intention may be so simple a one as that of getting us to do something practical about the cause of the suffering or to help actual sufferers, or at least to feel that we should;

or it may lead us to look beyond apparent causes to those which the author wishes us to think of as more real, such as Fate, or the will of the gods, or the will of God; or it may challenge our fortitude or intelligence or piety.

A sense of the necessity of some such intention animates all considerations of the strange paradox of tragedy. Aristotle is concerned to solve the riddle of how the contemplation of human suffering can possibly be pleasurable, of why its pleasure is permissible. He wanted to know what literary conditions were needed to keep a tragedy from being a display of horror. Here it is well to remember that the Greeks were not so concerned as we have been led to believe to keep all dreadful things off the stage — in the presentation of Aristotle's favorite tragedy, the audience saw Jocasta hanging from a beam, it saw the representation of Oedipus's bloody eyesockets. And so Aristotle discovered, or pretended to discover, that tragedy did certain things to protect itself from being merely cruel. It chose, Aristotle said, a certain kind of hero; he was of a certain social and moral stature; he had a certain degree of possibility of free choice; he must justify his fate, or seem to justify it, by his moral condition, being neither wholly good nor wholly bad, having a particular fault that collaborates with destiny to bring about his ruin. The purpose of all these specifications for the tragic hero is to assure us that we observe something more than mere passivity when we witness the hero's suffering, that the suffering has, as we say, some meaning, some show of rationality.

Aristotle's theory of tragedy has had its way with the world to an extent which is perhaps out of proportion to its comprehensiveness and accuracy. Its success is largely due to its having dealt so openly with the paradox of tragedy. It serves to explain away any guilty feelings that we may have at deriving pleasure from suffering.

But at the same time that the world has accepted Aristotle's theory of tragedy, it has also been a little uneasy about some of its implications. The element of the theory that causes uneasiness in modern times is the matter of the stature of the hero. To a society based in egalitarian sentiments, the requirement that the hero be a man of rank seems to deny the presumed dignity of tragedy to men of lesser status. And to a culture which questions the freedom of the will, Aristotle's hero seems to be a little beside the point. Aristotle's prescription for the tragic hero is clearly connected with his definition, in his *Ethics,* of the nature of an ethical action. He tells us that a truly ethical action must be a free choice between two alternatives. This definition is then wonderfully complicated by a further requirement — that the moral man must be so trained in making the right choice that he makes it as a matter of habit, makes it, as it were, instinctively. Yet it *is* a choice, and reason plays a part in its making. But we, of course, don't give to reason the same place in the moral life that Aristotle gave it. And in general, over the last hundred and fifty years, dramatists and novelists have tried their hand at the representation of human suffering without the particular safeguards against cruelty which Aristotle perceived, or contrived. A very large part of the literature of Western Europe may be understood in terms of an attempt to invert or criticize the heroic prescription of the hero, by burlesque and comedy, or by the insistence on the common-place, the lowering of the hero's social status and the diminution of his power of reasoned choice. The work of Fielding may serve as an example of how the mind of Europe has been haunted by the great image of classical tragedy, and how it has tried to lay that famous ghost. When Fielding calls his hero Tom Jones, he means that his young man is not Orestes or Achilles; when he calls him a foundling, he is suggesting that Tom Jones is not, all appearances to the contrary notwithstanding, Oedipus.

Edith Wharton was following where others led. Her impulse in conceiving the story of Ethan Frome was not, however, that of moral experimentation. It was, as I have said, a purely literary impulse, in the bad sense of the word "literary." Her aim is not that of Wordsworth in any of his stories of the suffering poor, to require of us that we open our minds to a realization of the kinds of people whom suffering touches. Nor is it that of Flaubert in *Madame Bovary,* to wring from solid circumstances all the pity and terror of an ancient tragic fable. Nor is it that of Dickens or Zola, to shake us with the perception of social injustice, to instruct us in the true nature of social life and to dispose us to indignant opinion and action. These are not essentially literary intentions; they are moral intentions. But all that Edith Wharton has in mind is to achieve that grim tableau of which I have spoken, of pain and imprisonment, of life-in-death. About the events that lead up to this tableau, there is nothing she finds to say, nothing whatever. The best we can conclude of the meaning of her story is that it might perhaps be a subject of discourse in the context of rural sociology — it might be understood to exemplify the thesis that love and joy do not flourish on poverty-stricken New England farms. If we try to bring it into the context of morality, its meaning goes no further than certain cultural considerations — that is, to people who like their literature to show the "smiling aspects of life," it may be thought to say, "This is the aspect that life really has, as grim as this"; while to people who repudiate a literature that represents only the smiling aspects of life it says, "How intelligent and how brave you are to be able to understand that life is as grim as this." It is really not very much to say.

And yet there is in *Ethan Frome* an idea of considerable importance. It is there by reason of the author's deficiencies, not by reason of her powers — because it suits Edith Wharton's rather dull intention to be content with telling a story about people who do not make moral decisions, whose fate cannot have moral reverberations. The idea is this: that moral inertia, the *not* making of moral decisions, constitutes a large part of the moral life of humanity.

This isn't an idea that literature likes to deal with. Literature is charmed by energy and dislikes inertia. It characteristically represents morality as positive action. The same is true of the moral philosophy of the West — has been true ever since Aristotle defined a truly moral act by its energy of reason, of choice. A later development of this tendency said that an act was really moral only if it went against the inclination of the person performing the act: the idea was parodied as saying that one could not possibly act morally to one's friends, only to one's enemies.

Yet the dull daily world sees something below this delightful preoccupation of literature and moral philosophy. It is aware of the morality of inertia, and of its function as a social base, as a social cement. It knows that duties are done for no other reason than that they are said to be duties; for no other reason, sometimes, than that the doer has not really been able to conceive of any other course, has, perhaps, been afraid to think of any other course. Hobbes said of the Capitol geese that saved Rome by their cackling that they were the salvation of the city, not because they were they but there. How often the moral act is performed not because we are we but because we are there! This is the morality of habit, or the morality of biology. This is Ethan Frome's morality, simple, unquestioning, passive, even masochistic. His duties as a son are discharged because he is a son; his duties as a husband are discharged because he is a husband. He does nothing by moral election. At one point in his story he is brought to moral crisis — he must choose between his habituated duty to his wife and his duty and inclination to the girl he loves. It is quite impossible for him to deal with the dilemma in the high way that literature and moral philosophy prescribe, by reason and choice. Choice is incompatible with his idea of his existence; he can only elect to die.

Literature, of course, is not wholly indifferent to what I have called the morality of habit and biology, the morality of inertia. But literature, when it deals with this morality, is tempted to qualify its dullness by endowing it with a certain high grace. There is never any real moral choice for the Félicité of Flaubert's story "A Simple Heart." She is all pious habit of virtue, and of blind, unthinking, unquestioning love. There are, of course, actually such people as Félicité, simple, good, loving — quite stupid in their love, not choosing where to bestow it. We meet such people frequently in literature, in the pages of Balzac, Dickens, Dostoievski, Joyce, Faulkner, Hemingway. They are of a quite different order of being from those who try the world with their passion and their reason; they are by way of being saints, of the less complicated kind. They do not really exemplify what I mean by the morality of inertia. Literature is uncomfortable in the representation of the morality of inertia or of biology, and overcomes its discomfort by representing it with the added grace of that extravagance which we denominate saintliness.

But the morality of inertia is to be found in very precise exemplification in one of Wordsworth's poems. Wordsworth is pre-eminent among the writers who experimented in the representation of new kinds and bases of moral action — he has a genius for imputing moral existence to people who, according to the classical morality, should have no moral life at all. And he has the courage to make this imputation without at the same time imputing the special grace and interest of saintliness. The poem I have in mind is ostensibly about a flower, but the transition from the symbol to the human fact is clearly, if awkwardly, made. The flower is a small celandine, and the poet observes that it has not, in the natural way of flowers, folded itself against rough weather:

> But lately, one rough day, this Flower I passed
> And recognized it, though in altered form,
> Now standing as an offering to the blast,
> And buffeted at will by rain and storm.
>
> I stopped, and said with inly-muttered voice,
> It doth not love the shower nor seek the cold;
> This neither is its courage nor its choice,
> But its necessity in being old.

Neither courage nor choice, but necessity: it cannot do otherwise. Yet it acts as if by courage and choice. This is the morality imposed by brute circumstance, by biology, by habit, by the unspoken social demand which we have not the strength to refuse, or, often, to imagine refusing. People are scarcely ever praised for living according to this morality — we do not suppose it to be a morality at all until we see it being broken.

This is morality as it is conceived by the great mass of people in the world. And with this conception of morality goes the almost entire negation of any connection between morality and destiny. A superstitious belief in retribution may play its part in the thought of simple people, but essentially they think of catastrophes as fortuitous, without explanation, without reason. They live in the moral universe of the Book of Job. In complex lives, morality does in some part determine destiny; in most lives it does not. Between the moral life of Ethan and Matty and their terrible fate we cannot make any reasonable connection. Only a moral judgment cruel to the point of insanity could speak of it as anything but accidental.

I have not spoken of the morality of inertia in order to praise it but only to recognize it, to suggest that when we keep our minds fixed on what the great invigorating books tell us about the moral life, we obscure the large bulking dull mass of moral fact. Morality is not only the high, torturing dilemmas of Ivan Karamazov and Captain Vere. It is also the deeds performed without thought, without choice, perhaps even without love, as Zeena Frome ministers to Ethan and Matty. The morality of inertia, of the dull unthinking round of duties, may, and often does, yield the immorality of inertia; the example that will most readily occur to us is that of the good simple people, so true to their family responsibilities, who gave no thought to the concentration camps in whose shadow they lived. No: the morality of inertia is not to be praised, but it must be recognized. And Edith Wharton's little novel must be recognized for bringing to our attention what we, and literature, so easily forget.

STUDY QUESTIONS

1. *Exactly what is meant by "the morality of inertia"? How does it differ from the usual concept of morality? Why does* Ethan Frome *present "no moral issue at all"?*
2. *Is "the morality of inertia" really morality? Is it possible to conceive of morality in the absence of choice? Can a person be moral if his course of action is compulsory? In considering these questions, refer to Milton's views about the freedom to read in evil books as he expresses them in* Areopagitica.
3. *What reasons does Trilling give for the decline of tragedy in modern times?*
4. *What importance is attributed to the presence of a "moral issue" in a work of literature? What does Trilling mean when he says the "mind can do nothing with" the suffering depicted in* Etham Frome?
5. *In what ways do some of the works mentioned by the author fulfill the requirement that they be concerned with a moral intention? What does Trilling mean when he speaks of a book as having or not having a "moral reverberation"?*
6. *Can you give some example from your experience of the kind of morality described by Trilling?*

E. M. Forster   What I Believe*

I do not believe in belief. But this is an age of faith, in which one is surrounded by so many militant creeds that, in self-defense, one has to formulate a creed of one's own. Tolerance, good temper, and sympathy are no longer enough in a world which is rent by religious and racial persecution, in a world where ignorance rules, and science, which ought to have ruled, plays the subservient pimp. Tolerance, good temper, and sympathy — well, they are what matter really, and if the human race is not to collapse they must come to the front before long. But for the moment they don't seem enough; their action is no stronger than a flower battered beneath a military jack-boot. They want stiffening, even if the process coarsens them. Faith, to my mind, is a stiffening process, a sort of mental starch, which ought to be applied as sparingly as possible. I dislike the stuff. I do not believe in it, for

* From *Two Cheers for Democracy*, copyright, 1938, 1939, 1947, 1949, 1951, by E. M. Forster. Reprinted by permission of Harcourt, Brace and Company, Inc. and Edward Arnold, Ltd.

its own sake, at all. My lawgivers are Erasmus and Montaigne, not Moses and St. Paul. My temple stands not upon Mount Moriah but in that Elysian Field where even the immoral are admitted.

I have, however, to live in an Age of Faith — the sort of thing I used to hear praised and recommended when I was a boy. It is damned unpleasant, really. It is bloody in every sense of the word. And I have to keep my end up in it. Where do I start?

With personal relationships. Here is something comparatively solid in a world full of violence and cruelty. Not absolutely solid, for psychology has split and shattered the idea of a "person" and has shown that there is something incalculable in each of us, which may at any moment rise to the surface and destroy our normal balance. We don't know what we're like. We can't know what we're like. We can't know what other people are like. How then can we put any trust in personal relationships, or cling to them in the gathering political storm? In theory we can't. But in practice we can and do. For the purpose of living one has to assume that the personality is solid, and the "self" is an entity, and to ignore all contrary evidence. And since to ignore evidence is one of the characteristics of faith, I certainly can proclaim that I believe in personal relationships.

Starting from them, I get a little order into the contemporary chaos. One must be fond of people and trust them if one isn't to make a mess of life, and it is therefore essential that they shouldn't let one down. They often do. The moral of which is that I must, myself, be as reliable as possible, and this I try to be. But reliability isn't a matter of contract. It is a matter for the heart, which signs no documents. In other words, reliability is impossible unless there is a natural warmth. Most men possess this warmth, though they often have bad luck and get chilled. Personal relationships are despised today. They are regarded as bourgeois luxuries, as products of a time of fair weather which has now passed, and we are urged to get rid of them, and to dedicate ourselves to some movement or cause instead. I hate the idea of dying for a cause, and if I had to choose between betraying my country and betraying my friend, I hope I should have the guts to betray my country. Such a choice may scandalize the modern reader, and he may stretch out his patriotic hand to the telephone at once, and ring up the police. It wouldn't have shocked Dante, though. Dante placed Brutus and Cassius in the lowest circle of Hell because they had chosen to betray their friend Julius Caesar, rather than their country, Rome.

This brings me along to democracy, "even Love, the Beloved Republic, which feeds upon Freedom and lives." Democracy isn't a beloved republic really, and never will be. But it is less hateful than other contemporary forms of government, and to that extent it deserves our support. It does start from the assumption that the individual is important, and that all types are needed to make a civilization. It doesn't divide its citizens into the bossers and the bossed, as an efficiency-regime tends to do. The people I admire most are those who are sensitive and want to create something or discover something, and don't see life in terms of power, and such people get more of a chance under a democracy than elsewhere. They found religions, great or small, or they produce literature and art, or they do disinterested scientific research, or they may be what are called "ordinary people," who are creative in their private lives, bring up their children decently, for instance, or help their neighbors. All these people need to express themselves, they can't do so unless society allows them liberty to do so, and the society which allows them most liberty is a democracy.

Democracy has another merit. It allows criticism, and if there isn't public criticism there are bound to be hushed-up scandals. That is why I believe in the press, despite all its lies and vulgarity, and why I believe in Parliament. The British Parliament is often sneered at because it's a talking-shop. Well, I believe in it *because* it is a talking-shop. I believe in the Private Member who makes himself a nuisance. He gets snubbed and is told that he is cranky or ill-informed, but he exposes abuses which would otherwise never have been mentioned, and very often an abuse gets put right just by being mentioned. Occasionally, too, in my country, a well-meaning public official loses his head in the cause of efficiency, and thinks himself God Almighty. Such officials are particularly frequent in the Home Office. Well, there will be questions about them in Parliament sooner or later, and then they'll have to mend their ways. Whether Parliament is either a representative body or an efficient one is very doubtful, but I value it because it criticizes and talks, and because its chatter gets widely reported.

So two cheers for democracy: one because it admits variety and one because it permits criticism. Two cheers are quite enough: there is no occasion to give three. Only Love, the Beloved Republic, deserves that.

What about force, though? While we are trying to be sensitive and advanced and affectionate and tolerant, an unpleasant question pops up; doesn't all society rest upon force? If a government can't count upon the police and the army how can it hope to rule? And if an individual gets knocked on the head or sent to a labor camp, of what significance are his opinions?

This dilemma doesn't worry me as much as it does some. I realize that all society rests upon force. But all the great creative actions, all the decent human relations, occur during the intervals when force has not managed to come to the front. These intervals are what matter. I want them to be as frequent and as lengthy as possible and I call them "civilization." Some people idealize force and pull it into the foreground and worship it, instead of keeping it in the background as long as possible. I think they make a mistake, and I think that their opposites, the mystics, err even more when they declare that force doesn't exist. I believe that it does exist, and that one of our jobs is to prevent it from getting out of its box. It gets out sooner or later, and then it destroys us and all the lovely things which we have made. But it isn't out all the time, for the fortunate reason that the strong are so stupid.

Consider their conduct for a moment in the Niebelungs' Ring. The giants there have the gold, or in other words the guns; but they do nothing with it, they do not realize that they are all-powerful, with the result that the catastrophe is delayed and the castle of Valhalla, insecure but glorious, fronts the storms for generations. Fafnir, coiled round his hoard, grumbles and grunts; we can hear him under Europe today; the leaves of the wood already tremble, and the Bird calls its warnings uselessly. Fafnir will destroy us, but by a blessed dispensation he is stupid and slow, and creation goes on just outside the poisonous blast of his breath. The Nietzschean would hurry the monster up, the mystic would say he didn't exist, but Wotan, wiser than either, hastens to create warriors before doom declares itself. The Valkyries are symbols not only of courage but of intelligence; they represent the human spirit snatching its opportunity while the going is good, and one of them even finds time to love. Brunhilde's last song hymns the recurrence of love, and since it is the privilege of art to exaggerate, she goes even further and proclaims the love which is eternally triumphant and feeds upon Freedom, and lives.

So that is what I feel about force and violence. I look the other way until fate strikes me. Whether this is due to courage or to cowardice in my own case I cannot be sure. But I know that if men hadn't looked the other way in the past nothing of any value would survive. The people I respect most behave as if they were immortal and as if society were eternal. Both assumptions are false: both of them must be accepted as true if we are to go on eating and working and loving, and are to keep open a few breathing holes for the human spirit. No millennium seems likely to descend upon humanity; no better and stronger League of Nations will be instituted; no form of Christianity and no alternative to Christianity will bring peace to the world or integrity to the individual; no "change of heart" will occur. And yet we needn't despair, indeed we cannot despair; the evidence of history shows us that men have always insisted on behaving creatively under the shadow of the sword, and that we had better follow their example under the shadow of the airplanes.

There is of course hero worship, fervently recommended as a panacea in some quarters. But here we shall get no help. Hero worship is a dangerous vice, and one of the minor merits of a democracy is that it does not encourage it, or produce that unmanageable type of citizen known as the Great Man. It produces instead different kinds of small men, and that's a much finer achievement. But people who can't get interested in the variety of life and can't make up their own minds get discontented over this, and they long for a hero to bow down before and to follow blindly. It's significant that a hero is an integral part of the authoritarian stock-in-trade today. An efficiency-regime can't be run without a few heroes stuck about to carry off the dullness — much as plums have to be put into a bad pudding to make it palatable. One hero at the top and a smaller one each side of him is a favorite arrangement, and the timid and the bored are comforted by such a trinity and, bowing down, feel exalted by it.

No, I distrust Great Men. They produce a desert of uniformity around them and often a pool of blood, too, and I always feel a little man's pleasure when they come a cropper. I believe in aristocracy though — if that's the right word, and if a democrat may use it. Not an aristocracy of power, based upon rank and influence, but an aristocracy of the sensitive, the considerate, and the plucky. Its members are to be found in all nations and classes, and all through the ages, and there is a secret understanding between them when they meet. They represent the true human tradition, the one permanent victory of our queer race over cruelty and chaos. Thousands of them perish in obscurity; a few are great names. They are sensitive for others as well as for themselves, they are considerate without being fussy, their pluck is not swankiness but the power to endure, and they can take a joke. I give no examples — it is risky to do that — but the reader may as well consider whether this is the type of person he would like to meet and to be, and whether (going further with me) he would prefer that the type should *not* be an ascetic one. I'm against asceticism myself. I'm with the old Scotchman who wanted less chastity and more delicacy. I don't feel that my aristocrats are a real aristocracy if they thwart their bodies, since bodies are the instruments through which we register and enjoy the world. Still, I don't insist here. This isn't a major point. It's clearly possible to be sensitive, considerate, and plucky and yet be an ascetic too, and if anyone possesses the first three qualities, I'll let him in! On they go — an invincible army, yet not a victorious one. The aristocrats, the elect, the chosen, the best people — all the words that describe them are false, and all attempts to organize them fail. Again and again authority, seeing their value, has tried to net them and to utilize them as the Egyptian priesthood or the Christian church or the Chinese civil service or the Group Movement, or some other worthy stunt. But they slip through the net and are gone; when the door is shut they are no longer in the room; their temple, as one of them remarked, is the holiness of the heart's imagination, and their kingdom, though they never possess it, is the wide-open world.

With this type of person knocking about, and constantly crossing one's path if one has eyes to see or hands to feel, the experiment of earthly life cannot be dismissed as a failure. But it may well be hailed as a tragedy, the tragedy being that no device has been found by which these private decencies can be transferred to public affairs. As soon as people have power they go crooked and sometimes dotty, too, because the possession of power lifts them into a region where normal honesty never pays. For instance, the man who is selling newspapers outside the House of Parliament can safely leave his papers to go for a drink, and his cap beside them: anyone who takes a paper is sure to drop a copper into the cap. But the men who are inside the houses of Parliament — they can't trust one another like that; still less can the government they compose trust other governments. No caps upon the pavement here, but suspicion, treachery, and armaments. The more highly public life is organized the lower does its morality sink; the nations of today behave to each other worse than they ever did in the past; they cheat, rob, bully, and bluff, make war without notice, and kill as many women and children as possible; whereas primitive tribes were at all events restrained by taboos.

The Savior of the future — if ever he comes — will not preach a new gospel. He will merely utilize my aristocracy; he will make effective the good will and the good temper which are already existing. In other words he will introduce a new technique. In economics, we are told that if there was a new technique of distribution, there need be no poverty, and people would not starve in one place while crops were dug under in another. A similar change is needed in the sphere of morals and politics. The desire for it is by no means new; it was expressed, for example, in theological terms by Jacopone da Todi over six hundred years ago. "Ordina questo amore, O tu che mi ami," he said. ("O thou who lovest me, set this love in order.") His prayer was not granted and I do not myself believe that it ever will be, but here, and not through a change of heart, is our probable route. Not by becoming better, but by ordering and distributing his native goodness, will man shut up force into its box, and so gain time to explore the universe and to set his mark upon it worthily.

Such a change, claim the orthodox, can only be made by Christianity, and will be made by it in God's good time: man always has failed and always will fail to organize his own goodness, and it is presumptuous of him to try. This claim leaves me cold. I cannot believe that Christianity will ever cope with the present world-wide mess, and I think that such influence as it retains in modern society is due to its financial backing rather than to its spiritual appeal. It was a spiritual force once, but the indwelling spirit will have to be restated if it is to calm the waters again, and probably in a non-Christian form.

These are the reflections of an individualist and a liberal who has found his liberalism crumbling beneath him and at first felt ashamed. Then, looking around, he decided there was no special reason for shame, since other people, whatever they felt, were equally insecure. And as for individualism — there seems no way out of this, even if one wants to find one. The dictator-hero can grind down his citizens till they are all alike, but he can't melt them into a single man. He can order them to merge, he can incite them to mass-antics, but they are obliged to be born separately and to die separately and, owing to these unavoidable termini, will always be running off the totalitarian rails. The memory of birth and the expectation of death always lurk within the human being, making him separate from his fellows and consequently capable of intercourse with them. Naked I came into the world, naked I shall go out of it! And a very good thing, too, for it reminds me that I am naked under my shirt. Until psychologists and biologists have done much more tinkering than seems likely, the individual remains firm and each of us must consent to be one, and to make the best of the difficult job.

STUDY QUESTIONS

1. Note that in this statement of his beliefs, Forster says almost nothing about the sort of questions that are generally considered religious. Yet he does express "faith," a belief in something unproveable, and, in fact, not likely to be true. Explain what this belief is.

2. What are the two reasons—the "Two Cheers for Democracy"—that Forster gives for approving of a democratic form of government? Explain the difference Forster sees in the idea of achievement as conceived by "the artist and the lover" and as conceived by the Great Man.

3. Underlying this discussion is the feeling that there are two opposing elements in life. What are they?

4. There is an easy, relaxed informality about Forster's writing. Can you detect what gives it this quality? Is it appropriate to his attitudes and beliefs? Explain.

5. What would a government be like in which Forster's "aristocracy" had the upper hand? Write a theme describing how such a government would operate.

6. Do you think Forster has given a full or fair treatment of Democracy, Great Men, or Christianity? Write a theme criticizing (or agreeing with) the opinions he has given on any one of these subjects.

3. RELIGIOUS BELIEF IN OUR TIME

Lord Balfour Science, Religion, and Reality *

*L*et us then consider, in the first place, some points on which all men are
agreed. No one practically doubts that the world in which we live
possesses a certain kind and measure of regularity. Every expectation that
we entertain, every action that we voluntarily perform, implies the belief.
The most fantastic fairy tale requires it as a background; there are traces of it
even in our dreams.

Again, we are all at one in treating with suspicion any statement which,
in our judgment, is inconsistent with the "sort of way things happen" in the
world as we conceive it. It seems to us more probable that this or that witness
should be mistaken or mendacious, than that the wonders to which he testified
should be true. If we have no antecedent ground for thinking him a liar, we
probably accept his statements when he confines his narrative to the familiar
or the commonplace; when he deals in marvels we begin to doubt; when his
marvels become too marvelous we frankly disbelieve — though well aware (if
we be men of sense) that what is exceedingly marvelous may nevertheless be
true.

Such, roughly speaking, has been, and is, the general procedure of mankind. But evidently it is ill-suited to satisfy historians, philosophers, or men of
science. It lacks precision. It rests on no clear principles. It depends too
obviously on personal predilections. We seek a criterion of credibility more
objective and more fundamental. We should like to know, for example,
whether there is any sort of statement which, without being self-contradictory,
may always be pronounced untrue.

This question will, to many high authorities, seem capable of the simplest
answer. Unbroken experience (they will tell us) establishes the uniformity of
Nature, and it is the uniformity of Nature which makes inferences from
experience possible. Were this disturbed by miraculous occurrences the very
foundations of science would be shaken. On broad general grounds therefore
"miracles" must be treated in this scientific age as intrinsically incredible.
They never have happened, and they never can happen. Many excellent
people have indeed professed to see them, and we need not doubt their

* From *Science, Religion, and Reality*, ed. by Joseph Needham, 1925. Reprinted
by permission of the Society for the Promotion of Christian Knowledge.

veracity. But illusion is easy, credulity is limitless, and there is nothing in their testimony which can absolve us from the plain duty of purifying or rejecting every narrative in which a taint of the "miraculous" can be detected.

In spite of its apparent precision all this is very loose talk, raising more questions than it answers.

What, for example, is meant by the uniformity of Nature? About the course of Nature we know little; yet surely we know enough to make us hesitate to call it uniform. Phase follows phase in a perpetual flow; but every phase is unique. Nature, as a whole, neither repeats itself, nor (according to science) can possibly repeat itself. Why, then, when we are considering it as a whole, should we describe it as uniform?

Perhaps it will be said that amidst all this infinite variety some fixed rules are always obeyed. Matter (for example) always gravitates to matter. Energy is never either created or destroyed. May we not — nay *must* we not — extend yet further this conception of unbroken regularity, and accept the view that nature, if not uniform as a whole, is nevertheless compounded of uniformities, of causal sequences, endlessly repeated, which collectively illustrate and embody the universal reign of unalterable law? Were any of these causal sequences to fail, we should no doubt be faced with a "miracle"; but such an event (it is urged) would violate all experience, and it need not be seriously considered.

Now this has always seemed to me a most unsatisfactory theory. It throws upon experience a load of responsibility which experience is quite unable to bear. No doubt, as I have already pointed out, the whole conduct of life depends upon our assuming, instinctively or otherwise, that the kind of thing which has happened once, will, under more or less similar circumstances, be likely to happen again. But this assumption, whether instinctive or reflective, whether wisely acted on or unwisely, supplies a very frail foundation for the speculative structure sometimes based upon it. Can it be denied, for example, that nature, uncritically observed, seems honeycombed with irregularities, that the wildest excesses of credulity may arise not from ignoring experience, but from refusing to correct it, that the most ruthless editing is required to force the uncensored messages we receive from the external world into the ideal mold which satisfies our individual convictions?

But what is this ideal mold? We sometimes talk as if by the help of Scientific Method or Inductive Logic we could map out all reality into a scheme of well-defined causes indissolubly connected with well-defined effects, together forming sequences whose recurrence in different combinations constitutes the changing pattern of the universe.

But can such hopes be realized? In the world of concrete fact nothing occurs through the action of a single cause, nor yet through the simple cooperation of many causes, each adding its own unqualified contribution to the total effect, as we picture horse helping horse to draw a loaded dray. Our world is a much more complicated affair. Sequences are never exactly repeated. Causes can never be completely isolated. Their operation is never unqualified. Fence round your laboratory experiments with what precautions you will, no two of them will ever be performed under exactly the same conditions. For the purpose in hand the differences may be negligible. With skilled observers they commonly are. But the differences exist, and they must certainly modify, however imperceptibly, the observed result.

It seems evident from considerations like these that no argument directly based on mere experience can be urged either for or against the possibility of "miracles." Common sense looks doubtfully upon anything out of the common; and science follows suit. But this is very different from the speculative assertion that, since "miracles" are a violation of natural law, their occurrence must be regarded as impossible. The intrusion of an unexpected and perhaps anomalous element into the company of more familiar factors in world development may excite suspicion, but it does not of necessity violate anything more important than our preconceived expectations.

I think it will be found that those who most vehemently reject this way of regarding the world are unconsciously moved not by their knowledge of scientific laws, but by preference for a particular scientific ideal. They are persuaded that if only we had the right kind of knowledge and adequate powers of calculation, we should be able to explain the whole contents of possible experience by applying mathematical methods to certain simple data. They refuse to believe that this calculable "Whole" can suffer interference at the hands of any incalculable power. They find no room in the close-knit tissue of the world process, as they conceive it, for any arbitrary element to find lodgment. They have a clear notion of what science ought to be, and that notion is incompatible with the "miraculous."

The conception of a material universe, overwhelming in its complexity and its splendor, yet potentially susceptible of complete explanation by the actions and the reactions of two very minute and simple kinds of electrical sub-atom, is, without doubt, extraordinarily fascinating. From the early days of scientific philosophy or (if you prefer it) of philosophical science, thinkers have been hungering after some form of all-embracing atomism. They have now apparently reached it (so far as matter is concerned) by the way of observation and experiment — truly a marvelous performance. Yet the very lucidity of the new conceptions helps to bring home to us their essential insufficiency as a theory of the universe. They may be capable of explaining the constitution and behavior of inanimate objects. They may go some (as yet unmeasured) distance towards explaining organic life. But they certainly cannot explain mind. No man really supposes that he personally is nothing more than a changing group of electrical charges, so distributed that their relative motions enable or compel them in their collective capacity to will, to hope, to love, to think, perhaps to discuss themselves as a physical multiplicity, certainly to treat themselves as a mental unity. No creed of this kind can ever be extracted by valid reasoning from the sort of data which the physics either of the present or the future can possibly supply.

The truth is that the immense advances which in modern times have been made by mechanical or quasi-mechanical explanations of the material world have somewhat upset the mental balance of many thoughtful persons who approach the problems of reality exclusively from the physical side. It is not that they formulate any excessive claims to knowledge. On the contrary, they often describe themselves as agnostics. Nevertheless they are apt unconsciously to assume that they already enjoy a good bird's-eye view of what reality *is*, combined with an unshaken assurance about what it is *not*. They tacitly suppose that every discovery, if genuine, will find its place within the framework of a perfected physics, and, if it does not, may be summarily dismissed as mere superstition.

After all, however, superstition may be negative as well as positive, and the excesses of unbelief may be as extravagant as those of belief. Doubtless the universe, as conceived by men more primitive than ourselves, was the obscure abode of strange deities. But what are we to say about a universe reduced without remainder to collections of electric charges radiating energy through a hypothetical ether? Thus to set limits to reality must always be the most hazardous of speculative adventures. To do so by eliminating the spiritual is not only hazardous but absurd. For if we are directly aware of anything, it is of ourselves as personal agents; if anything can be proved by direct experiment it is that we can, in however small a measure, vary the "natural" distribution of matter and energy. We can certainly act on our environment, and as certainly our action can never be adequately explained in terms of entities which neither think, nor feel, nor purpose, nor know. It constitutes a spiritual invasion of the physical world: — it is a miracle.

To me therefore it seems that in the present state of our knowledge or (if you prefer it) of our ignorance, we have no choice but to acquiesce provisionally in an unresolved dualism. Our experience has a double outlook. The first we may call material. It brings us face to face with such subjects as electricity, mass, motion, force, energy, and with such manifestations of energy as ethereal radiation. The second is spiritual. The first deals with objects which are measurable, calculable, capable (up to a point) of precise definition. The second deals with the immeasurable, the incalculable, the indefinable and (let me add) the all-important. The first touches the fundamentals of science; the second is intimately connected with religion. Yet different as they seem, both are real. They belong to the same universe; they influence each other; somewhere and somehow they must be in contact along a common frontier.

But where is that frontier to be drawn? And how are we to describe the relation between these co-terminous provinces of reality? This is perhaps a question for metaphysics rather than for religion or science; and some day, perhaps, metaphysics may provide us with a satisfying answer. In the meanwhile, I may conclude this Introduction at a less ambitious level — concerning myself rather with the relations between religion and science in the practice of life, than with any high problems of speculative philosophy.

I suggest then that in scientific research it is a wise procedure to press "mechanical" theories of the material world to their utmost limits. Were I, for example, a biologist I should endeavor to explain all the phenomena under investigation in terms of matter and motion. I should always be searching for what could be measured and calculated, however confident I might be that in some directions at least the hopeless limitations of such a view would very rapidly become apparent.

In the practice of life, on the other hand, and in the speculation of philosophy, we are free to move within wider horizons. In forming our estimate of the sort of beliefs which may properly be regarded as rationally acceptable, we ought not to be limited by mechanistic presuppositions, however useful these may be in our investigations of Nature. We are spiritual beings, and must take account of spiritual values. The story of man is something more than a mere continuation of the story of matter. It is different in kind. If we cannot calculate the flow of physical events, that is because our knowledge of natural processes is small, and our power of calculation feeble. If we cannot calculate the course of human history, that is because (among other reasons) it is inherently incalculable. No two specimens of humanity exactly resemble each other, or live in circumstances that are exactly comparable. The so-called "repetitions" of history are never more than vague resemblances. The science of history therefore, if there be one, is something quite different from (say) the science of physics. And this is true even when history is wholly divorced from religion. But when it is considered in a different setting, when man is regarded as a spiritual agent in a world under spiritual guidance, events of spiritual significance cannot be wholly judged by canons of criticism which seem sufficient for simpler cases. Unexampled invasions of the physical sphere by the spiritual are not indeed to be lightly believed. But they are certainly not to be rejected merely because historians cannot bring themselves to accept the "miraculous."

This point of view, for those who are prepared to take it, may help to eliminate some of the chief causes of conflict between science and religion. In times not far distant there were men devoted to religion who blundered ignorantly into science, and men devoted to science who meddled unadvisedly with religion. Theologians found their geology in Genesis; materialists supposed that reality could be identified with the mechanism of matters. Neither procedure is to be commended, nor is it by these paths that the unsolved riddle of the universe can best be approached. A science which declares itself incompatible with religion, a religion which deems itself a substitute for science, may indulge in controversies as interminable as they are barren. . . .

STUDY QUESTIONS

1. *What, exactly, does Balfour mean when he says that "superstition may be negative as well as positive"? Do you find any example of superstition in this sense in your experience?*
2. *What does Balfour think of the regularity of nature revealed by science? Why, according to Balfour, is it wrong to deny the possibility of miracles? What does science often unjustifiably assume, in Balfour's opinion?*
3. *Is there any relation between Balfour's view of the "uniformity of nature" and the views of Krutch in "The Colloid and the Crystal"? To what extent are his views of the limits of science like or unlike those of Cohen and Nagel?*
4. *How well do Balfour's concepts of the relations between science and philosophy agree with Russell's views of the value and aims of philosophy?*
5. *What double outlook does Balfour recommend? Do you think his views of the relations between science and religion do in fact eliminate some of the "chief sources of conflict" between the two? Are the conflicts deeper than he acknowledges? Consider the following selection by Huxley in making your answer here.*
6. *Many think that our inability to predict events is a defect in our knowledge, rather than a result of the existence of incalcuable factors, as Balfour believes. Which view do you consider correct? Would it be possible to increase our mastery of reality and to control it by increasing our knowledge? Or do we have to resign ourselves to limited knowledge?*

Thomas Henry Huxley

Agnosticism and Christianity*

The present discussion has arisen out of the use, which has become general in the last few years, of the terms "Agnostic" and "Agnosticism."

The people who call themselves "Agnostics" have been charged with doing so because they have not the courage to declare themselves "Infidels." It has been insinuated that they have adopted a new name in order to escape the unpleasantness which attaches to their proper denomination. To this wholly erroneous imputation, I have replied by showing that the term "Agnostic" did, as a matter of fact, arise in a manner which negatives it; and my statement has not been, and cannot be refuted. Moreover, speaking for myself, and without impugning the right of any other person to use the term in

* From *Essays on Some Controverted Subjects,* 1892.

another sense, I further say that Agnosticism is not properly described as a "negative" creed, nor indeed as a creed of any kind, except in so far as it expresses absolute faith in the validity of a principle which is as much ethical as intellectual. This principle may be stated in various ways, but they all amount to this: that it is wrong for a man to say that he is certain of the objective truth of any proposition unless he can produce evidence which logically justifies that certainty. This is what Agnosticism asserts; and, in my opinion, it is all that is essential to Agnosticism. That which Agnostics deny and repudiate, as immoral, is the contrary doctrine, that there are propositions which men ought to believe, without logically satisfactory evidence; and that reprobation ought to attach to the profession of disbelief in such inadequately supported propositions. The justification of the Agnostic principle lies in the success which follows upon its application, whether in the field of natural, or in that of civil, history; and in the fact that, so far as these topics are concerned, no sane man thinks of denying its validity.

Still speaking for myself, I add, that though Agnosticism is not, and cannot be, a creed, except in so far as its general principle is concerned; yet that the application of that principle results in the denial of, or the suspension of judgment concerning, a number of propositions respecting which our contemporary ecclesiastical "gnostics" profess entire certainty. And, in so far as these ecclesiastical persons can be justified in their old-established custom (which many nowadays think more honoured in the breach than the observance) of using opprobrious names to those who differ from them, I fully admit their right to call me and those who think with me "Infidels"; all I have ventured to urge is that they must not expect us to speak of ourselves by that title.

The extent of the region of the uncertain, the number of the problems the investigation of which ends in a verdict of not proven, will vary according to the knowledge and the intellectual habits of the individual Agnostic. I do not very much care to speak of anything as "unknowable." What I am sure about is that there are many topics about which I know nothing; and which, so far as I can see, are out of reach of my faculties. But whether these things are knowable by any one else is exactly one of those matters which is beyond my knowledge, though I may have a tolerably strong opinion as to the probabilities of the case. Relatively to myself, I am quite sure that the religion of uncertainty — the nebulous country in which words play the part of realities — is far more extensive than I could wish. Materialism and Idealism; Theism and Atheism; the doctrine of the soul and its mortality or immortality — appear in the history of philosophy like the shades of Scandinavian heroes, eternally slaying one another and eternally coming to life again in a metaphysical "Nifelheim." It is getting on for twenty-five centuries, at least, since mankind began seriously to give their minds to these topics. Generation after generation, philosophy has been doomed to roll the stone uphill; and, just as all the world swore it was at the top, down it has rolled to the bottom again. All this is written in innumerable books; and he who will toil through them will discover that the stone is just where it was when the work began.

Hume saw this; Kant saw it; since their time, more and more eyes have been cleaned of the films which prevented them from seeing it; until now the weight and number of those who refuse to be the prey of verbal mystifications has begun to tell in practical life.

It was inevitable that a conflict should arise between Agnosticism and Theology; or rather, I ought to say, between Agnosticism and Ecclesiasticism. For Theology, the science, is one thing; and Ecclesiasticism, the championship of a foregone conclusion as to the truth of a particular form of Theology, is another. With scientific Theology, Agnosticism has no quarrel. On the contrary, the Agnostic, knowing too well the influence of prejudice and idiosyncrasy, even on those who desire most earnestly to be impartial, can wish for nothing more urgently than that the scientific theologian should not only be at perfect liberty to thresh out the matter in his own fashion; but that he should, if he can, find flaws in the Agnostic position; and, even if demonstration is not to be had, that he should put, in their full force, the grounds of the conclusions he thinks probable. The scientific theologian admits the agnostic principle, however widely his results may differ from those reached by the majority of Agnostics.

But, as between Agnosticism and Ecclesiasticism, or, as our neighbours across the Channel call it, Clericalism, there can be neither peace nor truce. The Cleric asserts that it is morally wrong not to believe certain propositions, whatever the results of a strict scientific investigation of the evidence of these propositions. He tells us that "religious error is, in itself, of an immoral nature." He declares that he has prejudged certain conclusions, and looks upon those who show cause for arrest of judgment as emissaries of Satan. It necessarily follows that, for him, the attainment of faith, not the ascertainment of truth, is the highest aim of mental life. And, on careful analysis of the nature of this faith, it will too often be found to be, not the mystic process of unity with the Divine, understood by the religious enthusiast; but that which the candid simplicity of a Sunday scholar once defined it to be. "Faith," said this unconscious plagiarist of Tertullian, "is the power of saying you believe things which are incredible."

Now I, and many other Agnostics, believe that faith, in this sense, is an abomination; and though we do not indulge in the luxury of self-righteousness so far as to call those who are not of our way of thinking hard names, we do feel that the disagreement between ourselves and those who hold this doctrine is even more moral than intellectual. It is desirable there should be an end of any mistakes on this topic. If our clerical opponents were clearly aware of the real state of the case, there would be an end of the curious delusion, which often appears between the lines of their writings, that those whom they are so fond of calling "Infidels" are people who not only ought to be, but in their hearts are, ashamed of themselves. It would be discourteous to do more than hint the antipodal opposition of this pleasant dream of theirs to facts.

The clerics and their lay allies commonly tell us, that if we refuse to admit that there is good ground for expressing definite convictions about certain topics, the bonds of human society will dissolve and mankind lapse into savagery. There are several answers to this assertion. One is that the bonds of human society were formed without the aid of their theology; and, in the opinion of not a few competent judges, have been weakened rather than strengthened by a good deal of it. Greek science, Greek art, the ethics of old Israel, the social organisation of old Rome, contrived to come into being, without the help of any one who believed in a single distinctive article of the simplest of the Christian creeds. The science, the art, the jurisprudence, the chief political and social theories, of the modern world have grown out of those of Greece and Rome — not by favour of, but in the teeth of, the fundamental teachings of early Christianity, to which science, art, and any serious occupation with the things of this world, were alike despicable.

Again, all that is best in the ethics of the modern world, in so far as it has not grown out of Greek thought, or Barbarian manhood, is the direct development of the ethics of old Israel. There is no code of legislation, ancient or modern, at once so just and so merciful, so tender to the weak and poor, as the Jewish law; and, if the Gospels are to be trusted, Jesus of Nazareth himself declared that he taught nothing but that which lay implicitly, or explicitly, in the religious and ethical system of his people.

> "And the scribe said unto him, Of a truth, Teacher, thou hast well said that he is one; and there is none other but he and to love him with all the heart, and with all the understanding, and with all the strength, and to love his neighbour as himself, is much more than all the whole burnt offerings and sacrifices." (Mark xii: 32, 33.)

Here is the briefest of summaries of the teaching of the prophets of Israel of the eighth century; does the Teacher, whose doctrine is thus set forth in his presence, repudiate the exposition? Nay; we are told, on the contrary, that Jesus saw that he "answered discreetly," and replied, "Thou are not far from the kingdom of God."

So that I think that even if the creeds, from the so-called "Apostles'" to the so-called "Athanasian," were swept into oblivion; and even if the human race should arrive at the conclusion that, whether a bishop washes a cup or leaves it unwashed, is not a matter of the least consequence, it will get on very well. The causes which have led to the development of morality in mankind, which have guided or impelled us all the way from the savage to the civilized state, will not cease to operate because a number of ecclesiastical hypotheses turn out to be baseless. And, even if the absurd notion that morality is more the child of speculation than of practical necessity and inherited instinct, had any foundation; if all the world is going to thieve, murder, and otherwise misconduct itself as soon as it discovers that certain portions of ancient history are mythical; what is the relevance of such arguments to any one who holds by the Agnostic principle?

Surely, the attempt to cast out Beelzebub by the aid of Beelzebub is a hopeful procedure as compared to that of preserving morality by the aid of immorality. For I suppose it is admitted that an Agnostic may be perfectly sincere, may be competent, and may have studied the question at issue with as much care as his clerical opponents. But, if the Agnostic really believes what he says, the "dreadful consequence" argufier (consistently, I admit, with his own principles) virtually asks him to abstain from telling the truth, or to say what he believes to be untrue, because of the supposed injurious consequences to morality. "Beloved brethren, that we may be spotlessly moral, before all things let us lie," is the sum total of many an exhortation addressed to the "Infidel." Now, as I have already pointed out, we cannot oblige our exhorters. We leave the practical application of the convenient doctrines of "Reserve" and "Non-natural interpretation" to those who invented them.

I trust that I have now made amends for any ambiguity, or want of fulness, in my previous exposition of that which I hold to be the essence of the Agnostic doctrine. Henceforward, I might hope to hear no more of the assertion that we are necessarily Materialists, Idealists, Atheists, Theists, or any other ists, if experience had led me to think that the proved falsity of a statement was any guarantee against its repetition. And those who appreciate the nature of our position will see, at once, that when Ecclesiasticism declares that we ought to believe this, that, and the other, and are very wicked if we don't, it is impossible for us to give any answer but this: We have not the slightest objection to believe anything you like, if you will give us good grounds for belief; but, if you cannot, we must respectfully refuse, even if that refusal should wreck morality and insure our own damnation several times over. We are quite content to leave that to the decision of the future. The course of the past has impressed us with the firm conviction that no good ever comes of falsehood, and we feel warranted in refusing even to experiment in that direction.

STUDY QUESTIONS

1. *How does Huxley define "Agnosticism"? What misunderstanding about the beliefs of Agnostics does he attribute to his opponents?*
2. *What is the ecclesiastical argument which Huxley is attacking here? What evidence does Huxley offer to show that dogmatic religious belief is not essential to society?*
3. *What importance does Huxley attribute to faith and revelation as opposed to logic and evidence?*
4. *Do Huxley's opponents have the same concept of morality as he, or a different one?*
5. *What is the principal purpose of Huxley in this selection? Does he intend primarily to clarify his beliefs? To defend and argue for his position? Point out details and phrases which support your answer.*
6. *Compare the views of Huxley and Lord Balfour, especially with regard to the unknown.*

John Henry Newman   Knowledge and Faith *

*P*eople say to me that it is but a dream to suppose that Christianity should regain the organic power in human society which once it possessed. I cannot help that; I never said it could. I am not a politician; I am proposing no measures, but exposing a fallacy, and resisting a pretence. Let Benthamism reign if men have no aspirations; but do not tell them to be romantic, and then solace them with glory; do not attempt by philosophy what once was done by religion. The ascendancy of Faith may be impracticable, but the reign of Knowledge is incomprehensible. The problem for statesmen of this age is how to educate the masses, and literature and science cannot give the solution.

Not so deems Sir Robert Peel; his firm belief and hope is "that an increased sagacity will administer to an exalted faith; that it will make men not merely believe in the cold doctrines of Natural Religion, but that it will so prepare and temper the spirit and understanding, that they will be better qualified to comprehend the great scheme of human redemption." He certainly thinks that scientific pursuits have some considerable power of impressing religion upon the mind of the multitude. I think not, and will now say why.

Science gives us the grounds of premises from which religious truths are to be inferred; but it does not set about inferring them, much less does it reach the inference; — that is not its province. It brings before us phenomena, and it leaves us, if we will, to call them works of design, wisdom, or benevolence; and further still, if we will, to proceed to confess an Intelligent Creator. We have to take its facts, and to give them a meaning, and to draw our own conclusions from them. First comes Knowledge, then a view, then reasoning, and then belief. This is why Science has so little of a religious tendency; deductions have no power of persuasion. The heart is commonly reached, not through the reason, but through the imagination, by means of direct impressions, by the testimony of facts and events, by history, by description. Persons influence us, voices melt us, looks subdue us, deeds inflame us. Many a man will live and die upon a dogma: no man will be a martyr for a conclusion. A conclusion is but an opinion; it is not a thing which *is*, but which *we are "certain about"*; and it has often been observed, that we never say we are certain without implying that we doubt. To say that a thing *must* be, is to admit that it *may not* be. No one, I say, will die for his own calculations; he dies for realities. This is why a literary religion is so little to be depended upon; it looks well in fair weather, but its doctrines are opinions, and,

* From *The Tamworth Reading Room*, 1841.

when called to suffer for them, it slips them between its folios, or burns them at its hearth. And this again is the secret of the distrust and raillery with which moralists have been so commonly visited. They say and do not. Why? Because they are contemplating the fitness of things, and they live by the square, when they should be realizing their high maxims in the concrete. Now Sir Robert thinks better of natural history, chemistry, and astronomy, than of such ethics; but they too, what are they more than divinity *in posse?* He protests against "controversial divinity"; is *inferential* much better?

I have no confidence, then, in philosophers who cannot help being religious, and are Christians by implication. They sit at home, and reach forward to distances which astonish us; but they hit without grasping, and are sometimes as confident about shadows as about realities. They have worked out by a calculation the lie of a country which they never saw, and mapped it by means of a gazetteer; and like blind men, though they can put a stranger on his way, they cannot walk straight themselves, and do not feel it quite their business to walk at all.

Logic makes but a sorry rhetoric with the multitude; first shoot round corners, and you may not despair of converting by a syllogism. Tell men to gain notions of a Creator from His works, and, if they were to set about it (which nobody does), they would be jaded and wearied by the labyrinth they were tracing. Their minds would be gorged and surfeited by the logical operation. Logicians are more set upon concluding rightly, than on right conclusions. They cannot see the end for the process. Few men have that power of mind which may hold fast and firmly a variety of thoughts. We ridicule "men of one idea"; but a great many of us are born to be such, and we should be happier if we knew it. To most men argument makes the point in hand only more doubtful, and considerably less impressive. After all, man is *not* a reasoning animal; he is a seeing, feeling, contemplating, acting animal. He is influenced by what is direct and precise. It is very well to freshen our impressions and convictions from physics, but to create them we must go elsewhere. Sir Robert Peel "never can think it possible that a mind can be so constituted, that, after being familiarized with the wonderful discoveries which have been made in every part of experimental science, it can retire from such contemplations without more enlarged conceptions of God's providence, and a higher reverence for His name." If he speaks of religious minds, he perpetrates a truism; if of irreligious, he insinuates a paradox.

Life is not long enough for a religion of inferences; we shall never have done beginning, if we determine to begin with proof. We shall ever be laying our foundations; we shall turn theology into evidences, and divines into textuaries. We shall never get at our first principles. Resolve to believe nothing, and you must prove your proofs and analyze your elements, sinking further and further, and finding "in the lowest depths a lower deep," till you come to the broad bosom of skepticism. I would rather be bound to defend the reasonableness of assuming that Christianity is true, than to demonstrate a moral governance from the physical world. Life is for action. If we insist on proofs for everything, we shall never come to action: to act you must assume, and that assumption is faith.

Let no one suppose that in saying this I am maintaining that all proofs are equally difficult, and all propositions equally debatable. Some assumptions are greater than others, and some doctrines involve postulates larger than others, and more numerous. I only say that impressions lead to action, and that reasonings lead from it. Knowledge of premises, and inferences upon them, — this is not to *live*. It is very well as a matter of liberal curiosity and of philosophy to analyze our modes of thought; but let this come second, and when there is leisure for it, and then our examinations will in many ways even be subservient to action. But if we commence with scientific knowledge and argumentative proof, or lay any great stress upon it as the basis of personal Christianity, or attempt to make man moral and religious by Libraries and Museums, let us in consistency take chemists for our cooks, and mineralogists for our masons.

Now I wish to state all this as matter of fact, to be judged by the candid testimony of any persons whatever. Why we are so constituted that Faith, not Knowledge or Arguments, is our principle of action, is a question with which I have nothing to do; but I think it is a fact, and if it be such, we must resign ourselves to it as best we may, unless we take refuge in the intolerable paradox that the mass of men are created for nothing, and are meant to leave life as they entered it. So well has this practically been understood in all ages of the world, that no Religion has yet been a Religion of physics or of philosophy. It has ever been synonymous with Revelation. It never has been a deduction from what we know: it has ever been an assertion of what we are to believe. It has never lived in a conclusion; it has ever been a message, or a history, or a vision. No legislator or priest ever dreamed of educating our moral nature by science or by argument. There is no difference here between true religions and pretended. Moses was instructed, not to reason from the creation, but to work miracles. Christianity is a history, supernatural, and almost scenic: it tells us what its Author is, by telling us what He has done....

When Sir Robert Peel assures us from the Town Hall at Tamworth that physical science must lead to religion, it is no bad compliment to him to say that he is unreal. He speaks of what he knows nothing about. To a religious man like him, Science has ever suggested religious thoughts; he colours the phenomena of physics with the hues of his own mind, and mistakes an interpretation for a deduction. "I am sanguine enough to believe," he says, "that that superior sagacity which is most conversant with the course and constitution of Nature will be first to turn a deaf ear to objections and presumptions against revealed religion, and to acknowledge the harmony of the Christian dispensation with all that reason, assisted by revelation, tells us of the course and constitution of Nature." Now, considering that we are all of us educated as Christians from infancy, it is not easy to decide at this day whether science creates faith, or only confirms it; but we have this remarkable fact in the history of heathen Greece against the former supposition, that her most eminent empirical philosophers were atheists, and that it was their atheism which was the cause of their eminence. "The natural philosophies of Democritus and others," says Lord Bacon, "*who allow no God or mind* in the frame of things, but attribute the structure of the universe to infinite essays and trials of nature, or what they call fate or fortune, and assigned the causes of particular things to the necessity of matter, *without any intermixture of final causes*, seems, as far as we can judge from the remains of their philosophy, *much more solid*, and to have *gone deeper into nature*, with regard to physical causes, than the philosophies of Aristotle or Plato: and this only because they *never meddled with final causes*, which the others were perpetually inculcating."

Lord Bacon gives us both the fact and the reason for it. Physical philosophers are ever inquiring *whence* things are, not *why*; referring them to nature, not to mind; and thus they tend to make a system a substitute for a God. Each pursuit or calling has its own dangers, and each numbers among its professors men who rise superior to them. As the soldier is tempted to dissipation, and the merchant to acquisitiveness, and the lawyer to the sophistical, and the statesman to the expedient, and the country clergyman to ease and comfort, yet there are good clergymen, statesmen, lawyers, merchants, and soldiers, notwithstanding; so there are religious experimentalists, though physics, taken by themselves, tend to infidelity; but to have recourse to physics to *make* men religious is like recommending a canonry as a cure for the gout, or giving a youngster a commission as a penance for irregularities.

The whole framework of Nature is confessedly a tissue of antecedents and consequences, we may refer all things forwards to design, or backwards on a physical cause. La Place is said to have considered he had a formula which solved all the motions of the solar system; shall we say that those motions came from this formula or from a Divine Fiat? Shall we have recourse for our theory to physics or to theology? Shall we assume Matter and its necessary properties to be eternal, or Mind with its divine attributes? Does the sun shine to warm the earth, or is the earth warmed because the sun shines? The one hypothesis will solve the phenomena as well as the other. Say not it is but a puzzle in argument, and that no one ever felt it in fact. So far from it, I believe that the study of Nature, when religious feeling is away, leads the mind, rightly or wrongly, to acquiesce in the atheistic theory, as the simplest and easiest. It is but parallel to that tendency in anatomical studies, which no one will deny, to solve all the phenomena of the human frame into material elements and powers, and to dispense with the soul. To those who are conscious of matter, but not conscious of mind, it seems more rational to refer all things to one origin, such as they know, than to assume the existence of a second origin such as they know not. It is

Religion, then, which suggests to Science its true conclusions; the facts come from Knowledge, but the principles come of Faith.

There are two ways, then, of reading Nature — as a machine and as a work. If we come to it with the assumption that it is a creation, we shall study it with awe; if assuming it to be a system, with mere curiosity.... The truth is that the system of Nature is just as much connected with religion, where minds are not religious, as a watch or a steam-carriage. The material world, indeed, is infinitely more wonderful than any human contrivance; but wonder is not religion, or we should be worshipping our railroads. What the physical creation presents to us in itself is a piece of machinery, and when men speak of a Divine Intelligence as its Author, this god of theirs is not the Living and True, unless the spring is the god of a watch, or steam the creator of the engine. Their idol, taken at advantage (though it is *not* an idol, for they do not worship it), is the animating principle of a vast and complicated system; it is subjected to laws, and it is connatural and co-extensive with matter. Well does Lord Brougham call it "the great architect of nature"; it is an instinct, or a soul of the world, or a vital power; it is not the Almighty God....

I consider, then, that intrinsically excellent and noble as are scientific pursuits, and worthy of a place in a liberal education, and fruitful in temporal benefits to the community, still they are not, and cannot be, *the instrument* of an ethical training; that physics do not supply the basis, but only materials, for religious sentiment; that knowledge does but occupy, does not form, the mind; that apprehension of the unseen is the only known principle capable of subduing moral evil, educating the multitude, and organizing society; and that, whereas man is born for action, action flows not from inferences, but from impressions,— not from reasonings, but from Faith....

STUDY QUESTIONS

1. *What characteristic of human nature leads Newman to believe that religious belief performs a function which scientific belief cannot perform?*
2. *How do Newman and Huxley differ in their evaluation of logic and evidence?*
3. *What does Newman see as the proper relation between Knowledge and Religion? Would Balfour agree with Newman?*
4. *Who is the more democratic, or the more concerned with humanity in general, Newman or Huxley?*
5. *Do you agree with Newman that reasoning and analysis lead away from action, and serve merely to satisfy the curiosity?*
6. *Write a theme describing Newman's opinion of the limitation of science as a religious guide.*

W. T. Stace   Man Against Darkness*

1

The Catholic bishops of America recently issued a statement in which they said that the chaotic and bewildered state of the modern world is due to man's loss of faith, his abandonment of God and religion. For my part I believe in no religion at all. Yet I entirely agree with the bishops. It is no doubt an oversimplification to speak of *the* cause of so complex a state of affairs as the tortured condition of the world today. Its causes are doubtless multitudinous. Yet allowing for some element of oversimplification, I say that the bishops' assertion is substantially true.

M. Jean-Paul Sartre, the French existentialist philosopher, labels himself an atheist. Yet his views seem to me plainly to support the statement of the bishops. So long as there was believed to be a God in the sky, he says, men could regard him as the source of their moral ideals. The universe, created and governed by a fatherly God, was a friendly habitation for man. We could be sure that, however great the evil in the world, good in the end would triumph and the forces of evil would be routed. With the disappearance of God from the sky all this has changed. Since the world is not ruled by a spiritual being, but rather by blind forces, there cannot be any ideals, moral or otherwise, in the universe outside us. Our ideals, therefore, must proceed only from our own minds; they are our own inventions. Thus the world which surrounds us is nothing but an immense spiritual emptiness. It is a dead universe. We do not live in a universe which is on the side of our values. It is completely indifferent to them.

Years ago Mr. Bertrand Russell, in his essay *A Free Man's Worship*, said much the same thing.

> Such in outline, but even more purposeless, more void of meaning, is the world which Science presents for our belief. Amid such a world, if anywhere, our ideals henceforward must find a home.... Blind to good and evil, reckless of destruction, omnipotent matter rolls on its relentless way; for man, condemned today to lose his dearest, tomorrow himself to pass through the gate of darkness, it remains only to cherish, ere yet the blow falls, the lofty thoughts that ennoble his little day; ... to worship at the shrine his own hands have built; ... to sustain alone, a weary but unyielding Atlas, the world that his own ideals have fashioned despite the trampling march of unconscious power.

It is true that Mr. Russell's personal attitude to the disappearance of religion is quite different from either that of M. Sartre or the bishops or

* From *The Atlantic Monthly*, September, 1948. By permission of Walter T. Stace.

myself. The bishops think it a calamity. So do I. M. Sartre finds it "very distressing." And he berates as shallow the attitude of those who think that without God the world can go on just the same as before, as if nothing had happened. This creates for mankind, he thinks, a terrible crisis. And in this I agree with him. Mr. Russell, on the other hand, seems to believe that religion has done more harm than good in the world, and that its disappearance will be a blessing. But his picture of the world, and of the modern mind, is the same as that of M. Sartre. He stresses the *purposelessness* of the universe, the facts that man's ideals are his own creations, that the universe outside him in no way supports them, that man is alone and friendless in the world.

Mr. Russell notes that it is science which has produced this situation. There is no doubt that this is correct. But the way in which it has come about is not generally understood. There is a popular belief that some particular scientific discoveries or theories, such as the Darwinian theory of evolution, or the views of geologists about the age of the earth, or a series of such discoveries, have done the damage. It would be foolish to deny that these discoveries have had a great effect in undermining religious dogmas. But this account does not at all go to the root of the matter. Religion can probably outlive any scientific discoveries which could be made. It can accommodate itself to them. The root cause of the decay of faith has not been any particular discovery of science, but rather the general spirit of science and certain basic assumptions upon which modern science, from the seventeenth century onwards, has proceeded.

2

It was Galileo and Newton — notwithstanding that Newton himself was a deeply religious man — who destroyed the old comfortable picture of a friendly universe governed by spiritual values. And this was effected, not by Newton's discovery of the law of gravitation nor by any of Galileo's brilliant investigations, but by the general picture of the world which these men and others of their time made the basis of the science, not only of their own day, but of all succeeding generations down to the present. That is why the century immediately following Newton, the eighteenth century, was notoriously an age of religious skepticism. Skepticism did not have to wait for the discoveries of Darwin and the geologists in the nineteenth century. It flooded the world immediately after the age of the rise of science.

Neither the Copernican hypothesis nor any of Newton's or Galileo's particular discoveries were the real causes. Religious faith might well have accommodated itself to the new astronomy. The real turning point between the medieval age of faith and the modern age of unfaith came when the scientists of the seventeenth century turned their backs upon what used to be called "final causes." The final cause of a thing or event meant the purpose which it was supposed to serve in the universe, its cosmic purpose.

What lay back of this was the presupposition that there is a cosmic order or plan and that everything which exists could in the last analysis be explained in terms of its place in this cosmic plan, that is, in terms of its purpose.

Plato and Aristotle believed this, and so did the whole medieval Christian world. For instance, if it were true that the sun and the moon were created and exist for the purpose of giving light to man, then this fact would explain why the sun and the moon exist. We might not be able to discover the purpose of everything, but everything must have a purpose. Belief in final causes thus amounted to a belief that the world is governed by purposes, presumably the purposes of some overruling mind. This belief was not the invention of Christianity. It was basic to the whole of Western civilization, whether in the ancient pagan world or in Christendom, from the time of Socrates to the rise of science in the seventeenth century.

The founders of modern science — for instance, Galileo, Kepler, and Newton — were mostly pious men who did not doubt God's purposes. Nevertheless they took the revolutionary step of consciously and deliberately expelling the idea of purpose as controlling nature from their new science of nature. They did this on the ground that inquiry into purposes is useless for what science aims at: namely, the prediction and control of events. To predict an eclipse, what you have to know is not its purpose but its causes. Hence science from the seventeenth century onwards became exclusively an inquiry into causes. The conception of purpose in the world was ignored and frowned on. This, though silent and almost unnoticed, was the greatest revolution in human history, far outweighing in importance any of the political revolutions whose thunder has reverberated through the world.

For it came about in this way that for the past three hundred years there has been growing up in men's minds, dominated as they are by science, a new imaginative picture of the world. The world, according to this new picture, is purposeless, senseless, meaningless. Nature is nothing but matter in motion. The motions of matter are governed, not by any purpose, but by blind forces and laws. Nature on this view, says Whitehead — to whose writings I am indebted in this part of my paper — is "merely the hurrying of material, endlessly, meaninglessly." You can draw a sharp line across the history of Europe dividing it into two epochs of very unequal length. The line passes through the lifetime of Galileo. European man before Galileo — whether ancient pagan or more recent Christian — thought of the world as controlled by plan and purpose. After Galileo European man thinks of it as utterly purposeless. This is the great revolution of which I spoke.

It is this which has killed religion. Religion could survive the discoveries that the sun, not the earth, is the center; that men are descended from simian ancestors; that the earth is hundreds of millions of years old. These discoveries may render out of date some of the details of older theological dogmas, may force their restatement in new intellectual frameworks. But they do not touch the essence of the religious vision itself, which is the faith that there is plan and purpose in the world, that the world is a moral order, that in the end all things are for the best. This faith may express itself through many different intellectual dogmas, those of Christianity, of Hinduism, of Islam. All and any of these intellectual dogmas may be destroyed without destroying the essential religious spirit. But that spirit cannot survive destruction of belief in a plan and purpose of the world, for that is the very heart of it. Religion can get on with any sort of astronomy, geology, biology, physics. But it cannot get on with a purposeless and meaningless universe.

If the scheme of things is purposeless and meaningless, then the life of man is purposeless and meaningless too. Everything is futile, all effort is in the end worthless. A man may, of course, still pursue disconnected ends, money, fame, art, science, and may gain pleasure from them. But his life is hollow at the center. Hence the dissatisfied, disillusioned, restless, spirit of modern man.

The picture of a meaningless world, and a meaningless human life, is, I think, the basic theme of much modern art and literature. Certainly it is the basic theme of modern philosophy. According to the most characteristic philosophies of the modern period from Hume in the eighteenth century to the so-called positivists of today, the world is just what it is, and that is the end of all inquiry. There is no reason for its being what it is. Everything might just as well have been quite different, and there would have been no reason for that either. When you have stated what things are, what things the world contains, there is nothing more which could be said, even by an omniscient being. To ask any question about *why* things are thus, or what purpose their being so serves, is to ask a senseless question, because they serve no purpose at all. For instance, there is for modern philosophy no such thing as the ancient problem of evil. For this once famous question presupposes that pain and misery, though they seem so inexplicable and irrational to us, must ultimately subserve some rational purpose, must have their places in the cosmic plan. But this is nonsense. There is no such overruling rationality in the universe. Belief in the ultimate irrationality of everything is the quintessence of what is called the modern mind.

It is true that, parallel with these philosophies which are typical of the modern mind, preaching the meaninglessness of the world, there has run a line of idealistic philosophies whose contention is that the world is after all spiritual in nature and that moral ideals and values are inherent in its structure. But most of these idealisms were simply philosophical expressions of romanticism, which was itself no more than an unsuccessful counterattack of the religious against the scientific view of things. They perished, along with romanticism in literature and art, about the beginning of the present century, though of course they still have a few adherents.

At the bottom these idealistic systems of thought were rationalizations of man's wishful thinking. They were born of the refusal of men to admit the cosmic darkness. They were comforting illusions within the warm glow of which the more tender-minded intellectuals sought to shelter themselves from the icy winds of the universe. They lasted a little while. But they are shattered now, and we return once more to the vision of a purposeless world.

3

Along with the ruin of the religious vision there went the ruin of moral principles and indeed of all values. If there is a cosmic purpose, if there is in the nature of things a drive towards goodness, then our moral systems will derive their validity from this. But if our moral rules do not proceed from something outside us in the nature of the universe — whether we say it is God or simply the universe itself — then they must be our own inventions. Thus it came to be believed that moral rules must be merely an expression of our own likes and dislikes. But likes and dislikes are notoriously variable. What pleases one man, people, or culture displeases another. Therefore morals are wholly relative.

This obvious conclusion from the idea of a purposeless world made its appearance in Europe immediately after the rise of science, for instance in the philosophy of Hobbes. Hobbes saw at once that if there is no purpose in the world there are no values either. "Good and evil," he writes, "are names that signify our appetites and aversions; which in different tempers, customs, and doctrines of men are different....Every man calleth that which pleaseth him, good; and that which displeaseth him, evil."

This doctrine of the relativity of morals, though it has recently received an impetus from the studies of anthropologists, was thus really implicit in the whole scientific mentality. It is disastrous for morals because it destroys their entire traditional foundation. That is why philosophers who see the danger signals, from the time at least of Kant, have been trying to give to morals a new foundation, that is, a secular or nonreligious foundation. This attempt may very well be intellectually successful. Such a foundation, independent of the religious view of the world, might well be found. But the question is whether it can ever be a *practical* success, that is whether apart from its logical validity and its influence with intellectuals, it can ever replace among the masses of men the lost religious foundation. On that question hangs perhaps the future of civilization. But meanwhile disaster is overtaking us.

The widespread belief in "ethical relativity" among philosophers, psychologists, ethnologists, and sociologists is the theoretical counterpart of the repudiation of principle which we see all around us, especially in international affairs, the field in which morals have always had the weakest foothold. No one any longer effectively believes in moral principles except as the private prejudices either of individual men or of nations or cultures. This is the inevitable consequence of the doctrine of ethical relativity, which in turn is the inevitable consequence of believing in a purposeless world.

Another characteristic of our spiritual state is loss of belief in the freedom of the will. This also is a fruit of the scientific spirit, though not of any particular scientific discovery. Science has been built up on the basis of determinism, which is the belief that every event is completely determined by a chain of causes and is therefore theoretically predictable beforehand. It is true that recent physics seems to challenge this. But so far as its practical consequences are concerned, the damage has long ago been done. A man's actions, it was argued, are as much events in the natural world as is an eclipse of the sun. It follows that men's actions are as theoretically predictable as an eclipse. But if it is certain now that John Smith will murder Joseph Jones at 2.15 p.m. on January 1, 1963, what possible meaning can it have to say that when that time comes John Smith will be *free* to choose whether he will commit the murder or not? And if he is not free, how can he be held responsible?

It is true that the whole of this argument can be shown by a competent philosopher to be a tissue of fallacies — or at least I claim that it can. But the point is that the analysis required to show this is much too subtle to be understood by the average entirely unphilosophical man. Because of this, the argument against free will is generally swallowed whole by the unphilosophical. Hence the thought that man is not free, that he is the helpless plaything of forces over which he has no control, has deeply penetrated the modern mind. We hear of economic determinism, cultural determinism, historical determinism. We are not responsible for what we do because our glands control us, or because we are the products of environment or heredity. Not moral self-control, but the doctor, the psychiatrist, the educationist, must save us from doing evil. Pills and injections in the future are to do what Christ and the prophets have failed to do. Of course I do not mean to deny that doctors and educationists can and must help. And I do not mean in any way to belittle their efforts. But I do wish to draw attention to the weakening of moral controls, the greater or less repudiation of personal responsibility which, in the popular thinking of the day, result from these tendencies of thought.

4

What, then, is to be done? Where are we to look for salvation from the evils of our time? All the remedies I have seen suggested so far are, in my opinion, useless. Let us look at some of them.

Philosophers and intellectuals generally can, I believe, genuinely do something to help. But it is extremely little. What philosophers can do is to show that neither the relativity of morals nor the denial of free will really follows from the grounds which have been supposed to support them. They can also try to discover a genuine secular basis for morals to replace the religious basis which has disappeared. Some of us are trying to do these things. But in the first place philosophers unfortunately are not agreed about these matters, and their disputes are utterly confusing to non-philosophers. And in the second place their influence is practically negligible because their analyses necessarily take place on a level on which the masses are totally unable to follow them.

The bishops, of course, propose as remedy a return to belief in God and in the doctrines of the Christian religion. Others think that a new religion is what is needed. Those who make these proposals fail to realize that the crisis in man's spiritual condition is something unique in history for which there is no sort of analogy in the past. They are thinking perhaps of the collapse of the ancient Greek and Roman religions. The vacuum then created was easily filled by Christianity, and it might have been filled by Mithraism if Christianity had not appeared. By analogy they think that Christianity might now be replaced by a new religion, or even that Christianity itself, if revivified, might bring back health to men's lives.

But I believe that there is no analogy at all between our present state and that of the European peoples at the time of the fall of paganism. Men had at that time lost their belief only in particular dogmas, particular embodiments of the religious view of the world. It had no doubt become incredible that Zeus and the other gods were living on the top of Mount Olympus. You could go to the top and find no trace of them. But the imaginative picture of a world governed by purpose, a world driving towards the good — which is the inner spirit of religion — had at that time received no serious shock. It had merely to re-embody itself in new dogmas, those of Christianity or some other religion. Religion itself was not dead in the world, only a particular form of it.

But now the situation is quite different. It is not merely that particular dogmas, like that of the virgin birth, are unacceptable to the modern mind. That is true, but it constitutes a very superficial diagnosis of the present situation of religion. Modern skepticism is of a wholly different order from that of the intellectuals of the ancient world. It has attacked and destroyed not merely the outward forms of the religious spirit, its particularized dogmas, but the very essence of that spirit itself, belief in a meaningful and purposeful world. For the founding of a new religion a new Jesus Christ or Buddha would have to appear, in itself a most unlikely event and one for which in any case we cannot afford to sit and wait. But even if a new prophet and a new religion did appear, we may predict that they would fail in the modern world. No one for long would believe in them, for modern men have lost the vision, basic to all religion, of an ordered plan and purpose of the world. They have before their minds the picture of a purposeless universe, and such a world-picture must be fatal to any religion at all, not merely to Christianity.

We must not be misled by occasional appearances of a revival of the religious spirit. Men, we are told, in their disgust and disillusionment at the emptiness of their lives, are turning once more to religion, or are searching for a new message. It may be so. We must expect such wistful yearnings of the spirit. We must expect men to wish back again the light that is gone, and to try to bring it back. But however they may wish and try, the light will not shine again,— not at least in the civilization to which we belong.

Another remedy commonly proposed is that we should turn to science itself, or the scientific spirit, for our salvation. Mr. Russell and Professor Dewey both make this proposal, though in somewhat different ways. Professor Dewey seems to believe that discoveries in sociology, the application of scientific method to social and political problems, will rescue us. This seems to me to be utterly naïve. It is not likely that science, which is basically the cause of our spiritual troubles, is likely also to produce the cure for them. Also it lies in the nature of science that, though it can teach us the best means for achieving our ends, it can never tell us what ends to pursue. It cannot give us any ideals. And our trouble is about ideals and ends, not about the means for reaching them.

5

No civilization can live without ideals, or to put it in another way, without a firm faith in moral ideas. Our ideals and moral ideas have in the past been rooted in religion. But the religious basis of our ideals has been undermined, and the superstructure of ideals is plainly tottering. None of the commonly suggested remedies on examination seems likely to succeed. It would therefore look as if the early death of our civilization were inevitable.

Of course we know that it is perfectly possible for individual men, very highly educated men, philosophers, scientists, intellectuals in general, to live moral lives without any religious convictions. But the question is whether a whole civilization, a whole family of peoples, composed almost entirely of relatively uneducated men and women, can do this.

It follows, of course, that if we could make the vast majority of men as highly educated as the very few are now, we might save the situation. And we are already moving slowly in that direction through the techniques of mass education. But the critical question seems to concern the time-lag. Perhaps in a few hundred years most of the population will, at the present rate, be sufficiently highly educated and civilized to combine high ideals with an absence of religion. But long before we reach any such stage, the collapse of our civilization may have come about. How are we to live through the intervening period?

I am sure that the first thing we have to do is to face the truth, however bleak it may be, and then next we have to learn to live with it. Let me say a word about each of these two points. What I am urging as regards the first is complete honesty. Those who wish to resurrect Christian dogmas are not, of course, consciously dishonest. But they have that kind of unconscious dishonesty which consists in lulling oneself with opiates and dreams. Those who talk of a new religion are merely hoping for a new opiate. Both alike refuse to face the truth that there is, in the universe outside man, no spirituality, no regard for values, no friend in the sky, no help or comfort for man of any sort. To be perfectly honest in the admission of this fact, not to seek shelter in new or old illusions, not to indulge in wishful dreams about this matter, this is the first thing we shall have to do.

I do not urge this course out of any special regard for the sanctity of truth in the abstract. It is not self-evident to me that truth is the supreme value to which all else must be sacrificed. Might not the discoverer of a truth which would be fatal to mankind be justified in suppressing it, even in teaching men a falsehood? Is truth more valuable than goodness and beauty and happiness? To think so is to invent yet another absolute, another religious delusion in which Truth with a capital T is substituted for God. The reason why we must now boldly and honestly face the truth that the universe is non-spiritual and indifferent to goodness, beauty, happiness, or truth is not that it would be wicked to suppress it, but simply that it is too late to do so, so that in the end we cannot do anything else but face it. Yet we stand on the brink, dreading the icy plunge. We need courage. We need honesty.

Now about the other point, the necessity of learning to live with the truth. This means learning to live virtuously and happily, or at least contentedly, without illusions. And this is going to be extremely difficult because what we have now begun dimly to preceive is that human life in the past, or at least human happiness, has almost wholly depended upon illusions. It has been said that man lives by truth, and that the truth will make us free. Nearly the opposite seems to me to be the case. Mankind has managed to live only by means of lies, and the truth may very well destroy us. If one were a Bergsonian one might believe that nature deliberately puts illusions into our souls in order to induce us to go on living.

The illusions by which men have lived seem to be of two kinds. First, there is what one may perhaps call the Great Illusion — I mean the religious illusion that the universe is moral and good, that it follows a wise and noble plan, that it is gradually generating some supreme value, that goodness is bound to triumph in it. Secondly, there is a whole host of minor illusions on which human happiness nourishes itself. How much of human happiness notoriously comes from the illusions of the lover about his beloved? Then again we work and strive because of the illusions connected with fame, glory, power, or money. Banners of all kinds, flags, emblems, insignia, ceremonials, and rituals are invariably symbols of some illusion or other. The British Empire, the connection between mother country and dominions, is partly kept going by illusions surrounding the notion of kingship. Or think of the vast amount of human happiness which is derived from the illusion of supposing that if some nonsense syllable, such as "sir" or "count" or "lord" is pronounced in conjunction with our names, we belong to a superior order of people.

There is plenty of evidence that human happiness is almost wholly based upon illusions of one kind or another. But the scientific spirit, or the spirit of truth, is the enemy of illusions and therefore the enemy of human happiness. That is why it is going to be so difficult to live with the truth.

There is no reason why we should have to give up the host of minor illusions which render life supportable. There is no reason why the lover should be scientific about the loved one. Even the illusions of fame and glory may persist. But without the Great Illusion, the illusion of a good, kindly, and purposeful universe, we shall *have* to learn to live. And to ask this is really no more than to ask that we become genuinely civilized beings and not merely sham civilized beings.

I can best explain the difference by a reminiscence. I remember a fellow student in my college days, an ardent Christian, who told me that if he did not believe in a future life, in heaven and hell, he would rape, murder, steal, and be a drunkard. That is what I call being a sham civilized being. On the other hand, not only could a Huxley, a John Stuart Mill, a David Hume, live great and fine lives without any religion, but a great many others of us, quite obscure persons, can at least live decent lives without it.

To be genuinely civilized means to be able to walk straightly and to live honorably without the props and crutches of one or another of the childish dreams which have so far supported men. That such a life is likely to be ecstatically happy I will not claim. But that it can be lived in quiet content, accepting resignedly what cannot be helped, not expecting the impossible, and thankful for small mercies, this I would maintain. That it will be difficult for men in general to learn this lesson I do not deny. But that it will be impossible I would not admit since so many have learned it already.

Man has not yet grown up. He is not adult. Like a child he cries for the moon and lives in a world of fantasies. And the race as a whole has perhaps reached the great crisis of its life. Can it grow up as a race in the same sense as individual men grow up? Can man put away childish things and adolescent dreams? Can he grasp the real world as it actually is, stark and bleak, without its romantic or religious halo, and still retain his ideals, striving for great ends and noble achievements? If he can, all may yet be well. If he cannot, he will probably sink back into savagery and brutality from which he came, taking a humble place once more among the lower animals.

STUDY QUESTIONS

1. *In what way, according to Stace, did the development of science undermine religious belief? How did this lead to a destruction of moral values?*

2. *What does Stace see as the essential difference between the present situation in religion and that which obtained at the time of the decline of the pagan beliefs?*

3. *Although he feels that civilization can survive only if the mass of humanity is either religious or highly educated, Stace does not explain how an intense degree of education can become a substitute for religion. Can you explain this point?*

4. *Why does Stace think Truth is over-rated? Are there any good arguments against his view?*

5. *Do you agree with Stace that religion has begun an inevitable decline? Write a theme in which you offer evidence for or against his view, and follow this up by explaining what beliefs about the nature of the universe, the soul, immortality, the nature and existence of God, and the existence of evil underlie the condition you have described.*

6. *Discuss Stace's observation that ". . . human life in the past, or at least human happiness has almost wholly depended upon illusions."*

C. S. Lewis What Christians Believe*

I have been asked to tell you what Christians believe, and I am going to begin by telling you one thing that Christians don't need to believe. If you are a Christian you don't have to believe that all the other religions are simply wrong all through. If you are an atheist you do have to believe that the main point in all the religions of the whole world is simply one huge mistake. If you are a Christian, you are free to think that all these religions, even the queerest ones, contain at least some hint of the truth. When I was an atheist I had to try to persuade myself that the whole human race were pretty good fools until about one hundred years ago; when I became a Christian I was able to take a more liberal view. But, of course, being a Christian does mean thinking that where Christianity differs from other religions, Christianity is right and they are wrong. Like in arithmetic — there's only one right answer to a sum, and all other answers are wrong; but some of the wrong answers are much nearer being right than others.

The first big division of humanity is into the majority, who believe in some kind of God or gods, and the minority who don't. On this point, Christianity lines up with the majority — lines up with ancient Greeks and Romans, modern savages, Stoics, Platonists, Hindus, Mohammedans, etc., against the modern Western European materialist. There are all sorts of different reasons for believing in God, and here I'll mention only one. It is this. Suppose there was no intelligence behind the universe, no creative mind. In that case nobody designed my brain for the purpose of thinking. It is merely that when the atoms inside my skull happen for physical or chemical reasons to arrange themselves in a certain way, this gives me, as a by-product,

---

* From *The Case for Christianity* by C. S. Lewis. Copyright, 1947, by The Macmillan Company and used with their permission. Published by Geoffrey Bles Ltd. in England and Canada as *Broadcast Talks* and used with their permission.

the sensation I call thought. But if so, how can I trust my own thinking to be true? It's like upsetting a milk-jug and hoping that the way the splash arranges itself will give you a map of London. But if I can't trust my own thinking, of course I can't trust the arguments leading to atheism, and therefore have no reason to be an atheist, or anything else. Unless I believe in God, I can't believe in thought: so I can never use thought to disbelieve in God.

Now I go on the next big division. People who all believe in God can be divided according to the sort of God they believe in. There are two very different ideas on this subject. One of them is the idea that He is beyond good and evil. *We* call one thing good and another thing bad. But according to some people that's merely our human point of view. These people would say that the wiser you become the less you'd want to call anything good or bad, and the more clearly you'd see that everything is good in one way and bad in another, and that nothing could have been different. Consequently, these people think that long before you got anywhere near the divine point of view the distinction would have disappeared altogether. We call a cancer bad, they'd say, because it kills a man; but you might just as well call a successful surgeon bad because he kills a cancer. It all depends on the point of view. The other and opposite idea is that God is quite definitely "good" or "righteous," a God who takes sides, who loves love and hates hatred, who wants us to behave in one way and not in another. The first of these views — the one that thinks God beyond good and evil — is called Pantheism. It was held by the great Prussian philosopher Hegel and, as far as I can understand them, by the Hindus. The other view is held by Jews, Mohammedans, and Christians.

And with this big difference between Pantheism and the Christian idea of God, there usually goes another. Pantheists usually believe that God, so to speak, animates the universe as you animate your body: that the universe almost *is* God, so that if it didn't exist He wouldn't exist either, and anything you find in the universe is a part of God. The Christian idea is quite different. They think God *made* the universe — like a man making a picture or composing a tune. A painter isn't a picture, and he doesn't die if his picture is destroyed. You may say, "He's put a lot of himself into it," but that only means that all its beauty and interest have come out of his head. His skill isn't in the picture in the same way that it's in his head, or even in his hands. I expect you see how this difference between Pantheists and Christians hangs together with the other one. If you don't take the distinction between good and bad very seriously, then it's easy to say that anything you find in this world is a part of God. But, of course, if you think some things really bad, and God really good, then you can't talk like that. You must believe that God is separate from the world and that some of the things we see in it are contrary to His will. Confronted with a cancer or a slum the Pantheist can say, "If you could only see it from the divine point of view, you would realize that this also is God." The Christian replies, "Don't talk damned nonsense."[1] For Christianity is a fighting religion. It thinks God made the world — that space and time, heat and cold, and all the colors and tastes, and all the animals and vegetables, are things that God "made up out of His head" as a man makes up a story. But it also thinks that a great many things have gone wrong with the world that God made and that God insists, and insists very loudly, on our putting them right again.

And, of course, that raises a very big question. If a good God made the world why has it gone wrong? And for many years I simply wouldn't listen to the Christian answers to this question, because I kept on feeling "Whatever you say, and however clever your arguments are, isn't it much simpler and easier to say that the world was *not* made by any intelligent power? Aren't all your arguments simply a complicated attempt to avoid the obvious?" But then that threw me back into those difficulties about atheism which I spoke of a moment ago. And soon I saw another difficulty.

My argument against God was that the universe seemed so cruel and unjust. But how had I got this idea of *just* and *unjust?* A man doesn't call a line crooked unless he has some idea of a straight line. What was I comparing this universe with when I called it unjust? If the whole show was bad and senseless from A to Z, so to speak, why did I, who was supposed to be part of the show, find myself in such violent reaction against it? A man feels wet when he falls into water, because man isn't a water animal: a fish wouldn't feel wet. Of course I could have given up my idea of justice by saying it was nothing but a private idea of my own. But if I did that then my argument against God collapsed too — for the argument depended on saying that the world was really unjust, not that it just didn't happen to please my private fancies. Thus in the very act of trying to prove that God didn't exist — in other words, that the whole of reality was senseless — I found I was forced to assume that one part of reality — namely my idea of justice — was full of sense. Consequently atheism turns out to be too simple. If the whole universe has no meaning, we should never have found out that it has no meaning; just as if there were no light in the universe and therefore no creatures with eyes we should never know it was dark. *Dark* would be a word without meaning.

II

Very well then, atheism is too simple. And I'll tell you another view that is also too simple. It's the view I call Christianity-and-water, the view that just says there's a good God in Heaven and everything is all right — leaving out all the difficult and terrible doctrines about sin and hell and the devil, and the redemption. Both these are boys' philosophies.

---

[1] One listener complained of the word *damned* as frivolous swearing. But I mean exactly what I say—nonsense that is *damned* is under God's curse, and will (apart from God's grace) lead those who believe it to eternal death.

It is no good asking for a simple religion. After all, real things *aren't* simple. They *look* simple, but they're not. The table I'm sitting at looks simple: but ask a scientist to tell you what it's really made of — all about the atoms and how the light waves rebound from them and hit my eye and what they do to the optic nerve and what it does to my brain — and, of course, you find that what we call "seeing a table" lands you in mysteries and complications which you can hardly get to the end of. A child, saying a child's prayer, looks simple. And if you're content to stop there, well and good. But if you're not — and the modern world usually isn't — if you want to go on and ask what's really happening — then you must be prepared for something difficult. If we ask for something more than simplicity, it's silly then to complain that the some-thing more isn't simple. Another thing I've noticed about reality is that, besides being difficult, it's odd: it isn't neat, it isn't what you expect. I mean, when you've grasped that the earth and the other planets all go round the sun, you'd naturally expect that all the planets are made to match — all at equal distances from each other, say, or distances that regularly increased, or all the same size, or else getting bigger or smaller as you go further from the sun. In fact, you find no rhyme or reason (that we can see) about either the sizes or the distances; and some of them have one moon, one has four, one has two, some have none, and one has a ring.

Reality, in fact, is always something you couldn't have guessed. That's *one* of the reasons I believe Christianity. It's a religion you couldn't have guessed. If it offered us just the kind of universe we'd always expected, I'd feel we were making it up. But, in fact, it's not the sort of thing anyone would have made up. It has just that queer twist about it that real things have. So let's leave behind all these boys' philosophies — these over-simple answers. The problem isn't simple and the answer isn't going to be simple either.

What is the problem? A universe that contains much that is obviously bad and apparently meaningless, but containing creatures like ourselves who know that it is bad and meaningless. There are only two views that face all the facts. One is the Christian view that this is a good world that has gone wrong, but still retains the memory of what it ought to have been. The other is the view called Dualism. Dualism means the belief that there are two equal independent powers at the back of everything, one of them good and the other bad, and that this universe is the battlefield in which they fight out an endless war. I personally think that next to Christianity Dual-ism is the manliest and most sensible creed on the market. But it has a catch in it.

The two powers, or spirits, or gods — the good one and the bad one — are supposed to be quite independent. They both existed from all eternity. Neither of them made the other, neither of them has any more right than the other to call itself God. Each presumably thinks it is good and thinks the other bad. One of them likes hatred and cruelty, the other likes love and mercy, and each backs its own view. Now what do we mean when we call one of them the Good Power and the other the Bad Power? Either we're merely saying that we happen to prefer the one to the other — like preferring beer to cider — or else we're saying that, whatever *they* say about it, and whichever *we* happen to like, one of them is actually wrong, actually mistaken, in regarding itself as good. Now if we mean merely that we happen to prefer the first, then we must give up talking about good and evil at all. For good means what you ought to prefer quite regardless of what you happen to like at any given moment. If "being good" meant simply joining the side you happened to fancy, for no real reason, then good wouldn't *be* good. So we must mean that one of the two powers is actually wrong and the other actually right.

But the moment you say that, you are putting into the universe a third thing in addition to the two Powers: some law or standard or rule of good which one of the powers conforms to and the other fails to conform to. But since the two powers are judged by this standard, then this standard, or the being who made this standard, is farther back and higher up than either of them, and He will be the real God. In fact, what we meant by calling them good and bad turns out to be that one of them is in a right relation to the real ultimate God and the other in a wrong relation to Him.

The same point can be made in a different way. If Dualism is true, then the Bad Power must be a being who likes badness for its own sake. But in reality we have no experience of anyone liking badness just because it is bad. The nearest we can go to it is in cruelty. But in real life people are cruel for one of two reasons — either because they are sadists, that is, because they have a sexual perversion which makes cruelty a cause of sensual pleasure to them, or else for the sake of something they are going to get out of it — money, or power, or safety. But pleasure, money, power, and safety are all, as far as they go, good things. The badness consists in pursuing them by the wrong method, or in the wrong way, or too much. I don't mean, of course, that the people who do this aren't desperately wicked. I do mean that wickedness, when you examine it, turns out to be pursuit of some good in the wrong way. You can be good for the mere sake of goodness: you can't be bad for the mere sake of badness. You can do a kind action when you're not feeling kind and when it gives you no pleasure, simply because kindness is right; but no one ever did a cruel action simply because cruelty is wrong — only because cruelty was pleasant or useful to him. In other words, badness can't succeed even in being bad *in the same way* in which goodness is good. Goodness is, so to speak, itself: badness is only spoiled goodness. And there must be something good first before it can be spoiled. We called Sadism a sexual perversion; but you must first have the idea of a normal sexuality before you can talk of it being perverted; and you can see which is the perversion, because you can explain the perverted from the normal, and can't explain the normal from the perverted. It follows that the Bad Power, who is supposed to be on an equal footing with the Good Power, and to love badness in the same way as the good one loves goodness, is a mere bogey. In order to be bad he must have **good** things to want and then to pursue in the wrong way: he must have impulses which were originally good in order to be able to pervert them. But if he is bad he can't supply himself either with good things to desire or with good impulses to pervert. He must be getting both from the Good Power. And if so, then he is not independent. He is part of the Good Power's world: he was made either by the Good Power or by some power above them both.

Put it more simply still. To be bad, he must exist and have intelligence and will. But existence, intelligence, and will are in themselves good. Therefore he must be getting them from the Good Power: even to be bad he must borrow or steal from his opponent. And do you now begin to see why Christianity has always said that the devil is a fallen angel? That isn't a mere story for the children. It's a real recognition of the fact that evil is a parasite, not an original thing. The powers which enable evil to carry on are powers given it by goodness. All the things which enable a bad man to be effectively bad are in themselves good things — resolution, cleverness, good looks, existence itself. That's why Dualism, in a strict sense, won't work.

But I want to say that real Christianity (as distinct from Christianity-and-water) goes much nearer to Dualism than people think. One of the things that surprised me when I first read the New Testament seriously was that it was always talking about a Dark Power in the universe — a mighty evil spirit who was held to be the Power behind death, and disease, and sin. The difference is that Christianity thinks this Dark Power was created by God, and was good when he was created, and went wrong. Christianity agrees with Dualism that this universe is at war. But it doesn't think this is a war between independent powers. It thinks it's a civil war, a rebellion, and that we are living in a part of the universe occupied by the rebel.

Enemy-occupied territory — that's what this world is. Christianity is the story of how the rightful king has landed, you might say landed in disguise, and is calling us all to take part in a great campaign of sabotage. When you go to church you're really listening in to the secret wireless from our friends: that's why the enemy is so anxious to prevent us going. He does it by playing on our conceit and laziness and intellectual snobbery. I know someone will ask me, "Do you really mean, at this time of day, to reintroduce our old friend the devil — hoofs and horns and all?" Well, what the time of day has to do with it I don't know. And I'm not particular about the hoofs and horns. But in other respects my answer is, "Yes, I do." I don't claim to know anything about his personal appearance. If anybody really wants to know him better I'd say to that person. "Don't worry. If you really want to, you will. Whether you'll like it when you do is another question."

III

Christians, then, believe that an evil power has made himself for the present the Prince of this World. And, of course, that raises problems. Is this state of affairs in accordance with God's will or not? If it is, He's a strange God, you'll say: and if it isn't how *can* anything happen contrary to the will of a being with absolute power?

But anyone who has been in authority knows how a thing can be in accordance with your will in one way and not in another. It may be quite sensible for a mother to say to the children, "I'm not going to go and make you tidy the schoolroom every night. You've got to learn to keep it tidy on your own." Then she goes up one night and finds the Teddy bear and the ink and the French Grammar all lying in the grate. That's against her will. She would prefer the children to be tidy. But on the other hand, it is her will which has left the children free to be untidy. The same thing arises in any regiment, or trades union, or school. You make a thing voluntary and then half the people don't do it. That isn't what you willed, but your will has made it possible.

It's probably the same in the universe. God created things which had free will. That means creatures which can go wrong *or* right. Some people think they can imagine a creature which was free but had no possibility of going wrong, but I can't. If a thing is free to be good it's also free to be bad. And free will is what has made evil possible. Why, then, did God give them free will? Because free will, though it makes evil possible, is also the only thing that makes possible any love or goodness or joy worth having. A world of automata — of creatures that worked like machines — would hardly be worth creating. The happiness which God designs for His higher creatures is the happiness of being freely, voluntarily united to Him and to each other in an ecstasy of love and delight compared with which the most rapturous love between a man and a woman on this earth is *mere milk and water*. And for that they've got to be free.

Of course God knew what would happen if they used their freedom the wrong way: apparently He thought it worth the risk. Perhaps we feel inclined to disagree with Him. But there's a difficulty about disagreeing with God. He is the source from which all your reasoning power comes: you couldn't be right and He wrong any more than a stream can rise higher than its own source. When you are arguing against Him you're arguing against the very power that makes you able to argue at all: it's like cutting off the branch you're sitting on. If God thinks this state of war in the universe a price worth paying for free will — that is, for making a *real* world in which creatures can do real good or harm and something of real importance can happen, instead of a toy world which only moves when He pulls the strings — then we may take it it *is* worth paying.

When we've understood about free will, we shall see how silly it is to ask, as somebody once asked me: "Why did God make a creature of such rotten stuff that it went wrong?" The better stuff a creature is made of — the cleverer and stronger and freer it is — then the better it will be if it goes right, but also the worse it will be if it goes wrong. A cow can't be very good or very bad; a dog can be both better and worse; a child better and worse still; an ordinary man, still more so; a man of genius, still more so; a superhuman spirit best — or worst — of all.

How did the Dark Power go wrong? Well, the moment you have a self at all, there is a possibility of putting yourself first — wanting to be the centre — wanting to *be* God, in fact. That was the sin of Satan: and that was the sin he taught the human race. Some people think the fall of man had something to do with sex, but that's a mistake. What Satan put into the heads of our remote ancestors was the idea that they could "be like gods" — could set up on their own as if they had created themselves — be their own masters — invent some sort of happiness for themselves outside God, apart from God. And out of that hopeless attempt has come nearly all that we call human history — money, poverty, ambition, war, prostitution, classes, empires, slavery — the long terrible story of man trying to find something other than God which will make him happy.

The reason why it can never succeed is this. God made us, invented us as a man invents an engine. A car is made to run on petrol, and it won't run properly on anything else. Now God designed the human machine to run on Himself. He Himself is the fuel our spirits were designed to burn, or the food our spirits were designed to feed on. There isn't any other. That's why it's just no good asking God to make us happy in our own way without bothering about religion. God can't give us a happiness and peace apart from Himself, because it isn't there. There's no such thing.

That is the key to history. Terrific energy is expended — civilizations are built up — excellent institutions devised; but each time something goes wrong. Some fatal flaw always brings the selfish and cruel people to the top and it all slides back into misery and ruin. In fact, the machine konks. It seems to start up all right and runs a few yards, and then it breaks down. They're trying to run it on the wrong juice. That's what Satan has done to us humans.

And what did God do? First of all He left us conscience, the sense of right and wrong: and all through history there have been people trying (some of them very hard) to obey it. None of them ever quite succeeded. Secondly, He sent the human race what I call good dreams: I mean those queer stories scattered all through the heathen religions about a god who dies and comes to life again and, by his death, has somehow given new life to men. Thirdly, He selected one particular people and spent several centuries hammering into their heads the sort of God He was — that there was only one of Him and that He cared about right conduct. Those people were the Jews, and the Old Testament gives an account of the hammering process.

Then comes the real shock. Among these Jews there suddenly turns up a man who goes about talking as if He was God. He claims to forgive sins. He says He has always existed. He says He is coming to judge the world at the end of time. Now let us get this clear. Among Pantheists, like the Indians, anyone might say that he was a part of God, or one with God: there'd be nothing very odd about it. But this man, since He was a Jew, couldn't mean that kind of God. God, in their language, meant the Being outside the world Who had made it and was infinitely different from anything else. And when you've grasped that, you will see that what this man said was, quite simply, the most shocking thing that has ever been uttered by human lips.

I'm trying here to prevent anyone from saying the really silly thing that people often say about Him: "I'm ready to accept Jesus as a great moral teacher, but I don't accept His claim to be God." That's the one thing we mustn't say. A man who was merely a man and said the sort of things Jesus said wouldn't be a great moral teacher. He'd either be a lunatic — on a level with the man who says he's a poached egg — or else he'd be the Devil of Hell. You must make your choice. Either this man was, and is, the Son of God: or else a madman or something worse. You can shut Him up for a fool; you can spit at Him and kill Him as a demon; or you can fall at His feet and call Him Lord and God. But don't let us come with any patronizing nonsense about His being a great human teacher. He hasn't left that open to us. He didn't intend to.

STUDY QUESTIONS

1. *This selection is taken from a series of talks which Lewis originally gave on BBC. In his introduction, Lewis remarks that he thinks a radio "talk" should be "as like real talk as possible." What qualities of vocabulary, sentences, and organization help make this selection sound like "real talk"?*

2. *Why does Lewis say that the atheistic view of the universe is "too simple"? Why does he reject the Dualist view?*

3. *How does Lewis explain the existence of evil in a universe controlled by a good God?*

4. *It is obvious that Lewis does not make any attempt to offer evidence to support his views. Is evidence necessary? Or does his method succeed in being convincing without it?*

5. *Lewis says little about the place of man in the scheme of things he has described. If you find his argument convincing, extend it by explaining what place man has in his universe.*

6. *What are the moral implications of Lewis' views? If he is right, what sort of behavior is indicated as correct for this sort of a universe?*

Miguel de Unamuno My Religion*

A friend writing to me from Chile tells me that he has met people acquainted with my writings who have asked him: "What, in a word, is the religion of this Señor Unamuno?" I myself have several times been asked a similar question. And I am going to see if I cannot — I will not say, answer it, for that is a thing I do not pretend to be able to do, but endeavour at any rate to elucidate the meaning of the question.

Individuals as well as peoples characterized by intellectual inertia — and intellectual inertia is quite compatible with great productive activity in the sphere of economics and in other kindred spheres — tend to dogmatism, whether they know it or not, whether they wish it or not, whether they intend it or not. Intellectual inertia shuns the critical or sceptical attitude.

I say sceptical, taking the word scepticism in its etymological and philosophical sense, for the sceptic does not mean him who doubts, but him who investigates or researches, as opposed to him who asserts and thinks that he has found. The one is the man who studies a problem and the other is the man who gives us a formula, correct or incorrect, as the solution of it.

In the order of pure philosophical speculation it is premature to demand that an investigator shall produce a definite solution of a problem while he is engaged in defining the problem itself more exactly. When a long calculation does not work out correctly, it is no small step forward to rub it all out and begin afresh. When a house threatens to collapse or becomes completely uninhabitable, the first thing to do is to pull it down and not to demand that another shall be built on top of it. The new house may indeed be built with materials taken from the old one, but only after the old one has first been demolished. In the meantime, if there is no other house available, the people can find shelter in a hut or sleep in the open.

And it is necessary not to lose sight of the fact that in the problems of practical life we must seldom expect to find definite scientific solutions. Men live and always have lived upon hazardous hypotheses and explanations, and sometimes even without them. Men have not waited to agree as to whether or not the criminal was possessed of free will before punishing him, and a man does not pause before sneezing to reflect upon the possible injury that may be caused by the obstructing particle that provokes him to sneeze.

I think that those men are mistaken who assert that they would live evilly if they did not believe in the eternal pains of hell, and the mistake is all to their credit. If they ceased to believe in a sanction after death, they would

---

* From *Essays and Soliloquies* by Miguel de Unamuno, by permission of Alfred A. Knopf, Inc. Copyright, 1924, by Alfred A. Knopf, Inc.

not live worse, but they would look for some other ideal justification for their conduct. The good man is not good because he believes in a transcendental order, but rather he believes in it because he is good — a proposition which I am sure must appear obscure or involved to those inquirers who suffer from intellectual inertia.

I am asked, then: "What is your religion?" And I will reply: My religion is to seek truth in life and life in truth, even though knowing full well that I shall never find them so long as I live; my religion is to wrestle unceasingly and unwearyingly with mystery; my religion is to wrestle with God from nightfall until the breaking of the day, as Jacob is said to have wrestled with Him. I cannot accommodate myself to the doctrine of the Unknowable or to that of "thus far and no farther." I reject the everlasting *Ignorabimus*. And at all hazards I seek to scale the unattainable.

"Be perfect as your Father in heaven is perfect," Christ said to us, and such an ideal of perfection is, without doubt, unattainable. But He put the unattainable before us as the goal and term of our endeavours. And He attained to it, say the theologians, by grace. And I wish to fight my fight careless of victory. Are there not armies and even peoples who march to certain defeat? Do we not praise those who die fighting rather than surrender? This, then, is my religion.

Those who put this question to me want me to give them a dogma, a solution which they can accept without disturbing their mental inertia. Or rather it is not this that they want, so much as to be able to label me and put me into one of the divisions in which they classify minds, so that they can say of me: He is a Lutheran, a Calvinist, a Catholic, an atheist, a rationalist, a mystic, or any other of those nicknames whose exact meaning they do not understand but which dispense them from further thinking. And I do not wish to have myself labelled, for I, Miguel de Unamuno, like every other man who aspires to full consciousness, am a unique species. "There are no diseases, but only persons who are diseased," some doctors say, and I say that there are no opinions, but only opining persons.

In religion there is but little that is capable of rational resolution, and as I do not possess that little I cannot communicate it logically, for only the rational is logical and transmissible. I have, it is true, so far as my affections, my heart and my feelings are concerned, a strong bent towards Christianity, but without adhering to the special dogmas of this or that Christian confession. I count every man a Christian who invokes the name of Christ with respect and love, and I am repelled by the orthodox, whether Catholic or Protestant — the latter being usually as intransigent as the former — who deny the Christianity of those who interpret the Gospel differently from themselves. I know a Protestant Christian who denies that Unitarians are Christians.

I frankly confess that the supposed rational proofs — ontological, cosmological, ethical, etc. — of the existence of God, prove to me nothing; that all the reasons adduced to show that a God exists appear to me to be based on sophistry and begging of the question. In this I am with Kant. And in discussions of this kind, I feel that I am unable to talk to cobblers in the terms of their craft.

Nobody has succeeded in convincing me rationally of the existence of God, nor yet of His non-existence; the arguments of atheists appear to me even more superficial and futile than those of their opponents. And if I believe in God, or at least believe that I believe in Him, it is, first of all, because I wish that God may exist, and then, because He is revealed to me, through the channel of the heart, in the Gospel and in Christ and in history. It is an affair of the heart.

Which means that I am not convinced of it as I am of the fact that two and two make four.

If it were a question of something that did not touch my peace of conscience or console me for having been born, perhaps I should pay no heed to the problem; but as it involves my whole interior life and the spring of all my actions, I cannot quiet myself by saying: I do not know nor can I know. I do not know, that is certain; perhaps I can never know. But I want to know. I want to, and that is enough.

And I shall spend my life wrestling with mystery, and even without hope of penetrating it, for this wrestling is my sustenance and my consolation. Yes, my consolation. I have accustomed myself to wrest hope from despair itself. And let not fools in their superficiality shriek: Paradox!

I cannot conceive of a man of culture without this preoccupation, and in point of culture — and culture is not the same as civilization — I can hope but little from those who live without interest in the metaphysical aspect of the religious problem, and only study it in its social or political aspects. I can hope but very little for the enrichment of the spiritual treasury of mankind from those men or from those peoples who, whether it be from intellectual inertia, or from superficiality, or from scientificism, or from any other cause, are unmoved by the great and eternal disquietudes of the heart. I can hope nothing from those who say: "We must not think about these things!" I can hope even less from those who believe in a heaven and a hell such as those which we believed in when we were children; and still less can I hope from those who affirm with a fool's gravity: "All this is but myth and fable; he who dies is buried and there's an end of it." I can hope for something only from those who do not know, but who are not resigned not to know; from those who fight unrestingly for the truth and put their life in the fight itself rather than in the victory.

The greater part of my work has always been to disquiet my neighbours, to rob them of heart's ease, to vex them if I can. I have said this already in my commentary upon "The Life of Don Quixote and Sancho," in which I have confessed myself most fully. Let them seek as I seek, let them wrestle as I wrestle, and between us all we will tear some shred of secret from God, and at any rate this wrestling will make us more men, men of more spirit.

In order to accomplish this work — a religious work — among peoples like those that speak the Castilian tongue who suffer from intellectual inertia and superficiality, slumbering in the routine of Catholic dogma or in the dogmatism of free-thought or of scientificism, it has been necessary for me to appear sometimes shameless and indecorous, at other times harsh and aggressive, and not a few times perverse and paradoxical. In our pusillanimous literature it was a rare thing to hear anyone cry out from the depths of his heart, to get excited, to exclaim. The shout was almost unknown. Writers were frightened of making themselves ridiculous. They behaved and still behave like those who put up with an affront in the street for fear of the ridicule of being seen with their hat on the ground marched off by the police. But I, no! When I have felt like shouting I have shouted. Never have I been restrained by decorum. And this is one of the things for which I have never been forgiven by my colleagues of the pen, so discreet, so correct, so disciplined, even when they preach indiscretion and indiscipline. Literary anarchists are more punctilious about style and syntax than about anything else. And when they play out of tune they do so tunefully; their discords resolve themselves into harmonies.

When I have felt a pain I have shouted and shouted in public. The psalms which are to be found in my *Poesias* are simply the cries from the heart with which I have sought to make the heart-strings of the wounded hearts of others vibrate. If they have no heart-strings or only heart-strings that are too rigid to vibrate, then my cry will awaken no echo in them and they will declare that it is not poetry and they will proceed to investigate its acoustic properties. It is possible also to study acoustically the cry that is torn from the heart of a man who sees his son suddenly fall down dead — and he who has neither heart nor sons will understand no more of it than the acoustics.

These psalms, together with various other pieces in my *Poesias,* are my religion, a religion that I have sung, not expressed in logic and reasoning. And I sing it as best I can, with the voice and ear that God has given me, because I cannot reason it. And he to whom my verses appear to be more full of reasoning and logic and method and exegesis than of life, because they are not peopled with fauns, dryads, satyrs and the like or garbed in the latest modernist fashion, had better leave them alone, for it is evident that I shall not touch his heart whether I use a violin bow or a hammer.

What I fly from, I repeat, as from the plague, is any kind of classification of myself, and when I die I hope I shall still hear these intellectual sluggards inquiring: "And this gentleman, what is he?" Liberal or progressive fools will take me for a reactionary and perhaps for a mystic, without understanding of course what they may mean; and conservative and reactionary fools will take me for a kind of spiritual anarchist; and both of them will pity me as an unfortunate gentleman anxious to distinguish himself by singularity, hoping to be reputed an original, and with a bonnet full of bees. But no one need worry about what fools think of him, be they progressive or conservative, liberal or reactionary.

And since man is naturally intractable, and does not habitually thirst for the truth, and after being preached at for four hours usually returns to all his inveterate habits, these busy inquirers, if they chance to read this, will return to me with the question: "Well, but what solutions do you offer?" And I will tell them, once and for all, that if it is solutions they want, they can go to the shop opposite, for I do not deal in the article. My earnest desire has been, is and will be that those who read me should think and meditate on fundamental things, and it has never been to furnish them with thoughts ready made. I have always sought to agitate and to suggest rather than to instruct. It is not bread that I sell, not bread, but yeast, ferment.

I have friends, and good friends, who advise me to abandon this task and to concentrate upon what they call some objective work, something which will be, so they express it, definitive, something constructive, something that will last. They mean something dogmatic. I declare that I am incapable of it, and I claim my liberty, my holy liberty, even, if need be, the liberty of contradicting myself. I do not know whether anything that I have written or may write in the future is destined to live for years and centuries after I am dead; but I know that if anyone agitates the surface of a shoreless sea the waves will go radiating without end, even though at last they dwindle into ripples. To agitate is something. And if thanks to this agitation another who comes after me shall create something that will live, then my work will live in his.

It is a work of supreme mercy to awaken the sleeper and to shake the sluggard, and it is a work of supreme religious piety to seek truth in everything and to expose fraud, stupidity and ignorance wherever they are to be found.

STUDY QUESTIONS

1. *Unamuno asserts that the ultimate religious problems have not been solved. Further, he declares that they are especially valuable because they cannot be solved. How would you explain this paradox?*

2. *According to Unamuno, it is impossible to approach God through reason. What does he substitute for reason?*

3. *Although this essay is about Unamuno's religion, it also reveals a good deal about his personality. Judging from his opinions and the way he expresses them, what sort of a man would you say the author was? Do you find any qualities similiar to those of Santayana? Different from Santayana?*

4. *What is Unamuno's attitude toward religious and intellectual authority?*

5. *This statement of a man's religion is incomplete, for it says nothing about his ideas of the nature of the world, men's duty toward each other, the creation of the earth, the immortality of the soul, the nature of morality and other spiritual and religious questions. Without necessarily following Unamuno's method, write an essay using his title in which you explain your opinion about these or other spiritual questions.*

6. *This essay exemplifies an extreme position on the question of authority in religious matters. Write a theme giving your opinion of this question, and telling what you believe the relation between authority and individual conscience should be.*

6 Popular Culture

1. ON MOVIES, TELEVISION, AND THE COMICS

Martha Wolfenstein and Nathan Leites

British, French, and American Films*

$\mathcal{T}$he dramatic productions of a particular culture at a particular time, or even over a considerable period, tend to exhibit a distinctive plot configuration. This configuration gives the various individual dramas the distinctive atmosphere which we can recognize as pervading them all. Obviously a group of plots or even a single plot is exceedingly complex. Nevertheless a certain basic plan may be discerned: we can see that one pattern from among the range of dramatic alternatives has been chosen for major emphasis.

Looking back over the films which we have been discussing, we shall now indicate briefly the essential plot configuration which distinguishes each of the three groups of films with which we have been concerned, the British, the French, and the American.

The essential plot in British films is that of the conflict of forbidden impulses with conscience. Either one of the contending forces may win out and we may follow the guilt-ridden course of the wrong-doer or experience

* From *Movies: A Psychological Study* by Martha Wolfenstein and Nathan Leites. Copyright, 1950, by The Free Press. Reprinted by permission of The Free Press.

the regrets of the lost opportunity virtuously renounced. In the happy instance, wishes may coincide with the demands of virtue and a fatherly fate will reward the good children. The world is presided over by authorities who are wise and good and against whom the wilful and unlucky may contend. But the counterpart of these authorities is also implanted in the individual soul; the evil-doer will be self-condemned as well as pursued by the authorities.

British films evoke the feeling that danger lies in ourselves, especially in our impulses of destructiveness. In a cautionary way they show what happens if these impulses break through, particularly where the weak become the victims. Thus they afford a catharsis at the same time that they demonstrate the value of defenses by showing the consequences of their giving way. The character who embodies dangerous impulses is apt to be a superior person, one who should be able to control his own destructiveness, and in whom it is all the more terrible to see it get out of hand. Violence is not simply a destructive force but a breaking both of the pattern within the individual personality and of the order which prevails in his world. The complete murderer is one who disputes the rule of just authorities, in his pride setting himself up as an arbiter of life and death, and doomed by his own struggle. While violence is on one side related to a whole social framework, it has also another side of intimacy and isolation. The act of violence is slowly prepared and may be preceded by special closeness between murderer and victim. Violence is thus often pervaded by the tenderness which in ordinary circumstances serves to ward it off.

Self-accusation is prominent in British films and may be evoked by wishes no less than by acts. Characters feel guilty when circumstances beyond their control produce fatalities coinciding with unconscious wishes. Lovers tempted to overstep lawful bounds draw back alarmed by guilty apprehensions. However, the pure in heart find that the authorities of this world and the next are their allies. The hero, temporarily distressed by a false charge, discovers that the police know all along that he is innocent and are quietly working side by side with him. The fine young couple who for the moment fear that fate has brought them together only to separate them learn that even death can be set aside so that they can be joined.

British films preserve, in a modern idiom (the peculiarities of which we shall not analyze here), many of the themes of Shakespearean drama. There are heroes who like Macbeth are carried away by criminal impulses and then punished; heroes who like Hamlet suffer pangs of conscience for crimes they did not commit. And there are young couples briefly and playfully threatened by the same fate which intended all along to wed them as Prospero did with his daughter and Ferdinand. The image of a perfect father, like Hamlet Sr., still presides over the scene, and constitutes the model for an exacting conscience.

In the major plot configuration of French films, human wishes are opposed by the nature of life itself. The main issue is not one of inner or outer conflicts in which we may win or lose, be virtuous or get penalized. It is a contest in which we all lose in the end and the problem is to learn to accept it. There are inevitable love disappointments, the world is not arranged to collaborate with our wishes, people grow older, lovers become fathers, the old must give way to the young, and eventually everyone dies. The desire for justice is ranged alongside other human wishes which are more likely than not to be frustrated. French films repeatedly present these aspects of life so that we may inure ourselves to them and master the pain they cause us. It is the Mithridates principle of taking a little poison every day so that by and by one becomes less vulnerable to it.

It is in keeping with this tendency that French films so often take as their central character an aging man. He is not the triumphant hero whom we wish to become nor the criminal hero whom we fear to become, but simply what we must become: old. In him we see concentrated disappointment, lost hopes, change, decline of physical powers, and imminent death. We can observe his sadly comic struggle against his fate as he refuses to realize that he is no longer eligible to be the lover of a young girl, or learn from him the compensations of later life as he renounces the role of lover for that of father. He helps to reconcile us both to our past and to our future. We see in him our own father no longer dominant and powerful but a sharer of our common human fate. He who was in possession of things which we as children were denied is now seen suffering disappointments more grievous than we suffered then. In making peace with him we also make peace with our own future.

The young hero no less than the aging one in French films is likely to be disappointed. We see him in his pursuit of a beloved woman about whom he gradually learns much that is contrary to his wishes. He is not spared the discovery that this woman is involved with another man, and we in following his fate may work through our own similar disillusionments. Knowledge which at first glance increases sorrow in the end mitigates the pain which, we see, could not be avoided.

We must learn that the world is not arranged to fulfil our demands for justice any more than to satisfy our longings for happiness. Human agencies of justice are obtuse and inefficient, and there are no divine ones. We are shown how the innocent are convicted, how the guilty are exonerated; they may even confess without being believed. Where justice is done, it is made clear that this is a happy accident. A clue uncovered by chance a moment earlier or later makes the difference between life and death for an innocent man. No one is watching over him, nor is he able to be the master of his own fate. Things may turn out happily. The suicidal bullet misses, the brain tumor may be operable, the hostages facing execution may be rescued at the last moment, the aging couple may find an unexpected revival of pleasure in life. The pleasure, no less sweet for that, is tinged with sadness; we know it is only a reprieve.

The major plot configuration in American films contrasts with both the British and the French. Winning is terrifically important and always possible though it may be a tough fight. The conflict is not an internal one; it is not our own impulses which endanger us nor our own scruples that stand in our way. The hazards are all external, but they are not rooted in the nature of life itself. They are the hazards of a particular situation with which we find ourselves confronted. The hero is typically in a strange town where there are apt to be dangerous men and women of ambiguous character and where the forces of law and order are not to be relied on. If he sizes up the situation correctly, if he does not go off half-cocked but is still able to beat the other fellow to the punch once he is sure who the enemy is, if he relies on no one but himself, if he demands sufficient evidence of virtue from the girl, he will emerge triumphant. He will defeat the dangerous men, get the right girl, and show the authorities what's what.

When he is a child, he is the comic hero, showing off, blundering, cocky, scared, called on to perform beyond his capacities, and pulling through by surprising spurts of activity and with the help of favorable circumstances. He is completely harmless, free from sexual or aggressive impulses, and the world around him reflects his own innocuous character. Its threats are playful and its reproaches ridiculous. When he is a man he is the melodrama hero and the world changes to reflect his changed potentialities; it becomes dangerous and seriously accusing, and launches him on his fighting career. The majority of the melodramas show him coming through successfully. A minority reveal various perils which lie off the main track; they are cautionary tales. The hero may succumb to his attacker; this is his bad dream. The men around him may be less dangerous than he suspects. Under the delusion that he attacks in self-defense, he may initiate hostilities; then he will lose. In this case he is crazy. Without being deluded to this extent, out of greed and overconfidence, he may try to get away with murder; he commits the crime of which he is usually only suspected and he has to pay for it. The girl may turn out to be worse than he believed. He will have to go off without her; then he is lonely. He may not be able to produce anyone on whom to pin the blame for the crimes of which he is falsely accused; then he is a victim of circumstances. If circumstances fail to collaborate with his need to blame someone else, he may even end by blaming himself. These are the various hazards which the usual melodrama hero safely passes on the way.

The fantasy which provides for defeating dangerous men, winning the right girl, and coming out in the clear, is produced under the auspices of two major mechanisms: projection and denial. Self-accusations are embodied in the blundering police and destructive impulses in the unprovoked attacker. The beloved woman seems to be involved with another man but investigation ends in the gratifying demonstration that she never loved anyone but the hero. The love disappointment to which the French movie hero is repeatedly exposed is here denied.

The external world may be dangerous but manageable, or, at other times, uncontrollable but gratifying. Where things seem to get out of control the results turn out to be wish-fulfilling. The overturning automobile throws the girl into the hero's arms, the rocking boat tosses the heroine's rival into the waves. The world that is uncontrollable but gratifying expresses an omnipotence fantasy while at the same time eliminating guilt. As soon as an internal problem is replaced by an external one, we can see the promise of success. The hero suffering from kleptomania becomes involved in investigating the activities of a gang of thieves; the amnesiac hero pursues his memories only long enough to unearth clues of someone else's crime before he rises impatiently from the psychiatrist's couch to embark on a successful detective job.

The world, which is not effectively policed, does not need to be policed at all. The hero, the self-appointed investigator and agent of justice, is able to set things right independently. The world thus appears as a kind of workable anarchic arrangement where, although hostilities are far from eliminated, life need not be nasty, brutish, and short, at any rate not for anyone we care about. The unofficial supervisors of private morals, the comic onlookers, are just as superfluous as the police. No one has any intention of doing anything naughty; only the mistakenly suspicious onlooker fails to recognize the natural goodness of the clean-cut young people.

American film plots are pervaded by false appearances. In this shadowy but temporarily vivid guise, the content of what is projected and denied tends to reappear. It is in false appearances that the forbidden wishes are realized which the hero and heroine so rarely carry into action. In a false appearance the heroine is promiscuous, the hero is a murderer, the young couple carry on an illicit affair, two men friends share the favors of a woman. This device makes it possible for us to eat our cake and have it, since we can enjoy the suggested wish-fulfilments without empathic guilt; we know that the characters with whom we identify have not done anything. The contention of American films is that we should not feel guilty for mere wishes. The hero and heroine are threatened with penalties for the incriminating appearance but in the end are absolved. The misguided police or the foolish onlooker in comedies convey a self-accusation from which the hero and heroine struggle to dissociate themselves, a vestige of archaic conscience which is to be dispensed with.

What the plot unfolds is a process of proof. Something is undone rather than done: the false appearance is negated. The hero and heroine do not become committed to any irretrievable act whose consequences they must bear. Nor do they usually undergo any character transformation, ennoblement or degradation, gain or loss of hope, acceptance of a new role or the diminution and regrets of age. They succeed in proving what they were all along. They emerge from the shadow of the false appearance. What has changed is other people's impressions of them. In so far as the hero and heroine may be unsure of who or what they are except as they see themselves mirrored in the eyes of others, they have succeeded in establishing for themselves a desirable identity. In so far as they struggle against a projected archaic conscience that persecutes the wish as if it were the act, they win a victory for a more tolerant and discriminating morality.

STUDY QUESTIONS

1. *This selection is taken from a point very near the end of an entire book in which the authors have developed their analysis of films. They are concerned here to draw broad general conclusions. How do they support their generalizations here? Could different generalizations be supported by a different selection of evidence? Do the authors' generalizations seem reasonably valid? Explain.*

2. *In what ways do the authors find foreign films more realistic and mature than American ones?*

3. *It is pointed out in this discussion that representatives of morality and law-enforcement agents have a different character in the films of the different countries. What are these differences?*

4. *Do you see any relation between the American pattern of life and the plot characteristics of American movies? What can American movie heroes do that seems unnatural or forbidden for the heroes of foreign films?*

5. *Do you consider these generalizations about movie-plots largely correct or incorrect? Write a theme giving your opinion of one or all of them, basing your criticism, whether favorable or unfavorable, upon your own experience with movies.*

6. *Do the movies generally give a realistic or honest view of life? It is important, in discussing this subject to limit yourself to one or two aspects, such as the portrayal of love or old age or business or sports or family life.*

Robert Warshow The Gangster as Tragic Hero*

America, as a social and political organization, is committed to a cheerful view of life. It could not be otherwise. The sense of tragedy is a luxury of aristocratic societies, where the fate of the individual is not conceived of as having a direct and legitimate political importance, being determined by a fixed and supra-political — that is, non-controversial — moral order or fate. Modern equalitarian societies, however, whether democratic or authoritarian in their political forms, always base themselves on the claim that they are

* "The Gangster as Tragic Hero," by Robert Warshow, copyright, 1948, by *Partisan Review*. Reprinted by permission.

making life happier; the avowed function of the modern state, at least in its
ultimate terms, is not only to regulate social relations, but also to determine
the quality and the possibilities of human life in general. Happiness thus
becomes the chief political issue — in a sense, the only political issue — and
for that reason it can never be treated as an issue at all. If an American or a
Russian is unhappy, it implies a certain reprobation of his society, and therefore, by a logic of which we can all recognize the necessity, it becomes an
obligation of citizenship to be cheerful; if the authorities find it necessary,
the citizen may even be compelled to make a public display of his cheerfulness
on important occasions, just as he may be conscripted into the army in time
of war.

Naturally, this civic responsibility rests most strongly upon the organs of
mass culture. The individual citizen may still be permitted his private unhappiness so long as it does not take on political significance, the extent of
this tolerance being determined by how large an area of private life the society
can accommodate. But every production of mass culture is a public act and
must conform with accepted notions of the public good. Nobody seriously
questions the principle that it is the function of mass culture to maintain
public morale, and certainly nobody in the mass audience objects to having
his morale maintained.[1] At a time when the normal condition of the citizen
is a state of anxiety, euphoria spreads over our culture like the broad smile of
an idiot. In terms of attitudes towards life, there is very little difference between a "happy" movie like *Good News*, which ignores death and suffering,
and a "sad" movie like *A Tree Grows in Brooklyn*, which uses death and
suffering as incidents in the service of a higher optimism.

But, whatever its effectiveness as a source of consolation and a means of
pressure for maintaining "positive" social attitudes, this optimism is fundamentally satisfying to no one, not even to those who would be most disoriented
without its support. Even within the area of mass culture, there always exists
a current of opposition, seeking to express by whatever means are available
to it that sense of desperation and inevitable failure which optimism itself
helps to create. Most often, this opposition is confined to rudimentary or
semi-literate forms: in mob politics and journalism, for example, or in certain
kinds of religious enthusiasm. When it does enter the field of art, it is likely
to be disguised or attenuated: in an unspecific form of expression like jazz,
in the basically harmless nihilism of the Marx Brothers, in the continually
reasserted strain of homelessness that often seems to be the real meaning
of the soap opera. The gangster film is remarkable in that it fills the need

---

[1] In her testimony before the House Committee on Un-American Activities, Mrs.
Leila Rogers said that the movie *None But the Lonely Heart* was un-American because
it was gloomy. Like so much else that was said during the unhappy investigation of
Hollywood, this statement was at once stupid and illuminating. One knew immediately
what Mrs. Rogers was talking about; she had simply been insensitive enough to carry
her philistinism to its conclusion.

for disguise (though not sufficiently to avoid arousing uneasiness) without requiring any serious distortion. From its beginnings, it has been a consistent and astonishingly complete presentation of the modern sense of tragedy.[2]

In its initial character, the gangster film is simply one example of the movies' constant tendency to create fixed dramatic patterns that can be repeated indefinitely with a reasonable expectation of profit. One gangster film follows another as one musical or one Western follows another. But this rigidity is not necessarily opposed to the requirements of art. There have been very successful types of art in the past which developed such specific and detailed conventions as almost to make individual examples of the type interchangeable. This is true, for example, of Elizabethan revenge tragedy and Restoration comedy.

For such a type to be successful means that its conventions have imposed themselves upon the general consciousness and become the accepted vehicles of a particular set of attitudes and a particular aesthetic effect. One goes to any individual example of the type with very definite expectations, and originality is to be welcomed only in the degree that it intensifies the expected experience without fundamentally altering it. Moreover, the relationship between the conventions which go to make up such a type and the real experience of its audience or the real facts of whatever situation it pretends to describe is of only secondary importance and does not determine its aesthetic force. It is only in an ultimate sense that the type appeals to its audience's experience of reality; much more immediately, it appeals to previous experience of the type itself: it creates its own field of reference.

Thus the importance of the gangster film, and the nature and intensity of its emotional and aesthetic impact, cannot be measured in terms of the place of the gangster himself or the importance of the problem of crime in American life. Those European movie-goers who think there is a gangster on every corner in New York are certainly deceived, but defenders of the "positive" side of American culture are equally deceived if they think it relevant to point out that most Americans have never seen a gangster. What matters is that the experience of the gangster *as an experience of art* is universal to Americans. There is almost nothing we understand better or react to more readily or with quicker intelligence. The Western film, though it seems never to diminish in popularity, is for most of us no more than the folklore of the past, familiar and understandable only because it has been repeated so often. The gangster film comes much closer. In ways that we do not easily or willing define, the gangster speaks for us, expressing that part of the American psyche which rejects the qualities and the demands of modern life, which rejects "Americanism" itself.

The gangster is the man of the city, with the city's language and knowl-

---

[2] Efforts have been made from time to time to bring the gangster film into line with the prevailing optimism and social constructiveness of our culture; *Kiss of Death* is a recent example. These efforts are usually unsuccessful; the reasons for their lack of success are interesting in themselves, but I shall not be able to discuss them here.

edge, with its queer and dishonest skills and its terrible daring, carrying his life in his hands like a placard, like a club. For everyone else, there is at least the theoretical possibility of another world — in that happier American culture which the gangster denies, the city does not really exist; it is only a more crowded and more brightly lit country — but for the gangster there is only the city; he must inhabit it in order to personify it: not the real city, but that dangerous and sad city of the imagination which is so much more important, which is the modern world. And the gangster — though there are real gangsters — is also, and primarily, a creature of the imagination. The real city, one might say, produces only criminals; the imaginary city produces the gangster: he is what we want to be and what we are afraid we may become.

Thrown into the crowd without background or advantages, with only those ambiguous skills which the rest of us — the real people of the real city — can only pretend to have, the gangster is required to make his way, to make his life and impose it on others. Usually, when we come upon him, he has already made his choice or the choice has already been made for him, it doesn't matter which: we are not permitted to ask whether at some point he could have chosen to be something else than what he is.

The gangster's activity is actually a form of rational enterprise, involving fairly definite goals and various techniques for achieving them. But this rationality is usually no more than a vague background; we know perhaps, that the gangster sells liquor or that he operates a numbers racket; often we are not given even that much information. So his activity becomes a kind of pure criminality: he *hurts* people. Certainly our response to the gangster film is most consistently and most universally a response to sadism; we gain the double satisfaction of participating vicariously in the gangster's sadism and then seeing it turned against the gangster himself.

But on another level the quality of irrational brutality and the quality of rational enterprise become one. Since we do not see the rational and routine aspects of the gangster's behavior, the practice of brutality — the quality of unmixed criminality — becomes the totality of his career. At the same time, we are always conscious that the whole meaning of this career is a drive for success: the typical gangster film presents a steady upward progress followed by a very precipitate fall. Thus brutality itself becomes at once the means to success and the content of success — a success that is defined in its most general terms, not as accomplishment or specific gain, but simply as the unlimited possibility of aggression. (In the same way, film presentations of businessmen tend to make it appear that they achieve their success by talking on the telephone and holding conferences and that success *is* talking on the telephone and holding conferences.)

From this point of view, the initial contact between the film and its audience is an agreed conception of human life: that man is a being with the possibilities of success or failure. This principle, too, belongs to the city; one must emerge from the crowd or else one is nothing. On that basis the necessity of the action is established, and it progresses by inalterable paths to the point where the gangster lies dead and the principle has been modified; there is really only one possibility—failure. The final meaning of the city is anonymity and death.

In the opening scene of *Scarface*, we are shown a successful man; we know he is successful because he has just given a party of opulent proportions and because he is called Big Louie. Through some monstrous lack of caution, he permits himself to be alone for a few moments. We understand from this immediately that he is about to be killed. No convention of the gangster film is more strongly established than this: it is dangerous to be alone. And yet the very conditions of success make it impossible not to be alone, for success is always the establishment of an *individual* pre-eminence that must be imposed on others, in whom it automatically arouses hatred; the successful man is an outlaw. The gangster's whole life is an effort to assert himself as an individual, to draw himself out of the crowd, and he always dies *because* he is an individual; the final bullet thrusts him back, makes him, after all, a failure. "Mother of God," says the dying Little Caesar, "is this the end of Rico?"—speaking of himself thus in the third person because what has been brought low is not the undifferentiated *man*, but the individual with a name, the gangster, the success; even to himself he is a creature of the imagination. (T. S. Eliot has pointed out that a number of Shakespeare's tragic heroes have this trick of looking at themselves dramatically; their true identity, the thing that is not destroyed when they die, is something outside themselves— not a man, but a style of life, a kind of meaning.)

At bottom, the gangster is doomed because he is under the obligation to succeed, not because the means he employs are unlawful. In the deeper layers of the modern consciousness, *all* means are unlawful, every attempt to succeed is an act of aggression, leaving one alone and guilty and defenseless among enemies; one is *punished* for success. This is our intolerable dilemma: that failure is a kind of death and success is evil and dangerous, is—ultimately—impossible. The effect of the gangster film is to embody this dilemma in the person of the gangster and resolve it by his death. The dilemma is resolved because it is *his* death, not ours. We are safe; for the moment, we can acquiesce in our failure, we can choose to fail.

STUDY QUESTIONS

1. *What does Warshow think to be the relation of the gangster movie, which has considerable sadness in it, to the optimism that generally prevails in mass culture? Does his thesis seem reasonable to you? Why? Are other explanations possible? How do you think other standard types of movies or TV shows are related to our culture?*

2. *What does Warshow mean by saying that the gangster movie "creates its own field of reference"? Is this true of any other art or medium of entertainment?*

3. *What difference is suggested by Warshow's careful use of the two words, "criminal" and "gangster"?*

4. *What, according to Warshow, is the "style of life" the movie gangster represents, even to himself?*

5. *Do you agree with Warshow that it is the function of the movie gangster to reflect our feelings of guilt, and to enable us to satisfy the feeling that we should be punished for our successes? Or is it possible to apply a different interpretation to the plot of the gangster film? Write a theme explaining what emotions and attitudes you believe gangster films express.*

6. *Compare Warshow's conception of the tragic role of the movie gangster with Edith Hamilton's definition of tragedy.*

Alistair Cooke Epitaph for a Tough Guy*

And just what was this new sort of hero, whose originality I have hinted at in a menacing phrase or two? Looked at after twenty years' familiarity, it is a surprise to see that he is a direct descendant of Sherlock Holmes, as indeed are most fictional private detectives invented since Conan Doyle cast the original mold: a depressed, eccentric bachelor of vast, odd knowledge, whose intelligence is poised over the plot like a dagger, which in the moment of resolution slices through the butter of the surrounding confusion. This is the elementary recipe for all the moderns, from Perry Mason to Philip Marlowe. Where Holmes knew the soil classification of the Home Counties, Bogart — sharing an unfriendly drink with Sidney Greenstreet — sees a ship slink by on the horizon and calls off the full-load displacement, overall length, gun caliber, muzzle velocity. Holmes possessed an uncanny sense of the whereabouts of distressed gentlewomen and had memorized the Paddington train schedules against the day of their rescue. Bogart knows all about hotels, from Yokohama to New York: the tactical geography of suites, connecting doors, and fire escapes, how to confuse the room clerk and evade the house dick, determine the clientele by a glance around the lobby, know who is up to no good and where she is likely to be.

The field maneuvers may be different from those in Holmes's day, and the villain is more socially mobile, but since Sir Arthur we have not changed the three essential ingredients of the private eye. He must be a bachelor, with the bachelor's harum-scarum availability at all hours (William Powell's marriage to Myrna "Nora" Loy, a wistful concession to the family trade, fooled nobody.) He must have an inconspicuous fund of curious knowledge, which in the end is always crucially relevant. He must pity the official guardians of the law.

Of course, the twentieth century has grafted some interesting personality

* From *The Atlantic Monthly*, May, 1957. Reprinted by permission of *The Atlantic Monthly*.

changes on the original. Holmes was an eccentric in the Victorian sense, a man with queer hobbies — cocaine was lamentable but pardonably melodramatic — whose social code was essentially that of the ruling classes. He was, in a way, the avenging squire of the underworld ready to administer a horsewhipping to the outcasts who were never privileged by birth to receive it from their fathers. Bogart is a displaced person whose present respectability is uncertain, a classless but well-contained vagabond who is not going to be questioned about where he came from or where he is going. ("I came to Casablanca for the waters." "But there are no waters in Casablanca." "I was misinformed.")

As a Victorian bachelor-hero, Holmes must be presumed to be asexual. Bogart too is a lone wolf, but with a new and equal stress on the noun. His general view of women implies that he was brought up, sexually speaking, no earlier than the twenties. Hence he is unshockable and offhand, and, one gathers, a very devil with the women, who is saved from absurdity by never having time to prove it. ("Sorry, angel, I have a pressing date with a fat man.") Unlike Holmes, he cannot claim even the castle of a carefully cluttered set of rooms. He is always on the move, and his only domestic base is a fairly seedy hotel bedroom with an unmade bed (this is called audience identification, and to tell the truth is the sort of independent base of operations most college boys and many rueful husbands would like to have). Yet somehow, somewhere, in his baffling past he learned the habits of the *haut monde*. And his audience is constantly flattered by the revelation that a sudden call to dine with a jewel importer at the Ritz will find him shaved and natty and handling the right knives with easy boredom.

It is a gorgeous conception, fulfilling more fantasies in the male audience than a Freudian could shake a stick at, and it was given a very entertaining dry run in the appearances of Warren William as Perry Mason. But it was always thought of as B-film material until Bogart turned it into box office. The change may have been due in the first place to what Peter Ustinov has called his "enormous presence," the simple, inexplicable characteristic of natural stars: you cannot take your eyes off them. (No one in the history of the movies has made smoking a cigarette a more deadly and fascinating thing to watch.) It was also due to Bogart's graduation from mere gangster parts just when parliamentary Europe was caving in to gangsters on a grand scale. He is the first romantic hero who used the gangster's means to achieve our ends. And this character was suddenly very precious in the age of violence, for it satisfied a quiet, desperate need of the engulfed, ordinary citizen. When Hitler was acting out scripts more brutal and obscene than anything dreamed of by Chicago's North Side or the Warner Brothers, Bogart was the only possible antagonist likely to outwit him and survive. What was needed was no Ronald Colman, Leslie Howard, or other knight of the boudoir, but a conniver as subtle as Goebbels. Bogart was the very tough gent required, and to his glory he was always, in the end, on our side.

STUDY QUESTIONS

1. This brief selection is the central section from an essay of the same title in which Cooke describes and favorably evaluates the career and genuine contribution of Humphrey Bogart. Note and be prepared to discuss some of the differences in writing and purpose between this and the two preceding selections.

2. In what other ways besides his freedom does the character portrayed by Bogart offer his audience opportunities for "audience identification"?

3. In what way did the events of the time help Bogart become famous?

4. In what ways does the character portrayed by Bogart differ from other movie heroes? What can he do that other movie heroes never do? What sort of activities and ideas can he omit that would be required in another sort of hero? What conclusions do these observations suggest?

5. Write a theme describing the sort of character portrayed by another favorite movie star, telling why he appeals to (or is detested by) his audience.

6. Note that Alistair Cooke tries to give definite reasons for Bogart's popularity. Can the popularity of types of films and film personalities always be explained in this way? Write a theme giving definite reasons for the popularity of a particular type of movie, such as Westerns, family movies, science-fiction pictures or musicals, or a particular type of character, such as the earnest doctor, the hard-working girl singer, the tough outdoor man, or the poor little rich girl.

Norman Podhoretz   The Father on the Hearth*

At least fifty plays are produced on television every week. About a third of these are detective and mystery stories; another large slice is devoted to whimsical tales with surprise endings. But the remainder constitutes a genre peculiar to television. It has developed its own style, its own conventions, and to some extent its own subject matter.

These TV plays are theatrical rather than cinematic, taking their cue from Broadway, not Hollywood. Movie stars rarely appear in them, though prominent Broadway figures often do; the casts consist of extremely competent actors most of whom, I imagine, consider themselves theater people. The direction almost always betrays the influence of men like Kazan — which is to say that it tries to combine realism of surface with self-conscious, sometimes arty, arrangements, movement, and overtones. Both dialogue and acting are more sophisticated than is usual in the movies. In general the productions are on a surprisingly high level, considering the number of plays turned out every week.

* From Commentary, 1953. Reprinted by permission of Norman Podhoretz.

The tendency is toward low-key drama, a kind of domestic realism whose effect derives from its accuracy in reflecting the ordinary man's conceptions of the world. The very style of the acting — always plausible, always controlled, never permitting itself the least intimation of hamminess, rarely even admitting that it is artifice rather than actual conversation — restricts the drama to that level of reality which is easily accessible to common sense. A whole play may be based on a very trivial incident, chosen because everyone in the audience will have experienced something similar. For example, a teenage boy takes the family car without his father's permission, gets involved in a minor accident, and doesn't come home until three in the morning. His parents wait up for him, anxiety-ridden, and when he finally returns, all is forgiven and the whole family goes to bed with the sense of having got through another crisis. This play is "true to life" in a way that popular culture seldom is: the audience has never had the stuff of its daily existence taken so seriously, and it responds with a new feeling of self-importance and dignity. Unlike the soap operas, which betray a masochistic relish in minor troubles, the point here is the relief people feel in being able to resume their usual routine: trouble teaches gratitude for the humdrum.

Depending for its effectiveness on its ability to remain content with the world perceived and comprehended by common sense, this kind of drama must resist appealing either to escapist fantasy or to the critical intelligence, never wandering above or below the staples of experience. Nowadays, to be sure, that can include a great deal of surprising matter. In a play about the relation between a mother and her son, suggestions of an Oedipus complex are offered in much the same way as characters appear wearing clothes: the writer, the director, the actors, take it completely for granted as an ordinary element in the family. It isn't a mysterious, sinister force (as it tends to be in the movies) but a tangible factor existing almost wholly on the surface and demanding to be observed. This means, of course, that it needn't have consequences; in this particular instance, it counted for nothing in the plot. That a son should be in love with his mother is an index of his normality, not of his monstrousness. This must imply, I suppose, that the audience has been trained to regard it thus, or is well on its way to doing so.

Life in these plays, then, is non-heroic: a world governed by common sense is a world where "everyone has his faults and his good points." No insuperable moral problems are recognized, for, in a universe ruled exclusively by forces visible to the common-sense eye, there can be no dilemma which resists the touch of good will and a spirit of compromise. Often a play will open with a situation in which right seems to conflict with right, but in the end someone is proved wrong or neurotic or misguided, and the difficulty immediately resolves *itself*. A common-sense ethos must always hack its way through to the simple truths which are supposed to lie buried beneath the ugly and delusory overgrowths of experience.

Though everyone in these plays has weaknesses as well as virtues, we find the weaknesses far less in evidence. If a man sins, he does so almost accidentally, for sin is something that happens to people, not something they do. They make errors of judgment all the time, but they generally know nothing of pure or gratuitous malice. Only their virtues are essential to them; their sins are somehow external, reefs against which they have blundered in the fog. (The TV crime plays, on the other hand, become a repository of much that is omitted from domestic drama: crime is a violation of common-sense living, and therefore results in the criminal's exclusion from the sphere in which all slips can be made good.)

One would expect that a world made by common sense, ruled by common sense, and upheld by common sense, would be a pleasant world to live in. In many ways it is. It produces people whose passions are under control, who are well-bred, well-mannered, open, friendly, helpful, and above all, reasonable. More than anything else, they want to get along, they will do nearly anything to keep the peace.

And yet the optimism we find here is gray rather than flaming; it is overcast with a sadness that seems a new element in American popular culture. There is a distinct feeling that life is tough even for those who aren't harassed by the landlord and the grocer; and there is a shade of disillusion over the discovery that human possibility is not infinite — reverberations of Korea are in the air. The mood is more sober than what used to be called American optimism, and, as we shall see, far more honest.

Before the dislocations caused by 3D, Hollywood had been gravitating in several full-dress productions toward a similar form of drama. . . . But the features characterizing the new genre — an insistent interest in domestic life, a *dramatis personae* entirely composed of ordinary people, a strict fidelity to the appearance of things, a quiet tone (everything is underplayed), a paucity of plot, and much discussion and debate — made it apparent that its real home was in television. Going to the movies is still more or less an occasion for most people, and an occasion demands something extraordinary. Even the size of the cinema screen insures that the movie world shall be larger than life (indeed, in answer to the small television screen, movie screens have become larger); perhaps for this reason, movies reproduced on television lose their bite. Watching television, on the other hand, has become an integral part of domestic routine, and the new genre serves an impulse to make the program a relevant and appropriate presence in the living room.

The living room, in fact, is the favorite setting of these plays, just as the favorite cast is a family. It is a middle-class family, neither unusually happy nor (as in the soap operas) continually besieged with trouble. Its most remarkable quality as a group is a negative one — fear is absent from the relations of its members and power thus becomes a corollary of love: it can only be had by free consent. The father guides and administers his household; he does not rule it. The plot always turns on some crisis that has suddenly developed, often in the family relations themselves: as in any family, its members are continually in the process of losing their illusions about one another, and the effort at readjustment is constant. Ultimately they emerge from their difficulties as more of a family, having restored a workable balance of power.

Almost always the father comes through as a sharper figure than the mother, who is supposed to have her being in and through her husband and children. A good woman is not so much *by* as *on* the side of her husband. If she asserts her personality too forcefully, we may be sure that calamity will result. Evil, when it makes one of its rare visits to these plays, is likely to come in the shape of a domineering wife or an overly possessive mother. As for the father, he is an earnest man, but his earnestness is mellow compared with the fierce unyielding grimness of his children or his wife's firm, uncritical loyalty to her feelings. Soft-spoken, controlled, never glamorous-looking, but always carrying himself with great dignity and self-assurance, he exhibits the palpable scars of a long combat with life. His humility, patience, and sadness are the products of many frustrations, and he is thus extremely skeptical of any comprehensive schemes or over-ambitious plans. Sometimes he is portrayed as a great disappointment to his children — for we live in an era where parents rather than children are perennially on trial — and in such cases the guilt and bitterness he feels are tempered by his pity for the son who will soon learn that all human beings are disappointing to those who make excessive demands on them.

We practically never see this new American father (as we used to in the movies and as we still do in television soap operas) involved in the big business deal, or embroiled in the problems of earning money: a comfortable income is taken for granted, while his career is merely a shadowy presence in the background. The great reality of his life, the sphere in which things happen to him, is his family. He carries his responsibilities willingly, without a sense of oppression, and the fact that they occupy him so fully, challenging all his resources of character and mind, never allowing him to get bored, is his most powerful proof to his son that the ordinary life is worth living. For this is the great lesson he is intent upon teaching. We find him telling his daughter that marriage, children, and love are far more important than fame and wealth; we find him insisting to his son that there is no disgrace in compromise. He represents reasonableness, tolerance, and good will: the image of American maturity.

Preserving the family from disruption is the role he is most often called upon to play. One species of disruption is conflict with his children. The conflict never takes the form of youth's rebellion against parental authority because the father's authority over his children is not given in the nature of things. Since he is a constitutional leader rather than an absolute monarch, his authority must constantly be reaffirmed at the polls. Nor can he assert it forcefully or arbitrarily: he must win the right to participate in his son's problems by making himself sufficiently attractive in the boy's eyes — good "public relations" is essential to his position. Interference with his son's private affairs being a matter of the greatest delicacy, he only presumes to speak in crucial matters. Otherwise he is there, looking on, setting an example, communicating through the silent power of his personality.

In an encounter with his children, he confronts them with a flexibility that often seems to be weakness but in reality turns out to be a wisdom based on the knowledge that human beings cannot afford to be too hard either on themselves or others. One play (already mentioned above) was about a young man of twenty who discovers his mother committing adultery while his father is away on a business trip. After wandering around the streets all night, the son staggers into his house, dishevelled, distraught, and looking a little drunk; to his amazement, he finds his father waiting for him. "Now, listen, son, I know everything; your mother wired me and I took the next plane back. She told me the whole story."[1] The boy covers his face with his hands, unable to speak. "What are you going to do?" asks his father. "What do you mean, what am I going to do? What are you going to do?" "Well, what do you expect me to do — leave your mother and break up our home because she made a mistake?" At this suggestion that his father wants to forget the whole thing, the boy stares at him incredulously; it's impossible to go on living with an immoral mother and a weak-kneed father. Patiently and sympathetically, the father persists in trying to convince his son that their family is too important to be destroyed by a mistake. His wife, he explains, is going through a difficult phase; her son is grown up, she has nothing left to do, she thinks she isn't needed. Now she's upstairs suffering more than her son would believe, terrified that he may turn away from her. "Our job is to help her, not to kill her. I've got to be more loving, you've got to show that you understand her side of things. Will you do it?" And, of course, the play ends with the boy going upstairs to comfort his mother. This is an atmosphere in which adultery and betrayal breed not hatred, but new responsibility. Yet all this understanding disturbs one: is there no breaking point?

Occasionally there is, as when the father's worldliness becomes irrelevant (or worse) to his son's problems. A young man, caught violating the Honor System in his pre-graduation exams at college, is about to be expelled by a committee of his peers, when he offers to turn in the names of the others who had cheated with him. The list of names is confided to the chairman of the committee, a brilliant student who is planning to marry a sweet young classmate and to go into his father's business. On the list he finds his fiancée's name. Should he, before handing it in to the Dean, strike off her name? His father, guessing the boy's trouble, persuades him to do so: "You're going out into a tough world where nobody will care about you and your interests. You have to look out for yourself and the people you love. This is a small town, son; they never forget a scandal, they'll never let you forget that your wife was once expelled from college for cheating. Everybody cheats; the only

[1] I quote from memory throughout this article.

difference between a respectable man and a cheater is that the cheater has been caught. Son, don't let your 'principles' destroy your happiness. Use your head, boy!" At first the boy takes this advice, but later, to the consternation of his father, confesses while delivering his valedictory address, and proclaims his own expulsion. The two young people leave the small university town together to begin a new life.

Though repudiated, the father in this play is not unsympathetically portrayed. He realizes that the Honor System places too great a burden on young people, and that there is something absurd — something that violates common sense — in allowing a trivial matter to ruin a life. He does not, as his own father might have done, advise his son to give up this girl who will disgrace him: the highest value is still preservation of the family, even if it hasn't quite been formed yet. And in this play the idea of family takes on a special significance. The world outside is assumed to be hostile (like the outraged student body demanding the expulsion of the cheaters), or, like the kindly Dean, helpless in the face of circumstances and the Rules. The world outside is mechanical, rigid, governed by cold standards of no one's making: even the Dean can't protect the students he would like to forgive. Within the family, however, a man has resources, for the family rests on love and reasonableness, and it is in the nature of love to persist despite circumstance, while reasonableness provides flexibility to liberate the spirit from the tyranny of Rules. A person is most a person to those who love him; otherwise he is judged and disposed of.

That understanding and flexibility should be the father's greatest qualities is not surprising. What does surprise us, however, is that he rarely feels ambition for his children, merely wishing them to lead normal, contented lives. The only ambitious father I remember seeing is the one in the play just discussed, and he is also the only father who comes off badly in the end — as if ambitiousness were an act of *hubris* to be avenged. The drive for extraordinary achievement has always been considered notoriously American. An identity is something that must be earned, not inherited, and once earned it remains precarious and must be vigilantly maintained: if you lose your money, you also lose your name. This compulsion to prove that we are "saved" is probably a consequence of being born into a Puritan culture — many marks of status in America are simply secularized versions of what once were the symptoms of grace.

We seem, however, under the influence of psychoanalysis, to have reached a point where the most important mark of status has become not money, power, or fame, but a reasonably happy family life. Play after play insists that everyone is saved, that all are granted grace if they are but willing to accept it: adjustment is supposed to be available to all.

The way to justify the space you take up in the world is — as one father puts it — not to be *somebody,* but just to *be.* An adaptation of Dos Passos' *The Big Money* is used as a vehicle for showing the disastrous consequences of the pursuit of wealth; a young boxer who had been a foundling realizes that he needn't be compulsive about becoming a champion in order to give his infant son a "name"; a great soprano feigns the loss of her voice because she has learned that happiness lies in raising children and being supported by a responsible husband; a distinguished (divorced) actress gives up her career because she falls in love with a man who teaches her that what she really wants is a husband and family; a potentially great pianist is forced to admit that he is incapable of performing on the concert stage, and finds that being released from an immature ambition allows him for the first time to feel content in his marriage.

A particularly interesting example is a play about a widower, father of a fifteen-year-old daughter, who falls in love with a formerly great concert pianist. We are given to understand that some sort of illness interrupted her career, but now she is working steadily to stage a comeback. The woman is in her thirties, completely dedicated to music, living in a room which is stuffed with busts of great composers and that suggests the atmosphere of a mausoleum. Pressured into a date with the widower by a friendly neighbor, she reveals herself as socially inept. Her behavior is awkward, she can't dance, and she commits the great crime of being a killjoy by leaving the country club at midnight. ("I'm so sorry to have ruined your evening," she apologizes pathetically. "I knew I shouldn't have come. I'm just no good at this sort of thing. And now I have to get some sleep, because I have a long day of practice ahead of me.") The widower was an extremely good representative of his type: equable, quiet, observant (the camera kept finding excuses for giving us close-ups of his intently serious eyes), sensible, understanding, and completely at his ease in the many different situations the play showed him in. We soon discover that the widower's young daughter fancies herself a pianist too. Against the tactful urging of her father, she breaks a date for the junior prom in order to prepare for a high-school concert. Eventually, of course, the daughter and the ex-concert pianist become great friends. Father is disturbed, but for the moment does nothing, allowing her to study with the older woman. As soon as the high-school concert is over, he intends to be firm. The night before the concert, however, he is horrified to learn that great plans are being made for his daughter. "She reminds me so much of what I was like at her age. And she has talent. You can't stand in her way. I've sent for the Great Maestro to hear her tomorrow night. He'll convince you." After the concert, the Great Maestro tells his ex-pupil that her protégé is extremely talented, but that she'll never be anything more than a competent performer: the divine spark is missing. Father is pleased, but the woman refuses to accept this judgment as final. "There are other teachers. We'll get them to hear her. I *know* she has talent. She'll work hard, oh it will be very hard, but she'll make it, I know she will." The father shakes his head sadly. "Why did you stop giving concerts?" "Because I was ill." "No, you weren't ill. I know because I looked up the reviews. They said you had lost your genius, that you were a great child prodigy who never developed." "No, no, it's not true!" "But it *is* true, my darling. Why can't you face reality? Why won't you move out of this tomb and live?" Through her tears she whimpers, "But don't you understand? I have to be somebody." Then comes the clinching line of the play: "Why do you have to be *somebody?* Why can't you just *be?*" And she collapses into his arms. In the last act, the young girl tells her idol that she has to be somebody, but the redeemed artist repeats father's epigram, adding that "there are so many things in life for you. There's your first dance, and the first time you fall in love, and marriage and children." The child weeps hysterically and rushes out of the room, but father and stepmother-to-be embrace. "Don't worry. She'll be all right now."

The play hardly entertains the suggestion that there are circumstances in which a normal life is worth sacrificing, nor does the writer admit that there may be more than one way of finding happiness, or that there may be other forms of the good life which take place outside the family circle. All this is typical of serious television drama. It would be a mistake, however, to think that "conformity" is being urged, if we mean by that imposing a specific model of behavior. On the assumption that everyone really wants the same kind of things out of life, these plays argue, quite plausibly, that only childishness or neurosis (both of which are characterized by the excessive demands they foster) will prevent people from taking advantage of their inalienable right to pursue happiness. Nor is there any uncertainty about the content of happiness; the only problem is finding the surest, swiftest, and safest means to a predetermined end.

Yet, curiously enough, the most salient feature of this ethos remains its sadness. It presents itself as making a modest demand upon life, a demand so modest that life would be guilty of the cruelest perversity to deny it. Bearing in its countenance the lines and wrinkles of maturity, it is always opposed to the presumptuous, enthusiastic "idealism" of youth. Yet what could be more optimistic than the belief that contentment and security are within everyone's reach? When success is measured by money or fame, failure can be chalked up to bad luck; the whole man is rarely in the balance, for a certain distinction will be maintained between the private and public selves: the private self is there to fall back upon if the other turns out treacherous. But when success is conceived as an attribute of the personality rather than of the wallet, failure becomes the tenth circle of Hell. A new fortune can be made, but a man's personality is his essence — personality, in fact, is the modern word for soul — and if that proves befouled, then no good can come of it. In these plays personality itself figures as the goal of all striving; the object of ambition becomes not success but "successful living." The type of all failures is the neurotic, pictured writhing under his burdens like one of the damned; and appropriately so, for in this view of things, a failure of the personality is the last and most refined torture of the Devil. Perhaps some perception of this accounts for the resignation that overcomes the intrinsic cheeriness of the new ethos.

It would be foolish at this point to make any simple judgments of television drama as a whole. Its most notable achievements, I think, are the sharpness with which it has distinguished itself from the movies, the effort it has made to be honest, the success with which it has managed to be serious without being objectionably pretentious. Most important, perhaps, it gives pleasure as so many "serious" movies have failed to do — Hollywood's great fault is its inability to see any connection between "entertainment" and "significance." Apart from a few comic strips, television drama seems the only area of American popular culture that refuses to distinguish finally between the two. Because it isn't imitative, it gives a picture of American life whose accuracy may be difficult to measure but whose honesty is sometimes astonishing: there was a time when the play about the mother's adultery would have ended with the discovery that she hadn't really committed adultery at all.

It may be that this drama reflects the values and aspirations of the newly emerged middle class, now large enough to constitute a mass audience and powerful enough to set the stamp of its attitudes on an important segment of popular culture. Formed by psychoanalysis and nourished by the concepts of social work, this class shows a conspicuous distaste for violence and a remarkable lack of interest in the ungovernable passions of young love. It puts a very high value on the family, though not in order to retreat from the community. The family here is an expanding rather than a restrictive entity, the nucleus of community; it comes to mean all decent, sensible, and understanding people, "people like us," people, that is, who act as people and not as "forces." The retreat to the home, then, means a retreat from "environment" — from the competitive world of business and politics, which menaces amiable human relations and does not yield easily to compromise and good will.

Finally, this drama has contributed a new figure to the popular imagination. Attractive and disturbing as he is, the father may turn out to be a summation of the postwar ethos. In his benign firmness, in his mature sobriety, in his sad but determined sense of responsibility, in his unceasing efforts to keep the peace, we can detect the traces of the contemporary political climate. He reflects the feeling that the only safe oasis in a dangerous, cold-war world is our own home, a home which, though it may once have been taken lightly, must now be preserved at all costs if the battle is not to be lost everywhere. And in the long series of plays which turn on a rediscovery of the father by his son, we find, perhaps, the mark of a generation which has moved out of rebellion and skepticism into a patient and humble acquiescence; and we may here discover the role the new middle class seems to have marked out for its own.

STUDY QUESTIONS

1. *Why would not the father, as described in this article, qualify as a movie hero?*
2. *What are the elements of sadness in the basically optimistic picture of American life presented by the new TV drama?*

3. *In what ways are the TV dramas more realistic than the movies? Are there any ways in which they are less realistic?*

4. *Does this kind of drama make use of conventions peculiar to itself, as Warshow has pointed out the gangster film does? Is it different in this respect from other dramatic and fictional media?*

5. *Do you agree with the author that this is a new kind of popular drama, which reflects changes in American life? Write a theme on this subject.*

6. *Following Podhoretz' method, analyze another staple TV product, such as the adventure story, the detective chase or the animal-hero story.*

John Steinbeck

How to Tell Good Guys from Bad Guys*

Television has crept upon us so gradually in America that we have not yet become aware of the extent of its impact for good or bad. I myself do not look at it very often except for its coverage of sporting events, news, and politics. Indeed, I get most of my impressions of the medium from my young sons.

Whether for good or bad, television has taken the place of the sugar-tit, soothing syrups, and the mild narcotics parents in other days used to reduce their children to semiconsciousness and consequently to seminoisiness. In the past, a harassed parent would say, "Go sit in a chair!" or "Go outside and play!" or "If you don't stop that noise, I'm going to beat your dear little brains out!" The present-day parent suggests, "Why don't you go look at television?" From that moment the screams, shouts, revolver shots, and crashes of motor accidents come from the loudspeaker, not from the child. For some reason, this is presumed to be more relaxing to the parent. The effect on the child has yet to be determined.

I have observed the physical symptoms of television-looking on children as well as on adults. The mouth grows slack and the lips hang open; the eyes take on a hypnotized or doped look; the nose runs rather more than usual; the back-bone turns to water and the fingers slowly and methodically pick the designs out of brocade furniture. Such is the appearance of semiconsciousness that one wonders how much of the "message" of television is getting through to the brain. This wonder is further strengthened by the fact that a television-looker will look at anything at all and for hours. Recently I came into a room to find my eight-year-old son Catbird sprawled in a chair, idiot slackness on his face, with the doped eyes of an opium smoker. On the television screen stood a young woman of mammary distinction with ice-cream hair listening to a man in thick glasses and a doctor's smock.

"What's happening?" I asked.

Catbird answered in the monotone of the sleeptalker which is known as television voice, "She is asking if she should dye her hair."

"What is the doctor's reaction?"

"If she uses Trutone it's all right," said Catbird. "But if she uses ordinary or adulterated products, her hair will split and lose its golden natural sheen. The big economy size is two dollars and ninety-eight cents if you act now," said Catbird.

You see, something was getting through to him. He looked punch-drunk, but he was absorbing. I did not feel it fair to interject a fact I have observed — that natural golden sheen does not exist in nature. But I did think of my friend Elia Kazan's cry of despair, and although it is a digression I shall put it down.

We were having dinner in a lovely little restaurant in California. At the table next to us were six beautiful, young, well-dressed American girls of the age and appearance of magazine advertisements. There was only one difficulty with their perfection. You couldn't tell them apart. Kazan, who is a primitive of a species once known as men, regarded the little beauties with distaste, and finally in more sorrow than anger cried, "It's years since I've seen or smelled a dame! It's all products, Golden Glint, l'Eau d'Eau, Butisan, Elyn's puff-adder cream — I remember I used to like how women smelled. Nowadays it's all products!"

End of digression.

Just when the parent becomes convinced that his child's brain is rotting away from television, he is jerked up in another direction. Catbird has corrected me in the Museum of Natural History when I directed his attention to the mounted skeleton of a tyrannosaur. He said it was brontosaurus but observed kindly that many people made the same error. He argued with his ten-year-old brother about the relative cleanness of the line in Praxiteles and Phidias. He knows the weight a llama will bear before lying down in protest, and his knowledge of entomology is embarrassing to a parent who likes to impart information to his children. And these things he also got from television. I knew that he was picking up masses of unrelated and probably worthless information from television, incidentally the kind of information I also like best, but I did not know that television was preparing him in criticism and politics, and that is what this piece is really about.

I will have to go back a bit in preparation. When television in America first began to be a threat to the motion-picture industry, that industry fought back by refusing to allow its films to be shown on the home screens. One never saw new pictures, but there were whole blocks of films called Westerns which were owned by independents, and these were released to the television stations. The result is that at nearly any time of the day or night you can find a Western being shown on some television station. It is not only the children who see them. All of America sees them. They are a typically American conception, the cowboy picture. The story never varies and the conventions are savagely adhered to. The hero never kisses a girl. He loves his horse and he stands for right and justice. Any change in the story or the conventions would be taken as an outrage. Out of these films folk heroes have grown up — Hopalong Cassidy, the Lone Ranger, Roy Rogers, and Gene Autry. These are more than great men. They are symbols of courage, purity, simplicity, honesty, and right. You must understand that nearly every American is drenched in the tradition of the Western, which is, of course, the celebration of a whole pattern of American life that never existed. It is also as set in its form as the *commedia dell' arte*.

End of preparation.

One afternoon, hearing gunfire from the room where our television set is installed, I went in with that losing intention of fraternizing with my son for a little while. There sat Catbird with the cretinous expression I have learned to recognize. A Western was in progress.

"What's going on?" I asked.

He looked at me in wonder. "What do you mean, what's going on? Don't you know?"

"Well, no. Tell me!"

He was kind to me. Explained as though I were the child.

"Well, the Bad Guy is trying to steal Her father's ranch. But the Good Guy won't let him. Bullet figured out the plot."

"Who is Bullet?"

"Why, the Good Guy's horse." He didn't add "You dope," but his tone implied it.

"Now wait," I said, "which one is the Good Guy?"

"The one with the white hat."

"Then the one with the black hat is the Bad Guy?"

"Anybody knows that," said Catbird.

For a time I watched the picture, and I realized that I had been ignoring a part of our life that everybody knows. I was interested in the characterizations. The girl, known as Her or She, was a blonde, very pretty but completely unvoluptuous because these are Family Pictures. Sometimes she wore a simple gingham dress and sometimes a leather skirt and boots, but always she had a bit of a bow in her hair and her face was untroubled with emotion or, one might almost say, intelligence. This also is part of the convention. She is a symbol, and any acting would get her thrown out of the picture by popular acclaim.

The Good Guy not only wore a white hat but light-colored clothes, shining boots, tight riding pants, and a shirt embroidered with scrolls and flowers. In my young days I used to work with cattle, and our costume was blue jeans, a leather jacket, and boots with run-over heels. The cleaning bill alone of the gorgeous screen cowboy would have been four times what our pay was in a year.

The Good Guy had very little change of facial expression. He went through his fantastic set of adventures with no show of emotion. This is another convention and proves that he is very brave and very pure. He is also scrubbed and has an immaculate shave.

I turned my attention to the Bad Guy. He wore a black hat and dark clothing, but his clothing was definitely not only unclean but unpressed. He had a stubble of beard but the greatest contrast was in his face. His was not an immobile face. He leered, he sneered, he had a nasty laugh. He bullied and shouted. He looked evil. While he did not swear, because this is a Family Picture, he said things like "Wall dog it" and "You rat" and "I'll cut off your ears and eat 'em" which would indicate that his language was not only coarse but might, off screen, be vulgar. He was, in a word, a Bad Guy. I found a certain interest in the Bad Guy which was lacking in the Good Guy.

"Which one do you like best?" I asked.

Catbird removed his anaesthetized eyes from the screen. "What do you mean?"

"Do you like the Good Guy or the Bad Guy?"

He sighed at my ignorance and looked back at the screen. "Are you kidding?" he asked. "The Good Guy, of course."

Now a new character began to emerge. He puzzled me because he wore a gray hat. I felt a little embarrassed about asking my son, the expert, but I gathered my courage. "Catbird," I asked shyly, "what kind of a guy is that, the one in the gray hat?"

He was sweet to me then. I think until that moment he had not understood the abysmal extent of my ignorance. "He's the In-Between Guy," Catbird explained kindly. "If he starts bad he ends good and if he starts good he ends bad."

"What's this one going to do?"

"See how he's sneering and needs a shave?" my son asked.

"Yes."

"Well, the picture's just started, so that guy is going to end good and help the Good Guy get Her father's ranch back."

"How can you be sure?" I asked.

Catbird gave me a cold look. "He's got a gray hat, hasn't he? Now don't talk. It's about time for the chase."

There it was, not only a tight, true criticism of a whole art form but to a certain extent of life itself. I was deeply impressed because this simple explanation seemed to mean something to me more profound than television or Westerns.

Several nights later I told the Catbird criticism to a friend who is a producer. He has produced many successful musical comedies. My friend has an uncanny perception for the public mind and also for its likes and dislikes. You have to have if you produce musical shows. He listened and nodded and didn't think it was a cute child story. He said, "It's not kid stuff at all. There's a whole generation in this country that makes its judgments pretty much on that basis."

"Give me an example," I asked.

"I'll have to think about it," he said.

Well, that was in March. Soon afterward my wife and I went to Spain and then to Paris and rented a little house. As soon as school was out in New York, my boys flew over to join us in Paris.

In July, my producer friend dropped in to see us. He was going to take an English show to New York, and he had been in London making arrangements.

He told us all of the happenings at home, the gossip and the new jokes and the new songs. Finally I asked him about the McCarthy hearings. "Was it as great a show as we heard?" I asked.

"I couldn't let it alone," he said. "I never saw anything like it. I wonder whether those people knew how they were putting themselves on the screen."

"Well, what do you think will happen?"

"In my opinion, McCarthy is finished," he said, and then he grinned. "I base my opinion on your story about Catbird and the Westerns."

"I don't follow you."

"Have you ever seen McCarthy on television?"

"Sure."

"Just remember," said my friend. "He sneers. He bullies, he has a nasty laugh and he always looks as though he needs a shave. The only thing he lacks is a black hat. McCarthy is the Bad Guy. Everybody who saw him has got it pegged. He's the Bad Guy and people don't like the Bad Guy. I may be wrong but that's what I think. He's finished."

The next morning at breakfast I watched Catbird put butter and two kinds of jam and a little honey on a croissant, then eat the treacherous thing, then lick the jam from the inside of his elbow to his fingers. He took a peach from the basket in the center of the table.

"Catbird," I asked, "did you see any of the McCarthy stuff on television?"

"Sure," he said.

"Was he a Good Guy or a Bad Guy?" I asked.

"Bad Guy," said Catbird, and he bit into the peach.

And, do you know, I suspect it is just that simple.

STUDY QUESTIONS

1. *What advantages does Steinbeck gain from presenting his observations in the form he does? Would he have been able to accomplish the same end by straight explanatory prose of the kind that Podhoretz uses? Are there disadvantages to Steinbeck's method? Explain.*

2. *The tone of this essay is not consistent, but unless it is understood, the essay may not be clear. What is the prevailing tone? What parts of the essay seem to have a different tone?*
3. *What point is being made here about TV? About its audience?*
4. *Does Steinbeck's experience support the point made by Warshow about gangster films, that they "create their own field of reference"?*
5. *What conclusions about the influence of people's reading or TV-watching upon real life may be drawn from this essay?*
6. *Note that Steinbeck concedes that TV has some benefits and advantages as well as shortcomings. Write a theme which tries to reach a conclusion about whether the better or the worse prevails in the TV medium at the present time.*

Delmore Schwartz Masterpieces as Cartoons*

R ecently I have been trying hard to watch television and read comic books. I do not know whether this is an effort to keep in touch with the rest of the American population or an attempt to win the esteem and keep up with my brother-in-law, aged twelve, who regards me as a hideous highbrow and thinks that I am probably a defrocked high school English teacher. The effort is, at any rate, one which permits me moments of self-congratulation. I feel that no one can say that I have not tried my best to keep open the lines of communication between myself and others, and to share the intellectual interests of the entire community.

The bottom of the pit has been reached, I think, in the cartoon books which are called *Classics Illustrated,* a series of picture-and-text versions of the masterpieces of literature. Seventy-eight of them have been published, but so far I have only been able to obtain six of them, and they have been so exciting and fascinating and distracting that I have only been able to read three of them with any care: Dostoevsky's *Crime and Punishment,* Shakespeare's *A Midsummer Night's Dream,* and *Gulliver's Travels.* The intentions of the publishers and the editors of these illustrated classics are either good, or they feel guilty, or perhaps both, since at the end of *A Midsummer Night's Dream* there is a striking and entirely capitalized sentence: "NOW THAT YOU HAVE READ THE CLASSICS ILLUSTRATED EDITION, DON'T MISS THE ADDED ENJOYMENT OF READING THE ORIGINAL, OBTAINABLE AT YOUR SCHOOL OR PUBLIC LIBRARY." Notice how it is assumed that the reader has not read the original version of these works and it is taken for granted that he will not buy, he will only borrow, the original version from school or the public

* "Masterpieces as Cartoons," by Delmore Schwartz, copyright, 1952, by *Partisan Review.* Reprinted by permission of the *Partisan Review.*

library. An interesting and significant fact to discover would be: just how many readers who first encounter Shakespeare, Dostoevsky, or Jonathan Swift in their comic strip garb are moved by this encounter to read the original. It would take a good detective or a good pollster to find out. When one feels optimistic, it seems possible that some quality of the masterpiece may bring some readers to the original; but when one feels pessimistic, one remembers an analogous phenomenon: even when a reader goes from James M. Cain to William Faulkner and James Joyce because they are all available in pocket book form for twenty-five cents, most readers who come to Faulkner and Joyce by means of pocket books do not know the difference between James M. Cain and James Joyce or Dashiel Hammett and William Faulkner; and some of the time they do not remember the names of the authors, no matter how many of their works they read.

The good intentions, or the guilty conscience, of the publishers of *Classics Illustrated* show clearly at the end of the cartoon version of *Crime and Punishment*, where again, as with Shakespeare, they write sentences of bold apology and excellent advice: "BECAUSE OF SPACE LIMITATIONS, WE REGRETFULLY OMITTED SOME OF THE ORIGINAL CHAR-ACTERS AND SUB-PLOTS OF THIS BRILLIANTLY WRITTEN NOVEL. NEVERTHELESS, WE HAVE RETAINED ITS MAIN THEME AND MOOD. WE STRONGLY URGE YOU TO READ THE ORIGINAL." This explanation is more interesting and more inaccurate, the more one thinks about it and the more one remembers the novel which Dostoevsky wrote. For one of the characters who is omitted is Sonia, the heroine. She may have been omitted because of space limitations, but it is just as likely that her prostitution had something to do with her absence from the illustrated version. What remains after the deletion of some of the original characters and sub-plots is the thin line of a detective story in which a murderer is tracked down; as the publishers explain, at the end of the last slot in which Raskolnikov confesses his crime:

> This then was the story of the intelligent young man who committed a premeditated "perfect crime." His conscience and the efforts of a brilliant police attorney brought about the dramatic confession and a just punishment. Raskolnikov was sentenced to serve a long term at hard labor in a Siberian prison.

Not much is left of the profound affirmation of Christianity with which the original work concludes, although there are cartoon book versions of the Old and New Testaments.

The miracle, or perhaps one should say the triumph of Dostoevsky's genius, is that despite all the cuts and mutilations of the original, there are gleams and glitters throughout the illustrated version of the psychological insight which Dostoevsky possessed to so powerful a degree and which made so stern a judge as Freud declare that only Shakespeare surpassed him as an author and as a literary psychologist. The brilliance and the originality of Dostoevsky's psychologizing comes through mainly in the exchanges between

Raskolnikov and Porfiry the detective as the latter gradually traps the murderer into confessing his crime. There are also numerous moments in the illustrated edition which are unknowingly comic and probably the expression of deep unconscious attitudes upon the part of the illustrator and the editor. For example, Raskolnikov at times looks very much like a Russian delegate to the UN who is afraid that the NKVD is after him. At other times Raskolnikov has an unquestionable resemblance to Peter Lorre, the film star who has so often been a villain. At other moments the illustrations — but not the text — suggest a detestation of all intellectuals, not only Raskolnikov, and in general there is the sharp implication throughout that most Russians are either criminals or police agents, and all Russians are somehow fundamentally evil.

I tried to check on this impression which seemed possibly an overinterpretation by examining another cartoon series called *Crime Does NOT Pay* (an immortal aphorism which is not going to hold much weight when the readers and the children find out about Frank Costello); a series about true crimes in the United States. The results of the comparison are incontestable: American crimes and criminals do not resemble Russia's or Dostoevsky's in the least.

The illustrated "edition" of *A Midsummer Night's Dream* is much less of a distortion of the original work. There are none of the serious cuts and omissions which virtually reduce the cartoon version of *Crime and Punishment* to a trite detective story. And the reason is clear enough: Shakespeare's play was intended for an audience which was very much like the juvenile readers of *Classics Illustrated,* and *A Midsummer Night's Dream* is one of the most playful and child-like of plays. Nevertheless here too the medium of the cartoon tends to make this version misleading. For one thing, the title page presents the (juvenile) reader with boxed and oval portraits of four of the leading characters. Under them is a landscape — a lake, a grove of trees, a distant temple, and Puck flying through the air in front of an enormous rising moon — and at the foot of the page there is a scroll-like band of words which announces the leading elements of the plot: "A dark forest... An angry fairy king...His mischievous messenger...A magic flower... Four thwarted lovers...And a troupe of wretched actors make a merry mix-up on a midsummer night...," all of which is fair enough as a brief overture. The illustrated edition begins at the very beginning of the play (something which is certainly far from being the case in all cartoon versions of the classics) and it is at this point that the most important kind of distortion takes place. For, first, there is a slot which explains to the youthful reader the purpose of the scene: "In his palace, Theseus, Duke of Athens, and Hippolyta, Queen of the Amazons, discuss their coming wedding...," an explanation which interferes with the natural dramatic unfolding, although the intention, I suppose, is to help the reader as much as possible and keep him from being in the least perplexed or from feeling that he has to make any serious exertion beyond keeping his eyes open.

Second, and more important by far, the opening speeches, which are in blank verse, are printed as if they were prose. This occurs from beginning to end. There is no conceivable way in which the juvenile reader can find out from the illustrated edition itself that he is reading poetry and not prose, although one would guess that some sense of the movement of language in blank verse rhythms certainly must impinge upon every reader. This failure to make it clear that the speeches are often poetry and not prose may not seem as serious, at first glance, as in actuality it is. For the speeches are bound to be read incorrectly; and worse still, when the juvenile reader does at some later date encounter poetry printed as poetry he is likely to be annoyed, if not irritated to the point where he refuses to read whatever is printed as poetry at all. His illustrated edition will have given him an easy and pleasant experience which becomes an obstacle in reading poetry straight, that is to say, as it was written and as it was meant to be read.

Perhaps it is not as important as I think it is that there should be a certain number of readers of poetry. But the fear that disturbs me can be exemplified by what occurred in a class of freshmen at one of the best universities in the world. The instructor, who was teaching English composition, asked the students to define blank verse. No student volunteered an answer. The instructor expressed his dismay and asked his class if they had not studied Shakespeare and other poets in high school. The students admitted that they had, and finally one student, perhaps feeling sympathy for the clearly distressed teacher, raised his hand and attempted a definition of blank verse: "Sir," he said, hesitantly, tentatively, and unsurely, "isn't blank verse something which looks like poetry, but is not poetry?" It turned out that the well-meaning student supposed that unless there were rhymes at the end of each line, he was not reading poetry. Now this class of students represented what was probably the most intensively and expensively educated young man in America. And as I have said, the incident and others like it occurred at one of the best schools in the world. If such a systematic misunderstanding of the nature of literature and poetry can exist among such young men, what, after all, can be expected of a population which first comes upon great literature in the guise of cartoon editions? One can well imagine a student insisting to his instructor that *A Midsummer Night's Dream* cannot be a play in blank verse, since the student has seen with his own eyes that it was printed as prose. And it is certainly not fanciful to suppose that the day is swiftly approaching when one human being says to another: "Have you read *Hamlet?*" and is answered: "No, but I seen the comic book edition."

Yet certainly there is a good side to everything, however infamous. There always is. And the good side to Shakespeare's plays as cartoon strips might be that some juvenile readers who are oppressed and biased by the way in which Shakespeare is for the most part taught in high schools all over America will now come upon Shakespeare first of all as a cartoon and see that he is really a great deal of fun, he is not a painful assignment in homework and a difficult, outmoded, canonized ancient author who wrote strange plays which provide the teachers of English with inexhaustible and eminently respectable reasons for boring their students. But there must be other and less misleading ways of demonstrating the pleasures of poetry to juvenile readers.

It is true that to encounter a literary masterpiece in a dramatic or cinematic form sometimes gives the reader, juvenile or adult, a new view and a new interest in the work. The French films of Dostoevsky's *The Idiot* and *Crime and Punishment* not only gave me a new and clarified understanding of both novels, but it seemed to me that the changes that were made in the original text were often improvements. The same was true of the German film version of *The Brothers Karamazov*, even though the character of Alyosha and the fable of the Grand Inquisitor were omitted, probably for theatrical reasons. And it is even more true that when a Shakespearean film is made well, as *A Midsummer Night's Dream* and *Henry V* were, there is a great gain for the common reader of Shakespeare who is used to reading him in a book rather than grasping his plays as visual experiences.

The fundamental question, whether it is a matter of the filmed Shakespeare or the cartoon book Shakespeare, seems to me to be: will the juvenile reader ever arrive at the point where he wants to see the original as it was intended to be, in its full actuality as a work? And the answer which suggests itself is a depressing one. If you get used to getting literature with illustrations — "visualized" is the phrase, I think — then you are likely to feel deprived when there are no illustrations and you have to do all the work yourself, depending upon the book itself. Moreover, the vice of having your visualizing done for you is all too likely to make you unused if not unwilling to read books which have no pictures in them. The Chinese proverb, "A picture is worth a thousand words," is often quoted by American advertisers. But the Chinese meant something very different from what the advertisers are trying to say. The Chinese meant that the visual experience of an object was more likely to give the full concreteness of that object than many of the words about it, which are for the most part abstract, generalized, colorless, and the like. The advertisers mean that human beings are more interested in looking at things (and find it easier) than in reading about them, so that the pictures in an ad are more efficacious in increasing sales than the words that accompany the pictures.

This fact is relevant to *Classics Illustrated* in the most direct way: the reader finds it easy and pleasant to look at words-with-pictures, he finds it more difficult and less pleasant to look at words which have no pictures to make them clear and visual. There is a tendency among some readers to read so much that their capacity to look at the visual world is spoiled. But far worse and far more prevalent is the tendency (of which masterpieces in cartoon form are an apt example) to read as little as possible and to prefer a thousand pictures to a single paragraph of intelligent reading matter. The over-all picture of the state of literacy was formulated two years ago by Gilbert Seldes in *The Great Audience*, a book which did not receive the attention it deserved: "In fourteen million homes equipped with radios, *no* magazines are read; families with television sets read fewer magazines than those who do not have them; half the adults in America never buy books." It is simple to transpose this statement to the great juvenile audience and to their reading of comic books and of the classics in cartoon form.

When we turn to the cartoon book version of *Gulliver's Travels,* other aspects of juvenile literacy (I was about to write, delinquency!) become clear. Of course *Gulliver's Travels* has been a children's classic for a long time as well as one of the greatest works of English literature for those who have reached the age of reason and consent. In the past, however, it is unquestionably true that the children's version of Swift's best work did not become a barrier to the interest of the same children in that work when they were old enough to want to enjoy the masterworks of their native language. The cartoon book version, unlike the older children's edition of *Gulliver's Travels,* goes much further in mutilation. At the end of the cartoon version, there is no plea by the publisher, as there was in *Crime and Punishment,* and in *A Midsummer Night's Dream,* telling the reader that he ought to read this work in its original form. There is, however, as in all the *Classics Illustrated,* a biography of the author. These biographies vary in inaccuracy, but they are all inaccurate to some degree. Swift's cartoon biography contains a number of trivial errors — such as the statement that he began to write in 1704 — but the important distortion is a truth which is stated in such a way that it is likely to mislead and deceive anyone who wants to find out the truth and is limited in the resources and skills necessary to finding out what the truth is (as, obviously, most juvenile readers are, whether they are quiz kids or not). The truth which is stated in such a way as to be entirely misleading is set forth in the cartoon biography of Swift as follows:

> Gulliver's Travels was written by Swift as a savage commentary on the European world Swift knew, as a condemnation of the laws and customs of his own and other countries that led one of the characters in the story to describe the inhabitants of Europe as "the most pernicious race of little odious vermin that nature ever suffered to crawl upon the surface of the earth." In later years Swift's satire became more and more violently bitter, possibly the result of mental disease which, by 1736, caused him to become insane.

Whoever wrote the cartoon biography may not have a chance to read the cartoon version. For there is very little in the cartoon version to suggest that the original is a "savage commentary" in which human beings are condemned as "odious little vermin." Moreover, the cartoon biography suggests that Swift was commenting on the state of human nature in his own time, and not in all times and places which he knew about. There is also the suggestion that the bitterness and violence of his satire were probably due to the onset of mental disease. All of this apology is unnecessary, however, for the reader who only knows of Swift through the cartoon edition. And what the biography states is literally true, and as true, deceptive. Swift did suffer from mental disease, and the disappointment of his political ambition did inspire in part the savage indignation which makes *Gulliver's Travels* a masterpiece. But the juvenile reader has no need of reassurance as to the benign character of human nature and the one-sidedness of Swift's point of view. In the cartoon version Gulliver returns to England and we last see him as he stands at the wheel of the ship which is coming into an English harbor. The captain of the ship, who is standing next to him, says: "There she is! Good old Brittania!" and Gulliver expresses his own pleasure in returning to civilized Europe and merry England by saying: "I certainly am happy to be back ... but it will take me weeks to get used to moving among people my own size!" He has had strange and interesting adventures and now he is delighted to be home.

Surely no explanation that Swift was a disappointed man of genius who concluded in insanity is necessary if all the reader has read is the cartoon edition. If he reads the original, he is certainly bound to be disturbed. For the original concludes in a way which is very different from *Classics Illustrated*. Gulliver explains to the "Courteous Readers," on the next to the last page, that having lived among horses and among human beings, he still prefers horses to human beings. When he has just come back to his own house in England, his wife's kiss makes him faint: "My Wife took me in her Arms, and kissed me; at which, having not been used to the touch of that odious Animal for so many years, I fell in a Swoon for almost an hour," and he feels disgusted with himself at the thought that he has become the father of human beings: the fact strikes him "with the utmost Shame, Confusion, and Horror." For the first year after his return to England "I could not endure my Wife or Children in my Presence, the Smell of them was intolerable." (I am quoting at length because anyone who has not read *Gulliver's Travels* recently will probably think any synopsis or paraphrase an exaggeration of Swift's satire.) As to the purpose of the work, Gulliver declares that "I write for the noblest End, to inform and instruct Mankind, over whom I may, without Breach of Modesty, pretend to some superiority, from the Advantages I received by conversing among the most accomplished Houyhnhnms. I write without any View toward Profit or Praise," which is to say that, having dwelt with horses, Gulliver feels superior to mankind and capable of instructing human beings in how to improve. At the very end, having been back among civilized human beings for five years, Gulliver declares that he is now able to sit at the same dinner table with his wife, although since the smell of any civilized being is still offensive to him, he has to keep applying rue, lavender, or tobacco to his nose. And he adds that he would be able to accept human nature as it is in most of its follies and vices except for one unbearable trait, the vice of pride, which causes more viciousness than any other human trait. It is the viciousness of pride and vanity which make civilized existence insupportable.

Clearly there is little likelihood that the juvenile reader of the cartoon version of *Gulliver's Travels* will be corrupted by Swift's cynicism and nihilism (which was inspired, we ought to remember, by an intense idealism and an intense purity as well as by the disappointment of ambition and the distortion of growing neurosis.) But the important point here is not the juvenile reader himself or herself, but the adult publisher and editor who has exhibited a well-meaning solicitude for the juvenile reader's tender sensibility. For whoever is responsible for the cartoon version is very much aware of the true character of *Gulliver's Travels* and wishes to spare the feelings and the mind of the juvenile audience. But where does this solicitude stop?

I must turn to personal experience to show how far the solicitude and the censorship can go. When I taught English composition to freshmen and coeds ten years ago along with some twenty-five other instructors, a crisis occurred as a result of the modern novels which the students had been assigned to read. One of the coeds had been reading late at night at her English assignment, which was John Dos Passos' *U.S.A.* Dos Passos' savage indignation, which resembles Swift's, and his explicit account of the sexual experiences of his characters, terrified the young lady to the point where she had to waken her father (not her mother!) and tell him that she had been scared and shocked by her reading assignment in English. The unhappy father conferred with the head of the English staff, who in turn discussed the entire issue with the entire staff. The head of the staff was very much aware of both sides of the problem and he tried to be just to the interests and rights of his instructors as well as to the problems of adolescents who are in the first year of their undergraduate careers. But in such a situation, judiciousness and compromise can accomplish very little. Most of the instructors felt, whether rightly or wrongly, that they had been told not to assign Dos Passos, or Joyce, or Thomas Mann, or Proust, or Gide or Celine to their students. They felt that they probably would be fulfilling their duty as teachers of English composition and literature better if they went no further than such authors as Dickens, Thackeray, George Eliot, and George Meredith. Thomas Hardy was an ambiguous and questionable author, given the point of view which a shocked coed had brought to the fore, since *Jude the Obscure* and *Tess of the D'Urbervilles* were both books which might very well be shocking again as they had been when they first appeared (as a result of which scandal, the heartsick Hardy ceased to write novels).

The juvenile and adolescent reader certainly ought not to be scared and shocked. But he ought not to be cut off from the reality of great literature and of modern literature (the latter being, because of its contemporaneity, the best way of getting the ordinary adolescent reader interested in literature of any kind). And it is essential and necessary to remember that if a human being does not become interested in literature when he is an undergraduate, it is quite unlikely that he will become a devoted reader at any other time of life.

The teaching of English has a direct and continuous relationship to the kinds of books which juvenile, adolescent, and adult readers are likely to desire to read. The cartoon version of *Gulliver's Travels* suggests still another incident in the teaching of English literature. The text in this instance was Swift's *A Modest Proposal*, in which Swift proposes among other things that the economic problem of Ireland might be solved if the Irish bred children and then butchered them for food. In the seven years during which, at some point during the year, I had to assign this little classic of satire to freshman students, I naturally encountered a variety of impressions on their part. But the most frequent and representative comment was exemplified by a student of Armenian parents (he must have heard of the Turks) and a boy who was Irish (and who must have heard of the English in Ireland). Both students announced that Swift was "morbid." I was tempted to embark upon a self-indulgent excursion when I heard this comment and to say that I would not permit the greatest prose writer in English, except for Shakespeare, perhaps, to be called "morbid," and to recall to the students what they had heard about the Turks in Armenia, the English in Ireland, to say nothing of Buchenwald and Dachau. But I felt that the students would merely have concluded that I too was morbid. By questioning them with some degree of patience, I found out that after they had read comic books, listened to soap operas, and witnessed the sweetness and light of the motion pictures, they were inclined to regard anything which is serious satire as morbid sensationalism.

To return directly to the cartoon versions of the Classics: it is customary and habitual, when one has expressed the point of view I have suggested here, to be asked, *What is to be done?* I do not suffer from the delusion that I know what is to be done. But I confess that I sometimes entertain certain modest guesses, the practicality of which I cannot determine. The reading of comic books, and cartoon versions of the classics (and listening to the radio, looking at the motion pictures and listening and looking at television programs) cannot be stopped. Mass culture is here to stay: it is a major industry and a very profitable one, and one can no more banish it than one can banish the use of automobiles because thirty-four thousand people are killed by cars every year. And even if the reading of cartoon books might be stopped, it is probable the prohibition and censorship would have the usual boomerang effect.

What can be done, I think (or rather, I guess), is to set a good example, or perhaps I should say an example which is the least of all the possible evil examples, namely: each adult and literate human being who feels that literature is one of the necessary conditions of civilized existence can set the example of reading *both* the original classics and the cartoon versions. By doing both, he is keeping his hold on the literature at its best and at the same time he is remaining aware of the experience and thus the consciousness of any other reader: children, juveniles, adolescents, housewives, aged relatives, farmers, mechanics, taxi-drivers — in fact, everyone! For the products of mass culture preoccupy the minds of most human beings in America, whether they know it or not. And in setting the good or least evil example of maintaining his hold on great literature in the midst of forcing himself to be aware of the debased versions and mutilations and dilutions of it, he may make some other readers imitative enough to come or return to the classics in their full actuality. This proposal may seem very much like one of the labors of Hercules. But it is also a lot of fun, at least some of the time. Besides, Hercules was a hero, and as practically everyone knows, all human beings want to be heroic heroes and heroines, at least once in a while.

STUDY QUESTIONS

1. *Is there anything fundamentally wrong about putting a profound and complicated work into such a medium as the comic-strip? Or is it possible to imagine a superior comic-strip which does justice to the qualities of a great work, like the movie versions of Dostoevsky novels which, as Schwartz comments, were as good as or better than the originals?*

2. *Why does Schwartz feel that it is wrong to make things easy for the reader by means of pictures? Or that young readers should not be sheltered from the harsh realities some literature describes? Why does he feel it unlikely that the comic-book version of a classic will lead its readers to the original?*

3. *Why does Schwartz appear to be more concerned about the use of "masterpieces" as the subjects of cartoons than he would be if original scripts were used?*

4. *Select some short classic which has been published in comic-book form and compare the original in some detail with the comic-book version. Be prepared to explain to what extent your examination bears out or does not bear out Schwartz's conclusions.*

5. *Discuss some treatment of a classic in a popular culture medium such as TV or the movies. Were the original values retained? Did the interpretation do justice to the original? Was any improvement made?*

6. *There have always been objections to new forms of popular art. The stage, the movies and the novel were all criticized when they were new as vulgar and vulgarizing. Do you think that the criticism of the comics is a case of history repeating itself, and that they will eventually come to occupy an accepted and valuable place in civilized life?*

2. PERSPECTIVES ON POPULAR CULTURE

Alexis De Tocqueville

In What Spirit the Americans Cultivate the Arts*

It would be to waste the time of my readers and my own, if I strove to demonstrate how the general mediocrity of fortunes, the absence of superfluous wealth, the universal desire for comfort, and the constant efforts by which everyone attempts to procure it, make the taste for the useful predominate over the love of the beautiful in the heart of man. Democratic nations, among whom all these things exist, will therefore cultivate the arts which serve to render life easy, in preference to those whose object is to adorn it. They will habitually prefer the useful to the beautiful, and they will require that the beautiful should be useful.

But I propose to go further; and, after having pointed out this first feature, to sketch several others.

It commonly happens that, in the age of privilege, the practice of almost all the arts becomes a privilege, and that every profession is a separate domain into which it is not allowable for everyone to enter. Even when productive industry is free, the fixed character which belongs to aristocratic nations gradually segregates all the persons who practice the same art till they form a distinct class, always composed of the same families, whose members are all known to each other, and among whom a public opinion of their own and a species of corporate pride soon spring up. In a class or guild of this kind each artisan has not only his fortune to make, but his reputation to preserve. He is not exclusively swayed by his own interest or even by that of his customer, but by that of the body to which he belongs; and the interest of that body is that each artisan should produce the best possible workmanship. In aristocratic ages the object of the arts is therefore to manufacture as well as possible, not with the greatest dispatch or at the lowest rate.

When, on the contrary, every profession is open to all, when a multitude of persons are constantly embracing and abandoning it, and when its several members are strangers, indifferent to, and because of their numbers hardly

* Reprinted from *Democracy in America* (1835). Adapted from the Henry Reeve translation.

seen by, each other, the social tie is destroyed, and each workman, standing alone, endeavors simply to gain the most money at the least cost. The will of the customer is then his only limit. But at the same time a corresponding change takes place in the customer also. In countries in which riches, as well as power, are concentrated and retained in the hands of a few, the use of the greater part of this world's goods belongs to a small number of individuals, who are always the same. Necessity, public opinion, or moderate desires exclude all others from the enjoyment of them. As this aristocratic class remains fixed at the pinnacle of greatness on which it stands, without diminution or increase, it is always acted upon by the same wants and affected by them in the same manner. The men of whom it is composed naturally derive from their superior and hereditary position a taste for what is extremely well made and lasting. This affects the general way of thinking of the nation in relation to the arts. It often occurs, among such a people, that even the peasant will rather go without the objects he covets than procure them in a state of imperfection. In aristocracies, then, the handicraftsmen work for only a limited number of fastidious customers; the profit they hope to make depends principally on the perfection of their workmanship.

Such is no longer the case when, all privileges being abolished, ranks are intermingled and men are forever rising or sinking upon the social scale. Among a democratic people a number of citizens always exist whose patrimony is divided and decreasing. They have contracted, under more prosperous circumstances, certain wants, which remain after the means of satisfying such wants are gone; and they are anxiously looking out for some surreptitious method of providing for them. On the other hand, there are always in democracies a large number of men whose fortune is on the increase, but whose desires grow much faster than their fortunes, and who gloat upon the gifts of wealth in anticipation, long before they have means to obtain them. Such men are eager to find some short cut to these gratifications, already almost within their reach. From the combination of these two causes the result is that in democracies there is always a multitude of persons whose wants are above their means, and who are very willing to take up with imperfect satisfaction rather than abandon the object of their desires altogether.

The artisan readily understands these passions, for he himself partakes in them. In an aristocracy he would seek to sell his workmanship at a high price to the few; he now conceives that the more expeditious way of getting rich is to sell them at a low price to all. But there are only two ways of lowering the price of commodities. The first is to discover some better, shorter, and more ingenious method of producing them; the second is to manufacture a larger quantity of goods, nearly similar, but of less value. Among a democratic population all the intellectual faculties of the workman are directed to these two objects: he strives to invent methods which may enable him not only to work better, but quicker and cheaper; or, if he cannot succeed in that, to diminish the intrinsic quality of the thing he makes, without rendering it wholly unfit for the use for which it is intended. When none but the wealthy had watches, they were almost all very good ones; few are now made which are worth much, but everybody has one in his pocket. Thus the democratic principle not only tends to direct the human mind to the useful arts, but it induces the artisan to produce with great rapidity many imperfect commodities, and the consumer to content himself with these commodities.

Not that, in democracies, the arts are incapable, in case of need, of producing wonders. This may occasionally be the case, if customers appear who are ready to pay for time and trouble. In this rivalry of every kind of industry, in the midst of this immense competition and these countless experiments, some excellent workmen are formed who reach the utmost limits of their craft. But they rarely have an opportunity of showing what they can do; they are scrupulously sparing of their powers; they remain in a state of accomplished mediocrity, which judges itself, and though well able to shoot beyond the mark before it, aims only at what it hits. In aristocracies, on the contrary, workmen always do all they can; and when they stop, it is because they have reached the limit of their art.

When I arrive in a country where I find some of the finest productions of the arts, I learn from this fact nothing of the social condition or of the political constitution of the country. But if I perceive that the productions of the arts are generally of an inferior quality, very abundant, and very cheap, I am convinced that, among the people where this occurs, privilege is on the decline, and that ranks are beginning to intermingle and will soon be confounded together.

The handicraftsmen of democratic ages endeavor not only to bring their useful productions within the reach of the whole community, but strive to give to all their commodities attractive qualities that they do not in reality possess. In the confusion of all ranks, everyone hopes to appear what he is not, and makes great exertions to succeed in this object. This sentiment, indeed, which is but too natural to the heart of man, does not originate in the democratic principle; but that principle applies it to material objects. The hypocrisy of virtue is of every age, but the hypocrisy of luxury belongs more particularly to the ages of democracy.

To satisfy these new cravings of human vanity, the arts have recourse to every species of imposture; and these devices sometimes go so far as to defeat their own purpose. Imitation diamonds are now made which may be easily mistaken for real ones; as soon as the art of fabricating false diamonds shall become so perfect that they cannot be distinguished from real ones, it is probable that both will be abandoned, and become mere pebbles again.

This leads me to speak of those arts which are called, by way of distinction, the fine arts. I do not believe that it is a necessary effect of a democratic social condition and of democratic institutions to diminish the number of those who cultivate the fine arts; but these causes exert a powerful influence on the manner in which these arts are cultivated. Many of those who had already contracted a taste for the fine arts are impoverished; on the other hand, many of those who are not yet rich begin to conceive that taste, at least by imitation; the number of consumers increases, but opulent and fastidious consumers become more scarce. Something analogous to what I have already pointed out in the useful arts then takes place in the fine arts; the productions of artists are more numerous, but the merit of each production is diminished. No longer able to soar to what is great, they cultivate what is pretty and elegant, and appearance is more attended to than reality.

In aristocracies a few great pictures are produced; in democratic countries a vast number of insignificant ones. In the former, statues are raised of bronze; in the latter, they are modeled in plaster.

When I arrived for the first time at New York, by that part of the Atlantic Ocean which is called the East River, I was surprised to perceive along the shore, at some distance from the city, a number of little palaces of white marble, several of which were of classic architecture. When I went the next day to inspect more closely one which had particularly attracted my notice, I found that its walls were of whitewashed brick, and its columns of painted wood. All the edifices which I had admired the night before were of the same kind.

The social condition and the institutions of democracy impart, moreover, certain peculiar tendencies to all the imitative arts, which it is easy to point out. They frequently withdraw them from the delineation of the soul to fix them exclusively on that of the body, and they substitute the representation of motion and sensation for that of sentiment and thought; in a word, they put the Real in the place of the Ideal.

I doubt whether Raphael studied the minute intricacies of the mechanism of the human body as thoroughly as the draftsmen of our time. He did not attach the same importance as they do to rigorous accuracy on this point, because he aspired to surpass nature. He sought to make of man something which should be superior to man, and to embellish beauty itself. David and his scholars were, on the contrary, as good anatomists as they were painters. They wonderfully depicted the models which they had before their eyes, but they rarely imagined anything beyond them; they followed nature with fidelity, while Raphael sought for something better than nature. They have left us an exact portraiture of man, but he discloses in his work a glimpse of the Divinity.

This remark as to the manner of treating a subject is no less applicable to the choice of it. The painters of the Renaissance generally sought far above themselves, and away from their own time, for mighty subjects, which left to their imagination an unbounded range. Our painters often employ their talents in the exact imitation of the details of private life, which they have always before their eyes; and they are forever copying trivial objects, the originals of which are only too abundant in nature.

STUDY QUESTIONS

1. *According to Tocqueville, what are the factors present in an aristocracy that encourage the artist to do his best? What factors in a democracy encourage him to compromise?*

2. *In what way does Tocqueville relate the demand for the kind of art that imitates the real thing to the social situation in a democracy?*

3. *Apply Tocqueville's observation about the tendency of artists in a democracy to produce much at the expense of quality to the popular literature found in magazines, newspapers and detective stories. Does his generalization hold true in the field of music or architecture?*

4. *Is Tocqueville's closing observation about the preference for dealing with the real rather than the ideal true in the light of present-day movies, novels and TV plays?*

5. *Is Tocqueville's generalization about the useful arts applicable today? Write a theme discussing this question. (Remember that in spite of his criticisms, he does admit that democracy can produce "wonders" in this field.)*

6. *Do you think Tocqueville has failed to mention some of the ways in which a democracy favors the production of excellent art? Write a theme defending democracy against his objections, and showing how certain conditions present in a democracy work in the artist's favor.*

Lyman Bryson Art and Democracy*

I t will help us to understand the problem of taste in a technological society, in a society where man is free and in possession of machinery for mass production and mass sales, to look at the older factors in the determination of taste, the aristocrats, the patronized artists, and the folk. But we are making an effort to deal with facts and not with sentimental memories. Most statements about the days "when there was a very high level of taste" are meaningless because one does not know what population was the repository of that fine taste.

The comparative statement is often made, for example, about books. There is supposed to have been a time when the "whole reading public" was excited about Macaulay's next volume. The inference is left that the generations have backslid. The whole reading public of Macaulay's time was a small, expensively educated part of the expensively maintained upper and upper middle class of a small country; what the farmer or the shopkeeper's assistant or the factory worker read, if he read anything, was not considered.

Today, men and women, and indeed adolescents, roughly comparable to

* From *The Next America* by Lyman Bryson. Copyright, 1952, by Harper and Brothers. Reprinted by permission.

these neglected ones, are part of the "whole reading public." It is evident that the same proportion of the larger group does not respond to the best that is now being written or to the best of the past. But whether or not the absolute number of persons who read a book of high quality in America now is a larger or smaller proportion of the total population than was the number that read a good book in England in the nineteenth century might be hard to determine. Our taste in reading for entertainment seems to have changed little.[1] It seems probable, judging from the figures on the printing of books, that the good nonfiction book of today gets a larger proportion of readers out of the whole population in either England or America, although a much smaller proportion of the general reading public, than it would have had a hundred years ago. None of this really makes a great deal of difference unless one believes that great books are not now being written because there is no public for them. This is a not impressive kind of nostalgia.

There were three factors in the older situation: the aristocracy, the patronized artist, and the folk. What did each contribute and what did each enjoy? The aristocracy and its aesthetic camp followers did undoubtedly enjoy good things appreciatively and we can generously admit that a large number of them took full advantage of their training and their wealth. Some even sacrificed their comfort to their taste, as did Edward Fitzgerald, who was a great connoisseur and a great gentleman but a humble man. These real zealots of taste were few, of course, but probably roughly as numerous as their counterparts, the eccentrics, who took advantage of their social security to defy all taste.

The social role of the eccentric aristocrat, the man who would be a tramp if he were not endowed to be a gentleman, has never been well studied; it is not trivial. And it is possible that some mild eccentrics who happened also to be greatly gifted, as Walter Savage Landor was, for example, may contribute far more to the growth and variation of taste than is realized. The real eccentric aristocrat is often a moralist and even a reformer. Of Landor, Harriet Martineau said: "He was passionate and prejudiced, but usually in some great cause, and on the right side of it..." Wilfrid Scawen Blunt would be another good British example. The range of eccentrics, from rich rascals to eremites of good taste, is wide. It is, of course, also unpredictable, and the breeding and protection of all kinds of eccentrics is one of the prerogatives of an aristocracy that we, in our fashion, would give up. Leaving them aside, the steady educated taste of established families in most European countries has been a conservative but appreciative safeguard of good things. The real accumulation of culture has depended on it. The deviants and the scamps have had too much license behind their social protection but have done little harm. They are not the real price that is paid for the aristocratic system; they are only a minor cost.

The second factor in this older stock situation, to which some modern critics

_____
[1] James D. Hart, *The Popular Book*. New York: Oxford University Press, 1950.

think they long to go back, was the patronage of new artists by the powerful and the wealthy. This does not include ordinary connoisseurship, which is patronage by merchants. Patronage of artists is now becoming, like so many other old cultural functions, the business of democratic government. In the past it has been a concomitant of power, whether governmental or feudal or merely personal. The Medicis, who spent so many millions in their job of being a prime factor in creating the greatest art period of modern times, were both bankers and tyrants. They can be seen as a kind of peak in the possible usefulness of deliberate bounty to creative brains.

If we should try to estimate the general run of patrons as factors in taste, we should have to be generous, I think, to countless men and women who took a decent respect for established art fashions to be a necessary part of their duty. They upheld the taste of their communities in art and music and letters in much the same spirit as nerved them to dispense justice and defend the peace. They seldom discovered or paid for the birth of new genius. In that they did no better, perhaps, than the boards of tax-supported museums today. The trouble with the really new in any art is that it offends taste and we are discussing taste, not creative greatness. There was a rough justice to taste in the patronage that privileged wealth and power could give.

These two factors in the older typical situations, aristocratic appreciation and patronage, did not in any way touch most of the people of the time. Matters of taste were the concern and pleasure of a small, fairly homogeneous social elite which was intelligent enough to be also an elite in refined judgment. The peasantry, the clerks, and the journeymen were not involved although the aesthetic aspects of their lives were marked by good taste, far more so probably than in the democratic present. It is that fact, in part, which accounts for the homesickness for a time of beauty that infects so many critics. Those who want to return to a culture of rigid class levels and those who, for aesthetic reasons, want to go back to the "folk," both argue that the old stratification was better because folk art is simple and substantial and pure. The question to be asked both of them is how much they would be willing to pay in other values, including the aesthetic, in order to get the old times back again. The fact is that the days of a powerful elite, moving circumspectly in the high levels of taste while the peasantry produces honest pots and fine embroidery, could not be recaptured, but that can be for the moment ignored since we are discussing comparative values, not possible reforms.

The folk art that is largely anonymous, conventional, and variant only in the handicraft of the single maker is often beautiful. It is almost never mean or vulgar. It was once worth having. What did it cost? The paradox is that it gave little play to the really creative impulses of the artist and his joy in it was that of the craftsman, which is admirable but different. It gave no scope to inventiveness or imagination. The folk artist created nothing; he made things. I have in several places in this book paid homage to the fine humanity of the craftsman; his use of skill with honesty and devotion is a great social contribution. But into the life of every man, the craftsman and all others, the good society would bring a chance at doing things not by the ancient designs, no matter how beautiful, but by his own invention, his own whim, his own self-developing experiments in freedom. Folk art is nearly always in good taste, not because the craftsman who makes it has creative taste but because he is bound to the old designs.

In all taste there is a dialectic effect; good taste means the standards arrived at in the past by thorough argument among those who are trying to find what is enduring and honest in experience. This dialectic has worked, through generations, in folk art and has produced its wonderful effect. But the folk artist is not, by reason of his craftsmanship, able to carry it on. If he does sometimes invent, that is because all men are artists when given a chance; he is all too likely to be afraid of his own inventions for fear of sacrilege. Folk art is good and its excellences are paid for by the tight restraint that a social system of the old type lays on the craftsman who makes it.

We can have a certainty of good taste if only the trained and sensitive have any freedom to choose; following them, the elites will make wise choices and the peasants will stay in their grooves. The cost of such a system, in so far as it works, is that it denies, to all but the few, any experience at all in aesthetic choice, in real aesthetic creation, in any inventive change. In the past this cost has been paid cheerfully enough, but by men and women who did not know what they were buying at what price.

In these days, and more in America than anywhere else, we have developed a new pattern. The uniformity ascribed to a machine age democracy is a myth, or a misstatement of cultural patterns, but the vulgarity we are accused of is a fact. The rich vulgarity of the taste of the American people is the natural result of freedom for commonplace invention, for the small independence of choice in so many aspects of his life that an American enjoys. Instead of presenting to the eye of perspective a firm mosaic of rigid spot patterns, it presents a vast single pattern of dizzy variations. The aristocratic eccentric escaped being vulgar by being singular; there was only one of each kind at a time. The craftsman of folk art cannot show anything but dignity and good taste under the restraint of custom. The modern industrialized democrat shows all kinds of trivial inventions of his own and chooses freely in a wild profusion of the trivial, mass-produced inventions of others.

This kind of variation distresses the social aristocrat, as well as the aristocrat of taste, because it blurs hopelessly the distinctions of caste such as those that are publicly declared in dress. Even now, a peasant woman in her best costume on the streets of Paris is stigmatized for her class and identified for her province. But on Madison Avenue in New York, or Market Street in San Francisco, or anywhere else where this kind of culture has been established, the shopgirl at five o'clock comes into the street in a cheaper version of the same costume her lady customer just purchased. The clerk and the capitalist are hard to distinguish. This is true, of course, only if they want to be alike. In the older systems they could not be alike if they so desired. Now a man may, especially in summer, give a fair indication of his own estimate of his own position by the clothes he wears, the test being almost entirely one of quantity; but it is his own decision that he follows, not a sumptuary prescription of invariant costume or a class-imposed prohibition. He follows his bent.

Vulgarity is the result because vulgarity is the inventiveness of small or inexperienced or too numerous minds. The question that democracy poses is whether or not the restraint of peasant custom is better than the vulgarity of popular choice. To the fastidious onlooker the peasant's good taste is better, of course; there is never any doubt that restraint of those who differ from ourselves in standards of taste is pleasant to the fastidious. Is it better for the persons who must either wear the costumes and use the utensils of their ancestors or pick casually among the products of mass production? In one case, they use with indifferent habit the simple and beautiful things that ages have refined. In the other, they choose. The ease with which the shoddiest commercial gadgets invade a market of peasant buyers shows, first, how little attached they are by anything but habit to the fine old things and, second, how much pleasure they get out of choosing.

The act of choice, the experience of seeing several ways of expressing a need and considering them, and taking one that appeals to some trait of one's own character, is important even in trivial things. The fact that the choice when made will be the vagary of a passing momentary convention, rather than of an ancient one, does not matter. It will be a choice.

Do we dare affirm a hope that long practice in the freedom of small details of personal behavior will lead in the long run to something better than vulgarity? Not, I think, if by "something better" we continue to mean something stylized and localized like a peasant costume. Freedom of mass manufacture which leads to trivial but real differences in what is offered to the mass market, and to freedom for the customers to choose, will not lead to fixed styles. If the question is put in another way, can it get a more hopeful answer? Does industrial designing improve in time and do the customers respond to better ranges of choice? No one can offer anything but an impression on this, of course, but my impression is the hopeful one. The costumes of women in a modern American town today, compared with what their own peasant ancestors wore in Ireland or Poland or Sicily a few generations ago, will serve to give what reasons there are for optimism.

There is first the great gain in self-respect to women in all industrial societies that has come in the fact that their dress is no longer an enforced badge of status. There is also the fact that the present fashion is one of those waves of comparative good sense in which women's fashions are loose and free and healthy. Peasant clothing, in a variable climate, runs to caps and petticoats. But our present fashions run strongly to summer nakedness, and that brings up another aspect of this subject in which so many of the most important aspects of cultural democracy lie hidden in trivialities.

The worship of the sun, which is no doubt exaggerated as far as its hygienic value is concerned, the manners of the beach, and the fond romanticism of the middle-aged Midwesterners who have gone to Southern California and Florida, have all combined to make nakedness in public too common to be noticed, thus disappointing the pioneers. When a brilliantly colored and almost completely exposed young couple come into a roadside restaurant, one may frown in behalf of decorum but be persuaded into amused tolerance by the shapeliness and health of impersonally exhibited bodies. It is possible then to remember that we have talked for years about slavery to clothing, and the neglect of simple naturalness. An involuntary close association with a fat, middle-aged body of either sex, presented with equal assurance, is more disconcerting. One gets himself out of disdain then by hoping that a cult of nakedness may bring on a cult of health. It might even reform our laziness and gluttony until all bodies could be exposed without indecency or ugliness. What supports that hope? Not much perhaps. If there is to be freedom for people to be undressed, the only result one has any rational right to expect is the vulgar display of a good deal of ugliness. Most people are ugly just as most people are vulgar. We define ugliness and vulgarity, whether consciously or not, both in the same way. They are both failures to vary, in the direction of superiority, from the average.

The choice is philosophically simple: we can have men restrained from showing their commonness or we can see them as they are. I say philosophically because the practical choice is more complicated. In an industrial society, where material prosperity depends on inciting and satisfying an endless flood of small choices, difference in consuming interest between one man and another or, as is more common between a woman today and the same woman next week, is as essential to mass production as deeper differences are to democracy.

There are philosophers and poets of freedom who want freedom for all men, provided its beneficiaries express freedom in the way their patrons like. But here, again, we have to be realists and stand by our faith. This is the way men and women are; that is our realism. Freedom is the means by which they will be the best personalities they are capable of being; that is our faith. There is no contradiction between faith and realistic knowledge here but the compromises are seductive to most reformers because their love of mankind is poisoned with disdain.

Do we pay too great a price for freedom by losing little things that add up to good taste? The price paid by the older systems, all of them in fact that have been above savage manners, has been in a tolerance of eccentrics and bigots of judgment among the aristocrats, a sycophancy in the hope of survival among the artists, and a compulsory simplicity among the peasants. What we pay for our system is to tolerate a vast rich vulgarity that covers up the peripheral fossils of aristocracy and patronage still left.

What of the artists? There is a common myth that they have only succeeded in substituting fawning upon the crowd for the older need to flatter a lord. This has to be discussed elsewhere at greater length. I happen to believe that the artist is not damaged by living in our kind of society if he has the artist's real vocation of creative independence.

Moreover, we are a democracy. I am urging that we undertake to make ourselves into a true democracy of culture and of the spirit. The aim of a democracy of culture is to enrich the cultural experience of persons; it corresponds functionally to the political democracy whose end is the political experience of persons. A political democracy is successful not in terms of its political decisions but in the degree that it uses political experience to give every citizen the best chance to be his best self. A democracy of culture (using the word here, of course, in the narrower sense of the enduring things in any society that are sought for their own sake) must be measured by its success in giving its citizens the greatest chances to grow in their appreciation and, still more, in their creative capacities. We have to be brave enough to say, in the face of aesthetes and timid decorous critics, that justification of freedom of taste is not in what a free citizen chooses to wear, or how he builds his house, so much as in the reality of his freedom to follow his own taste whatever it is. The result in human experience is worth having now, and if it be true that taste grows by experience and by the dialectic of free social life, in the long run future taste will be better, also, for better reasons.

STUDY QUESTIONS

1. *How does Bryson show that the formation of good taste in the general public is at odds with democratic principles? Do you agree with his argument?*
2. *In what way were artists better off under the old social situation described by Bryson?*
3. *What significance does Bryson attach to the fact that the social classes in a democracy are not distinguishable by their clothes?*
4. *Note that Bryson sees the vulgarity of popular culture as the result of the nature of the mass of people. Compare his cause-effect interpretation of the situation with that of Mills.*
5. *Write a theme explaining what Bryson means by "vulgarity" in popular art, giving examples from your own experience.*
6. *Social classes in modern America are much less clearly distinguished than they have been in other times and countries, but we are still aware of general differences among large groups of people depending, roughly, upon income, occupation and education. Bryson has pointed out that clothes are not a good index to these differences. Does the same near-uniformity apply in other fields where taste plays a part? Have you noticed any correlation between particular entertainments (movies, the different kinds of music, libraries, museums), and "types" of people? If you have, you are in a position to write a theme supporting (or denying) the proposition that even in America taste is a matter of class, being sure to tell what you mean by "taste" and what you mean by "class."*

C. Wright Mills Some Effects of Mass Media*

Early observers believed that the increase in the range and volume of the formal means of communication would enlarge and animate the primary public. In such optimistic views — written before radio and television and movies — the formal media are understood as simply multiplying the scope and pace of personal discussion. Modern conditions, Charles Cooley wrote, "enlarge indefinitely the competition of ideas, and whatever has owed its persistence merely to lack of comparison is likely to go, for that which is really congenial to the choosing mind will be all the more cherished and increased." Still excited by the break-up of the conventional consensus of the local community, he saw the new means of communication as furthering the conversational dynamic of classic democracy, and with it the growth of rational and free individuality.

No one really knows all the functions of the mass media, for in their entirety these functions are probably so pervasive and so subtle that they cannot be caught by the means of social research now available. But we do now have reason to believe that these media have helped less to enlarge and animate the discussion of primary publics than to transform them into a set of media markets in mass-like society. I do not refer merely to the higher ratio of deliverers of opinion to receivers and to the decreased chance to answer back; nor do I refer merely to the violent banalization and stereotyping of our very sense organs in terms of which these media now compete for "attention." I have in mind a sort of psychological illiteracy that is facilitated by the media, and that is expressed in several ways:

I. Very little of what we think we know of the social realities of the world have we found out first-hand. Most of "the pictures in our heads" we have gained from these media — even to the point where we often do not really believe what we see before us until we read about it in the paper or hear about it on the radio. The media not only give us information; they guide our very "experience it," and in terms of this experience, that they would all debunk be set by these media rather than by our own fragmentary experience.

Accordingly, even if the individual has direct, personal experience of events, it is not really direct and primary: it is organized in stereotypes. It takes long and skillful training to so uproot such stereotypes that an individual sees things freshly, in an unstereotyped manner. One might suppose, for example, that if all the people went through a depression they would all "experience it," and in terms of this experience, that they would all debunk

* From *The Power Elite* by C. Wright Mills. © 1956, by Oxford University Press, Inc. Reprinted by permission.

or reject or at least refract what the media say about it. But experience of such a *structural* shift has to be organized and interpreted if it is to count in the making of opinion.

The kind of experience, in short, that might serve as a basis for resistance to mass media is not an experience of raw events, but the experience of meanings. The fleck of interpretation must be there in the experience if we are to use the word experience seriously. And the capacity for such experience is socially implanted. The individual does not trust his own experience, as I have said, until it is confirmed by others or by the media. Usually such direct exposure is not accepted if it disturbs loyalties and beliefs that the individual already holds. To be accepted, it must relieve or justify the feelings that often lie in the back of his mind as key features of his ideological loyalties.

Stereotypes of loyalty underlie beliefs and feelings about given symbols and emblems; they are the very ways in which men see the social world and in terms of which men make up their specific opinions and views of events. They are the results of previous experience, which affect present and future experience. It goes without saying that men are often unaware of these loyalties, that often they could not formulate them explicitly. Yet such general stereotypes make for the acceptance or the rejection of specific opinions not so much by the force of logical consistency as by their emotional affinity and by the way in which they relieve anxieties. To accept opinions in their terms is to gain the good solid feeling of being correct without having to think. When ideological stereotypes and specific opinions are linked in this way, there is a lowering of the kind of anxiety which arises when loyalty and belief are not in accord. Such ideologies lead to a willingness to accept a given line of belief; then there is no need, emotionally or rationally, to overcome resistance to given items in that line; cumulative selections of specific opinions and feelings become the pre-organized attitudes and emotions that shape the opinion-life of the person.

These deeper beliefs and feelings are a sort of lens through which men experience their worlds, they strongly condition acceptance or rejection of specific opinions, and they set men's orientation toward prevailing authorities. Three decades ago, Walter Lippmann saw such prior convictions as biases: they kept men from defining reality in an adequate way. They are still biases. But today they can often be seen as "good biases"; inadequate and misleading as they often are, they are less so than the crackpot realism of the higher authorities and opinion-makers. They are the lower common sense and as such a factor of resistance. But we must recognize, especially when the pace of change is so deep and fast, that common sense is more often common than sense. And, above all, we must recognize that "the common sense" of our children is going to be less the result of any firm social tradition than of the stereotypes carried by the mass media to which they are now so fully exposed. They are the first generation to be so exposed.

II. So long as the media are not entirely monopolized, the individual can play one medium off against another; he can compare them, and hence resist what any one of them puts out. The more genuine competition there is among the media, the more resistance the individual might be able to command. But how much is this now the case? *Do* people compare reports on public events or policies, playing one medium's content off against another's?

The answer is: generally no, very few do: (1) We know that people tend strongly to select those media which carry contents with which they already agree. There is a kind of selection of new opinions on the basis of prior opinions. No one seems to search out such counter-statements as may be found in alternative media offerings. Given radio programs and magazines and newspapers often get a rather consistent public, and thus reinforce their messages in the minds of that public. (2) this idea of playing one medium off against another assumes that the media really have varying contents. It assumes genuine competition, which is not widely true. The media display an apparent variety and competition, but on closer view they seem to compete more in terms of variations on a few standardized themes than of clashing issues. The freedom to raise issues effectively seems more and more to be confined to those few interests that have ready and continual access to these media.

III. The media have not only filtered into our experience of external realities, they have also entered into our very experience of our own selves. They have provided us with new identities and new aspirations of what we should like to be, and what we should like to appear to be. They have provided in the models of conduct they hold out to us a new and larger and more flexible set of appraisals of our very selves. In terms of the modern theory of the self, we may say that the media bring the reader, listener, viewer into the sight of larger, higher reference groups — groups, real or imagined, up-close or vicarious, personally known or distractedly glimpsed — which are looking glasses for his self-image. They have multiplied the groups to which we look for confirmation of our self-image.

More than that: (1) the media tell the man in the mass who he is — they give him identity; (2) they tell him what he wants to be — they give him aspirations; (3) they tell him how to get that way — they give him technique; and (4) they tell him how to feel that he is that way even when he is not — they give him escape. The gaps between the identity and aspiration lead to technique and/or to escape. That is probably the basic psychological formula of the mass media today. But, as a formula, it is not attuned to the development of the human being. It is the formula of a pseudo-world which the media invent and sustain.

IV. As they now generally prevail, the mass media, especially television, often encroach upon the small-scale discussion, and destroy the chance for the reasonable and leisurely and human interchange of opinion. They are an important cause of the destruction of privacy in its full human meaning. That is an important reason why they not only fail as an educational force, but are a malign force: they do not articulate for the viewer or listener the broader sources of his private tensions and anxieties, his inarticulate resentments and half-formed hopes. They neither enable the individual to transcend his narrow milieu nor clarify its private meaning.

The media provide much information and news about what is happening in the world, but they do not often enable the listener or the viewer truly to connect his daily life with these larger realities. They do not connect the information they provide on public issues with the troubles felt by the individual. They do not increase rational insight into tensions, either those in the individual or those of the society which are reflected in the individual. On the contrary, they distract him and obscure his chance to understand himself or his world, by fastening his attention upon artificial frenzies that are resolved within the program framework, usually by violent action or by what is called humor. In short, for the viewer they are not really resolved at all. The chief distracting tension of the media is between the wanting and the not having of commodities or of women held to be good looking. There is almost always the general tone of animated distraction, of suspended agitation, but it is going nowhere and it has nowhere to go.

STUDY QUESTIONS

1. *What are the four components of the "psychological illiteracy" that, according to Mills, is promoted by the mass media?*

2. *What values, actual or potential, does Mills recognize in the mass media? Why, if he recognizes these values, does he disapprove of the media?*

3. *Is Mills justified in expecting mass media to live up to such high standards? Can you find any evidence in his comments on television for saying that he is expecting too much? What would Mills say of Podhoretz' relatively favorable evaluation of one kind of TV drama?*

4. *Mills sees a chain of relationships leading from the individual's experience to one's loyalties and beliefs, to the mass media. Describe these connections.*

5. *Describe a book, movie or television show that portrays something or someone (a family, a businessman, soldiers, teen-agers, students) as "what we should like to be." Compare the portrayal with the actual reality, as you have experienced it or know about it. Do you think the portrayal did harm or good or neither?*

6. *Write an essay doing the following: first, describe a book, movie or television show that gives its audience the experience of "being correct without having to think." Tell what pre-formed attitude it exploited. Then, describe a statement you have found that seems intended to correct the reader's beliefs, or to challenge him. These are usually easier to find in textbooks, serious magazines, and sometimes in newspaper editorials. Describe the attitude that it tries to attack or correct. Then conclude with some observation in which you compare these two examples.*

Richard Weaver The Great Stereopticon*

A great point is sometimes made of the fact that modern man no longer sees above his head a revolving dome with fixed stars and glimpses of the *primum mobile*. True enough, but he sees something similar when he looks at his daily newspaper. He sees the events of the day refracted through a medium which colors them as effectively as the cosmology of the medieval scientist determined his view of the starry heavens. The newspaper is a man-made cosmos of the world of events around us at the time. For the average reader it is a construct with a set of significances which he no more thinks of examining than did his pious forebear of the thirteenth century — whom he pities for sitting in medieval darkness — think of questioning the cosmology. This modern man, too, lives under a dome, whose theoretical aspect has been made to harmonize with a materialistic conception of the world. And he employs its conjunctions and oppositions to explain the occurrences of his time with all the confidence of the now supplanted disciple of astrology.

The Great Stereopticon, like most gadgets, has been progressively improved and added to until today it is a machine of three parts: the press, the motion picture, and the radio. Together they present a version of life quite as controlled as that taught by medieval religionists, though feeble in moral inspiration, as we shall see....

If we are pleading for unity of mind and if we admit the necessity for some degree of subjective determination, it might appear that this machine, with its power to make the entire environment rhetorical, is a heaven-sent answer to our needs. We do not in the final reckoning desire uninterpreted data; it is precisely the interpretation which holds our interest. But the great fault is that data, as it passes through the machine, takes its significance from a sickly metaphysical dream. The ultimate source of evaluation ceases to be the dream of beauty and truth and becomes that of psychopathia, of fragmentation, of disharmony and nonbeing. The operators of the Stereopticon by their very selection of matter make horrifying assumptions about reality. For its audience that overarching dome becomes a sort of miasmic cloud, a breeder of strife and degradation and of the subhuman. What person taking the affirmative view of life can deny that the world served up daily by press, movie, and radio is a world of evil and negation? There is iron in our nature sufficient to withstand any fact that is present in a context of affirmation, but we cannot remain unaffected by the continued assertion of cynicism and brutality. Yet these are what the materialists in control of publicity give us.

The sickly metaphysical dream is not the creation solely of those who have cast restraint to the winds to seek profit in sensationalism. It is the work, too, of many who profess higher ideals but who cannot see where their assumptions lead. Fundamental to the dream, of course, is the dogma of progress, with its postulate of the endlessness of becoming. The habit of judging all things by their departure from the things of yesterday is reflected in most journalistic interpretation. Hence the restlessness and the criteria of magnitude and popularity. The fact that capitalism seems to flourish only by expansion is no doubt connected with this; but, whatever the cause may be, there is no law of perfection where there are no standards of measure. The touchstone of progress simply schools the millions in shallow evaluation.

Somewhere, moreover, the metaphysicians of publicity have absorbed the idea that the goal of life is happiness through comfort. It is a state of complacency supposed to ensue when the physical appetites have been well satisfied. Advertising fosters the concept, social democracy approves it, and the acceptance is so wide that it is virtually impossible today, except from the religious rostrum, to teach that life means discipline and sacrifice. It means, in the world picture of press agency, a job, domesticity, interest in some harmless diversion such as baseball and fishing, and a strong antipathy toward abstract ideas. This is the Philistine version of man in pursuit of happiness. Even Carlyle's doctrine of blessedness through work has overtones of strenuousness which are repungant to the man of today. Because the journalist-philosophers evaluate the multifarious objects and events of the world by their appeal to the greatest possible number of this type, it is not to be expected that they will recommend the arduous road of spiritualization.

As for the latter, it cannot be said too emphatically that the operators of the Great Stereopticon have an interest in keeping people from breaking through to deeper significances. Not only is the philosopher a notoriously poor consumer; he is also an unsettling influence on societies careless of justice. That there are abysses of meaning beneath his daily routine, the common man occasionally suspects; to have him realize them in some appocalyptic revelation might well threaten the foundations of materialist civilization. It is no wonder that experienced employers advertise for workers who are married and sober, for the other type sometimes begins to wonder which is the *real* reality, and they cannot afford help which might behave as Santayana, when he reportedly deserted the Harvard lecture room at the voice of spring, or Sherwood Anderson, when he left without adieu the Ohio paint factory.

The speculations of journalism seldom go beyond the confines of business and propriety, and its oracles have been quick to assail those who come with disturbing notions — quick and unscrupulous, too, if they sense that the notions contain some necessary truth. In this they bear out the observation of Socrates that society does not mind an individual's being wise; only when he begins to make others wise does it become apprehensive. This is to say that they fear the spread of what has truth and reason on its side. Has any brilliant social critic of the last century received something better than a sneer from the pundits of journalism until his appreciation by the thoughtful forced a grudging recognition? A Nietzsche, a Kierkegaard, a Péguy, a Spengler — it is impossible for journalism to take these people seriously. The existence of the one threatens the existence of the other. The proprietors of the Stereopticon have a pretty clear idea of the level at which thinking is safe for the established order. They are protecting a materialist civilization growing more insecure and panicky as awareness filters through that it is over an abyss.

Thus, by insisting upon the dogma of progress, by picturing physical sufficiency as the goal of living, by insulating the mind against thoughts of an immanent reality, the Great Stereopticon keeps the ordinary citizen from perceiving "the vanity of his bookkeeping and the emptiness of his domestic felicities." It is the great projection machine of the bourgeois mentality, which we have already seen to be psychopathic in its alienation from reality.

It is curious to see how this mentality impresses those brought up under differing conditions. I recall with especial vividness a passage from Walter Hines Page's *The Autobiography of Nicholas Worth*. Page, who grew up in the Reconstruction South and later went North to school, had received his earliest impressions in a society where catastrophe and privation had laid bare some of the primal realities, including the existence of evil — a society, too, in which the "primitive infection" of the African race, to use a term employed by Jung, had developed in the white man some psychological cunning. It seemed to Page that his northern acquaintances had "minds of logical simplicity."[1] Such, I think, must be the feeling of anyone who comes out of a natural environment into one in which education, however lengthy and laborious, is based on bourgeois assumptions about the real character of the world. It is a mind which learns to play with counters and arrives at answers which work — in a bourgeois environment. If we reverse this process and send the "mind of logical simplicity" into regions where mystery and contingency are recognized, we re-enact the plot of Conrad's *Lord Jim*. There is a world of terrifying reality to which the tidy moralities of an Anglican parsonage do not seem applicable.[2]

[1] In his novel *The Bostonians*, which deserves to be better known, Henry James sends the "southern" type of mind into a northern environment, with consequences that corroborate Page's thesis.

[2] An anthropologist related to me that certain Negro tribes of West Africa have a symbol for the white man consisting of a figure seated on the deck of a steamer in a position of stiffest rigidity. The straight, uncompromising lines are the betrayal; the primitive artist has caught the white man's unnatural rigor, which contrasts, ominously for him, with the native's sinuous adaptation.

Seen from another point of view, the Great Stereopticon is a translation into actuality of Plato's celebrated figure of the cave. The defect of the prisoners, let us recall, is that they cannot perceive the truth. The wall before them, on which the shadows play, is the screen on which press, motion picture, and radio project their account of life. The chains which keep the prisoners from turning their heads are the physical monopoly which the engines of publicity naturally possess. And is it not pathetically true that these victims, with their limited vision, are "in the habit of conferring honors among themselves to those who are quickest to observe the passing shadows and to remark which of them went before and which followed after, and which were together"?

The result is that insulation by technology has made the task of disseminating wisdom more difficult since Plato's day. In Athenian sophistry and demagoguery Plato faced evils of the same kind, but they could not work behind such strategic entrenchment, and it was hardly as difficult for the wise man to make himself heard in centers of influence. Nothing is more natural than that, in an age dominated by materialism, authority should attach to those who possess. What chance today, to make the situation concrete, has a street-corner preacher, without means and without institutional sponsorship, in competition with the glib assertions of a radio oracle? The denizens of the cave have never been so firmly enchained as in this age, which uses liberty as a veritable incantation.

There are, it is true, certain hopeful signs of restiveness growing out of our condition. Most of us have observed among ordinary people a deep suspicion of propaganda since the first World War. The lesson of that disillusionment has lasted surprisingly. So intense has been this distrust that during the recent conflict the most authentic stories of outrages, documented and proved in every possible way, either were met with outright disbelief or were accepted gingerly and with reservations. The common man realizes that he has been misled and that there are those who would mislead him again; but, lacking analytical power, he tends to group every instance of organized expression with propaganda. In times of peace, too, he has exhibited a certain hard-headed resistance to attempts to drive or cajole him. We have seen in this country politicians elected in the face of almost unanimous press opposition; we note oftentimes a cagey dismissal of the obvious falsification in advertising, and I have heard simple men remark that newspapers should not print items of a private and distressing nature such as we have classified as obscene.

In serious writing, too, there are some hopeful portents of change. It has been noted how modern poets have reacted against the debased coinage of cliché language; and indications appear in other types of literature that the

---

A mind nurtured on press, motion picture, and radio cannot be otherwise in relation to the complexity of the world. Its instructors do not teach it to use the "proper reticences and proprieties" toward different things, and so its ideas may be comical simplifications.

middle-class world picture is being abandoned. Perhaps Arthur Koestler is right: as the bourgeois novel flickers out, an entirely new type of writer is destined to appear: "airmen, revolutionaries, adventurers, men who lead the dangerous life." Such, indeed, seem Silone, Saint-Exupéry, Hemingway. They will carry the gift for reflection into experiences of intense physical distress, and they will emerge with a more genuine contempt for materialist explanations than has been seen for centuries. When Saint-Exupéry, for example, declares that "the physical drama itself cannot touch us until some-one points out its spiritual sense," he makes an affirmation of tragedy and significance. In a way, these men have the same recourse as medieval mystics, who, in suffering, caught the vision. And, since their faith has been tested by fire, they cannot be intimidated by those things which reduce the armchair philosopher to meekness. They have broken through the falsity and have returned to tell that the world is not at all what it has been made to seem — not after one has cut loose from security and comfort and achieved a kind of freedom far different from that promised by political liberals, who are themselves pushing slides into the Stereopticon. In reflecting on what is taught by extremities, one is reminded of Yeats's saying that saints and drunkards are never Whigs.

It will certainly have to be asked whether European fascism was not just this impulse vulgarized and perverted. The rebellion of youth, the repudiation of bourgeois complacency, the attempt to renew the sense of "holiness and heroism," appear the beginning of a revolt at least as deep-seated as that which made the French Revolution. The revolt was led by ignorant spirits who were impelled from behind by resentment and who, through their determination to invert the Christian ethic, made an unexampled fiasco. There is no reason to believe, however, that the deep dissatisfaction with the superficiality of Western life has been removed or even mitigated. And this is why we wonder how long the Stereopticon can preserve the inane world which the bourgeois finds congenial. It is, after all, only a mechanical means of unifying empirical communities.

In summary, the plea that the press, motion picture, and radio justify them-selves by keeping people well informed turns out to be misleading. If one thinks merely of facts and of vivid sensations, the claim has some founda-tion, but if he thinks of encouragement to meditation, the contrary rather is true. For by keeping the time element continuously present — and one may recall Henry James's description of journalism as criticism of the moment at the moment — they discourage composition and so promote the fragmentation already reviewed. We have seen in other connections how specialization is hostile to all kinds of organization, whether that organization is expressed as image, as whole, or as generalization. In the last analysis this reveals itself as an attempt to prevent the simultaneous perception of successive events, which is the achievement of the philosopher. Materialism and success require the "decomposed eternity" of time for their operation, and this is why we have these hidden but persistent attacks on memory, which holds successive events in a single picture. The successive perception of successive events is empiricism; the simultaneous perception is idealism. Need we go further to account for the current dislike of long memories and for the hatred of the past?

Recurring to Plato's observation that a philosopher must have a good memory, let us inquire whether the continuous dissemination of news by the media under discussion does not produce the provincial in time. The constant stream of sensation, eulogized as lively propagation of what the public wants to hear, discourages the pulling-together of events from past time into a whole for contemplation. Thus, absence of reflection keeps the individual from being aware of his former selves, and it is highly questionable whether anyone can be a member of a metaphysical community who does not preserve such memory. Upon the presence of the past in the present depends all conduct directed by knowledge.

There can be little doubt that this condition of mind is a large factor in the low political morality of our age. Oswald Garrison Villard, a political journalist of the old school, who spent half a century crusading for standards of probity in public administration, once declared that he has never ceased to marvel at the shortness of the public's memory, at the rapidity with which it forgets episodes of scandal and incompetence. It sometimes appeared to him of little use to attack a party for its unethical conduct, for the voters would have no recollection of it. The glee with which the epithet "ancient history" is applied to what is out of sight is of course a part of this barbarous attitude. The man of culture finds the whole past relevant; the bourgeois and the barbarian find relevant only what has some pressing connection with their appetites. Those who remember alone have a sense of relatedness, but whoever has a sense of relatedness is in at least the first grade of philosophy. Henry Ford's statement that history is bunk is a perfectly proper observation for a bourgeois industrialist, and it was followed with equal propriety by another: "Creeds must go." Technology emancipates not only from memory but also from faith.

What humane spirit, after reading a newspaper or attending a popular motion picture or listening to the farrago of nonsense on a radio program, has not found relief in fixing his gaze upon some characteristic bit of nature? It is escape from the sickly metaphysical dream. Out of the surfeit of falsity born of technology and commercialism we rejoice in returning to primary data and to assurance that the world is a world of enduring forms which in themselves are neither brutal nor sentimental.

STUDY QUESTIONS

1. *In what way, according to Weaver, does the modern consciousness resemble the medieval one?*

2. What two beliefs in particular does Weaver think are primarily responsible for the distortions of the mass media? What conditions of modern life are responsible for these distortions?

3. What specific points of disagreement exist between Weaver's views and Bryson's? Note that some of these disagreements relate to the underlying assumptions, and are not openly stated.

4. This and the preceding three selections offer several perspectives on popular culture, from different points of view. Which of them seems to you the most "objective" analysis? If you feel that any of the writers are biased, how would you describe their particular bias? Which writer seems to you to present the most optimistic analysis? Which the most pessimistic?

5. Do you agree with Weaver that the role of the press, movies and radio (and TV) is primarily one of evil and negation? If you do, explain what you mean, giving examples from your own experience. If you do not, defend at least one of these mass media against Weaver's charges.

6. Weaver blames two beliefs for the disorders he is describing, but he never tries to explain why these beliefs are wrong. Write a theme on one of them, either supporting Weaver's point of view or defending the belief against his criticisms.

7 Literature and the Arts

1. THE NATURE AND MEANING OF ART

Eric Newton The Nature of the Arts*

A postage stamp, the overture to "The Magic Flute," No. 7, Acacia
Grove, Guerlain's latest perfume, Leonardo's "Last Supper," an innings
by Don Bradman, Shakespeare's "Hamlet," a performance of "Sylphides,"
a dish of "homard à la cardinal," St. Paul's Cathedral, a Walt Disney cartoon
— all these are (or can be) works of art.

There are other things that are not works of art. Niagara Falls is not a work
of art, nor is the afterglow of the snows of Monte Rosa, nor the sound of
breakers against a cliff, nor the dance executed by washing hanging on a
clothes line in a stiff breeze, nor the scent of a pine wood on a summer day.

These two classes of phenomena are different in kind. The first are man-
made and man-designed. They had to be conceived in the mind of a man

* From *European Painting and Sculpture* by Eric Newton, by permission of Penguin
Books, Ltd. Copyright, 1950, by Penguin Books, Ltd.

(or group of men) and then made communicable to other men by the skill of the designer, working in some medium that could be perceived by the senses of other men — the eye, the ear, the nose, the palate.

The other set of phenomena — Niagara Falls, the sound of breakers and so on — are not man-made or man-designed. They may be equally beautiful or equally pleasurable. They may even be the result of design by God or the Laws of Nature or what you will, but they have not that double element in them of conception and parturition. They were not imagined first and then made manifest through the medium of visible materials, visible movements, audible sounds, perceptible smells.

Art has always fascinated the makers of definitions, and has always baffled them; the makers of definitions are never content to define what a thing *is*: they usually attempt to describe what it is *for*. And though I myself have no doubt at all about what art *is*, no sequence of words known to me will describe what art is *for*.

In trying to tell the story of art I shall therefore start with an initial advantage. I have no preconceived theories about the artist's purpose: therefore I have no prejudice against the artist who runs counter to such theories. If the artist tells me a story I shall exclaim "how interesting!"; if he wishes to overawe me with mystical conceptions of the Godhead I am ready to be impressed; if he wants to construct a purely formal pattern of line and colour or mass or sound, I will say "how beautiful!"; if he preaches I am ready to be converted; if he wants to be of use to me I shall say "thank you." Art has done all these things at various times in the history of civilization.

But if the story of art is to be told it is certainly necessary to know what art is, and if I define it briefly as a human conception made manifest by the use of a medium: and if I define good art (and no one wants to waste his time telling the story of bad art) as a noble (or arresting, or interesting, or valuable) conception made manifest by the skilful use of a medium, I can then have done with definitions and get on with the story. . . .

The artist, then, is a man of double activity. He has to have imagination and he has to have craftsmanship. He has to imagine (in his mind's eye, or his mind's ear, or his mind's nose) the thing he is going to make; and he must also have the power to translate the thing he has imagined into terms of his medium. Those are not separate activities. On the contrary, they affect one another in unpredictable and unanalysable ways, so that when an artist is at work he cannot possibly say at a given moment which part of himself he is using. Is the fact that he is working with a soft pencil on rough paper giving a breadth to Tintoretto's line, or had the image in his mind's eye already formed itself with that breadth of sweep? Did Mozart, in his mind's ear, conjure up a quality of sound that could be translated into music only by a certain combination of bassoons and strings? Or did his memory of that combination, heard perhaps by chance while an orchestra was tuning up, prompt him to make further experiments with it? No one can possibly answer these questions, since no one but Tintoretto himself knew the precise quality of the image in his mind's eye and no one but Mozart ever heard what was in Mozart's mind's ear. The work of art, the drawing or the overture, is all we have to judge by. We can only say, "this man *seems* to have found an adequate means of expression for the thing he had to say." A marriage has taken place between the visionary and the craftsman and one can judge of the success of the marriage only by examining the fruits of it — the work of art.

But this artistic activity — this making of drawings and overtures and books and postage stamps — is not a thing done just for the fun of doing it. No doubt it *is* fun to write a book or compose an overture, but no artist was ever content to have his fun and then throw the result of it away. The book has to be read, the overture performed, the ballet or picture seen. Art is a communication. Behind every work of art is the artist's appeal to his fellows, "Don't you see what I mean? Don't you see what I'm getting at?"

The story of art is therefore not merely the story of men who make things and of the kind of things they make. It is also the story of the relationship — the very complicated and always shifting relationship — between these men and their fellow men. It is a relationship full of contradictions and difficulties. For no workman can afford to produce unless he is paid to do so: therefore the artist has to have an employer. And no employer can afford to pay a workman unless he is producing something that he (the employer) needs. It follows, therefore, that (except in the rare case of artists of independent means) the artist's work of art is not merely the child of his own personal fancy, the thing he personally wants to communicate. It must also be something that his employer wants him to communicate to himself or to others. The work of art must be not only the result of an urge on the part of the producer, but also of a need on the part of the consumer. Here is a strange state of things indeed! For how can the consumer feel a need of something so personal and so (on the face of it) unnecessary as an artist's expression of his inner vision? And even supposing he does feel that need sufficiently strongly to induce him to pay an artist to produce a work of art, how is the artist going to reconcile his personal and private desire to communicate his own personal and private vision with his employer's or patron's specification of what he wants the artist to produce? In any other branch of human activity the question would not arise. No maker of chisels would say to his employer, "My whole nature rebels against the idea of making the kind of chisels you want. You wish me to make sharp chisels. I, on the other hand, can only express myself to the full by making blunt chisels. You want steel chisels; I, as a craftsman, feel irresistibly drawn to the use of lead as medium."

The more materially useful a man-made thing is, the more chance there is of complete agreement between artist and employer. But material usefulness is not the only kind of usefulness; there is such a thing as spiritual usefulness. To the maker of chisels the employer can justifiably say, "Make your chisels exactly thus," but to the maker of crucifixes he must say, "Let your crucifix conform to the minimum requirements of all crucifixes — a cross, a male human body, an impression of suffering, but also a sense of nobility. Beyond that I leave it to you. Add your own personal thoughts and feelings. Embody your own vision."

So as long as the artist is an employed workman he must compromise, never losing touch with life and its requirements yet never sacrificing his own integrity in doing so. And that is almost always a good thing, for compromise of that kind is not a concession to a lower order of things. It is a dangerous holding of the balance between two sets of forces. The artist, like the maker of chisels, serves a master (Palestrina served the Pope, Shakespeare wrote his plays for a touring company), but in doing so he gives his master something he never bargained for. When Rembrandt painted the "Night Watch" he was ostensibly painting the portraits of a certain Captain Banning Cocq and the members of his shooting company. Presumably something corresponding to a group photograph of the school hockey team would have satisfied the club, but Rembrandt had things to say that had nothing to do with the likenesses of the captain and his friends — things about how light falls in dark places, and how it strikes hard here and gently caresses there — and he insisted on saying them. In doing so he began to lose sight of the original purpose of his picture. Banning Cocq and his friends became mere excuses for an essay in chiaroscuro. The club was offended; certain members of it complained that their faces had been plunged into semi-darkness; they were more interested in themselves than in chiaroscuro. We, on the other hand, are delighted. We have lost interest in seventeenth-century shooting clubs, but what Rembrandt has to say about the play of light on flesh is as fascinating today as it was in 1642. A similar controversy, it will be remembered, arose a few years ago in connection with the statue of Sir Douglas Haig in Whitehall. Michelangelo, faced with the same kind of criticism of his statues of Lorenzo and Giuliano de Medici, answered that in a thousand years' time nobody would know what the two Medicis were really like. Pope Clement VII, however, who ordered the statues, *did* know; he asked for portraits of two men and he was given symbols of mankind. Michelangelo was unwilling to make the compromise. We may be glad of his unwillingness, but his employer was anything but pleased.

This necessity of serving two masters has always been one of the artist's difficulties. He must deliver the goods he is asked for, and he must also be true to himself. And rightly so. Whenever either is sacrificed to the other the work of art suffers in quality. There are plenty of instances of both kinds of sacrifices in the art of to-day. There are commercial artists who produce flavourless trash in an attempt to give their employers what they want; and there are artists who, through lack of employers or through unwillingness to be employed, have nothing to serve but their own impulses, and whose work can only be described as psychological exhibitionism.

It is not by chance that the greatest periods of art have usually occurred when the artist was most firmly harnessed to a master or to a cause. Necessarily the pace of a man in harness is slower than that of a free man. He is less free to choose his own direction, but he has the satisfaction of knowing that he is an indispensable member of society — or of a portion of society — and the further satisfaction of knowing that because society needs him, society will understand him — at any rate that portion of him that is in service. His double service gives him a double message and a double appeal. A Palestrina, left to himself, will merely further the cause of music: employed by the Pope, he also enriches the texture of Christian ritual and enlarges the meaning of Christianity.

The present-day cleavage of artists into two groups, those who are so enslaved to their employers that they "can't call their souls their own," and those unfettered spirits whose souls are so much their own that they are no use to anyone but themselves, is a comparatively new thing. It has led to the division of artists into two kinds known as "commercial" and "fine artists" — i.e., men who work only to please the man who pays them and men who have no one to please but themselves — though these latter always hope that they will happen to please someone else sufficiently to induce him to pay them enough to go on pleasing themselves without starving. Three-quarters of the films made, about a quarter of the books published, ninety per cent of the music composed are "commercial" in the true sense that they were created primarily in order to be turned into money. The bulk of the remainder, the "fine" works of art, are genuine attempts at self-expression without reference to the requirements of society. In some cases they succeed so well in impressing themselves on society that society begins to require them. In others they are so personal and so remote from average human experience that society, far from requiring them, complains of their uselessness, their unintelligibility, their divorce from "life." That complaint, so often heard nowadays, is not a criterion of the genuineness or sincerity of the works of art in question. It is an index of the unfamiliarity of the language in which those works of art are couched. For a personal vision demands a personal set of idioms to express it. Usually a generation or so must pass before those idioms become understood and accepted by the average man and pass into general currency. The time-lag between the appearance of an unfamiliar artistic message couched in an unfamiliar artistic idiom, and its acceptance by the average man can be reduced only when the artist can be harnessed to a cause that the average man understands. Giotto was as violent an innovator as Picasso, but as Giotto's innovations were harnessed to Christianity (while Picasso's are harnessed to nothing more stable than Picasso) the average contemporary of Giotto, shocked though he may have been by the new Giottesque idiom, felt that he could at least understand the cause that idiom served, and could dimly see how the new idiom somehow served the cause in a new and valuable way. To-day the same phenomenon can be observed. The more the artist is willing to compromise between making what *he* wants (in Rembrandt's case, a study of light) and what his employer wants (in Banning Cocq's case, a set of recognizable portraits) the more immediately acceptable his work will be. A cubist whose picture conveys nothing but the cubiness of things in general is apt to leave the average man cold and puzzled. But a cubist who uses his cubism to advertise the merits of A's petrol or B's beer is understood at once. A cubized egg is, to the average man, simply a bad egg; but a cubized glass of beer grasped in a cubized hand is interesting and arresting. The one is merely an artist's visual adventure, the other is a voyage of discovery that carries the spectator along with it and deposits him surprisingly at his destination. Once the artist has harnessed himself to society, society at once begins to regard him as a workman performing a useful function and not as a playboy amusing himself in a vacuum.

In the same way a scientist's discovery that an electric current passed through metal coil will heat the metal leaves most people uninterested, but the man who uses that discovery to boil a kettle arouses an immediate interest.

This double function of the artist is the key to the story of art. Many learned books about art have been written which fail to tell the story because they lose sight of the perpetual adjustment that goes on in the artist between art-as-expression and art-as-service.

Meanwhile, before going on to examine the particular kinds of adjustments that take place when the artist happens to be a painter or a sculptor, one other thing must be said about the arts in general. A work of art may be an expression of the artist's inner vision, and it may also be a thing useful to society, but beyond both these it is a thing-in-itself. Apart from its function as a means of communion between one human being and another it exists in its own right. It consists of a series of sounds or words or movements or of a set of shapes made of pigment applied to canvas or of a set of masses carved out of stone or modelled out of clay. In a word, it has form; and it must obey the laws of form as dictated by whatever medium the artist uses. A sentence may embody an idea in the writer's mind, but it must also obey grammatical laws. A drawing may say what the draughtsman wanted it to say but it must also say it in the pencil's way. A statue may represent a man in a lounge suit, but, if it is made of stone, both flesh and cloth must be translated into terms of stone: stone must not be tortured into an imitation of flesh and cloth. Every medium has its own set of laws, and the work of art must obey them or perish. When the word is made flesh it ceases to have the qualities of word-ness. It must behave like flesh.

Moreover, the work of art is self-contained. A picture must have four edges, a play or piece of music must have a beginning and an end, whereas the experience it embodies has no edges, no beginning or end. It is just an indeterminate slice of an endless ebb and flow. But the work of art must be a thing that can be isolated from all surrounding things. A picture occupies a square yard of space, a symphony three-quarters of an hour of time, a play several cubic yards of space and a couple of hours of time. Having "edges," therefore, in space or time, it follows that it must also have a shape. E. M. Forster, in his remarkable essay on the novel, points out that Anatole France's "Thaïs" is shaped like an hour-glass. ("We do not see it as an hour-glass — that is the hard jargon of the lecture room — but if it was not for this hour-glass the story, the plot and the characters of Thaïs and Paphnuce would none of them exert their full force, they would none of them breathe as they do.") Percy Lubbock's "Roman Pictures" is shaped like a "grand chain." ("What is so good in 'Roman Pictures' is not the presence of the 'grand chain' pattern — anyone can organize a grand chain — but the suitability of the pattern to the author's mood.") Observe the word *pattern*. The arts are difficult things to write about because there is no adequate terminology that fits them all. "Pattern" is a word taken from graphic art, "rhythm" from music, "phrasing" from literature. But they all have their counterparts in one another and they have all been invented by people who want (as I do) to talk about the work of art as a thing-in-itself, a thing with form, as opposed to a thing with content. Pattern, for example, is visual rhythm; a set of relationships set up in the eye of the beholder. A drawing of a flower is just a drawing of a flower, a thing that imparts a certain amount of botanical information. But repeat that drawing three times side by side on a square of paper and you have a pattern. You have established a relationship between three things and not only between three things but also between them and the four edges of the paper, and that relationship can be pleasant or unpleasant without any reference to botany. As long as a work of art has a shape it must also have a pattern. Pattern is a subdivision of shape. The parts within the shape must be related to the shape and to one another.

The artist's feeling for form and shape has given birth, in all the arts, to a host of conventions that are on the face of them fantastic. Why should poets have invented a shape called the sonnet? Why should the ear have to be tickled with an elaborate system of rhymes? What is the virtue of fourteen iambic pentameters if thirteen or fifteen would equally well express the poet's thought? Why should Edward Lear, in recounting the brief but poignant story of the old man of Aosta, have decided to fit his story into the strange shape of a Limerick with its attendant pattern of lines — long, long, short, short, long — and its parallel pattern of rhymes — *a, a, b, b, a*? What gave birth to the Sonata form? One can only answer that deep down in mankind is a thirst for something we have agreed to call aesthetic pleasure, a thirst for order, harmony, balance, rhythm, pattern.

Each art has its own set of conventions, but this brief chapter is not the place to examine them in detail.... It is sufficient to remember that the artist, in the act of creation, is perpetually obsessed with this question of the form his work of art is taking. His picture is not merely a representation of an object, or an expression of his feeling about an object. It is a thing-in-itself, equally valid if it is turned upside down; equally valid if it is an inaccurate representation, or a representation of something that lies outside the spectator's experience (as, say, a picture of a snow scene would be to an inhabitant of the Sahara desert); a thing that justifies itself by its shape alone and the obedience of that shape to the laws of the medium in which it is made.

STUDY QUESTIONS

1. What, according to Newton, is the difference between pleasant things that are works of art and pleasant things that are not works of art? What are the three major considerations involved in the creation of a work of art that Newton discusses?

2. Do you see any danger in Newton's recommendation that the artist seek to make his work "acceptable" by working out a compromise between the demands of self-expression and the requirements of his public? What advantages does such a compromise have for the artist? For the public? What might the public lose?

3. What reasons does Newton give for saying that a work of art must have a "shape" or "pattern"? Compare the comments of Daiches in "The Literary Use of Language" in the first section of this anthology.

4. Newton's essay is, at least in part, a definition. What devices does he use to make clear exactly what he means by art? How is the selection organized? How does he develop it?

5. Do you agree with Newton that "double service" is a good requirement for an artist to have to meet? Or is something to be said for situations where only one type of service is necessary? Can you cite examples of artists who (a) would have done better with only one master to serve, or (b) did good work because they had only a single aim?

6. Describe an episode involving some work of art—a book, a movie, a painting, a piece of music or an example of architecture—which reflected a disagreement between an artist and his public. Exactly what was the cause of the misunderstanding? How was it settled?

Percy C. Buck   The Meaning of Appreciation*

You will have noticed that in my previous lectures I have been at pains to make certain words, which we use loosely in conversation, carry a more definite meaning, believing as I do that shallow thinking is more often due to vagueness of terms than to incapacity of mind. I have tried to make you see that a critical mind is not one that adopts a rather querulous and censorious attitude to everything presented to it, but that true criticism is, in the words

* From *The Scope of Music*, 1923. Reprinted by permission.

of a recent writer, a hunt for buried treasure. And I have tried to show that the discriminating mind is not necessarily one provided with the most exact apparatus for classifying things, but that taste is the result of thought guiding feeling.

I now ask you to consider whether you really give the right meaning to the word appreciation, and I will begin by discussing imagination.

If a man is of a certain type of mind, if he is generally dreamy and un-practical, we are apt to label him imaginative. It does not much matter, so long as we understand one another, that we use words loosely in daily life. But when we are definitely inquiring into a branch of life where imagination assumes importance, it becomes imperative that the connotation of the word should be definite. And if you possess imagination, there are two types of it, either of which may be yours; but the two are so distinct, and in some ways so much in opposition, that I think no one can possess both in any full measure.

Imagination may be receptive or creative. If your type is receptive you will "follow" quickly. If I tell you the story of a railway accident you will see "in your mind's eye" the sudden catastrophe, the overturned carriages, and all the attendant confusion. You will probably even imagine the spot and the sur-rounding country so vividly that, if you are taken to the scene of the accident, you will say, "I hadn't thought of it as a bit like that." For the receptive imagination is primarily reconstructive, and deals with things that are con-crete and particular; it is objective, and works by mental images.

All of us have this form of imagination in some degree, and most of us when young have it in a high state of perfection. Most children actually form mental images of the lions and tigers of the storyteller. All of us, how-ever, listen with less concentration as we grow older, and the power of reconstruction dwindles from atrophy. You should all strive to keep it alive and develop it, in yourselves and especially in your children, for the value to you of any speech, any book, any piece of music depends on your power of holding it in your mind by giving it your concentrated attention. If one of my children is so absorbed in a book that he does not hear what I say to him, then I am delighted, for that is the way in which a book should be read; but I think a good many less sophisticated parents would be annoyed and blame the child.

Creative imagination is definitely constructive; it deals with general and abstract ideas and is subjective. It works through technique, because without the power of presentation in some medium the artist's idea remains for ever in his head. The early stages of everybody's artistic attempts are due to his receptive imagination. If you or I try for the first time to draw a man or write a tune we have to rely on our memory of men and tunes, and will really only be reproducing. But if either of us is endowed with the creative imagina-tion, our pictures and our compositions will leave the ruts and gradually acquire a distinction, an "originality," which is due solely to our constructive as distinct from reconstructive powers. Consequently the more creative imagination we have the less we use the receptive, and indeed there is a danger of our losing it entirely. Few great creative artists have been good admirers of other people's work.

Now for appreciation. I will take for my text the remark made to me by a man to whom I was maintaining that mind had a part to play in enjoyment. He replied, "If I could appreciate anything as much as a dog does a bone, I should be happy." The question of "as much as" I shall deal with in my next lecture, and so will leave alone now. At the moment I want to claim that the various forms of appreciation can be graded, and that it is reasonable to say that one end of the scale is a lower type, qualitatively, than the other. Lecture VI will discuss the quantitative side.

Appreciation falls into three main groups. They are not, of course, water-tight, for there is every conceivable step in a range which is continuous. But the three types will serve as landmarks.

1. *Crude Appreciation* is when we are concerned with almost pure sensation. The cat finds the sensation of warmth, when she sits by the fire, to be pleasant, and memory will suggest her making a habit of it. The child is pleased with the sound of the trumpet and wants the sensation to be repeated. But every experience in this opening stage is a result of simple sensation, and "liking" is a more appropriate term than "appreciating." If the latter word is to have any distinctive connotation to separate it from 'liking' it must be through the addition of the intellectual process of comparison and appraisement. If I have only once in my life tasted an apple I may like it or dislike it, but I cannot "appreciate" it *qua* apple unless I have an apple-standard in my mind for comparison; though I may appreciate it *qua* food, if I find it nicer than other kinds of food. So I think it is not a quibble to say that the first time the cat sits by the fire she "likes" the warmth, and later on may or may not appreciate the experience according as she does, or does not, compare it with other experiences. Appreciation only begins when she says to herself, "This is a nicer fire than usual" or "This is better than being outside."

2. *Intelligent Appreciation* is established when the rudimentary intelligence hitherto scarcely brought into play has become the cardinal feature in the experience, as when a child listens to a story. It won't even "like" the story if it does not understand what happens; but having understood, it will compare the story with others, and its appreciation depends on its judgement. If you remember I am leaving aside entirely, for the moment, the comparison of the various *quantities* of enjoyment — the cat may, for all I know, enjoy the fire more than the child enjoys the story — I think you will admit that we may claim this "intelligent appreciation" to be of a "higher" type than crude appreciation, and that the steps by which the one merges into the other are steps upward. They certainly seem to follow the laws of evolutionary progress, for they develop in an unbroken line, and always in the same

direction as we grow from the simple sensational infant to the developed intellectual adult. And if you will admit that these steps are steps upward, and that "intelligent" is a higher form of appreciation than crude, you are admitting that the controlling factor, the element in appreciation that makes one form better than another, is judgement.

3. Given, then, that we wish to increase our powers of appreciation, as distinct from the quantity of our enjoyment, we must set out to improve our powers of judgement and discrimination. And if we develop these to their limit we attain the third and final stage, the goal of all serious art-lovers, *Critical Appreciation*.

I think that all questions of this kind are made difficult for us because the circumstances of their discussion nearly always arouse the suspicion that some one is trying to "improve" us. However much we desire improvement in our inner soul, we resent the man who volunteers to undertake the job. So take a case, for your comfort, where you yourself are "top dog," and I think you will allow that the truth of what I have argued is obvious. Supposing some one told you that your errand boy, aged nine, appreciated as much as you do *Paradise Lost*, or the "Forty-eight," or some such miraculous testimony to the greatness of man. You resent, and this time quite rightly, the suggestion that mysteries which are only beginning to raise their veil for you, who have spent a lifetime at their shrine, are an open book to a child who has not lived long enough to have formed a standard of anything. He may enjoy the noble sounds, the rolling rhythms, the feeling of splendour and pageantry they evoke, and his enjoyment may be as great as you like; but as to appreciation, that, you will maintain, is not a gift of the senses but a reward of the mind.

True appreciation, then, is no isolated elementary thing, but a nexus. It is feeling combined with understanding, it is our verdict when the appeal to our feelings has been modified by our realization of value, it is "liking" corrected by judgement.

Should any one deny that "valuation" is a factor in appreciation, we come, of course, to a standstill. We use language in a different way. If he seriously maintains that a pig can appreciate port wine, we can only ask him what word he uses to express the fact that to a man one port is better than another. Once he admits the validity of the claim that "appraisement" is essential, he must allow the importance of the quality of judgement involved in valuation. It is not, as I explained when speaking *de gustibus,* a question of whether we can say the opinion of Mr. Jones on a glass of port is better than that of Mr. Brown, but whether the opinion of either of these gentlemen becomes more valuable as their judgement becomes riper by experience. So we come back to my original postulate that the better the understanding the greater the appreciation.

The corollary is simple. Improvement in taste means education in understanding. If you want your children to grow up to love great literature you must see to it that they acquire right standards of judgement. They may be by nature sensitive, even over-sensitive, to the emotional appeal of pictures or music or books, and they can only acquire discrimination by the education of their judgement. If we undertake the education our task lies in raising them from the mire of crude appreciation which is the common starting-point for all of us, and leaving them as near as we can to the goal where the power of critical appreciation makes life an inexhaustible well of joy. It is a road every one can travel, and all of us do travel some distance along it; for even the appreciation of a tale or a tune involves a rudimentary form of "intelligent appreciation." Only a fool will ever think the end of the road has been reached, for there is no end, and only conceit will allow any one to think he has gone as far as he might have gone. And the going a little farther, which is possible to all of us, will not only result in an increase of our own enjoyment of life, but will also prevent that atrophy of our power of enjoyment which, as Darwin so pathetically lamented, may make our later years emotionless and grey.

Hitherto, as you will have noticed, I have assumed in pleading the importance of the intellectual side in art that I was addressing people who wished to deny it. In general, especially when talking with young painters or poets or musicians, that assumption is necessary. But the danger that most people ignore or at all events never apprehend this truth, is scarcely greater than the converse danger that those earnest folk who have once realized it carry it to an extreme that defeats its purpose. There is some Puck-like gargoyle in the structure of the human mind that delights, when once it finds us taking a thing seriously, in making us suspect that any deviation from solemnity smacks of flippancy. We acquiesce in our sermons being long and austere, our leading articles being pompous and verbose, our art being pretentious and above our heads, until the acquiescence, if we are too intensely serious, becomes a demand. We like our medicines to be nasty.

There is more than a little danger, in this age of specialization, of those who take music seriously falling into this heresy and preaching the over-intellectualization of their art until the red blood has gone out of it. They forget that the appeal of music is to the feelings, and only to the feelings, and that the one function of the understanding is to act as the link, because there is no other possible link in existence. The intellectual factors in a work of art are only merits in so far as they are facilities in bridging the gulf to the feelings. The cleverness of a fugue, the structural complexity of a symphony, the masked unity of a set of variations, are only justifiable in so far as they help to establish the emotional connexion. It is true that we must not place the standard of intelligence on which the composer may count too low; it has been my main object to insist on our duty of educating this intelligence-link to its utmost limit. But it is equally true that it is easy and common to look on intellectualism in art as an end in itself. If you discuss a theatrical performance with an actor, a picture with an artist, a concert with a musician, another man's poem with a poet, I think you will in most cases be astonished at how much a thing which to you is a matter of feeling, is to them a matter of pure technique. I would remind you of what I said once before: we cannot "understand" art, because the part we understand is not art.

There is a *cliché* in common use, amongst people whose talk tends towards "journalese," which I should like you to examine and then dismiss from your vocabulary. An artist is often said to "construct a work of imagination." At best this is no more than a half-truth. The artist does, it is true, produce his work by the exercise of his creative imagination. His catharsis sets his creative powers to work, almost unconsciously, in that medium in which he has acquired technique. His function in life for you and me, however, is not to construct a work of imagination, but to make us do so. From the purely personal and selfish point of view, of course, the poet's work is ended when his poem is signed, sealed, and delivered. But our concern is with appreciation of the poem, and the function of the poem is to compel us to reconstruct in order that we may feel. It may be so overcharged with the sensuous element as compared with its grip on the understanding — like, for instance, some of Swinburne's poems — that we pronounce it, for our individual selves, a failure. Or it may — like Browning's *Sordello* — put so great a strain on our understanding that we cannot "reconstruct" anything at all, and our "feeling" is never called into play. Even the least competent judge of poetry has acquired some standard of judgement, however elementary, to which he will bring the poem for a verdict: a standard acquired from his experience of poems, however limited, which he uses to justify his verdicts even if it is too unorganized to be formulated.

If, then, you would "appreciate" anything, aim at the enlarging and defining of your standard of judgement. If you think when you listen — or, better still, think after you have listened — you will find inevitably that security of judgement arrives. It has arrived, I should think, to every one in the world in some branch of life. The most unmusical woman here probably feels certain as to the merits of pieces of needlework, and she knows that I, who am now in complete ignorance, would before long attain her certainty of judgement if I devoted time to the study of it. Gradually, but beyond doubt, it would "come." The reward is within the reach of every one who desires it, the danger being, indeed, that when it arrives we are apt to feel so self-satisfied that we progress no further. For we must always bear in mind that art is not stagnant, and that we are called on to recast and develop as art changes, recognizing that art is also testing us.

As an antidote to the danger of this self-satisfaction, let me tell you the story of the tourists in the gallery of masterpieces. After "doing" the gallery in half an hour they disdainfully remarked to the attendant, on leaving, that they did not think very much of his pictures. "Gentlemen," replied the attendant, "these pictures are not here for judgement; it is the spectators who are on their trial."

STUDY QUESTIONS

1. *What two kinds of imagination does Buck recognize? Explain and illustrate each kind.*

2. *Buck notes three degrees of appreciation arranged on a scale from lower to higher. What are these three degrees of appreciation? What standard of measurement does he use? Do you find this an acceptable standard?*

3. *Buck observes that we cannot "understand" art. What does he mean by this observation? Do you agree with him? Support your answer with illustration from your own experience.*

4. *What place do experience and observation have in Buck's definition of appreciation?*

5. *In this selection Buck has defined "appreciation" by analyzing it and suggesting that the term really has various meanings. Could a different analysis have been made? Would there be any value in suggesting more than three kinds of appreciation? Choose some similar term and approach its definition by Buck's method.*

6. *Write an "appreciation" of some work of art you have seen (or heard) recently, evaluating it by comparing it with other examples of this art, and making clear what feelings it aroused in you.*

Rainer Maria Rilke   Letters to a Young Poet*

You ask whether your verses are good. You ask me. You have asked others before. You send them to magazines. You compare them with other poems, and you are disturbed when certain editors reject your efforts. Now (since you have allowed me to advise you) I beg you to give up all that. You are looking outward, and that above all you should not do now. Nobody can counsel and help you, nobody. There is only one single way. Go into yourself. Search for the reason that bids you write; find out whether it is spreading out its roots in the deepest places of your heart, acknowledge to yourself whether you would have to die if it were denied you to write. This above all — ask yourself in the stillest hour of your night: *must* I write? Delve into yourself for a deep answer. And if this should be affirmative, if you may meet this earnest question with a strong and simple "I *must*," then build your life according to this necessity; your life even into its most indifferent and slightest hour must be a sign of this urge and a testimony to it. Then draw near to Nature. Then try, like some first human being, to say what you see and experience and love and lose. Do not write love-poems;

* From *Letters to a Young Poet* by Rainer Maria Rilke, by permission of W. W. Norton and Company, Inc. Copyright, 1934, 1954, by W. W. Norton and Company, Inc.

avoid at first those forms that are too facile and commonplace: they are the most difficult, for it takes a great, fully matured power to give something of your own where good and even excellent traditions come to mind in quantity. Therefore save yourself from these general themes and seek those which your own everyday life offers you; describe your sorrows and desires, passing thoughts and the belief in some sort of beauty — describe all these with loving, quiet, humble sincerity, and use, to express yourself, the things in your environment, the images from your dreams, and the objects of your memory. If your daily life seems poor, do not blame it; blame yourself, tell yourself that you are not poet enough to call forth its riches; for to the creator there is no poverty and no poor indifferent place. And even if you were in some prison the walls of which let none of the sounds of the world come to your senses — would you not then still have your childhood, that precious, kingly possession, that treasure-house of memories? Turn your attention thither. Try to raise the submerged sensations of that ample past; your personality will grow more firm, your solitude will widen and will become a dusky dwelling past which the noise of others goes by far away. — And if out of this turning inward, out of this absorption into your own world *verses* come, then it will not occur to you to ask anyone whether they are good *verses*. Nor will you try to interest magazines in your poems: for you will see in them your fond natural possession, a fragment and a voice of your life. A work of art is good if it has sprung from necessity. In this nature of its origin lies the judgment of it: there is no other. Therefore, my dear sir, I know no advice for you save this: to go into yourself and test the deeps in which your life takes rise; at its source you will find the answer to the question whether you *must* create. Accept it, just as it sounds, without inquiring into it. Perhaps it will turn out that you are called to be an artist. Then take that destiny upon yourself and bear it, its burden and its greatness, without ever asking what recompense might come from outside. For the creator must be a world for himself and find everything in himself and in Nature to whom he has attached himself.

But perhaps after this descent into yourself and into your inner solitude you will have to give up becoming a poet; (it is enough, as I have said, to feel that one could live without writing: then one must not attempt it at all). But even then this inward searching which I ask of you will not have been in vain. Your life will in any case find its own ways thence, and that they may be good, rich and wide I wish you more than I can say.

What more shall I say to you? Everything seems to me to have its just emphasis; and after all I do only want to advise you to keep growing quietly and seriously throughout your whole development; you cannot disturb it more rudely than by looking outward and expecting from outside replies to questions that only your inmost feeling in your most hushed hour can perhaps answer....

Very dear Mr. Kappus: I have left a letter from you long unanswered, not that I have forgotten it — on the contrary: it was of the sort that one reads again, when one finds them among one's correspondence, and I recognized you in it as though you had been close at hand. It was the letter of May 2nd, and you surely remember it. When I read it, as now, in the great quiet of these distances, I am touched by your beautiful concern about life, more even than I had felt it in Paris, where everything resounds and dies away differently because of the too great noise that makes things vibrate. Here, where an immense country lies about me, over which the winds pass coming from the seas, here I feel that no human being anywhere can answer for you those questions and feelings that deep within them have a life of their own; for even the best err in words when they are meant to mean most delicate and almost inexpressible things. But I believe nevertheless that you will not have to remain without a solution if you will hold to objects that are similar to those from which my eyes now draw refreshment. If you will cling to Nature, to the simple in Nature, to the little things that hardly anyone sees, and that can so unexpectedly become big and beyond measuring; if you have this love of inconsiderable things and seek quite simply, as one who serves, to win the confidence of what seems poor: then everything will become easier, more coherent and somehow more conciliatory for you, not in your intellect, perhaps, which lags marveling behind, but in your inmost consciousness, waking and cognizance. You are so young, so before all beginning, and I want to beg you, as much as I can, dear sir, to be patient toward all that is unsolved in your heart and to try to love the *questions themselves* like locked rooms and like books that are written in a very foreign tongue. Do not now seek the answers, which cannot be given you because you would not be able to live them. And the point is, to live everything. *Live* the questions now. Perhaps you will then gradually, without noticing it, live along some distant day into the answer. Perhaps you do carry within yourself the possibility of shaping and forming as a particularly happy and pure way of living; train yourself to it — but take whatever comes with great trust, and if only it comes out of your own will, out of some need of your inmost being, take it upon yourself and hate nothing. Sex is difficult; yes. But they are difficult things with which we have been charged; almost everything serious is difficult, and everything is serious. If you only recognize this and manage, out of yourself, out of your *own* nature and ways, out of your *own* experience and childhood and strength to achieve a relation to sex wholly your own (*not* influenced by convention and custom), then you need no longer be afraid of losing yourself and becoming unworthy of your best possession.

Physical pleasure is a sensual experience no different from pure seeing or the pure sensation with which a fine fruit fills the tongue; it is a great unending experience, which is given us, a knowing of the world, the fullness and the glory of all knowing. And not our acceptance of it is bad; the bad thing is that most people misuse and squander this experience and apply it as a stimulant at the tired spots of their lives and as distraction instead of a rallying toward exalted moments. Men have made even eating into something else: want on the one hand, superfluity upon the other, have dimmed the distinctness of this need, and all the deep, simple necessities in which life renews itself have become similarly dulled. But the individual can clarify them for himself and live them clearly (and if not the individual, who is too dependent, then at least the solitary man). He can remember that all beauty in animals and plants is a quiet enduring form of love and longing, and he can see animals, as he sees plants, patiently and willingly uniting and increasing and growing, not out of physical delight, not out of physical suffering, but bowing to necessities that are greater than pleasure and pain and more powerful than will and withstanding. O that man might take this secret, of which the world is full even to its littlest things, more humbly to himself and bear it, endure it, more seriously and feel how terribly difficult it is, instead of taking it lightly. That he might be more reverent toward his fruitfulness, which is but *one*, whether it seems mental or physical; for intellectual creation too springs from the physical, is of one nature with it and only like a gentler, more ecstatic and more everlasting repetition of physical delight. "The thought of being creator, of procreating, of making" is nothing without its continuous great confirmation and realization in the world, nothing without the thousandfold concordance from things and animals — and enjoyment of it is so indescribably beautiful and rich only because it is full of inherited memories of the begetting and the bearing of millions. In one creative thought a thousand forgotten nights of love revive, filling it with sublimity and exaltation. . . .

Think, dear sir, of the world you carry within you, and call this thinking what you will; whether it be remembering your own childhood or yearning toward your own future — only be attentive to that which rises up in you and set it above everything that you observe about you. What goes on in your innermost being is worthy of your whole love; you must somehow keep working at it and not lose too much time and too much courage in clarifying your attitude toward people. Who tells you that you have one anyway? — I know, your profession is hard and full of contradiction of yourself, and I foresaw your complaint and knew that it would come. Now that it has come, I cannot comfort you, I can only advise you to consider whether all professions are not like that, full of demands, full of enmity against the individual, saturated as it were with the hatred of those who have found themselves mute and sullen in a humdrum duty. The situation in which you now have to live is no more heavily laden with conventions, prejudices and mistakes than all the other situations, and if there are some that feign a greater freedom, still there is none that is in itself broad and spacious and in contact with the big things of which real living consists. Only the individual who is solitary is like a thing placed under profound laws, and when he goes out into the morning that is just beginning, or looks out into the evening that is full of happening, and if he feels what is going on there, then all status drops from him as from a dead man, though he stands in the midst of sheer life. What you, dear Mr. Kappus, must now experience as an officer, you would have felt just the same in any of the established professions; yes, even if, outside of any position, you had merely sought some light and independent contact with society, this feeling of constraint would not have been spared you. — It is so everywhere; but that is no reason for fear or sorrow; if there is nothing in common between you and other people, try being close to things, they will not desert you; there are the nights still and the winds that go through the trees and across many lands; among things and with the animals everything is still full of happening, in which you may participate; and children are still the way you were as a child, sad like that and happy, — and if you think of your childhood you live among them again, among the solitary children, and the grownups are nothing, and their dignity has no value....

I believe that almost all our sadnesses are moments of tension that we find paralyzing because we no longer hear our surprised feelings living. Because we are alone with the alien thing that has entered into our self; because everything intimate and accustomed is for an instant taken away; because we stand in the middle of a transition where we cannot remain standing. For this reason the sadness too passes: the new thing in us, the added thing, has entered into our heart, has gone into its inmost chamber and is not even there any more, — is already in our blood. And we do not learn what it was. We could easily be made to believe that nothing has happened, and yet we have changed, as a house changes into which a guest has entered. We cannot say who has come, perhaps we shall never know, but many signs indicate that the future enters into us in this way in order to transform itself in us long before it happens. And this is why it is so important to be lonely and attentive when one is sad: because the apparently uneventful and stark moment at which our future sets foot in us is so much closer to life than that other noisy and fortuitous point of time at which it happens to us as if from outside. The more still, more patient and more open we are when we are sad, so much the deeper and so much the more unswervingly does the new go into us, so much the better do we make it ours, so much the more will it be *our* destiny, and when on some later day it "happens" (that is, steps forth out of us to others), we shall feel in our inmost selves akin and near to it. And that is necessary. It is necessary — and toward this our development will move gradually — that nothing strange should befall us, but only that which has long belonged to us. We have already had to rethink so many of our concepts of motion, we will also gradually learn to realize that that which we call destiny goes forth from within people, not from without into them. Only because so many have not absorbed their destinies and transmuted them within themselves while they were living in them, have they not recognized what has gone forth out of them; it was so strange to them that, in their bewildered fright, they thought it must only just then have entered into them, for they swear never before to have found anything like it in themselves. As people were long mistaken about the motion of the sun, so they are even yet mistaken about the motion of that which is to come. The future stands firm, dear Mr. Kappus, but we move in infinite space.

How should it not be difficult for us?

And to speak of solitude again, it becomes always clearer that this is at bottom not something that one can take or leave. We *are* solitary. We may delude ourselves and act as though this were not so. That is all. But how much better it is to realize that we are so, yes, even to begin by assuming it. We shall indeed turn dizzy then; for all points upon which our eye has been accustomed to rest are taken from us, there is nothing near any more and everything far is infinitely far. A person removed from his own room, almost without preparation and transition, and set upon the height of a great mountain range, would feel something of the sort: an unparalleled insecurity, an abandonment to something inexpressible would almost annihilate him. He would think himself falling or hurled out into space, or exploded into a thousand pieces: what a monstrous lie his brain would have to invent to catch up with and explain the state of his senses! So for him who becomes solitary all distances, all measures change; of these changes many take place suddenly, and then, as with the man on the mountaintop, extraordinary imaginings and singular sensations arise that seem to grow out beyond all bearing. But it is necessary for us to experience *that* too. We must assume our existence as *broadly* as we in any way can; everything, even the unheard-of, must be possible in it. That is at bottom the only courage that is demanded of us: to have courage for the most strange, the most singular and the most inexplicable that we may encounter. That mankind has in this sense been cowardly has done life endless harm; the experiences that are called "visions," the whole so-called "spirit-world," death, all those things that are so closely akin to us, have by daily parrying been so crowded out of life that the senses with which we could have grasped them are atrophied. To say nothing of God. But fear of the inexplicable has not alone impoverished the existence of the individual; the relationship between one human being and another has also been cramped by it, as though it had been lifted out of the riverbed of endless possibilities and set down in a fallow spot on the bank, to which nothing happens. For it is not inertia alone that is responsible for human relationships repeating themselves from case to case, indescribably monotonous and unrenewed; it is shyness before any sort of new, unforeseeable experience with which one does not think oneself able to cope. But only someone who is ready for everything, who excludes nothing, not even the most enigmatical, will live the relation to another as something alive and will himself draw exhaustively from his own existence. For if we think of this existence of the individual as a larger or smaller room, it appears evident that most people learn to know only a corner of their room, a place by the window, a strip of floor on which they walk up and down. Thus they have a certain security. And yet that dangerous insecurity is so much more human which drives the prisoners in Poe's stories to feel out the shapes of their horrible dungeons and not be strangers to the unspeakable terror of their abode. We, however, are not prisoners. No traps or snares are set about us, and there is nothing which should intimidate or worry us. We are set down in life as in the element to which we best correspond, and over and above this we have through thousands of years of accommodation become so like this life, that when we hold still we are, through a happy mimicry, scarcely to be distinguished from all that surrounds us. We have no reason to mistrust our world, for it is not against us. Has it terrors, they are *our* terrors; has it abysses, those abysses belong to us; are dangers at hand, we must try to love them. And if only we arrange our life according to that principle which counsels us that we must always hold to the difficult, then that which now still seems to us the most alien will become what we most trust and find most faithful. How should we be able to forget those ancient myths that are at the beginning of all peoples, the myths about dragons that at the last moment turn into princesses; perhaps all the dragons of our lives are princesses who are only waiting to see us once beautiful and brave. Perhaps everything terrible is in its deepest being something helpless that wants help from us.....

STUDY QUESTIONS

1. *How does Rilke's advice to the young poet compare with Newton's attitude that it is up to the artist to reach a compromise with his public?*

2. *What does Rilke mean by his advice not to seek the answers to questions, but to "love" problems and "live" them? What is the value, for a poet or an artist, in doing this?*

3. *To what aspects of life does Rilke call attention? How do you account for his omission of parts of life that are generally considered important, such as relationships with others, earning a living and being successful?*

4. *What is Rilke's philosophy of insecurity?*

5. *Write a theme summarizing the part of Rilke's ideas that seems most original to you, and tell whether or not this original idea seems to have any value for you.*

6. *Note that Rilke has assured the young poet that he himself is the best source of inspiration for his work and the best judge of it. Has Rilke omitted some of the important considerations an artist must face? Whether your answer to this question is positive or negative, write a theme expressing and explaining your opinion.*

2. ON MUSIC AND PAINTING

Susanne K. Langer The Essence of Music*

W hat, then, is the essence of *all* music? The creation of virtual time,** and
its complete determination by the movement of audible forms. The
devices for establishing this primary illusion of time are many; the recognition of related tones (fundamental and overtones, and by derivation our
entire harmonic system) is the most powerful structural principle that has
ever been employed, if artistic power be judged by the range and expressiveness of the structures to which the principle gives rise; but other musical traditions have used other devices. The drum has been used with wonderful effect
to enthrall the ear, to push away, as it were, the world of practical time, and
create a new time image in sound. In our own music the drum is a subsidiary
element, but there are records of African music in which its constructive
power is paramount.[1] The voice, in such performances, serves essentially to
contrast with the steady tone of the drum — to wander and rise and fall where
the purely rhythmic element goes on like Fate. The effect is neither melody
nor harmony, yet it is music: it has motion and autonomous form, and anyone
familiar with many works of that sort would probably feel their structure
and mood almost from the opening beat.

Another ruling principle of music has been the intonation of speech. If
chant, in its oldest sense, has a protomusical line, that line is not constructed
harmonically, like Schenker's *Urlinie*, but rests on some other principle.

* From *Feeling and Form* by Susanne Langer, copyright, 1953, by Charles Scribner's
Sons. Reprinted by permission of the publisher.

** "Virtual time" is a special term used by Professor Langer to mean the time shaped
and organized by a piece of music. This is not the time of practical experience, but an
abstraction from time as we feel it. A musical work organizes time into forms peculiar
to itself. "Music," explains Professor Langer, "spreads out time for our direct and complete apprehension, by letting our hearing monopolize it. . . . It creates an image of
time measured by the motion of forms that seem to give it substance, yet a substance
that consists entirely of sound . . ." (Editors' note.)

[1] For example, Victor P10-12 (89b), "Secret Society Drums, Bini Tribe" (5 drums).
It is customary among Europeans to call all drum music "primitive"; but this drumming
is not primitive at all—it is highly developed, the sophisticated product of a living
tradition. If such African drumming be compared with the drummed dance accompaniments of European peasants (*L'anthologie sonore*, 16 [a, "Thirteen Century Music";
b, "Fourteenth Century"]), the latter will sound truly "primitive," i.e. undeveloped, by
contrast.

Yet choric chant, no matter what its poetic content, is essentially music. It creates a dynamic form, purely sonorous movement, that metes out its own audible Time even to a person who cannot understand the words, though that person inevitably misses some of the richness of the musical texture. But this is a subject for future discussion. The point at issue here is merely that music is more universal than any one artistic tradition, and the difference between music and noise is not the absence of this or that constructive prin ciple, but of any commanding form whatever. Even noise may happen to furnish musical phenomena; hammers on anvils, rotary saws, dripping faucets are very apt to do so; but real music comes into being only when someone seizes on the motif and uses it, either as a form to be developed, or as an element to be assimilated to a greater form.

The essence of all composition — tonal or atonal, vocal or instrumental, even purely percussive, if you will — is the semblance of *organic* movement, the illusion of an indivisible whole. Vital organization is the frame of all feeling, because feeling exists only in living organisms; and the logic of all symbols that can express feeling is the logic of organic processes. The most characteristic principle of vital activity is rhythm. All life is rhythmic; under difficult circumstances, its rhythms may become very complex, but when they are really lost life cannot long endure. This rhythmic character of organism permeates music, because music is a symbolic presentation of the highest organic response, the emotional life of human beings. A succession of emotions that have no reference to each other do not constitute an "emotional life," any more than a discontinuous and independent functioning of organs collected under one skin would be a physical "life." The great office of music is to organize our conception of feeling into more than an occasional awareness of emotional storm, i.e. to give us an insight into what may truly be called the "life of feeling," or subjective unity of experience; and this it does by the same principle that organizes physical existence into a biological design — rhythm.

There have been countless studies of rhythm, based on the notion of periodicity, or regular recurrence of events. It is true that the elementary rhythmic functions of life have regularly recurrent phases: heartbeat, breath, and the simpler metabolisms. But the obviousness of these repetitions has caused people to regard them as the essence of rhythm, which they are not. The ticking of a clock is repetitious and regular, but not in itself rhythmic; the listening ear hears rhythms *in* the succession of equal ticks, the human mind organizes them into a temporal form.

The essence of rhythm is the preparation of a new event by the ending of a previous one. A person who moves rhythmically need not repeat a single motion exactly. His movements, however, must be complete gestures, so that one can sense a beginning, intent, and consummation, and see in the last stage of one the condition and indeed the rise of another. Rhythm is the setting-up of new tensions by the resolution of former ones. They need not be of equal duration at all; but the situation that begets the new crisis must be inherent in the denouement of its forerunner.

Breathing is the most perfect exhibit of physiological rhythm: as we release the breath we have taken, we build up a bodily need of oxygen that is the motivation, and therefore the real beginning, of the new breath. If the release of one breath is not synchronous with the growth of the need for the next — for instance, if physical exertion exhausts our oxygen faster than we can exhale, so the new need grows imperative before the present breath is completed — breathing is not rhythmic, but gasping.

The heartbeat illustrates the same functional continuity: the diastole prepares the systole, and vice versa. The whole self-repair of living bodies rests on the fact that the exhaustion of a vital process always stimulates a corrective action, which in turn exhausts itself in creating conditions that demand new spending.

The principle of *rhythmic continuity* is the basis of that organic unity which gives permanence to living bodies — a permanence that ... is really a pattern of changes. Now, the so-called "inner life" — our whole subjective reality, woven of thought and emotion, imagination and sense perception — is entirely a vital phenomenon, most developed where the organic unity of the precarious, individual form is most complete and intricate, i.e. in human beings. What we call mind, soul, consciousness, or (in current vocabulary) experience, is an intensified vitality, a sort of distillate of all sensitive, teleological, organized functioning. The human brain, with all its ramifications, is wide open to the world outside, and undergoes profound, more or less permanent changes by impressions that the "older," less variable organs record only by transient responses, the bodily symptoms of emotion. In animals, the intellect is almost as selective as the mouth in what it will receive; and what it does admit is apt to set the entire organism in motion. But the human brain is incomparably more tolerant of impressions, because it has a power of handling stimuli which must not be allowed to affect the total metabolic process deeply at all, on pain of death: that power is the *symbolic transformation* of perceptions.

Where the symbolic process is highly developed it practically takes over the domain of perception and memory, and puts its stamp on all mental functions. But even in its highest operations, the mind still follows the organic rhythm which is the source of vital unity: the building-up of a new dynamic *Gestalt* in the very process of a former one's passing away.

There are such genuine rhythms in inorganic nature, too; rhythm is the basis of life, but not limited to life. The swing of a pendulum is rhythmic, without our organizing interpretation (which is what makes a mere succession of sounds — all we perceive in listening to a watch, for instance — rhythmic for us). The kinetic force that drives the pendulum to the height of its swing builds up the potential that will bring it down again; the spending of kinetic energy prepares the turning point and the fall. The gradual decrease

of the pendulum's arc due to friction is not usually visible in direct observation, so the motions seem exactly repetitious. A bouncing ball, on the other
hand, shows rhythmic performance without equal measure. But the most
impressive example of rhythm known to most people is the breaking of waves
in a steady surf. Each new comber rolling in is shaped by the undertow flowing back, and in its turn actually hurries the recession of the previous wave by
suction. There is no dividing line between the two events. Yet a breaking
wave is as definite an event as one could wish to find — a true dynamic
Gestalt.

Such phenomena in the inanimate world are powerful *symbols* of living
form, just because they are not life processes themselves. The contrast between the apparently vital behavior and the obviously inorganic structure of
ocean waves, for instance, emphasizes the pure semblance of life, and makes
the first abstractions of its rhythm for our intellectual intuition. That is the
prime function of symbols. Their second function is to allow us to manipulate
the concepts we have achieved. This requires more than a recognition of what
may be termed "natural symbols"; it demands the deliberate making of expressive forms that may be deployed in various ways to reveal new meanings.
And such created *Gestalten,* that give us logical insight into feeling, vitality
and emotional life, are works of art.

The commanding form of a piece of music contains its basic rhythm,
which is at once the source of its organic unity and its total feeling. The
concept of rhythm as a relation between tensions rather than as a matter of
equal divisions of time (i.e. meter) makes it quite comprehensible that
harmonic progressions, resolutions of dissonances, directions of "running"
passages, and "tendency tones" in melody all serve as rhythmic agents. Everything that prepares a future creates rhythm; everything that begets or intensifies expectation, including the expectation of sheer continuity, prepares the
future (regular "beats" are an obvious and important source of rhythmic
organization); and everything that fulfills the promised future, in ways foreseen or unforeseen, articulates the symbol of feeling. Whatever the special
mood of the piece, or its emotional import, the vital rhythm of subjective
time (the "lived" time that Bergson adjures us to find in pure experience)
permeates the complex, many-dimensional, musical symbol as its internal
logic, which relates music intimately and self-evidently to life.

And what about repetition of forms, equal divisions, if recurrence is not
the real basis of rhythm? What is the function of the countless regularities
of accent, phrase, figure, and bar in the greatest masterpieces?

Repetition is another structural principle — deeply involved with rhythm,
as all basic principles are with each other — that gives musical composition
the appearance of vital growth. For what we receive, in the passage of sound,
with a sense of recognition, i.e. as a recurrence, is oftentimes a fairly free
variant of what came before, a mere analogy, and only logically a repetition;
but it is just the sort of play on a basic pattern, especially the reflection of
the over-all plan in the structure of each part, that is characteristic of organic

forms. This is Schenker's principle of "diminution,"[2] Roger Sessions' "principle of association."[3] The fullest recognition of its "vitalizing" function that I know is in the article by Basil de Selincourt from which I have already had occasion to quote at length, and I cannot refrain from letting the author of that masterly little essay speak again:

"Repetition begins with the bar, and continues in the melody and in every phrase or item into which we can resolve it. The growth of a musical composition may be compared to that of a flowering plant, ... where not only the leaves repeat each other, but the leaves repeat the flowers, and the very stems and branches are like un-folded leaves. ... To the pattern of the flower there corresponds a further pattern developed in the placing and grouping of flowers along the branches, and the branches themselves divide and stand out in balanced proportions, under the controlling vital impulse. ... Musical expression follows the same law."[4]

As soon as a musical idea acquires organic character (no matter by what device this is achieved), it expresses the autonomous form of a *work*, the "commanding form" that controls its entire subsequent development. It is the comprehension of this organic unity and individuality that enables a composer to carry out a protracted piece of work on the strength of one initial "inspiration," and make the product more and more integral, instead of less and less so, by the constant importation of new ideas — sometimes even themes that occurred to him long ago, developments he has used elsewhere, traditional preparations — all to be assimilated and transfigured by the unique composition. As long as he can keep the musical organism alive in his imagination he needs no other rule or goal.

There are countless references in musicological literature and among the utterances of great musicians that bear witness to the central importance of living form, the semblance of spontaneous movement, in music; one could quote almost at random from Marpurg, Goddard, Tovey, Schweitzer, Schenker, Lussy, or from the notes and letters of Mozart, Chopin, Mendelssohn, Brahms — anyone, almost, who has written seriously and knowingly about music at all. One is forcibly reminded of the insistent note of vitalism, the universal agreement on the organic quality of all space composition, that runs through the comments of the masters of visual art, collected at the close of Chapter 5; and it would be hard, indeed, not to entertain at least the hypothesis that all art works, no matter in what special domain, are "organic" in the same sense. But let us be content with the hypothesis, until the proof takes care of itself; and without prematurely generalizing musical form, study it further.

Perhaps the most striking thing about it is the *objective* character already mentioned. Once a matrix of musical thought, a "commanding form," has been grasped by one's artistic imagination, it assumes a peculiarly impersonal

[2] See especially *Das Meisterwerk in der Musik, passim*.
[3] *Op. cit.*, pp. 129 ff.
[4] "Music and Duration," p. 288.

status, like an impression from outside, something "given." Great musicians have spoken of the musical "Idea" with an unmistakable feeling of moral obligation toward it, a sense of responsibility for its development and perfection. Thus Mendelssohn wrote to his friend Ferdinand Hiller, a gifted but superficial composer: "Nothing seems to me more reprehensible than to carp at a man's natural endowments ... but if it be that, as here in your piece, all the themes, all that depends on talent or inspiration (call it what you will) is good and beautiful and moving, but the workmanship is not good, then, I think, one has no right to let it pass.... As I believe that a man of great capacities is duty-bound to become an excellent person, and is to be blamed if he does not develop to the full the powers he has been given, so, I maintain, it is with a piece of music.... I am quite aware that no musician can make his ideas and his talents other than what heaven has sent him; but just as surely do I know that if heaven has sent him great ideas he is bound to carry them out properly. Don't try to tell me ... that your work is as good as your compositions are!" [5]

An even clearer statement, however, is Beethoven's, if we may trust Bettina Brentano's report to Goethe, which she assured him, on the strength of her extraordinary memory, was very nearly verbatim: "It takes spiritual [geistigen] rhythm to grasp music in its essence.... All genuine [musical] invention is moral progress. To submit to its inscrutable laws, and by virtue of these laws, to overcome and control one's own mind, so it shall set forth the revelation: that is the isolating principle of art....

"Thus every true creation of art is independent, mightier than the artist himself.... Music gives the mind a relation to the [total] harmony. Any single, separate idea has in it the feeling of the harmony, which is Unity." [6]

I stress this objectivity and potency of the commanding form in a piece of music so heavily because I believe it is the key to almost all the moot problems of performance, understanding, adaptation, and even that dry old bone of contention, self-expression. From the matrix, the greatest movement, flows the life of the work, with all its contingencies, its powers and perils in the community of human minds.

STUDY QUESTIONS

1. *According to the author, what is the difference between noise that gives musical effects and true music?*

2. *The idea presented here, that a work of art takes on the qualities of a living organism and achieves a kind of "life," is a favorite one among philosophers and artists. What resemblances does Langer point out between a piece of music and an organism? In what important ways would you say they were different?*

3. *Read carefully the rather difficult explanation of the nature of symbols. How*

[5] *Meisterbriefe*, II: "Felix Mendelssohn-Bartholdy," edited by Ernst Wolff. See pp. 128-129.

[6] Ludwig van Beethoven, *Briefe und Gespräche*, p. 146.

do such rhythmic but non-living phenomena as a bouncing ball or waves on
a beach act as symbols? In what way is their resemblance to life valuable or
useful?

4. What does the author mean by the "matrix" or "commanding form"? What
function does it perform in the mind of the composer?

5. This essay shows how music makes use of one of the important aspects of life,
rhythm. Write an essay showing how some other art with which you are
familiar makes use of an aspect of life. Good possibilities here are painting,
architecture, literature and dancing.

6. Probably one of the most difficult tasks a writer can try is that of expressing
his reactions to a work of art. Nevertheless, it is often an interesting exercise,
and can give surprising results. Take some specific work of art which has had
an effect on you, and describe your reaction to it. Among the things you may
want to mention are: a description of the work, the emotions you feel, the
things about the work that arouse these emotions, and any associations the
work has for you.

Charles Baudelaire   Imagination and Painting*

In recent years we have heard it said in a thousand different ways: "Copy
nature; only copy nature. There is no greater delight, no finer triumph
than an excellent copy of nature." And this doctrine, the enemy of art,
was to be applied not only to painting, but to all the arts, even the novel,
even poetry. To these doctrinaires, so satisfied with Nature, a man of
imagination would certainly have had the right to reply: "I find it worthless
and tedious to imitate that which *is*, because nothing that *is* satisfies me.
Nature is ugly, and I prefer the monsters of my fancy to trivial reality."
Yet, it would have been more philosophical to ask them first if they were so
certain of the existence of external nature, or, if this question might seem
calculated to invite their sarcasm, if they were so sure they understood *all*
of nature, all that is contained in nature. A "yes" would have been the most
arrogant and extravagant of answers. So far as I have been able to understand these singular and degrading contradictions, the doctrine meant — at
any rate, I do it the honor of believing that it meant — the artist, the true
artist, the true poet ought to record only what he sees and feels. He ought
to be *really* faithful to his own nature. He ought to avoid like death borrow-
ing the eyes or emotions of another man, however great he be; for thus
the productions that he would give us would be, relative to himself, lies
and not realities. But, if the pedants of whom I speak (there is pedantry
even in the mean-spirited) and who have representatives everywhere (for
their theory flatters both incapacity and laziness) do not wish the matter

* From *Curiosités Esthétiques* by Charles Baudelaire. Translated for this anthology by
David Gordon.

to be understood thus, let us believe simply that they want to say: "We do not have imagination and we decree that no one should have any."

How mysterious a faculty is this Queen of the faculties! It touches all the others; it rouses them; it sends them into combat. It resembles them sometimes to the point of being confused with them; yet it is always itself, and the men that it does not stimulate are easily recognizable by some strange curse which withers their productions like the Biblical fig-tree.

It is analysis, it is synthesis; yet only some of those men who are apt in taking things apart and putting them together are gifted with imagination. So it is that, yet not entirely that. It is sensitivity, yet only some sensitive persons, too sensitive perhaps, are gifted with it. It is the imagination which has taught man the moral significance of color and contour, of sound and scent. It created, at the beginning of the world, analogy and metaphor. It decomposes all of creation and, reassembling and ordering the material according to laws whose origins can be discovered only in the depths of the soul, it creates a new world; it produces the sensation of the new. Because it has created the world (one can say this, I think, even in a religious sense) it is fitting that it governs it. What would we say of a warrior without imagination? That he may be an excellent soldier, but, if he is put in command of armies, he will not make conquests. The case can be compared to that of a poet or a novelist who takes away the command of the faculties from the imagination in order to give it, for example, to his knowledge of languages or his observation of facts. What would we say of a diplomat without imagination? That he may be very familiar with the past history of treaties and alliances but he will not be able to sense what treaties or alliances are contained in the future. Of a scholar without imagination? He may have learned all that can be learned from instruction, but he will not discover any laws which have not yet been imagined. The imagination is the queen of the truth, and the possible is one of the provinces of truth. It is married to the infinite.

Without imagination, all the faculties, however strong or penetrating they may be, are as if they did not exist, whereas weakness of secondary faculties when they are stimulated by a vigorous imagination is only a secondary misfortune. None of them can do without it, but it can make up for lack in them. Often, what our other faculties seek for and find only after repeated attempts, using various methods ill-adapted to the nature of things, the imagination can proudly and simply intuit. And finally it plays a powerful role even in morality; for let me ask what is virtue without imagination? You might as well say virtue without pity, virtue without heaven; something hard, cruel and sterilizing which in certain countries has become bigotry, in others protestantism.

In spite of all the magnificent prerogatives which I have assigned to the imagination, I will not insult your readers by explaining to them that the better it is assisted, the more powerful it is, and that nothing is more potent in battle with the ideal than a fine imagination with an immense armory of observations at its disposal. Nevertheless, to return to what I was saying a moment ago concerning its prerogative to make up for deficiency, which the imagination owes to its divine origin, I wish to cite you an example, a little example, which I hope you will not scorn. Do you think that the author of *Antony*, of *Comte Hermann*, of *Monte-Cristo* was a scholar? No, you would say. Do you think he was steeped in the practice of the arts and had made a patient study of them? No, again. That would even be, I believe, antipathetic to his nature. He is an example, then, which proves that the imagination even when unassisted by practice and a knowledge of technical terms, cannot produce nonsense in a matter which, for the most part, is of its own making. Recently I was riding in a train and was thinking about the article that I am now writing; I was thinking especially of the singular reversal of values which has permitted (in a century, to be sure, in which for the chastisement of man, everything has been permitted him) the disdain of the most honorable and valuable of the moral faculties. Then I noticed lying along a nearby cushion a stray issue of the *Indépendance Belge*. In it Alexander Dumas had undertaken this year's account of the works in the Salon. The circumstance caught my attention. You can guess my delight when I discovered my reflections amply verified by an example furnished me by chance. That this man who seems to represent universal vitality should praise an epoch which was full of life; that the creator of the romantic drama should sing (in a tone which, I assure you, did not lack grandeur) of the happy time in which alongside the new school of literature flourished a new school of painting — Delacroix, the Devéria brothers, Boulanger, Poterlet, Bonnington, etc. — a fine cause for surprise, you will say! That is just what you would expect. *Laudator temporis acti.* But that he should praise Delacroix sensitively, that he should explain clearly the nature of his opponents' madness, that he should go ever further and show in what ways the most famous of recent painters were deficient; that he, Alexander Dumas, so reckless and fluent, should demonstrate so well, for example, that Troyon did not have genius and lacked even the ability to simulate genius — tell me, my good friend, do you find that so simple? All this, of course, was written in that informal dramatic style which he has gradually adopted in talking to his innumerable audience; nevertheless, what grace and quickness in the expression of the truth! You have anticipated my conclusion: if Alexander Dumas, who is not a scholar, did not fortunately possess a rich imagination, he would have written only nonsense; he has written intelligently and effectively because... (one must conclude) because the imagination, thanks to its comprehensive nature, contains the spirit of criticism....

THE RULE OF THE IMAGINATION

Yesterday evening, after having sent you the last pages of my letter in which I had written, but not without a certain scruple: "Because it is

imagination which has created the world, it is imagination which rules it,"
I was leafing through the *Night Side of Nature* and my eyes fell on these
lines which I cite only because they are a corroborating paraphrase of the
statement that bothered me.

> By imagination, I do not simply mean to convey the common notion
> implied by that much abused word, which is only fancy, but the constructive
> imagination, which is a much higher function and which, in as much as man
> is made in the likeness of God, bears a distant relation to that sublime
> power by which the Creator projects, creates, and upholds his universe.

I am not at all ashamed but on the contrary very happy to coincide on this
point with the excellent Madame Crowe whom I have always admired and
envied for her capacity for *belief*, which is as developed in her as that of
doubt is in others.

I was saying that a long time ago I had heard a man truly wise and
learned in his art expressing on this subject the grandest and yet the
simplest ideas. When I saw him for the first time, I had no further experience than that granted by a consuming love and no other basis for reasoning
than instinct. It is true that this love and this instinct were rather strong; for
in early youth my eyes had never been able to drink their fill of painted
or sculpted images, and I felt that worlds would end, *impavidum ferient*,
before I would become an iconoclast. Evidently he wanted to be indulgent
and obliging, for we chatted right away about commonplaces, that is to say,
about the grandest and profoundest questions. About nature, for example.
"Nature is only a dictionary," he repeated frequently. To really understand
the scope of meaning implied in this phrase, one must consider the numerous,
ordinary uses of the dictionary. In it one seeks the meaning of words, their
genealogy and their etymology; in short, one extracts from it all the elements
which make up a sentence or a narrative; but no one has ever considered the
dictionary a composition in the poetic sense of the world. Painters who obey
the imagination seek in their dictionary the elements which fit their conception and, in adjusting them with a certain art, give them an entirely
new appearance. Those who do not have imagination copy the dictionary.
From that practice results a great vice, the vice of banality to which those
painters are particularly prone who work more closely with external nature,
for example, landscape painters, who generally consider it a triumph not
to show their personality. Preoccupied with observing, they forget to feel
and think.

For this great painter, however, all the elements of art, of which one
man takes this, another that as the most important, were — I should say
are — only the humble servants of a unique and superior faculty.

If a very neat execution is called for, it is in order that the language of
dream may be very neatly translated; if it should be very rapid, that is lest
anything be lost of the extraordinary vividness which accompanied the conception; if the attention of the artist should extend even to the material

cleanliness of his tools, that is easily understandable, seeing that every pre-caution must be taken to render his execution both deft and exact.

With such a method, which is essentially logical, all the figures, their relative disposition on the canvas, the landscape or interior which provides them with horizon or background, their garments — all, in short, ought to serve to illuminate the generating idea, and to wear its original color, its livery, so to speak. Even as a dream inhabits an atmosphere that is appro-priate to it, so a conception which has become a composition needs to move in a setting colored to fit it particularly. Clearly, a particular color is given to that part of a picture which becomes the key and which governs the others. Everyone knows that yellow, orange, and red inspire and express ideas of joy, riches, glory and love; but there are thousands of yellow or red atmospheres and all other colors will be affected naturally and to a pro-portionate degree by the dominant atmosphere. The art of the colorist evidently resembles in certain ways that of mathematics and music. Yet its most delicate operations are done by a certain feeling to which long exercise has given an absolute sureness. One sees that this grand law of overall harmony condemns much of the brilliant or crude color even in the work of the most illustrious painters. There are paintings of Rubens which not only make one think of a colored firework but even of several fireworks set off at one place. The larger a picture is, the broader must be its color strokes — that goes without saying — but it is well that they not be materially fused; they will fuse naturally at a distance determined by the law of sympathy which has brought them together. The color thus achieves more energy and freshness.

A good picture, faithful and equal to the dream which gave it birth, should be brought into being like a world. Just as the creation which we see is the result of several creations in which the preceding ones are ever completed by the following, so a picture harmoniously designed consists of a series of superimposed pictures, each new layer giving to the dream more reality and raising it a degree toward perfection. An entirely contrary pro-cedure I remember having seen followed in the studios of Paul Delaroche and Horace Vernet where there were large pictures, not sketched but actually begun, that is to say absolutely finished in certain parts while certain others were still only indicated in black or white outline. One could compare this kind of work to a purely manual labor — so much space to be covered in a given time — or to a long road divided into a number of stages. When one stage is covered, it is finished with, and when the whole road is trav-elled, the artist is delivered of his picture.

All of these rules are obviously more or less modifiable by the varying temperaments of artists. However, I am convinced that what I have de-scribed is the surest method for men of rich imagination. Consequently, too great divergences from the method in question testify to an abnormal and undue importance given to a secondary aspect of art. I am not afraid of the possible objection that it is absurd to suppose a like education fit for a crowd of different individuals. For it is evident that systems of rhetoric and prosody are not arbitrarily invented tyrannies, but a collection of rules required by the very constitution of the spiritual being. And never have systems of prosody and rhetoric prevented originality from clearly emerging. The contrary, namely that they have assisted the birth of originality, would be infinitely truer.

To be brief, I am obliged to omit a host of corollaries following from my principal formula, in which is contained, so to speak, the entire formulary of a true esthetic and which can be expressed thus: The whole visible universe is only a storehouse of images and signs to which the imagination assigns a relative place and value; it is a kind of fodder which the imagination must digest and transform. All the faculties of the human soul ought to be subordinated to the imagination, which puts them in requisition all at once. As a good knowledge of the dictionary does not necessarily imply a knowledge of the art of composition, and as the art of composition does not itself imply universal imagination, so a good painter need not be a great painter. But a great painter is of necessity a good painter, because universal imagination contains the understanding of all means of expression and the desire to acquire them.

As a result of the ideas which I have just elucidated as well as I could (so much remains to be said particularly concerning the concordant aspects of all the arts and the resemblances in their methods!), it is clear that the vast family of artists — that is to say men who are dedicated to artistic expression — can be divided into two distinct camps. There is one which calls itself *realist,* a word of double meaning, the sense of which is not well-determined, and which we will call, the better to characterize its error, *positivist.* This says: "I wish to represent things such as they are, or rather, as they would be, supposing that I did not exist." In other words, the universe without man. And the other, the *imaginative,* says: "I wish to illuminate things with my mind and to project their reflection upon other minds." Although these two absolutely contrary methods can magnify or diminish all subjects, from a religious scene to a modest landscape, nevertheless the man of imagination has generally tended to express himself in religious paintings and in fantasy, while landscape and the type of painting called "genre" would appear to offer enormous opportunities to minds which are lazy and sluggish.

Besides the imaginative and the self-styled realist, there is a third class of painters who are timid and servile and put all their pride into obeying a code of false dignity. Whereas the realists believe in representing nature, and the men of imagination wish to paint their own souls, this class conforms to a purely conventional set of rules, entirely arbitrary rules, not derived from the human soul but simply imposed by the procedure of a celebrated studio. In this very numerous but very uninteresting class are found the false amateurs of the antique, the false amateurs of style — in a word, all those men who, by their incapacity, have elevated triteness to the honors of a style.

STUDY QUESTIONS

1. *In what respect does Baudelaire agree with Rilke? What part of Spender's account of his development as a poet is a discovery of the value of Baudelaire's doctrine that the imagination must prevail?*
2. *Is there any evidence in the article on perception by Ittelson and Kilpatrick which supports Baudelaire's statement that the imagination creates a new world unlike the actual one? Reread the selections in the first part of this anthology by Herbert Read, Steinbeck and Ricketts, and Daiches. What relation do you find between these essays and Baudelaire's concept of the imagination?*
3. *What is Baudelaire trying to show in the example involving Alexander Dumas? Is his argument here really a sound one?*
4. *What is Baudelaire's objection to the partly finished paintings he saw in the artists' studios?*
5. *Does Baudelaire's idea that a painting should be primarily devoted to expressing the idea in which it originated, help to explain why so much modern painting is "non-representational" and does not even attempt to achieve a resemblance to the objects it is supposed to picture? If you see a connection, explain it, using at least one painting or syle of painting as an example.*
6. *Write a theme about a painting you did or did not like, giving the reader a clear impression of the painting itself and explaining the reasons for your opinion of it.*

Richard Neutra Utility and Beauty*

If a hotel is built with the help of labor-saving devices, the resulting economy will, of course, be reflected in the price charged for a room. But financial considerations cannot fully account for the satisfaction of watching such devices in operation. A similar economy could be achieved by the use of cheap labor and backbreaking working methods, such as were customary, for instance, in colonial metropolises like Shanghai.

Mere financial considerations are beside the point in question. The way a thing is produced seems to matter a great deal in our evaluation of the result, even though we ourselves may not be the exploited slaves, or foot the bill. But in its psychological effect upon us or in its aesthetic appeal the

* From *Survival Through Design* by Richard Neutra. © 1954, by Oxford University Press, Inc. Reprinted by permission.

ultimate product is not independent of an implicit interpretation of the processes that brought it about.

As to pure form, there is great similarity between the scroll of an Ionic column, carved in limestone, and the spiral of a thin steel spring which, because of its material characteristics, perfectly and speedily rolls up by itself. The two spiralic lines may be equal, but the formative process automatically contributes different psychological accents to each of these products, and the distinction is felt by the beholder.

Aesthetic gratification, seemingly concerned with form in space only, deals with implications of development in time, unless this form is lifted out of practical context for the sake of simplified theory.

We seem physiologically made to see things always in a genetic time perspective. Moreover, we unconsciously look at things as if they had been produced by a human maker; we tend to sense at work a creative being with nervous equipment and behavior similar to those of man. This naïve, anthropomorphic attitude is natural. It, too, is physiologically determined, because any creative experiences that we can possibly have ourselves are correlated with our own nervous reactions, such as accompany our labors to produce a thing.

Viewing hand-formed pottery, or the lines of a draftsman, or the lettering of a calligraphist, we unconsciously identify ourselves with their makers: We seem to follow vicariously the imagined muscular exertion in the nervous experience of the craftsman, as if experiencing it ourselves. In the same way, our tongue is slightly innervated when we only think of a word; our muscles tighten while we watch a wrestler or a tightrope walker, however comfortably we ourselves may be seated. Our emphatic experience of the pains of creation, unconsciously inferred when we look at a product, may add or detract, heighten or reduce, our enjoyment of it.

Precision — that is, minimum deviation from the theoretical aim — has at all times been a major human aspiration; in fact, as we shall see, it has been considered the object of a basic urge. For thousands of years, precision of production could be achieved only by laborious methods. Our attitude toward precision has thus been closely linked to the idea of a slow, long and painstaking process, and, as already noted, the quality of precise workmanship has in turn become associated with the characteristic of rarity, sometimes even of uniqueness.

The Chinese emperor would send for a famous craftsman in a distant province, and give him unlimited time to produce a lacquer bowl with twenty coats, smoothly ground, or a handkerchief of exquisitely spun and woven silk, or a miracle of ceramic glaze. This work, and the craftsmanship required to produce it, would become a legend for millions. Such admiring appraisal goes far back to primitive society.

The Stone Age collection of the anthropological laboratory at Santa Fe,

New Mexico, contains specimens of amazingly perfect rotational pottery, made without a turning wheel, a contraption that originated in a later period. The ideal of perfect shape and texture was present in human hearts much earlier. It corresponded to a need of the nervous system which existed long before tools were invented to satisfy it. In fact, the ambition for perfect form, or the nervous pressure toward it, must have led to the invention of the potter's wheel. Yet, today, in the bazaars of Santa Fe, tourists are offered artificially misshaped, bumped-up pottery as charmingly primitive souvenirs. The truth is that perfect roundness was a perhaps rare but well-recognized desideratum even in the most ancient pueblo.

With the coming of machines, however, the concept of quality has undergone a profound change, as far as our nervous responses are concerned. The productive processes have often become puzzling, and we can no longer vicariously share in them. The formative background, the genetic perspective, is now blurred and clouded. This is like traveling in an unfamiliar country. If all empathy has its original precedent in reading facial expressions and thus experiencing the motives behind them, this ability seems to fail us when we are among the natives of an utterly strange place. Our customary clues no longer fit. Precision in workmanship meant one thing when the work was done by craftsmen; it means another when it is inhuman, done by strange machines.

Mechanical precision was initiated in the munitions industry, which was also one of the first to use mass-production methods. Munitions must be produced in enormous quantities, since consumption here frequently approaches the level of complete waste, even from a military point of view. The exact fitting of projectiles to gun barrels required great mechanical precision in the shop and made operation on the battlefield more foolproof. This precision was later extended for similar reasons to other mass manufacturers. Automobile production is perhaps the most striking example.

But here another important factor had to be taken into account. Although the motor car was made as foolproof as possible to allow for careless and wasteful handling by drivers ignorant of mechanical exigencies, unavoidable repairs on the road had to be foreseen and facilitated. This problem was solved by the interchangeability of parts. Worn-out pieces of the engine can be easily replaced by substitute parts, which are stocked in thousands of far-flung depots. The necessary repairs are made without hand-fitting and without too much dependence on the worker's skill. The new part cannot easily be misplaced even by a poorly trained mechanic, or despite fidgety human nerves.

In order to achieve interchangeability of parts, the highest degree of accuracy became imperative in the production of good automobiles, and only the minutest dimensional deviations from the norm could be tolerated. As early as the 1920's, the margin of error in the production of some cars could not exceed: 1/1000 of an inch for 5000 processes; 1/2000 of an inch for 1200 processes; 1/4000 of an inch for 300 processes; and 1/10,000 of an inch in bearing balls.

All this precise workmanship was marshaled to produce not a refractor for astronomical use, but a common, almost ubiquitous article. The concept of rarity or uniqueness is as foreign to this new type of precision as it is to this new type of quality. The entire issue grew into a matter of broad popular impressiveness; it thoroughly re-educated us and reconditioned our attitudes. Precision, formerly a luxury, has turned into a prerequisite for economical production and maintenance, because the possible market, the scope of consumption, depends on it.

As precision became commonplace in an industrialized civilization, however, it inevitably lost much of its charm and mysterious prestige. Those uniquely balanced innervations in a master craftsman were here no longer required, nor could they be admiringly re-experienced by the consumer.

It was within the very historical decades which produced machine precision that precision itself lost face and was arbitrarily abandoned for "beauty's" sake. Precision was discredited; it seemed vulgar, and was combated by various romantic antidotes. For instance, contrivances such as *Jazz-plaster,* or picturesque false ceiling beams, crudely surfaced, began to infest American domestic architecture. This was also the time when wheel-turned pottery was kinked out of shape just to make it look primitive. Precision was equated with coldness, imperfection with warmth; exactness of detail was discarded, and haphazard "rustic" forms were introduced by the speculative psychologists of the real-estate market.

Moreover, these introductions proved to be cheap, wherever lingering remnants of neat handicraft could be abandoned. While formerly a plasterer had to serve a long, exacting apprenticeship, now — especially in a temperate climate like that of California — any laborer seemed capable of doing a plasterer's job quickly and, of course, for less. While in bygone days paint had to be applied with skill in flawlessly uniform coats and tones, now wild irregularities and accidental discolorations became an asset of the Hollywood bungalow.

It is true that the machine has ruined handicraft. This, however, did not come about because, as Ruskin and Morris sadly noted, the first machine products were crude and primitive, but rather because the machine soon proved superior in precision, the quality that craftsmen had proudly regarded as their prerogative for thousands of years and that had inspired consumers with awe. The machine introduced an entirely new psychology of precision, by changing and sometimes directly reversing, the accents. Thanks to it, irregular, imprecise forms have become unusual, and almost morbidly attractive.

In abstract aesthetics, the method of producing an object may possibly be ignored as a factor of evaluation. But the practical situation and the daily workings of our brain are never so purely one-track. Whenever we are confronted by a product, our attitude toward it is more or less consciously motivated first by considerations of performance and consumption. How is the form of the object related to the manner in which it operates? Is there any obnoxious discrepancy between appearance and immediate function? Secondly, considerations enter concerning the genesis of this form. How was it produced? How did it grow and reach this particular materialization? How far is the consumer able to follow? Can he at least vicariously, nervously, empathically share in the production process?

The first group of questions is concerned with functional significance, and the second with the "constructivistic" background, with constructive procedures, sensed behind the appearance. Any appraisal of design, then, has these two vital aspects: the constructivistic — how is it made? how can it be fabricated? — and the functionalistic — how will it operate and be used?

Also, the concrete beauty of an organism, say a plant, is not understood as just a static non-operational phenomenon, looming in space. Here, too, a dynamic time perspective is indispensable and unavoidable. In our minds, beauty is related, on the one hand, to the process by which this organism seems to have grown to its present state and, on the other, to the manner in which it will function to fulfill its obvious biological requirements. Much of this can be intuitively perceived without analytical knowledge, and even erroneous judging does not alter the principle. If we look at a pine tree bent by the wind on a coastal bluff, the concept of it does not remain within the bounds of mere *sensual impressionism*. The fused conductive structure of our own mental-nervous apparatus, its rich operation as an integrated whole, makes this impossible.

Sensory perception merely ushers in an automatic process of higher brain activity. The entire associative machinery of the mind is bound to be set in motion. From beginning to end our emotions are co-activated. We feel in a flash those struggles our tree has had with storms. The genetic past, the present function in relation to external forces, the telling expression of *functional preparedness* — the tree bracing itself in the direction of prevailing winds — all this is hardly separable from what we look upon as the form and beauty of a grown tree. Any doctrinaire division of the total concept into the aesthetic and the non-aesthetic aspect would be artificial and cloud rather than clear the insight into this truly unified phenomenon. No such division is possible from a physiological point of view; and no other view, we feel, could be valid today.

In animals, or in human beings who are underdeveloped or who have regressed, the activity of the higher brain centers is limited, associations are of lesser scope. But it is absurd to reduce aesthetics for normal human beings to the level of animals or morons.

We shall consider the undoubtedly existing primitive aesthetic comfort of birds and insects equipped with exquisite sense apparatus. But there can be no doubt that the human nervous equipment, through the associative powers of the forebrain, has developed incomparably more differentiated demands and solutions.

It is an unfortunate roaming of theory that favors a separation, even an antithesis, of beauty and utility, and places an accent of additive extravagance and uselessness on the first of this pair. Once such a contrast has been established, the self-respecting adult, the practical man, cannot but vote for "utility first," with perhaps a few occasional self-conscious concessions to "beauty" second.

An artificial, abrupt contrast has been set up where, by nature, oneness and an uninterrupted continuum are true to fact. Where does the utility of a tree stop and its beauty start? Our dualism has dangerously harmed, not helped, an understanding of design and of the architecture of a well-integrated environment. The direct result is that harmful turmoil we know so well, that disintegration conspicuously spreading and sprawling around us in so-called civilized areas which are biologically blighted.

STUDY QUESTIONS

1. *What does Neutra mean by "the genetic time perspective" which is one of the sources of satisfaction in art?*

2. *How does Neutra explain the paradox that machine production has put a premium on irregularity of form?*

3. *What are the two considerations that, according to Neutra, operate when we observe an object? Do you agree with Neutra? Discuss this with reference to your own experience.*

4. *Compare Neutra's observations about the feelings aroused by the pine tree with Langer's statement about the importance of "vital organization" in musical composition.*

5. *Take some familiar object—a screwdriver, a pair of scissors, a can opener, a fountain pen, a lamp—and discuss its functional qualities. How well is it designed to perform its function? Would any changes in its design be desirable?*

6. *Does Neutra's discussion explain why the design of buildings has a psychological effect on people? Does it suggest principles which should be followed in designing or furnishing a home?*

3. PROSE, POETRY, AND DRAMA

Arnold Bennett On Literary Taste*

THE AIM

At the beginning a misconception must be removed from the path. Many people, if not most, look on literary taste as an elegant accomplishment, by acquiring which they will complete themselves, and make themselves finally fit as members of a correct society. They are secretly ashamed of their ignorance of literature, in the same way as they would be ashamed of their ignorance of etiquette at a high entertainment, or of their inability to ride a horse if suddenly called upon to do so. There are certain things that a man ought to know, or to know about, and literature is one of them: such is their idea. They have learnt to dress themselves with propriety, and to behave with propriety on all occasions; they are fairly "up" in the questions of the day; by industry and enterprise they are succeeding in their vocations; it behooves them, then, not to forget that an acquaintance with literature is an indispensable part of a self-respecting man's personal baggage. Painting doesn't matter; music doesn't matter very much. But "everyone is supposed to know" about literature. Then, literature is such a charming distraction! Literary taste thus serves two purposes: as a certificate of correct culture and as a private pastime. A young professor of mathematics, immense at mathematics and games, dangerous at chess, capable of Haydn on the violin, once said to me, after listening to some chat on books, "Yes, I must take up literature." As though saying: "I was rather forgetting literature. However, I've polished off all these other things. I'll have a shy at literature now."

This attitude, or any attitude which resembles it, is wrong. To him who really comprehends what literature is, and what the function of literature is, this attitude is simply ludicrous. It is also fatal to the formation of literary taste. People who regard literary taste simply as an accomplishment, and literature simply as a distraction, will never truly succeed either in acquiring the accomplishment or in using it half-acquired as a distraction; though the one is the most perfect of distractions, and though the other is unsurpassed by any other accomplishment in elegance or in power to impress the universal snobbery of civilised mankind. Literature, instead of being an accessory,

* From *Literary Taste* by Arnold Bennett. Copyright, 1927, by Doubleday and Co., Inc. Reprinted by permission of the publishers, the Trustee for the Bennett Estate, and Jonathan Cape, Ltd.

is the fundamental *sine qua non* of complete living. I am extremely anxious to avoid rhetorical exaggerations. I do not think I am guilty of one in asserting that he who has not been "presented to the freedom" of literature has not wakened up out of his prenatal sleep. He is merely not born. He can't see; he can't hear; he can't feel, in any full sense. He can only eat his dinner. What more than anything else annoys people who know the true function of literature, and have profited thereby, is the spectacle of so many thousands of individuals going about under the delusion that they are alive, when, as a fact, they are no nearer being alive than a bear in winter.

I will tell you what literature is! No — I only wish I could. But I can't. No one can. Gleams can be thrown on the secret, inklings given, but no more. I will try to give you an inkling. And, to do so, I will take you back into your own history, or forward into it. That evening when you went for a walk with your faithful friend, the friend from whom you hid nothing — or almost nothing...! You were, in truth, somewhat inclined to hide from him the particular matter which monopolized your mind that evening, but somehow you contrived to get on to it, drawn by an overpowering fascination. And as your faithful friend was sympathetic and discreet, and flattered you by a respectful curiosity, you proceeded further and further into the said matter, growing more and more confidential, until at last you cried out, in a terrific whisper: "My boy, she is simply miraculous!" At that moment you were in the domain of literature.

Let me explain. Of course, in the ordinary acceptation of the word, she was not miraculous. Your faithful friend had never noticed that she was miraculous, nor had about forty thousand other fairly keen observers. She was just a girl. Troy had not been burnt for her. A girl cannot be called a miracle. If a girl is to be called a miracle, then you might call pretty nearly anything a miracle...That is just it: you might. You can. You ought. Amid all the miracles of the universe you had just wakened up to one. You were full of your discovery. You were under a divine impulsion to impart that discovery. You had a strong sense of the marvelous beauty of something, and you had to share it. You were in a passion about something and you had to vent yourself on somebody. You were drawn towards the whole of the rest of the human race. Mark the effect of your mood and utterance on your faithful friend. He knew that she was not a miracle. No other person could have made him believe that she was a miracle. But you, by the force and sincerity of your own vision of her, and by the fervour of your desire to make him participate in your vision, did for quite a long time cause him to feel that he had been blind to the miracle of that girl.

You were producing literature. You were alive. Your eyes were unlidded, your ears were unstopped, to some part of the beauty and the strangeness of the world; and a strong instinct within you forced you to tell someone. It was not enough for you that you saw and heard. Others had to see and hear. Others had to be wakened up. And they were! It is quite possible — I am not quite sure — that your faithful friend the very next day, or the next month, looked at some other girl, and suddenly saw that she, too, was miraculous! The influence of literature!

The makers of literature are those who have seen and felt the miraculous interestingness of the universe. And the greatest makers of literature are those whose vision has been the widest, and whose feeling been the most intense. Your own fragment of insight was accidental, and perhaps temporary. *Their* lives are one long ecstasy of denying that the world is a dull place. Is it nothing to you to learn to understand that the world is not a dull place? Is it nothing to you to be led out of the tunnel on to the hillside, to have all your senses quickened, to be invigorated by the true savour of life, to feel your heart beating under that correct necktie of yours? These makers of literature render you their equals.

The aim of literary study is not to amuse the hours of leisure; it is to awake oneself, it is to be alive, to intensify one's capacity for pleasure, for sympathy, and for comprehension. It is not to affect one hour, but twenty-four hours. It is to change utterly one's relations with the world. An understanding appreciation of literature means an understanding appreciation of the world, and it means nothing else. Not isolated and unconnected parts of life, but all of life, brought together and correlated in a synthetic map! The spirit of literature is unifying; it joins the candle and the star, and by the magic of an image shows that the beauty of the greater is in the less. And, not content with the disclosure of beauty and the bringing together of all things whatever within its focus, it enforces a moral wisdom by the tracing everywhere of cause and effect. It consoles doubly — by the revelation of unsuspected loveliness, and by the proof that our lot is the common lot. It is the supreme cry of the discoverer, offering sympathy and asking for it in a single gesture. In attending a University Extension Lecture on the sources of Shakespeare's plots or in studying the researches of George Saintsbury into the origins of English prosody, or in weighing the evidence for and against the assertion that Rousseau was a scoundrel, one is apt to forget what literature really is and is for. It is well to remind ourselves that literature is first and last a means of life, and that the enterprise of forming one's literary taste is an enterprise of learning how best to use this means of life. People who don't want to live, people who would sooner hibernate than feel intensely, will be wise to eschew literature. They had better, to quote from the finest passage in a fine poem, "sit around and eat blackberries." The sight of a "common bush afire with God" might upset their nerves....

WHERE TO BEGIN

I wish particularly that my readers should not be intimidated by the apparent vastness and complexity of this enterprise of forming the literary taste. It is not so vast nor so complex as it looks. There is no need whatever for the inexperienced enthusiast to confuse and frighten himself with thoughts of "literature in all its branches." Experts and pedagogues (chiefly pedagogues) have, for the purpose of convenience split literature up into divisions and sub-divisions — such as prose and poetry; or imaginative, philosophic, historical; or elegiac, heroic, lyric; or religious and profane, etc., *ad infinitum.* But the greater truth is that literature is all one — and indivisible. The idea of the unity of literature should be well planted and fostered in the head. All literature is the expression of feeling, of passion, of emotion, caused by a sensation of the interestingness of life. What drives an historian to write history? Nothing but the overwhelming impression made upon him by the survey of past times. He is forced into an attempt to reconstitute the picture for others. If hitherto you have failed to perceive that an historian is a being in strong emotion, trying to convey his emotion to others, read the passage in the *Memoirs* of Gibbon, in which he describes how he finished the *Decline and Fall.* You will probably never again look upon the *Decline and Fall* as a "dry" work.

What applies to history applies to the other "dry" branches. Even Johnson's Dictionary is packed with emotion. Read the last paragraph of the preface to it: "In this work, when it shall be found that much is omitted, let it not be forgotten that much likewise is performed ... It may repress the triumph of malignant criticism to observe that if our language is not here fully displayed, I have only failed in an attempt which no human powers have hitherto completed ..." And so on to the close "I have protracted my work till most of those whom I wish to please have sunk into the grave, and success and miscarriage are empty sounds: I therefore dismiss it with frigid tranquillity, having too little to fear or hope from censure or from praise." Yes, tranquility; but not frigid! The whole passage, one of the finest in English prose, is marked by the heat of emotion. You may discover the same quality in such books as Spencer's *First Principles.* You may discover it everywhere in literature, from the cold fire of Pope's irony to the blasting temperature of Swinburne. Literature does not begin till emotion has begun.

There is even no essential, definable difference between those two great branches, prose and poetry. For prose may have rhythm. All that can be said is that verse will scan, while prose will not. The difference is purely formal. Very few poets have succeeded in being so poetical as Isaiah, Sir Thomas Browne, and Ruskin have been in prose. It can only be stated that, as a rule, writers have shown an instinctive tendency to choose verse for the expression of the very highest emotion. The supreme literature is in verse, but the finest achievements in prose approach so nearly to the finest achievements in verse that it is ill work deciding between them. In the sense in which poetry is best understood, all literature is poetry — or is, at any rate, poetical in quality. Macaulay's ill-informed and unjust denunciations live because his genuine emotion made them into poetry, while his *Lays of Ancient Rome* are dead because they are not the expression of a genuine emotion. As the literary taste develops, this quality of emotion, restrained or loosed, will be more and more widely perceived at large in literature. It is the quality that must be looked for. It is the quality that unifies literature (and all the arts).

It is not merely useless, it is harmful, for you to map out literature into divisions and branches, with different laws, rules, or canons. The first thing is to obtain some possession of literature. When you have actually felt some of the emotion which great writers have striven to impart to you, and when your emotions become so numerous and puzzling that you feel the need of arranging them and calling them by names, then — and not before — you can begin to study what has been attempted in the way of classifying and ticketing literature. Manuals and treatises are excellent things in their kind, but they are simply dead weight at the start. You can only acquire really useful general ideas by first acquiring particular ideas, and putting those particular ideas together. You cannot make bricks without straw. Do not worry about literature in the abstract, about theories as to literature. Get at it. Get hold of literature in the concrete as a dog gets hold of a bone. If you ask me where you ought to begin, I shall gaze at you as I might gaze at the faithful animal if he inquired which end of the bone he ought to attack. It doesn't matter in the slightest degree where you begin. Begin wherever the fancy takes you to begin. Literature is a whole.

There is only one restriction for you. You must begin with an acknowledged classic; you must eschew modern works. The reason for this does not imply any depreciation of the present age at the expense of past ages. Indeed, it is important, if you wish ultimately to have a wide, catholic taste, to guard against the too common assumption that nothing modern will stand comparison with the classics. In every age there have been people to sigh: "Ah, yes. Fifty years ago we had a few great writers. But they are all dead, and no young ones are arising to take their place." This attitude of mind is deplorable, if not silly, and is a certain proof of narrow taste. It is a surety that in 1959 gloomy and egregious persons will be saying: "Ah, yes. At the beginning of the century there were great poets like Swinburne, Meredith, Francis Thompson, and Yeats. Great novelists like Hardy and Conrad. Great historians like Stubbs and Maitland, etc. etc. But they are all dead now, and whom have we to take their place?" It is not until an age has receded into history, and all its mediocrity has dropped away from it, that we can see it as it is — as a group of men of genius. We forget the immense amount of twaddle that the great epochs produced. The total amount of fine literature created in a given period of time differs from epoch to epoch, but it does not differ much. And we may be perfectly sure that our own age will make a favourable impression upon that excellent judge, posterity. Therefore, beware of disparaging the present in your own mind. While temporarily ignoring it, dwell upon the idea that its chaff contains about as much wheat as any similar quantity of chaff has contained wheat.

The reason why you must avoid modern works at the beginning is simply that you are not in a position to choose among modern works. Nobody at all is quite in a position to choose with certainty among modern works. To sift the wheat from the chaff is a process that takes an exceedingly long time. Modern works have to pass before the bar of the taste of successive generations. Whereas, with classics, which have been through the ordeal, almost the reverse is the case. *Your taste has to pass before the bar of the classics.* That is the point. If you differ with a classic, it is you who are wrong, and not the book. If you differ with a modern work, you may be wrong or you may be right, but no judge is authoritative enough to decide. Your taste is unformed. It needs guidance, and it needs authoritative guidance. Into the business of forming literary taste faith enters. You probably will not specially care for a particular classic at first. If you did care for it at first, your taste, so far as that classic is concerned, would be formed, and our hypothesis is that your taste is not formed. How are you to arrive at the stage of caring for it? Chiefly, of course, by examining it and honestly trying to understand it. But this process is materially helped by an act of faith, by the frame of mind which says: "I know on the highest authority that this thing is fine, that it is capable of giving me pleasure. Hence I am determined to find pleasure in it." Believe me that faith counts enormously in the development of that wide taste which is the instrument of wide pleasures. But it must be faith founded on unassailable authority.

STUDY QUESTIONS

1. *To what extent, according to Bennett, is a knowledge of literature useful as a social accomplishment? Do you agree with his view? Does he seem to agree on this point with Rilke?*

2. *To what extent do Buck and Bennett agree about the place of emotion in art? What similar point do they make about established or classical works?*

3. *Bennett explains that literature is the result of a writer's impulse to express some intense feeling that is nearly inexpressible. Do you know some story or poem that seems to be the product of such an impulse?*

4. *Do Bennett's remarks about the formal study of literature help to explain the fact pointed out by Phyllis McGinley in "The Consolations of Illiteracy" that people generally dislike the books they have to read in school?*

5. *Describe your experience in reading a book, play or poem generally considered a classic, telling whether you passed or failed the test of good judgment mentioned by Bennett, and analyzing the situation.*

6. *Do you agree with Bennett that the right way for a beginner to approach the reading of a classic is with a feeling of faith in its greatness? Or is some other attitude more constructive?*

Virginia Woolf   How Should One Read a Book?*

*I*n the first place, I want to emphasise the note of interrogation at the end of my title. Even if I could answer the question for myself, the answer would apply only to me and not to you. The only advice, indeed, that one person can give another about reading is to take no advice, to follow your own instincts, to use your own reason, to come to your own conclusions. If this is agreed between us, then I feel at liberty to put forward a few ideas and suggestions because you will not allow them to fetter that independence which is the most important quality that a reader can possess. After all, what laws can be laid down about books? The battle of Waterloo was certainly fought on a certain day; but is *Hamlet* a better play than *Lear*? Nobody can say. Each must decide that question for himself. To admit authorities, however heavily furred and gowned, into our libraries and let them tell us how to read, what to read, what value to place upon what we read, is to destroy the spirit of freedom which is the breath of those sanctuaries. Everywhere else we may be bound by laws and conventions — there we have none.

But to enjoy freedom, if the platitude is pardonable, we have of course to control ourselves. We must not squander our powers, helplessly and ignorantly, squirting half the house in order to water a single rose-bush; we must train them, exactly and powerfully, here on the very spot. This, it may be, is one of the first difficulties that faces us in a library. What is "the very spot"? There may well seem to be nothing but a conglomeration and huddle of confusion. Poems and novels, histories and memoirs, dictionaries and blue-books; books written in all languages by men and women of all tempers, races, and ages jostle each other on the shelf. And outside the donkey brays, the women gossip at the pump, the colts gallop across the fields. Where are we to begin? How are we to bring order into this multitudinous chaos and so get the deepest and widest pleasure from what we read?

It is simply enough to say that since books have classes — fiction, biography, poetry — we should separate them and take from each what it is right that each should give us. Yet few people ask from books what books can give us. Most commonly we come to books with blurred and divided minds, asking of fiction that it shall be true, of poetry that it shall be false, of biography that it shall be flattering, of history that it shall enforce our own prejudices. If we could banish all such preconceptions when we read, that would be an admirable beginning. Do not dictate to your author; try to become him. Be his fellow-worker and accomplice. If you hang back, and reserve and criticise at first, you are preventing yourself from getting the fullest possible value from what you read. But if you open your mind as widely as possible, then signs and hints of almost imperceptible fineness, from the twist and turn of the first sentences, will bring you into the presence of a human being unlike any other. Steep yourself in this, acquaint yourself with this, and soon you will find that your author is giving you, or attempting to give you, something far more definite. The thirty-two chapters of a novel — if we consider how to read a novel first — are an attempt to make something as formed and controlled as a building: but words are more impalpable than bricks; reading is a longer and more complicated process than seeing. Perhaps the quickest way to understand the elements of what a novelist is doing is not to read, but to write; to make your own experiment with the dangers and difficulties of words. Recall, then, some event that has left a distinct impression on you — how at the corner of the street, perhaps, you passed two people talking. A tree shook; an electric light danced; the tone of the talk was comic, but also tragic; a whole vision, an entire conception, seemed contained in that moment.

But when you attempt to reconstruct it in words, you will find that it breaks into a thousand conflicting impressions. Some must be subdued; others emphasized; in the process you will lose, probably, all grasp upon the emotion itself. Then turn from your blurred and littered pages to the opening pages of some great novelist — Defoe, Jane Austen, Hardy. Now you will be better able to appreciate their mastery. It is not merely that we are in the presence of a different person — Defoe, Jane Austen, or Thomas Hardy — but that we are living in a different world. Here, in *Robinson Crusoe*, we are trudging a plain high road; one thing happens after another; the fact and the order of the fact is enough. But if the open air and adventure mean everything to Defoe they mean nothing to Jane Austen. Hers is the drawing-room, and people talking, and by the many mirrors of their talk revealing their characters. And if, when we have accustomed ourselves to the drawing-room and its reflections, we turn to Hardy, we are once more spun round. The moors are round us and the stars are above our heads. The other side of the mind is now exposed — the dark side that comes uppermost in solitude, not the light side that shows in company. Our relations are not towards people, but towards Nature and destiny. Yet different as these worlds are, each is consistent with itself. The maker of each is careful to observe the laws of his own perspective, and however great a strain they may put upon us they will never confuse us, as lesser writers so frequently do, by introducing two different kinds of reality into the same book. Thus to go from one great novelist to another — from Jane Austen to Hardy, from Peacock to Trollope, from Scott to Meredith — is to be wrenched and uprooted; to be thrown this way and then that. To read a novel is a difficult and complex art. You must be capable not only of great fineness of perception, but of great boldness of imagination if you are going to make use of all that the novelist — the great artist — gives you.

But a glance at the heterogeneous company on the shelf will show you that writers are very seldom "great artists"; far more often a book makes no claim to be a work of art at all. These biographies and autobiographies, for example, lives of great men, of men long dead and forgotten, that stand cheek by jowl with the novels and poems, are we to refuse to read them because they are not "art"? Or shall we read them, but read them in a different way, with a different aim? Shall we read them in the first place to satisfy that curiosity which possesses us sometimes when in the evening we linger in front of a house where the lights are lit and the blinds not yet drawn, and each floor of the house shows us a different section of human life in being? Then we are consumed with curiosity about the lives of these people — the servants gossiping, the gentlemen dining, the girl dressing for a party, the old woman at the window with her knitting. Who are they, what are they, what are their names, their occupations, their thoughts, and adventures?

Biographies and memoirs answer such questions, light up innumerable such houses; they show us people going about their daily affairs, toiling, failing, succeeding, eating, hating, loving, until they die. And sometimes as we watch, the house fades and the iron railings vanish and we are out at sea; we are hunting, sailing, fighting; we are among savages and soldiers; we are taking part in great campaigns. Or if we like to stay here in England, in London, still the scene changes; the street narrows; the house becomes small, cramped, diamond-paned, and malodorous. We see a poet, Donne, driven from such a house because the walls were so thin that when the children cried their voices cut through them. We can follow him, through the paths that lie in the pages of books, to Twickenham; to Lady Bedford's Park, a famous meeting-ground for nobles and poets; and then turn our steps to Wilton, the great house under the downs, and hear Sidney read the *Arcadia* to his sister; and ramble among the very marshes and see the very herons that figure in that famous romance; and then again travel north with that other Lady Pembroke, Anne Clifford, to her wild moors, or plunge into the city and control our merriment at the sight of Gabriel Harvey in his black velvet suit arguing about poetry with Spenser. Nothing is more fascinating than to grope and stumble in the alternate darkness and splendour of Elizabethan London. But there is no staying there. The Temples and the Swifts, the Harleys and the St. Johns beckon us on; hour upon hour can be spent disentangling their quarrels and deciphering their characters; and when we tire of them we can stroll on, past a lady in black wearing diamonds, to Samuel Johnson and Goldsmith and Garrick; or cross the channel, if we like, and meet Voltaire and Diderot, Madame du Deffand; and so back to England and Twickenham — and how certain places repeat themselves and certain names! — where Lady Bedford had her Park once and Pope lived later, to Walpole's home at Strawberry Hill. But Walpole introduces us to such a swarm of new acquaintances, there are so many houses to visit and bells to ring that we may well hesitate for a moment, on the Miss Berrys' doorstep, for example, when behold, up comes Thackeray; he is the friend of the

woman whom Walpole loved; so that merely by going from friend to
friend, from garden to garden, from house to house, we have passed from one
end of English literature to another and wake to find ourselves here again in
the present, if we can so differentiate this moment from all that have gone
before. This, then, is one of the ways in which we can read these lives and
letters; we can make them light up the many windows of the past; we can
watch the famous dead in their familiar habits and fancy sometimes that we
are very close and can surprise their secrets, and sometimes we may pull out
a play or a poem that they have written and see whether it reads differently
in the presence of the author. But this again rouses other questions. How
far, we must ask ourselves, is a book influenced by its writer's life — how far
is it safe to let the man interpret the writer? How far shall we resist or give
way to the sympathies and antipathies that the man himself rouses in us —
so sensitive are words, so receptive of the character of the author? These
are questions that press upon us when we read lives and letters, and we must
answer them for ourselves, for nothing can be more fatal than to be guided
by the preferences of others in a matter so personal.

But also we can read such books with another aim, not to throw light on
literature, not to become familiar with famous people, but to refresh and
exercise our own creative powers. Is there not an open window on the right
hand of the bookcase? How delightful to stop reading and look out! How
stimulating the scene is, in its unconsciousness, its irrelevance, its perpetual
movement — the colts galloping round the field, the woman filling her pail
at the well, the donkey throwing back his head and emitting his long, acrid
moan. The greater part of any libary is nothing but the record of such fleeting
moments in the lives of men, women, and donkeys. Every literature, as it
grows old, has its rubbish-heap, its record of vanished moments and forgotten
lives told in faltering and feeble accents that have perished. But if you give
yourself up to the delight of rubbish-reading you will be surprised, indeed
you will be overcome, by the relics of human life that have been cast out to
moulder. It may be one letter — but what a vision it gives! It may be a few
sentences — but what vistas they suggest! Sometimes a whole story will come
together with such beautiful humor and pathos and completeness that it seems
as if a great novelist had been at work, yet it is only an old actor, Tate
Wilkinson, remembering the strange story of Captain Jones; it is only a
young subaltern serving under Arthur Wellesley and falling in love with a
pretty girl at Lisbon; it is only Maria Allen letting fall her sewing in the
empty drawing-room and sighing how she wishes she had taken Dr. Burney's
good advice and had never eloped with his Rishy. None of this has any
value; it is negligible in the extreme; yet how absorbing it is now and again to
go through the rubbish-heaps and find rings and scissors and broken noses
buried in the huge past and try to piece them together while the colt gallops
round the field, the woman fills her pail at the well, and the donkey brays.

But we tire of rubbish-reading in the long run. We tire of searching for
what is needed to complete the half-truth which is all that the Wilkinsons,

the Bunburys, and the Maria Allens are able to offer us. They had not the artist's power of mastering and eliminating; they could not tell the whole truth even about their own lives; they have disfigured the story that might have been so shapely. Facts are all that they can offer us, and facts are a very inferior form of fiction. Thus the desire grows upon us to have done with half-statements and approximations; to cease from searching out the minute shades of human character, to enjoy the greater abstractness, the purer truth of fiction. Thus we create the mood, intense and generalised, unaware of detail, but stressed by some regular, recurrent beat, whose natural expression is poetry; and that is the time to read poetry when we are almost able to write it.

> Western wind, when wilt thou blow?
> The small rain down can rain.
> Christ, if my love were in my arms,
> And I in my bed again!

The impact of poetry is so hard and direct that for the moment there is no other sensation except that of the poem itself. What profound depths we visit then — how sudden and complete is our immersion! There is nothing here to catch hold of; nothing to stay us in our flight. The illusion of fiction is gradual; its effects are prepared; but who when they read these four lines stops to ask who wrote them, or conjures up the thought of Donne's house or Sidney's secretary; or enmeshes them in the intricacy of the past and the succession of generations? The poet is always our contemporary. Our being for the moment is centered and constricted, as in any violent shock of personal emotion. Afterwards, it is true, the sensation begins to spread in wider rings through our minds; remoter senses are reached; these begin to sound and to comment and we are aware of echoes and reflections. The intensity of poetry covers an immense range of emotion. We have only to compare the force and directness of

> I shall fall like a tree, and find my grave,
> Only remembering that I grieve,

with the wavering modulation of

> Minutes are numbered by the fall of sands,
> As by an hour glass; the span of time
> Doth waste us to our graves, and we look on it;
> An age of pleasure, revelled out, comes home
> At last, and ends in sorrow; but the life,
> Weary of riot, numbers every sand,
> Wailing in sighs, until the last drop down,
> So to conclude calamity in rest,

or place the meditative calm of

> whether we be young or old,
> Our destiny, our being's heart and home,

> Is with infinitude, and only there;
> With hope it is, hope that can never die,
> Effort, and expectation, and desire,
> And something evermore about to be,

beside the complete and inexhaustible loveliness of

> The moving Moon went up the sky,
> And no where did abide;
> Softly she was going up,
> And a star or two beside—

or the splendid fantasy of

> And the woodland haunter
> Shall not cease to saunter
>   When, far down some glade,
> Of the great world's burning,
> One soft flame upturning
> Seems, to his discerning,
>   Crocus in the shade.

to bethink us of the varied art of the poet; his power to make us at once actors and spectators; his power to run his hand into character as if it were a glove, and to be Falstaff or Lear; his power to condense, to widen, to state, once and for ever.

"We have only to compare" — with those words the cat is out of the bag, and the true complexity of reading is admitted. The first process, to receive impressions with the utmost understanding, is only half the process of reading; it must be completed, if we are to get the whole pleasure from a book, by another. We must pass judgment upon these multitudinous impressions; we must make of these fleeting shapes one that is hard and lasting. But not directly. Wait for the dust of reading to settle; for the conflict and the questioning to die down; walk, talk, pull the dead petals from a rose, or fall asleep. Then suddenly without our willing it, for it is thus that Nature undertakes these transitions, the book will return, but differently. It will float to the top of the mind as a whole. And the book as a whole is different from the book received currently in separate phrases. Details now fit themselves into their places. We see the shape from start to finish; it is a barn, a pig-sty, or a cathedral. Now then we can compare book with book as we compare building with building. But this act of comparison means that our attitude has changed; we are no longer the friends of the writer, but his judges; and just as we cannot be too sympathetic as friends, so as judges we cannot be too severe. Are they not criminals, books that have wasted our time and sympathy; are they not the most insidious enemies of society, corrupters, defilers, the writers of false books, faked books, books that fill the air with decay and disease? Let us then be severe in our judgments; let us compare each book with the greatest of its kind. There they hang in the mind the shapes of the books we have read solidified by the judgments we have passed on them

— *Robinson Crusoe*, *Emma*, *The Return of the Native*. Compare the novels with these — even the latest and least of novels has a right to be judged with the best. And so with poetry — when the intoxication of rhythm has died down and the splendour of words has faded, a visionary shape will return to us and this must be compared with *Lear*, with *Phèdre*, with *The Prelude*; or if not with these, with whatever is the best or seems to us to be the best in its own kind. And we may be sure that the newness of new poetry and fiction is its most superficial quality and that we have only to alter slightly, not to recast, the standards by which we have judged the old.

It would be foolish, then, to pretend that the second part of reading, to judge, to compare, is as simple as the first — to open the mind wide to the fast flocking of innumerable impressions. To continue reading without the book before you, to hold one shadow-shape against another, to have read widely enough and with enough understanding to make such comparisons alive and illuminating — that is difficult; it is still more difficult to press further and to say, "Not only is the book of this sort, but it is of this value; here it fails; here it succeeds; this is bad; that is good." To carry out this part of a reader's duty needs such imagination, insight, and learning that it is hard to conceive any one mind sufficiently endowed; impossible for the most self-confident to find more than the seeds of such powers in himself. Would it not be wiser, then, to remit this part of reading and to allow the critics, the gowned and furred authorities of the library, to decide the question of the book's absolute value for us? Yet how impossible! We may stress the value of sympathy; we may try to sink our own identity as we read. But we know that we cannot sympathise wholly or immerse ourselves wholly; there is always a demon in us who whispers, "I hate, I love," and we cannot silence him. Indeed, it is precisely because we hate and we love that our relation with the poets and novelists is so intimate that we find the presence of another person intolerable. And even if the results are abhorrent and our judgments are wrong, still our taste, the nerve of sensation that sends shocks through us, is our chief illuminant; we learn through feeling; we cannot suppress our own idiosyncrasy without impoverishing it. But as time goes on perhaps we can train our taste; perhaps we can make it submit to some control. When it has fed greedily and lavishly upon books of all sorts — poetry, fiction, history, biography — and has stopped reading and looked for long spaces upon the variety, the incongruity of the living world, we shall find that it is changing a little; it is not so greedy, it is more reflective. It will begin to bring us not merely judgments on particular books, but it will tell us that there is a quality common to certain books. Listen, it will say, what shall we call *this*? And it will read us perhaps *Lear* and then perhaps *Agamemnon* in order to bring out that common quality. Thus, with our taste to guide us, we shall venture beyond the particular book in search of qualities that group books together; we shall give them names and thus frame a rule that brings order into our perceptions. We shall gain a further and a rarer pleasure from this discrimination. But as a rule only lives when it is perpetually broken by contact with the books themselves — nothing is easier and more stultifying than to make rules which exist out of touch with facts, in a vacuum — now at last, in order to steady ourselves in this difficult attempt, it may be well to turn to the very rare writers who are able to enlighten us upon literature as an art. Coleridge and Dryden and Johnson, in their considered criticism, the poets and novelists themselves in their unconsidered sayings, are often surprisingly relevant; they light up and solidify the vague ideas that have been tumbling in the misty depths of our minds. But they are only able to help us if we come to them laden with questions and suggestions won honestly in the course of our own reading. They can do nothing for us if we herd ourselves under their authority and lie down like sheep in the shade of a hedge. We can only understand their ruling when it comes in conflict with our own and vanquishes it.

If this is so, if to read a book as it should be read calls for the rarest qualities of imagination, insight, and judgment, you may perhaps conclude that literature is a very complex art and that it is unlikely that we shall be able, even after a lifetime of reading, to make any valuable contribution to its criticism. We must remain readers; we shall not put on the further glory that belongs to those rare beings who are also critics. But still we have our responsibilities as readers and even our importance. The standards we raise and the judgments we pass steal into the air and become part of the atmosphere which writers breathe as they work. An influence is created which tells upon them even if it never finds its way into print. And that influence, if it were well instructed, vigorous and individual and sincere, might be of great value now when criticism is necessarily in abeyance; when books pass in review like the procession of animals in a shooting gallery, and the critic has only one second in which to load and aim and shoot and may well be pardoned if he mistakes rabbits for tigers, eagles for barndoor fowls, or misses altogether and wastes his shot upon some peaceful cow grazing in a further field. If behind the erratic gunfire of the press the author felt that there was another kind of criticism, the opinion of people reading for the love of reading, slowly and unprofessionally, and judging with great sympathy and yet with great severity, might this not improve the quality of his work? And if by our means books were to become stronger, richer, and more varied, that would be an end worth reaching.

Yet who reads to bring about an end however desirable? Are there not some pursuits that we practice because they are good in themselves, and some pleasures that are final? And is not this among them? I have sometimes dreamt, at least, that when the Day of Judgment dawns and the great conquerors and lawyers and statesmen come to receive their rewards — their crowns, their laurels, their names carved indelibly upon imperishable marble — the Almighty will turn to Peter and will say, not without a certain envy when He sees us coming with our books under our arms, "Look, these need no reward. We have nothing to give them here. They have loved reading."

STUDY QUESTIONS

1. *Note that, unlike Bennett, Virginia Woolf sees some value in an awareness of the different classes of books. What value? What two kinds of classes does she mention?*
2. *What importance does Virginia Woolf attribute to personal preference? What relation do her views here have to those of Holbrook Jackson in "Writer and Reader" in Part One of this anthology?*
3. *What is the point of the open window next to the book-case? What suggestion is the author making here about the use of literature?*
4. *Virginia Woolf divides reading into two steps. What are they? How well does her account of them agree with Buck's definition of "appreciation"?*
5. *Follow Virginia Woolf's suggestion to write an account of some everyday incident that made a clear impression upon you, trying to convey this impression to the reader accurately and simply.*
6. *Describe a book which you feel gave you a clear insight into a time or a place you knew little about before you read it. Good subjects for this would be biographies, historical works or historical novels.*

Archibald MacLeish

Why Do We Teach Poetry?*

There is something about the art of poetry which induces a defensive posture. Even in the old days when the primacy of poetry was no more challenged than the primacy of Heaven, which is now also challenged, the posture was habitual. If you published your reflections on the art in those days you called them a *Defense*. Today, when the queen of sciences is Science, you do not perhaps employ that term but you mean it. It is not that the gentlemen at the long table in the Faculty Club whose brains have been officially cleared to serve as depositories of scientific secrets of the eighth and thirteenth classes are patronizing in their manner. They are still gentlemen and therefore still modest no matter how great their distinction or how greatly certified. But one knows one's place. One knows that whereas the teachers of science meet to hear of new triumphs which the newspapers will proudly report, the teachers of poetry meet to ask old questions — which no one will report: such questions as, why teach poetry anyway in a time like this?

It is a relief in this general atmosphere to come upon someone who feels

* From *The Atlantic Monthly*, March, 1956. Reprinted by the kind permission of the author.

no defensiveness whatever: who is perfectly certain that poetry ought to be taught now as at any other time and who is perfectly certain also that he knows why. The paragon I have in mind is a young friend of mine, a devoted teacher, who was recently made headmaster of one of the leading American preparatory schools, and who has been taking stock, for some time past, of his curriculum and his faculty. Poetry, as he sees it, ought to be taught "as a most essential form of human expression as well as a carrier throughout the ages of some of the most important values in our heritage." What troubles him is that few teachers, at least in the schools he knows, seem to share his conviction. He is not too sure that teachers themselves have "an abiding and missionary faith in poetry" which would lead them to see it as a great clarifier — a "human language" capable of competing with the languages and mathematics and science.

But though teachers lack the necessary faith, the fault, as my young friend sees it, is not wholly theirs. The fault is the fault of modern criticism, which has turned poetry into something he calls "poetry itself" — meaning, I suppose, poetry for poetry's sake. "Poetry itself" turns out to be poetry with its meanings distilled away, and poetry with its meanings distilled away is difficult if not impossible to teach in a secondary school — at least *his* secondary school. The result is that secondary school teachers have gone back, as to the lesser of two evils, to those historical and anecdotal practices sanctified by American graduate schools in generations past. They teach "poets and not poetry." With the result that "students become acquainted with poets from Homer to MacLeish" (quite a distance no matter how you measure it!) "but the experience doesn't necessarily leave them with increased confidence in what poetry has to offer." I can well believe it.

The reason why modern criticism has this disastrous effect, the reason why it produces "an almost morbid apathy toward 'content' or 'statement of idea,'" is its excessive "preoccupation with aesthetic values." Modern criticism insists that poems are primarily works of art; and when you insist that poems are primarily works of art you cannot, in my friend's view, teach them as carriers "throughout the ages of some of the most important values in our heritage." What is important about Homer and Shakespeare and the authors of the Bible is that they were "realists with great vision ... whose work contains immensely valuable constructions of the meaning of life"; and if you talk too much about them as artists, those constructions of the meaning of life get lost.

Now this, you will observe, is not merely another walloping of the old horse who was once called the New Criticism. It goes a great deal farther. It is a frontal attack upon a general position maintained by many who never accepted the New Criticism or even heard of it. It is an attack upon those who believe — as most poets, I think, have believed — that a poem *is* primarily a work of art and must be read as a work of art if it is to be read at all. It is a high-minded and disinterested attack delivered for the noblest of purposes, but an attack notwithstanding — and an effective one. What it contends is that an approach to poetry which insists that a poem is a work of art blocks off what the poem has to say, whereas what the poem has to say is the principal reason for teaching it. What the argument comes down to, in other words, is the proposition that it is a mistake, in teaching poetry, to insist that poetry is art, because, if you do so insist, you will not be able to bring your students to the meaning of the poem, the idea of the poem, what the poem has to tell them about man and world and life and death — and it is for these things the teaching of the poem is important.

Now, I can understand this argument and can respect the reasons for making it. Far too many of those who define poetry in exclusively artistic terms use their definition as a limiting and protective statement which relieves them of all obligation to drive the poem's meanings beyond the meanings of the poem: beyond the mere translation of the symbols and metaphors and the classical or other references — the whole apparatus of *explication du texte.* Far too many, indeed, of those who have to do with literature generally in our time, and particularly with modern literature, consider that meanings in any but a literary (which includes a Freudian) sense are not only outside, but beneath, their proper concern — that the intrusion of questions of morality and religion into the world of art is a kind of trespass and that works of literary art not only should but *can* be studied in a moral vacuum. Literature in the hands of such teachers is well on the way to becoming again that "terrible queen" which the men of the nineties raised above life and which Yeats, when he outgrew the men of the nineties, rejected.

But although I can understand this argument, and although I can respect its reasons, and although I believe it raises a true issue and an important issue, I cannot accept it; for it rests, or seems to me to rest, on two quite dubious assumptions. The first is the assumption, familiar in one form or another to all of us, that the "idea" of a work of art is somehow separable from the work of art itself. The most recent — and most egregious — expression of this persistent notion comes from a distinguished Dean of Humanities in a great institution of learning who is reported by the New York *Times* to have argued in a scholarly gathering that "the idea which the reader derives from Ernest Hemingway's *The Old Man and The Sea* comes after the reader has absorbed some 60,000 words. This takes at least an hour.... A similar understanding could come after a few minutes study of a painting by a skillful artist." Precisely, one imagines, as the Doré illustrations gave one the "idea" of the *Inferno* in a few easy looks!

2

It is the second assumption, however, which divides me most emphatically from my young friend. For the second assumption seems to be that *unless* idea and work of art are distinguished from each other in the teaching of a poem, the idea — and so the effectiveness of the teaching — will be lost. At this point my friend and I part company. I am ready, and more than ready, to agree that it is for the meanings of life that one reads (and teaches) poetry. But I am unable to see how there can be a distinction between a poem as a conveyer of such meanings and a poem as a work of art. In brief, the distinction between art and knowledge which is made throughout my friend's argument seems to me wholly without foundation. That it is a distinction almost universally recognized in our epoch I know well enough. Science makes it. Poetry makes it. And the world agrees with both. "Whatever can be *known*," says Bertrand Russell, "can be known by means of science." Poetry, say its professors, has no "messages" to deliver. And no one dissents from either. The exclusive proprietary right of science to know and to communicate knowledge is not only commonly recognized in our civilization: in a very real sense it is our civilization. For the characteristic of our civilization — that which distinguishes it from the civilizations which have preceded it — is the characteristic which knowledge-by-science has conferred upon it: its abstractness.

But though the agreement is general, the proposition is not one I can accept. I argue that the apologists for science are not justified in claiming, nor the apologists for poetry in admitting, the sole right of science to know. I insist that poetry is also capable of knowledge; that poetry, indeed, is capable of a kind of knowledge of which science is not capable; that it is capable of that knowledge *as poetry;* and that the teaching of poetry as poetry, the teaching of poem as work of art, is not only not incompatible with the teaching of poetry as knowledge but is, indeed, the only possible way of teaching poetry as knowledge.

To most of us, brought up as we have been in the world of abstractions which science has prepared for us, and in the kind of school which that world produces — schools in which almost all teaching is teaching of abstractions — the notion of poetry as knowledge, the notion of art as knowledge, is a fanciful notion. Knowledge by abstraction we understand. Science can abstract ideas about apple from apple. It can organize those ideas into knowledge about apple. It can then, by some means, introduce that knowledge into our heads — possibly because our heads are abstractions also. But poetry, we know, does not abstract. Poetry presents. Poetry presents the thing as the thing. And that it should be possible to *know* the thing *as the thing it is* — to *know* apple *as* apple — this we do not understand; this, the true child of the time will assure you, cannot be done. To the true child of abstraction you can't know apple as apple. You can't know tree as tree. You can't know man as man. All you can *know* is a world dissolved by analyzing intellect into abstraction — not a world composed by imaginative intellect into itself. And the result, for the generations of abstraction, is that neither poetry nor art can be a means to knowledge. To inspiration, yes: poetry can undoubtedly lead to that — whatever it is. To revelation, perhaps: there may certainly be moments of revelation in poetry. But to knowledge, no. The only connection between poetry and knowledge we can see is the burden of used abstractions

— adages and old saws — which poetry, some poetry, seems to like to carry
— adages most of which we knew before and some of which aren't even true.

But if all this is so, what then is the "experience of art" — the "experience
of poetry" — which all of us who think about these things at all have known?
What is the experience of *realization* which comes over us with those apples
on a dish of Cézanne's or those three pine trees? What is the experience of
realization which comes over us with Debussy's *Nuages*? What is the experience of realization which comes over us when Coleridge's robin sits and sings

> Betwixt the tufts of snow on the bare branch
> Of mossy apple-tree, while the nigh thatch
> Smokes in the sun thaw; . . .

or when his eave-drops fall

> Heard only in the trances of the blast,
> Or if the secret ministry of frost
> Shall hang them up in silent icicles,
> Quietly shining to the quiet Moon.

And if all this is so, why does one of the most effective of modern definitions
of poetry (Arnold's in his letter to Maurice de Guérin) assign to that art the
peculiar "power of so dealing with *things* as to awaken in us a wonderfully
full, new and intimate sense of them and of our relation with them"?

The answer is, of course, that the children of abstraction are wrong — and
are impoverished by their error, as our entire time is impoverished by it. They
are wrong on both heads. They are wrong when they think they *can* know
the world through its abstractions: nothing can be known through an abstraction but the abstraction itself. They are wrong also when they think
they *cannot* know the world as the world: the whole achievement of art is a
demonstration to the contrary. And the reason they are wrong on both heads
is the reason given, quite unintentionally, by Matthew Arnold. They are
wrong because they do not realize that all true knowledge is a matter of relation: that we *really* know a thing only when we are filled with "a wonderfully full, new and intimate sense of it" and, above all, of "our relation with"
it. This sense — this *knowledge* in the truest meaning of the word knowledge — art can give but abstraction cannot.

There are as many proofs as there are successful works of art. Take, for
obvious example, that unseen mysterious phenomenon, the wind. Take any
attempt, by the familiar processes of abstraction, to "know" the wind. Put
beside it those two familiar lines of George Meredith: —

> Mark where the pressing wind shoots javelin-like
> Its skeleton shadow on the broad-backd wave!

What will be the essential difference between the two? Will it not be that the
first, the analytical, statement is or attempts to be a wholly objective statement
made without reference to an observer (true everywhere and always), whereas
an observer — *one's self* as observer! — is involved in the second? And will not

the consequential difference be that a relation involving one's self is created by the second but not by the first? And will not the end difference be that the second, but not the first, will enable us to know the thing itself — to know what the thing is *like?*

It would be quite possible, I suppose, to semanticize this difference between knowledge by poetry and knowledge by abstraction out of existence by demonstrating that the word, know, is being used in two different senses in the two instances, but the triumph would be merely verbal, for the difference is real. It is indeed the realest of all differences, for what it touches is the means by which we come at reality. How are we to find the knowledge of reality in the world without, or in the shifting, flowing, fluid world within? Is all this a task for the techniques of abstraction — for science as it may be or as it is? Is it through abstraction alone that we are to find what is real in our experience of our lives — and so, conceivably, what is real in ourselves? Or do we need another and a different way of knowing — a way of knowing which will make that world out there, this world in here, available to us, not by translating them into something else — into abstractions of quantity and measure — but by bringing us ourselves to confront them as they are — man and tree face to face in the shock of recognition, man and love face to face?

The question, I beg you to see, is not what we *ought* to do. There is no ought. A man can "live" on abstractions all his life if he has the stomach for them, and many of us have — not the scientists only, but great numbers of the rest of us in this contemporary world, men whose days are a web of statistics, and names, and business deals, held together by the parentheses of a pair of commuting trains with three Martinis at the close. The question is not what we ought to do. The question is what we have the choice of doing — what alternatives are open to us. And it is here and in these terms that the issue presents itself to the teacher of poetry.

3

Colleges and universities do not exist to impose duties but to reveal choices. In a civilization like ours in which one choice has all but overwhelmed the other, a civilization dominated by abstraction, in which men are less and less able to deal with their experience of the world or of themselves unless experience and self have first been translated into abstract terms — a civilization like a foreign language — in such a civilization the need for an understanding of the alternative is urgent. What must be put before the generation of the young is the possibility of a knowledge of experience *as* experience, of self *as* self; and that possibility only the work of art, only the poem, can reveal. That it is so rarely, or so timidly, presented in our schools is one of the greatest failures of our educational system. Young men and young women graduate from American schools and colleges by the hundreds of thousands every year to whom science is the only road to knowledge, and to whom poetry is little more than a subdivision of something called "literature" — a kind of writing printed in columns instead of straight across the page and primarily intended to be deciphered by girls, who don't read it either.

This sort of thing has consequences. Abstractions are wonderfully clever tools for taking things apart and for arranging things in patterns but they are very little use in putting things together and no use at all when it comes to determining what things are *for*. Furthermore, abstractions have a limiting, a dehumanizing, a dehydrating effect on the relation to things of the man who must live with them. The result is that we are more and more left, in our scientific society, without the means of knowledge of ourselves as we truly are or of our experience as it actually is. We have the tools, all the tools — we are suffocating in tools — but we cannot find the actual wood to work or even the actual hand to work it. We begin with one abstraction (something we think of as ourselves) and a mess of other abstractions (standing for the world) and we arrange and rearrange the counters, but who we are and what we are doing we simply do not know — above all what we are doing. With the inevitable consequence that we do not know either what our purpose is or our end. So that when the latest discoveries of the cyclotron are reported we hail them with the cry that we will now be able to control nature better than ever before — but we never go on to say for what purpose, to what end, we will control her. To destroy a city? To remake a world?

It was something of this kind, I imagine, that Adlai Stevenson had in mind when he startled a Smith Commencement last spring by warning his newly graduated audience of prospective wives that the "typical Western man — or typical Western husband — operates well in the realm of means, as the Roman did before him. But outside his specialty, in the realm of ends he is apt to operate poorly or not at all.... The neglect of the cultivation of more mature values," Mr. Stevenson went on, "can only mean that his life, and the life of the society he determines, will lack valid purpose, however busy and even profitable it may be."

As he has so often done before, Mr. Stevenson there found words for an uneasiness which has been endemic but inarticulate in the American mind for many years — the sense that we are getting nowhere far too fast and that, if something doesn't happen soon, we may arrive. But when he came to spell out the causes for "the neglect of the cultivation of more mature values" Mr. Stevenson failed, or so it seems to me, to identify the actual villain. The contemporary environment in America, he told his young listeners, is "an environment in which 'facts,' the data of the senses, are glorified and value judgments are assigned inferior status as 'mere matters of opinion.' It is an environment in which art is often regarded as an adornment of civilization rather than a vital element of it, while philosophy is not only neglected but deemed faintly disreputable because 'it never gets you anywhere.'" It is true that philosophy is neglected, and even truer that art is regarded in this country generally as it seems to be regarded by the automobile manufacturers of Detroit: as so much enamel paint and chromium to be applied for allegedly decorative purposes to the outside of a car which would run better without it. But the explanation is not, I think, that we set facts — even facts in quotation marks — above values, or that we glorify the data of the senses, unless one means by that latter phrase not what the senses tell us of the world we live in but what the statistics that can be compiled out of the data of the senses would tell us if we were ever in touch with our senses.

In few civilizations have the senses been less alive than they are with us. Look at the cities we build and occupy — but look at them! — the houses we live in, the way we hold ourselves and move; listen to the speaking voices of the greater part of our women. And in no civilization, at least in recorded time, have human beings been farther from the *facts* if we mean by that word, facets of reality. Our indifference to ends is the result of our obsession with abstractions rather than facts: with the ideas of things rather than with things. For there can be no concern for ends without a hunger for reality. And there can be no hunger for reality without a sense of the real. And there can be no sense of the real in the world which abstraction creates, for abstraction is incapable of the real: it can neither lay hold of the real itself nor show us where to find it. It cannot, that is to say, create the *relation* between reality and ourselves which makes *knowledge* of reality possible, for neither reality nor ourselves exist in abstraction. Everything in the world of abstraction is object. And, as George Buttrick pointedly says, *we* are not objects: we are subjects.

4

But all this is a negative way of saying what a defender of poetry should not be afraid of saying positively. Let me say it. We have lost our concern with ends because we have lost our touch with reality and we have lost our touch with reality because we are estranged from the means to reality which is the poem — the work of art. To most members of our generation this would seem an extravagant statement but it is not extravagant in fact and would not have seemed so in another time. In ancient China the place of poetry in men's lives was assumed as matter of course; indeed, the polity was based on it. The three hundred and five odes or songs which make up the Song-word Scripture survived to the fourth century B.C., when Confucius is said to have collected them because they were part of the government records preserved in the Imperial Archive. For thousands of years the examinations for the Chinese civil service were examinations in poetry, and there is no record that the results were more disappointing to the throne than examinations of a different character might have been. Certainly there is no record that a Chinese civil servant ever attempted to deny an honor student in a military academy his commission in the imperial army *or* navy because he was friendly with his own mother! Idiocies which the study of science and of other abstractions in contemporary institutions of naval education in the United States seem to nourish were apparently cauterized from the mind by the reading of poems.

It was not for nothing that Confucius told his disciples that the three hundred and five songs of the Song-word Scripture could be boiled down to the commandment: "Have no twisty thoughts." You cannot have twisty thoughts if you are real and if you are thinking about real things. But if a mother is merely a biological event to you and if you yourself are merely a military event called an admiral, anything may happen: you may make your country ridiculous, humiliate a promising boy, and deprive the navy of a good officer, all in the twisted belief that you are being a wise man and a patriot.

One can see, not only in the three hundred and five songs, but in Chinese poetry of other periods, what Confucius meant. Consider two Chinese poems of the second century B.C. and the sixth of our era, both written by Emperors. The first is a poem of grief — of the sense of loss of someone loved: a poem therefore of that inward world of feeling, of emotion, which seems to us most nearly ourselves and which, because it is always in flux, always shifting and changing and flowing away, is, of all parts of our experience of our lives, most difficult to know. We cannot know it through science. We cannot know it by knowing things *about* it — even the shrewdest and most intelligent things, helpful though they may be to us in other ways. We cannot know it either by merely feeling it — by uttering its passing urgencies, crying out "I love" meaning "I think of myself as loving" or sobbing "I grieve" meaning "I think of myself as grieving." How then can we know it?

The Emperor Wu-ti wrote (this is Arthur Waley's beautiful translation): —

> The sound of her silk skirt has stopped.
> On the marble pavement dust grows.
> Her empty room is cold and still.
> Fallen leaves are piled against the doors.
>
> > Longing for that lovely lady
> > How can I bring my aching heart to rest?

Four images, one of sound, two of sight, one of feeling, each like a note plucked on a stringed instrument. Then a question like the chord the four would make together. And all at once we *know*. We know this grief which no word could have described, which any abstraction the mind is capable of would have destroyed. But we know more than this grief: we know our own — or will when it shall visit us — and so know something of ourselves.

The second is a poem of that emotion, that feeling, which is even more difficult to know than grief itself. The second is a poem of delight: youth and delight — the morning of the world — the emotion, of all emotions, most difficult to stop, to hold, to see. "Joy whose hand is ever at his lips bidding adieu." How would you *know* delight in yourself and therefore yourself de-

lighting? Will the psychiatrists tell you? Is there a definition somewhere in
the folios of abstraction by which we attempt to live which will capture it for
you? The Emperor Ch'ien Wen-ti (again Waley's translation) knew that
there is only one mirror which will hold that vanishing smile: the mirror of
art, the mirror of the poem: —

> A beautiful place is the town of Lo-yang:
> The big streets are full of spring light
> The lads go driving out with harps in their hands:
> The mulberry girls go out to the fields with their baskets
> Golden whips glint at the horses' flanks,
> Gauze sleeves brush the green boughs.
> Racing dawn the carriages come home—
> And the girls with their high baskets full of fruit.

In this world within, you see, this world which is ourselves, there is no
possibility of knowing by abstracting the meaning out — or what we hope will
be the meaning. There we must know things *as* themselves and it must be
we who know them. Only art, only poetry, can bring about that confronta-
tion, because only art, only poetry, can show us what we are and ourselves
confronting it. To be ignorant of poetry is to be ignorant therefore of the
one means of reaching the world of our experience of the world. And to be
ignorant of *that* world is to be ignorant of who and what we are. And to be
ignorant of who and what we are is to be incapable of reality no matter what
tools we have, or what intelligence, or what skills. It is this incapacity, this
impotence, which is the tragedy of the time we live in. We are spiritually
impotent because we have cut ourselves off from the poem. And the crown-
ing irony is that it is only in the poem that we can know how impotent we
have become.

Why do we teach poetry in this scientific age? To present the great alternative not to science but to that knowledge by abstraction which science
has imposed. And what is this great alternative? Not the "messages" of poems,
their interpreted "meanings," for these are abstractions also — abstractions
far inferior to those of science. Not the explications of poetic texts, for the
explication of a poetic text which goes no farther ends only in abstraction.

No, the great alternative is the poem as itself, the poem as a poem, the
poem as a work of art — which is to say, the poem in the context in which
alone the work of art exists: the context of the world, of the man and of the
thing, of the infinite relationship which is our lives. To present the great alternative is to present the poem not as a message in a bottle, and not as an
object in an uninhabited landscape, but as an action in the world, an action
in which we ourselves are actors and our lives are known.

STUDY QUESTIONS

1. *To what characteristics of modern life does MacLeish attribute the distrust
   of poetry as a method of knowledge? Do you agree that there is such a distrust?
   Do you agree with MacLeish's analysis of its causes?*

2. *MacLeish says that poetry conveys knowledge by bringing the reader face to face with concrete reality. Is this how language is usually used? What does MacLeish's point suggest about the difference between poetry and other uses of language?*

3. *In what way does MacLeish think a familiarity with poetry will help to ameliorate the present spiritual confusion?*

4. *Why does MacLeish think poetry better qualified than, for example, science or social science, as a medium of knowledge?*

5. *Try to explain to a friend who has read this essay and failed to understand it very well what MacLeish means by saying "we have lost our touch with reality." In order to do this you will have to explain the part played in this process by abstraction and "twisty thoughts."*

6. *Do you agree with MacLeish that poetry is the main way to satisfactory knowledge? If not, write a theme criticizing his opinion and pointing out alternatives.*

Stephen Spender The Young Poet*

*M*y conception of the poet had now shifted from my boyish idea of the simple nature-loving Wordsworth to that of Milton, with the "last infirmity" of his noble mind, the thirst for fame. The poet now became for me someone whose mind rejects the preoccupations of the day, news, struggles for material gain, the machinery of society and even the apparatus of scholarship, by which men add stature to themselves, and who makes for himself a world out of timeless things, nature, and the beauty that he can create with his own imagination. He creates by virtue of the power that comes from the fullest realization of his own being. He does not add anything external to his personality: only that which will develop his inner life. However, my view of the poet was not solipsist. For I remember the thought striking me that to realize oneself to the fullest extent of one's powers means an entering into that which is beyond oneself. So it seemed to me that the point of my writing poetry might be to understand other poetry, to enter Shakespeare's mind as it were across the threshold of lines and images of my own creation which at some point were simply "poetry." If I could write a line which was "poetry," then it would be like a key by which I could enter into the poetry of Shakespeare as far as the limits of my imagination enabled me to go. And after all, what can the aim of life be, beyond attaining, at certain moments, the height of oneself so as to gain a view of heights attained by minds in the past?

At these best moments a great humility fused with a great ambition: to be only what I was, but to the utmost of what I was, in order to enter into the

* From *World Within World*, copyright, 1948, 1949, 1951, by Stephen Spender. Reprinted by permission of Harcourt, Brace and Company, Inc., and A. D. Peters.

being of the poets. And if I could not do so, to accept that I had failed after
I had tested my own being against that of others, upon the level of naked
existence.

When I was young I did not like the poems of every poet, and I recognized that some were better than others. Yet I had nothing which could be
called critical sense. I assumed that every poem published in anthologies like
The Oxford Book of English Verse and *Poems of Today* was good, because
competent authorities had selected them. It was my own fault if I did not appreciate all the poems which editors admired. Often my excitement about
the idea of poetry created, as it were, a poetry beyond the words themselves,
so that words which conveyed little to me were surrounded by the aura of
what others had found in them. Thus:

> "Charm'd magic casements, opening on the foam
>   Of perilous seas, in faery lands forlorn,"

conveyed no attractive picture to me. But that they were often quoted as
"pure poetry" illuminated them nevertheless, and just as getting out of a
boat at a quayside and seeing some ships, I was later one day to cover my disappointment by saying to myself, "This is France," bringing my whole conception of France to bear on my glimpse of Calais or Dieppe, so when I read
these lines, I said to myself: "This is poetry."

Other poetry, as soon as I had read it became identified with an experience
which seemed already to have existed unconsciously within myself. When I
read certain sonnets of Shakespeare, Wordsworth, Keats, I seemed to know
them at once as though I had known them before: and yet I had not done
so. The inevitability of the words in the poetry had such force that it created
in my mind an illusion of its own past history there. What is meant by
"inevitability" in poetry is surely a time-illusion produced by a certain order
of words, which, while striking one as original, seem at the same time to have
been said, and said in this way, always. This illusion exists also in music:
Mozart can open a symphony or quartet with a tune which seems quite fresh
and yet eternally familiar.

Some poetry, which I should have liked, actually repelled me: Milton's
Allegro and *Il Penseroso*, Gray's *Elegy*, Wordsworth's *Ode on Intimations of
Immortality*, Dryden's Odes. What repelled me about these wonderful
achievements was that the poetry in them seemed to strive to become monumental. I felt barred out of these great architectural constructions.

I liked much that was bad. The young accept the bad, not through bad
judgment, but through lack of experience. They like the good as well as the
bad, and they cannot distinguish between an effect which a writer indicates
that he is trying to make, and one that is actually made. Thus although I was
conscious of the ravishing beauty of the poems of de la Mare, I thought his
virtue lay in a dream-like atmosphere which he shared in common with
other writers. I did not understand that this very vagueness was achieved by

methods as precise as those by which a watchmaker screws the jewels into a watch. I was deceived by the will to make a thing of beauty which betrays itself in some poems by the excessive use of words such as "beauty" itself.

The thread which led me through the maze of poetic experiences to a truer sense of poetry was the concern, which I have already mentioned, with the single line. For what I remembered were not whole works, but lines — "His silver skin laced with his golden blood," or "The multitudinous seas incarnadine." Gradually I came to see that such single lines crystallized an image which was the very core of the poetry: and to realize that there is a difference between the poets who allow their imaginations to lead them into a pleasant garden of poetic phrases, and those who use language as an instrument to hew a replica of their experience into words. I began to realize how much audacity, patience and solitude are required to express one's experiences. For the imagination suggests to the poet the undefined sensation of a metaphor which explains to him the quality of some experience. But to feel his way beyond this vague sensation to the exact image of the metaphor, to pursue it through solitude to places where it is hidden from all that has been put into words before, and then to mold it within all the hazards of language, reconciled with grammar and form, is extremely difficult. Most writers allow their ideas to lead them back from terrifying solitude to the consolatory society of approximate and familiar phrases. An experience to them is the beginning of a journey where they soon arrive at already expressed ideas. The writer who clings to his own metaphor is facing his own loneliness; in fighting to distinguish a new idea from similar ideas which have already been expressed, he may find that his most hidden experience brings him in conflict with current ideas among people surrounding him, and face to face with the terrifying truth of his own isolated existence. For he is revealing a fragment of the ultimate truth of his loneliness.

Gradually I saw that the true poets are not just "poetic." They also have an audacity of the imagination which enables them to pursue an idea even when it may seem unpoetic, a desperateness in clinging to their own vision wherever it may seem to lead. This realization prepared me for the moderns. Thus while I was still at school I read *Troy Park* and other early volumes of Edith Sitwell. I was immediately attracted by a poet who transforms everything into pure hard images. Edith Sitwell wrote of the "stalactites of the hard rain," light in one of her poems "brays," and when a kitchen maid holds a candle in her hand the flame is compared with a carrot.

Until I met Auden, my idea of poetry remained still that of a separate poetic world apart from the real world. I thought of it as word-pictures and word-music outside everyday life. You look out of a window on to a lawn: beyond the lawn there is a stream running parallel with the house and the horizon, and, barring the horizon, rising like a pillar whose top is dark against the fiery wheel of the moon, is a poplar tree whose leaves, absorbing the darkness, are filled with the music of nightingales. My idea of a poem was the imitation of some such picture. It was the extension within music and imagery of the great "O" of pure invocation.

Once, many years after this, when traveling in Greece, I dined out of doors at a restaurant on a small island which lies in the Bay of Chalcis. The tables were under the stars, and a few yards from them lay the sea like a black flapping flag, beyond which in a vast ring around the waters the mountains stood like huge green-gray transparent stones. At the table next to me sat a young Englishman — whose face I could not see — and with him a girl. After we had eaten, this young man pushed his chair back from the table, and, without affectation, looking up at the stars, recited lines which began with a great "O." Some vague recollection from my school days told me that these were the address of the watchman to the night in the *Agamemnon*. I did not understand the lines, but the Greek words in the clear English voice were filled with the stars, the seas and the mountains. This is the effect which was my idea of pure poetry, an invocation which one understands imperfectly but which is yet expressed exactly, filled with the stars, the mountains, the tables and the chairs.

When I was at Oxford, I changed my view of poetry. I ceased to think of it creating a special world in which the poet enjoys Keatsian imaginings shutting out the real word. Nor did I think of the poet as a kind of shadowy prophet behind the throne of power, Shelley's unacknowledged legislator of mankind. Instead, he was now a translator of the world which man projects around him through the actions of his will, back into language of the inner life of dreams and fantasy which has projected this materialistic external actuality. I believed now that everything which men make and invent is to some degree a symbol of an inner state of consciousness within them, as they are conditioned by their generation. Poetry was a use of language which revealed external actuality as symbolic inner consciousness.

I began to realize that unpoetic-seeming things were material for poetry. What seemed petrified, overwhelming and intractable could be melted down again by poetry into their symbolic aspects. The fantasy at the back of actuality could be imagined, and the imagination could create its order.

What excited me about the modern movement was the inclusion within new forms, of material which seemed ugly, anti-poetic and inhuman. The transformation of the sordid scene and life of the Dublin of Stephen Dedalus and Bloom into the poetic novel whose title, *Ulysses*, sets its aim beside that of the most timeless epic; the juxtaposition of scenes of European decline with ones recalling the greatest glories of the past tradition, in Eliot's *The Waste Land;* these showed me that modern life could be material for art, and that the poet, instead of having to set himself apart from his time, could create out of an acceptance of it.

Some of the writers who now came to interest me were: James Joyce, T. S. Eliot, Virginia Woolf, Robert Graves, Laura Riding, Ernest Hemingway, Osbert, Edith and Sacheverell Sitwell, Ezra Pound, Henry Green, Herbert

Read — to name a few. What I admired was their hard clear imagery, their boldness of experimentation, and their search for means of expressing complicated states of consciousness and acute sensibility.

At Oxford I started writing poems containing references to gasworks, factories and slums. I understood the significance beneath the affectation of Auden's saying that the most beautiful walk in Oxford was that along the canal, past the gasworks, and that the poet must go dressed like "Mr. Everyman." I used to try experiments in prose to express several levels of consciousness going on at the same time. For example, my taking up a book of history or philosophy and beginning to read a paragraph of facts or abstract speculation whilst all the time a part of my mind was thinking of a conversation with a friend. I studied how such a double layer of two streams of thought flowing simultaneously could be expressed.

Joyce, Virginia Woolf and Hemingway revealed to me areas of sensibility of which I had hardly been conscious before reading them. For example, the sensibility which can enable one to think about what one is thinking while one is thinking it. Hemingway made me aware of a quality and texture in the words upon a page which are like the rough surface of a plaster wall.

What differentiated these from previous writers seemed, above all else, to be that they drew attention to the processes of thinking and perceiving. Other writers have made their readers aware of the significance of a stain on a wall. Virginia Woolf makes them aware of the moment in which an observer becomes conscious of the stain: the stain is made vivid by the description of the state of mind of perceiving.

The tendency of these writers was to extend the material of literature and at the same time to clarify the processes whereby the outside world becomes an inner world within the mind of the individual. On the whole, the result of their writing was to direct the literary sensibility inwards. It was as though the twentieth-century writer had extended the range of his material, but in so doing had made the external world an object of interior sensibility. He had cast away the husk of its outwardness in attempting to digest it in his mind, and he had often become sick in the process. The hero of this literature was inevitably the exceptionally sensitive person, that is to say he who was most capable of receiving a wide range of impressions, most conscious of himself as a receiver of impressions, and most likely to make use of his impressions as a means of cultivating himself rather than of acting upon the world. Joyce, Proust, Eliot and Virginia Woolf had turned a hero or heroine into a passive spectator of a civilization falling into ruins.

One writer whom I began to read at Oxford challenged the passive sensibility which was characteristic of this literature. He was D. H. Lawrence. Lawrence, despite his artistic defects, wrote poetry and prose which turned outwards from himself towards men and women, and towards nature. He had an abhorrence for the isolation of certain modern writers within their own highly developed sensibility. He had a sense that the distinctions between outer and inner are sacred: that whilst the inner life should meet the outer, the outer world should not become the inner world of the writer. To him the idea of the separateness of perceiving from what is perceived, of man from nature and from other men, is sacred. Meeting is a dark mystery, a kind of godliness, and even within the fusion of the sexual act the separateness of man and woman remain. This paradox of a fusion of existences which cannot become one another is for him the creative mystery. For from the contact of the individual with what is outside him, with nature, and with other people, there is a renewal of himself.

No attempt to resume Lawrence's ideas can explain the influence he had over me. This was an immediate reaction when I read a page of his descriptive prose, or one of his poems. At once I was aware of nature as a life-and-death force, existing independently of man's existence but containing energies capable of renewing him. Lawrence's birds, beasts and flowers were marvelously themselves, marvelously outside Lawrence, even where his intuition of them had an uncanny animal or vegetable quality. They stubbornly refused to become ideas or to be colored by his own mental preoccupations. Lawrence could not have cerebralized the sea in the manner of Joyce calling it the "snot-green sea." Nor could he, like Eliot, have described the evening sky as "a patient etherized upon a table."

Lawrence, besides opening my eyes to a world that was just not potential literature, also seemed to challenge my own existence, my mind and my body. I felt the force of his criticism of his contemporaries and did not feel that I myself was spared his condemnation of Oxford undergraduates and namby-pamby young men. Worst of all, I felt that my work must suffer from that which was lacking in my own physical and mental being.

STUDY QUESTIONS

1. *What is the important distinction that Spender failed to make in his early reading of poetry?*
2. *The mark of a true poet is not novelty or vividness, according to Spender, but something else. What is it?*
3. *Actually, in describing how he corrected his early misconceptions about poetry, Spender tells how he rejected one "other world" for a second "other world." What were these two realms?*
4. *How did Spender's experiences with reading exemplify his early conception of the nature of self-fulfillment?*
5. *Write a theme describing your experience with a book or author whose discovery seemed to you to open new areas of thought or suggest new ideas.*
6. *Follow Spender's method in describing in detail a change of mind or development of thought which you experienced.*

Edith Hamilton   The Idea of Tragedy*

*T*he great tragic artists of the world are four, and three of them are Greek. It is in tragedy that the pre-eminence of the Greeks can be seen most clearly. Except for Shakespeare, the great three, Æschylus, Sophocles, Euripides, stand alone. Tragedy is an achievement peculiarly Greek. They were the first to perceive it and they lifted it to its supreme height. Nor is it a matter that directly touches only the great artists who wrote tragedies; it concerns the entire people as well, who felt the appeal of the tragic to such a degree that they would gather thirty thousand strong to see a performance. In tragedy the Greek genius penetrated farthest and it is the revelation of what was most profound in them.

The special characteristic of the Greeks was their power to see the world clearly and at the same time as beautiful. Because they were able to do this, they produced art distinguished from all other art by an absence of struggle, marked by a calm and serenity which is theirs alone. There is, it seems to assure us, a region where beauty is truth, truth beauty. To it their artists would lead us, illumining life's dark confusions by gleams fitful indeed and wavering compared with the fixed light of religious faith, but by some magic of their own, satisfying, affording a vision of something inconclusive and yet of incalculable significance. Of all the great poets this is true, but truest of the tragic poets, for the reason that in them the power of poetry confronts the inexplicable.

Tragedy was a Greek creation because in Greece thought was free. Men were thinking more and more deeply about human life, and beginning to perceive more and more clearly that it was bound up with evil and that injustice was of the nature of things. And then, one day, this knowledge of something irremediably wrong in the world came to a poet with his poet's power to see beauty in the truth of human life, and the first tragedy was written. As the author of a most distinguished book on the subject says: "The spirit of inquiry meets the spirit of poetry and tragedy is born." Make it concrete: early Greece with her godlike heroes and hero-gods fighting far on the ringing plains of windy Troy; with her lyric world, where every common thing is touched with beauty — her twofold world of poetic creation. Then a new age dawns, not satisfied with beauty of song and story, an age that must try to know and explain. And for the first time tragedy appears.

* From *The Great Age of Greek Literature* by Edith Hamilton. By permission of W. W. Norton and Company, Inc. Copyright 1943, by W. W. Norton and Company, Inc.

A poet of surpassing magnitude, not content with the old sacred conventions, and of a soul great enough to bear new and intolerable truth — that is Æschylus, the first writer of tragedy.

Tragedy belongs to the poets. Only they have "trod the sunlit heights and from life's dissonance struck one clear chord." None but a poet can write a tragedy. For tragedy is nothing less than pain transmuted into exaltation by the alchemy of poetry, and if poetry is true knowledge and the great poets guides safe to follow, this transmutation has arresting implications.

Pain changed into, or, let us say, charged with, exaltation. It would seem that tragedy is a strange matter. There is indeed none stranger. A tragedy shows us pain and gives us pleasure thereby. The greater the suffering depicted, the more terrible the events, the more intense our pleasure. The most monstrous and appalling deeds life can show are those the tragedian chooses, and by the spectacle he thus offers us, we are moved to a very passion of enjoyment. There is food for wonder here, not to be passed over, as the superficial have done, by pointing out that the Romans made a holiday of a gladiator's slaughter, and that even to-day fierce instincts, savage survivals, stir in the most civilized. Grant all that, and we are not a step advanced on the way to explaining the mystery of tragic pleasure. It has no kinship with cruelty or the lust for blood.

On this point it is illuminating to consider our everyday use of the words tragedy and tragic. Pain, sorrow, disaster, are always spoken of as depressing, as dragging down — the dark abyss of pain, a crushing sorrow, an overwhelming disaster. But speak of tragedy and extraordinarily the metaphor changes. Lift us to tragic heights, we say, and never anything else. The depths of pathos but never of tragedy. Always the height of tragedy. A word is no light matter. Words have with truth been called fossil poetry, each, that is, a symbol of a creative thought. The whole philosophy of human nature is implicit in human speech. It is a matter to pause over, that the instinct of mankind has perceived a difference, not of degree but of kind, between tragic pain and all other pain. There is something in tragedy which marks it off from other disaster so sharply that in our common speech we bear witness to the difference.

All those whose attention has been caught by the strange contradiction of pleasure through pain agree with this instinctive witness, and some of the most brilliant minds the world has known have concerned themselves with it. Tragic pleasure, they tell us, is in a class by itself. "Pity and awe," Aristotle called it, "and a sense of emotion purged and purified thereby." "Reconciliation," said Hegel, which we may understand in the sense of life's temporary dissonance resolved into eternal harmony. "Acceptance," said Schopenhauer, the temper of mind that says, "Thy will be done." "The reaffirmation of the will to live in the face of death," said Nietzsche, "and the joy of its inexhaustibility when so reaffirmed."

Pity, awe, reconciliation, exaltation — these are the elements that make up tragic pleasure. No play is a tragedy that does not call them forth. So the philosophers say, all in agreement with the common judgment of mankind, that tragedy is something above and beyond the dissonance of pain. But what it is that causes a play to call forth these feelings, what is the essential element in a tragedy, Hegel alone seeks to define. In a notable passage he says that the only tragic subject is a spiritual struggle in which each side has a claim upon our sympathy. But, as his critics have pointed out, he would thus exclude the tragedy of the suffering of the innocent, and a definition which does not include the death of Cordelia or of Deianira cannot be taken as final.

The suffering of the innocent, indeed, can itself be so differently treated as to necessitate completely different categories. In one of the greatest tragedies, the *Prometheus* of Æschylus, the main actor is an innocent sufferer, but, beyond this purely formal connection, that passionate rebel, defying God and all the powers of the universe, has no relationship whatever to the lovely, loving Cordelia. An inclusive definition of tragedy must cover cases as diverse in circumstance and in the character of the protagonist as the whole range of life and letters can afford it. It must include such opposites as Antigone, the high-souled maiden who goes with open eyes to her death rather than leave her brother's body unburied, and Macbeth, the ambition-mad, the murderer of his king and guest. These two plays, seemingly so totally unlike, call forth the same response. Tragic pleasure of the greatest intensity is caused by them both. They have something in common, but the philosophers do not tell us what it is. Their concern is with what a tragedy makes us feel, not with what makes a tragedy.

Only twice in literary history has there been a great period of tragedy, in the Athens of Pericles and in Elizabethan England. What these two periods had in common, two thousand years and more apart in time that they expressed themselves in the same fashion, may give us some hint of the nature of tragedy, for far from being periods of darkness and defeat, each was a time when life was seen exalted, a time of thrilling and unfathomable possibilities. They held their heads high, those men who conquered at Marathon and Salamis, and those who fought Spain and saw the Great Armada sink. The world was a place of wonder; mankind was beauteous; life was lived on the crest of the wave. More than all, the poignant joy of heroism had stirred men's hearts. Not stuff for tragedy, would you say? But on the crest of the wave one must feel either tragically or joyously; one cannot feel tamely. The temper of mind that sees tragedy in life has not for its opposite the temper that sees joy. The opposite pole to the tragic view of life is the sordid view. When humanity is seen as devoid of dignity and significance, trivial, mean, and sunk in dreary hopelessness, then the spirit of tragedy departs. "Sometime let gorgeous tragedy in sceptred pall come sweeping by." At the opposite pole stands Gorki with *The Lower Depths*.

Other poets may, the tragedian must, seek for the significance of life. An error strangely common is that this significance for tragic purposes depends, in some sort, upon outward circumstance, on

> pomp and feast and revelry,
> With mask, and antique pageantry—

Nothing of all that touches tragedy. The surface of life is comedy's concern; tragedy is indifferent to it. We do not, to be sure, go to Main Street or to Zenith for tragedy, but the reason has nothing to do with their dull familiarity. There is no reason inherent in the house itself why Babbitt's home in Zenith should not be the scene of a tragedy quite as well as the Castle of Elsinore. The only reason it is not is Babbitt himself. "That singular swing toward elevation" which Schopenhauer discerned in tragedy, does not take any of its impetus from outside things.

The dignity and the significance of human life — of these, and of these alone, tragedy will never let go. Without them there is no tragedy. To answer the question, what makes a tragedy, is to answer the question wherein lies the essential significance of life, what the dignity of humanity depends upon in the last analysis. Here the tragedians speak to us with no uncertain voice. The great tragedies themselves offer the solution to the problem they propound. It is by our power to suffer, above all, that we are of more value than the sparrows. Endow them with a greater or as great a potentiality of pain and our foremost place in the world would no longer be undisputed. Deep down, when we search out the reason for our conviction of the transcendent worth of each human being, we know that it is because of the possibility that each can suffer so terribly. What do outside trappings matter, Zenith or Elsinore? Tragedy's preoccupation is with suffering.

But, it is to be well noted, not with all suffering. There are degrees in our high estate of pain. It is not given to all to suffer alike. We differ in nothing more than in our power to feel. There are souls of little and of great degree, and upon that degree the dignity and significance of each life depend. There is no dignity like the dignity of a soul in agony.

> Here I and sorrows sit;
> Here is my throne, bid kings come bow to it.

Tragedy is enthroned, and to her realm those alone are admitted who belong to the only true aristocracy, that of all passionate souls. Tragedy's one essential is a soul that can feel greatly. Given such a one and any catastrophe may be tragic. But the earth may be removed and the mountains be carried into the midst of the sea, and if only the small and shallow are confounded, tragedy is absent.

One dark page of Roman history tells of a little seven-year-old girl, daughter of a man judged guilty of death and so herself condemned to die, and how she passed through the staring crowds sobbing and asking, "What has she done wrong? If they would tell her, she would never do it again" — and so on to the black prison and the executioner. That breaks the heart, but is not tragedy, it is pathos. No heights are there for the soul to mount to, but only the dark depths where there are tears for things. Undeserved suffering is not in itself tragic. Death is not tragic in itself, not the death of the beautiful and the young, the lovely and beloved. Death felt and suffered as Macbeth feels and suffers is tragic. Death felt as Lear feels Cordelia's death is tragic. Ophelia's death is not a tragedy. She being what she is, it could be so only if Hamlet's and Laertes' grief were tragic grief. The conflicting claims of the law of God and the law of man are not what make the tragedy of the *Antigone*. It is Antigone herself, so great, so tortured. Hamlet's hesitation to kill his uncle is not tragic. The tragedy is his power to feel. Change all the circumstances of the drama and Hamlet in the grip of any calamity would be tragic, just as Polonius would never be, however awful the catastrophe. The suffering of a soul that can suffer greatly — that and only that, is tragedy.

It follows, then, that tragedy has nothing to do with the distinction between Realism and Romanticism. The contrary has always been maintained. The Greeks went to the myths for their subjects, we are told, to insure remoteness from real life which does not admit of high tragedy. "Realism is the ruin of tragedy," says the latest writer on the subject. It is not true. If indeed Realism were conceived of as dealing only with the usual, tragedy would be ruled out, for the soul capable of a great passion is not usual. But if nothing human is alien to Realism, then tragedy is of her domain, for the unusual is as real as the usual. When the Moscow Art Players presented the *Brothers Karamazov* there was seen on the stage an absurd little man in dirty clothes who waved his arms about and shuffled and sobbed, the farthest possible remove from the traditional figures of tragedy, and yet tragedy was there in his person, stripped of her gorgeous pall, but sceptred truly, speaking the authentic voice of human agony in a struggle past the power of the human heart to bear. A drearier setting, a more typically realistic setting, it would be hard to find, but to see the play was to feel pity and awe before a man dignified by one thing only, made great by what he could suffer. Ibsen's plays are not tragedies. Whether Ibsen is a realist or not — the Realism of one generation is apt to be the Romanticism of the next — small souls are his dramatis personæ and his plays are dramas with an unhappy ending. The end of *Ghosts* leaves us with a sense of shuddering horror and cold anger against society where such things can be, and these are not tragic feelings.

The greatest realistic works of fiction have been written by the French and the Russians. To read one of the great Frenchmen's books is to feel mingled despair and loathing for mankind, so base, so trivial and so wretched. But to read a great Russian novel is to have an altogether different experience. The baseness, the beast in us, the misery of life, are there as plain to see as in the French book, but what we are left with is not despair and not loathing, but a sense of pity and wonder before mankind that can so suffer. The Russian sees life in that way because the Russian genius is primarily poetical; the French genius is not. *Anna Karénina* is a tragedy; *Madame Bovary* is not.

Realism and Romanticism, or comparative degrees of Realism, have nothing to do with the matter. It is a case of the small soul against the great soul and the power of a writer whose special endowment is *"voir clair dans ce qui est"* against the intuition of a poet.

If the Greeks had left no tragedies behind for us, the highest reach of their power would be unknown. The three poets who were able to sound the depths of human agony were able also to recognize and reveal it as tragedy. The mystery of evil, they said, curtains that of which "every man whose soul is not a clod hath visions." Pain could exalt and in tragedy for a moment men could have sight of a meaning beyond their grasp. "Yet had God not turned us in his hand and cast to earth our greatness," Euripides makes the old Trojan queen say in her extremity, "we would have passed away giving nothing to men. They would have found no theme for song in us nor made great poems from our sorrows."

Why is the death of the ordinary man a wretched, chilling thing which we turn from, while the death of the hero, always tragic, warms us with a sense of quickened life? Answer this question and the enigma of tragic pleasure is solved. "Never let me hear that brave blood has been shed in vain," said Sir Walter Scott; "it sends an imperious challenge down through all the generations." So the end of a tragedy challenges us. The great soul in pain and in death transforms pain and death. Through it we catch a glimpse of the Stoic Emperor's Dear City of God, of a deeper and more ultimate reality than that in which our lives are lived.

STUDY QUESTIONS

1. Note that the author finds that the word "tragedy" is used in two ways, a common or familiar one, and a more literary one. What is the distinction in meaning between these two uses?
2. Using the information provided in this essay, write an accurate one-sentence definition of the term "tragedy."
3. What is the philosophy of life upon which tragedy is based?
4. What methods does the author use for rejecting unsatisfactory definitions of tragedy and for arriving at a good one?
5. Take some novel or play with which you are familiar and write a theme telling why it is or is not a genuine tragedy.
6. Is our present civilization congenial to the expression of genuine tragic feeling as it is defined by Edith Hamilton? Since this is a rather abstract subject, you should be as explicit as possible in explaining your answer to this question.

Appendixes

1. THE METHODS AND AIMS OF PROSE

THE METHODS OF PROSE

All writing is an attempt to make something clear to someone. The methods which the writers in this anthology use to attain this end are in one sense as numerous as the selections in the anthology, for the skillful writer is always trying to choose that combination of methods which will best communicate *his* unique material and ideas. In this sense, therefore, there are as many "methods of prose" as there are writers.

But in another sense all writing relies upon certain almost unavoidable means of organization and development. Modern and earlier rhetoricians have classified these methods of organization and development in many ways, and it may well be argued that the more conscious a writer becomes of the variety of techniques he can use, the easier will be his search for the forms most appropriate to any particular writing task he faces. The majority of elaborate classifications, however, derive from subdivision of five basic ways of organizing and developing our information, emotions, and ideas: development by analysis, classification, comparison and contrast, example or illustration, and by definition. A brief explanatory comment on each of these will be helpful as a guide to the use of the selected examples of each method which are listed below.

Analysis. We can clarify an action, the construction of a mechanism, our interpretation of a character or an experience, the steps in a process, or the structure of an idea by indicating to the reader its parts as we see them. By dividing the whole into segments and explaining in turn the nature of each segment, we explain the whole. An automatic toaster, thus, can be explained in part by noting that it has receptacles for the bread, a heating element, and a timing device controlling the length of time the bread is exposed to the heating element. Writing can be described as consisting of observing and collecting information, interpreting that information, and then recording it. The ends of education can be conceived as being liberal, vocational, or professional. And so on. In many ways expository writing, if not in fact all writing, depends upon the method of analysis, for although our observations, experiences, and concepts exist within our minds as total entities, the nature of language requires that our communication of them be spread out over time. If we are to be clear to our readers, this spread must almost inevitably be in some graspable segments of time, space, or logic into which we have analyzed our experience or ideas. It is for this reason, in part, that clear writing and clear thinking are virtually inseparable.

Classification. Classification may be thought of as a special kind of analysis, but it is profitably examined separately. Whenever we *sort* things into *groups,* as we might sort the apple harvest into large good apples, small good apples, and poor apples; or housing into low, middle, and upper income housing; or governments into dictatorships and democracies, we are *classifying*. All science, and all ordered knowledge for that matter, depends heavily upon the method of classification, for it is the method which allows us to group infinitely varying particulars under abstract headings so that we may see their similarities and thus retain them in our minds. A student asked to describe his professors is very likely to begin by suggesting that they fall generally into three groups: good, bad, and indifferent. A professor asked to define the C student may begin by suggesting that there is the C student who is average or mediocre in ability, and the C student who is able but lazy. In this anthology, John Dewey clarifies the nature of *thought* by suggesting different kinds or classes of thought; and Percy Buck clarifies the nature of *appreciation* by dividing appreciation into three different kinds.

Comparison and contrast. In our daily life, the value of experiences and relationships is frequently driven home to us by unexpectedly enforced comparisons, and previously unperceived aspects of things are frequently brought into focus when we are invited to put them beside others. Thus the living room which we had come to think of as cramped and shabby falls into a different perspective when something forces us to visit someone less fortunate; or the sister who seemed a quarrelsome competitor seems suddenly more like a genial companion after she has been away at camp for two weeks. The nature of poetry as a particular form of literature is clarified by the instructor who invites us to think of it in relation to fiction, history, and philosophy; or the special function of social science is defined more precisely when someone lines it up against natural science. In writing, we can capitalize upon this natural device for rendering experience sharper and ideas clearer. Thus, in this anthology Jesse Stuart intensifies our appreciation both of the child's sense of time as defined by daylight and dark and the winds of the four seasons, and the adult's time of man-made schedule by juxtaposing the two. By setting the colloid and the crystal against each other, Joseph Wood Krutch brings into focus the limitations of science when it is applied to animate things. And by inviting us to think of the laws of nature and opinion together, Dorothy Sayers clarifies for us the nature of moral law.

A special kind of comparison, *analogy,* is sometimes classified as a separate rhetorical method. This name is usually applied to an extended comparison and more frequently to a comparison in which something unfamiliar—and frequently abstract—is explained by comparing it to something familiar—and frequently concrete. Thus, in this anthology, Richard Weaver explains his concept of the effects of mass media upon contemporary culture by comparing the media to a "great stereopticon."

Example. A piece of writing is usually said to be developed or organized by example when a general statement is defined by citing a particular representative instance of a type or a particular application of a principle, or several such instances or applications. Thus, Chafee explains what he means by the "inquiring mind" by pointing out how Darwin, Pasteur, Kepler, Einstein, and Maitland illustrate such a mind at work. Similarly, Podhoretz supports his general statements about contemporary television by describing particular TV dramas; and Richard Neutra clarifies his conception of the relation between utility and beauty by providing numerous examples. Although in rhetoric the term *example* is frequently reserved for the kind of development or organization just described, the method of making things clear by example is almost inseparable from clear and vivid writing. Whether the "examples" be the activities of the kitchen-maid and laborer with which Herbert Read gives substance to the "intense bustle" of the farm kitchen, the instances with which Ortega y Gasset supports his contention that modern man is "mass man," or the more extended illustrations which Podhoretz and Chafee use, the concreteness of specific instances is a large part of the life of writing.

Definition. The basic procedure of definition is to assign a thing to a class or genus, and then to set up differentiae which distinguish the thing defined from other members of its class. Since this is a specialized procedure, definition may usefully be considered as an independent method of organization. All definition, however, depends largely upon the basic principles of analysis and classification. And beyond *formal* or *logical definition,* all *extended definition,* concerned as it is to set unmistakably and unambiguously the bounds within which a writer wishes his reader to understand such words as "democracy," "thought," or "love," inevitably depends upon development by one of the methods outlined above. Thus, among the selections in this anthology, Bernard DeVoto defines his concept of skill by providing examples and illustrations, and John Dewey defines thought by classifying various kinds of thought.

It is worth noting that one of the principal objectives of the expository writer is to define the limits and precise meanings of abstract terms and concepts, as he understands them. Sound argument, clear understanding of explanations, and appreciation of evaluative judgments all rest largely upon agreement between writer and reader as to the meaning of the terms used. The mature and ethical writer usually intends less to argue for a particular meaning which he has assigned to a term than to clarify that meaning as he understands it, and is using it. By so doing he frequently provides his reader with new perspectives and insights, as do DeVoto in defining "skill," Mill in defining "liberty," and Santayana in defining "understanding, imagination, and mysticism."

It may not be amiss at the conclusion of this brief explanation of rhetorical methods to repeat the warning of the introductory generalization. No piece of writing which extends beyond a few hundred words will illustrate any of these techniques purely. To some extent, as we have noted, all writing depends upon the use of examples, it being difficult to develop a meaningful comparison or classification without resort to detail which always tends to grow into example or illustration. And comparison and classification, in their very nature, are particular varieties of the analysis which is always either explicit or implicit in a well ordered piece of writing.

In the following tables the editors have made no attempt to categorize every selection in the anthology. They have rather selected representative pieces which provide relatively clear-cut examples of each of the methods of prose outlined above.

Analysis

Wendell Johnson	"You Can't Write Writing"
Robert E. Sherwood	"A Speech is Written"
Everett Dean Martin	"The Educational Value of Doubt"
D. W. Brogan	"The New American"
Clinton Rossiter	"The Conservative View of Man and Society"
C. E. Ayres	"Society in the Light of Reason"
Morris R. Cohen and Ernest Nagel	"The Limits and Value of the Scientific Method"
Edward Westermarck	"The Emotional Origin of Moral Judgments"
E. M. Forster	"What I Believe"
C. S. Lewis	"What Christians Believe"
Miguel de Unamuno	"My Religion"
Alexis de Tocqueville	"In What Spirit the Americans Cultivate the Arts"
Arnold Bennett	"On Literary Taste"

Classification

Phyllis McGinley	"The Consolations of Illiteracy"
Charles Morris	"A Primer of Semantics"
John Dewey	"What is Thinking?"
Newman and Genevieve Birk	"Persuasion by Logical Argument"
C. Wright Mills	"Some Effects of Mass Media"
W. H. Ittelson and F. P. Kilpatrick	"Experiments in Perception"
George Santayana	"Understanding, Imagination, and Mysticism"
Lord Balfour	"Science, Religion, and Reality"
Martha Wolfenstein and Nathan Leites	"British, French, and American Films"
Eric Newton	"The Nature of the Arts"
Percy C. Buck	"The Meaning of Appreciation"

Comparison and Contrast

Jesse Stuart	"Child's Time and Clock Time"
David Daiches	"The Literary Use of Language"
Harold Whitehall	"Writing and Speech"
H. L. Mencken	"American Culture"
David Riesman	"Americans and Kwakiutls"
Edward Hallett Carr	"From Individualism to Mass Democracy"
José Ortega y Gasset	"The Mass Man"
Joseph Wood Krutch	"The Colloid and the Crystal"
Plato	"Allegory of the Cave"
Herman Melville	"Chronometricals and Horologicals"
John Henry Newman	"Knowledge and Faith"
Richard Weaver	"The Great Stereopticon"

Example

Winifred Welles	"The Attic"
Graham Greene	"The Lost Childhood"
Zechariah Chafee, Jr.	"The Inquiring Mind"
Jacques Barzun	"The Teaching Process"
Gilbert Highet	"The Tutorial Method"
Thomas Henry Huxley	"All Men are Scientists"
Henri Poincaré	"Mathematical Creation"
Delmore Schwartz	"Masterpieces as Cartoons"
Richard Neutra	"Utility and Beauty"

Definition

Bernard DeVoto	"The Value of Observation"
William Hazlitt	"On Familiar Style"
John Dewey	"What is Thinking?"
Zechariah Chafee, Jr.	"The Inquiring Mind"
D. W. Brogan	"The New American"
John Stuart Mill	"On Liberty"
Clinton Rossiter	"The Conservative View of Man and Society"
Thomas Henry Huxley	"All Men Are Scientists"
Arthur S. Eddington	"The Nature of the Physical World"
Dorothy Sayers	"The 'Laws' of Nature and Opinion"
Eric Newton	"The Nature of the Arts"

Percy C. Buck   "The Meaning of Appreciation"
Susanne K. Langer   "The Essence of Music"

THE AIMS OF PROSE

Writing varies not only in its rhetorical methods but also in its aims, and the student can learn much from studying the ways in which experienced writers have gone about achieving their specific intentions. The main intentions of prose have dictated its division into the four classical types of discourse — narration, description, exposition, and argument — and it would be possible to arrange all the selections in this anthology under those headings, the selections of Part One falling for the most part under the first two, and the bulk of the remainder falling under the last two. Since this text stresses the prose of exposition and argument, however, a grouping of selections which distinguishes more exact expository aims will be useful, and such an arrangement has been followed in the lists below.

It should be noted that, just as any analysis of the methods of prose shows few pure examples of one method, so an analysis of prose according to its aims will show that most pieces have a mixture of aims. Autobiographic narrative may be very heavily descriptive; a definition may seem at times to be persuading us to subscribe to its particular understanding of a term; or a reasoned argument may devote much time to explaining information upon which its conclusions are based. Hence some of the selections in the following list may appear under more than one heading, since they may be usefully examined as models of several kinds of writing. A brief description of each of the headings the editors have used will serve as a guide to the use of the selections as models for study.

Narration. Narration in the sense of a story or incident for its own sake has not been included in this collection of readings; but the opening section of the book has several examples of *autobiographical* writing, which is partly narrative and partly descriptive. A few narratives of varied purpose appear later in the anthology.

Description. The term *description* is traditionally used to mean *suggestive description,* which is concerned with conveying the qualities of a thing, the impression it has made on the writer's senses, as distinguished from *expository* and *technical description,* which are more objective. Suggestive description as an independent type of writing was considerably more common in the nineteenth century than in our time, and no pure examples of the form have been included in this collection, although Lafcadio Hearn's "Creole Carrier-Girl" and Robert Louis Stevenson's description of Monterey are close to it. But nearly all the autobiographical selections in Part One rely heavily upon this kind of description, as do most of the descriptions of places.

Exposition of process and technique. A good deal of our writing and reading is mainly informative, its intention being not to set limits, to convince us, or to evaluate something, but merely to explain how a thing is done, or how something came about. Most "how-to-do-it" books and most technical report writing today fall within this category. In this anthology, selections placed under this heading are both objective and subjective, many of the latter being interpretations of processes and techniques about which there may be wide differences of opinion.

Reasoned argument and persuasion. The intention of a goodly share of our writing and talking is essentially to convince someone that we are right, that our point of view is sound, or to persuade someone to act or believe in a certain way. In a time of conflicting political and philosophical beliefs we need both as readers and as writers to be aware of the devices of argument and persuasion, and to be alert to the logic of a writer and the reliability of his evidence. A line is sometimes drawn between *reasoned argument* and *persuasion.* The term *argument* is then reserved for those attempts at persuasion which first carefully define their assumptions and then draw their conclusions logically from those assumptions. *Persuasion* connotes a heavier reliance upon the appeal of slanted evidence, loaded language, or unexamined analogy. In the hands of dictators, demagogues and other unscrupulous men the devices of persuasion can become deadly instruments, as is attested by the history of our century; but we should not forget that they can be equally forceful instruments for good. Since this anthology is concerned to present only mature and honest argument, there are no examples of what the editors would regard as dishonest persuasion. Nonetheless, the reader will do well to be alert to such differences as those between John Stuart Mill's carefully reasoned definition of and argument for liberty, and Milton's impassioned plea; between the weighed evaluation of the scientific method presented by Cohen and Nagel, and the persuasiveness of Chesterton; and between the reasoned analysis of the effects of mass media by C. Wright Mills, and the loaded analogy upon which Richard Weaver builds his case against these same media in "The Great Stereopticon."

Evaluation. Much of the most valuable writing of all times is less concerned to inform or persuade us, than to weigh and evaluate. Because the respect for differences of view, and the relatively unbiased search for truth which this kind of writing embodies are qualities which have traditionally marked the liberally educated person, this kind of selection is heavily represented in this collection.

As with the representation of methods of prose, the editors have made no attempt in the following lists to classify every selection in the anthology, but rather have selected a representative cross-section of pieces illustrating the various types of writing defined above.

Autobiographical Narrative

Herbert Read	"The Vale and the Farm"
Dylan Thomas	"Reminiscences of Childhood"
Winifred Welles	"The Attic"
Henry Adams	"A New England Boyhood"
Henry Miller	"On Dictionaries and Encyclopedias"
H. L. Mencken	"I Discover *Huckleberry Finn*"
Graham Greene	"The Lost Childhood"
Phyllis McGinley	"The Consolations of Illiteracy"
Stephen Spender	"The Young Poet"

Description

Herbert Read	"The Vale and the Farm"
Dylan Thomas	"Reminiscences of Childhood'
Henry Adams	"A New England Boyhood"
Jesse Stuart	"Child's Time and Clock Time"
George Orwell	"Visiting a Coal Mine"
Lafcadio Hearn	"Creole Carrier-Girl"
Samuel Butler	"Dr. Skinner"
Mark Twain	"Steamboat Town"
John Richard Green	"Elizabeth"
R. P. T. Coffin	"Whistling Wings"
Robert Louis Stevenson	"The Old Pacific Capital"
Albert Camus	"The Wind at Djémila"

Exposition of Process and Technique

John Steinbeck and Edward Ricketts	"Observation and Interpretation"

2. BIOGRAPHICAL NOTES

HENRY ADAMS (1838–1918), descendant of two Presidents and son of a diplomat, studied at Harvard and spent many years in Europe as a young man. Later he became a Washington journalist, a magazine editor, and professor of history at Harvard. The author of a number of historical works, essays, and novels, he is best known for his autobiography, *The Education of Henry Adams* (1906).

CLARENCE EDWARD AYRES (1891–   ) has taught philosophy and economics at a number of universities, and has been Professor of Economics at the University of Texas since 1930. He has held several government posts, including that of director of the Federal Reserve Bank, and has written books on philosophy and economics.

ARTHUR JAMES BALFOUR (1848–1930), English Conservative politician and philosopher, was Prime Minister from 1902 to 1905. He wrote a number of books on economic and philosophic subjects.

JACQUES BARZUN (1907–   ) teaches history at Columbia University, where he is also Dean of the Graduate Faculty. Born in France, he came to America with his family in 1919 and studied at Columbia. His first books dealt with race, but he has since become well-known as a writer on a variety of subjects, including history, music, and literature. Among his books are *Darwin, Marx, Wagner* (1941) and *Berlioz and the Romantic Century* (1950).

CHARLES BAUDELAIRE (1821–1867), the great French poet, came near failing in his school-work when he was a boy, and after graduating with difficulty, went on a trip to the east and lived on the island of Mauritius. He then returned to Paris to live on a dwindling inheritance and to become a great writer. His masterpiece, a book of poems called *Les Fleurs du mal* (1857), was written while he lived in acute poverty. He is also famous for his art criticism and reviews, which expressed an esthetic philosophy that has become very influential today.

MONROE BEARDSLEY (1915–   ), Professor of Philosophy at Swarthmore College, has also taught at Yale and Mount Holyoke. He has written on logic, language, and the problems of poetic expression.

CARL BECKER (1873–1945) taught history at Dartmouth College, the University of Kansas, and, from 1917 until his death, at Cornell University. Among recent historians, he was noted for his unusual clarity and ease of style. Among his best known works are *The Heavenly City of the Eighteenth Century Philosophers* (1932), *Every Man His Own Historian* (1935) and *Modern Democracy* (1941), the latter consisting of lectures delivered at the University of Virginia in 1940.

ARNOLD BENNETT (1867–1931), English novelist and playwright, began his career as a clerk in his father's law office. After a family disagreement, he went to London, where he supported himself for a time by hack journalism. In 1896 he gave up this employment to write. After earning money by reviews, stories, and articles, he sold a novel, and began his long career as a realistic novelist. Though he was more interested in making money than in producing art, Bennett produced many novels that are highly admired as examples of realistic fiction.

NEWMAN P. BIRK (1906–   ) studied at Centre College, Kentucky; and at

Tufts and Harvard Universities in Massachusetts. Since 1933 he has taught English at Tufts University, where he has been Director of Freshman English since 1940. He and his wife, Genevieve, are co-authors of a widely used freshman English text, *Understanding and Using English*.

Max Black (1909–   ), Professor of Philosophy at Cornell University, is a specialist in the philosophy of language. Born in Baku, Russia, he studied at the Universities of Cambridge, Goettingen, and London, and came to the United States in 1940 to teach at the University of Illinois. He has been co-editor of the *Journal of Symbolic Logic* and the *Philosophy Review*.

Denis William Brogan (1900–   ), British political scientist, is an authority on America and France. After spending two years at Harvard as a graduate student, he returned to England, where he taught at Oxford and Cambridge. He has written several books on American life and government.

Lyman Bryson (1888–   ), American educator, was born in Nebraska, attended the University of Michigan, and worked as a newspaper man in Omaha before coming to Columbia University as Professor of Education. He has been active in adult education, and is well known as director of the radio program "Invitation to Learning."

Sir Percy Carter Buck (1871–1947) was an English musical scholar, composer, organist, and educationist noted for his careful scholarship, his skill as a contrapuntist, and his contributions to the teaching of music. After studying at the Guildhall School of Music and the Royal College of Music, he became successively organist at Worcester College, Oxford; Wells Cathedral; and Bristol Cathedral. From 1901 to 1927 he served as Director of Music at Harrow School, serving part of this time also as Professor of Music at the University of Dublin. In 1925 he became King Edward Professor of Music at the University of London, a position which he held until his retirement. He was knighted in 1935. He is the composer of a variety of music for strings, orchestra, and organ, and the author of numerous works on the method and history of music.

Samuel Butler (1835–1902), English novelist and satirist, was educated at Cambridge and went to New Zealand as a young man, where he made a comfortable fortune. He returned to England to pursue his interests, which included music and painting as well as writing. His first important book, *Erewhon* (1872), is a Utopian romance that satirizes European institutions. After writing it, Butler became interested in evolution and wrote a series of books taking issue with some of Darwin's theories. Butler also translated Homer, wrote some travel books, and a single novel, *The Way of All Flesh* (1903), which was not published until after his death, but is considered his greatest work.

Albert Camus (1913–   ) was born in Algeria and spent the early part of his life there. After working as a journalist in Algiers and Paris, he played an important part in the French Resistance and emerged after the war as one of France's leading philosophical writers. He has been editor of the periodical, *Combat*, and director of a publishing house. He is the author of many essays and some plays, but is best known for his novels, *The Stranger* (1946), *The Plague* (1948) and *The Fall* (1956). He won the Nobel Prize for Literature in 1957.

Edward H. Carr (1892–   ), British diplomat and political scientist, studied at Cambridge and worked in the foreign service for twenty years before becoming Professor of International Politics at the University of Wales. During World

War II he returned to government service as director of the Ministry of Information. He has written numerous books about international affairs, is a specialist on Russia, and is working on a comprehensive *History of Soviet Russia.*

ZECHARIAH CHAFEE, JR. (1885–1956) was born in Providence, studied at Brown University, and taught law at Harvard from 1913 on. He helped to write a number of important laws, was active as a delegate to United Nations committees, and wrote a number of books on law and related subjects for the general public.

GILBERT KEITH CHESTERTON (1874–1936) was an English essayist, novelist, and journalist who became a Roman Catholic convert in 1922 and devoted much of his writing to the vigorous expression of his religious views. He wrote a tremendous number of essays, travel books, studies of literary figures, poems, and novels, his best-known works being the stories about the detective-priest, Father Brown.

MARCHETTE CHUTE (1909–   ) was born in Minnesota and educated at the University of Minnesota. She is well known for her biographies of Chaucer, Shakespeare, and Ben Jonson.

ROBERT PETER TRISTRAM COFFIN (1892–1955) was born in Maine and spent much of his life there as a student and Professor of English at Bowdoin College. He wrote both poetry and prose for magazines, and was the author of books of verse, biographies, novels, and a volume of history. He lectured widely on poetry and his book of poems, *Strange Holiness,* won the Pulitzer Prize in 1936.

MORRIS RAPHAEL COHEN (1880–1947), American philosopher and professor, spent most of his life as a student and Professor of Philosophy at the City College of New York. He also taught at the University of Chicago and many of the leading American universities and served as president of the American Philosophical Association.

ALISTAIR COOKE (1908–   ) is a journalist and television personality who was born in England, but came to America, first as a student, then as a correspondent for British newspapers, and has remained to become an American citizen. He is master of ceremonies of the television program "Omnibus" and has written a number of books on public figures, as well as *One Man's America* (1952), a book on the American scene.

DAVID DAICHES (1912–   ), English author and educator, was educated at the University of Edinburgh and at Balliol College, Oxford. After teaching for short periods in both of these universities, he taught in the United States, at the University of Chicago from 1937–1943, and at Cornell University from 1946 to 1951. In the intervening years he served in World War II with the British Information Services. Since 1951 he has been University Lecturer in English at Cambridge University. He is the author of several books of literary criticism, including *The Novel and the Modern World* (1939), *Virginia Woolf* (1942), and *A Study of Literature* (1948), and a contributor of poetry, essays, and articles to various periodicals.

BERNARD DE VOTO (1897–1956) was born in Utah, but spent most of his life in Cambridge, Massachusetts and New York City as a writer and critic. Primarily interested in American literature and civilization, he wrote books on these subjects, served as editor of the *Saturday Review,* and conducted the monthly Easy Chair column of *Harper's.*

JOHN DEWEY (1859–1952) has been an important influence in American education and philosophy. Born in Vermont, he taught philosophy at various midwestern universities before coming to Columbia University, where he stayed until his retirement. He wrote a number of books in the fields of philosophy and education, including *School and Society* (1899), *Reconstruction in Philosophy* (1920), and *Art as Experience* (1934).

BARROWS DUNHAM (1905–   ), for several years a Professor of Philosophy at Temple University, was born in New Jersey and studied at Princeton University. He has written on esthetics and social philosophy, his best-known book being *Man Against Myth*.

ARTHUR S. EDDINGTON (1882–1944), British astrophysicist, was for many years Professor of Astronomy at Cambridge and Director of the Cambridge Observatory. He lectured at many universities and wrote several books on relativity and astronomy, including *The Nature of the Physical World* (1928) and *The Expanding Universe* (1933).

LOREN EISELEY (1907–   ), Chairman of the Department of Anthropology at the University of Pennsylvania and Curator of the Museum of Early Man there, was born in Lincoln, Nebraska and educated at the University of Pennsylvania. He has been active on a number of archaeological expeditions and has been President of the Institute of Human Paleontology.

EDWARD MORGAN FORSTER (1879–   ), English novelist, was educated at Cambridge and began to write short stories soon after his graduation. His best novel, *A Passage to India* (1924), was the result of his visits to India with a Cambridge teacher, G. Lowes Dickinson. In addition he has written essays, literary criticism, biography, and a travel book on Alexandria.

JOHN RICHARD GREEN (1837–1883), an English historian, was educated at Magdalen College School, and at Jesus College, from which he graduated in 1859. After some years as a cleric, he resigned to devote himself to history and politics. His *Short History of the English People* was written with a view to making historical knowledge easily available to ordinary people, and although not infallible in detail, has been much praised for its vividness. Its great success led to its expansion into the four-volume *History of the English People* (1877–1880).

GRAHAM GREENE (1904–   ) is an English novelist who occasionally writes essays. He was educated at Oxford, worked as an editor of the London *Times*, served in Africa during World War II, and has been director of a publishing house. A well-known Roman Catholic convert, he writes novels on religious themes as well as suspense stories. His best-known serious novels are *The Power and the Glory* (1940), *The Heart of the Matter* (1948), and *The Quiet American* (1955).

EDITH HAMILTON (1869–   ), a specialist in Latin and Greek literature, founded the Bryn Mawr School in Baltimore, and was director of it for twenty years. She studied at Bryn Mawr College and at the Universities of Leipzig and Munich. After retiring from teaching she wrote *The Greek Way* (1930) and *The Roman Way* (1932), accurate accounts of ancient civilizations.

WILLIAM HAZLITT (1778–1830), English critic and essayist, earned his living by writing theater and art criticism for London periodicals and by giving lectures on art and literature. He had tried studying both theology and painting before he turned to writing. He is best known as a literary critic, and his writing is admired for its clear and vigorous style.

LAFCADIO HEARN (1850–1904) was born of mixed Greek and Irish parentage in Greece, was for a time a journalist in America, but eventually, after wide travels, became attracted by the culture of Japan, and settled down there to marry, become a citizen, and teach at the Imperial University of Tokyo. Hearn, one of the most exotic figures in American literature, transformed himself into a Japanese and is known as the leading interpreter of the culture of Japan.

GILBERT HIGHET (1906–   ), born in Scotland, was educated at Glasgow University and Oxford University, in the latter of which he taught classics until 1938. Since that date he has been Professor of Greek and Latin at Columbia University. He is now an American citizen. Among his best-known recent books are *The Art of Teaching* (1950), *The Classical Tradition* (1949), *Man's Unconquerable Mind* (1954) and *Talents and Geniuses* (1957). He is also well known for his radio book-talks, some of which have been published as *People, Places, and Books* (1953).

SIDNEY HOOK (1902–   ) is chairman of the Department of Philosophy at New York University. Born in New York City, he was a student of Morris R. Cohen and John Dewey. He has written a number of books on contemporary social and philosophical problems, contributes often to periodicals, and is a specialist in Marxism.

FRED HOYLE (1915–   ), British astronomer, was educated at Cambridge, where he now teaches astronomy. He is a member of the Royal Astronomic Society, gives talks in his field over the BBC, and has written some popular interpretations of the difficult concepts involved in present-day astrophysics.

THOMAS HENRY HUXLEY (1825–1895) was a biologist by profession, but he is remembered today as a great English stylist and advocate of Darwin's theories in the evolution controversy. Huxley wrote some studies of marine zoology while on a four-year voyage on a naval vessel, and these made him famous. He served as Professor of Natural History at the Royal School of Mines and did much teaching in other institutions while writing on evolution and biology, contributing to periodicals, and taking a leading part in the controversy between scientific and religious interests that had been stirred up by Darwin's theories.

W. H. ITTELSON (1920–   ), Professor of Psychology at Brooklyn College, is co-author of *Perception: A Transactional Approach*. Educated at Columbia and Princeton, he served in the navy and taught psychology at Princeton from 1948 to 1955. He is resident consultant at the Veterans Hospital at East Orange, New Jersey.

HOLBROOK JACKSON (1874–1948), English essayist and journalist, was self-educated and began his career as a free-lance London journalist in 1907. He contributed many articles to periodicals while also writing books on Edward Fitz-Gerald and George Bernard Shaw. As an active journalist, he served on the staffs of a number of magazines and became editor of several of them. He has made some important contributions to literary history, notably his book *The Eighteen Nineties* (1913).

WENDELL JOHNSON (1906–) is a specialist in speech pathology. He was educated at the University of Iowa and is now Director of the Speech Clinic there. He is an associate editor of *Etc.*, the journal of semantics, and has been president of the Speech and Hearing Association and the Society of General Semantics.

JOSEPH WOOD KRUTCH (1893–   ), American drama critic, essayist, and teacher, was born in Nashville, Tennessee, and educated at the University of Tennessee and Columbia, where he later became Brander Matthews Professor of Drama. He was drama critic of *The Nation* and one of the founders of the Literary Guild. His works include literary studies, nature writing, dramatic criticism, and discussions of moral and cultural problems. They include *Samuel Johnson* (1944), *The Modern Temper* (1929), and *The Measure of Man* (1955).

OLIVER LA FARGE (1901–) is a novelist and student of the American Indian. Born in New York City and educated at Harvard, he has made a number of archaeological expeditions and has been president of the Association on Indian Affairs for many years. Most of his writing, including his Pulitzer Prize novel, *Laughing Boy* (1929), has been about Indians.

SUSANNE K. LANGER (1895–) studied at Radcliffe and the University of Vienna and taught philosophy at Radcliffe as well as at other colleges and universities before she went to her present post as professor of philosophy at Connecticut College. She is the author of *Philosophy in a New Key* and *Feeling and Form*.

GEORGE HENRY LEWES (1817–1878) was an English critic and philosophical writer, considerably influenced in his work by the French philosopher Auguste Comte. His connection with Marian Evans (George Eliot) was regarded by both partners as a marriage. He was the first editor of the *Fortnightly Review* (1865–66), and the author of a variety of books including the *Biographical History of Philosophy* (1845–46), *Actors and the Art of Acting* (1875), and *Physical Basis of Mind* (1877). His *Life of Goethe* continues to have more than historical interest.

CLIVE STAPLES LEWIS (1898–) studied and taught at Oxford and is now Professor of English Literature at Cambridge. Known as a vigorous Christian apologist, he is the author of a number of philosophical science-fiction novels, essays on religion, and studies of literature, including *The Screwtape Letters* (1942), and *The Allegory of Love* (1936).

ARCHIBALD MACLEISH (1892–), American poet, went to Yale and Harvard Law Schools. He has served as an editor of *Fortune*, was Librarian of Congress, and worked as an Assistant Secretary of State. He is now Professor of Rhetoric at Harvard. He has written a number of volumes of verse including *Conquistador* (1930), which won the Pulitzer Prize, and he sometimes contributes essays to periodicals.

EVERETT DEAN MARTIN (1880–1941) was a Congregationalist minister and educator who taught social philosophy at the People's Institute of New York, where he became Director in 1922. He has written a number of books on social questions, including *The Meaning of a Liberal Education*.

PHYLLIS MCGINLEY (1905–) was educated at the universities of Utah and California. She has been a teacher and editor, but is best known as a prolific writer of light verse.

HERMAN MELVILLE (1819–1891), the American novelist and author of *Moby Dick* (1851), spent his early years at sea working on merchant ships. In 1844 he left the sea, and began to write novels based on his experiences as a sailor. He had little recognition during his lifetime, and had to earn his living as a customs official, but is now considered one of the greatest American writers.

HENRY LOUIS MENCKEN (1880–1956) was a newspaper man whose active crusading in a number of social and literary causes made him a national figure. He wrote memoirs, literary studies, commentary on current affairs, and his own brand of philology, but is most famous for *The American Language*, which is both the best and the most entertaining work of scholarship in its field.

JOHN STUART MILL (1806–1873), English philosopher, economist, and politician, was a remarkable child prodigy who was educated by his father, James Mill. During most of his life he worked as an official of the East India Company. He served in Parliament from 1865 to 1868. Mill, one of the leading thinkers of his time, contributed articles to periodicals on such subjects as economics, social reform, the rights of women, and literature, and wrote a number of works on politics, logic, and economics that were of primary importance. His most popular books today are *On Liberty* (1859) and his *Autobiography* (1873).

HENRY MILLER (1891–   ), who has been called "the most controversial writer of our time," is the author of a number of eccentric novels as well as more conventional works of non-fiction. Born in the United States, he had an extremely miscellaneous youth, including some college study and a large number of jobs which proved little except that he was incapable of earning a living. He began to write in 1924, but was unsuccessful until his *Tropic of Cancer* was published in Paris in 1931. He returned to California in 1942 after traveling widely and editing some European reviews, and is earning a growing reputation in America.

C. WRIGHT MILLS (1916–   ) is Professor of Sociology at Columbia University. Educated at the Universities of Texas and Wisconsin, he has served as a consultant on labor and small business matters with the government.

JOHN MILTON (1607–1674) is best known as the great English poet, author of *Paradise Lost* (1667), but he was also a government official and vigorous controversialist on the side of civil liberties. Educated at Cambridge, he traveled in Italy and after the English revolution became an official in Cromwell's government. His *Areopagitica* (1644) is one of the classical defenses of freedom of the press.

SAMUEL ELIOT MORISON (1887–   ) is Professor of American History at Harvard. A graduate of Harvard, he studied in England and France before returning to teach at California and Harvard. He has won a number of distinctions, including the Pulitzer Prize, given in 1943 for his biography of Columbus, *Admiral of the Ocean Sea*. He has been a delegate to international conferences, and has written numerous books on American history, notably *The Growth of the American Republic* (1930), a work written in collaboration with Henry Steele Commager.

CHARLES MORRIS (1901–   ) is Professor of Philosophy at the University of Chicago. He has also taught at Northwestern University and has been lecturer in Social Relations at Harvard. He has written on semantics and the theory of value.

HERBERT J. MULLER (1905–   ) teaches English at Purdue University. He was born in New York State, was educated at Cornell University, and has taught at the University of Istanbul. He is a literary critic who has also written a book on history, *The Uses of the Past* (1952).

RICHARD J. NEUTRA (1892–   ), American architect and city planner, was born in Vienna and educated there and in Switzerland. He has lectured on architecture throughout the Western Hemisphere, is active as a leading designer and innovator, and has received many awards. He has also served as a consultant on numerous government bodies.

JOHN HENRY NEWMAN (1801–1890), English author and churchman, was educated and taught at Oxford and was active as a reformer in the Anglican church until 1846 when he became a convert to Catholicism. He was for a time rector of the Catholic University in Dublin, and was made a Cardinal in 1875. Much of his writing resulted from the controversies in which he became involved, but he also wrote on educational theory, and produced some poetry. His most famous book is his autobiographical *Apologia Pro Vita Sua* (1864).

ERIC NEWTON (1893–   ), British art critic, was educated at the University of Manchester. After serving nearly four years in World War I, he returned to the family business in mosiac designing, from which he resigned in 1922 to devote his full time to art criticism. He has served as art critic of the Manchester *Guardian* and of the London *Sunday Times,* and currently writes for various British periodicals. He is known to American audiences by his frequent articles in the Sunday Art section of the New York *Times,* and by his lecture tours of the United States and Canada. His best known books are his *Introduction to European Painting* (1949), *In My View* (1950), and *The Meaning of Beauty* (1950).

JOSE ORTEGA Y GASSET (1883–   ) is a leading Spanish philosopher. As a philosophy professor and periodical editor he fought against the Spanish monarchy, but when the Civil War broke out in Spain, he went into exile in France. After living and teaching in South America for many years, he returned to Spain in 1949. His best-known book is *The Revolt of the Masses* (1932).

GEORGE ORWELL (1903–1950) was the pen name of Eric Blair, whose *Animal Farm* (1946) and *Nineteen Eighty-Four* (1949) made him famous as a social prophet and satirist. After graduating from Eton College, Orwell spent five years in Burma as a policeman and then returned to England where, after a period spent doing odd jobs, he began to write articles, reviews, and then books. Always interested in social problems, Orwell at first specialized in clear and straightforward reporting designed to reveal little-known facts about the lives of working people.

WALTER PATER (1839–1894) studied at Oxford and intended at first to enter the church, but settled down at Oxford as a life-time fellow. He wrote essays on art and cultural history, philosophical works, and some fiction. Pater is famous as a stylist and also as the originator of esthetic theories that were extremely influential in his time and remain important today.

PLATO (about 428–346 B.C.), the great Greek philosopher, was a student of Socrates, who is the leading speaker in his *Dialogues.* After Socrates was executed, Plato left Athens to travel, and then returned to found a school called the Academy. He has probably had more influence on thought than any other philosopher, and his work is also admired for its literary quality. *The Republic* is generally considered his greatest work.

NORMAN PODHORETZ (1929–   ), now associate editor of *Commentary,* was born in Brooklyn, New York, and educated at Columbia University and Cambridge University, England. In addition to his editorial work, Mr. Podhoretz has been a frequent reviewer and contributor of critical articles to such magazines as the *New Yorker,* the *New Leader, Midstream,* and others.

JULES HENRI POINCARÉ (1854–1912) was a French mathematician and theorist who taught at the University of Paris beginning in 1881. He made many important contributions to mathematical thought and to theoretical physics.

SIR HERBERT EDWARD READ (1893–   ) was born in Yorkshire of a farming family. His writing career began with poetry and fiction about his experiences in World War I. He then turned to literary and art criticism, and held positions as a museum curator and university lecturer. He has written many books on art and literature as well as poetry and novels.

DAVID RIESMAN (1909–   ) is professor of social science at the University of

Chicago. He studied law at Harvard and taught law at the University of Buffalo and at Yale. He has been teaching social science at Chicago since 1949. He often contributes to periodicals and has written a number of books on the social sciences, the best known being *The Lonely Crowd*.

RAINER MARIA RILKE (1875–1926) was an Austrian poet born in Prague who studied philosophy and art at the universities of Prague and Munich with only fair success. He published his first book of poems in 1894, traveled in various parts of Europe, served as secretary to the great sculptor, Rodin, and began to write his greatest poetry in the years 1906–1908. He was forced to leave Paris by World War I, and served for a time in the German army. His best-known group of poems is the "Duino Elegies."

CLINTON ROSSITER (1917–   ) is Professor of Government at Cornell University. He was educated at Cornell and Princeton and is a specialist in the problems of American government.

BERTRAND RUSSELL (1872–   ), English essayist, philosopher, and mathematician, has made important contributions to mathematical theory, but is also the foremost living writer of the short essay and won the Nobel Prize for literature in 1950. His book *Principia Mathematica* (1913), written in collaboration with A. N. Whitehead, is a leading work in its field.

GEORGE SANTAYANA (1863–1952) taught philosophy at Harvard from 1889 to 1912 and was the author of a large number of distinguished books on philosophy, literature, and related subjects, as well as a single novel, *The Last Puritan*. Santayana was born in Spain and never gave up his Spanish citizenship. After retiring from Harvard in 1912 he lived in Rome and continued to write and to give lectures at European universities.

DOROTHY SAYERS (1893–   ) is a British writer of detective stories who has recently turned to religion and theology. She was one of the first women to take a degree at Oxford, where she specialized in medieval literature. She has written a translation of Dante and a series of radio plays on the life of Christ, but is best known as the author of a long succession of popular detective novels.

DELMORE SCHWARTZ (1914–   ) is an American poet and critic. Born in New York City and educated at various universities, he began literary work by writing translations and editing a little magazine. He has published several books of verse, often writes criticism for periodicals, and has taught English at Harvard.

ROBERT E. SHERWOOD (1896–   ) is a leading American playwright who has won the Pulitzer Prize three times. He was born in New Rochelle, New York, graduated from Harvard, and worked as a drama critic and editor of two periodicals. After the success of his first play, *The Road to Rome* (1927), he became prominent as a dramatist. He has been president of several theatrical organizations and has been active in national politics.

STEPHEN SPENDER (1909–   ), English poet and critic, was educated at Oxford and traveled widely on the Continent. He has been active in political movements and was at one time co-editor of the magazine *Horizon*. He is the author of several volumes of verse and criticism.

W. T. STACE (1886–   ) is an Englishman who is Professor of Philosophy at Princeton. He studied at universities in Scotland and Ireland and worked as a civil servant in Ceylon for twenty-two years. He has written on Greek philosophy and on the theories of morals and esthetics.

JOHN STEINBECK (1902–   ) was born in California and went to Stanford University where he studied marine biology. After a number of years at odd jobs, including fruit-picking, fishing, and reporting, he began to publish novels and stories, including *The Grapes of Wrath* (1939), the novel about migrant workers which became one of the best-known books of its time.

Robert Louis Stevenson (1850–1894) studied engineering and law at the University of Edinburgh, but turned to writing, beginning as an author of travel books and a contributor of essays to periodicals. After falling in love, Stevenson followed his future wife, an American, to California, married her, and brought her back to England. His health soon forced him to leave England, and after living in various parts of the United States and Honolulu, he moved to Samoa, where he spent the rest of his life. Although he is most famous for such novels as *Treasure Island* (1883), and *The Strange Case of Dr. Jekyll and Mr. Hyde* (1886), he also wrote many fine essays and critical works.

Jesse Stuart (1907–   ) was born on a remote Kentucky farm and went to a one-room school. He ran away from home as a boy and worked his way through school and Vanderbilt University. After graduating, he went back to farming, but continued to write poems which were eventually published as the volume *Man With a Bull-Tongue Plow* (1934). After his poems attracted attention, he began to write stories and novels, and his work often appeared in periodicals.

Dylan Thomas (1914–1953) was a Welsh poet who was a journalist for a time and worked for the British Broadcasting Corporation. He published his first book of poems at the age of nineteen. After his poetry had attracted wide attention, he began to give readings and lectures in America. In addition to his poetry, Thomas wrote short stories, essays, a movie-script, and a verse play.

Henry David Thoreau (1817–1862), American essayist and nature writer, is most famous for having left civilization to live alone in a cabin in the woods where he read, wrote, meditated, and provided for himself. He recorded this experience in his most famous book, *Walden* (1854). Thoreau was a great defender of freedom and individualism, and his essay *Civil Disobedience* (1894), has had world-wide influence.

Alexis de Tocqueville (1805–1859) came to the United States as a young French magistrate to make a study of law enforcement agencies. The result of this trip was his book *Democracy in America* (1835), one of the great books in the social sciences and the most perceptive study of America ever written.

Arnold J. Toynbee (1889–   ), leading British historian, was educated at Oxford and taught at the University of London. He served in the government in both World War I and World War II. His ten-volume *A Study of History,* which was completed in 1954, is generally considered one of the major historical works.

Lionel Trilling (1905–   ) is an American critic who teaches English at Columbia University. He was educated at Columbia, has contributed frequently to periodicals, and has written on Matthew Arnold and E. M. Forster. In addition, he is the author of a novel, *The Middle of the Journey* (1947), and some short stories.

Mark Twain (1835–1910) is the pen-name of Samuel Langhorne Clemens, the famous American humorist. Born in Missouri, Twain worked as a traveling printer and Mississippi River pilot in his youth, and went west as a prospector when the Civil War made traveling impossible. He began to write feature articles for the Virginia City *Enterprise,* then moved to San Francisco and continued to send correspondence to California papers as he traveled around the Pacific and the Mediterranean. After two years as editor of the Buffalo *Express,* Twain moved in 1871 to Hartford, Connecticut, where he wrote most of his famous books, including *Tom Sawyer* (1876), and *Huckleberry Finn* (1884).

MIGUEL DE UNAMUNO (1864–1936), former Professor of Greek and Rector of the University of Salamanca, was a leading Spanish scholar, poet, and novelist. He was active in political affairs until 1924, when the Spanish Republican government exiled him, and he moved to Paris. His works are characterized by his love of the people and landscape of Spain.

ROBERT WARSHOW (1917–1955), literary critic, graduated in 1937 from the University of Michigan where he edited *Contemporary*, a literary magazine. He wrote numerous reviews for such magazines as the *New Yorker*, the *New Leader*, *Commentary*, and the *Partisan Review*, and for the latter regularly wrote the "Film Chronicle" for several years. For a number of years prior to his death he was on the staff of *Commentary*, first as managing editor and later as associate editor.

RICHARD WEAVER (1910–   ), now an Associate Professor of English at the University of Chicago, was educated at the University of Kentucky, Vanderbilt, and Louisiana State, from the latter of which he received his Ph.D. in 1943. Prior to joining the faculty of the University of Chicago in 1944, he taught at various universities including Vanderbilt and Louisiana State. His special fields are the theory of rhetoric, American literature and culture, and problems of modern civilization. His best known books are *Ideas Have Consequences* and *The Ethics of Rhetoric*.

WINIFRED WELLES (1893–1939) was a New England poet, author of several volumes such as *Hesitant Heart* (1919), *This Delicate Love* (1935), and *The Shape of Memory*, published posthumously in 1944. She wrote, in addition, several juvenile prose works, and one adult prose work, *The Lost Landscape*, a group of memoirs based upon family history and letters. Both her poetry and her prose were praised by such critics as Stephen Vincent Benet and Padraic Colum for their charm and quiet clarity.

EDWARD WESTERMARCK (1862–1939) was a Finnish anthropologist who spent most of his life in England, first to gather material for his important work on marriage, and then as professor of sociology at the University of London, where he taught from 1907 to 1930. He wrote a number of scholarly works on morals, ethics and religion.

HAROLD WHITEHALL (1905–   ) was born and educated in England, but took his doctorate at the University of Iowa. He has taught linguistics at a number of colleges and universities, and is now chairman of the Department of Linguistics at the University of Indiana. He has written many works on language and served on the boards of some important reference works in the field of English.

MARTHA WOLFENSTEIN (1911–   ), psychologist, was educated at Radcliffe, from which she received her A.B. in 1932, and her doctorate in 1939. From 1943 to 1950 she taught and did research at Hunter College and Columbia University. Since 1952 she has been a visiting professor at the College of the City of New York. Her special fields are clinical research and child psychology, culture, and personality.

VIRGINIA WOOLF (1882–1941), English novelist, was the daughter of Leslie Stephen, a Victorian writer, and got the most important part of her education from her father's friends. She began writing in 1915, and produced many novels in experimental form, as well as a number of essays and reviews. Her best-known works are *Mrs. Dalloway* (1925), *To the Lighthouse* (1927), and *Orlando* (1928).

Index

609